To Jacqueline, whose suggestion this book was,
and whose encouragement and support
made possible its achievement.

Eric Gill: a barrister's wig on a wig-stand, from his typographical monograph, 1926, reprinting Hilary Pepler, *The law the lawyers know about*, 1915 [BL].

Gill's connection with the Inn is noted in 12.1. and Pepler's in 27.2. below.

A LINCOLN'S INN *COMMONPLACE* BOOK

The buildings and grounds of an Inn of Court, its dependencies and neighbourhood over eight centuries: in art, literature, reportage and music

Preface by

Sir William Blackburne

Treasurer of the Honourable Society of Lincoln's Inn for 2015

Foreword by

The Rt Hon Lord Walker of Gestingthorpe, PC

Formerly a Justice of the Supreme Court of Great Britain and Northern Ireland
A Past Treasurer of the Honourable Society of Lincoln's Inn
An Honorary Fellow of Trinity College, Cambridge

Historical Essay on the origin and early character of Lincoln's Inn, and
Glossary of Inns of Court terminology, especially as used in Lincoln's Inn, by

Sir John Baker, QC, LLD, FBA

Sometime Downing Professor of the Laws of England in the University of Cambridge
A Fellow and sometime President of St Catharine's College, Cambridge
An Honorary Bencher of the Honourable Societies of the Inner Temple and Gray's Inn

Words and pictures compiled and edited by

Graham S Brown, LLM

Formerly Senior Partner of Payne Hicks Beach, Solicitors in Lincoln's Inn
An Honorary Bencher of the Honourable Society of Lincoln's Inn

Third Millennium
Publishing

2011

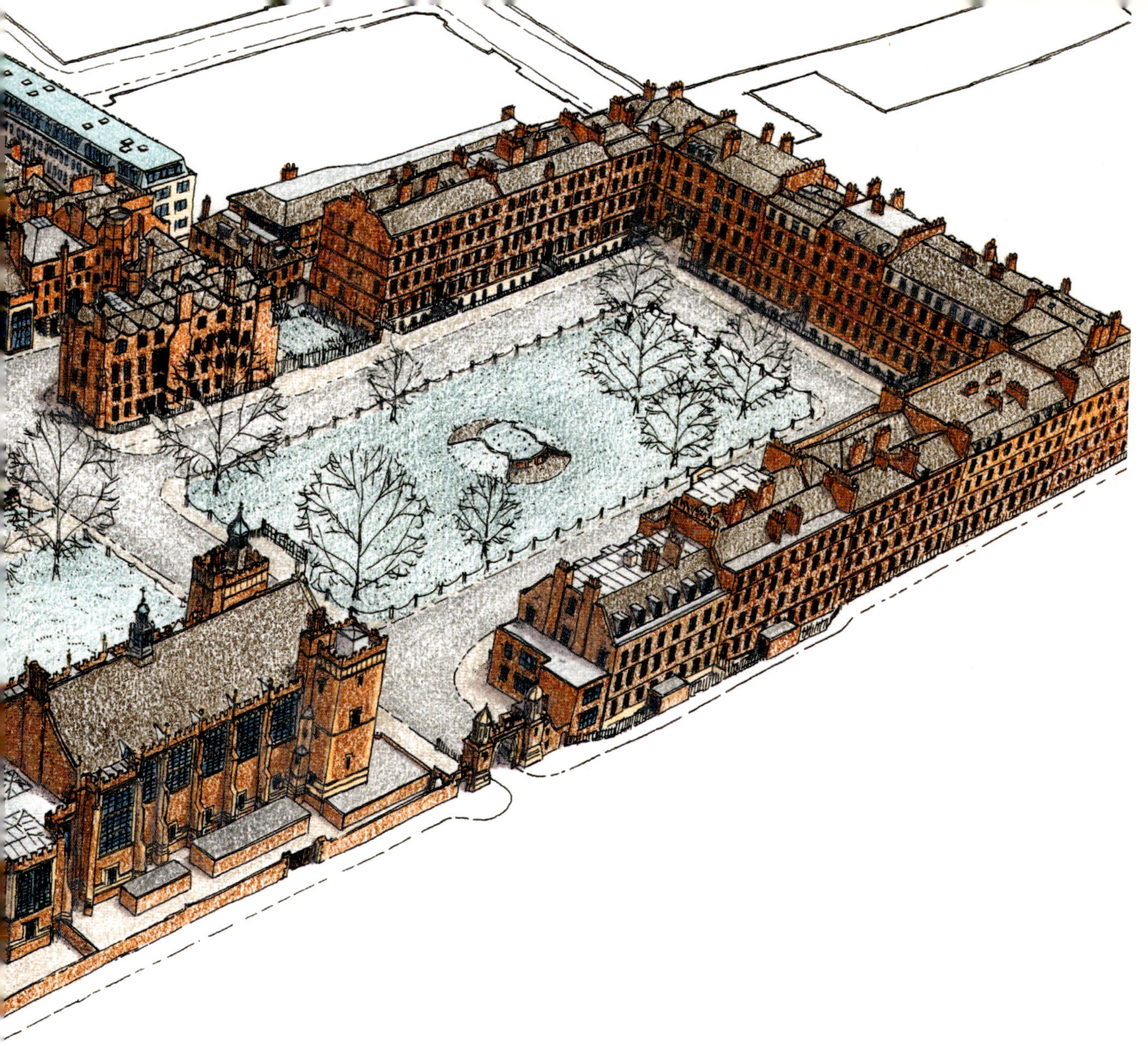

First published in Great Britain in 2016 by Third Millennium Publishing, an imprint of Profile Books Ltd

3 Holford Yard, Bevin Way
London WC1X 9HD, United Kingdom
www.tmiltd.com

A CIP catalogue record for this book is available from The British Library.

ISBN: 978 1 908990 54 9

Design: Matthew Wilson and Susan Pugsley

Reprographics by Studio Fasoli, Italy
Printed and bound in Italy by Printer Trento srl
on acid-free paper from sustainable forestry

TABLE OF CONTENTS

In the Table of Contents and Topography, and in the corresponding headings in the text:

- 'Court' indicates law-court, and 'Court' within the Inn indicates a square or enclosure of buildings, as in the Cambridge usage. This nomenclature has almost fallen out of use in this Inn, but remains in the other three. Outside the Inn, it may also mean a passage or footpath.
- 'Rents' means a passageway with tenements or shops along it.
- 'Row' indicates a line of contiguous chambers or houses. The term has almost gone in all four Inns, and remains in occasional use on their periphery in, for example, Bedford Row.
- the use of *italics* indicates, both within the Inn and without, a former building or structure, passage or footpath, or the former use or name for an existing building or structure or place.

- The chambers within the original footprint of the Inn (not now as to the majority the oldest chambers) are viewed from a starting point (formerly marked by the projecting *turret spiral staircase* of *3, Old Buildings*) at the e. end of the Chapel: the visual division between the n. and the s. courts, under their successive names. From there, 11.1.–11.2. look clockwise around Old Buildings as far as the Old Hall; and 12. continues s.w. of the Old Hall, viewing their front elevations. Then, from the same starting point, 13. surveys Old Square (as it is now called) anti-clockwise: the original chambers being *4-9 Old Buildings* and the existing chambers 14-11 Old Square. In 14., the chambers in the former w. court, *Dial* or *Chapel Court*, are seen clockwise in ascending numerical order. Finally, the rear elevations of 18-20, Old Buildings are seen in 17.1., after New Square, whence they are visible, framing the Kitchen Garden. The idiosyncrasies of numbering of these chambers at the present day have been explained in other books. Understanding them is not necessary for this perambulation.
- *Courts* & *Judges' Chambers* within the Inn are viewed or noted in the paragraphs for their respective buildings or courts: *the Master of the Rolls', the Lord Chancellor's* and *the Lords Justices' Courts* in the Old Hall; *the Lord Chancellor's Chambers* and *the Vice-Chancellor's Court* in *Library Row*; *the junior Vice-Chancellors' Courts* in Gatehouse Court; and *Fry J's Court* below the Library.

§ 18. Stone Buildings (originally *Stone Building Court*):

18.1. *The Stone Building*: the Society's chambers for members, in 1-6; *the old Library*, in 2; and the *Plaint Office* in 4.

18.1.1. Their elevations

18.1.2. The view from their chambers

18.1.3. William Pitt, the younger, PM

18.2. *Offices of the Courts* in *Stone Building Court*:

18.2.1. *The Record & Writ Office* and *the Register* (or *Registrar*) *& Report Office,* in 8-9

18.2.2. *The Office of the Corporation of the Six Clerks,* in 10

18.2.3. *The Inrolment* (or *Enrolment*) *Office of Chancery,* and *the Accountant-General's Office,* in 11

18.2.4. *The Masters' Chambers* and *the Pleas Office of the Court of Exchequer*, in 7 (formerly in *8 & 9, Old Buildings*)

18.3. *The Officers' Training Corps* (now the Inns of Court and City & Essex Yeomanry: the ICCEY), in 10 (the former *Six Clerks' Office*)

· See 43.1.5: the Volunteers in and after the First World War

§ 19. Doorways and staircases, fireplaces and chimneys, and curtains:

19.1. Some doorways and staircases

19.2. Some fireplaces and chimneys

19.3. Some curtains and textiles in chambers, five centuries apart

§ 20. Other chambers, *offices* and *shops* in the Inn, or of the Society outside, of the C19th to the C21st:

20.1. More House (*the Yemen Coffee House*, before incorporation into the Inn), on Carey Street and Serle Street:

20.1.1. The building

20.1.2. Sir Thomas More, LC

20.2. The Garden House: 14-15, New Square (originally *the new law stationer's shop*)

20.3. Hardwicke Building (originally *Hale Court chambers* and *the Lincoln's Inn Post Office*):

20.3.1. The building

20.3.2. Sir Matthew Hale, CJ

20.4. 16, New Square (originally *Hardwicke Building*):

20.4.1. The building

20.4.2. The first Earl of Hardwicke, LC

20.5. 30, Lincoln's Inn Fields (originally *Erskine Chambers*), on Newman's Row

20.5.1. The building

20.5.2. Lord Erskine, LC

20.6. 76A, Chancery Lane, and *its python*

20.7. 33, Chancery Lane (*Law Courts Chambers*, before incorporation into the Inn)

§ 21. *The Walks* (now the Cherry Tree Walk, the North Lawns, the Benchers' Border, and Parker's Piece):

21.1. The flora: trees, blossom and flowers

21.2. The fauna: promenaders, men seeking women, litigants, garden-party goers and dogs

21.3. *The Jakes*

21.4. The Terrace wall (formerly *Lincoln's Inn Wall*); and *the Terrace* (now the Cherry Tree Walk) and its prospect over the Fields

21.5. The spirituality of the Gardens

21.6. Gentlemen gardeners of the Society, and their philosophies

---

THIRD PART: DEPENDENCIES OF THE INN

---

§ 22. The Society's *Inns of Chancery*:

22.1. *Thavies Inn*, and its associations with St Andrew's church

22.2. *Furnival's Inn*:

D. CHILDREN

§ 33. **Children of the neighbourhood in the Inn:**
i. their playtimes
ii. their treats

SIXTH PART: PLACES OF WORK: COURTS AND THEIR CHAMBERS & OFFICES ON THE PERIPHERY OF THE INN

§ 34. ***Courts, Chambers* and *Court Offices* on the periphery of the Inn, and some of their personnel**

• *The High Court of Chancery:*

34.1. *The Office of the Corporation of the Six Clerks*, and *the Inrolment* (or *Enrolment) Office of Chancery*, in Chancery Lane

34.2. *The Master of the Rolls' Court*, in *the Rolls House*, in Chancery Lane

34.3. *The Examiners' Office* and *the Petty Bag Office*, in *the Rolls Yard*

34.4. *The Register* (or *Registrar*) and other *Court Offices* in *Symond's Inn*, in Chancery Lane

34.5. *The Office of the Corporation of Cursitors of Chancery*, on Chancery Lane and Cursitor *Alley* (now Street)

34.6. *The Office of the Masters in Ordinary in Chancery*, on Southampton Buildings and Quality Court (accommodated with *the Offices of the Secretaries of Bankrupts* and *of Lunatics*)

34.7 *The Office of the Taxing Masters in Chancery*, in Staple Inn

• *The Courts of Common Law:*

34.8 *The Fire Court* in *Clifford's Inn*, off Chancery Lane, Fleet Street and Fetter Lane

• *The Courts of Common Law:*

34.9 *The Chambers of the Judges of the Queen's Bench* and *of Common Pleas*, and *the offices of the latter Court*; and *the Court* & *Chambers of the Chief Baron of Exchequer*, in *Serjeants' Inn* and *the Rolls Garden*

34.10. *The Insolvent Debtors' Court*, in Portugal Street

• *The Supreme Court of Judicature* (now the Senior Courts):

34.11. *The Royal Courts of Justice,* between Carey St. and the Strand

34.12. *The Bankruptcy Courts*, on Carey Street and Grange Court

SEVENTH PART: PLACES OF ENTERTAINMENT, FELLOWSHIP, RECREATION AND RESORT IN THE PURLIEUS OF THE INN

§ 35. **The distractions to bar students around the Inn:**

35.1. Their multiplicity

35.2. Seeking to resist them

§ 36. **The attractions of *Playhouse Street*:**

36.1. *The real tennis court*

36.2. *The Lincoln's Inn Fields Theatre*, and David Garrick's performances

§ 37. ***Coffee-houses* and *clubs:***

37.1. *Coffee-houses* adjacent to the Inns of Court and Chancery

37.2. *Clubs* and *literary taverns* in the neighbourhood of the Inn:
i. *The Apollo Club*
ii. *The Kit-Cat Club*

§ 38. **Freemasons' lodges in the vicinity of and in the Inn**

§ 39. ***Drinking-houses* and *chop-houses* close to the Inn:**

39.1. Their premises, proprietors and personnel:
i. *Newman's Tipple House*
ii. *St John's Coffee House*
iii. *The Gin House in Lincoln's Inn Back Side*
iv. The Cock

39.2. Their Inn clientèle

§ 40. ***Music halls***

§ 41. ***Bawdy-houses* in proximity to the Inn**

EIGHTH PART: FURTHER COMINGS AND GOINGS

§ 42. **The exodus from the Inn in the long vacation:**

42.1. The law terms

42.2. The deserted Inn

PREFACE

Lincoln's Inn has seen out many centuries, just how many no one quite knows. Its Treasurers, by contrast, each serving for a single year, make a brief appearance in the ever-unfolding drama which is the life of the Inn.

This commonplace book, as it is accurately and, I think, self-deprecatingly entitled, is truly a labour of love. It is the fruit of years of painstaking research, deep contemplation, careful authorship and scholarly devotion to the extraordinary place which is this Inn. And what better person could there be to undertake the task than Graham Brown? From his many years in practice as a member and latterly senior partner of Payne Hicks Beach working from his office in New Square and since 2009 as one of the Society's Honorary Benchers, Graham knows his subject as well as anyone can. To this must be added his love of literature, music and the visual arts, and a willingness to find the time both when in practice and now in retirement to put together this magnificent picture of the Inn and those who have inhabited it as expressed in the thoughts or as seen through the eyes of so many persons, from all walks of life, drawn from London's colourful past right down to the present day. The Foreword by Lord Walker of Gestingthorpe, who, as he explains, has lived or worked for most of his adult life within the Inn, introduces the reader to the author and sets the scene for what is to come. Sir John Baker's masterly historical essay on the origin and early character of the Inn is an intriguing glimpse into the past. Coming from the leading expert on English legal history, it is a most significant contribution to this tantalising subject.

Anyone who takes an interest in Lincoln's Inn should acquire a copy of this book. It will remain an everlasting and treasured source of interest and amusement for the reader. I commend it without reservation.

Sir William Blackburne

1 Accountant-General
2 Pleas of Exchequer
3 Six Clerks' Office
4 Register Office
5 Taxing Master in Chancery
6 Great Seal Patent Office
7 Masters in Chancery
8 Quality Court
9 Cursitors' Office
10 Stamp Office
11 New Court, Lincoln's Inn
12 Insolvent Debtors' Court
13 Lincoln's Inn Fields Theatre
14 Clement's Inn
15 New Inn
16 Lyons Inn
17 Sardinian Chapel
18 St Mary-le-Strand Ch.
19 St Clement's Ch.
20 Temple Bar
21 Royal Courts of Justice
22 Bankruptcy Court
23 Temple Stairs
24 Middle Temple
25 Serjeants' Inn, Chancery Lane
26 Law Society's Hall
27 Rolls House and Chapel
28 Inner Temple
29 St Dunstan's-in-the-West Ch.
30 Serjeants' Inn, Fleet Street
31 Clifford's Inn
32 Symond's Inn
33 St Andrew's Ch.
34 Thavies Inn
35 Barnard's Inn
36 Furnival's Inn
37 Holborn Bars
38 Staple Inn
39 Middle Row, Holborn
40 Gray's Inn
41 St Alban's Ch.
42 Gray's Inn Walks
43 Whetstone Park
44 HM Land Registry
45 Snow Hill
46 Serle's Coffee House

FOREWORD

THIS REMARKABLE BOOK, SINGLE-HANDEDLY EDITED BY Graham Brown, is the mature fruit of his devoted interest in Lincoln's Inn, where he has worked throughout his long and distinguished career as a solicitor. His interest in the Inn, sustained through almost five decades, extends to its architecture, history, collegiate life, governance, scandals, literary associations and much else; to its great men (and, for about the last tenth of its history, women) and to the extraordinary variety of less famous people (barristers, solicitors, litigants and others) who have, either in fact or in fiction, practised or taught or studied law, or sought legal advice, or lived within the Inn.

If the reader looks at the list of the book's contents, it is immediately apparent that the editor has undertaken a formidable task. And as the reader starts on the book it quickly becomes clear that the editor has brought to the task exacting standards of scholarship, unfailing enthusiasm, and an eye for the unexpected. But the Editor's Note is characteristically modest and self-effacing, and gives few hints as to where the scholarship, the enthusiasm and the eclectic taste come from. I have had the privilege of knowing Graham, first as a professional client, latterly as a fellow bencher, and at all times as a friend, for at least forty years. But for those who do not know him, a bit of background is not out of place.

Graham's family roots have links not only with the law, but also with mathematics and science. He took a first degree in law at Bristol University and a master's at King's College, London. His master's degree was achieved by part-time study when he was already an articled clerk (as it was then called) in the Inn. Later he spent a year studying civil law at Louvain.

His articles were with Payne Hicks Beach & Co, a well-known firm which is one of the Inn's most long-established tenants. He had thought that he might move on to the City or even to practise overseas, but in the event he stayed with Payne Hicks Beach for the whole of his professional career, from articled clerk to assistant solicitor, to partner, senior partner and consultant, a position from which he finally retired in 2014. In 2009 the Benchers of Lincoln's Inn wisely decided to elect him as an Honorary Bencher—believed to be the first practising English solicitor to have been so.

Graham first saw the Inn when he came from Bristol to an interview at the offices of what became his firm in New Square. He found his way from the tube station to the great gate in Chancery Lane and he was immediately struck—as many others have been struck: see for instance Douglas Newton, writing in 1951, in section 11.2.1. below—by the calm and quiet and beauty of the Inn. This was the beginning of his wish to learn more about the Inn. As a sort of *hors d'œuvre* to his researches he used the Law Society's archives to trace the history of his own firm. He succeeded in tracing it, through various permutations, to the first half of the eighteenth century. The end result is an impressive diagram, a sort of professional pedigree of Payne Hicks Beach and its ancestors, which hangs in their offices.

As regards the Inn, Graham has undertaken a prodigious amount of research, and what he has achieved is truly remarkable. As the list of libraries, galleries and collections shows, his researches have taken him to many of the great repositories of knowledge in England, and also to the United States of America and to Belgium. The list includes libraries and galleries in Washington, New York, Philadelphia and New Haven. It was at the Yale Center for British Art at New Haven that Graham found what is believed to be the oldest known or surviving oil painting of the Inn: a view of Gatehouse Court, by an unknown artist, of 1725 (see illustration *7.a*).

Having lived or worked in the Inn for most of my adult life, I complacently supposed that I knew quite a bit about its architecture and history, and the achievements of its members either in the law, or in other fields such as literature.

Indeed, I contributed two essays to *A Portrait of Lincoln's Inn*, an illustrated book edited by Angela Holdsworth (Lady Neuberger) which Graham mentions kindly in his Editor's Note. But reading the manuscript of Graham's book has brought home to me the superficiality and sketchiness of my knowledge. Here is real scholarship, but always presented with grace, charm and a light touch.

One of the signs of increasing age (overtaking the conviction that not only policemen and silks, but even judges, are getting younger all the time) is when you observe the demolition of large buildings that you saw in course of construction. That is happening on the east side of Chancery Lane opposite the Great Gate, and to the outstandingly ugly building enclosed by Portugal Street, Carey Street and Serle Street, and adjacent to the south-west corner of New Square. It used to be called New Court (see section 24. in the Third Part of this book). In 1961 I was a pupil in chambers in New Court, which was then a red-brick building designed by Alfred Waterhouse (also the architect of the better-known Prudential premises north of Holborn). I now learn that it was described as 'Not rose-red, half as old as time, more neo-Gothic-brick-sublime' in the verse by Nathaniel Micklem, then a busy junior in the chambers, and later a learned county court judge. Waterhouse's building was demolished in 1961, soon after I completed my pupillage. This vandalism cannot be laid at the door of the benchers, since New Court is what Graham calls a 'dependency', and does not belong to the Inn.

Lincoln's Inn does not demolish and reconstruct its buildings every fifty years.

It has been there, in good times and bad, for over six hundred years, and it is showing itself well able to go forward—partly by going back to its roots and having the education and training of advocates as its paramount concern. This remarkable book celebrates six centuries of history, and it will be cherished as a unique contribution to the Inn's literature.

Lord Walker of Gestingthorpe

A DEDICATION TO THE INNS OF COURT

from Ben Jonson, *Every man out of his own humour*, 1599.

'To the Noblest Nurseries of Humanity and Liberty in the Kingdom:
The Inns of Court

I understand you, gentlemen, not your houses: and a worthy succession of you, to all time, as being born the judges of these studies. When I wrote this poem, I had friendship with divers in your societies; who, as they were great names in learning, so they were no less examples of living. Of them and then (that I say no more) it was not despised. Now that the printer, by a doubled charge, thinks it worthy a longer life than commonly the air of such things doth promise, I am careful to put it a servant to their pleasures who are the inheritors of the first favour born of it. Yet, I command it lie not in the way of your more noble and useful studies to the public. For so I shall suffer for it. But, when the gown and cap is off, and the Lord of Liberty reigns, then, to take it in your hands perhaps may make some bencher, tincted with humanity, read; and not repent him.'

EDITOR'S NOTE

'... Lincoln's Inn... is... an Inn of Court... now lately encreased with fair Buildings, and replenished with Gentlemen, studious on the common Laws... And this Inn, taken in the whole, is a curious Pile of Buildings, not inferiour to any of the four Inns of Court.'

—John Stowe, from *The Survey of London*, second edn., 1603

THIS BOOK IS A COMPILATION OF HISTORICAL IMAGES AND WORDS relating to one of the four Inns of Court in London, Lincoln's Inn, and its neighbourhood. It is an essay in historical topography, but it is not a history of the Inn.

First, this book depicts—principally through the images made by artists and architects—the development, building, demolition, destruction by fire, bombing and rebuilding of Lincoln's Inn, its dependencies and environs over some eight centuries, and evokes the types of people living or working there over that time. In a few instances, a photograph has been used where no other image could be found. Most of the images here have not previously been reproduced in print. Some have, however, been made accessible on the Web in recent years. They constitute the most extensive collection of artists' views of the buildings and grounds of an Inn of Court yet published in one book.

Lawrence Baker's plans of the development of the Inn over the centuries—a labour of love on his part—should enable each of those illustrations from past centuries to be put into their time and place.

Second, the individual buildings, and their courtyards and gardens, are where possible matched with a contemporary or intermediate description or evocation of them, or of an event taking place in them, or of a person or people working in or associated with them. Those chambers buildings named in honour of distinguished members of the Society were built long after their deaths. In these instances one or more brief quotations relevant to that man is included in the paragraph referable to that building. Where available, quotations are from recognised figures in English literature, some of whom may have been lawyers, failing which they may be from a diary or letter written by a member or resident of the Inn who was there, or the reportage of a visitor, or a guide to visitors. Some of the writing quoted is fact and some fiction, but there is no reason to imagine that the fiction, with rare exceptions, is not founded on fact. Which is which will be self-evident. Where I have had a choice between poetry or prose, I have usually chosen the former: always for its powers of evocation, and sometimes for its brevity. In consequence, there is here a wide range of poetry, verse, rhyme and doggerel. The association of a piece of literature or reportage with a building or space or a person working, living or visiting there, does not provide a history of the building, etc. For that, reference may be had to the books mentioned later in this Note.

The eclectic character and diverse quality of the quotations reprinted here do not justify their being called an anthology. Some pieces are, indeed, flowers of English literature, but more are not. Thus I use a term from legal history—commonplace book—to describe this compilation. By contrast, much of the material would fit into the meaning, closest to its etymology, of anecdotes: hitherto unpublished details of history. But legal anecdotes have a particular character, and this is not another book of those. What I hope that the quotations have in common is that they are readable.

Before looking at the Inn itself, there are some pictures and literary evocations of the approaches to the Inn in past centuries. There was a striking difference between the squalor—and often danger—outside the walls of the Inn, and the dignity and peace within. The squalor is suggested by the short section on the ragged children occasionally let into the Inn, in the C19th. The danger is illustrated by the specific hazards of crossing Lincoln's Inn Fields, and more generally the civil disorders which intermittently, over the centuries, came close or up to the very gates of the Inn. The approaches do, of course, offer the means of seeing the Inn in the context of its neighbourhood, as once it was.

By contrast with the comings in, there is an evocation of the extraordinary exodus from, and almost total evacuation of, the Inn, which occurred every summer in the long vacation of the courts.

The Inn is also placed in its geographical and professional context by a rapid *tour d'horizon* of some of the numerous law courts, chambers and court offices which over several centuries were closely grouped around the perimeter of the Inn—and in which the bar of, and solicitors and their clerks in, the Inn will have appeared or transacted business. The sooty exteriors and greasy interiors of a few of them were memorably evoked by Dickens in his writing, but this book has brought together descriptions of rather more of them, with images of some, of which none appears in Dickens. Many of these buildings were imposing, and were the work of the country's most notable architects—Inigo Jones, Colen Campbell, Sir Robert Taylor, Sir William Chambers or his studio, Sir John Soane, Sir Robert Smirke, Sir James Pennethorne and Sir John Taylor. Almost all have been demolished and lost to memory. Books on legal London—if not on the Inns of Court and Chancery—seem to have focused on the criminal courts and prisons, to the exclusion of the civil courts.

By contrast to the working buildings of the law, there is a bird's-eye view of some of those buildings and establishments which also stood on the periphery of the Inn, and formerly offered a great variety of recreation and entertainment to those visiting or studying, practising and living in it. It is not suggested, however, that members of the Society availed themselves of every one of those possibilities!

Self-evidently, the pictorial and literary material relating to the approaches to the Inn and to these last two categories of buildings is not specific to the Inn, and does not form part of the history of the Honourable Society. That relating to the long vacation is both specific to the Inn, and generic to all four.

I have sought to give a structure to the book by means of which the reader—if reader there be—may be able physically or mentally to walk through the Inn, its dependencies and its neighbourhood. But that structure has been imposed on me no less by the images or writings themselves, and their existence or their absence.

'The figures in a townscape' who peopled the buildings and spaces of the Inn and the lanes outside it are looked at in other sections of the book, after the peregrination. They were, most significantly for the focus of this book, the members of the Society at the successive stages of their studies and careers, within the Inn and its dependencies. The first was that of being a law student in an Inn of Chancery (or preparatory school), whether one of the two dependent on Lincoln's or another. There are a few quotations from literature and from collegiate records which offer impressions of the life and habits—seemingly of some luxury and indolence—of students in the larger of them, Furnival's. By accident of history, fragmentary records of the business of that Inn predate by some years those of the mother house. The second was that of being a law student in Lincoln's Inn. That is evoked in the Historical Essay, while *pointilliste* impressions of student life are provided in the Glossary by the numerous special words used in the Inn, relating to their studies, food, clothing and official recreations. The third was that of practice at the Bar. This is seen, specifically in an Inn environment, by the selection of material from novels, and a few verses, evoking the Bar in their chambers here, their work and their practice specialisations. The fourth was either the summit of the profession: the judiciary, or in parallel the holding of office as a minister of the Crown. For these, most of their work will have been outside the walls of the Inn, with the exception in the C18th and C19th of the hearing of some cases in the Courts of Chancery or Exchequer, when those were housed within the Inn. Those categories of member therefore appear here only fleetingly.

There is a further categorisation of lawyers of and in the Inn. They are the judges, barristers, solicitors and clerks under arms—the Volunteers. These have a long association with the buildings and grounds of the Inn, which has accommodated their orderly room, office and drill hall, provided parade grounds, and on occasions lent the use of the Chapel and the Halls. Many books on this Inn or the Inns of Court generally—unless written by an old soldier—have taken the reasonable view that they fell outside the scope of a study of the practice of law, or of a legal institution. They have accordingly either omitted reference to the Volunteers' history entirely, or limited it to the world wars, when their membership was swollen by recruitment from outside the law, and thus less representative of the legal profession. This book therefore takes the opportunity of recording something of the continuity of the military life of the Society by means of a few quotations evoking the training in the Inn and the thoughts of these men, matched with some illustrations of them in uniform.

Notwithstanding its having come into existence as a professional home of bar and bench, the Inn has been a microcosm in which a broad range of humanity, and all human activity, were to be found. Having regard to its origins, some books on the Inn have overlooked, or glanced only in passing at, those who were not bar students, barristers or judges. But their doing so lost sight of that rich variety, which was such a distinctive feature of the Inn. The compilation of words and pictures therefore seeks to recapture something of it here.

Two books specific to the Inn have appeared in recent years, and I wish to express my admiration for each. The first, *A Portrait of Lincoln's Inn*, under the editorship and part authorship of Angela Holdsworth (Lady Neuberger of Abbotsbury) succeeded, among other things, in both fully describing and depicting for the first time the Inn's buildings and collegiate life, past and present. It also contained biographical material on many distinguished members of the Society: judicial, political, ecclesiastical and otherwise, at home and abroad. The treatment of these topics could scarcely be bettered, and therefore with specific exceptions for matters not treated in that book neither the collegiate life of the Inn nor biography of eminent members appears here. The second is a monograph, *The Chapels of Lincoln's Inn since 1422*, by Dr Stella Baker. That book sprang from her long and close association with the Chapel, and reflects far more knowledge, with corresponding information and dates, than is to be found in the relevant section of this book.

All books on the Inn stand in the shadow of *The Black Books*: six volumes comprising some three and a half thousand pages of edited and reprinted records of the domestic business of the Society since 1422, with scholarly introductions by their successive editors, plus two volumes of lists of admissions of members, published at intervals over the last hundred years. A few quotations here have, with due acknowledgement, been borrowed from those books. Conversely, most of the words quoted and images reproduced here fall outside the scope of *The Black Books*, and do not appear there.

Many people have been selfless in their help to me in compiling this book. Almost no-one to whom I wrote ever failed to respond. I wish to thank here a small number of them above all. The successive Treasurers of the Society over the years of my assembling material for this book unprecedentedly and unconditionally gave me free access to the Society's library, archives and art. Among them, Lord Walker of Gestingthorpe has always discreetly encouraged my research into the visual history of the Inn and my hope to publish the results, and he has graciously lent his name to this book by contributing a Foreword. Correspondingly the present Treasurer, Sir William Blackburne, has written a generous Preface and made a number of suggestions as to the text, upon which I have been glad to act. Professor Sir John Baker of Cambridge University has unstintingly helped me on points of legal history, both general and specific to this Inn. He has written an historical essay and compiled a glossary especially for this book, which have the learning and authority to which my compilation manifestly does not aspire. My old friend George C White of the Eugene O'Neill Theater Center in Waterford, Connecticut, took time and trouble to introduce me and my wife to and guide us around the Yale Center for British Art at his *alma mater* in New Haven. He and his wife Betsy generously offered us accommodation and hospitality while on our visit. That fine gallery possesses the earliest oil painting, and original watercolours, of the Inn—all unknown here and their significance unrecognised there until found in the course of research for this book—and a version of the oil painting by Hogarth of the Lincoln's Inn Fields Theatre. The owner of an English Private Collection readily agreed to my reproducing his fine Samuel Scott of the Inn in *ca.* 1740, without which the visual record of the Inn would have been incomplete. Angela Holdsworth very kindly discussed the contents of the book, then in the course of preparation, under her editorship. This helped me to focus my accumulated material and reduce to a minimum the areas of duplication. Mark Ockelton, a bencher of the Society, kindly read the typescript and made helpful comments. The Society's learned librarian, Guy Holborn, has always been willing to share his extensive knowledge of the Inn and guide my researches in the Society's library and archives, and impart his experience of book production. Recently, the Inn's archivist, Robert Athol, has been most helpful. Last—and as a representative of others—the New England antiquarian bookseller who was happy to trudge through the snow of a winter's afternoon to find a rare first edition in her shop and post it to me. To each I am greatly indebted, for without them this compilation could not exist.

I hope that for those to whom this Inn has special meaning, or to whom the Inns of Court generally are of interest, this book may inform, surprise, gladden the heart, or even move to shed a tear. It will not, I trust, diminish the honour of the Society, and may even enhance it.

Izaak Walton—in his day a close friend of several members of the Society and a resident nearby in Chancery Lane—made a number of pithy observations in his preface to *The Compleat Angler*, 1653, of which I borrow two for this book. One was: 'I wish the reader also to take notice that… it might… not read dull and tediously, I have in several places mixt… some innocent, harmless mirth; of which if thou be a severe, sowre-complexion'd man, then I here disallow thee to be a competent judge…'. The other was: 'And next let me add this, that he that likes not the book, should like the excellent picture[s]… which I may take the liberty to commend, because [they] concern not myself'.

The research for and compilation of this book have been a personal occupation, but the publication has been made possible by the support of the officers and staff of the Society, among whom I would particularly like to thank the present Under-Treasurer, Mary Kerr, and Deputy Under-Treasurer, Murray Campbell. All errors of historiography or topography are to be laid—or, should I rather say, piled up—at my door.

Graham S Brown

ALPHABETICAL LIST OF AUTHORS, PERIODICALS & BOOKS QUOTED OR CITED

The references are to the section or sub-section in which the quotation appears. Where appropriate, a note in brackets indicates the subject matter, not invariably by repeating the section heading under which it appears in this book. Intermediate sources (which may be cited in the text) are omitted. Names of persons known to have been members of the Society are asterisked. It may be surmised that most of the anonymous pieces were also by members. Where more than one work by the same author is quoted, the works are in alphabetical order of title, and then by paragraph number of this book. For serial publications, and for anonymous writings, multiple entries are in date order. The underlining of a single letter indicates the same meaning as *sic*. Some titles have been shortened for reasons of space.

Addison, Joseph	*Spectator*, 1711	(dancing)	6.3.3.i.
		(lawyers in playhouses)	36.2.
	Tatler, 1709	(LI Gardens)	21.5.
Albery, Michael*, QC	'Eros in LI', mid-C20th	(New Squ., LI)	16.5.2.
	'Registrar in Bankruptcy', mid-C20th	(Bankruptcy Courts)	34.11.
	'Trumpets Again', 1939-1940	(Second World War)	44.1.5.i.
Aldington, Richard	*Wellington*, 1946	(Duke of Wellington in LI)	43.3.4.
Ames, Richard*	*Folly of Love, or an Essay... Against Woman*, 1691	(LI Gardens)	21.2.
	Lawyerus Bootatus and Spurratus..., 1691	(long vacation)	42.4.
Anderson, Sir Henry, Bart*	'On Charls the Porter of LI', 1631	(porters)	31.2.
Annual Register, The	[chimneys falling in storm] 1790		19.2.
Arbuthnot, Dr John	'The Kit Cat Club', C18th	(clubs adjacent to LI)	37.2.
Archer Shee, Martin*	'Lay of the Lincoln's Inn Legion', 1848	(Chartists at the gates of LI)	43.3.5.
Ashworth, Margaret	'On Living in LI', 1930	(Stone Bldgs., LI)	18.1.2.
		(LI Gardens)	21.1.
		(Épée Club)	44.1.5.i.
		(aerial bombing)	44.2.1.
Asquith, H H*, PM	Speech of Dedication of War Memorial, 1921		44.3.
Aubrey, John	*Brief Lives*, 1679-80	(a LI bricklayer)	31.1.
		(drinking: Sir John Denham*)	39.2.
Baker, Sir John H	'Origin and early character of LI'		Hist. Essay
	Glossary of terms used in LI		Appx.
Banks, Prof A Leslie	*LI Fields*, 1980	(solicitors' clerks)	30.
Barr, David	'Country Solicitor visits his London Agents', 1989	(LI solicitors' practices)	28.5.
Barrett-Lennard, Rev Sir Hugh, Bt.	*Last week we had a dreadful strike...*, 1926	(General Strike)	43.3.6.
Batt, John*	Letter, 1780	(Gordon riots)	43.3.3.
Bennett, Arnold	*A Man from the North*, 1898	(New Court, LI)	24.

Bennett, Richard Rodney	*Five Carols*, 1967	(LI carol)	6.3.2.
Betjeman, John	'Lord Cozens-Hardy'*, 1958	(spirits of members)	45.3.
Black Books, The	Minutes of Council, 1565	(laundresses)	31.4.i.
	'Naparye in the Buttrye', 1570	(kitchen utensils)	12.2.ii.
	Minutes of Council, 1613	(appointment of porter)	31.2.
	Minutes of Council, 1675	(a LI bricklayer)	31.1.
	Report of the Poor Children's Treat Committee, 1893	(children in Gardens)	33.ii.
Blackmore, Sir Richard	'The Kit-Cats', 1708	(clubs adjacent to LI)	37.2.
Bladen, Nathaniel	[Six Clerks] 1701		34.1.
Bloomsbury and Inns of Court Assoc. Minutes, 1798		(LI Volunteers)	44.1.2.
British Architect, The	'Street Architecture', 1889	(More's Passage, LI)	3.7.
		(More Ho., LI)	20.1.1.
Buc, Sir George	'England's Third University', 1615	(Thavies Inn)	22.1.
Builder, The	[wall painting in Old Bldgs., LI] 1885		11.1.
	[New Squ., LI] 1891		15.1.4.
Burney, Fanny	Letter, 1821	(Accountant-General's Office in LI)	18.2.3.
Bush, Geoffrey	'Fog', mid-C20th	(LI Old Hall)	6.5.1.
Butler, Samuel	*Hudibras*, 1680	(LI Chapel Undercroft)	5.2.2.
	*William Prynne**, 1669	(LI Chapel Undercroft)	5.2.3.
Byrd, William	*London Diary*, 1717-21	(lewd gentry)	2.4.4.
		(LI coffee house)	15.3.
Campbell, Lord	*Lives of the Lord Chancellors*, 1847	(Hardwicke*)	20.4.2.
'Caudwell, Sarah' (Sarah Cockburn*)	*The Sirens sang of Murder*, 1989	(Queen's Counsel)	27.1.
	Thus was Adonis Murdered, 1989	(Clerks)	29.
Canning, George*	*The Pilot that weathered the storm*, 1802	(Pitt*)	18.1.3.
Cavendish, George	*Life of Cardinal Wolsey, ca.* 1557	(Chancery La.)	2.3.3.i.
Chamberlain, John	Letter to Dudley Carleton, 1623	(LI Chapel)	4.2.1.i.
Church, Richard	'The Bonfire', 1936	(LI gardeners)	31.3.
	Green Tide, 1945	(Chancery La.)	2.3.1.
		(Old Squ., LI)	13.1.
	The Voyage Home, 1964	(Old Squ., LI)	13.1.
Clare, John	*Autobiographical Notes*, 1824	(Chancery La.)	2.3.1.
Cockayne, Sir Aston	'On Mr Francis Lenton* refusing Wine', 1658		39.2.
Cole, Arthur*	'Dogs Only', C20th	(LI Gardens)	21.2.
Coleridge, Samuel Taylor	'To the Hon Mr Erskine'*, 1794		20.5.2.
Collyer, James	*An Historical Record of the Light Horse...*, 1843	(LI Volunteers)	44.1.2.
Congreve, William	*Love for Love*, 1695	(Lisle's tennis court off LI Fields)	36.1.
Cook, Mrs E T	*Highways and Byways in London*, 1902	(LI Fields)	2.4.
		(Quality Ct.)	34.6.
'Copywell, Jemmy' (William Woty)	*Vacation in Lincoln's Inn*, 1758		42.2.
Cottle, Basil	*Lincoln's Inn*, 1993	(LI Chapel)	4.2.4.
Courrier de l'Europe, Le	'News from London', 1845	(LI New Hall)	8.2.

Fortescue, Sir John*	*De Laudibus Legum Anglie*, *ca.* 1470	(Inns of Chancery)	22.
	Who wyll be ware, mid-C15th	(conveyancers)	27.2.
Galsworthy, John*	*In Chancery—The Forsyte Saga*, 1920	(LI Volunteers)	44.1.4.
	'Youth's Own', 1934	(dead of First World War)	44.1.5.ii.
Gay, John	*Trivia*, 1716	(Strand)	2.2.i.
		(LI Fields)	2.4.5.
Gentleman's Magazine, The	[Fires] 1752		15.6.
	[Thomas Wildman] 1796		28.1.ii.
Gilbert, Michael	*Smallbone Deceased*, 1950	(LI solicitors)	28.3.
Gill, Eric	*Autobiography*, 1940	(Old Bldgs., LI)	12.1.
Goldsmith, Oliver	'A Description of the Courts of Justice in Westminster Hall', 1760	(long vacation)	42.2.
	'Retaliation', 1774	(Garrick*)	36.2.
Graham, Prof David	*Bankruptcy, Insolvency and Corporate Rescue*, 2009	(Bankruptcy Courts)	34.11.
Grant Duff, Sir Mountstuart	*Notes from a Library*, 1897	(worship in LI Chapel)	4.2.1.ii.
Granville-Barker, Harley	*The Voysey Inheritance*, 1903	(LI solicitors)	28.3.
Gray, Thomas	*Elegy*, 1751	(long vacation)	42.2.
Greenaway, Walter and Lee, Alfred	*Serjeant Sharp of Lincoln's Inn*, 1872	(music halls)	40.
Greene, John*	*Diary*, 1635	(dancing in LI Hall)	6.3.3.
Griffiths, Elizabeth	*School for Rakes*, 1769	(LI coffee house)	15.3.
Habington, William	*To my worthy Cousin Mr E C In Praise of the City Life…*, 1634	(long vacation in Inns)	42.3.
Hailsham of St Marylebone, Lord*, LC	*Legal Ghosts*, 1968		45.2.
	'Sidi Rezegh', 1968	(dead of Second World War)	44.1.5.ii.
Hakewill, William*	*Middle Temple Manuscript*, 1620-38	(the bishop's Hall)	6.
		(beating parish bounds in LI)	16.1.
		(watchwords in Furnival's Inn)	22.2.2.
		(feasts in Furnival's Inn)	22.2.2.
Hale, Sir Matthew*	Will	(Old Library Bldg., LI)	14.2.1.
Hamilton, James	*Arthur Rackham, A Life with Illustration*, 1990	(New Ct., LI)	24.
Harington, Sir John*	*The Metamorphosed A Jax*, 1596	(LI Privy)	21.3.
Harwood, Miles	'Lincoln's Inn Fields', 1999	(music)	2.4.
Hawthorne, Nathaniel	*English Notebook*, 1853-58	(entering gates of an Inn)	3.1.
		(worship in LI Chapel)	4.2.1.ii.
Hayman, Richard*	*Quodlibets*, 1628	(dancing in LI Hall)	6.3.3.
Haynes, E S P	*The Lawyer, a conversation piece*, 1951	(12-13, New Squ., LI)	12.3.
		(dissolution of LI solicitors' partnership)	28.2.
Heckethorn, C W	*Lincoln's Inn Fields*, 1896	(Bankruptcy Court)	34.11.
Henley, W E	'London Voluntary', 1908	(Fleet St.)	2.2.i.
Herbert, W	*Antiquities of the Inns of Court and Chancery*, 1804	(fountain, New Squ., LI)	16.4.
		(New Squ. staircases)	19.1.
		(prospect of LI Fields)	21.4.
		(Furnival's Inn)	22.2.1.
Hollams, Sir John	*Jottings of an Old Solicitor*, 1906	(Chancery Masters' Office)	34.6.

Hook, Theodore	*Ass-ass-Ination*, 1809	(Erskine*)	20.5.2.
Hughes, Thomas*	*Journal*, 1845	(Serle's Gate, LI)	3.6.
Hunt, Leigh	*Town*, 1848	(Chancery La.)	2.3.3.ii.
Hurst, Sir Gerald*	*Short History of LI*, 1946	(tolling LI Chapel bell)	4.2.6.
Husee, John	*Letters* to Lady Lisle, 1534/5	(textiles in chambers in LI)	19.3.
Ireland, Samuel	*Picturesque Views of the Inns…*, 1800	(Stone Bldgs., LI)	18.1.1.
James I	*Letters Patent*, 1617	(volunteers in Inns)	44.1.1.
James, Henry	*Notebooks*, 1907	(More's Gate, LI)	3.7.
Johnson, Edward	*Letter*, 1902	(post box in LI)	32.1.
Johnson, Richard	'London's Description', 1607	(law terms)	42.1.
Jones, E and Woodward, C	*Architecture of London*, 1983	(Stone Bldgs., LI)	18.1.1.
Jones, Sydney R	*Thames Triumphant*, 1942	(New Squ., LI)	15.1.2.
Jonson, Ben	*Devil is an Ass*, 1616	(Baptist's Head Yard)	11.2.2.
		(LI Gardens)	21.1.
	Every man out of his own humour, 1599	(benchers of the Inns)	Dedic.
	Leges Convivales, Sociable Rules for the Apollo, ca. 1619	(clubs)	37.2.
	Witticism, *ca.* 1590		31.1.2.
Kingsley, Rev Charles*	*Invitation (to Tom Hughes*)*, 1856	(long vacation)	42.4.
Kyd, Thomas	*In Cygneam Cantionem Chideochi Tychborne*	(executions in LI Fields)	2.4.2.
Lach-Szyrma, Krystyn	*Reminiscences of a Journey Through England and Scotland*, 1820-24	(Eldon LC in Old Hall, LI)	6.5.2.
Lamb, Charles	'A Complaint of the Decay of Beggars in the Metropolis', 1823	(outside LI Wall)	2.4.5.
	'Old Benchers of the Inner Temple', 1821	(fountain, New Squ.)	16.4.
Lancaster, Osbert	*Homes Sweet Homes*, 1964	(decoration and furnishing of chambers)	13.3.
Langley, Batty	*Grub St. Journal*, 1735	(LI Chapel Undercroft)	5.1.
Lease, 17th June, 1745	Inventory of Chambers	(New Squ., LI)	15.1.1.
Lenton, Francis*	*Young Gallant's Whirligigg*, 1629	(life of students)	35.1.
Levy, Amy	'A London Plane Tree', 1899	(Garden, New Squ.)	16.5.1.
'Limner, Luke' (John Leighton)	*The Cries of London*, 1851	(itinerant traders in LI)	32.4.
Lincoln's Inn Act, 1860	Preamble	('flying freeholds' in New Sq., LI)	15.2.
Lloyd's News	'Old Apple Stall at LI', 1912		32.3.
Luttrell, Narcissus	*Diary*, 1692	(New Squ.)	18.2.
Lydgate, John	*London Lickpenny*, C14th	(Master of the Rolls' Court)	34.2.
M'Leod, Addison	*A Window in LI…*, 1897	(New Squ., LI)	15.1.2.
McLeod, Mona	*London Observed: A Polish Philosopher at Large…*, 2009	(Eldon LC in Old Hall, LI)	6.5.2.
Macaulay, Thomas, Lord*	*Indian Penal Code*, 1860		27.3.
	*Lines to the Memory of Pitt**, 1813		18.1.3.
Marriott, N M	Letters to the Benchers, 1940-1	(aerial bombing in LI)	44.2.1.
Marston, John	*What you will*, 1607	(LI Privy)	21.3.
Mathew, Theo*	*For Lawyers and Others*, 1937	(Six Clerks' Office in LI)	18.2.2.
Mayhew, Henry	*London Labour and the London Poor*, 1851	(street sweeper of Chancery La.)	2.3.2.
		('dress-lodger-follower')	40.
Mayhew, Henry and Binney, John	*Scenes of London Life*, 1862	(gates)	3.1.
		(Chichester Rents Gate)	3.4.2.ii.
		(doorways)	19.1.

Melville, Herman	*The Paradise of Bachelors and the Tartarus of Maids*, 1855	(approaching the Inns)	3.1.
Micklem, Nathaniel, HH*	'Homage to Chambers', 1983	(New Court, LI)	24.
	'Spring in LI', 1958	(LI Gardens)	21.1.
Mirror of Literature, Amusement and Instruction, 1838		(Serjeants' Inn)	34.8.
Moore, Thomas	*Lines on the Death of Mr P-R-C-V-L*, 1812	(LI Chapel Memorials)	4.2.5.
More, Sir (St) Thomas, LC*	*(see Roper, William)*		
Moreland, Arthur	*Dickens Landmarks in London*, 1928	(Thavies Inn)	23.2.
Moser, Joseph	'Vestiges', 1803	(coffee-houses)	37.1.
Nairn, Ian	*Nairn's London*, 1966	(Stone Bldgs., LI)	3.2.
Napoléon I	Will, 1821	(LI solicitors' practices)	28.1.iii.b.
Newbolt, Sir Henry*	'The Non-Combatant', 1898	(LI Volunteers)	44.1.4.
	The Twymans, 1892	(entering the Inns)	3.1.
Newman, Blessed John*	*The Dream of Gerontius*, 1865	(worship in LI Chapel)	4.2.1.ii.
Newton, Douglas	*London West of the Bars*, 1951	(Old Squ., LI)	11.2.1.
Nugee, Rose	'I do not know', 2015	(Chancery Counsel in LI)	27.2
Ockelton, Mark*	*A Portrait of Lincoln's Inn*, 2007	(Watts' fresco)	8.4.
Ord, Robert*	Letter, 1752	(fires)	15.6.
OED	'Base Court'		17.4.
	'Bog House'		17.4.
	'Chancery'		32.2.
	'Epithalamion'		6.3.4.
	'Laundress'		31.4.
	'Masque'		2.2.3.
	'Purlieu'		3.1.
	'Snob'		43.3.5.
	'Toucher'		23.2.
Pall Mall Budget, The	'Piper and the Poor Children', 1891	(children in LI Gardens)	33.i.
Partridge, Eric	*Dictionary of Slang and Unconventional English*, 1984	('Lincoln's Inn')	32.2.
Payne, Joseph*	'Lines on… the opening of LI New Hall', 1845	(LI New Hall)	8.2.
Penn, William*	*Frame of Government of the Free Society of Traders of Pensilvania*, 1682		27.3.
Pepler, Hilary	'The Devil's Devices', 1915	(conveyancers)	27.2.
Pepys, Samuel	*Diary*, 1663	(approaches to LI)	2.1.
		(LI Gardens)	21.1.
		(LI Chapel Undercroft)	5.2.2.
	Diary, 1660	(Six Clerks)	34.1.
		(Master of the Rolls' Court)	34.2.
	Diary, 1669	(Master of the Rolls' Court)	34.2.
Peterborough, Earl of	Letter, C17th	(Laws of Pennsylvania)	27.3.
Piper, David	*Companion Guide to London*, 1992	(Chancery counsel)	27.2.
Pitt, William, yngr*., PM	Letter, 1780	(rioters outside LI)	43.3.3.
Playfair, William	*British Family Antiquity*, 1809-11	(LI solicitors' practices)	28.1.i.
Playford, John	*LI*, in *The English Dancing Master*, 1703	(LI dance)	6.3.3.
Pope, Alexander	*The Dunciad*, 1728	(Chancery La.)	2.3.1.
	The Dunciad, 1742	(dancing in LI Hall)	6.3.3.
	First Ode of the Fourth Book of Horace, ca. 1740	(Lord Mansfield*, LCJ)	11.1.

Summerson, Sir John	*Architecture in Britain 1530-1830*, 1991	(Stone Bldgs., LI)	18.1.
Surtees, R S	*Handley Cross, or Mr Jorrocks's Hunt*, 1843	(barristers' clerks)	29.
Swift, Jonathan	'Description of a City Shower', 1710	(coffee houses adjacent to Inns)	37.1.
Tearle, Christian (ET Jaques)	'The Ghosts of LI', 1911		45.2.
Tennyson, Alfred, Lord	*In Memoriam*, 1850	(purlieus of LI)	3.1.
	'To the Rev F D Maurice', 1854	(Chaplain of LI)	43.1.
	'Will Waterproof's Lyrical Monologue, made at the Cock', 1842	(taverns)	39.1.
Thackeray, William Makepeace	*The History of Pendennis*, 1850	(Inns of Chancery)	23.1.
Thoresby, Ralph	*Diary*, 1714	(foundation of SPCK in LI)	15.4.
Tichborne, Chidiock	'Elegy, written with his own hand in the Tower…', 1586	(executions in LI Fields)	2.4.2.
Times, The	'Division of Parishes', 1840	(extra-parochiality of LI)	16.2.
	[Junior V-Cs' Courts in LI] 1841		11.3.
	'Polygamy in LI', 1930	(ducks in New Squ., LI)	16.5.2.
	[Trees, New Squ.]		16.5.1.
Torriano, Giovanni	*Commonplace of Italian Proverbs and Phrases*, 1666	(Furnival's Inn students)	22.2.2.
Trollope, Anthony	*Can you forgive her?*, 1864	(purlieus of LI)	
		(Accountant-General's Office in LI)	18.2.3.
		(Symond's Inn)	34.4.
	The Eustace Diamonds, 1872	(solicitor consulting counsel in LI)	28.4.
	Orley Farm, 1862	(counsel's chambers in LI)	27.1.
		(barristers' clerks)	29.
	Phineas Finn, 1868	(barristers' choices of careers)	25.2.
	The Prime Minister, 1875	(V-C's Court)	14.2.2.
		(Stone Bldgs., LI)	18.1.2.
	'The Spotted Dog', 1870	(LI Gates)	3.2.2.
Vaughan, Henry	*A Rhapsody, written… at the Globe*, 1641	(approaches to LI)	2.2.1.i.
Vitoria, Mary, QC*	*The Conveyancer and Property Lawyer*, 1977	(flying freeholds)	15.2.
Walton, Izaak	*The Compleat Angler*, 1653		Editor's Note
Warburton, William, Bishop	*Epigram*, C18th	(worship in LI Chapel)	4.2.1.ii.
Ward, Ned	*The London Spy*, 1703	(LI Fields)	2.4.5.
	A Vade Mecum for Malt-Worms, 1712	(taverns)	39.1.
Weedon, Cavendish	[Offices of Chancery]	18.2.	
Wellington, Duke of, PM	Eulogy to Eleanor Louise Brougham, 1834	(LI Chapel Undercroft)	5.2.3.
Whetstone, George	'Fifty Apples of Admonition… to… Gentlemen of Furnivall's Inn', 1576	(law students)	22.2.2.
Whitelocke, Bulstrode	*Memorials of The English Affairs*, 1682	(masques)	2.3.3.i.
Whitney, Isabella	*A Sweet Nosegay*, 1573	(distractions to law students)	35.1.
'W.I.'	*The Whipping of the Satyre*, 1601	(revels in Inns)	6.3.1.
Wither, George*	*A Collection of Emblems*, 1635	(planting of gardens)	21.6.
Woolf, Virginia	*Diary*, 1941	(aerial bombing)	44.2.2.
Wordsworth, William	*Prelude*, 1805	(approaching Inns)	3.1.
Wynne, Edward	*Eunomus*, 1774	(location of Inns)	1.2.

Anon. (? J Stephens*)	'Satire', in *Poems on the Affairs of State 1640-1704*	(LI Wall)	2.4.5.
Anon.	Simile, ? C18th	(LI Gates)	3.1.
Anon. words and music	'Nowell, Nowell, Nowell!' (or 'Out of your slepe'), C15th	(LI carol)	6.3.2.
Anon. words and music	'Mirth and Solace', 1625	(LI song)	6.3.2.
Anon. music	'The Howe of the House', C16th	(LI dance)	6.3.3.
Anon.	Epigram, *ca.* 1815	(LC and V-C)	6.5.2.
Anon.	*Brief and Papers, Sketches of the Bar and Press*, 1872	(junior V-Cs' courts)	11.3
Anon.	Epigram, *ca.* 1820	(LC and V-C)	14.2.2.ii.
Anon.	'A Litany wrote in a LI Boghouse', 1672	(LI Privy)	17.4.
Anon.	Inscription, All Saints', Chitterne, Wilts	(chimneys)	19.2.
Anon.	Doggerel	(LI Gardens)	21.1.
Anon.	'The Fair Shoot at a Foul Mark, or a New Way of Wooing', 1741	(LI Gardens)	21.2.
Anon.	Doggerel	(LI Wall)	21.4.
		(Conveyancers)	27.2.
Anon.	Inscription, St Peter's, Iver, Bucks	(LI bricklayer)	31.1.
Anon.	'On the Three Dukes Killing the Beadle On Sunday Morning, Feb. the 26th 1670/1', 1671	(bawdy houses adjacent to LI)	40.
Anon.	*A True relation of a most Desperate Murder…*, 1617	(murder in LI)	43.2.
Anon.	'The Barriers', 1616	(masques, etc.)	44.1.1.
Anon. words and music	'Nancy Dawson', 1727 or earlier	(LI Volunteers)	44.1.2.
Anon. words and music	'Molly put the kettle on', *ca.* 1790	(LI Volunteers)	44.1.2.

LIST OF PROSPECTS, MAPS AND PLANS

ABBREVIATIONS & SYMBOLS, AND PREFATORY NOTES

December 2015

TOPOGRAPHICAL & COLLEGIATE

- HSLI — The Honourable Society of Lincoln's Inn
- of LI, of GI, of MT and of IT — a member of one of those four Inns of Court, including those who enrolled and did not pursue their career and proceed to call, or those who were called but did not practise; and those enrolled but in former times not permitted on religious grounds (as Catholics or Jews) to be called and practise as barristers, but did so as equity draftsmen or special pleaders; or those who were attorneys and not permitted also to be called to the Bar
- the Society — the collegiate body of benchers, barristers and students of HSLI
- the Inn — is normally used here to mean the buildings (and the grounds within the gates) owned or occupied by the Society
- Inn — an Inn of Court or Chancery or Serjeants—not, unless suitably qualified, a tavern or coaching inn
- OTC — Officers' Training Corps
- n., s., e. and w. — refer to the points of the compass, taking the Inn to be aligned n.-s.
- n., s., e. and w. view — a view *towards* that point of the compass
- St. — Street

GENERAL

- C — century
- c. — chapter (of an Act of Parliament)
- *ca.* — *circa*
- coll. — collection of
- ed. — editor/ed
- edn. — edition
- *fo.* — folio (page)
- *ibid* — the same
- *ILN* — *Illustrated London News*
- *JSPTL* — *Journal of the Society of Public Teachers of Law*
- *loc. cit.* — in the place already mentioned
- *LQR* — *Law Quarterly Review*
- *N & Q* — *Notes and Queries*
- *ODNB* — *Oxford Dictionary of National Biography*
- *OED* — *Oxford English Dictionary*

- *op. cit.* — in the book of which the title is given elsewhere in this book
- posth. — posthumously
- publ. — published
- *r.* and *v.* — *recto* (front of a page or leaf of a manuscript), *verso* (back of *ditto*)
- *sic* — written or printed thus
- St or S — Saint

PROFESSIONAL

- CB — Chief Baron (of the Court of Exchequer)
- CJ — Chief Justice
- HH — His Honour
- J — holder of any judicial office not otherwise designated here, but usually a High Court Judge
- LC — Lord Chancellor
- LCI — Lord Chancellor of Ireland
- LCJ — Lord Chief Justice
- MR — Master of the Rolls
- PM — Prime Minister
- PPLS — Past President of the Law Society of England and Wales
- PPRIBA — Past President of the Royal Institute of British Architects
- V-C — Vice-Chancellor (of the High Court of Chancery)

LIBRARIES, GALLERIES & COLLECTIONS

- BL — British Library
- BM — British Museum
- Bodleian — Bodleian Library, Oxford
- CCC — Corpus Christi College, Cambridge
- CLHL — Camden Local History Library, London
- CUL — Cambridge University Library
- CWA — City of Westminster Archives
- Folger — Folger Library, Washington, DC, USA
- GL — City of London Guildhall Library
- ICCEY — Inns of Court & City and Essex Yeomanry: the name of the Inn's Volunteers at the present day (and its museum and archives in the Inn)
- *ILN* — *Illustrated London News* [for the *ILN*, the varying picture credits are determined by the location of the printed illustration photographed and by the date of the permission. Where no credit is given, the photograph is a press-cutting in a library, which required no acknowledgement.]
- *ILN*PL — *Illustrated London News* Picture Library
- LMA — City of London Metropolitan Archives (amalgamating the City of London Guildhall Library Prints & Drawings collection with that of the Greater London Record Office)
- LS — Law Society's Library
- LT — Lindum Trust (Charity 328240 England)
- Mary Evans — Mary Evans Picture Library, Blackheath, London
- MoL — Museum of London

- MRBB — Musées royaux des Beaux-Arts de Belgique, Bruxelles
- NPG — National Portrait Gallery, London
- NYCPL — New York City Public Library, New York, NY, USA
- PHB — Payne Hicks Beach, solicitors in Lincoln's Inn
- PLMC — Pepysian Library, Magdalene College, Cambridge
- PML — Pierpont Morgan Library, New York, NY, USA
- PRO — Public Record Office, Kew, London
- RCHM — Royal Commission on Historic Monuments
- RCJ — Royal Courts of Justice, in the Strand, London
- RIBA — Royal Institute of British Architects, or a Fellow or Associate thereof
- RSA — Royal Society of Arts, London
- SoAL — Society of Antiquaries of London
- SoFP — Society of Friends, Philadelphia, PA, USA
- SM — Sir John Soane's Museum, London
- V&A — Victoria and Albert Museum, London
- YCBA — Yale Center for British Art, New Haven, CT, USA

•	Text printed in Univers indicates Minutes or Orders of Council of the Society, written in the MS Black Books or re-printed in *The Black Books*.
•	Numbers alone, printed in ordinary (roman) type indicate paragraph or sub-paragraph sections or sub-sections, and numbers followed by a letter, both printed in italic type, indicate an illustration.
>	Where a quotation or illustration would not have come to the Editor's notice but for being reprinted in a modern book or journal, that intermediate source is indicated thus. Where the material is widely reprinted, no such acknowledgement is given. The symbol is also used to credit the person who was the source of an explanation printed as a footnote to a quotation or a caption to an illustration reprinted here.
>>	Indicates the Editor's indebtedness to a person who has drawn the quotation or picture to his attention, when otherwise he would not have found it; or who has given him a copy of the book or image.
[ ]	A bracket: at the end of a picture caption indicates the owner or custodian of the illustration reproduced and in most instances the giving of copyright permission to reprint here. The copyright may be either in the original art work or in the photograph of it. In respect of images created by living artists, or those who have died within the last seventy years, their name at the beginning of the picture caption should be taken to indicate their copyright and the giving of consent by them or their representatives as the case may be and for which due acknowledgement and thanks are given. Most holders of copyright in images or words have given permission either gratuitously or at a nominal fee and for which the Editor's gratitude is recorded. In the case of literary works, the intermediate source from which the Editor has found the piece is, wherever possible, named and credited.
{ }	A brace: indicates the grantor of copyright permission, if that is not apparent from the acknowledgement of the holder of the writing or art work.
¶	A pilcrow: an editorial explanation or introduction to a quotation.

PREFATORY NOTES

Commonplace books

These, in a legal context, were note books in which law students were expected to record material of value which they had encountered in their reading or in observing the legal practices of their elders. This is an extract from the advice on doing so from an older member of Lincoln's Inn to a student of the Inn:

'23 November 1659

For my nephew Maurice Eustace, Student at Lincolns Inne

My dear nephew I receaved yours of the 9th. instant wherein you propound these following doubts unto me viz

First how I would have you provide materialls for a future common place book & for this you must collect your materials out of the books you read & reduce them under apt heads & and lay them up in store as the painfull bees doe the honey they gather of severall flowers in their proper cells to which they by instinct of nature know when to goe upon occasion.

Secondlie whether in reading… you should make an index or abridgn of principall causes & for this you are to reduce your cases under apt & fit heads for it is already abridged to your handes.

Your very loving unkle Mau. E.'

> F W X Fincham, from *English Historical Review, CXXXVII*, January 1920.

The calendar

Two reasons contribute to confusion over English dates prior to 1751. The first is that the adoption of the more accurate Gregorian calendar in place of the Julian was later here than in many continental countries and so that when effected by the Calendar Act 1750, it required ten days on the calendar to be jumped to synchronise with those countries on the continent who were already using that calendar. The second is that from the C12th to that date, the English *legal* year began on 25th March, Lady Day, and thus, for example, 24th March 1720 was followed by 25th March 1721. Alternatively, to reduce confusion at the time, the days between 1st January and 24th March might have been written 1720/1. These are the combined reasons for the UK tax year's beginning on 6th April, in order not—in the year of change—to levy taxes or tithes twice for those ten days.

The confusion may have extended to the Editor, and some dates in the text may therefore be wrongly stated by a year.

THE ORIGIN AND EARLY CHARACTER OF LINCOLN'S INN

PROFESSOR SIR JOHN BAKER, QC, LLD, FBA

NO ONE KNOWS, AND NO ONE IS EVER LIKELY TO DISCOVER, the precise origin of the four inns of court. This is because, although they are in a sense colleges, they were not founded in the same way as colleges at the universities. The history of every Cambridge college is visible in its muniment room, stacked with charters and licences to purchase in mortmain, and in the historical recitation of its major endowments in the annual commemoration of the founder and benefactors. The inns of court have nothing comparable, for they had no founders or early benefactors to pray for, they have never sought charters of incorporation, and for centuries they did not own the freehold property in their sites. It is chiefly for want of such records that their origins are obscure, though the question of origin is also partly a question of definition. To the outside observer the inns of court are quiet havens from the bustle of the metropolis, full of fine and curious buildings and well-kept gardens, forming a legal quarter of London. Most of the buildings now standing can be dated with some precision. But the buildings and gardens were created by and for societies, with aims and purposes which are perhaps less well known to the general public than their visible possessions. The history of those societies is longer than that of any of the existing buildings. Even the story of the societies as we know them is not the whole story, for they have a prehistory.[1]

There were lawyers attending the king's courts at Westminster, and advising clients in London, by the 1230s, a century before the societies in the inns of court came into being. Not long after that there were students attending the courts to learn the law by observation. These 'apprentices of the Bench' are mentioned by that name in the 1280s. We know that such students had teachers who devised lectures, practical instruction and disputations; but who those teachers were, and how the education was organised, remain dark mysteries. If the law school was in a sense the court itself, we may safely guess that both practitioners and students required term-time accommodation in the suburbs of London, and it is certain that by the middle of the fourteenth century at the latest some of them were living in communities in the very places still associated with the law. On the other hand, there is no mention of any particular inn of court by name before 1388, and no evidence for the existence of distinct collegiate societies before about 1340. The reason is almost certainly that until that period the royal courts were not permanently stationed at Westminster. Troubles in Scotland took the administration (including the courts of law) on several occasions under Edward I to York, and its last sojourn there ended in 1338 when Scotland was abandoned to deal with France. Whenever these migrations occurred the lawyers moved north in force, much to the distress of the shopkeepers and landlords in Holborn and Fleet Street. It is not yet clear what happened to legal education when the courts were at York, but it is hardly likely that it could have remained behind, and it is even more unlikely that settled collegiate institutions could have grown up around movable courts. When a contract was made in 1323 to support a law student, it is noteworthy that the document does not mention any fixed institution or place but provides that he should be found for four years among the apprentices 'at our lord the king's court of Common Bench, wherever the said Bench should be in England'.[2] From 1339, however, it was apparently the accepted understanding that in future Westminster Palace would be the permanent home of royal justice: as indeed it remained until 1882, when the Royal Courts of Justice were opened in the Strand. The 'men of court'—the colloquial term for the lawyers and students attending the king's courts—no longer had to 'follow' the court in a mobile sense, wherever it should be in England, but could count on a permanent station for the foreseeable future. That may well have been what prompted the evolution of societies, groups of lawyers who combined to share lodgings and servants, and to nurture and develop the old exercises of learning. There are references from around 1340 to apprentices of the law living in the legal quarter of London, including the Temple, and to manciples, a term used only for servants employed by academical institutions.[3] The town-houses of the men of

1 The following account of the origins of the inns is based on the fuller essay in the introduction to J H Baker ed., *Readings and Moots at the Inns of Court in the Fifteenth Century,* ii (Selden Soc. vol. 105, 1990). The theme is enlarged upon in *The Third University of England* (Selden Soc. lecture, 1990), reprinted without the Latin texts in *Collected Papers on English Legal History* (2013), i, ch. 7. There is further relevant information in *The Men of Court* (2012).

2 M J Bennett, 'Provincial Gentlefolk and Legal Education' (1984), 57 *Bulletin of the Institute of Historical Research* 203 at 207. The Common Bench (later called the Common Pleas) usually sat in Westminster Hall, but with proper long notice it could be moved elsewhere.

3 For fourteenth-century manciples see Baker, *Third University of England*, 11-12; *Collected Papers*, i. 155-7.

court (*hospicia hominum curiae*) acquired by the early fifteenth century their present English description, 'inns of court'. But the Anglo-French word for *hospicia* is *hostels*, and as early as 1355 there is a reference in the law reports to pleading exercises taking place *en hostelles*. From that period, then, we may suppose the inns to have come into being as collegiate institutions of learning. As it happens, this was also the first major period of college foundation in the universities. Our lawyers' inns had contemporary academical parallels.

The present four inns of court were themselves only the most prominent of an indeterminate number of legal societies, some of which disappeared long ago, others of which survived until the nineteenth century, known collectively if puzzlingly as 'inns of chancery'.[4] There are no surviving domestic records for any of these inns, great or small, from the fourteenth century. It is therefore not in itself of significance that Lincoln's Inn is the last to be mentioned in extant sources. Its three sisters, however, are all mentioned in a manuscript year book which recorded a call of serjeants at law in 1388. Five of the new serjeants came from the Inner Temple, two from Gray's Inn and one from the Middle Temple.[5] The note is of great interest as showing not only that the lawyers in the Temple formed two societies in 1388, but also (by strong inference) that already the greater inns—those soon to be known as inns of court—had a general primacy over the inns of chancery and other lesser inns when it came to the selection of leading advocates. It has been argued by Sir Ronald Roxburgh that, if the inns of court had achieved such special status by 1388, it is probable that Lincoln's Inn was in existence at the same time. The argument is that it seems counter-intuitive to suppose that another society was added to the select group at a later stage.[6] But there may not yet have been a precise distinction between the greater and lesser inns, for we know that in 1417 a serjeant was called from Clifford's Inn and in 1425 another from the Outer Temple.

All we know for sure is that Lincoln's Inn was in existence as a society immediately prior to 1422, when its records begin. These records, known as the 'Black Books', are the oldest inns of court records remaining, and their main contents have been calendared in print. The first entry in those records contains a list of members appointed to stay in the Inn over the Christmas vacation in the first year of King Henry VI (1422), and indicates that for twelve of them it was their third Christmas. That takes the story back to December 1420. Moreover, in the second Black Book there is a caption for some lost steward's accounts of the Inn in the seventh year of Henry V (1419-20).[7] Assuming that the steward must have been in office for a year before rendering an account, the Society was therefore in existence by Michaelmas 1419. Since there is nothing in the Black Books to suggest a recent origin, it could be older than that. Indeed there is evidence of a slightly earlier existence in the mention of one Thomas Brown as a manciple of 'Lyncolnesynne' in 1417.[8] That, however, is as far back as explicit sources will take us.

Speculation can carry us further, but the journey is not necessarily a safe one. Roxburgh argued that since some of the apprentices who refused the coif in 1417 appear as members of Lincoln's Inn in 1422, and since the governors and other members mentioned from 1422 onwards were quite senior, there must have been a Lincoln's Inn by the 1390s;[9] and he considered it a further piece of evidence that Lincoln's Inn boasted members who were described in 1421 as 'apprentices of the law', supposing that this had come to mean well-established lawyers.[10] But the argument is a *non sequitur*, since at some stage there must have been a first contingent of members. The senior members mentioned above could have migrated from elsewhere. The term 'apprentice of the law', moreover, even if it had lost its student connotations, was still quite vague in meaning. There were, it is true, some 'great apprentices of the law' (as mentioned in the poll-tax commission of 1379), but there were also some very obscure ones, the 'apprentices de meindre estate'.[11] Roxburgh attached much weight to the evidence which the Black Books afford of a settled constitution and customs, and the absence of any written orders introducing them, as indicating their continuance from some good time before 1422.[12] This is more persuasive but far from conclusive, because it assumes that the Black Books were intended to be a comprehensive record. In fact they were primarily concerned with routine business, especially of a financial nature, and omit many things which would greatly interest us now—such as the duties of readers, the appointment of readers and benchers prior to 1465, or calls to the Bar prior to 1518. It is not

4 By the fifteenth century the inns of chancery were primarily for younger students, but also for practising attorneys who lived in them and kept their offices there. Nine survived after medieval times, and two of them (Furnival's Inn and Thavies Inn) came to be associated with Lincoln's Inn.

5 J H Baker, *The Order of Serjeants at Law* (1984), 256; *Collected Papers*, i. 168-72.

6 *Two Postscripts to the Black Books Vol. V* (1977), 24; 94 *LQR* (1978), p. 376. Sir Ronald gave warm encouragement to the present writer's earlier researches and showed an endless curiosity in all aspects of the history of the Inn. It is regrettable that it has not proved possible to support all his conclusions about its origins.

7 MS Black Book II, fo. 64v, reversing ('Expensa hospicii de Lincoln. Inne facta per J… …er seneschallem ejusdem hospicii anno regni regis Henrici quinti post conquestum Anglie septimo'). Nothing follows the heading, but the hand is of the early fifteenth century and it seems beyond doubt that this relates to an actual stewardship. This fragment was omitted from the printed Black Books and has been generally overlooked.

8 Williams, *Early Holborn*, nos. 688, 1080, citing the City of London Letter Books. The reference is not, however, to be found in the printed *Calendar of Letter-Books* compiled by R R Sharpe. Williams thought the reference was to Serjeant Lincoln's Inn in Holborn (below); but this was a mere guess. The office of manciple is not mentioned in the Black Books until 1464, but thereafter it is common.

9 *Two Postscripts*, 24-25; 94 *LQR* 379-380.

10 One John Forster is described as an apprentice of the law in 'Lyncolnesynne' in August 1421: A H Thomas, *Calendar of Plea and Memoranda Rolls of the City of London 1413-37* (1943), 112. He is mentioned on fo. 7 of MS Black Book I (*BB*, i. 1).

11 See *The Men of Court*, i. 15. There are two instances from the 1420s of attorneys being described as apprentices of the law.

12 *The Origins of Lincoln's Inn* (1963), 28-31.

inconceivable that a newly founded Lincoln's Inn would have based its usages on those of older societies, especially since all the inns had inherited a pre-existing educational system. Given the unlikelihood that the four inns of court all came into being at the same time, the general congruence of their customs must indicate mutual emulation. In any case, none of the other inns of court had written constitutions. Roxburgh's further speculations therefore add little or nothing to his 1388 theory. There is a better argument, perhaps, from silence: there are hardly any references to the other inns of court between 1388 and 1422 either, whereas the creation of a major new society *ab initio* at so late a date is something which might have found mention in external sources.

Which Lincoln?

The principal clue to the origin of Lincoln's Inn, if only we could interpret it correctly, must be the name itself. By the time of its first known mention, at the end of Henry V's reign, there was no living person called Lincoln likely to have been associated with it. The name must therefore point back to an earlier age. The clue, however, is ambiguous, since there were two other places called Lincoln's Inn with legal associations in the western suburbs of London. The name Lincoln was even associated with a third pre-1400 *hospicium* in Holborn, in or near the Old Temple. This was the town-house or manor of the bishop of Lincoln,[13] which John Stow still referred to in the 1590s as the Bishop of Lincoln's Inn, though by his time it was usually called Southampton House. There is no evidence of any connection with the law, and it is probably safe to eliminate it from our enquiry. But the identification of the Lincoln from whom the legal inn takes its name remains in dispute.

Ancient tradition within the Inn derived the name from Henry de Lacy (1251-1311), earl of Lincoln, whose arms (*Or, a lion rampant Purpure*) were set over the gateway in Chancery Lane in 1518[14] and were probably in the hall windows in the previous century.[15] Sir William Sulyard (1488-1540), who was admitted to the Inn in 1512 and became a bencher in 1527, said the arms had 'always been set up in this House', and that it was a tradition among the older members of the Inn that the earl had 'brought a company to this House'.[16] Sulyard's father Edward (1459-1516) had been admitted to Lincoln's Inn in 1477, and Edward's father Sir John Sulyard (d. 1488) had been admitted in 1451 and served as a governor from 1459. The Sulyards might therefore have had a family memory stretching back to within thirty years of 1422. The repeated use of Lacy's coat of arms, and their incorporation in the arms still used by the Inn, ensured the continuance of the tradition long after the time of Henry VIII. A version was published in print by John Stow in his *Survey of London* (1598), and it was repeated by Sir William Dugdale and other writers up to the twentieth century. Stow said only that the house had been built by Lacy for his own lodging, using materials from the old Blackfriars in Holborn. The notion that Lacy had founded an inn of court on the premises, which was hinted at by Sulyard, was propagated by Francis Thynne, in a discourse delivered before the Elizabethan society of antiquaries in 1601. Dugdale said that this had become 'the tradition still current amongst the antients here... but direct proof thereof from good authority, I have not yet seen any'.[17]

The traditional explanation appeared to suffer a blow in 1902, when W P Baildon pointed out that the earl's inn was not on the site of the present Lincoln's Inn at all, but at the northern end of Shoe Lane, and that it was called the manor of Holborn or Holborn Hall.[18] The site of the present Lincoln's Inn, which was formerly part of the estate of the knights Templar, had been since the thirteenth century the property of the bishops of Chichester. Baildon hazarded a guess that a society had been founded by Lacy elsewhere, and migrated to the bishop's inn shortly before 1422, bringing their old name with them.[19] Elijah Williams, writing four years later, hinted that this society had begun in Lacy's own inn in Shoe Lane. The latter suggestion was made largely on the strength of an account roll for 1314-15, which showed that 1,714 lb. of wax, with vermilion and turpentine to make red seals, had been consumed in Lacy's household during one year:[20] evidence, it is true, of prodigious business and clerical activity, but not of legal study or the presence of apprentices. Williams later abandoned the Shoe Lane theory, but we shall return to it later.

Four years after Baildon's discovery, G J Turner took speculation in a new direction by announcing the existence of a third Lincoln's Inn in medieval Holborn, named after Thomas de Lincoln, a serjeant at law in

13 In 1342 it is called *manerium episcopi Lincolniensis* on the south side of what is now High Holborn: KB 27/330, Rex m. 58d.

14 A W B Simpson, 'Heraldic Evidence and the early History of Lincoln's Inn' (1979) 95 *LQR* 201. They were actually used by Henry de Lacy: see G J Brault ed., *Rolls of Arms: Edward I* (1997), ii. 247; *Dictionary of British Arms: Medieval Ordinary*, i, ed. D H B Chesshryre and T Woodcock (1992), i. 137.

15 J Baker, *The Men of Court* (2012), i. 193 (tricked in the 1590s as *Or, a lion rampant sable*; the purple may well have looked black by then). The hall was built in the 1490s.

16 Lost manuscript cited in Middle Temple Library MS 97 (*ca.* 1635), fo. 2v; Roxburgh, *Origins of Lincoln's Inn*, 39. The Middle Temple MS is part of an historical account of all the inns formerly attributed to Robert Brerewood (d. 1654), bencher of the Middle Temple, though a more plausible case has been made for authorship by William Hakewill (d. 1655), bencher of Lincoln's Inn.

17 *Origines Juridiciales* (1666; 3rd edn., 1680), 231. Dugdale was the basis of most accounts of the inns of court until recent times.

18 *BB*, iv. 266-79. Baildon traced its devolution down to the seventeenth century. See also G J Turner, *Lincoln's Inn* (1903); E Williams, *Staple Inn* (1906), 45-50; *Early Holborn: the Legal Quarter of London* (1927), nos. 676-752.

19 *BB*, iv. 291-297. His theory of a migration from Thavies Inn, via Furnival's Inn, is somewhat wild and has not commended itself to anyone else.

20 *Staple Inn*, 49-50, 53-54. It seems hardly credible that all the wax was used for seals; presumably most of it was for lighting.

the early part of Edward III's reign.[21] This property lay between Staple Inn and Barnard's Inn, and might have housed a legal community in the serjeant's own time. In June 1339 (only months after the return of the courts from York) four apprentices of the law were accused of attacking two Chancery clerks in the high street opposite the rent of Thomas de Lyncoln, *narrator*, as a result of which they died 'in the said rent'.[22] Now, the term 'rent' (*redditus* in the Latin of the original roll) indicates a let tenement, and although the record does not state that it was let to apprentices or Chancery clerks this was a plausible inference. What Turner did not know is that the law students fled to Thavies Inn, further along Holborn, and so it is possible that the location of the assault was fortuitous.[23] Although this newer discovery weakens the argument based on Turner's discovery, there is still an argument to be made from the nomenclature alone. Serjeant Lincoln died in the 1360s, and his inn was acquired by the abbot of Malmesbury,[24] who subsequently rebuilt part of it. The name Lincoln's Inn continued in use,[25] and in an abbey rental of 1399 or 1400 it was still *hospicium vocatum Lyncolnesynne*.[26] It was at that date let, the income being applied to support the chapel of St Mary in Malmesbury Abbey. A note added to the rental in the early 1400s shows that the 'tenements within the rent (*infra firmam*) of the great inn' consisted of four shops[27] and also 'the esquire's inn within the great inn, which is ruinous'. The significance of the phrase 'esquire's inn' (*hospicium armigeri*) has been the subject of inconclusive debate, and it has even been translated (incorrectly) as 'the serjeant's inn'; but since *armiger* is in the singular it does not obviously assist the quest for a society.

Although Serjeant Lincoln's inn belonged to Malmesbury Abbey until the Dissolution of the Monasteries, it was renamed several times in the interim, and no reference to it as Lincoln's Inn has been found subsequent to 1400, nor is there any evidence of lawyers being tenants. These circumstances led Turner and others to propose an adaptation of the Baildon theory, namely that it was the tenants of this Lincoln's Inn who migrated to the bishop of Chichester's inn, keeping their name as they went. Turner thought the migration might have occurred as early as the time of Edward III, with the serjeant personally taking the Society with him when the abbey acquired his original inn.[28] A few years later, Odgers suggested that the move occurred shortly before 1422.[29] And in 1927 Williams, abandoning his earlier theory, suggested a third variant, guessing at a merger with some pre-existing legal society in the bishop of Chichester's inn.[30] If the bishop's inn had indeed been let to lawyers in the previous century, a likely moment might have been soon after 1340, when—the courts having just returned to Westminster for good—a bishop of Chichester (Robert de Stratford) became chancellor of England for the second time. This is, indeed, probably when the legal societies were formed in the Temple. But there is no evidence whatever that apprentices at law were in the bishop's inn before the time of Henry V. If they had been, it seems likely they would have called their house Chichester Inn. There is in fact contemporary evidence for the use of that name during the episcopal occupation. In the diocesan records there survives a rental of the gardens of the bishop of Chichester's inn, by that name, in 1379:[31]

> London'
> Firma gardinorum Hospicii Episcopi Cicestrie ibidem anno regni Regis Ricardi tercio et consecrationis Willelmi episcopi decimo.
>
> Hospicium ibidem edificatum partim in parochia Sancti Dunstani et pars in parochia Sancti Andree de Holebourne *ut dicitur* in vico vocato Chauncelereslane inter Vetus Templum et Holbourne continens per estimationem [*blank*]
>
> Henry Prount pro firma gardini ex parte boriali hospicii predicti continente per estimationem [*blank*] in parochia Sancti Andree de Holbourne
> vjs viijd [*a quarter*]
> Idem Henricus pro firma domus et gardini ex parte orientali sub hospicio vocato Convers[32] ex parte australi continente per estimationem [*blank*] in parochia Sancti Dunstani
> xs [*a quarter*]

21 G J Turner, 'The Origins of Lincoln's Inn' (1906) The Athenaeum no. 4117, p. 335. Lincoln became a *narrator* (serjeant at law) in 1329: Baker, *Serjeants at Law*, 155. He probably came from Lincolnshire; his feoffees included another Lincolnshire serjeant, John Claymond. Further details concerning Thomas de Lincoln's inn were discovered by Elijah Williams: see W B Odgers, in *Essays in Legal History*, ed. P Vinogradoff (1913), at 251-2 (acknowledging unpublished information supplied by Williams); Williams, *Early Holborn*, no. 33; ii. 1127-34.

22 Corporation of London Record Office, Coroners Roll G, no. 35 ('in redditu Thome de Lyncoln narratoris in parochia Sancte Andree de Holebourne'); printed in Baker, *Third University of England*, 38-39.

23 Baker, *Collected Papers*, 154-5. Thavies Inn had been let to apprentices of law before 1349.

24 Williams abstracted the licence in mortmain of 1387 from BL Cotton MS Faustina B. VIII, fo. 195v: *Early Holborn*, ii. 1153. There is another copy in BL MS Lansdowne 217, fo. 218v.

25 Williams found a reference to it as 'Lyncolnesynne' in a deed of 1380: *Early Holborn*, ii. 1134.

26 Cartulary of the Abbey of Malmesbury, BL Cotton MS Faustina B. VIII, fo. 253v ('De firmario novi hospicii apud London vocati Lyncolnesynne'). This reference occurs in a rental dated 11th June 1399 at the head (fo. 250); but the Lincoln's Inn entry may be from the following year. At fo. 162v of the same cartulary is a copy of a charter identifying Thomas de Lincoln as the *narrator*. (In another charter on fo. 162 he has the addition 'serjaunt'.) There is a copy of the licence to purchase in another chartulary of the abbey, BL MS Lansdowne 417, fo. 216v.

27 The word *celda* puzzled Roxburgh, but is the same as *selda* (a shop or booth).

28 Turner supposed that the serjeant himself sold the inn to the abbey, but that is unclear because of the use of feoffees. The amortisation did not occur until around twenty years after his death.

29 *Essays in Legal History*, ed. Vinogradoff, at 252-3.

30 *Early Holborn*, no. 1081.

31 West Sussex Record Office, MS Ep. VI/1/3, fo. 165v. In the same volume, fo. 9v, a tax assessment of about 1290 shows London rents of 20s. in St Dunstan's, 50s. in St Andrew's, and 5s. in St Mary Strand.

32 I.e. the House of Converts (later the Rolls).

Robertus Camele pro firma domus et gardini ex parte australi dicti hospicii in predicta parochia Sancti Dunstani continente per estimationem [*blank*]
iijs iiijd [*a quarter*]
Summa totalis - iiij li.

No rent is shown for the inn itself, most of the leased property having been on the east side of Chancery Lane. Moreover, the garden on the north, let to Henry Prount for £2. 6s. 8d. a year, was part of the property let to the legal society in the fifteenth century. In 1392 the bishop's London rents amounted only to £2, which is substantially less than the £6. 13s. 4d. paid by the legal society half a century later.[33] These are both strong indications that the legal society was not yet in occupation. There is evidence, moreover, that the bishop of Chichester was still in occupation himself in 1413,[34] probably until the death of Bishop Reade in 1415, which was followed by a three-year hiatus until 1418.[35] The vacancy coincides with our earliest mention of the lawyers' society. But the destruction of the other early records of the diocese by parliamentary forces in 1642 means that there is little likelihood of any more light being thrown on this question.

In the most recent survey of the arguments, Sir Ronald Roxburgh argued for a return to the original tradition of foundation by Henry de Lacy in the time of Edward I.[36] His principal new suggestion was that Lacy might have been the minister primarily responsible for the writ of 1292 'concerning attorneys and apprentices' which had been associated since Dugdale's time with the origins of the inns of court. But his arguments, though backed by formidable learning, are unconvincing. The writ of 1292 is now believed to have been mainly if not entirely concerned with regulating the number of attorneys,[37] and was not directly relevant to the history of education for the Bar, as so many writers have supposed. Also, for the reasons given above, the reign of Edward I seems too early a period in which to seek the origins of settled societies. As Dugdale himself acknowledged, there is in fact little direct evidence to associate Lacy with the legal profession, let alone with the 1292 writ. Roxburgh's argument, 'It is improbable that if lawyers had remained in [Thomas of Lincoln's] Inn after 1369, there would have been no mention anywhere of their presence', is answered by the virtual absence of references to lawyers in any of the other inns at this period; and the same argument could be turned with greater force against his own solution, since there is no mention of their presence on the Chancery Lane site either.

The Strange Solution

The notion of a migration may be inherently difficult to believe, and especially the notion that a migrating society would take with them the name of their previous domicile.[38] But it makes even less sense to suppose that the new tenants of Chichester Inn chose the name Lincoln out of mere caprice. The name must have been taken from somewhere, and if we exclude the bishop of Lincoln it must have been either the serjeant or the earl. Both are eligible candidates. The ruinous condition of Serjeant Lincoln's Inn might explain a move to new accommodation between 1400 and 1419 and the consequent disappearance of that name for the Holborn premises. On the other hand, the ancient tradition of a connection with Henry de Lacy, earl of Lincoln, may point to a more satisfying solution, if modified to mean a connection with his inn rather than with his person.

Lacy bought the old Blackfriars in Shoe Lane, with a hall, chapel and garden, in 1286. It had not long been devoted to religion, since it had belonged in the 1220s to John Bucuinte, one of the earliest known professional common lawyers. Nor was it long connected with the earls of Lincoln, for it was inherited by Henry's daughter Alice Lacy (*suo jure* countess of Lincoln and Salisbury) on the death of her brother in 1322, and after her marriage to Ebulo le Strange it became the inheritance of the Barons Strange of Knockin.[39] It was later called Holborn Manor and Derby House. In 1417, however, there is mention in the London husting rolls of 'Straungesyn', anciently called the manor or inn of the earl of Lincoln in Holborn.[40] In other words, it was at that date called Strange's Inn, anciently Lincoln's Inn. And there is evidence that two years before that date it housed a legal society.

In 1415 a malefactor, possessed of various aliases, was indicted under the description, 'pretending to be an apprentice of the law in the inn called Strange's Inn in Holborn'.[41] There is no other mention of this society,[42] but the fraudulent pretence could only have been effective

33 A K McHardy, *The Church in London 1375-1392* (London Record Soc., 1977), 43, no. 414.

34 Roxburgh, *Origins of Lincoln's Inn*, 75-6.

35 Robert Reade died before 21st June 1415. A successor, Stephen Patrington, was appointed by papal provision on 15th December 1417 but died on 22nd December before consecration; his successor Henry Ware was consecrated on 17th July 1418. See *Handbook of British Chronology*, 3rd edn. by E B Fryde and others (1986), 239.

36 *Origins of Lincoln's Inn* (1963); repeated in 'Lincoln's Inns of the Fourteenth Century' (1978) 94 *LQR* 363-82. He took some encouragement from Sir Frederick Pollock, who had suggested in an after-dinner speech that both theories might be reconcilable: 'The Origins of the Inns of Court' (1932) 48 *LQR* 163 at 167, 169.

37 See P Brand, 5 Law & History Review at 42; 60 Historical Research at 150-1; R C Palmer, 11 Irish Jurist at 139; Baker, *Collected Papers*, i. 112, 148-50, 240. Although the writ was entered on the parliament roll with the heading 'De attornatis et apprenticiis', there is no mention of apprentices in the writ itself.

38 N L Ramsay, *The English Legal Profession ca. 1340-ca. 1450* (unpublished Cambridge Ph.D. dissertation, 1985), App. 5, p. xxv.

39 Williams, *Early Holborn*, i. 680-7, 717-31; *Calendar of Charter Rolls*, iv. 199, 213; *Calendar of Inquisitions post Mortem*, vii. 463, no. 681. It was settled in 1331 on Alice and her husband Ebulo le Strange and the heirs of Ebulo.

40 Williams, *Early Holborn*, i. 688, 733. This was a conveyance to Richard le Strange's feoffees on 3 May, enrolled in the Hustings on 12th July.

41 *R v Travers* (1415) KB 9/21/2/9 (formerly KB 9/212/57) ('pretendens se fore apprenticium legis in hospicio vocato Straungesyn in Holburne London'; noted in Williams, *Early Holborn*, i. 688 (misdated 1416), 732.

42 This is insignificant, since there are hardly any mentions of the other inns at or before this date.

if there was a known community of apprentices of law in Strange's Inn. The Society may even have been of some antiquity. Yet it did not survive to become one of the settled inns of chancery in the mid-fifteenth century, and so it must have reverted to being an ordinary house. Perhaps it is significant for the chronology of the change that when the malefactor of 1415 was pursued towards outlawry in 1419 he was 'pretending to be a clerk of the lord king's Chancery', with no mention of an inn.[43] It is possible, therefore, that Lord Strange decided to take up residence—or perhaps to maximum his income with different tenants—some time between 1415 and 1419, perhaps on the expiry of a lease. He was certainly in London by Easter Day 1417 (11th April), when he was involved in a notorious brawl in the church of St Dunstan's-in-the-East with Sir John Trussell, apparently started by their two ladies, but with armed adherents summoned on both sides, which ended in the death of a London fishmonger. Lord Strange, who had been present, was arrested and spent some time in the Tower until he was bailed on 10th May. Trussell was seriously wounded in the arm and fingers, in consequence of which he brought an appeal of mayhem against Lord and Lady Strange and their chaplain John Audeley (the blind poet)—who did not appear—and against thirteen of their household, including a cook. The thirteen were found guilty and condemned to pay 800 marks damages and 200 marks costs. It is perhaps telling that all but two of them (together with Audeley) were described as being of Knockin, Shropshire, which suggests that they had only recently moved to London.[44] And the fact that Lord Strange had been worshipping in the church where the incident occurred suggests that he was then resident in that parish, where Trussell also lived, rather than the old house in Holborn. No doubt it became utterly intolerable for them to share the same parish after Easter 1417, though nothing is known about the subsequent residence of the Stranges. It may not be a mere coincidence that less than a month after the incident Lord Strange conveyed Strange's Inn to his feoffees on undisclosed trusts. And it will be recalled that 1417 is the first year in which Lincoln's Inn is mentioned as a legal society, a mere two years after the allusion to apprentices at law in Strange's Inn.

If the lawyer tenants were in fact eased out around this time, and found a new home in the Chancery Lane house recently vacated by the bishop of Chichester, it is obvious that they could not have taken the name Strange's Inn with them.[45] Strange's Inn was still Lord Strange's inn. Given that they chose not to use the name Chichester Inn but to retain a nominal connection with their former abode, it would have made sense for them to take the previous (but still remembered) name of Strange's Inn. There was by that time no other Lincoln's Inn with which it might be confused. If that is what happened, then they were indeed named after Henry de Lacy, earl of Lincoln, and they had indeed migrated from the Blackfriars. Those were the two principal elements of the legend recounted by Stow in 1598. Stow confused matters by supposing the Blackfriars to have been at the north end of Chancery Lane, and Thynne confused them still further by supposing the inn of court to have been founded by Lacy himself. But Stow did not say that Lacy founded the inn of court. The legend, as he had received it, simply mistook the exact nature of the connection between the Blackfriars (*alias* Strange's Inn) and Lincoln's Inn. Those who speculated about the presence of Lacy's arms in the inn during the reigns of Henry VII and Henry VIII, being closer to the event, knew that the explanation lay in a migration, although the chronology of the migration had been distorted by conjecture. Legends can be notoriously fickle and they have the tendency to change slightly with every repetition. The historian is rightly cautious of placing too much weight on them; but they often have a basis in fact. Whether the origin of Lincoln's Inn truly lies in Strange's Inn, as the ancient legends had it, can no longer be a matter of proof beyond reasonable doubt. But the facts seem to fit.

Life in Fifteenth-Century Lincoln's Inn

After 1422 we move from the world of conjecture to a world of minute detail, since the Black Books provide a keyhole view of life in an inn of court for some eighty years before anything comparable is available for the other inns. We see a community of lawyers, law students and young lay gentlemen, governed by ancient customs which, though capable of being changed by democratic agreement, convey a flavour both of courtly and of academical life. It is perhaps not too surprising, since lawyers tend to a natural conservatism of manners, that their mode of life reflected the social life of the fourteenth century as much as the fifteenth. There is reason to believe that similar customs were common to all the inns even if the details differed. Lincoln's Inn was ruled at the outset by four elected governors, decisions of principle being taken by the whole fellowship; it was only in Tudor times, as in the other inns, that the power of government would effectively pass to the benchers.[46] The governing body was known as the 'Council', a term used in most of the inns of chancery but not in the other inns of court. The officers were chiefly financial: a steward and a pensioner are mentioned early in the Black Books. The steward was an employee responsible principally for providing 'commons', and collecting the payments for them, and a pensioner was a member who collected the 'pensions'. The first treasurer was appointed in 1455, though it was at least two centuries before this office came to achieve its present primacy. The treasurer, nowadays appointed for one year only, is the nearest the inns of court have to the master of a college. But that was not so from the beginning. It seems more likely that the Council was presided over by the senior

43 KB 27/631, Rex m. 7. He was, however, finally outlawed at Chelmsford in 1420 under the original description: KB 29/55, m. 28d.

44 KB 27/624, m. 76; KB 9/210, m. 39. The story is fully recounted by M Bennett, 'John Audelay: Life Records and Heaven's Ladder' in *My Wyl and my Wrytyng: Essays on John the Blind Audelay*, ed. S Fein (Kalamazoo, 2009), 30-53, at 31-7.

45 It is notable that no fewer than six members of the Strange family of Hunstanton, Norfolk, belonged to Lincoln's Inn after 1472: Baker, *The Men of Court*, ii. 1470-2. But they were a cadet branch of the Strange family and not descended from Ebulo le Strange.

46 See A W B Simpson, 'The Early Constitution of the Inns of Court' (1970), 28 C.L.J. 241-56. For benchers see below, **.

governor, the early treasurers being of distinctly lower rank.[47] The first under-treasurer—now the principal administrative officer of the Inn—was appointed in 1567.

The whole body of the inns of court and chancery in the fifteenth century was not much smaller in numbers than Cambridge University, and Lincoln's Inn had a resident membership of about 130 to 140 during most of the century.[48] It was usual before joining the Inn to spend some time in one of the inns of chancery,[49] and the usual age of migration from the latter was around 21. Many and various were the conditions of admission, which were a matter for bargaining; a barrel of wine or a haunch of venison might excuse the donor from attendance at learning exercises or from an onerous office. These bargains reflect the variety of the membership. The majority of members did not intend to learn or practise the law; indeed, of the 576 who were recorded as joining Lincoln's Inn between 1450 and 1500, half are never mentioned in the Black Books again.[50] Some members, of course, were legal practitioners, and some were officials of the courts or of the government, but most of them were the sons of landed gentlemen bent on meeting others of their kind and acquainting themselves with the metropolis before settling into country life.[51] Those who were uncertain of their destiny would soon learn, from their interaction with men of considerable intellect and talent, whether they were suited for the challenge of legal practice. The organised law school, to which we shall return, was more demanding of its graduands than the arts schools in the universities.

New members entered as 'clerks' and remained in clerks' commons until they became 'fellows' (*socii*), a form of graduation mentioned in the records long before any references to call to the Bar. The fellows were divided into benchers, barristers and (as we should say) students. Below the clerks were the 'yeomen' (*valetti*), consisting chiefly of the servants and clerks of the benchers and barristers. Members took an oath of obedience to the governors, and bound themselves to two main duties: the duty of paying the Inn's charges, and the duty of 'continuance'. The principal charges were the pension (a termly payment for residence in chambers), commons (a weekly payment for meals), and dues (such as the contributions to fuel, chapel and revels). The pension was fixed at 12d. a term in 1461, but raised to 16d. in 1464; commons were 20d. a week in the 1480s. From time to time a special levy or tax would be imposed on all the members for extraordinary charges, such as building work or leaving-presents to fellows who became serjeants at law. Continuance was the obligation of remaining in residence at certain seasons of the year, principally during the Lent and Summer vacations when the readings took place, and during Christmas, for a certain period of time after admission. It was a strict duty, not pardoned in earlier days even by plague, bereavement or the need for a young heir to go home and fight for his inheritance.[52] Both learning and pleasure were essential features of community life, to be kept up, if need be, by coercion. For the present we will confine our attention to social life, returning afterwards to the forms of learning.

Prior to 1431 there had been nine festival periods during which revels were held, in addition to Christmas. In that year the Society decided to reduce the number to four: Candlemas (in February), St Erkenwald (30th April), Midsummer (24th June) and All Hallows (2nd November). Little is known of their character, but they included exceedings at table, entertainments and dancing. The greatest of the celebrations by far were those which took place at Christmas and lasted until Twelfth Night. It will be recalled that keeping Christmas is the subject of the very first entry in the Black Books. The festivities—and we must here generalise from references scattered over a century—were under the control of the Marshal (who wore a distinctive red gown) and a Master of the Revels. There was an elected 'King' with officers of state, doubtless younger students, and we hear also at various times of a King of the Cockneys and a Lord of Misrule. Seasonal fare included such delicacies as boar and venison, marchpanes and jellies, accompanied by sweet and spiced wines. The hall was decorated with holly, and there was a relaxation of normal discipline to the extent that cards and dice were allowed. Waits (minstrels) and players were hired, to provide song and dramatic diversion. Carols, associated with the ancient 'hove' or ring-dance, were a distinctive feature of Christmas in the inns of court, preserved long after they went out of general fashion.[53] In a fifteenth-century moot-book belonging to successive butlers of Lincoln's Inn there survive the words and music of an early polyphonic carol (*Nowell, nowell, out of your sleep*),[54] together

47 The first known treasurer (1455-8), Thomas Humfrey (or Umfrey), was only an attorney of the Exchequer, though he was also one of the governors. In 1461, when the obscure Richard Isham was elected treasurer, the governors included Nicholas Statham (author of the abridgment), William Jenney (soon to become a serjeant and later a King's Bench judge) and Roger Towshend (law reporter and later a Common Pleas judge): *BB*, i. 36.

48 In 1481-2 the pensioner received 555 pensions (*BB*, i. 75); since these were paid quarterly, the resident membership must have been about 139. In 1478 money was collected from 129 members for the new serjeants, and in 1495 from 130 (*ibid.*, 65, 105). As late as 1574 there were only ninety-two sets of chambers, housing 160 members: *Calendar of Inner Temple Records*, i. 468. Lists of members vary in size from 151 in 1442 to 245 in 1454; but these must have included some non-residents. The rate of admission in the middle of the century was about eleven a year.

49 Not necessarily one of the two 'belonging' to the Inn. These connections were not fully established until the reign of Henry VIII.

50 There may also have been as many as fifty members before 1550 who are not mentioned in the Black Books either: Baker, *The Men of Court*, i. 12.

51 They have nearly all now been identified, partly with the help of the records of lawsuits brought to collect their dues: see Baker, *The Men of Court*. Around a third of all members before 1550 were sued at some point, and in 1564 a pension suit was brought against four knights and 374 gentlemen of London: *ibid.* i. 107.

52 See *BB*, i. 21, 31 (fines reduced but not pardoned). These excuses were all allowed later in the century: *ibid.* 42, 86.

53 For the early context see R Mullally, *The Carole: A Study of a Medieval Dance* (Aldershot, 2011).

54 Printed below, **.

with choreographical notes on the 'hove of the house'.[55] Music and dancing were, according to Sir John Fortescue (a governor of the Inn in the 1420s), part of the education of the men of court in the fifteenth century; and even as late as 1610 the students were put out of commons by decimation as a punishment for failing to dance at the Candlemas revels.[56] The ring-dance was kept up at least until that period, and involved walking solemnly around the fire in the centre of the hall, linking hands and singing the old song of mirth and solace.[57] There were also stage-plays, known as 'interludes' or 'disguisings'.[58] Historians of drama have attached some significance to these activities; but it would be anachronistic to infer from them a devotion to art or high culture in a modern sense. The students were having fun. The rumbustious side of the Christmas festivities could sometimes turn to excess, at any rate in Tudor times. In 1519 it was found necessary to end the election of a traitor, Jack Straw, with his 'adherents', while five years after that the Lord of Misrule actually killed someone.[59]

Life between the great festivals was doubtless more simple, at any rate for the poor and studious. Some chambers did not even possess fireplaces, and for their inhabitants the most comfortable place of refuge in winter was the hall. The hall has been the focal point of life in the inns of court down to the present day, and in essence communal dining in academic institutions continues to serve much the same purposes as it always has. The lawyers in Lincoln's Inn took over the old hall of the medieval bishops of Chichester, probably quite small and plain, the floor strewn with rushes or mats. The trestles and forms were arranged as in any college, with a high table at one end for the benchers, about twenty-four feet in length,[60] and trestles for the barristers, 'clerks' and yeomen. Meals were served on pewter dishes and platters, the drink in earthenware beer-pots and 'goddards', some of which have been excavated in recent years.[61] Bread and beer seem to have been the basis of the diet, and their supply was controlled by the two principal hall servants, the pannierman and the butler. Benchers and barristers had the privilege of a daily livery-pot of ale, called 'boyer', from the buttery. (Even within living memory, commons at lunch in the inns of court consisted simply of bread and cheese, with beer, any supplementation being charged for specially.) At dinner, then the mid-day meal, meat and fish were also available, supplemented by rabbits from the coneygarth, and fruit, nuts and herbs from the garden. Occasionally there would be a buck or a doe, or a hogshead of wine, given to the Society as the price for a special admission, or as a bequest;[62] more rarely the company might enjoy a special feast for a distinguished visitor, as when the duke of Buckingham dined in Lincoln's Inn in 1512. Members of the Inn who did not reside were excused commons payments and allowed to be 'at repasts', which meant that they only paid for the meals which they actually took.

The life of the Inn must also have centred to a considerable extent on the Chapel. Dedicated to St Richard of Chichester, who had lived or stayed in the Inn when it was the bishop's palace, it was used for meetings of the Society throughout the fifteenth century and until the Council Chamber was built around 1508. It was also used, at any rate in the sixteenth century, for vacation moots.[63] But it can hardly be doubted that it was primarily used for divine service. The Inn was not itself a parish, but had always provided services and claimed in later centuries to be extraparochial.[64] Nevertheless, the Inn also had its own chapel in St Andrew's parish church,[65] perhaps because the old chapel was inadequate for a growing community, and was at one time thought to be within that parish.[66] The Chaplain of Lincoln's Inn, also known as the Rector,[67] was paid a stipend by the Inn and provided with vestments, plate and service books. Besides ministering to the Society he also had chantries to keep.[68] One of the benchers was assigned to oversee the Chapel; from 1504 the office was known as the Dean of Chapel, and it still continues. There were, however, no regulations about chapel attendance before the 1570s, when tighter government policy required explicit attempts to enforce religious conformity.

These public gatherings apart, life for the students was far from monastic. Relations with women were a constant problem. They were so prevalent a problem by 1489 that the fine for fornicating in chambers was raised to £5—though only £2 if committed in the

55 Baker, *Collected Papers*, 335-41. There is a reference to a singer of the carol in 1498: MS Black Book II, fo. 50.

56 *BB*, ii. 131. The reference is to 'under barristers', which probably means inner barristers rather than utter barristers.

57 R Hayman, *Quodlibets* (1628), 44 (printed below, **); Baker, *Collected Papers*, i. 341.

58 Lincoln's Inn MS Hale 46(2), fly-leaf (1489); *BB*, i. 121 (1500), 132 (1503/4); *Lisle Letters*, ed. M S Byrne (1981), ii. 20 (1533/4).

59 *BB*, i. 190; *Letters and Papers of Henry VIII*, iv. 390.

60 The table-cloth in 1508 measured 6½ ells: *BB*, i. 156.

61 See L G Matthews and H J M Green, 'Post-medieval Pottery of the Inns of Court' (1970) 3 *Post-Medieval Archaeology* 1-17 (including some late-medieval finds).

62 E.g. in 1513 Walter Roudon, a past treasurer, left 'to the company of Lincolne Inne an hoggeshed of good Gascone wyne': will registered in the Prerogative Court of Canterbury [PCC], 1 Holder. (The PCC registers are now in the PRO, class PROB 11.)

63 *BB*, i. 305 (1553); C I Hammer, 'Bolts and Chapel Moots at Lincoln's Inn in the 16th Century' (1970) 11 *JSPTL* 24-8.

64 Waterhouse's reports, BL MS Add. 25200, fo. 83 (held in 1594 that an outlawry could not be proclaimed at Lincoln's Inn, 'car coment que ils avoyent un liew de prayers la uncore nest esglise ne chappell'); *Annual Register 1774*, p. 169 (part of the Inn found to be in the parish of St Clement Danes); private Act of Parliament, 14th May 1829 (most of the Inn made extraparochial).

65 Francis Sulyard in 1542 asked to be buried in 'Lincoln Inne chappell within Sainte Andrewes churche': PCC 1 Pynnyng.

66 In *Jenney v Wolvesby* (1458) CP 40/790, m. 325, two benchers sued for a trespass to the Jenney family chamber 'apud parochiam Sancti Andree in Holborne videlicet in hospicio Lyncolnes Inne extra barras Veteris Templi'.

67 Baldwin Hyde, a clerical master in Chancery admitted in 1466, left his furred gown and hood to the Rector ('rectori de hospicio de Lyncolnes Inne') in 1472: PCC 6 Wattys.

68 E.g. a chantry was established for John Nethersole (d. 1504/5), from whose residuary estate the Library was built in 1505-9: below, **.

garden[69]—and in 1565 it was felt necessary to take the preventative measure of forbidding the employment in chambers of any laundresses or bedmakers aged between twelve and forty.[70] No doubt many senior members of the profession came to regret the completeness of the Black Books in recording their youthful lapses, for it still remains on record that four future benchers—one of them destined to be a chief justice—were punished for misbehaving with loose women. Violent disorder had also been a lamentable tendency of the less bookish members of the inns since their beginnings, and in the later fifteenth century we read of battles between Lincoln's Inn and the members of other communities, such as the King's Household (1477), the household of Lord Darcy (1504) and Gray's Inn (1505).[71] Even quarrels within the walls might be violent, as when Sir Thomas More's father, a future King's Bench judge, drew a dagger on a future baron of the Exchequer in 1477. Student violence resulted at times in blood, but rarely in death. Death from disease, on the other hand, was an ever-present threat; the Black Books are full of references to plague, and the burial registers of St Andrew's church list many members of Lincoln's Inn, some of them young men dying within months of their arrival from more salubrious parts of the country.

Legal Education: Benchers and Barristers

Given the emphasis in the early Black Books on financial accounting and social arrangements, one might be forgiven for overlooking the fact that Lincoln's Inn was first and foremost a law school. Some historians have, indeed, deduced from the silences in the books that the educational routine was only grafted on to the social routine at a late stage, perhaps in the later fifteenth century: in this view, the inns of court began merely as lodging-places, and found an educational role in their maturity. This is now known to have been mistaken. The system of readings (lectures) and moots (disputations) was in place in the fourteenth century, and had developed continuously from the lectures and disputations of the thirteenth century. In other words, it is older than the inns, just as the schools at Oxford and Cambridge were older than the colleges. The Tudor moot-books, containing set problems upon which pleading exercises were based, still contained cases set in the time of Edward III,[72] and it is difficult to imagine that the practice had changed in the interim. It was a customary system which contained its own inducements and sanctions, and the Inn was obliged to intervene with written orders and financial penalties only when standards were perceived to be slipping. By the customs established in the fourteenth and fifteenth centuries one could only become a judge after becoming a serjeant; one could only become a serjeant after lecturing in an inn of court; one could only be chosen to lecture in an inn of court after some years as an utter barrister; and one could only become an utter barrister by taking part in moots. Advancement in the law was thus inextricably linked to the educational system in the inns; there was no judge who had not been a professor there.

Medieval lectures were always on a text and, since there was no text of the common law, the readings in the inns were given on the statutes, beginning with Magna Carta and ending with the legislation of Edward I. When details of the arrangements emerge in the fifteenth century we find that two readers were appointed each year, one for the Autumn or Lammas vacation (in August) and the other for the Lent Vacation (in February or March).[73] The latter was frequently a reader's second course of lectures (a 'double reading'), and on that account more esteemed; it would be attended by serjeants and judges who had formerly been members of the inn. Each course of lectures, illustrated with hypothetical cases, and challenged by discussion, lasted at least four weeks. Moots involved taking a complicated set of facts and turning them into a mock lawsuit; the students drew an appropriate writ, using each other's names as parties, and framed apt pleadings which were subdivided if necessary to raise all the different issues. The questions raised by the pleadings were then argued: first points of form, then points of substance. A good case might last as long as a term. The whole procedure was modelled closely on that of the fourteenth-century Common Pleas, and the hall was rearranged for the purpose by placing forms in front of the high table (the 'bench') to represent the Bar. Those who sat on the bench were the benchers, and those who argued at the Bar as if they were serjeants were the utter barristers. The most junior participants were called inner barristers, perhaps because they sat within the Bar as if they were officers of the court. These functions in the fifteenth century gave their names to the ranks or degrees to which members were 'called' when qualified. It was a mode of graduation closely resembling, and presumably modelled on, that in the universities. In academical parlance bachelors were the disputants or mooters, the masters and doctors those who sat on the bench. The degree of bachelor was taken by responding to a *quaestio*, the degree of master or doctor by giving lectures. The notion of 'call' in the inns of court represented the imposition of control, by the governing body of each Inn, over a system of exercises in which it was for participants to make themselves graduates by playing the appropriate part when ready to do so.[74] It was only by arguing a bar moot that one became a barrister, and originally it was only possible by lecturing to become a

69 *BB*, i. 89-90. This followed the discovery of nine such offences in one year: *ibid.* 86.

70 *BB*, i. 349. The title of 'laundress' had been in use since the fifteenth century: *ibid.* 78 (1482).

71 *BB*, i. 63, 135, 141; C G Bayne and W H Dunham ed., *Select Cases in the Council of Henry VII* (75 Selden Soc., 1958), 36-7.

72 For a fifteenth-century Lincoln's Inn moot-book, now in Cambridge, see Baker, *Collected Papers*, i. 336-40. It seems to be mentioned in *BB*, i. 219: 'that the utter barresters and inner barresters gyffe ther attendaunce for to assygne the mote and tymes accustumyd, and the butlers to wayte upon them with the booke and candell.' The Cambridge manuscript belonged to Richard Lyndesell (d. 1540) and John Lutwich (d. 1615), butlers of Lincoln's Inn.

73 The first known readings from Lincoln's Inn are those by John Sulyard (1466 or earlier) on advowsons, and Nicholas Statham (1472 or earlier) on the Statute of Marlborough. There is a complete list of readers, and their texts, in J H Baker, *Readers and Readings in the Inns of Court and Chancery* (13 Selden Soc. Supplem. Series, 2000), 106-41.

74 *Readings and Moots at the Inns of Court*, II, 105 Selden Soc. liv-lvii. 'Call' to the bench is mentioned in 1466, call to the bar in 1516. It may be noted that the creation of a serjeant at law was also a form of self-graduation, in his case the recitation of a 'count' (the plaintiff's opening pleading) in a semi-fictional case at the bar of the Common Pleas; this was both an exercise in pleading and a taking seisin of the right to be heard.

bencher. The graduation took on public significance when the degrees of bencher and utter barrister (or barrister at law) were recognised by the courts as necessary qualifications for rights of audience.[75] In remembrance of their origin, however, calls to the Bar in Lincoln's Inn were still published at moots as late as the 1670s.

By then the old system was disappearing. Lectures had ceased in 1642, and were resurrected after the Restoration only with difficulty and only for a few years. The chance to modernise the system was lost; like the law itself, it was entrenched in precedent. Money was not found to pay lecturers, and the old incentives to read were disappearing as advancement ceased to depend on having done so.[76] Mooting became ossified, first as a recognisable medieval relic and then as a piece of nonsense, which in Lincoln's Inn involved reading from a slip of paper supplied by the butler and containing an unintelligible fragment of some argument about a widow's dower. By slow stages a learned and severe method of professional training had degenerated to the level of post-prandial amusement. This last vestige of an 'exercise' finally disappeared in 1856. Mooting in the original sense has since been revived, as a way of testing the skills needed for legal argument in the present. And lectures have been provided since the 1850s under the auspices of the Council of Legal Education.

Much of a law student's education was, and still is, a matter of watching lawyers in action. This is why the readings were always in vacation: in term-time the students were expected to attend Westminster Hall to listen to the serjeants and judges. In the Common Pleas, and by the seventeenth century in the other courts as well, the students had a wooden pen into which they were herded to learn the law. Known in Edward II's time as 'the crib', it became in law-student jargon the mysterious 'pekynnes' to which Lincoln's Inn contributed 40s. in 1483.[77] The more industrious students and barristers kept notes of what they heard; in the absence of printed law reports,[78] everyone could be his own reporter. Two of the earliest known law reporters were members of Lincoln's Inn in the fifteenth century; and the will of a judge who died in 1487 mentioned an abridgment 'of Lincoln's Inn labour'.[79] Although there was no system of indentured apprenticeship, or formal pupillage, direction could be obtained from senior members of the profession with whom a student had connections. The Paston letters contain a reference to something like pupillage in Lincoln's Inn in 1478: the addressee is exhorted to keep a close eye on a young student, who is 'to be occupied under a dread of displeasure under subjection, with early rising accustomed, for sloth is the mother and nourisher of all vice'.[80] A student would spend much of his time at his desk, reading, copying and common-placing manuscripts or (after the 1480s) printed books. The earliest printed abridgment of case-law, though without title-page, has always been known by the name of Nicholas Statham, a bencher of Lincoln's Inn who died in 1472; it was printed in Rouen around 1490. The Inn had a library from 1509,[81] built through the good offices of the then lord chief justice, who happened to be the father-in-law of the treasurer when the funds were found in 1504.[82] None of the earliest contents has survived, but we know they included year books and a copy of *Bracton*. In 1517 John le Strange left to the Library a collection of 'borded bokes', which he wished to have chained and inscribed under horn with his name and the fact that he was 'a felawe and twyes redar and thryse thresaurar of the same place'.[83] There is no evidence that they were ever received, but a similar collection bequeathed by Randle Cholmeley in 1563 still survives, complete with inscriptions under horn. The Library was greatly augmented by gifts and purchases in the sixteenth and later centuries, and is now one of the finest libraries of common law in the world.[84]

A Glimpse at the Inn's Later History

Despite changes in legal education, the constitution and social customs of the inns of court in the twenty-first century remain recognisably similar to those of Tudor times. They still control the admission, education, graduation and professional discipline of barristers. Student life has, of course, changed with the cessation of student residence. The ancient and boisterous Christmas festivities have gone. They were kept up until the Stuart period, but by then the old forms of entertainment were giving way to newer fashions: the mock courts and interludes to masques and tragedies, the hove-dance to almains and pavanes.[85] But the halls of the inns still resound on occasion to the music of concerts and balls, or to the voices of thespians, and Christmas revels have enjoyed a successful renaissance in a new guise. The present requirement that students keep a number of terms before call to the Bar is met—as it always has been—by dining in hall. Without regular

75 See 'Audience in the Courts' in Baker, *Collected Papers*, i. 112-23 at 118-19.

76 In the seventeenth century the rank of king's counsel was often given to men who had not read, or were not even benchers. And judges could be appointed from outside the order of serjeants, the coif being conferred a few days beforehand as a formal qualification.

77 MS Black Book II, fo. 57v ('…pur lez pekynnes noviter fact.'); 'The Pekynnes' in Baker, *Collected Papers*, i. 308-14.

78 The first contemporaneous series of printed law reports began publication as late as 1785.

79 94 Selden Soc., intro., *165, 173*. Some of the reports by Roger Townshend (d. 1493), admitted 1454, treasurer 1459-60, and later a Common Pleas judge, were printed among the year books of Edward IV.

80 *Paston Letters and Papers*, ii, ed. N Davis (1976), 423 (spelling modernised).

81 There is mention in 1475 of a payment of 30s. 'pro bibliotheca' (*BB*, i. 59, 61), which has been misinterpreted to mean a library. It seems far more likely to be a bible for the Chapel.

82 The funds came from a deceased attorney called John Nethersole, a member of the Inn, who made no mention of this purpose in his will (PCC 25 Holgrave, dated 12th September 1504, proved 20th February 1505) but had perhaps made informal arrangements in trust. His chief residuary legatee was Sir John Fyneux CJ (formerly of Gray's Inn), whose son-in-law John Rooper was treasurer of Lincoln's Inn in 1504.

83 PCC 36 Holder.

84 For a brief history of the Library, see Baker, *English Legal Manuscripts*, ii (1978), 1-29; *Collected Papers*, ii. 702-4.

85 J P Cunningham, *Dancing in the Inns of Court* (1965), 4-5, 14 (for the 'measures' danced in Lincoln's Inn). The 1703 edition of John Playford's *The English Dancing Master* included a country dance called 'Lincoln's Inn'.

conversation and good fellowship between its members, most easily but no longer primarily arranged through dining, an inn of court could hardly claim to be a society. The adornment of each hall with the armorial bearings of former readers and treasurers, with portraits of distinguished judges who have been members of the Inn, and the regular use at table of silver given as tokens of affection by benchers of many generations, all induce a strong sense of continuity.

A vestige of earlier social discipline remains in the customs as to formal dress. Dress was not the subject of written regulation before Tudor times, any more than it was for university undergraduates, but at that period dark colours became de rigueur, and piecemeal regulations were introduced to prevent foppery, discourage long hair and maintain a decent conformity. By 1600 distinct forms of gown indicated the different ranks: barristers were distinguished by black velvet facings and two vertical strips of velvet above the arms, benchers by more elaborate black lace and tufts. All wore the black skull-cap. Gowns were not ceremonial dress, but everyday dress to be worn not only in hall and chapel but anywhere in public in London or Westminster.[86] Gowns are still required for dining in hall, and are the same in all four inns of court. Students wear a distinctive sleeveless gown with wings on the shoulders. The present barrister's gown with three buttons catching up each sleeve and a black mourning hood on the left shoulder—introduced in mourning for Charles II in 1685[87]—is worn also by those benchers who are not entitled to the plainer gown of Tudor fashion adopted around the same time by senior judges and Queen's Counsel.

The principal changes in the life of the inns of court during later centuries were the virtual cessation of organised legal education in the seventeenth century, and the disappearance after that period of resident students; the development of the informal arrangements for professional accommodation into the chambers system; the admission of solicitors and attorneys, and other non-members, as tenants of the Inn; and, of course, a steady expansion in membership, matched by a steady progress in building and the provision of amenities. The expansion is nowhere more evident than in the size of the governing body itself, which has grown with the numbers of Queen's Counsel, and with the retention (since the sale of Serjeants' Inn in 1877) of the superior judges,[88] so that by the 1990s there were as many benchers as there were members of the entire Inn in the 1490s. The long association between Lincoln's Inn and the Court of Chancery is well known to readers of Dickens, because *Bleak House* begins in Lincoln's Inn Hall, 'at the very heart of the fog' which not only enveloped London in dank November but which metaphorically enveloped the equity jurisdiction at the time of Lord Eldon's chancellorship. The use of the hall for the Lord Chancellor's vacation sittings, from the early eighteenth century until the abolition of the old Court of Chancery in 1875,[89] and the erection of courts in the Inn for the vice-chancellors during the nineteenth century, had the effect of attracting Chancery counsel to chambers in the Inn. Many sets of Lincoln's Inn chambers have retained a close connection with the Chancery Bar to the present day.

The legal, academical, political, literary and religious associations of Lincoln's Inn and its members are too numerous and important to survey in a short space, and they have in any case been the subject of several books which may be read with profit. The membership roll of an inn of court is more impressive than that of most individual colleges at Oxford or Cambridge, since so many of its members have been close to the intellectual or administrative heart of the nation; to attempt a biographical survey would be to survey much of English history. Lincoln's Inn can boast not only countless eminent judges and advocates, but many officers of state, several prime ministers, two kings and even a saint.

Brief History of the Site and Buildings

Lincoln's Inn occupies a large rectangle about 1,000 feet in length along the west side of what is now Chancery Lane. This was originally the New Street leading from the Old Temple in Holborn to the New Temple by the River Thames, and at the beginning of the thirteenth century was probably little more than a muddy lane passing through open fields. It was not paved until 1540. But few streets in England have been trodden by so many distinguished feet.

The principal site of the Inn was obtained in the 1220s by Ralph Neville (d. 1244), bishop of Chichester and chancellor of England. Baildon said it was granted by King Henry III to the bishop in 1227, relying on a charter in the possession of the Inn, a facsimile of which was inserted in the printed Black Books;[90] but it seems more likely that this grant was of land on the east side of Chancery Lane. The Lincoln's Inn site, according to Williams, was held by the knights Templar of the abbot of Westminster as a single unit with the Middle Temple, and subinfeudated directly by them to Bishop Neville (d. 1244). This must be a matter for conjecture, because no written grant is extant;[91] but a fourteenth-century book belonging to the diocese relates that Neville gave the inn 'amongst other great gifts' to his successors as

86 *BB*, ii. 8 (1588). In 1555 a member was fined 20d. for wearing his study gown in Cheapside and in Westminster Hall: *BB*, i. 312. *Cf.* the Judges' Rules of 1557, *ibid.* 320. Presumably the study gown was less formal than the gown to be worn outside.

87 Baker, *Collected Papers*, ii. 857-67.

88 Before 1877, when a bencher became a serjeant at law, which was a necessary qualification for a judgeship in the three common-law courts, he was required to leave the inn. There was a solemn leave-taking, and the chapel bell was tolled as if for a funeral.

89 Between 1875 and the opening of the Royal Courts of Justice (just next to Lincoln's Inn) in 1882, both halls in Lincoln's Inn were used for sittings of the new Court of Appeal.

90 *BB*, iv. 279. The property is described as a place and garden in New Street, forfeited by John Herlizun, opposite the bishop's land in the same street. Another part of Herlizun's estate became the House of Converts, later the Rolls Chapel, rebuilt as the Public Record Office, and now the library of King's College London.

91 Williams, *Staple Inn*, 51-4; *Early Holborn*, nos. 1520-1521.

bishops of Chichester in 1232.[92] It is Neville who is generally supposed to have built the lodgings, hall and chapel of the original bishops' inn in Chancery Lane. Indeed, the contemporary chronicler Matthew Paris says that he died 'in his noble palace which he had built not far from the New Temple'.[93] His immediate successor, Richard Wich (d. 1253), a canon lawyer, and the last English prelate to be canonised (in 1262), acted as tutor to Henry de Lacy's father, Edmund. Another successor, Robert de Stratford (d. 1362), was in 1340 sworn as lord chancellor in his inn in Chancery Lane.[94] It was at the beginning of Stratford's bishopric that the site was augmented by a grant from the Knights Hospitaller (as successors to the Knights Templar) of twenty-one acres of land, comprising the garden to the north of the inn and Fickett's Field to the south-west.[95] The legal society would pay rent to the bishop for this entire property, as Lincoln's Inn, throughout the fifteenth and early sixteenth centuries, though no written leases have been found. In 1535 Bishop Sherburne granted a written ninety-nine-year lease to the William Sulyard already mentioned, and two years later his successor granted the reversion to William and Eustace Sulyard. Eustace, the survivor, granted the fee simple in 1580 to Richard Kingsmill and the other benchers of the Inn, and it has been vested in groups of named benchers as trustees for the Society ever since. The benchers also acquired in the middle of the sixteenth century the freehold of Furnival's Inn (1547) and Thavies Inn (1551), the two inns of chancery over which Lincoln's Inn had come to exercise a general superintendence.

The history of the earliest buildings is impossible to trace with precision, because the details do not appear in the Black Books. No doubt the lawyers took over the existing apartments of the bishop's household, and only altered and extended them as it became necessary. Finance for building was raised either by *ad hoc* assessments on members, or (perhaps more usually) by private enterprise: members who built at their own expense retained rights to nominate incoming tenants.[96] Some of these privately built chambers once contained the arms of the builders in the windows, though none has survived.[97] An example of such private enterprise is provided by the office which Thomas Shotbolt, filazer of the Common Pleas, built in the garden in 1457. The first mention of major new work occurs three years before that, in 1454, when eleven new chambers were erected in a building of timber and plaster with a tiled roof. There was perhaps another in 1470.[98] In 1490 the old hall was pulled down and a new one erected, the first hall to be erected by lawyers in any of the inns of court; its windows contained the arms of some of the members who paid for it.[99] After extensive restoration, it still stands and is in regular use for lectures and meetings. In the first decade of the sixteenth century some further public buildings were erected near the hall, including the library and a new council chamber. The work continued during that and the following century, so that Old Buildings and Old Square were gradually rebuilt in brick. The gatehouse in Chancery Lane was erected between 1518 and 1520, renovated in the late seventeenth century, and rebuilt in replica in 1967. The stone carving dated 1518 over the great arch—part of which has been removed to Hale Court to preserve it from further erosion, and replaced in facsimile—bears in the centre the arms of King Henry VIII ensigned by a crown. On the left are the arms of Henry de Lacy, to which reference has already been made. On the right are those of Sir Thomas Lovell KG (d. 1524), senior governor of the Inn and a benefactor. On the ground floor (north) of the gateway was kept the office of the Chief Prothonotary of the Common Pleas until 1557. The oldest chambers now surviving in the Inn are thought to date from 1524.

The old chapel was demolished in the seventeenth century and the present edifice—doubtfully attributed to Inigo Jones—was consecrated in 1623 by the bishop of London: a memorable ceremony at which Dr John Donne, recently Preacher to the Inn, delivered the sermon. The colonnaded Undercroft or crypt was used in the seventeenth century, like the cloisters in the Temple, as a place where clients might consult counsel. Beneath their feet was the Inn's burial ground, consecrated as such in 1623. The badly worn memorial slabs conceal the resting-places of over 150 deceased servants and members of the Inn, from washpots and panniermen to benchers and judges, lying side by side.

The area now called New Square, on the south-west side of the oldest buildings, is part of what was formerly called Fickett's Fields, or Little Lincoln's Inn Fields. Here in the fourteenth century the Chancery clerks and the apprentices of law resorted for relaxation;[100] and it was still an open square in the 1670s when a famous running-down

92 West Sussex Record Office, MS Ep. VI/1/3, fo. 9v (memorandum at foot).

93 *Historia Anglorum*, ed. F. Madden (Rolls Series, 1866-9), ii. 480.

94 *BB*, iv. 281, quoting the Close Roll.

95 Williams, *Early Holborn*, nos. 1530, 1531, 1544.

96 A building agreement of 1534 survives in the H E Huntington Library, San Marino, California, MS Stowe Temple (Personal) Box 1, no. 10. Peter Temple was admitted to the upper chamber for life as kinsman of Thomas Heritage, who paid for the building, though Heritage himself seems not to have been admitted until 1536.

97 The arms of Sir Robert Townshend (d. 1557), justice of Chester, were in a window panel dated 1568 in the Townshend chamber: *The Men of Court*, ii. 1544. Those of William Ayloffe, later a Queen's Bench judge (d. 1584), were noted in Thomas Thornton's chamber in the 1590s: *ibid*. i. 247.

98 *BB*, i. 24-25, 51, 53.

99 College of Arms MS Vincent 94, p. 283, identified in Baker, *The Men of Court*, i. 192-4 (and partly illustrated in plate 3). The following members (with their dates of admission) were commemorated: William Gurney [1454], Sir Edmund Jenney [1463], Sir Thomas Lovell [1464], Thomas Butside (or Budockshead) [1468], Richard Heigham [1469], John Thornborough [1469], Sir Christopher Willoughby (later Lord Willoughby d'Eresby) [1470], Sir Robert Drury [1473], Robert Constable [1477], Thomas Marler [1485], Richard Blount [1485] and Sir Ralph Eure [1485]. Some of the other panels have not yet been identified. The Vincent MS dates from the 1590s. The windows were not noted by Dugdale and had presumably been destroyed before his time.

100 *BB*, iv. 281, quoting the Close Roll for 1375 ('Fikettesfeld juxta hospicium episcopi Cicestrensis… ubi dicti clerici [de cancellaria] et apprenticii ac alii civitatis predicte communem deductum suum habere solebant…'). The entry refers later to walking and games.

accident occurred there.[101] The first chambers here were erected in the 1680s, under an agreement between the benchers of Lincoln's Inn and Henry Serle, one of their number who owned part of the land. The arms of Henry Serle, and the date 1697, are still to be seen on the archway leading into Carey Street. The inside of the archway has been associated since 1830 with Wildy's, perhaps the oldest law bookshop in the world.

The northern part of the site—extending as far as the back yards of the houses in High Holborn—originally formed a large garden, including a coneygarth (or rabbit warren). This was sometimes called Coterell Garden, from the name of a twelfth-century owner (William Coterell), and was subject to a quit-rent of 9s. paid to the Hospital of St Giles-in-the-Fields until the Dissolution of the Monasteries. The conveyance of the bishop of Chichester's inn in 1536 included 'the coneygarth anciently called Coterell Garden'. In Tudor times it was walled with brick and gradually beautified; during the sixteenth and seventeenth centuries both garden and warren were laid out with terraces and trees, flower beds and a fountain. During the last two centuries, however, it has been extensively built upon. Stone Buildings, originally called The Stone Building, was begun in 1780 on the eastern part of the garden. The architect adopted a neo-classical style, but so situated the building as to avoid a clash with the more homely brick of the old buildings. The New Hall and Library, designed by Charles Hardwick in a grand Tudor style and intended to surpass in size the equivalent buildings in the other inns,[102] were opened by Queen Victoria in 1845. The general appearance of the Inn has not greatly changed since the removal of the various Chancery courts near the hall in the early 1880s. Unlike the other inns of court, the Inn was fortunate to escape major damage in the air raids of 1940-1. The buildings are now well known to the public, even if their identity is not, as a result of their many television and cinema appearances. But the Inn remains first and foremost, as it has been continuously for six centuries, a thriving place of work and study for members of the English legal profession.

101 It resulted in the celebrated case of *Mitchil v Allestree* (1676), which has been regarded (incorrectly) as the first action on the case for non-contractual negligence.

102 The Middle Temple previously had the largest hall, at 100 feet in length. The new hall of Lincoln's Inn is 120 feet in length: longer by five feet than that of Christ Church, Oxford.

SELECT BIBLIOGRAPHY

Archer, J A, Goldring, E and Knight, S, ed., *The Intellectual and Cultural World of the Early Modern Inns of Court* (Manchester, 2011).

Baildon, W P, *The Quincentenary of Lincoln's Inn 1422-1922* (1923).

Baker, J H, *The Third University of England* (Selden Soc. lecture, 1990); *Readers and Readings in the Inns of Court and Chancery* (13 Selden Soc. Suppl. Series, 2000); *The Men of Court 1440 to 1550: A Prosopography of the Inns of Court and Chancery and the Courts of Law* (18 Selden Soc. Suppl. Series, 2012), two volumes; *Collected Papers on English Legal History* (Cambridge, 2013), three volumes, especially vol. i.

Ball, W V, *Lincoln's Inn: its History and Traditions* (1947).

Bellot, H H L, *Gray's Inn and Lincoln's Inn* (1925), 113-210.

Dugdale, W, *Origines Juridiciales* (3rd edn., 1680), 231-70.

Holdsworth, A, ed., *A Portrait of Lincoln's Inn* (2007).

Hurst, G, *A Short History of Lincoln's Inn* (1946); *Lincoln's Inn Essays* (1947).

Lemmings, D, *Gentlemen and Barristers: The Inns of Court and the English Bar 1680-1730* (Oxford, 1990).

Megarry, R E, *Introduction to Lincoln's Inn* (1971).

Prest, W R, *The Inns of Court 1590-1640* (1972); *The Rise of the Barristers: A Social History of the English Bar 1590-1640* (Oxford, 1986).

Readings and Moots at the Inns of Court in the Fifteenth Century: vol. i, Readings, ed. S E Thorne (71 Selden Soc., 1952) and vol. ii, Moots and Readers' Cases, ed. J H Baker (105 Selden Soc., 1990).

Records of the Honorable Society of Lincoln's Inn: *Admissions* [1420-1893], two volumes (1897); *The Black Books* [1422-1965], six volumes (ed. W P Baildon, J D Walker, R Roxburgh and P V Baker, 1897-2001), with *Two Supplements* (R Roxburgh, 1977).

Ringrose, C W, *The Bench Book of Lincoln's Inn* (1973), reproduced from typescript.

Roxburgh, R, *The Origins of Lincoln's Inn* (Cambridge, 1963); summarised and augmented in 'Lincoln's Inns of the Fourteenth Century' (1978) 94 *LQR* 363-382; 'Lincoln's Inns of the Fifteenth Century' (1980) 96 *LQR* 51-72.

Simpson, J W, *Some Account of the Old Hall of Lincoln's Inn* (1928).

Spilsbury, W H, *Lincoln's Inn, its Ancient and Modern Buildings* (2nd edn., 1873).

Turner, G J, *Lincoln's Inn* (1903), a rare pamphlet printed by F E Robinson & Co., Great Russell Street; 'The Origins of Lincoln's Inn' (1906) *The Athenaeum*, no. 4117, p. 335.

Williams, E, *Early Holborn and the Legal Quarter of London: A Topographical Survey of the Beginnings of the District known as Holborn and of the Inns of Court and of Chancery* (1927), two volumes.

A. THE DEVELOPMENT OF THE INN

¶ The Inns of Court and the former Inns of Chancery are—to transpose a term from New York City—located mid-town, in an area which, apart from the Inns themselves, lacks the sense of identity, cohesiveness or character each possessed in its own way by the City of London, Westminster and the West End. This section evokes the origins of this area, leading to the presence of the Inns here.

1. THE INN'S LOCATION:

i. Where it was established

'On the western edge of medieval London where the suburbs ended at the outworks of Temple Bar and Holborn Bars and the open country of fields and scattered villages began, the Guilds of the lawyers formed a closely knit and well-defined community. Along the Thames, which had given it birth, the commercial city, crowded within the circuit of its walls, raised a cluster of spires and towers to the crowning spire of Old St Paul's Cathedral on its hill. Round the bend of the river and linked with the City by the waterside palaces and gardens of the magnates of Church and State, lay royal Westminster, seat and burial place of kings, its tremendous Abbey matched by the vast Hall where the Lord Chancellor and the Judges of England had their Courts. Between the two and independent of both, the Inns of Court and Chancery were taking shape. Independent likewise of the Universities of Oxford and Cambridge, they themselves constituted at once a legal university and an autonomous professional organisation unique in Christendom.'

—Francis Cowper [of GI and LI], from *A Prospect of Gray's Inn*, 1961.

>> D N Barnard [of GI].

The question not fully addressed by this quotation is 'why a *bishop's* town-house?' As Cowper indicates, the area between London and Westminster (to the extent that it was settled) was taken up by the houses of magnates of the State and Church. Not the least of them in numbers or wealth, were the latter who were summoned periodically from their provinces, dioceses, abbeys or estates to Parliament. The archbishop of York, twelve bishops and seven abbots were here. The only prelates to have their town-houses on the s. bank of the Thames were two of the most senior: Canterbury at Lambeth and Winchester at Southwark.

To the e., w. and n.w. of the City of London, encircling these town-houses, were numerous other houses dedicated to the service of God: the buildings and gardens of abbeys, priories and nunneries, among which may be numbered the Old and the New Temple of the Knights Templar (until that Order was suppressed); the Priory of St John Clerkenwell; the great Carthusian house of Charterhouse; St Bartholomew's Priory; the houses of the Carmelites (the White Friars), the Dominicans (the Black Friars), and within the City walls, the Franciscans (the Grey Friars).

By accident of topography, Lincoln's Inn is the only one of the Inns of Court or former Inns of Chancery which took over a bishop's town house.

I.a. The 'Ralph Agas' view of London (n. prospect), *ca.* 1560-70, redrawn by Geo. Vertue, for *Civitas Londinium*, 1737 [BM].

The Inn's demesne is shown in the centre, two-fifths of the distance from the river. W. of the Inn is the open land of Cup Field and Purse Field, later to become Lincoln's Inn Fields. The three boats moored in the river suggest Temple Stairs, and thence the route to the Inn up Middle Temple La. and Chancery La. On Holborn are the Society's daughter houses of Furnival's Inn (e. of Gray's Inn La.) and Thavies Inn (w. of St Andrew's).

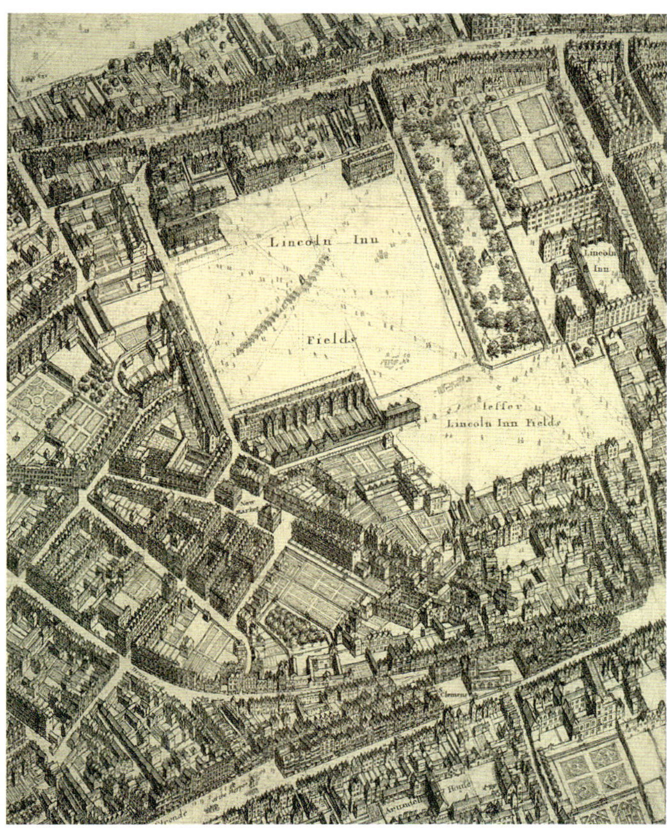

1.b. Wenceslas Hollar: Prospect of central London, from St Giles' to Lincoln's Inn, *ca.* 1658 [BM].

This very remarkable work shows, among many other things, the buildings of the Inn, its walks and gardens, with great accuracy. It has been debated as to whether the Fields are shown as they then were, or largely as built and partly as projected.

ii. Why it was there

'There are some circumstances however respecting their situation and establishment, I cannot altogether pass over. They seem to have been fixed in this spot, to be as much as could be in the centre of the town, and yet out of the noise and hurry of it. And it must be owned their situation is admirably calculated, with this mixed view. They are, at this day, between the cities of London and Westminster; and by their squares, courts, and spacious buildings, answer very well the various purposes of health, study, business and retirement. You may think perhaps they should have been nearer Westminster Hall, the great field of practice; and that their situation does not justify what, I said, was one end of fixing it, to be as near as could be in the centre of the town. The times in which the inns of court were established will answer both objections. If we view London, as the map exhibits it even in Queen Elizabeth's time, it will from thence appear, that noblemen's houses occupied all the intermediate space between Westminster Hall and the extremity of the city. But could the inns of court have been fixed nearer the hall, they would only have accommodated the profession in one respect, and too much at the expense of every other convenience. After this slight observation on the convenience, reflect a moment on the delightfulness and the dignity of the situation. Two of them on the bank of the river; and in those days the whole bank from the Temple to Westminster was lined with palaces of the king and some of the first noblemen of the kingdom: what the other two wanted in the view of the river, they made up in the extent of their gardens.'

—Edward Wynne [of MT], from *Eunomus*, 1774 [BL].

>> D S Bland, *A Bibliography of the Inns of Court and Chancery*, 1965.

1.c. Simon Gribelin: Cavendish Weedon's project for laying out Lincoln's Inn Fields, 1699 (detail: the Inn, omitting the Fields) (e. prospect of the Inn) in Colen Campbell, *Vitruvius Britannicus*, 1715-25 [BM].

The project included the building of a church in the Fields, which was never put in hand. The design for the church ('St Marie's') to be in the centre of the Fields was seemingly copied from one of Inigo Jones. The Fields must have been at what then seemed destined to be the heart of the best quarter of London, and the parishes of St Giles-in-the-Fields and St Andrew were too large, eventually being divided on the building of other churches, as the population increased. The Inn is clearly shown as it was at that date, shortly after the completion of Serle's Court, to the s. This is the earliest known prospect specific to the Inn and the Fields. The sun is shining from the n.!

1.e. G C Woodward: 'The Charm of Lincoln's Inn' (s. prospect), in *The Graphic*, 1922 [press cutting, HSLI].

From this perspective (unusually, one from the n.) little seems to have changed in the Inn from then to now, except in the area of the Kitchen Garden, Hardwicke Building and Bog House Court. On the perimeter, the most visible difference is that Alfred Waterhouse's New Court, between Carey St. and Portugal St., was demolished, and rebuilt to the designs of Richard Seifert and Partners in the 1960s, and is being demolished and rebuilt again.

1.d. J Kip: 'The Prospect of Lincoln's Inn', drawn *ca.* 1705 (n. prospect), in Strype's *Survey*, ed. of 1755.

The hand-colouring is of a later date. This well-known engraved prospect exists in two versions, for the 1720 and 1755 editions (the former without and the latter with a pond in the Fields). The Inn's Walks were then adorned with classical statues. This Society, unlike the other Inns, seems always to have avoided placing statues of distinguished members in its grounds.

B. THE APPROACH AND ENTRY INTO THE INN

2. APPROACHING THE INN:

¶ This section first evokes, by a choice of poetry and prose, the appearance and atmosphere of the approaches to this Inn or the experience of travelling along them. In past centuries, clients or their attorneys needed to travel from all corners of the kingdom to take legal advice in the Inns of Court, or to prepare cases for hearing in the courts or judges' chambers at Westminster or in the neighbourhood of the Inns. This constituted a secular pilgrimage which, until the Reformation, would have rivalled those to religious shrines. If the establishment of higher courts around the country and the corresponding growth of provincial bars has reduced the absolute necessity for this travelling within England, that has been matched by the great influx of those who choose to come from overseas.

Then, with a selection of literature which refers to the Inn, and to its immediate neighbourhood, there is an evocation of the often sordid access to the Inns, and thence the admission through a gate into their separate world—sometimes seen as dusty and gloomy, and sometimes verdant and bright—always very different from the world around them.

2.1. By water: by wherry or barge to Temple Stairs, and thence up Middle Temple Lane

¶ For centuries, one of the ways—usually the preferred way—to the Inn from Westminster or Whitehall or from the City of London was by water. For this reason, two well-known quotations are included here, inspired by the journey downstream past Westminster and the Inns to the City. Although not written as journeys to the Inn, for present purposes the reader may imagine being rowed down- or up-stream and alighting at the Temple (as in the third quotation, which *is* a journey to the Inn).

At length they all to mery London came,
To mery London, my most kyndly Nurse.
That to me gave this Lifes first native sourse:
Though from another place I take my name,
An house of auncient fame.
There when they came, whereas those bricky towres,
The which on Themmes brode aged backe doe ryde,
Where now the studious Lawyers have their bowers,
There whylome wont the Templer Knights[1] *to byde,*
Till they decayed through pride:

—Edmund Spenser, from *Prothalamion, or a Spousall Song*, 1595.

---

[1] The Knights Templar are associated with the sites of three of the Inns of Court. Their original home in London was the Old Temple on Holborn just e. of Chancery La., from which they removed in or before 1162 to the New Temple, on the river. The Order was dissolved in 1312, and the site of Inner and Middle Temples is largely co-extensive with their former home. The site occupied by New Square Lincoln's Inn was once part of their land holding.

Then Westminster next great Tames doth entertaine;
That vaunts her Palace large, and her most sumptuous Fane:[1]
The Land's tribunall seate[2] *that challenge for hers,*
The crowning of our Kings, their famous sepulchers.
Then goes he on along by that more beauteous Strand,[3]
Expressing both the wealth and bravery of the Land.
(So many sumptuous Bowres,[4] *within so little space,*
The All-beholding Sun scarse sees in all his race.)
And on by London leads, which like a Crescent lies,
Whose windowes seem to mock the Star-befreckled skies…

—Michael Drayton, from *Polyolbion,*[5] 1612.

> Peter Yapp, *The Travellers' Dictionary of Quotation*, 1983.

[1] Fane: temple, i.e. the Abbey.

[2] tribunall seat: Westminster Hall, housing the Courts of King's Bench, Common Pleas, and Chancery.

[3] Strand: the n. river shore of the Thames between Westminster and the City, whence the name of the street running w. from the Temple.

[4] Bowres (=bowers): the gardens and courts of the palaces and state-houses on the n. bank of the Thames, among which in particular those of the Temple.

[5] *Polyolbion*: much-blessed.

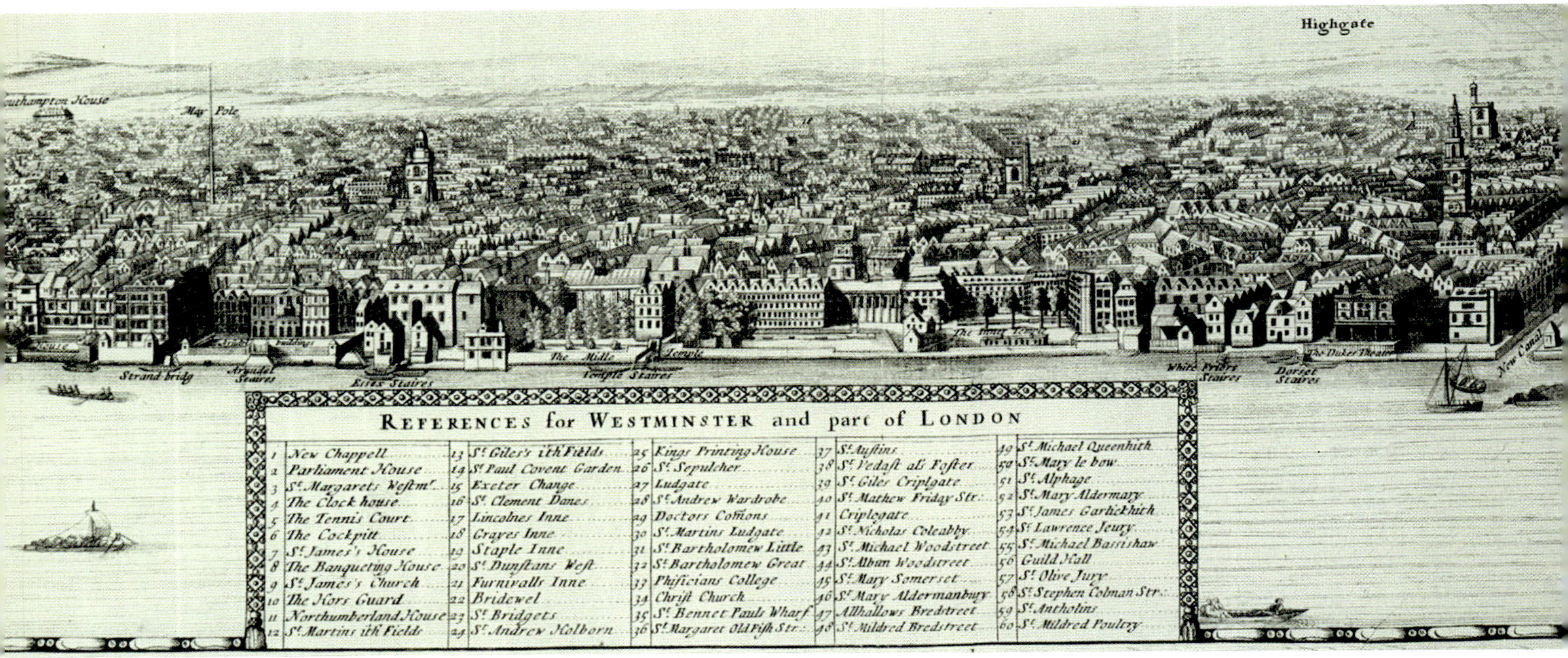

Highgate
May Pole
Arundel Staires
Essex Staires
Temple Staires
White Friers Staires
REFERENCES for WESTMINSTER and part of LONDON
1 New Chappell
2 Parliament House
3 St. Margarets Westmr.
4 The Clock house
5 The Tennis Court
6 The Cockpitt
7 St. James's House
8 The Banqueting House
9 St. James's Church
10 The Hors Guard
11 Northumberland House
12 St. Martins ith Fields
13 St. Giles's ith Fields
14 St. Paul Covent Garden
15 Exeter Change
16 St. Clement Danes
17 Lincolnes Inne
18 Grayes Inne
19 Staple Inne
20 St. Dunstans West
21 Furnivalls Inne
22 Bridewel
23 St. Bridgets
24 St. Andrew Holborn
25 Kings Printing House
26 St. Sepulcher
27 Ludgate
28 St. Andrew Wardrobe
29 Doctors Comons
30 St. Martins Ludgate
31 St. Bartholomew Little
32 St. Bartholomew Great
33 Phisicians College
34 Christ Church
35 St. Bennet Pauls Wharf
36 St. Margaret Old Fish Str:
37 St. Austins
38 St. Vedast als Foster
39 St. Giles Cripplgate
40 St. Mathew Friday Str:
41 Criplegate
42 St. Nicholas Coleabby
43 St. Michael Woodstreet
44 St. Albun Woodstreet
45 St. Mary Somerset
46 St. Mary Aldermanbury
47 Allhallows Bredstreet
48 St. Mildred Bredstreet
49 St. Michael Queenhith
50 St. Mary le bow
51 St. Alphage
52 St. Mary Aldermary
53 St. James Garlickhith
54 St. Lawrence Jeury
55 St. Michael Bassishaw
56 Guild Hall
57 St. Olive Jury
58 St. Stephen Colman Str:
59 St. Antholins
60 St. Mildred Poultry

2.a. William Morgan: 'Prospect of London and Westminster', 1682 (detail of panorama, n.)

The way which Pepys would have taken from the Thames two decades earlier is clearly drawn. The buildings of the Inn can just be discerned. Temple Stairs is marked.

¶ Clients and their lawyers travelling by water downstream from Westminster or Whitehall or upstream from the City of London by water alighted at the steps and jetty of Temple Stairs if they wished to walk up Middle Temple La. to Lincoln's Inn. The lane opened (and opens) through Middle Temple Gatehouse onto Fleet St., opposite Bell Yard. Having crossed Fleet St., the traveller had three choices: Shire La. and Bell Yard, both diagonally opposite that gatehouse and immediately to the e. of Temple Bar, and Chancery La., which lay a few yards yet further e. The choice may have been influenced by, among other considerations, the gate through which the visitor wished to enter the Inn, or the shops along the way to it.

'Thence, it raining hard, by water to the Temple and so to Lyncolns Inne…'

—Samuel Pepys, from *Diary*, for 27th June 1663.

> H B Wheatley, revised edn. of P Cunningham, *London Past and Present*, 1891.

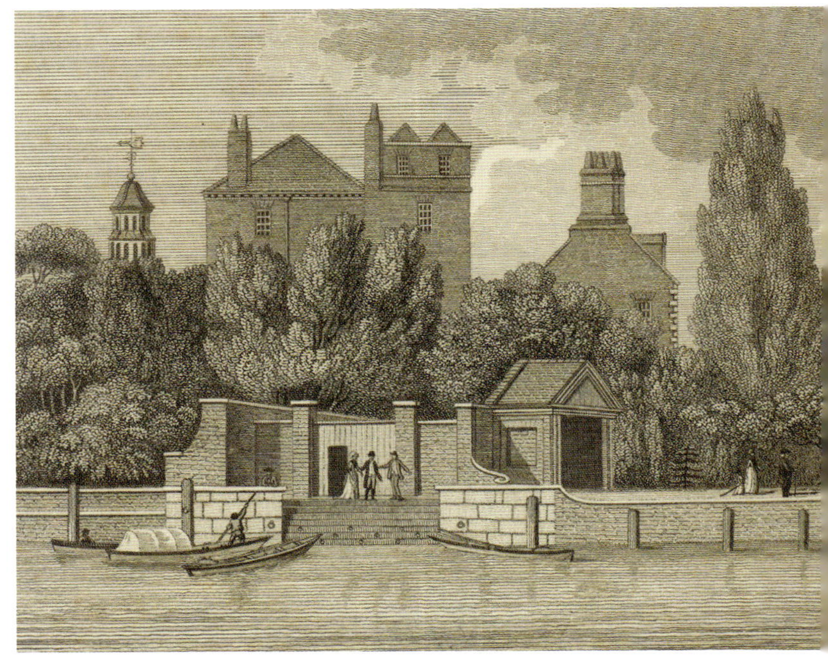

2.b. Charles Tomkins: Temple Stairs, 1801 (n. view) [LMA].

Passengers on the river were carried by wherry—a long, shallow-draft clinker-built boat—of which there were many hundreds in service, rowed by one or two of the fraternity of Thames watermen, or by the larger barge. A number of them were based at Temple Stairs. Other stairs, just upstream or downstream of the Temple, may also have served for access to the Inn.

2.c. Emile Claus: 'Derniers rayons vers Black Friars Bridge, mars 1917' [MRBB].

This e. view of the Thames, downstream, is taken from the terrace of Somerset House. It shows the modern transformation of the river bank at Temple Stairs (its location marked by the tall monument on the water's edge). Temple Gardens, a grandiose chambers building of 1879 in Portland stone, now forms the river end of Middle Temple La. Visitors to the Inn coming this way from the City of Westminster no longer have an adjacent pier, but—besides the road on the Victoria Embankment—have Temple Station on the Underground, beneath the Embankment Gardens, in the foreground of this painting.

2.d. William Macdonald: 'In Middle Temple Lane', 1904 [LMA].

This is the middle section of the La., as it ascends from the river.

2.e. William Macdonald: 'Middle Temple Lane', 1912 [LMA].

This is the upper section of the La., with the opening onto Fleet St.

2.f. Paul Sandby: Temple Bar and Fleet Street, 1790s (e. view) [BM].

Temple Bar marked the boundary of the City, on Fleet St. It was designed by Sir Christopher Wren, and erected *ca.* 1670. It was dismantled in 1870 but rescued and reconstructed in Paternoster Square in 2004. The boundary hereabouts remains visible at the present day in street signs, and in policemen's uniforms, as well as being marked by the Temple Griffin. The projecting clock of St Dunstan's is visible beyond the archway of Temple Bar.

2.2. By road: the bustle of people and vehicles:

i. Along Fleet Street and the Strand

¶ Fleet St. and its western continuation, the Strand, follow the ancient land route out of the City, leaving it at Ludgate, to the royal and ecclesiastical centre of Westminster. The C18th and C19th development of St James's, Mayfair, Belgravia and Kensington added those areas of London to the available destinations, and thus contributed to the overcrowding of these thoroughfares. The quotations which follow are drawn from evocations of Fleet St. and the Strand, not in context journeys along them to the Inn. The reader is, therefore, invited to follow the writers in his or her mind w. along Fleet St., or e. along the Strand and then leave them at the point where those roads converge, and turn n. from them into Chancery La., or Bell Yard, or Shire La., towards the Inn.

2.g. Herbert Marshall, RWS: 'Fleet Street, London', *ca.* 1885 (w. view) [LMA].

This artist was one of the most notable atmospheric painters of London scenes in the Edwardian era. In this view, on the r. is St Dunstan-in-the-West and the RCJ beyond. Between the two is the turning into Chancery La.

The projecting clock of St Dunstan's, with it's automata of Gog and Magog, was a sight of the street from 1671 until 1828 when the medieval church was demolished and a new one built further back to accommodate the widening of Fleet St. It was reinstated on the front of the new church in 1935. In consequence, it has inspired a number of literary references. One such was this:

When labour and when dullness, club in hand,
Like the two figures at St. Dunstan's stand,
Beating alternately in measured time
The clockwork tintinnabulum of rhyme,
Exact and regular the sounds will be,
But such mere quarter-strokes are not for me.

—William Cowper, from *The Task*, 1785.

• Fleet Street

Should we now go a-wandering, we should meet
With catchpoles,[1] *whores, and carts in every street;*
Now when each narrow lane, each nook and cave,
Sign-posts and shop doors, pimp for every knave,
When riotous sinful plush, and telltale spurs
Walk Fleet Street and the Strand, when the soft stirs
Of bawdy, ruffled silks, turn night to day;
And the loud whip and coach scolds all the way;
When lust of all sorts, and each itchy blood
From the Tower-Wharf to Cymbeline and Lud[2]
Hunts for a mate, and the tired footman reels
'Twixt chairmen, torches, and the hackney wheels.

—Henry Vaughan ('the Silurist'), from *A Rhapsody, written upon his meeting with some of his friends at The Globe Tavern in Fleet Street,* 1641.

> Lawrence Manley, *London in the Age of Shakespeare*, 1986.

1 catchpole: a low bailiff.

2 Cymbeline and Lud: statues of these mythical figures of early British history stood on Ludgate.

¶ A quarter-millennium later, the clothes and carriages had changed, as had some of the callings, but the ebb and flow tide of people and vehicles continued unabated:

Wings and rags of cloud in a withered sky,
A strip of pallid azure, at either end,
Above Ludgate obelisk, above
The Temple griffin, widening with the width
Below, and parallel with the street that counts
Seven hundred paces of tesselated road
From Ludgate Circus west to Chancery Lane[1]
By concrete pavement flanked and precipice
Of windowed fronts on this side and on that,
A thoroughfare of everything that hastes,
The sullen tavern-loafers notwithstanding
And hawkers in the channel hunger-it.
Interfluent night and day the tides of trade,
Labour and pleasure, law and crime, are sucked
From every urban quarter: through this strait
All business London pours.

—John Davidson,[2] from 'Fleet Street', 1909.

> John Arlott, *op. cit.*, 1988.

1 Chancery La.: just past the La., to the w., is the point at which Fleet St. becomes the Strand, formerly marked by Temple Bar, and now by the statue of the Temple Griffin.

2 Davidson: a poet very much associated with this street, and the author of *Fleet Street Eclogues*. He was a member of one of the last literary flowerings of Fleet St. (if newspaper journalists are taken to represent a different form of writing), centred on The Rhymers, founded by W B Yeats, and meeting in *The Old Cheshire Cheese*.

From north and south, from east and west,
Here in one shrieking vortex meet
These streams of life, made manifest
Along the shaking quivering street,
Its pulse and heart that throbs and glows
As if strife were its repose.

I shut my ear to such rude sounds
As reach a harsh discordant note,
Till, melting into what surrounds,
My soul doth with the current float;
And from the turmoil and the strike
Wakes all the melody of life.

The stony buildings blindly stare
Unconscious of the crime within,

While man returns his fellow's glare
The secrets of his soul to win.
And each man passes from his place,
None heed. A shadow leaves such trace.

—Isaac Rosenberg, 'Fleet Street', 1916.

Rosenberg was killed in action, aged 27, serving in a 'bantam' battalion of the British army. An authoritative survey of English First World War poetry adjudged his poem 'Break of Day in the Trenches' as the greatest of the war. His name is inscribed in Poets' Corner, in Westminster Abbey, and his self portraits are in the NPG and Tate Britain.

• The Strand

¶ Two evocations of the same street, separated by two centuries:

Where the fair columns of St Clement[1] *stand*
Whose straiten'd bounds encroach[2] *upon the Strand;*
Where the low penthouse bows the walker's head,
And the rough pavement wounds the yielding tread;
Where not a post protects the narrow space,
And strung in twines, combs dangle in thy face;
Summon at once thy courage, rouze thy care,
Stand firm, look back, be resolute, beware.
Forth issuing from steep lanes, the colliers' steeds
Drag the black load; another cart succeeds,
Team follows team, crouds heap'd on crouds appear,
And wait impatient, 'till the road grow clear.
Now all the pavement sounds with trampling feet

2.h. Henry Tidmarsh: St Clement Danes, 1920 (e. view) [LMA].

[1] St Clement Danes: the church to the s.w. of the Inn, in whose parish that corner of New Square lies. The RCJ now stand on the n. side of the Strand, diagonally opposite the church.

[2] encroach: for a reader unfamiliar with this neighbourhood, it should be explained that the church stands on an island in the road, with traffic passing it on either side, and with only a few square feet of paving railed around it. Its burial ground lay some distance away, to the n.

[3] *Trivia*: used in its original etymology, to mean a road from which three roads diverge (a *patte d'oie* in Parisian topography), hence metaphorically a choice of routes.

And the mixt hurry barricades the street.
Entangled here, the waggon's lengthen'd team
Cracks the tough harness; here a pond'rous beam
Lies over-turn'd athwart; for slaughter fed
Here lowing bullocks raise their horned head.
Now oaths grow loud, with coaches coaches jar,
And the smart blow provokes the sturdy war;
From the high box they whirl the thong around,
And with the twining lash their shins resound...

—John Gay, from *Trivia,*[3] *or the Art of Walking the Streets of London*, 1716.

Gay is particularly associated with this corner of London on account of his *The Beggar's Opera*, 1728, first presented at the Lincoln's Inn Fields Theatre (see *36.a.*).

Down through the ancient Strand
The spirit of October, mild and boon
And sauntering, takes his way
This golden end of afternoon,
As though the corn stood yellow in all the land
And the ripe apples dropped to the harvest-moon.

Lo! the round sun, half-down to the western slope—
Seen as along an unglazed telescope—
Lingers and lolls, loth to be done with day:
Gifting the long, lean, lanky street
And its abounding confluences of being
With aspects generous and bland;
Making a thousand harnesses to shine
As with new ore from some enchanted mine,
And every horse's coat so full of sheen
He looks new-tailored, and every 'bus to 'bus feels clean,
And never a hansom but it worth the feeing.
And every jeweller between the pale
Offers a real Arabian Night for sale
And even the roar
Of the strong streams of toil, that pause and pour
Eastward and westward, sounds suffused—
Seems as it were bemused
And blurred, and like the speech
Of lazy seas on a lotus-haunted beach—
......
Till Clement's,[1] *angular and cold and staid,*
Gleams forth in glamour's very stuffs arrayed;
And Bride's[2] *her aëry, unsubstantial charm*
Through flight on flight of springing, soaring stone
Grown flushed and warm,
Laughs into life full-mooded and fresh-blown;
And the high majesty of Paul's
Uplifts a voice of living light, and calls—
Calls to his millions to behold and see
How goodly this his London Town can be!

—W E Henley, from 'London Voluntary', 1893.

> John Arlott, *op. cit.*, 1988

[1] Clement's: St Clement Danes.

[2] Bride's: St Bride's, at the e. end of Fleet St., notable for its 'wedding cake' stone spire.

Henley's standing in the literary world of his day has been compared to that of Samuel Johnson in his. In recent times, his short poem 'Invictus', 1875, has proved an inspiration to, among others, one commonwealth and one foreign president, and one British prince.

---

ii. On Holborn and High Holborn, and to their *coaching inns*

¶ The street named Holborn from the tributary stream of the river Fleet, the Holbourne (whence the name of the immediate neighbourhood and then of the former Metropolitan Borough within the LCC), forms part of the ancient main route out of London (through Newgate) to the w. Under the Romans it was the Praetorian Way which, among other destinations, led w. to the military towns of Calleva Atrebatum (Silchester) and Corinium (Cirencester). Later, it formed part of the Roman-Saxon way called Watling St., and in recent centuries led towards the Bath Rd., latterly known as the Great West Rd. Despite all this, the street seems not to have inspired the same quality of literature as Fleet St. and its most distinctive theme was that of the doleful journey along it from Newgate to Tyburn.

The boundary here of the City was just e. of the intersection with Gray's Inn La., marked by and known as 'Holborn Bars'.

2.i. W Allen: Holborn Bars and the s. side of Holborn (e. view), 1860 [LMA].

This is the first glimpse of the City—unprepossessing though it is—which a traveller, coming from the w. along High Holborn would have had, after passing through the constriction of Middle Row, or having come from the n. down Gray's Inn La. The full width of Holborn lay ahead of him. Staple Inn (of Chancery) is on the r. The boundary of the extended city 'liberties' was marked by two stone pillars (of which one on the edge of the pavement is visible here): insignificant in comparison with the equivalent entrance at Temple Bar, which was always the ceremonial entrance to the City—as when the Monarch entered and the Lord Mayor came to welcome him or her. The inner boundary of the City on this route was at Newgate, which did indeed have a stone structure until the C18th.

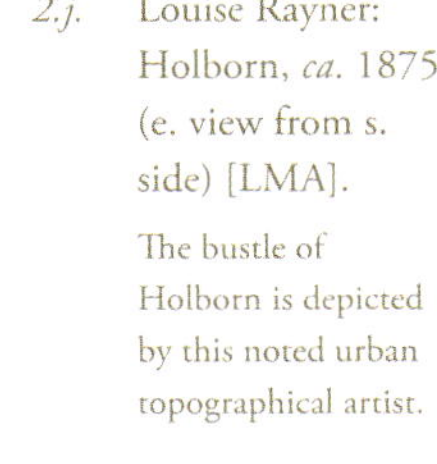

2.j. Louise Rayner: Holborn, *ca.* 1875 (e. view from s. side) [LMA].

The bustle of Holborn is depicted by this noted urban topographical artist.

'Holborn, or Holbourn hill, so called from its ascent from Holbourne Bridge: a very spatious Street, well built and inhabited by Tradesmen; as being a Place of so great a Resort for Stage Coaches[1] and Wagons; as also by Gentry, and others, that come to Town, induced thereunto from the Accommodation of the several Inns, not only in this Part, but likewise in High Holbourn; besides the several Inns of Chancery[2] here seated, are no small Advantage to the Place.'

—John Strype, from *Survey of London*, 1720.

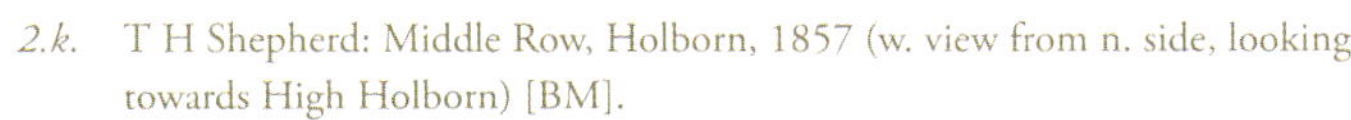

2.k. T H Shepherd: Middle Row, Holborn, 1857 (w. view from n. side, looking towards High Holborn) [BM].

This is the view of the route towards the Inn to be followed by a traveller who had arrived at one of the coaching inns in Holborn. The junction with Gray's Inn La. is at the end of the building on the r. (n.). Chancery La. is some yards ahead to the s. (l.), hidden by Middle Row, which comprised shops and houses and also the Inquest House of the parish. The space on its s. side was wide enough to allow passage to a pedestrian or a chair. All wheeled vehicles would have passed on its n. side. It was demolished soon after this watercolour was made. This action had been advocated two centuries earlier by James Howell in *Londinopolis*, 1657: 'Southward of Gray's Inn Lane there is a row of small houses, which is a mighty hindrance to Holborn in point of prospect, which if they were taken down there would be from Holborn Conduit to St Giles-in-the-Fields one of the fairest rising streets in the world'.

> quotation: Caroline M Barron, *The Parish of St Andrew Holborn*, 1979.

i.

ii.

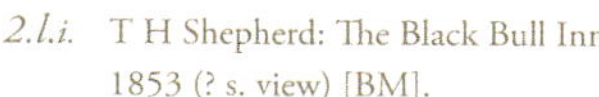

2.1.i. T H Shepherd: The Black Bull Inn, 1853 (? s. view) [BM].

2.1.ii. T H Shepherd: The French Horn Inn, 1853 [BM].

2.1.iii. T H Shepherd: The Old Bell Inn, 1853 (? s. view) [BM].

2.1.iv. T H Shepherd: The Bull & Gate Inn, on the s. side of High Holborn, 1855 (? n. view) [BM].

iii.

iv.

1 Stage Coaches and Wagons: as implied by Strype, the difference between Fleet St. and Holborn lay in the unusual breadth of Holborn and the large number of its inns and stables—whether coaching inns, working to timetables, or stables from which light carriages or livery horses (for riding) could be hired. High Holborn and Holborn, and to the e., Holborn Hill and Snow Hill descending into and out of the valley of the river Fleet, contained the greatest congregation of such equine establishments in London. On High Holborn and its continuations to the e. were the Bell and Crown, the Old Bell, the Black Bull, the Black Swan, the Bull and Gate, the King's Arms, the Saracen's Head and the George & Blue Boar. Intersecting that thoroughfare, on Fetter La., stood the White Horse, and on Gray's Inn La. was the Spread Eagle.

From early times, Holborn had been an important entry point to the City for wagons bringing food; feed for horses; and other products of the countryside, notably timber, wool and hides. The volume of the traffic and the scale of the business activity were remarkable. An early-C19th timetable of the George & Blue Boar, for example, lists times of departure daily for twenty coaches, from 5.30 a.m. to 6.00 p.m.—some forty movements a day into or out of one inn yard. The coaches from that inn served three points of the compass: including Bath and Bristol, Shrewsbury and Holyhead (for Dublin), Manchester and Liverpool, Newcastle and Edinburgh, Ramsgate and Dover (for Calais) as well as the university cities and many of the principal business cities and towns in the Midlands. Other inns in Holborn completed the points of the compass and served, among other destinations, East Anglia, the s. coast and the s.w. of England.

Supporting those inns and stables would have been the establishments of corn factors and hay merchants, farriers, saddlers and harness makers, coachbuilders and painters, wheelwrights, veterinary surgeons, horse infirmaries, knackers, horse-butchers, tanners and manure carters.

No vestiges above ground of any of the inns can now been seen, the last of them having been demolished at the turn of the C19th and C20th.

Dickens, in his sketch 'The Streets—Morning', evokes the passengers arriving at a Holborn inn yard in the early morning, having travelled all night: shaken, deprived of sleep, and having lost all sense of time. At much the same hour the passengers preparing to depart on the early coach are met by a throng of pedlars crowded into this yard and selling what were called *articles de voyage* which they might need, and many which they might not.

2 Inns of Chancery: see 22. and 23.

¶ A traveller, arriving at a coaching inn in High Holborn, would have chosen between entering the Inn from the e. through Chancery La. (treated in 2.3. below) or from the w. through Great Turnstile—a footpath which still exists, but was completely rebuilt in the last decade of the C20th and the first two of the C21st:

'on the North side is great Turnstile Alley, a great thoroughfare which leadeth into Holborn, a Place inhabited by Shoemakers, Sempsters, and Milliners; for which it is of a considerable Trade and well noted…'

—John Strype, *Survey*, 1720.

2.3.2. The mud and mire

¶ Mud was always a problem in the streets until they were paved or tarred, but Chancery La. seems to have had a worse problem than most.

'This Chancellor's Lane (now called Chancery Lane), in Edward I's time, was so foul and miry, that John Briton, *Custos*[1] of London, had it barred up, to hinder any harm that might happen in passing that way: and the Bishop of Chichester, whose house was there, kept up the bar for many years...'

—John Strype, *Survey*, 1720.

---

[1] *Custos Rotulorum*: Master of the Rolls.

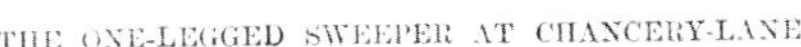

THE ONE-LEGGED SWEEPER AT CHANCERY-LANE.

2.r. The one-legged sweeper at Chancery Lane, in Henry Mayhew, *op. cit.*, 1851.

Mayhew does not locate the sweeper along the La., but it may be conjectured that he may have worked mid-way, where pedestrians would have crossed from the judges' chambers in Serjeants' Inn, or the Rolls (court), or the public legal offices in Symond's Inn or Quality Court, all on the e.; to Lincoln's Inn, or to the offices of the Paymaster-General, or those of the Accountant-General, or the Law Society's Hall, on the w., and vice-versa.

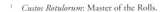

¶ The early C20th disappearance of horses from the streets removed what by then had become a primary component of 'mud'.

'It is quite dark now, and the gas-lamps have acquired their full effect. Jostling against clerks going to post the day's letters, and against counsel and attorneys going home to dinner, and against plaintiffs and defendants, and suitors of all sorts, and against the general crowd, in whose way the forensic wisdom of ages has interposed a million of obstacles to the transaction of the commonest business of life—diving through law and equity, and through that kindred mystery, the street mud, which is made of nobody knows what, and collects about us nobody knows whence or how; we only knowing in general that when there is too much of it, we find it necessary to shovel it away...'

—Charles Dickens, from *Bleak House*, 1852.

'That portion of the London street-folk who earn a scanty living by sweeping crossings constitute a large class of the Metropolitan poor. We can scarcely walk along a street of any extent, or pass through a square of the least pretensions to "gentility", without meeting one or more of these private scavengers. Crossing sweeping seems to be one of those occupations which are resorted to as an excuse for begging; and, indeed, as many expressed it to me: "it was the last chance left of obtaining an honest crust.

"...I don't know what induced me to take that crossing, except it was that no one was there, and the traffic was so good—fact is, the traffic is too good, and people won't stop as they cross over, they're very glad to get out of the way of the cabs and the omnibuses.

"Tradespeople never give me anything—not even a bit of bread. The only thing I get is a few cuttings, such as crusts of sandwiches and remains of cheese, from the publichouse at the corner of the court. The tradespeople are as distant to me now as they were when I came, but if I should pitch up a tale I should soon get acquainted with them.

"We have lived in this lodging two years and a half, and we pay oneandninepence a week, as you may see from the rentbook, and that I manage to earn on Sundays. We owe four weeks now, and, thank God, it's no more.

"I was born, sir, in — street, Berkeleysquare, at Lord —'s house, when my mother was minding the house. I have been used to London all my life, but not to this part; I have always been at the west-end, which is what I call the best end.

"I did not like the idea of crossing-sweeping at first, till I reasoned with myself, Why should I mind? I'm not doing any hurt to anybody. I don't care at all now—I know I'm doing what I ought to do".'

—Henry Mayhew, 'The one-legged sweeper at Chancery Lane', in *London Labour and the London Poor*, 1851.

2.3.3. The traffic of bench, bar and law students to, from and past the Inn:

i. Equestrian

¶ In the entire history of the Lane, the one man to have created the greatest spectacle must have been Cardinal Wolsey. This would in large part have been a manifestation of his being Lord Chancellor, but predated by some two centuries any association of the Chancellors with this Inn by sitting in their court within it. He was the last of the ecclesiastical Lord Chancellors. He made his way in procession from the bishop of Lincoln's inn or town-house near the corner of High Holborn and Chancery La. (as to which see the Historical Essay) down the Lane to the river at Temple Stairs on his way to conduct judicial business in Westminster Hall, or when embarking thence on a state barge bound downstream to Greenwich or upstream to his palace of Hampton Court:

'Now will I declare unto you his order in going to Westminster Hall, daily in the term season. First, before his coming out of his privy chamber, he heard most commonly every day two masses in his privy close… And after mass he would return in his privy chamber again, and being advertised of the furniture of his chambers without, with noblemen, gentlemen, and other persons, would issue out into them, apparelled all in red, in the habit of a cardinal; which was either of fine scarlet, or else of crimson satin, taffety, damask, or caffa, the best that he could get for money: and upon his head a round pillion, with a Noble of black velvet set to the same in the inner side; he had also a tippet of fine sables about his neck; holding in his hand a very fair orange, whereof the meat or substance within was taken out, and filled up again with the part of a sponge, wherein was vinegar, and other confections against the pestilent airs; the which he was most commonly smelt unto, passing among the press, or else when he was pestered with many suitors. There was also borne before him first, the great seal of England, and then his cardinal's hat, by a nobleman or some worthy gentleman, right solemnly, bareheaded. And as soon as he was entered into his chamber of presence, where there was attending his coming to await upon him to Westminster Hall, as well noblemen and other worthy gentlemen, as noblemen and gentlemen of his own family; thus passing forth with two great crosses of silver borne before him; with also two great pillars of silver, and his pursuivant at arms with a great mace of silver gilt. Then his gentlemen ushers cried, and said: "On, my lords and masters, on before; make way for my Lord's Grace!" Thus passed he down from his chamber through the hall; and when he came to the hall door, there was attendant for him his mule, trapped all together in crimson velvet, and gilt stirrups.

When he was mounted, with his cross bearers, and pillar bearers, also upon great horses trapped with fine scarlet. Then marched he forward, with his train and furniture in manner as I have declared, having about him four footmen, with gilt pollaxes in their hands; and thus he went until he came to Westminster Hall door. And there alighted, and went after this manner, up through the hall into the chancery; howbeit he would most commonly stay awhile at a bar, made for him, a little beneath the chancery on the right hand, and there commune sometime with the judges, and sometime, with other persons. And that done he would repair into the chancery…'

—George Cavendish, from *The Life of Cardinal Wolsey*, *ca.* 1557, publ. 1626 (modernised spelling), ed. R S Sylvester, 1959.

¶ An even greater spectacle to have been seen processing down Chancery La., since it involved numerous participants from all four Inns, was this:

'On Candlemas Day in the afternoon, the maskers, horsemen, musicians, dancers, and all that were actors in this business, according to order, met at Ely House[1] in Holborn. There the grand committee sat all day to order all affairs; and when the evening was come, all things being in full readiness, they began to set forth in this order down Chancery Lane to Whitehall.

The first that marched were twenty footmen, in scarlet liveries with silver lace, each one having his sword by his side, a baton in his hand, and a torch lighted in the other hand; these were the marshal's men, who cleared the streets, made way, and were all about the marshal, waiting his commands. After them, and sometimes in the midst of them, came the marshal, then Mr Darrel, afterwards knighted by the king; he was of Lincoln's Inn, an extraordinary handsome proper gentleman. He was mounted upon one of the king's best horses, and richest saddles, and his own habit was exceedingly rich and glorious; his horsemanship very gallant; and besides his marshal's men, he had two lackeys, who carried torches by him, and a page in livery that went by him, carrying his cloak.

After him followed one hundred gentlemen of the Inns of Court, five and twenty chosen out of each house, of the most proper and handsome young gentlemen of the societies. Every one of them was gallantly mounted on the best horses, and with the best furniture that the king's stable and the stables of all the noblemen in town would afford, and they were forward on this occasion to lend them to the Inns of Court.

Every one of these hundred gentlemen was in very rich clothes, scarce anything but gold and silver lace to be seen of them; and each gentleman had a page and two lackeys waiting on him in his livery by his horse's side; the lackey carried torches, and the page his master's cloak. The richness of their apparel and furniture glittering by the light of a multitude of torches attending on them, with the motion and stirring of their metalled horses and the many and various gay liveries of their servants; but especially the personal beauty and gallantry of the handsome young gentlemen, made the most glorious and splendid show that ever was beheld in England…

Then came the first chariot of the grand maskers, which was not so large as those that went before, but most curiously framed, carved, and painted with exquisite art, and purposely for this service and occasion. The form of it was after that of the Roman triumphal chariots, as near as could be gathered by some old prints and pictures extant of them. The seats in it were made of an oval form in the back end of the chariot, so that there was no precedence in them, and the faces of all that sat in it might be seen together…

In the third chariot rode the grand maskers of the Inner Temple, and in the fourth chariot went those of Lincoln's Inn according to the lot of each of them.

The habits of the sixteen grand maskers were all the same, their persons most handsome and lovely, the equipage so full of state and height of gallantry that it was never outdone by any representation mentioned in our former stories.

2.s. Inigo Jones: Design for a masquer's costume, 1633 [Duke of Devonshire's Chatsworth Settlement].

The artist had designed a masquer's costume for the masque of 1614, in the style of an American Indian's dress. Fashions had moved on in two decades.

The torches and flaming huge flambeaux borne by the sides of each chariot made it seem lightsome as at noonday, but more glittering, and gave a full and clear light to all the streets and windows as they passed by. The march was slow in regard of their great number but more interrupted by the multitude of the spectators in the streets, besides the windows, and they all seemed loth to part with so glorious a spectacle.'

—Bulstrode Whitlocke, from 'Candlemas, 1633/4', in *Memorials of The English Affairs*, 1682 [BL].

> D S Bland, *A Bibliography of the Inns of Court and Chancery*, 1965.

[1] Ely House: The town-house of the bishop of Ely, on the n. side of Holborn, across from Thavies Inn.

The quotation above is but a small segment of the original, which meticulously details each of the groups of masquers in the procession: on horseback, in chariots and on foot. Candlemas is 2nd February, usually the end of the Christmas festivities in the Inns.

Masque is defined by the *OED* as 'a form of amateur histrionic entertainment, originally consisting of acting and dancing in a dumb show, the performers being masked; afterwards including dialogue and song'.

Under the first three Stuart kings, masques (in which, by this time, the words and music were of great importance) were a form of entertainment at or of the royal Court (whether gathered at Whitehall or elsewhere) in which the members of the four Inns were prominent. These performances were seen by the first two of those kings as an adjunct to the divine character of the monarchy.

This masque, entitled *The Triumph of Peace*, was presented at Whitehall Banqueting House, on the occasion of the birth of James, Duke of York, the future James II. The poet was James Shirley [of GI], the composers William Lawes and Simon Ives, and the designer Inigo Jones.

One other of the masques processed down part of Chancery La., and is recorded by George Chapman [of GI] in *The Memorable Masque of the Middle Temple and Lyncolns Inne performed before the King at Whitehall 15 February 1613* (=1614)... *with a description of their whole show, in the manner of their march on horse-back to the Court from the Maister of the Rolls' house: with all their right noble comforts and most showfull attendents* [a tract, BL].

---

ii. Pedestrian

'Chancery Lane is the greatest legal thoroughfare in England. It leads from the Temple, passes by Sergeants' Inn, Clifford's Inn, Lincoln's Inn, and the Rolls, and conducts to Gray's Inn. Of the world of vice and virtue, of pain and triumph, of learning and ignorance, truth and chicanery, of impudence, violence, and tranquil wisdom, that must have passed through this spot, the reader may judge accordingly. There all the great and eloquent lawyers of the metropolis must have been, at some time or other, from Fortescue[1] and Littleton,[2] to Coke,[3] Ellesmere,[4] and Erskine.[5] Sir Thomas More[6] must have been seen going down with his weighty aspect; Bacon[7] with his eye of intuition; the coarse Thurlow;[8] and the reverend elegance of Mansfield[9]...'

—Leigh Hunt, from *The Town, its memorable characters and events,* 1848.

---

[1] Fortescue: Sir John [of LI] (*ca.* 1385-1477).

[2] Littleton: Sir Thomas [of IT] (*ca.* 1415-81).

[3] Coke: Sir Edward [of IT] (1552-1634), CJ of the Common Pleas, and then of the King's Bench.

[4] Ellesmere: Sir Thomas Egerton, Baron Ellesmere and Viscount Brackley [of LI] (1541-1617), LC.

[5] Erskine: Thomas, first Baron Erskine [of LI] (1750-1823), LC.

[6] More: Sir (St) Thomas [of LI] (1477-1535), LC.

[7] Bacon: Sir Francis [of GI] (1561-1626), LC.

[8] Thurlow: Edward, first Lord Thurlow [of IT] (1731-1806), LC, who will have sat in Lincoln's Inn Old Hall out of term, and who should not be confused (which indeed Hunt has not) with John Thurloe [of LI], Cromwell's spymaster, who lodged in the Inn.

[9] Mansfield: William Murray, first Earl of [of LI] (1705-1793), LCJ.

2.t. William M'Connell: 'Types of the Thoroughfares: Chancery Lane', *ca.* 1870 [LMA].

The scene is set in front of 34-33, Chancery La. on the e. side, the site soon after occupied by 'Law Courts Chambers' of 1874 (that building now having been purchased by the Society). It faces Bishop's Court and Chichester Rents, and is thus very close to the former courts of Chancery within the Inn, whence the name.

2.4. The Fields; and the approach to the Inn across them:

¶ John Strype's *Survey*, 1720, called the Fields 'a very curious spacious Place, with an excellent Air…' Henry Kingsley (the brother of Charles) in *Ravenshoe*, 1862, described the Fields as 'dry and dusty' and full of 'parched lilacs and laburnums'. Mrs E T Cook in *Highways and Byways in London*, 1902, observed that 'Lincoln's Inn Fields, though perhaps hardly rural, is still the largest and shadiest square in London.'

These various descriptions evoke the Fields as they were before and after being railed, planted and laid out with walks pursuant to an Act of Parliament of 1735. In 1820, they were laid out and planted afresh, and assumed an appearance which lasted for three-quarters of a century or more. They remained private, accessible only to residents of the town-houses around the Fields, or to key-holders. Despite periodic vicissitudes in the maintenance of the Fields, they remain a green oasis, and one which owes its existence to the enlightened self-interest

2.u. An encounter in Chancery La., *Punch*, 1864 [Editor's coll.].

Besides its weak joke about barristers' fees, the cartoon is interesting for the indication that at this period lawyers displayed business cards in shop windows—a practice inconceivable for most of the C20th. Professional life continued in London notwithstanding the carnage of the American Civil War—the subject of the newsvendor's placard—although the cotton trade from Savannah and Charleston to Manchester was severely disrupted. A consequence of the ending of the war not long after was the arrival in Lincoln's Inn of Judah P Benjamin, the former Secretary of State of the Confederacy, fleeing the threat of imprisonment as had been the fate of his President, Jefferson Davis. He was enrolled and was called, eventually becoming a QC. His majesterial work *Sale of Goods* is still in print, in its eighth edition.

Tomkins looking too long at the *cartes de visite* of the lawyers in Chancery Lane, is seized with a sudden involuntary panic. "Don't be alarmed, my boy," said his friend Wigsby, who happened to be passing at the time, "Your *coat* pockets are quite safe; we don't do it that way!"

2.v. William Lodge [of LI]: 'Lincoln's Inn, London', third quarter of C17th (e. view) [BM].

This unfinished drawing gives a view of the Fields before enclosure and planting, with the Inn in the background, rising over the trees in the Walks. It may well be the earliest view encompassing the whole Inn.

of the benchers of Lincoln's Inn over the centuries, in protecting the neighbourhood of the Inn and the outlook from the Walks of the Inn. Indeed, their present-day charm inspired a composer, Miles Harwood, to write and publish a piece of music entitled 'Lincoln's Inn Fields', having been inspired by a walk through them in the spring of 1999.

But their past character was sometimes, if not always, very different. This section of the book evokes some of the horrors, hazards and hardships (and occasional pleasures) which could have been encountered there over the centuries by a traveller in a coach, a chair, on horseback or on foot on his way to the Inn.

2.4.1. The view of the Fields towards the Inn, and from them of *Lincoln's Inn Wall* and *the Walks*

2.w. Thomas Rowlandson & Augustus Pugin: 'Lincoln's Inn Fields' (e. view) in T Ackermann, *The Microcosm of London*, 1808 [GL].

This view across the Fields to the Inn beyond, was transmuted gradually by the effects of replanting and some evolution of garden design, until the débacle of the 1980s.

2.4.2. The public executions

¶ From medieval times, the Fields (and the open land extending w. from them towards the former leper hospital of St Giles-in-the-Fields) were on occasion used as a place of execution. In the C16th–17th a few gentlemen and priests famously convicted of treason were put to death

2.x. R D Chantrell: View of London from 13, Lincoln's Inn Fields, 1813 (e. prospect) [SM].

This watercolour is of the view from the top floor of Sir John Soane's house, and was made by one of his pupils. In the foreground is the e. end of the gardens in the Fields, beyond which is Lincoln's Inn Wall and rising above, the trees of the Walks and Gardens of the Inn. In the middle distance, peeping over the trees into the r. of Stone Buildings, are the distinctive double ranks of dormer windows in the n. side of the roofs of Garden Row. To the s. is the Chapel and the cupola (with its bell wheel) over the Council Chamber in Library Row, and then the lantern over the Old Hall.

in the Fields, the last such execution being in 1683 (by which date the Fields had been built around with houses on the n., w. and s. sides, and Lincoln's Inn Wall on its e. side) of William, Lord Russell, who had been found guilty of complicity in the Rye House Plot.

These lines were written by one of those unfortunates:
My prime of youth is but a frost of cares,
My feast of joy is but a dish of pain;
My crop of corn is but a field of tares,
And all my good is but vain hope of gain.
The day is past, and yet I saw no sun;
And now I live, and now my life is done.

My tale was heard, and yet it was not told,
My fruit is fall'n, and yet my leaves are green;
My youth is spent, and yet I am not old,
I saw the world, and yet I was not seen.
My thread is cut, and yet it is not spun;
And now I live, and now my life is done.
I sought my death, and found it in my womb,
I looked for life and saw it was a shade;
I trod the earth, and knew it was my tomb,
And now I die, and now I was but made.
My glass is full, and now my glass is run;
And now I live, and now my life is done.

—Chidiock Tichborne,[1] 'Elegy, written with his own hand in the Tower before his execution', 1586.

> Emrys Jones, *New Oxford Book of Sixteenth Century Verse*, 1991.

[1] Tichborne (? 1558-86): a Roman Catholic and member of the conspiracy, which included Anthony Babington from whom history has given it its name, to kill Elizabeth I. These lines were reputedly written the night before he was brought to the Fields—he and thirteen other conspirators being put to death in succession over two days. This ancient Hampshire family had the undeserved misfortune to gain legal fame once more in the 1870s in the civil and criminal cases concerning the Tichborne Claimant, who pretended to membership of the family, and to inheritance accordingly.

A riposte to Tichborne, and to the treason for which he had been condemned, was written by 'TK', suggested by scholars to be the playwright Thomas Kyd, entitled *Hendecasyllabon in Cygneam Cantionem Chideochi Tychborne* ('verses against CT's swan song'):

Thy prime of youth is frozen with thy faults,
Thy feast of joy is finisht with thy fall;
Thy crop of corn is tares availing naughts,
Thy good God knows thy hope, thy hap and all.
Short were thy days, and shadowed was thy sun,
T'obscure thy light unluckily begun.
Time trieth truth, and truth hath treason tripped;
Thy faith bare fruit as thou hadst faithless been:
Thy ill spent youth thine after years hath nipt;
And God that saw thee hath preserved our Queen.

Her thread still holds, thine perished though unspun,
And she shall live when traitors lives are done.
Thou soughtst thy death, and found it in desert,
Thou look'dst for life, yet lewdly forc'd it fade:
Thou trodst the earth, and now on earth thou art,
As men may wish thou never hadst been made.
Thy glory and thy glass are timeless run;
And this, O Tychborne, hath thy treason done.

2.4.3. The 'no popery' mobs

¶ In the s.w. corner of the Fields, a few feet outside and through an arch, stood what is believed to have been the first Roman Catholic chapel accessible to the public to have been built in London since the reign of Henry VIII. It was therefore vulnerable for longer than any other to periodic outbursts of anti-popery, and suffered several misfortunes.

The first such was on 11th December 1688 when, on the flight from London of James II, mobs attacked all the Roman Catholic places of worship which had been allowed during his reign, and all chapels in the embassies of Catholic countries. The chapel, which at that period was attached to a small Franciscan monastery, was gutted and its fittings and chattels taken into the Fields and burned.

> C W Heckethorne, *Lincoln's Inn Fields and the Localities Adjacent*, 1896. [Editor's coll. >> Messrs B J and C M David].

2.y. G Bower: design for silver medallion, with an impression—albeit inaccurate—of Arch Row in the background, and the burning of the accoutrements of Roman Catholic worship in the Fields, in the foreground, 1688 [PLMC].

2.z. A Quinton: 'The Old Sardinian Chapel' in 'Bits of Old London', *Illustrated London News*, 1887 [*ILN*PL].

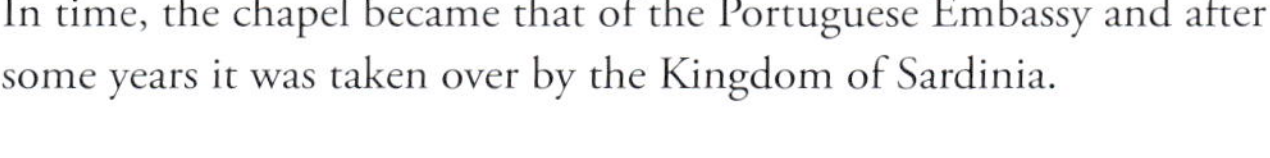

In time, the chapel became that of the Portuguese Embassy and after some years it was taken over by the Kingdom of Sardinia.

On 30th November 1759, the chapel was burnt to the ground and rebuilt soon after, enlarged and embellished, in a very Italian architectural style, and becoming usually known as the Oratory, on account of the excellence of its choral music. During the Gordon Riots, on 2nd June 1780, much the same thing occurred as nearly a century earlier, and the artefacts and ornaments of the chapel were taken out and burned in the Fields.

These former embassies and the chapel are remembered by the names still in use of Portugal St. and Sardinia St.

2.4.4. The gentry in pursuit of nocturnal adventure

¶ A hazard to be encountered in the Fields—certainly in the last quarter of the C17th and the first half of the C18th, if not for longer—was from gentry in pursuit of their own or others' nocturnal adventure.

This phenomenon was all too graphically recorded in the writings of the period, including for example the verses by or attributed to John Wilmot, Earl of Rochester, *In the Fields of Lincoln's Inn*, 1680 and in William Byrd II of Virginia, *London Diary*, for 1717-21.

The specialist reader may wish to consult those original texts. Neither is reprinted here.

2.4.5. The mumpers, rufflers and linkboys in the Fields; and the wig-snatchers on, and the blind beggars against, *the Wall*

¶ A mumper was a beggar; a ruffler was a vagabond; and a linkman or linkboy was one who lit the way for pedestrians with a torch of tow and pitch.

'...a parcel of wretches hopping about by the assistance of their crutches, like so many Lincoln's Inn Fields mumpers, drawing into a body to attack the coach of some charitable Lord.'

—Ned Ward, from *The London Spy*, 1703 [BL].

> H B Wheatley, *op. cit.*, 1891.

2.aa. John Crowther: The archway into Lincoln's Inn Fields from Duke St. (later, when reconfigured, Sardinia St.), with the flank wall of the chapel on the r., 1883 (n.e. view) [LMA].

Where Lincoln's Inn wide space, is railed around,
Cross not with venturous step; there oft is found
The lurking thief, who while the daylight shone,
Made the wall echo with his begging tone:
That crutch, which late compassion moved, shall wound
Thy bleeding head, and fell thee to the ground.
Though thou art tempted by the linkman's call,
Yet trust him not along the lonely wall;
In the midway he'll quench the flaming brand,
And share the booty with the pilfering band.
Still keep the public streets, where oily rays,
Shot from the crystal lamp, o'erspread the ways.

—John Gay, from *Trivia, or the Art of Walking the Streets of London,* 1716.

Upon the lofty walls of Lincolns-Inn
Coming from Holborn, I have often seen
A Tongs, which closely lay at the Command
Of this our Hero's most unnerving Hand
And when a flutt'ring Spark did walk that way,
It did its Master tenderly obey,
And snap the Hat and Perriwig for a Prey.

—Anon. (? John Stephens [of LI]), 'A Satire' in *Poems on Affairs of State 1640-1704*, III.

> William Henry Irving, *John Gay's London*, 1928.

At the n. end of the wall there were remnants once of old, decorative but very sharply spiked railings of the C18th or early C19th. Were they the remains of those placed there in the C17th to deter not only intruders but also wig-snatchers? In the 1990s those vestiges were removed, and the 100-yard length of wall, down to the Garden Gate, re-railed to the same pattern.

'The Mendicants of this great city were so many of her sights, her lions. I can no more spare them than I could the Cries of London. No corner of a street is complete without them. They are as indispensable as the Ballad Singer; and in their picturesque attire as ornamental as the signs of old London. They were the standing morals, emblems, mementoes, dial mottoes, the spital sermons, the books for children, the salutary checks and pauses to the high and rushing tide of greasy citizenry—

> "…look
> Upon that poor and broken bankrupt there."

Above all, those old blind Tobits that used to line the wall of Lincoln's Inn Garden, before modern fastidiousness had expelled them, casting up their ruined orbs to catch a ray of pity, and (if possible) of light, with their faithful Dog Guide at their feet,—whither are they fled? or into what corners, blind as themselves, have they been driven, out of the wholesome air and sunwarmth? Immersed between four walls, in what withering poorhouse do they endure the penalty of double darkness, where the chink of the dropt halfpenny no more consoles their forlorn bereavement, far from the sound of the cheerful and hopestirring tread of the passenger? Where hang their useless staves? and who will farm their dogs?'

—Charles Lamb, from 'A Complaint of the Decay of Beggars in the Metropolis', in *Essays of Elia*, 1823.

The Merry BEGGARS
of Lincolns-*Inn*-Fields.
O R, The Beggers Art to get Money.
Shewing all the Pranks and Tricks they uſe, to make people believe they are Poor. Alſo, How a Gentleman ſerved two Beggers that ſtood on the High-way craving his Charity, whereby their Roguery was diſcovered.
The Begger all the day makes moan, at night is brisk and jolly; And ſpends his gains upon good Beer, to drown his Melancholly.
To the Tune of, *A begging we will go.*
This may be Printed, R. P.

Three Beggars met together,
that uſed Lincolns-Inn,
To take off their good Liquor,
and tell where they had been.
And ſo merry we will be,
we'l be, we'l be,
And ſo merry we will be.

Let's drink our Liquor Harry,
although that we do beg,
I've got good ſtore of Silver
and by my wooden Leg.
And ſo, &c.

Good Maſter ſpare a farthing,
it is my daily cry,
But when I'm at the alehouſe,
no man ſo great as I.
And ſo, &c.

Pray ceaſe thy tattle Harry,
for I tye up my Leg,
And get by thy way face Sir,
good money when I beg.
And ſo merry we will be,
we'l be, we'l be,
And ſo merry we will be.

2.bb. *The Merry Beggars of Lincoln's-Inn Fields*, a broadside, *ca.* 1665 (detail) [PLMC].

'The Second Part, to the Same Tune', comprising fourteen further verses, is omitted here. The woodcut illustration may have been borrowed from an earlier broadside—there have never been hills in the Fields, and the women and children do not seem altogether apt.

2.dd. Liam Martin: 'Canvas City', 1991 (e. view of the Fields towards Lincoln's Inn Wall) [LT].

This noted Irish topographical artist made a number of drawings expressly for this book, having previously published a monograph *Legal Dublin,* and come to London in the hope of doing the same for this city.

2.cc. Clement Fowler: Lincoln's Inn Fields, in *The Sphere,* 1905. (w. view) {*ILN*PL/Mary Evans}.

The caption read: 'Lincoln's Inn Fields on a Sunday Evening. The summer months (especially Sunday evenings) are welcomed by the denizens of Drury Lane and that poor neighbourhood for the fact that music is supplied by bands playing in the middle of Lincoln's Inn Fields'.

AUGUST 26, 1905] *THE SPHERE* 185

LINCOLN'S INN FIELDS ON SUNDAY EVENING

The Band Playing to the Poor People of the Neighbourhood.

DRAWN BY CLEMENT FLOWER

2.4.6. The holiday crowds

¶ 'Holiday' is used here in its traditional sense of a day on which work is suspended, a day of recreation or amusement.

In 1735, pursuant to the Lincoln's Inn Fields Act of that year, trustees were elected and steps taken to enclose and embellish the Fields, and preserve their private character for the benefit of the occupiers of the houses enclosing them.

However, some 250 years later, a campaign to restore public access was successful. The trustees granted a 560-year lease to the London County Council, running from 1894 and for the purposes of public access.

The bandstand in the middle of the Fields (shown in the accompanying drawing) was erected immediately thereafter. It is still standing.

Thus it was that the inhabitants of the neighbourhood—most living in modest tenements or 'industrial dwellings'—had access to air and space, and to trees, shrubs and grass, and, on occasions, to the music of military bands.

2.4.7. The homeless and the hungry

¶ As suggested above, the Fields had for long been one of the more attractive public squares in London. During the 1980s, there was a marked deterioration. The planting of flower beds and ground maintenance were drastically reduced, as a result of the problems of local authority finance—and, it was suggested, the politics of the local authority in opposition to the policies of Margaret Thatcher. Most significantly, the two or three tramps who had always passed the night under the eaves of park buildings in the Fields were joined by up to 150 homeless people sleeping in cardboard boxes, or camping in small tents and bivouacs on the grass. The result was to present to the passer-by an image, unequalled at that time in any other western European capital, of a serious social problem. In 1992-3 the local authority—under threat of legal action by some of the occupiers of houses in the Fields—began the process of fencing in the Fields, and fencing out the homeless. Then charitable soup kitchens operated on the pavements outside the gardens, on the e. and w. sides, as still they do.

3. THE GATES OF THE INN

3.1. Approaching and entering the gates of an Inn of Court or Chancery; and specifically those of this Inn

¶ The quotations in this section evoke the contrast between the noise and bustle of the streets: the Strand, Fleet St., High Holborn, Holborn and Chancery La., which frame or intersect the neighbourhood of the Inns; and the alley-ways leading towards the gates of an Inn; and last the experience of walking through an Inn's gatehouse or a subsidiary gate, and of entering its collegiate world.

Meanwhile the roar continues, till at length,
Escap'd as from an enemy, we turn
Abruptly into some sequestered nook,
Still as a sheltered place when winds blow loud!
At leisure, thence, through tracts of thin resort,
And sights and sounds that come at intervals,
We take our way... ...Private courts,[1]
Gloomy as coffins, and unsightly lanes
Thrill'd by some female vendor's scream, belike
The very shrillest of all London cries,
May then entangle our impatient steps;
Conducted through those labyrinths, unawares,
To privileg'd regions and inviolate,
Where from their airy lodges studious lawyers
Look out on waters, walks, and gardens green.

—William Wordsworth, from *The Prelude*, 1805.

---

[1] courts: courtyards, or squares or quads.

Wordsworth stayed in the Inn on several occasions, when visiting his friend Basil Montagu, at 7, New Square.

'It lies not far from Temple-Bar.

Going to it, by the usual way, is like stealing from a heated plain into some cool, deep glen, shady among harboring hills.

Sick with the din and soiled with the mud of Fleet Street—where the Benedick tradesmen are hurrying by, with ledger-lines ruled along their brows, thinking upon rise of bread and fall of babies—you adroitly turn a mystic corner—not a street—glide down a dim, monastic way flanked by dark, sedate, and solemn piles, and still wending on, give the whole care-worn world the slip, and, disentangled, stand beneath the quiet cloisters of the Paradise of Bachelors.

Sweet are the oases in Sahara; charming the isle-groves of August prairies, delectable pure faith amidst a thousand perfidies: but sweeter, still more charming, most delectable, the dreamy Paradise of Bachelors, found in the stony heart of stunning London. Quite sequestered from the old city's surrounding din; and every thing about the place being kept in most bachelor-like particularity, no part of London offers to a quiet wight so agreeable a refuge.'

—Herman Melville, from 'The Paradise of Bachelors and the Tartarus of Maids', 1855.

These are the opening lines of an essay, one of a pair, by the author of *Moby Dick*, 1851, in which he described a visit to wine and dine in chambers—not in hall—in Inner Temple as the guest of a bencher. Those present included barristers who were members of Inner Temple, Lincoln's and Gray's or resident in Furnival's Inn. The experience would have been comparable if entering Lincoln's through one of the rents or courts off Chancery Lane.

'It is very strange to see so much of ancient quietude right in the Monster-city's very jaws, which yet the monster shall not eat up; right in its very belly, indeed, which yet, in all these ages, it shall not digest and convert into the same substance as the rest of its bustling streets. Nothing else in London is so like the effect of a spell, as to pass under one of these archways, and find yourself transported from the bustle, jumble, mob, tumult, uproar, as of an age of week-days intensified into the present hour, into what seems an eternal Sabbath.'

—Nathaniel Hawthorne, from *English Notebooks, 1853-58*, ed. Sophia Hawthorne [BL].

Hawthorne, having admired Lincoln's (as quoted below in 4.2.1.ii.), was reflecting here on his walking into Gray's: the effect created on entering the gates of each of the Inns being very similar, as he implies.

'How odd... are the desolate-looking legal alleys or courts adjoining these Inns, with nothing but a pump or a cane-bearing street-keeper to be seen in the midst of them, and occasionally at one corner, beside a crypt-like passage, a stray dark and dingy barber's shop, with its seedy display of powdered horsehair wigs of the same dirty-white hue as London snow.

Who... while threading his way through the monastic-like byways of such places, has not been startled to find himself suddenly light upon a small enclosure, comprising a tree or two, and a little circular pool, hardly bigger than a lawyer's inkstand, with a so-called fountain in the centre, squirting up the water in one long thick thread, as if it were the nozzle of a fire-engine.

Then how peculiar are the tidy legal gardens attached to the principal Inns, with their close-shaven grass-plots looking as sleek and bright as so much green plush, and the clean-swept gravel walks thronged with children, and nursemaids, and law-students.'

—Henry Mayhew and John Binney, from *Scenes of London Life*, 1862.

'Behind the most ancient part of Holborn… is a little nook composed of two irregular quadrangles. … It is one of those nooks the turning into which out of the clashing street imparts to the relieved pedestrian the sensation of having put cotton in his ears, and velvet soles on his boots. It is one of those nooks where a few smoky sparrows twitter in smoky trees, as though they called to one another, 'Let us play at country,' and where a few feet of garden-mould and a few yards of gravel enable them to do that refreshing violence to their tiny understandings. Moreover, it is one of those nooks which are legal nooks, and it contains a little hall, with a little lantern in its roof, to what obstructive purposes devoted, and at whose expense, this history knoweth not.'

—Charles Dickens, from *The Mystery of Edwin Drood*, 1870.

This is Staple Inn.

'…into the vast dark warren of the Inns of Court.'

—Henry Newbolt, QC [of LI], from *The Twymans*, 1892.

> Susan Chitty, *Playing the Game*, 1997.

…fresh from brawling Courts
And dusty purlieus of the law…

—Alfred, Lord Tennyson, from *In Memoriam,*[1] *Canto lxxxix*, 1850.

[1] This work was written to remember Arthur Henry Hallam, whose association was with IT. One of the shades of meaning of 'purlieu' in the *OED* is 'the meaner streets about some main thoroughfare; a mean, squalid, or disreputable street or quarter'.

'The gates of Lincoln's Inn are as numerous as those of Thebes.'

—Anon. simile, ? early C18th.

Thebes: the reference is to Homer and to his description of the city gates of Egyptian Thebes—Karnak, in modern nomenclature. The writer might have read him in Alexander Pope's celebrated verse translation of 1715-20.

As a collegiate institution ringed with perimeter walls, and locked at night, the Inn is well furnished with gates, most of which are open to all in the day. By accident of its topography, the Inn seems always—or certainly since building of Serle Court alongside it in the late C17th—to have possessed more than any other Inn.

3.2. Two gates in Chancery Lane:

3.2.1. North Gate

'Much of the Inn is too demonstratively picturesque to be memorable; the visitor reels from all the diapered brickwork and grossly pointed windows. The best part is the northeast corner, near Chancery Lane, where Robert Taylor's Stone Buildings of 1774 look across a long court to a later block in Mylne's style though still apparently done by Sir Robert's firm. Taylor at his best was a true Roman and set out his attached columns with real gusto and exquisite masonry technique—he began as a sculptor. There is an exit from the north-east corner of the court through a narrow arch into Chancery Lane, and this in reverse is one of the most delicious bits of Georgian London. It begins as an unprepossessing passage beside 76a Chancery Lane which leads to the back of the arch, set on the diagonal and giving just a glimpse of the courtyard beyond. Above it the Stone Buildings have a grandiose pedimented elevation to welcome you in, like finding a tiara under a factory girl's headscarf. The base and the arch itself are rusticated, and the channelling on the stonework is some of the best in London. The textures and shapes are countercharged with a verve which in another country would have led to a crop of *putti*. This is the English stiff upper lip ingested, and paying a splendid dividend in controlled power.'

—Ian Nairn, from *Nairn's London*, 1966.

3.a. Liam Martin: North Gate Passage and the e. pediment of Stone Buildings, 1991 (w. view) [LT].

3.b. Liam Martin: Stone Buildings Gate, with a porter's lodge (now disused), 1991 (w. view) [LT].

3.2.2. Stone Buildings Gate

'…and there is generally a little porter's lodge, not unlike a French *conciergerie*, adjoining the gate, about which loiter livened street-keepers to awe off little boys, who would otherwise be sure to dedicate the tranquil spots to the more innocent pursuit of marbles or leap-frog.'

—Henry Mayhew and John Binney, *op. cit.*, 1862.

'We passed on… down Chancery Lane, through the little iron gate into Lincoln's Inn, round through the old square,—than which we know no place in London more conducive to suicide; and the new square,—which has a gloom of its own, not so potent, and savouring only of madness…'

—Anthony Trollope, from 'The Spotted Dog', in *An Editor's Tales*, 1870.

>> Edward Ebden.

Trollope was born in the chambers of his father (a member of the Society) in the Inn. Of his father, Thomas, the *ODNB* said that he 'ruined himself by a scheme for selling fancy goods at Cincinnati'. A previous occupant of those same chambers had committed suicide.

3.3. The Great Gatehouse, in Chancery Lane: *the Tudor building*, and the C20th reconstruction:

¶ The Gatehouse was built during 1518-20 and was the principal entrance until the erection of the Fields Gate in the 1840s. Two members are principally associated with the work: William Sulyard, who supervised the building, and Sir Thomas Lovell, who made the largest contribution to its cost, and whose name is thus sometimes given to it.

3.d. James Basire: Heraldic carving over the Gate, on the Chancery La. side [cutting, HSLI].

A small part of the original of this carving has since been relocated for preservation in the corridor of 21, Old Buildings, and a reproduction of the whole placed over the rebuilt Gate.

3.c. Samuel Ireland: Lincoln's Inn Gate, *ca.* 1799 (w. view) [YCBA].

This is the earliest watercolour view of the Gate to have been found. A slightly earlier monochrome view is the engraving (not reproduced here) by J T Smith in his *Antiquities of London*, 1791. The reproduction here is of one of Ireland's original watercolours, from which the etchings in his *Picturesque Views of the Inns of Court and Chancery*, 1800, were made, as are the other views over his name here—having been located during the research for this book. Through the Gate may be glimpsed the Old Hall, and Screen Passage.

3.e. Constance Potts: 'Old Gateway, Lincoln's Inn', *ca.* 1897 (w. view) [V&A].

Perhaps this is the most meticulous and yet atmospheric representation of the Gatehouse ever made. It has now the added interest of preserving the patina of the Gatehouse before the rebuilding of the 1960s. The side gate on the n. side, for pedestrian traffic, still in daily use on week-days, was created in 1834.

3.3.2. The inside; and *its shop*

3.g. Richard Winsper's trade token for his stationer's shop in Lincoln's Inn Gate, mid-C17th [BM, Dept. of Coins and Medals].

Tokens such as this were issued to supplement the insufficiency of small change in the coin of the realm. *The Black Books* record the granting of a tenancy of the shop to Winsper's widow after his death. The shop is clearly shown in *7.a.* Its removal enabled the side gate for pedestrians to be created.

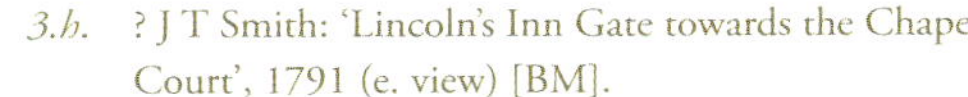

3.h. ? J T Smith: 'Lincoln's Inn Gate towards the Chapel Court', 1791 (e. view) [BM].

This view is of Chapel Court, and the inside of the Gate, and seems to correspond, in style and date, with that in Pennant, *Some Account of London*, 1790, of the outside of the Gate, although the original drawings are in different libraries.

3.3.1. The outside

3.f. Geoffrey Fletcher: The Gatehouse being rebuilt, 1967 (n.w. view from the La.) in his *London Dickens Knew*, 1970 [BL] {estate of artist}.

The major part of the Gatehouse was rebuilt at this time, following very closely the external appearance of the Tudor original. The n. tower had been rebuilt in 1956.

3.i. John Crowther: The Gatehouse, from Gatehouse Court, 1879 (n.e. view) [LMA].

This is the first of several watercolours of the Inn by this gifted artist, reproduced here. He had been commissioned by Sir Charles Chadwyck-Healey, Bt., QC [of LI], when still relatively unknown. He began work for Chadwyck-Healey in 1879 and continued, depicting the Inn and other picturesque or threatened buildings in London, for more than fifteen years. The best of his watercolours combine accuracy with poignancy for a vanishing world.

3.j. J P Emslie: View of 77-82 Chancery La. and the back of Old Buildings, Lincoln's Inn (n.w. view), 1880s [LMA].

The entrance to Bishop's Court is just visible. The buildings between that entrance and Old Buildings stand on the site now occupied by the Chancery La. front of Hardwicke Building.

3.k. Bishop's Court, 1887 (e. view) *Illustrated London News* [an offprint HSLI].

This is taken a few steps out from the Inn, and has the interest of showing the light reflectors then used in narrow passages.

3.4. Two gates in courts off Chancery Lane:

¶ These two pedestrian gates were approached by narrow, straight, public footpaths, some 100 yards in length, leading to them from Chancery La.

Access to each of these paths from the Lane in the C19th, and doubtless in earlier times, was through openings at street level in the frontages of privately owned buildings, which continued over them at first- and second-storey level. Being public pedestrian rights of way, they had no doorways or gates. There seems to be no one precise term for such passages, which were a common feature of the streets in the City and Westminster, and of which a good number survive to this day in Fleet St. and the Strand. In a city in which they are very commonly found and their name prominently signed—Venice—there is a specific dialect term for them: *sotoportegi*.

3.4.1. Bishop's Court Gate, and the approach through the Court

'Bishops Court, new built, with good Houses, having a Freestone Pavement, and a Passage into Lincoln's Inn. Where there is a pair of Gates with open Iron Bars.'

—John Strype, *Survey*, 1720.

3.l. John Crowther: Bishop's Court, with the York Coffee House, *ca.* 1880 (e. view) [LMA].

This view is taken from a point midway along the Court, showing the back of the York Coffee House on the w. side of Chancery La. and the foot passage into that lane.

3.m. T C Dibdin: View in Chichester Rents, *ca.* 1850 (w. view, towards the Gate) [LMA].

3.n. J P Emslie: Chichester Rents, seen from the Gate, with the Old Ship Inn in the foreground and the passage into Chancery La. in the distance (e. view) [LMA].

3.4.2. *Chichester Rents Gate*, and ways to it through the Rents or up Star Yard (formerly Lincoln's Inn Grange or Lincoln's Inn Back side)

'Chichester Rents, a pretty broad Court, with a Passage also into Lincoln's Inn, through a pair of Gates, shut up at Nights as those at Bishops Court. It is a Place not over well Inhabited, nor neatly kept, although it might be otherwise, as having a good Freestone Pavement.'

—John Strype, *Survey*, 1720.

i. The Rents

'...to nearly every one of these legal nooks and corners the entrance is through some arch way or iron gate that has a high bar left standing in the middle, so as to obstruct the passage of any porter's load into the chancery sanctuary...'

[1] 'a high bar...' is shown in *17.a.*

—Henry Mayhew and John Binney, *op. cit.*, 1862.

3.o. Ian Whadcock: Chichester Rents (w. view, looking towards Chichester Rents Gate), 1991 [Guardian Properties Limited].

Chichester Rents was redesigned and rebuilt, with small shops at street level along each side (as there had been until rebuilding a century earlier), in 1990-1. The Gate – a massive timber door – is now incorporated in the wall of 16, New Square, but not usable. This is an artist's impression (commissioned by its insurance company owner) of how the Rents were intended to look when completed and let, and as, indeed, on a winter's afternoon they did look, until redevelopment began in 2013.

3.p. Herbert Railton: Star Yard (n. view) in W J Loftie, *Picturesque Views of the Inns of Court*, 1893 [Editor's coll.].

The building with a roundel on the r. side of the Yard was the imposing Union Bank, and was the subject of an essay by Samuel (*Erewhon*) Butler. It is now a gastro-pub on the ground floor and Counsel's chambers above. Between it and the President of the Law Society's House, Star Yard runs n., to where it meets Chichester Rents and Bishop's Court, from the second of which the eponymous gate opens into the Inn, on the e.

ii. The Yard, past the *Iron Duke*

¶ This former Victorian urinal or 'public convenience' shelters against the outside of the perimeter wall of the Inn, and close to the former Chichester Rents Gate. The particular style is known to experts as an 'Iron Duke'. The term—a reference to their cast iron construction—was perhaps inspired by the iron shutters fitted by the Duke of Wellington to the windows of Apsley House. A plan of the Inn published by the Society in the 1990s rather picturesquely gave it the colloquial (not the formal) French name.

This facility, although outside the perimeter of the Inn, seems in the past to have been associated with the Inn, and to have been designated by the Society as an easement for its outdoor staff, and in consequence intermittently maintained by it. It was disused for many years, and latterly has been converted to storage for an adjacent building in Chancery La.

3.q. Geoffrey Fletcher: 'Star Yard, Holborn', 1962 (n.w. view), in his *The London Nobody Knows*, 1962 [Editor's coll.] {estate of artist}.

This drawing also shows the small windows and roof of the former Bog House inside the Inn.

Star Yard, Holborn

3.r. J Long: 'A plott for all Thickett Field', 1592 [SoAL].

The cardinal points of the compass are shown. Chancery La. is delineated as horizontal across the top of the plan, with n. on the l. The plan is more readily appreciated if rotated clockwise by about 120°. The small indentation is the Field Gate—not named there—from out of which runs 'The waye from Lincolns Inn leading threwe Sheyre Lane to Temple Barre'. Another path turns hard r. (that is w.), presumably towards Drury La.

Other legal institutions are Clement's Inn (of Chancery) and the Six Clerks' Office (their original home—now covered by part of the Law Society's Hall—before rebuilding on the same site in the C17th, and their subsequent move in the late C18th to Stone Buildings, within the Inn).

3.5. *Field Gate* (or the *Postern Gate*), and the ways to it across *Fickett's Fields* from the w. or up *Shire Lane* (otherwise *Great Shire Lane*), from the s.

¶ The location of the Postern Gate was midway along the s. perimeter (enclosed by a fence and ditch) of the Inn's demesne. It may be deduced that this corresponds to a position just s.e. of the Brewster Gates and n.w. of 13, New Square, at the present day.

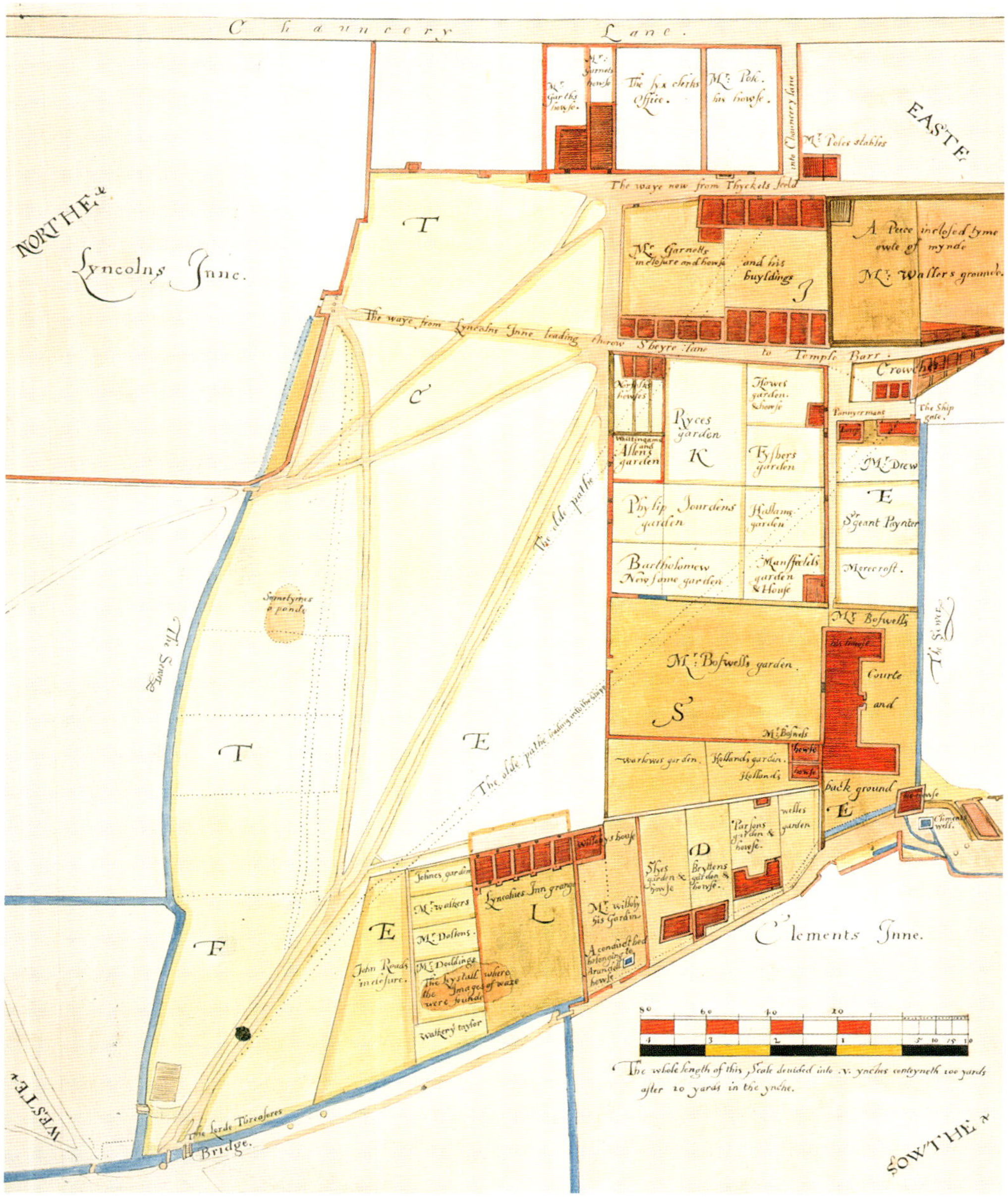

3.s. The plan forming part of the Agreement between representatives of the Society and the owners of Cup Field, 1657 (detail) [HSLI Archives].

The location of the Postern Gate (there called the 'backgate') is recorded in this plan. The perimeter of the Inn is edged red, creating the 'L' shape on the r. of the plan. At the n.w. corner of the Inn's Walks is 'Turne Stile', that is Great Turnstile, depicted in *2.m.* This agreement was intended to regulate, for the benefit of the Society and the protection of the view from the Walks, the future development of the houses around Lincoln's Inn Fields. Thus the s.e. end of the area edged in green on the plan corresponds to the site of New Square, and is there marked 'An open square'.

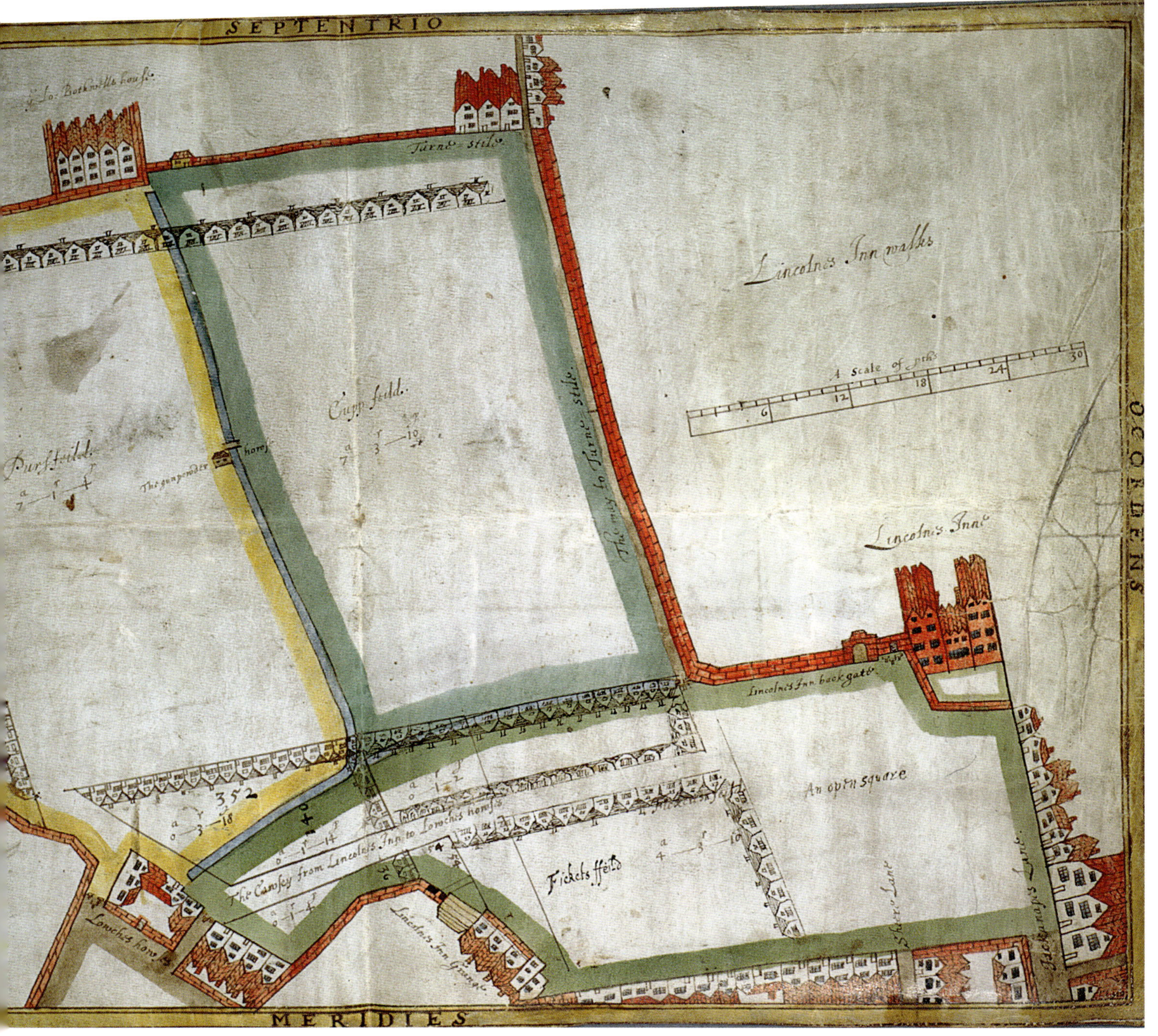

3.t. G S Shepherd: 'Bell Yard, near Chancery La. and Fleet St.', 1835 [LMA].

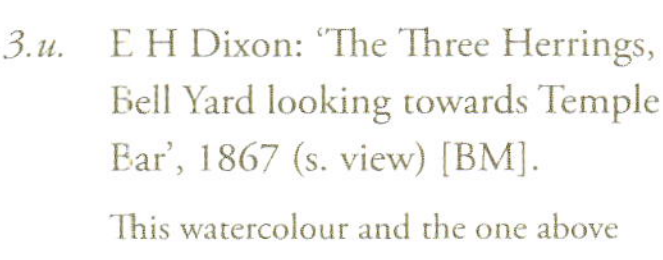

3.u. E H Dixon: 'The Three Herrings, Bell Yard looking towards Temple Bar', 1867 (s. view) [BM].

This watercolour and the one above are of the e. side of Bell Yard, the w. side of which was demolished for the construction in the 1880s, being the perimeter of the RCJ. The barrister, robed and with brief in hand, might have been making his way from a hearing in one of the Chancery Courts within the Inn, back to chambers in the Temple.

3.6. Serle's Gate into 4, New Square and its bookshops; and the approaches from Carey Street (formerly *Jackanapes Lane* and latterly *Weedon Street*), or up Bell Yard or *Shire Lane*, or through *the slum alleys w. of Shire Lane*

'I passed daily, twice at least, through the horrible nests of squalor and vice which then stood on the site of the New Law Courts. I soon found that (with the exception of thieves and beggars) these nests were peopled by shop workers—poor men, women and children, who if their employers could have flogged them, would have been in a far worse case than any negro slave. I say that the competitive struggle for life had brought them to this pass; and yet the most approved teachers, in reviews and newspapers, which I had begun to read, and even in Parliament, were insisting on 'free competition' as a corollary to 'free trade', and a necessary pillar of industrial prosperity.'

—Thomas Hughes, QC [of LI] (author of *Tom Brown's Schooldays*), from *Journal*, for 1845.

> Ian Ousby, *Literary Britain and Ireland*, second edn., 1990.

3.v. Entrance to New Boswell Court (n. view) in *Illustrated London News*, 1866 [*ILN* PL].

This drawing is one of the court-yards through which it was possible to approach this gate of the Inn from Fleet St. and Middle Temple, in the midst of the congeries which were swept away by the building of the RCJ. The upper doorway lead into Carey St., just w. of New Squ. Its flights of steps to accommodate the difference in height between Fleet St. and Carey St. correspond to those now within the RCJ or its precincts. New Boswell Court lay just to the w. of Shire La.

3.w. Unidentified artist and engraver: Great Shire La., (n. view) 1793 [LMA].

Shire La. lay immediately to the w. of Bell Yard, and marched with the boundary of the City and the county of Middlesex.

3.x. Dorothy Thomas: Serle's Gate, 1993 (s.e. view) {the artist}.

Wildy's shop-front proclaims the establishment of the bookshop in 1830, but surviving law books published in the name of the firm date from the 1820s.

3.y. Title page of *Drunken Barnaby's Four Journeys*, published in the Inn by S. Illidge, 1716 [BL].

This is the earliest book published in New Square yet identified as such. Illidge's premises were 'under Serle's arch'.

Drunken Barnaby's

Four Journeys

to the

North of England.

In Latin and English Verse.

Wittily and Merrily (tho' near One Hundred Years ago) compos'd; found among some old musty Books, that had a long time lain by in a Corner; and now at last made publick.

To which is added,

BESSY BELL.

Hic est quem quæris, ille quem requiris,
Toto notus in Orbe Britannus. Hor.
Barnabas *Ebrius.*

LONDON

Printed for *S. Illidge*, under *Searle's* Gate *Lincolns-Inn New-square*: and Sold by *S. Ballard* in *Little-Britain*, *J. Graves* in St. *James's-street*, and *J. Walthoe* over-against the *Royal Exchange*. 1716.

'Jackanapes Lane lately a bad, as well as frequent, Passage for Coaches and Carts into Lincoln's Inn fields… being very troublesome by reason of its narrowness, that two could not pass by one another. But now by a late Act of Parliament this lane is widened.'

—John Strype, *Survey*, 1720.

The Parliamentary Bill had been promoted by Cavendish Weedon, a resident in Serle Court (as to whom, see 16.4.).

¶ The Agreement between the Society and Henry Serle [of LI] of 1682 for the development of New Square (Serle Court) provided for 'a convenient, handsome and proportionable gate' to be made 'to go under an arch to be turned for that purpose.' And thus it was.

3.7. More's Gate into More's Passage and 7, New Square; and the approach from Carey Street and the Royal Courts of Justice

¶ The passage was created by cutting through from 7, New Square to Carey St. The Gate visible here became another entrance to the Inn, much used by judges and counsel walking between the Inn and the Royal Courts of Justice.

'I have come out of it into the big newish public green or garden beside the W. side of the Law-Courts—where you see the rich architecture and whence the tower and spire of St Clement's in profile are pleasing. But newness—large dull legal newness builds in this little expanse, spaciously, all round. There are highish steps at the end, to which I've climbed, and it's all very enlightened and commodious (reverse order) and the grey stone of the Law-Courts is in a good stage of that dusky-silvering which is the best that London buildings can look for in the so operative, so

3.z. Liam Martin: Keystone over archway of the Gate, 1991 [LT].

The date of 1848 is that of the remodelling of the passageway on its being closed to vehicular traffic, following the opening of the Fields Gate in 1845, and the enclosure of what had been the pedestrian passageways on either side of this gate.

tormenting (no, find the right kindly, affectionate word) air—which so deals with things (as a [fussy] family tone [no, not fussy]) deals with its members. The steps terminate in big stone and iron screen or *grille* opening into other grave clear Law precincts, into Serle St., with its dear old square windowed, square paned 18th century backs (of old chambers) all dingy red brick—more delectable than the new red (Butterfieldian) priggish (self-conscious—*why* self-conscious?) architecture of New Court all perpendicular round-about, but this a.m. rather charming with vivid green and geraniums at the centre. I have walked on to Lincoln's Inn Fields and am writing this in the large central garden or square, where, this moist summer, the lawns, the turf, are extraordinary and where some of the trees are more magnificent (are they the ash?) than I knew. But Lincoln's Inn Fields and the Soane Museum are a bit by themselves—they will give me something, the right little page, when I want it. … New Square, Lincoln's Inn, still delightful; *do* New Square…'

—Henry James, from his notes for *London Town*, in Notebooks, 1907.

> Leon Edell and Lyall H Powers, *The Complete Notebooks of Henry James*, 1987.

¶ The Passage as it was when newly built and as it has remained:

'…there is also a right of way, styled "More's Passage", through to the older buildings at the back. The first thing that attracts one's notice on passing through this main entrance is the admirable design and workmanship of the wrought-iron gates which bar the entrance to the building at night. About half-way down the corridor, which in common with all the other corridors in the building is laid in black and white marble squares, are a pair of carved oak doors, from which the corridor leads on into a circular hall-space lighted by a clerestory of little rectangular lights. From this circular hall, access to the suites of offices on the first floor is gained by projecting dwarf staircases on either side of the hall. Stairs also lead down under these staircases again to the basement offices…'

—from 'Street Architecture', in *The British Architect*, 13th September 1889.

3.aa. Raffles Pearson: 'The Yeman Coffee House' (n. view) in *The British Architect*, 1889 [coll. PHB].

Yem*a*n is the artist's error for Yem*e*n, the early home of the cultivated coffee bush.

3.bb. Sir Albert Richardson PPRIBA: The open doorway of No. 7, through which Serle Passage enters the Square [V&A].

Richardson had practised as an architect from chambers in the Inn, one of a number of men in the arts or creative professions who were allowed to rent chambers in the Inn in the late C19th and first half of the C20th.

3.cc. Charlotte Halliday, NEAC: The footpath formerly leading to and from the Passage (to the r.), and the steps in front of No. 10, down to the 'area', 1995 (s.e. view) [LT].

The artist's accurate delineation and delicate rendering of London scenes are distinctive. This is the first of several of her drawings commissioned for this book.

3.dd. Annabel Wilson: Lincoln's Inn Fields Gate, 1993 (e. view) [coll. PHB] {the artist}.

3.8. *Serle Street Passage* and *its shops* in 10, New Square; and the way out from the Inn to *the theatre* on Portugal Street (formerly *the Playhouse Street*)

¶ This vanished passageway ran from Serle's Court through a round-headed arch in No. 10 to Serle St., opposite Portugal St. (formerly the Playhouse St.). There were minuscule shops (law stationers, wig-makers, etc.) inside the passage. A plaque with a Latin inscription was placed over the passage on the Inn side, and probably recorded the name of Henry Serle, the landowner, or Nicholas Barbon, the developer. It is shown in the enlarged detailed of *15.b.* The passage was bricked up, and its space incorporated into No. 10, when the Lincoln's Inn Fields Gate was created.

3.9. Lincoln's Inn Fields Gate and its Gatehouse; and the approach along Portugal Row in the Fields

¶ Early prospects of the Fields showing the routes to be taken to the Inn are in 1.2.

¶ This gate, now the principal entrance to the Inn, and the only vehicular entrance in regular use, was designed by Philip Hardwick, and formed part of the project for the building of the New Hall and Library. There had previously been a wicket gate for pedestrians only at about this point. On either side of the carriage gate are small side gates for pedestrians.

Contemporary with the Gate, and in the same style, is 11a, New Square—separated from the Gatehouse only by the s. pedestrian gate—which now serves as the Chief Porter's Lodge.

'The square was as still as if an eternal Sabbath had reigned there for ages. Only three persons were to be seen, a young lady and two children, who had just entered the enclosure from Lincoln's Inn Fields.'

—Sarah Doudney, from *A Romance of Lincoln's Inn*, 1894 [BL].

3.ee. Hanslip Fletcher: 'The Guard Room, Lincoln's Inn Gate House', *ca.* 1930, from his *Changing London* [LMA].

3.ff. Unidentified artist: View of Surgeons' Hall and adjacent buildings (e. view), 1813 [LMA].

3.gg. The Garden Gate, and beyond it the corner of the Under-Treasurer's house—a building of the 1960s now scheduled for demolition: photograph G. Rodrigues (e. view), 2011 [LT].

3.hh. Theodore Ruoff: 'A Corner of Lincoln's Inn Fields today', 1956 {the artist}.

The artist was the Chief Land Registrar and co-author of Ruoff and Roper, *Registered Conveyancing*.

From the late C19th, the way for pedestrians crossing the Fields to the Inn has been marked by a tall water fountain in classical style, erected in memory of Philip Twells [of LI] MP for the City of London, d.1880. Twells is also remembered by a water trough on the w. of Smithfield Market, erected by the Metropolitan Drinking Fountain and Cattle Trough Association.

3.ii. Liam Martin: Sign in Lincoln's Inn, 1991 [LT].

3.10. The Garden Gate and Newman's Row Gate, on Lincoln's Inn Fields; and the ways onto the North Lawns

¶ These are *ad hoc* names given here to wooden doors set into the Wall, at the s. and n. ends respectively of the Cherry Tree Walk. The former is adjacent to the Under-Treasurer's house, and is occasionally used to give public access to events on the North Lawns, while the latter was designed to give private access to the North Lawns for the benefit of 30, Lincoln's Inn Fields, which are one of the few sets of chambers or offices not entered from within the Inn, but from without.

3.jj. Ken Day, RIBA: The Under Treasurer's House (s.w. view) 1948 {the architect}.

This watercolour depicts the original house, designed by Philip Hardwick, which formed part of the development of the New Hall and the Library, and stood just n. of the latter building, adjacent to the Under Treasurer's Gate. Indeed, its design was evidently inspired by that of a gate lodge. The single-storey extension on the r. (the n.) is seemingly of later date, and may have been the accommodation made available as a study to the Treasurer in his year of office. This building was demolished in 1961 and a new house built—in the design of a modern family house but with diapered brickwork, in deference to that of Hardwick's buildings.

C. THE COLLEGIATE BUILDINGS OF THE INN

4. THE CHAPELS:

4.1. *The bishops' Chapel*, and worship in it from the mid-C13th to the early C17th

¶ As noted in the Historical Essay, the association of Richard of Wych, St Richard, is with the site and original buildings of the Inn, inasmuch as the Society took over the bishop of Chichester's town house, and Richard, as bishop, lived here when in residence in London. Richard of Wych was born in 1197, became chancellor of Oxford University in 1235 and bishop of Chichester in 1244. He was the friend of St Edmund, Archbishop of Canterbury, and of Robert Grosseteste, bishop of Lincoln.

The chapel of the bishops continued to serve as the chapel of the Society, and is thought to have occupied an adjacent site to the present chapel. Lawrence Baker's plans, in the Appendices, show it somewhat further west. Two surviving fragments from the building are illustrated here.

4.a. Liam Martin: The C14th arch on the n. wall of the Old Hall, 1991 [LT].

This arch, the remains of which are incorporated into the Old Hall, is now the only building fragment visible above ground dating from the town-house of the bishops of Chichester, and in particular may be the only such remnant of the structure of the bishops' Chapel.

O most merciful redeemer,
friend and brother,
May we know thee more clearly,
Love thee more dearly,
And follow thee more nearly,
for Thine own sake. Amen.

—'The Prayer of St Richard of Chichester',[1] C13th.

---

[1] There is no evidence that St Richard wrote this prayer in the Inn, but it would be pleasurable to imagine that he might have recited it here, in his chapel. Tradition has it that he recited it on his death bed. The prayer was given a new life and became an inspiration to a worldwide congregation, by having been set to music by Stephen Schwartz in the rock opera *Godspell*, 1971.

THE TWO VERY ANCIENT FIGURES, AS ABOVE REPRESENTED, WERE FOUND IN 1822, WHILST DIGGING CONSIDERABLY BELOW THE FOUNDATION OF THE CHAPEL OF LINCOLNS INN.

4.b. T Wooddal: Carved C15th alabaster figures of the Annunciation, disinterred in 1822 below the foundations of the New Chapel, in Lane, *The Students' Guide through Lincoln's Inn*, 1823 [HSLI].

This is a fragment from the altar or reredos of the Old Chapel. *The Black Books* have a minute of 4th June 1559: paid by the Pensioner... for mending the pavement and carrieng awaie the rubbishe after the alter taken down in the Chapple. In 1995, the Society was granted an ecclesiastical faculty to authorise it to incorporate this carving into the fabric of the New Chapel, and it is now mounted on the wall behind the pulpit.

4.c. Thomas Cowlishaw: The Chapel, and the Old Hall, 1895 (e. view) [HSLI].

The new w. extension and staircase, made possible by the demolition of Chapel Court, are prominent. The Withdrawing Rooms, linking the Chapel and the Old Hall, have not yet been built.

¶ In the old Chapel of the Inn, John Donne delivered a sermon entitled 'A sermon of valediction, on my going into Germany, given at Lincoln's Inn', in 1619, as he left with the Earl of Doncaster's expedition, at the beginning of the horrors of the Thirty Years' War, to those kingdoms and principalities. The theme of that sermon was reworked by him into the poem 'A Hymn to Christ at the Author's last going into Germany', 1619. It is included in some modern anthologies of metaphysical or of devotional verse, but is perhaps of specialist interest and is not reprinted here. Its historical value to the Inn is that it is a literary record of a religious service conducted in the old Chapel, not long before its demolition.

4.2. The Society's Chapel:

¶ The earliest known representations of the elevations of the Chapel are those in a stained-glass window of *ca.* 1622 by the Van Linge brothers, and the engraving of Geo. Vertue of 1751, the other part of which is reproduced below. They have been widely reproduced and accordingly neither is so here. The anonymous oil painting of *ca.* 1725 in 7. has not previously been reproduced in a book. It conveys the same impression, and in colour. Being a view of the Chapel's s. elevation, it has the added value of showing its sundial.

4.2.1. The consecration of, and worship in, the Chapel: i. Its consecration

¶ In 1609, *The Black Books* first record the Society's need to build a new and larger chapel, but only in 1618 was an architect, Inigo Jones, requested to make a 'modull' for a new chapel. Whether the design finally adopted was by Jones has been much debated, but the matter seems to have been settled by Sir John Summerson in favour of George Clarke. Although the Society provided the organisation and—by a levy on members—the funds, it was the spirit of John Donne which was behind the achievement of the project. In the middle of that year, he delivered a sermon known as that 'Preached at Lincoln's Inne, preparing them to build their Chappell'. Thus it was fitting that, when in 1623, the bishop of London consecrated the new building, Donne should have delivered the sermon, entitled when published 'Encaenia. The Feast of Dedication. Celebrated at Lincolnes Inne, in a sermon there upon Ascension Day, 1623. At the dedication of the new Chappell there.'

'Lincoln's Inn new Chapel was consecrated with much solemnity by the bishop of London on Ascension Day where there was a great concourse of nobleman and gentlemen; whereof two or three were endangered, and taken up dead for the time, with the extreme press and thronging. The Dean of St Paul's made an excellent sermon, they say, about dedications.'

—John Chamberlain, from Letter to Dudley Carleton, Viscount Dorchester, 30th May 1623, in *State Papers, Domestic.*

---

ii. The worship

• Form and substance

'Orthodoxy, my Lord, is my doxy
Heterodoxy is the other man's doxy.'

—Bishop William Warburton,[1] Epigram, of unascertained date.

---

[1] Warburton (1698-1779) began life as an attorney, but turning to the Church, was appointed Preacher of the Inn in 1746, and later after a succession of steps up the ecclesiastical ladder, with the help of friends, bishop of Gloucester. His name lives on in the Inn for having founded and initially endowed a lecture (which bears his name) 'to prove the truth of revealed religion and the apostasy of Papal Rome…'. A number of distinguished men from the C18th to the C21st have delivered a Warburton (or Warburtonian) Lecture, including in recent years Lord Hailsham and Anthony Kenny: the contents of the lectures often now being philosophical in character, and conforming in part to the spirit if not wholly to the letter of the founder's wishes.

The epigram quoted above is said to have been a spontaneous whispered reply to Lord Sandwich, who asked the meaning of those two words in the course of a debate in the House of Lords. This was on one of the Indemnity Bills, modifying the scope of the Test Acts of 1673-8 (which had restricted civil and military offices to communicant members of the Church of England). Warburton's antipathies ranged from the Roman Catholics to the Methodists and thence to the Quakers. His reply is the more pithy when it is remembered that in the C18th, 'doxy' could carry both the Greek-derived meaning of 'belief' and the alternative meaning, of uncertain etymology, of 'trollop'.

¶ The Chapel uses the King James Bible of 1611 and the Book of Common Prayer of 1662.

In the language of the C17th: 'It hath been the wisdom of the Church of England, ever since the first compiling of her Publick Liturgy, to keep the mean between the two extremes, of too much stiffness in refusing and of too much easiness in admitting any variation from it'.

In that of the early C21st, it steers a course between the 'bells and smells' and the 'happy clappy' of each end of the broad spectrum of Anglican worship.

• Prayers

¶ This extract is from one of the letters comprising a novel which is both one of the longest written in English and one of the earliest in the epistolary style:

'Thursday, July 27
My dearest Miss Howe,

…You must know then, that this great town, wicked as it is, wants not opportunities of being better; having daily prayers at several churches in it; and I am desirous, as my strength will admit, to embrace those opportunities. The method I have proposed to myself (and was beginning to practise, when that cruel arrest deprived me both of freedom and strength), is this: when I was disposed to gentle exercise, I took a chair to St Dunstan's Church in Fleet Street, where are prayers at seven in the morning: I proposed, if the weather favoured to walk (if not, to take [a] chair) to Lincoln's Inn Chapel; where, at eleven in the morning, and at five in the afternoon, are the same desirable opportunities; and at other times to go no farther than Covent Garden Church, where are early morning prayers likewise.

This method pursued, I doubt not will greatly help, as it has already done, to calm my disturbed thoughts, and to bring me to that perfect resignation which I aspire after…
Your ever-affectionate and obliged,
Clarissa Harlowe.'

—Samuel Richardson, from *Clarissa, or the History of a Young Lady*, 1748.

4.d. J P Emslie: The Chapel, *ca.* 1881 (s. view) [LMA].
S. views seem to be rare. This was made shortly before the addition of a fourth bay to the w. (the r.). The rear of Library Row can be seen attached to the w. end of the Chapel.

• Sermons

¶ One of the most famous and humane of the Society's clergy was the Rev J F D Maurice, who is noted more fully below. Not everyone understood his sermons, however:

'I went, as usual about this time, to hear F D Maurice preach at Lincoln's Inn. I suppose I must have heard him, first and last, some thirty or forty times, and never carried away one clear idea, or even the impression that he had more than a faintest conception of what he himself meant.

Aubrey de Vere was quite right when he said that listening to him was like eating peasoup with a fork, and Jowett's[1] answer was no less to the purpose, when I asked him what a sermon which Maurice had just preached before the University was about, and he replied—"Well all that I could make out was that today was yesterday, and this world is the same as the next".'

—Sir Mountstuart Grant Duff, from *Notes from a Library*, 1897.

---

[1] Jowett: Benjamin Jowett (1817-93), Master of Balliol College, Oxford.

> James Sutherland, *The Oxford Book of Literary Anecdotes*, 1975.

• Choral singing

'Thence we went to the Chapel of Lincoln's Inn, where, on entering, we found a class of young choristers receiving instructions from their music master, while the organ accompanied their strains. These young, clear, fresh, elastic voices are wonderfully beautiful; they are like those of women, yet have something more birdlike and aspiring;—more like what one conceives of the singing of angels. As for the singing of saints and blessed spirits, that have once been human, it never can resemble that of these young voices; for no duration of heavenly enjoyments will ever quite take the mortal sadness out of it.'

—Nathaniel Hawthorne, from *English Notebooks, 1853-58*, ed. Sophia Hawthorne [BL].

In 1854-75, and thus at the time of Hawthorne's visit, there was a Choir School for the choristers of Lincoln's Inn Chapel and Temple Church, supported by those three Inns.

¶ The verses quoted below, written by a member of the Society, are reprinted, as Hymn 185, and set to music by Elgar, in *Hymns Ancient and Modern Revised*, the hymn-book used in the Chapel. They have thus been absorbed into the Anglican heritage:

Praise to the Holiest in the height,
And in the depth be praise:
In all His words most wonderful
Most sure in all his ways

O loving wisdom of our God
When all was sin and shame
A second Adam to the fight
And to the rescue came.

O wisest love that flesh and blood
Which did in Adam fail,
Should strive afresh against their foe,
Should strive and should prevail;

And that a higher gift than grace
Should flesh and blood refine,
God's Presence and His very Self,
And Essence all-divine.

O generous love that He who smote
In man for man the foe,
The double agony in man
For man should undergo;

And in the garden secretly,
And on the cross on high,
Should teach His brethren and inspire
To suffer and to die.

—The Blessed John, Cardinal Newman [of LI],
'The Fifth Choir of Angelicals', from *The Dream of Gerontius*, 1865.

John Newman's father had intended him for the law, and enrolled him as a member of the Society. But Newman found himself out of sympathy with the law and the profession, and did not pursue his legal studies. He may, therefore, stand here as a representative of that large body of men and women who, on account of family influences, have begun legal studies and then abandoned them, having found their true vocation elsewhere.
His celebrated autobiography, *Apologia Pro Vita Sua*, 1864, was written with the express purpose of explaining himself in the face of a journal article by Charles Kingsley [of LI] on the alleged indifference to the virtue of truthfulness of the Church of Rome, and linking Newman to that attitude. Perhaps not surprisingly, its account of his life's religious journey gives no credit to the Society. His work in the 1830s and 1840s for the Oxford Movement of the Church of England, and his conversion to Rome in 1845 caused great controversy. Newman was beatified by the Vatican in 2010.

4.e. Geo. Vertue: 'Lincoln's-Inne Chappel', 1751 (e. view of stairs) [BL].

The cartouche reads: 'Lincoln's-Inn Chappel Being erected at the expense of the Honble. Gentlemen of this Inn from a Plan of Mr Inigo Jones Surveyor of his Majesties Works and Buildings, *A.Dni.* DDCXXIII. It was compleated with the Ambulatory or Walk underneath, the Roof of which is adorned with ye. Arms of ye. members of ye. Society. The skill of that famous Architect is shewn in this particular Structure, having therein adapted the Old Gothick way of Building to the Manner of the Tuscan Order. Within the Chapel are no Pillars. The North and South Windows are adorned with Beautiful Painted Glass very justly admired for the best Performance of Skill in that Art'.

This is one half of the original two-part engraving, the other being a s.e. view of the exterior.

4.2.2. The exterior of the Chapel (as seen from the n. and the w.)

4.2.3. The Chapel stairs

¶ The building of the Chapel over an undercroft required, of course, stairs to lead up to it. As is clearly shown in Vertue's engraving, these were at the mid-C18th double stairs, each having a half-landing. When the Chapel was first built the stairs were, it is thought, spiral, and simpler.

4.f. Anon. artist: 'Lincoln's Inn Chapel, Doorway of', late C18th [LMA].

This is presumably the original door at the e. of the Chapel, at the head of the stairs. The extension of 1883, to seat a larger congregation, demolished this wall and door and justified the provision of a pair of doors, which remain in place, leading onto the stairs.

4.g. J P Emslie: 'Staircase of Lincoln's Inn Chapel', 1881 [CLHL].

This and the following image of the Chapel stairs show them as remodelled by Philip Hardwick in 1843 before the Chapel was lengthened to the w., with the consequent demoliton of those stairs, and new stairs constructed to the design of Stephen Salter, in 1883.

4.2.4. The interior of the Chapel

Within, a sombre rainbow floods the sight;
Five hundred rich escutcheons trap the light.
The Treasurers' bright arms are witness still
To the high office that they rose to fill,
And the van Linghe brothers glazed the grave
Prophets and rapt apostles of the nave
In dainty glass, and suit of gold and green.
The corbelled roof is coved in grey and red.
The pews are rich with many a poppyhead;
No central walk impedes their handsome ranks.
The pillared organ shouts its praise and thanks.
Up to the great threedecker pulpit came
Preachers whose faith was paralleled in fame:
Donne,[1] *hearing as they tolled the Chapel bell*
The Benchers' obsequies, and ours as well;
Ussher,[2] *who know the date when God created,*
But wouldn't have Erse liturgy instated;
Tillotson,[3] *moving from his young dissent*
To primacy and preaching eloquent;
Van Mildert,[4] *who could humbly deprecate*
The temporal lure of a Palatinate;
Heber,[5] *the brilliant don who left his land*
And early died on 'India's coral strand'.
Their voices echo in this Chapel, where
The usage is the Book of Common Prayer;
O Church misled, which elsewhere fails to see
The trite concoction of the A.S.B.!
Now to the west a raw Victorian bay
And vestibule and flights of stairs, betray
The heavy fist of old Lord Grimthorpe, him
who marred St Alban's Abbey at his whim.
The staircase holds the sad memorial
Of the brief murdered Premier, Perceval,
And the great western wheel glows with the warm
'Achievement' of the brilliant Viscount Maugham.

—Basil Cottle, from *Lincoln's Inn*, unpubl. verses, 1993 [LT].

---

1 John Donne (1572?-1631) the Preacher whose name has the most lasting fame, largely on account of his published sermons and his verse—devout, amorous and erotic—still in print. He became Dean of St Paul's.

2 James Ussher (1581-1656), became (Anglican) Archbishop of Armagh and Primate of All Ireland. His fame in his day was his chronology of the world, based on his research and analysis of extensive historical and biblical material, and which concluded that the world was created by God on Sunday 23 October 4004 BC.

3 John Tillotson (1630-1694) became Archbishop of Canterbury.

4 William Van Mildert (1765-1836) became the last Palatine bishop of Durham, and a force in the creation of University College Durham, the third university in England.

5 Reginald Heber (1783-1826) became Anglican bishop of Calcutta, and wrote many hymns of which a few are still in use, notably 'Holy, Holy, Holy, Lord God Almighty'. His hymn 'From Greenland's Icy Mountains' was once his most famous, but some of its sentiments are now out of sympathy with modern values.

This distinguished historian, architectural historian, linguist, Bletchley code-breaker and verse-writer composed the lines from which these are extracted in the year before his death.

4.h. John Crowther: Foot of the Chapel Stairs, 1881 [LMA].

4.i. W Herbert: Interior of Lincoln's Inn Chapel (e. view) in his *Antiquities of the Inns of Court*, 1804 [HSLI].

This engraving is the earliest such known of the interior, and shows the 'gothick' vaulted roof designed by James Wyatt, in the course of his repairs and renewals of the 1790s. The image exists in two versions: one with (as here) and one without the two figures.

4.j. Hanslip Fletcher: Interior of the Chapel, looking towards the east window, from the *Sunday Times*, 1934 [press cutting, HSLI].

The e. window is that designed by James Wyatt in 1793. A German bomb dropped in the First World War had caused some windows on one side to blow in and some on the other side to blow out. The barrel vault roof replaced its predecessor when the Chapel was lengthened.

4.k. A E Pearce: The pew ends, in W J Loftie, *op. cit.*, 1893 [Editor's coll.].

The majority of the pew ends of the front rows are contemporary with the building of the 1620s: *The Black Books* record the contract for them.

4.2.5. The Chapel memorials

¶ Spencer Perceval [of LI] (1762-1812) has an elaborate Latin memorial tablet which was originally in the Chapel, but has since been removed to the ante-chamber. Only two further such tablets to individual members have been erected, and those also in the ante-chamber. Thus Scott's observation quoted below remains substantially true. Spencer Perceval is the only British Prime Minister to have been assassinated, although two other members of the Society, Henry Addington, Viscount Sidmouth, a former PM, in the Cato St. Conspiracy of 1820, and Margaret Thatcher, in office as PM, in the Brighton hotel bombing of 1984, each came very close to it. Perceval's personal qualities were much praised. His performance as a Prime Minister, however, was such that there was widespread public rejoicing at his death, and the verses quoted below take the same view.

'Breakfasted with Dr. Maltby, preacher in Lincoln's Inn. … I heard service in the chapel, which is a very handsome place of worship; it is upstairs, which seems extraordinary, and the space beneath forms cloisters, in which the ancient Benchers of the Society of Lincoln's

are inter'd… There was only one monument in the chapel, being an handsome tablet to the memory of Perceval. The circumstance that it was the only monument in the chapel of a society which had produced so many men of talents and distinction was striking—it was a tribute due to the suddenness of his strange catastrophe.'

—Sir Walter Scott, from *Journal*, for 11th May 1828.

> ed. J G Tait, 1939, from the MS in the PML.

In the dirge we sung o'er him no censure was heard,
Unembittered and free did the teardrop descend;
We forgot in that hour how the statesman had erred,
And wept, for the husband, the father and friend.

Oh! proud was the meed his integrity won,
And generous indeed were the tears that we shed,
When in grief we forgot all the ill he had done,
And though wronged by him living, bewailed him when dead.

Even now, if one harsher emotion intrude,
'Tis to wish he had chosen some lowlier state—
Had known what he was, and, content to be good,
Had ne'er for our ruin aspired to be great.

So, left through their own little orbit to move,
His years might have rolled inoffensive away;
His children might still have been blessed with his love,
And England would ne'er have been cursed with his sway.

—Thomas Moore, *Lines on the Death of Mr P-R-C-V-L*, 1812.

> Lord Baker of Dorking, *English History in Verse*, 1988.

This is the first of several historical verses related to Lincoln's Inn or to its members, with their explanatory notes, included in that anthology with the notes reprinted here (verbatim or rephrased) with that editor's kind permission, for which grateful acknowledgement is given.

4.2.6. The Chapel bell

¶ The sound of the Chapel bell is to be heard in the Inn for three purposes: to ring the hour, to summon to prayer and to toll the passing of a bencher. A former and fourth reason is noted in the Historical Essay.

'No man is an Iland, intire of itselfe;
every man is a peece of the Continent, a part of the maine;
If a Clod bee washed away by the Sea, Europe is the lesse,
as well as if a Promontorie were,
as well as if a Mannor of thy friends or of thine owne were;
any mans death diminishes me, because I am involved in Mankinde;
And therefore never send to know for whom the bell tolls;
It tolls for thee.'

—John Donne [of LI], from *Devotions upon Emergent Occasions and severall steps in my sicknes*, 1624.

It has long been said in the Inn that these famous and powerful lines—some words of which having been made familiar to a world readership in the C20th by Ernest Hemingway—were inspired by the tolling of the Chapel bell. They were written soon after Donne resigned as the Society's Preacher, on becoming Dean of St Paul's. The theme is one which other divines before Donne had used, but there is no reason to doubt that the Inn was in his thoughts when writing.

'It is an old custom in Lincoln's Inn, when a Bencher dies, to toll the bell between 12.30 and 1, and to hoist half-mast the Inn's blue and gold standard from the turret on the new Hall. A barrister who then happens to be in chambers will ask his clerk or boy to find out who is dead. On hearing who it is, he mourns his friend's passing, wonders who will succeed to his practice or appointment, and then applies his mind again to the day's work. Life is like that.'

—Sir Gerald Hurst KC [of LI], from *A Short History of Lincoln's Inn*, 1946.

Ringing the Curfew.

4.1. Will Owen: 'Ringing the Curfew', in his *Old London Town*, 1921 [LMA].

5.a. John Crowther: The Undercroft seen through the 1737 archway, 1881. (e. view towards Chancery La. Row) [LMA].

This archway was dismantled, not demolished—testimony to a consciousness that it was, in its small way, a piece of architecture of interest and quality. It seems to have been the only example in the Inn in the style of William Kent's Palladian-inspired architecture. The elegantly incised initials record the treasurership of Marmaduke Alington.

5. THE CHAPEL UNDERCROFT AND AMBULATORY:

5.1. The architecture and atmosphere

'The Chapel was built with an Ambulatory,[1] or Walk, underneath, paved with Free Stones, very convenient for standing or walking in wet Weather…'

—John Strype, *Survey*, 1720.

---

[1] Ambulatory: no record exists of the elevations of the Old Chapel, and it is not known whether it was built in this way. It is to be regretted that Matthew Paris, when making a drawing of the Rolls Chapel in Chancery La. in *ca.* 1260, did not also make one of this chapel, the only other such in the La.

Mark Ockelton [of LI] in 2007 made the novel yet very persuasive suggestion that the Chapel was built on an arcade because that would have been the design of the Bishops' chapel, in common with those in a number of other bishops' palaces or town-houses in England.

An alternative, long-standing, theory is that the inspiration was the Temple, where at that date there remained a medieval cloister adjacent to the Church, built as part of the knights' and squires' quarters, and long since adapted to lawyers' and clients' meetings and perambulations. That cloister had a storey built over it in 1612, producing—a few years before the design for this chapel—an elevation of open arcade with enclosed room above.

The Temple's cloisters were burnt down in 1679, and replaced by smaller ones in classical style to the design of Sir Christopher Wren, echoed in the post-Second World War rebuilding.

A further element in this discussion—which seems not to have been cited in the discussions—is that the design for a baroque church, proposed by Cavendish Weedon to be built in the Fields, was to be 'on pillars'.

¶ If the inspiration for the Ambulatory were a cloister, its design and the atmosphere thereby created have a character more sepulchral than cloistral—a consequence perhaps of the three rows of arcades supporting the Chapel, and of their heavy branching vaults.

Two C18th commentators recorded the impression which the Undercroft made on them. One such, a noted architect and architectural writer, was inspired to suggest that its gothic (or 'gothick') effect could be improved by being made into:

'the most beautiful grotto in the kingdom… incrusted with all the varieties of artificial rock work, the ends and sides except the two middle arches being closed up; having water introduced so as to be constantly dropping from the capitals of the pillars into subterranean drains; and the whole intermix'd with moss, fossils, vitrifications, &c.'

—Batty Langley, from *Grub Street Journal*, 12th September 1735.

'The raising of this chapel on pillars affords a pleasing melancholy walk underneath; and by night particularly, when illuminated by the lamps, it has an effect that may be felt, but cannot be described.'

—James Ralph, from *A Critical Review of the Public Buildings… in and about London and Westminster*, 1783 [BL].

5.2. The quick and the dead:

5.2.1. New-born babies

¶ The Chapel Undercroft was a place for babies to be abandoned—or 'dropp'd' to use the term of art—by mothers who could not care for them, but who trusted that they would be saved, and not left to die. Babies thus accepted were sometimes given the surname 'Lincoln', as babies similarly abandoned in Temple Church might be named 'Temple'.

The most famous Lincoln of history, Abraham, was not of this lineage—his ancestors are believed to have come from Norfolk, not far from the county boundary with Lincolnshire.

The entries in *The Black Books* referring to the wide variety of arrangements made and expenditure incurred by the Society have been extensively quoted in books on the Inn and do not call to be so again here. Mark Ockelton [of LI] has suggested, however, that the foundling dropped in the Inn on 14th February 1774 and later baptised in the Chapel and named George Lincoln, was exceptionally well treated in order to demonstrate that the Inn had no need of the parish system of poor relief, and hence no need to be assessed to Poor Rates.

The Foundling Hospital, established in 1742 by Capt. Thomas Coram, some three-quarters of a mile n. of the Inn provided a more structured refuge—but some mothers who resorted to the Inn's Chapel may well have done so, having found that they could not meet the Hospital's stringent moral requirements (thus a first, but not a second, illegitimate baby could be eligible) or that if they could, they had failed in its ballot of white, red and black balls.

5.2.2. Lawyers, lay clients and professional perjurers

'To Lyncoln's Inn… and so to walk under the Chapell by agreement, whither Mr Clerke our Solicitor came to me; and he fetched Mr Long our Attorney in the Exchequer in the business against Field…'

—Samuel Pepys, from *Diary* for 27th June 1663.

¶ In these searing lines, an observer depicts the professional witnesses (that is to say professional *perjurers*) plying for hire under the Chapel. The better their clothes, the greater the weight of their evidence in court:

Retain all sorts of witnesses
That ply i' th' Temples under trees,[1]
Or walk the Round[2] *with Knights o' th' Posts,*
About their crosslegg'd Knights,[3] *their Hosts;*
Or wait for Customers between
The Pillar Rows of Lincoln's Inn
Where Vouchers, Forgers, Commonbail,
And Affidavitmen, ne'er fail
T'expose to sale, all sorts of Oaths,
According to their Ears and Cloaths,
Their only necessary Tools,
Besides the Gospel, and their Souls.

—Samuel Butler, from *Hudibras, III*, 1680.

1 Temples under trees: at this date the Temple Gardens had rows of trees ornamenting them, in the Dutch style.

2 Round: the earliest part of Temple Church is round, in the style adopted by the Knights Templar in remembrance of the Church of the Holy Sepulchre.

3 Knights: in that part of the Church are several carved effigies on tombs—those crossed-legged popularly said to be of crusaders.

These lines have been quoted in several books on the Inn or the Inns in an abbreviated form which, by accident or design, suggests that they refer to barristers' consulting with their clients—which manifestly they do not.

5.b. John Carter, FSA: The Ambulatory, 1779 (s.w. view towards the Old Hall) [BM].

This charming, naïve watercolour poses the question as to what the man in the foreground is doing. Is he a friend of the artist, posing as though for a photograph? Or is he one of the professional perjurers—soberly and well dressed in the manner of a business- or professional man—standing in the hope of being engaged to appear in court? The tombstones of members of the Society, set in the paving, are clearly shown.

5.2.3. Members of the Society lately departed

¶ Customarily, members of the Society, or in later years benchers only, were accorded the privilege of burial in the Undercroft, if their families requested it.

These lines recall one such member buried here:

Here lies the corpse of William Prynne,
A bencher late of Lincoln's Inn,
Who restless ran through thick and thin.

This grand scripturient paper-spiller,
This endless, needless margin-filler,
Was strangely tost from post to pillar.

His brain's career was never stopping,
But pen with rheum of gall still dropping,
Till hand o'er head brought ears to cropping.

Nor would he yet surcease such themes,
But prostitute new virgin reams
To types of his fanatic dreams.

But whilst he this hot humour hugs,
And for more length of tedder tugs,
Death fang'd the remnant of his lugs

—Samuel Butler, *William Prynne*, 1669.

This is a literary, not a lapidary, epitaph: Prynne's gravestone in the paving under the Ambulatory remains legible, but it is in Latin and has less to say about him. Prynne (1600-69) was a virulent and compulsive pamphleteer—writing what became represented by many thousands of printed pages. Those of them which offended the King led to his being sentenced on two successive occasions to have his ears cropped, whence the reference to 'lugs'. Prynne once walked in the Undercroft where now he lies. It was here, in May 1659, that he convened a group of MPs who had sat in the Long Parliament from 1648 to 1653, as a significant step in the reasserting of the power of the Commons and towards the deposing of the Lord Protector Richard Cromwell [of LI], and the Restoration of the Stuarts.

He became Treasurer of the Society, and Charles II appointed him Keeper of the Records in the Tower.

> Lord Baker of Dorking, *op. cit.*, 1988.

¶ An exceptional and particularly tragic interment was that of a daughter of Henry Brougham, first Baron Brougham and Vaux, LC, a Treasurer of the Society.

He had married a widow and there were two daughters of his marriage. Brougham's wife became reclusive after the birth of the second of their children, the first of whom died in infancy and the second in her teens. Surviving accounts by visitors to Brougham Hall refer to the younger daughter as 'interesting'. Brougham was heart-broken by her death and persuaded his fellow benchers to permit his daughter's body, having been brought up from Sussex where she died, to be buried in the Undercroft, and a memorial to be placed in the entrance to the Chapel: both contrary to the custom of the Society and the only non-member and female known ever to have been thus honoured.

The inscription on the monument—so finely chiselled as now scarcely to be legible—comprises a eulogy attributed to 'Wellesley' (Brougham's friend, the Duke of Wellington) followed by an epitaph, the second of which is loosely translated here from the Latin:

'Sacred to the memory of Eleanor Louise Brougham, only and most delightful daughter of Henry Baron Brougham and Vaux, lately Lord High Chancellor of England and of his wife Mary Anne. She died on the last day of November in the year of our Lord 1834, in her eighteenth year.'

Brougham was a difficult and overbearing man. The Society, when offered a portrait of him after his death, declined it. His architectural knowledge was extensive, and led him into excesses: that of proposing to rebuild the Great Gatehouse in a similar style to the Scott chambers in Old Square, and to heavy-handed 'restoration' at St Alban's Abbey (Cathedral). To his credit, however, he was one of a heterogeneous coterie (including Anglicans, Non-conformists, Catholics, Jews and atheists) who promoted the foundation of University College London and thus of London University.

6. THE OLD HALL OF THE SOCIETY:

¶ The Society occupied the bishop's Hall from the mid-C14th to the late C15th. Nothing of it is visible above ground; no artefacts from it appear to have survived; and no image is thought to exist. Of it *The Middle Temple Manuscript* said:

'Before the erecting of the said Hall, w[ch] was *Anno* 11 H.7., the Old Hall of this House stood somewhat nere unto the southwest end of the newe Chappell before yt was finished...'

¶ The Society built its own Hall and demolished the bishop's, in 1499.

'The old Hall of Lincoln's Inn has seen more and survived more than any of the other Halls of the Inns. It is the oldest of them all. It was built in the fifteenth century and it not only survived the perils of two wars in which explosive and fire bombs fell quite close to it; it survived also and, by a major surgical operation, eventually recovered from an almost fatal attack of uptodate architectural good taste, as understood by the eighteenth-century Benchers. Set in an ancient quiet court with an early Tudor gateway, overshadowed by the Chapel, neighboured by chambers with narrow winding staircases like those in the older Oxford quadrangles, simple in conception and far smaller than Middle Temple Hall with its splendid Elizabeth elaborations, it reflects more closely the collegiate intimacy of the mediaeval origins of the Inns.

......

In this small Hall, only sixty feet by thirty-two feet in its original dimensions, one can visualize the simple intimacy of [its] domestic occasions, the tiled floor thickly strewn with rushes, the central fire whence the smoke rose to escape through the louver above the sturdy, solid beams supporting the roof. In 1624 the Hall was lengthened at its lower end by twelve feet and a magnificently carved screen and gallery were introduced. The eighteenth century saw a revolution in domestic taste. The outer walls were thickly coated with cement. The roof beams were concealed and a heavy plaster ceiling was suspended from them. The lovely linenfold panels were either stowed away as lumber or destroyed. The screen was barbarously mutilated and varnished. In 1818 it was pushed back further to enlarge the floorspace of the Hall, an extension badly needed since in 1734 the Court of the Lord Chancellor with benches and other permanent fittings had been established at its upper end and the members when they dined were uncomfortably cramped and crowded at its lower end.

Then, when in 1883 the new Law Courts in the Strand were opened, the old Hall ceased to be used as a court of justice and was left without a function. In 1924 it was found to be in an advanced state of disintegration. Under the weight of the plaster ceiling the roof was pushing the walls out of the perpendicular. The plaster itself was rotten and heavily coated with mildew fungus. The mutilated roof timbers were dislocated and bent by the immense strain to which they had been improperly subjected. The stonework, which had been recklessly maltreated in fixing on the cement coating, was much decayed.

The original eightsided oak louver or lantern was found to be still existing and sound beneath a cupola of painted deal put up in 1818. Restoration and meticulous rebuilding took four years to complete, and on 22nd November, 1928 the old Hall, restored to its former character and personality, was reopened by King George V, as senior Bencher of the Inn. No machine work was used in the rebuilding and nothing was new but the mortar in the walls and such material as was required to replace what had been destroyed. Since then the windows have been filled with excellent modern glass, armorial bearings, and the figures of St Richard of Chichester, who occupied as his town house the mansion which afterwards became Lincoln's Inn, and of Sir Thomas More, saint, scholar, wit, and Chancellor, whose memory is still most highly honoured here, where he first rose to fame in the law.'

—Francis Cowper [of GI and LI], from *Topolski's Legal London*, 1961 {JML Stone}.

6.1. The exterior of the Old Hall and the Withdrawing Rooms (as seen from the w.)

¶ The Withdrawing Rooms were created as part of the rebuilding of the Old Hall in 1928, and now serve as kitchens for the service of food and beverages in the Old Hall.

6.a. Anon. artist: 'Hall of the Society of Lincoln's Inn', ? early C19th (w. view) [CWA].

One of a pair of simple elevations of the Hall, showing the two sides, perhaps done fairly soon after the Tudor brickwork had been rendered in cement, in 1819. At this date, there was no side door into the Hall. This may be one of a series of similar small watercolours of the Inns of Court by the same artist.

6.c. Annabel Wilson: The Old Hall (e. view), 1993 [coll. PHB] {the artist}.

The Withdrawing Rooms and the passageway at ground level are shown.

6.b. Charles E Flower: 'The Hall, Lincoln's Inn', *ca.* 1905 (s.e. view) [Editor's coll.] {Raphael Tuck}.

This provides a good view of the Hall, before the restoration of 1928, the exterior being still rendered in cement. The wicket gate on the l. (one of several which once stood in the Inn) evidently was removed when the archway between the Hall and the Chapel was created in 1928, and the tree has gone.

6.2. The interior of the Old Hall: *the Tudor building, the classical remodelling*, and the C20th restoration, in its collegiate and former parochial use

¶ In the late C18th, the internal appearance of the Hall was transformed by the creation of a plaster vaulted ceiling in classical style. No view of the interior before this alteration has been found, although its architectural appearance may be imagined to have been broadly similar to what it is today: that being the intention of the restoration in the 1920s, when the plaster was removed. It has been suggested that the master carpenter who designed and built the C15th roof had also been responsible for the similar one at Hatfield Old Palace.

6.e. T H Shepherd: The Old Hall, in use for dining, first half of C19th (n. view) [LMA].

At the period depicted here, the Old Hall served both for its primary collegiate purpose of a dining hall, and additionally as the Lord Chancellor's Court, when he was not sitting at Westminster Hall in law terms.

No. 79

The Natives of St. ANDREWS Holborn doe here-by desire you to meet them at their Parish Church on Thurs-day ye 23th of July at 10 in ye morning & after Sermon to accompany them to Lincolns Inn Hall to dinner where

This Ticket shall give you admittance.

Edward Orton, John Blow junr,
Benedict Ithell Jr, James Lawson, Stewards
James Johnson, Ralph Neale junr

Pay the Bearer 2s 6d

6.d. An invitation to a St Andrew's Parish Feast, in Lincoln's Inn (Old) Hall, C17th [PLMC].

As noted elsewhere, the ancient buildings of the Inn lay in the parish of St Andrew, Holborn. The Old Hall at this period must have been the best hall, not in a private town-house, within the parish.

> Caroline Barron, *The Parish of St Andrew, Holborn*, 1979.

6.f. The Old Hall, 1915 (n. view): anon. photographer [RCHM].

The furnishing would seem to be consistent with use as a lecture-theatre.

6.g. Arthur Moreland: The Old Hall, under restoration, 1928 (s. view), in his *Dickens Landmarks in London,* 1928 [GL].

The Old Hall was completely rebuilt at this date, to its original design, where possible reusing the old materials. The C18th plaster vaulted ceiling was removed, the original timbers of the roof restored, the cement rendering on the exterior walls of the Hall taken off, and the large cupola replaced with a lantern on the roof, truer to the original.

6.h. The Old Hall, interior, *ca.* 1940 (s. view): photograph A F Kersting {the photographer}.

This photograph was taken by one of the most distinguished English architectural photographers of the C20th, whose collected photographs became a unique archive. It was made as a record in case of later war damage, and shows the Hall as restored in 1928, and as it substantially remains, refurbished in 1991. The Old Hall and the Great Hall were the only halls in the four Inns not to be severely damaged or totally destroyed in the next four years.

6.i. Feliks Topolski: 'A lecture in Lincoln's Inn Old Hall', in *Topolski's Legal London,* 1961 {J M L Stone}.

The Old Hall is not now normally used for students' lectures (as here), but may be so for more special addresses. At the period of the introduction of the modern form of law lectures for bar students, and until the creation of the Inns of Court School of Law in Gray's Inn, it was much used as a classroom. The lecturer depicted was C H S Fifoot, the distinguished co-author of Cheshire and Fifoot's *Law of Contract.*

The Hall had also been used as an examination room for the Bar finals.

6.3. The Old Hall, in use for the revels:

6.3.1. The revels, and the importance attached to them in the Inns

¶ The Historical Essay explains the revels in the context of this Inn. These few ironic and punning lines—one of many comments on the revels—serve to emphasise the significance, in their day, of revels in each of the Inns:

You kept such revels with your careless pen
As made me thinke you of the Innes of Court:
For they use Revels more than any man.
So what doe in any evill sort,
You may defend it, and buy'd therupon,
That you were taught by revelation.

—'W.I.', from *The Whipping of the Satyre*, 1601.

> Robert W Wienpahl, *Music at the Inns of Court*, 1979.

6.3.2. The Society's music and song

¶ The Society's collegiate carol was sung in the Old Hall at Christmas:

Out of your slepe arise and wake,
For God mankynd now hath take
Al of a mayd with[out] make;
Nowell!
Of al women she berith the bell.

That ere was thrall nowe is made free;
That ere was small, nowe grete is she;
He shall deme bothe thee and me
Nowell!
And kepe us fromme the fynde of hell.

And thurghe that may both ware and wyse
Man is made of full grete pryse
To wynne the joye of paradyse
Nowell!
And be with Oure Ladye, emperesse of hell.

—from 'Nowell, Nowell, Nowell!', C15th
[MS LI.I.II., *fo.* 32 & 33, CUL].

> J H Baker, 'The Old Moot Book of Lincoln's Inn', (1979) 95 *LQR*.

The carol survives in a somewhat earlier MS in the Bodleian [MS Arch. Selden B.26 *f.* 14.*v*]. In that version, with three additional verses, it merited selection as one of the 'Anonymous lyrics of the C15th' in two scholarly American works: Edith Rickert, *Ancient English Christmas Carols 1400-1700*, 1914; and *The Norton Anthology of Poetry*, fifth edn., 2005—a book of two thousand pages, enjoying a wide circulation in the colleges and universities of the USA.

It has also been given a new life by the English composer, Richard Rodney Bennett, who included it in his setting of *Five Carols*, 1967, under the title 'Out of Your Sleep'.

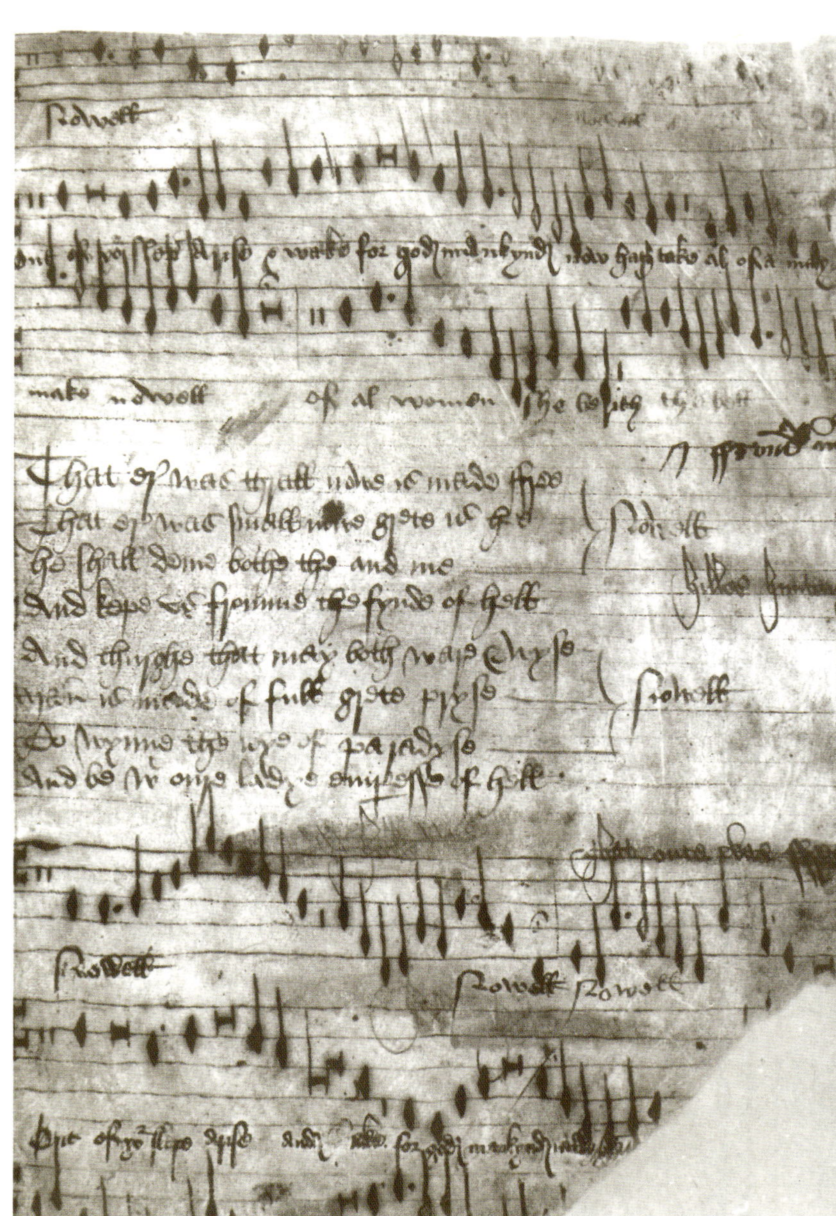

6.j. *Nowell, Nowell out of your slepe*, in old musical notation, in the handwriting of a butler of the Society, C16th [*loc. cit.*].

6.k.i. Nowell, Nowell out of your sleep, in modern notation.

> R L Greene, *The Early English Carols*, 2nd edn., 1977.

& 6.k.ii.

¶ Lincoln's Inn had its own song, which was also performed in the Old Hall as part of the Revels, a practice which continued until the C18th:

Some Mirth & Solace now let us make
To Cheer our hearts & Sorrow Slake

If thou beginst to be oppress'd
With any Malady in breast
Mirth of all Medecines is best
Such phantasies away to take

Some Mirth & Solace now let us make
To Cheer our hearts & Sorrow slake

For where ere Sorrow doth remain
It doth ingender grievous pain
Wherefore in time such things refrain
And Exercise mirth for healths Sake

Some Mirth &c.
To Cheer &c.

All Mirth I mean in honest Wise
Whereby there may no harm arise
Such Mirth to good men may suffice
And other Mirth we may not take

Some Mirth &c.
To Cheer &c.

Forsaking all that may annoy
A Peaceful Conscience to enjoy
Priant a Dieu Que *il octroy*[1]
That we in heaven may Solace take

Some Mirth & Solace now let us make
To Cheer our hearts & Sorrow Slake.

—'An Excellent Song, made 1000 [sic] Years ago Sung in Lincolns Inne Hall on Candlemas Day, 1725' (=1625) [HSLI MS. Misc. 718/11].

> J H Baker, 'The Old Songs of the Inns of Court' (1974) 90 *LQR*.

Sir John Baker, in *An Inner Temple Miscellany* (2004) 234-5, quotes an Inner Temple song which is not dissimilar. The expression 'mirth and solace' appears in *The Canterbury Tales* and in the morality play *Everyman*.

[1] *Priant…*: Praying to God that He grant.

6.3.3. The Society's dance and 'measures'

¶ The importance attached by the authorities of the Society (and those of the other Inns) to dancing has been noted in the Historical Essay.

The seeming incongruity of dancing in the Inns generally was the subject of widespread ironic observation. Joseph Addison, for example, in an essay in *The Spectator* (from which a longer extract appears later) refers to the men who 'live peaceably in their habitations, eating once a day, and dancing once a year, for the honour of their respective societies'. Referring to the senior end of the profession, Alexander Pope, in *The Dunciad iv*, 1742, has the line: 'The Judge to dance, his brother serjeant call'.

As respects this Inn, dancing was the subject of this sceptical comment, in the preceding century:

'When I was of Lincolns Inne, the fashion was (and I thinke is still) after dinner, upon grand and festivall dayes, some young gentleman of the house would take the best guest by the hand, and he the next, and so hand in hand, they did solemnly passe about the fire, the whole company, each after other, in order, to every staffe a song (which I could never sing), did the whole company then with a joyn'd voyce sing this burthen—

Some mirth and solace now let us make
To cheare our hearts, and sorrowes slake.

Upon this kind of commencement of these Revels, I conceited this:

When wise, rich Lawyers dance about the fire,
Making grave needlesse mirth sorrowes to slacke,
If clyents (who doe them too dearely hire,
Who want their money, and their comfort lacke)
Should for their solace, dance about the Hall:
I judge their dance were more methodicall.'

—Richard Hayman [of LI], from *Quodlibets*, 1628 [BL].

¶ And this more benign one by a participator, from the same century:

'On fryday being the 16th Mr Bladwell and I were admitted in the dancing school.

On Saturday Tindall admitted in the dancing schoole, and Smith paid quarteridge and began to learne. On monday also I had my new neate Leatherbottes and galossoos… On the 31, being all Saints Eve, wee had fire in the hall, noe gameing, none revells. We had musicke and mirth and solace and the measures. It was fasting night.

[Nov.] On the first of this month, being sonday and also All Saints day the judges dined here. Solace was song and measures danst, and alsoe after supper. I danst the measure after dinner.

[10th] I at lottery and dance. Corrante in musicke.

21 I saw the revells.

[Dec.] On the 4th of this month being saterday after supper wee had noe mirth and solace, but Mr Chamber and 4 couples danst the measure. After they were done 4 benchers came into the hall and we had songs as usual; nothing else noe gameing.'

—John Greene [of LI], from *Diary*, for 1635.

> E M Symonds, 'The Diary of John Greene', *English Historical Review*, 43, 1928.

¶ Lincoln's Inn had its own dance, performed in the Old Hall. These were the steps:

'Fyrst half turn and undo yt agayn, flower, iij forth; the first man and the second folowe, flower and roll into other placys, hole turn, flower, and then roll into other placys'.

—'The Howe of the House', C16th.

> J H Baker, 'The Old Moot Book of Lincoln's Inn', *loc. cit.*, 1979.

Sir John Baker observes that this manuscript addition to the Moot Book is in the handwriting of the time of Henry VII or VIII, perhaps of a butler of the Society, and that 'Howe' suggests 'hovedance' (or *hof dans*), a courtly dance. 'Flower' is presumably a flourish.

'Lincolns-Inn.
Longways for as many as will.
First take all four hands quite round, then the first man goes back to back with the second woman, then all four hand quite back again, the first woman and second man goes back to back. The first co[uple] takes both hands and half round and back again, then right hands and left, then lead down the third co[uple] and then through the first co[uple]. Each Strain play'd twice.'

—John Playford, from *The English Dancing Master*, 12th edn., 1703.

> Jeremy Barlow, combined edition of *The English Dancing Master*, 1985.

6.1. John Playford: *Lincoln's Inn*, in *The Dancing Master*, 12th edn., 1703, ed. Jeremy Barlow, 1985 {J Barlow}.

These were the steps of the Inn's dance. As might be conjectured, the Inn was not unique in having its own house dance—the other Inns of Court had theirs, and Playford even lists one for an Inn of Chancery, *Clifford's Inn*.

6.3.4. Entertainment of the Society's students' own devising

The Sun beames in the East are spred,
Leave, leave, faire Bride, your solitary bed,
No more shall you return to it alone,
It nourseth sadnesse, and your bodies print,
Like to a grave, the yielding down doth dint,
You and your other you meet there anon;
Put forth, put forth that warme balmebreathing thigh,
Which when next time you in these sheets will smother,
There it must meet another,
Which never was, but must be, oft, more nigh;
Come glad from thence, go gladder than you came,
To day put on perfection, and a womans name.

Daughters of London, you which bee
Our Golden Mines, and furnish'd Treasurie,
You which are Angels, yet still bring with you
Thousands of Angels on your marriage daies,
Help with your presence and devise to praise
These rites, which also unto you grow due;
Conceitedly dresse her, and be assign'd,
By you, fit place for every flower and jewell,
Make her for love fit fewell
As gay as Flora, and as rich as Inde;
So may shee fair, rich, glad, and in nothing lame,
To day put on perfection, and a womans name.

And you frolique Patricians,
Sonnes of these Senators, wealths deep oceans,
Ye painted courtiers, barrels of others wits,
Ye country men, who but your beasts love none,
Ye of those fellowships whereof hee's one,
Of study and play made strange Hermaphrodits,
Here shine; This Bridegroom to the Temple bring.
Loe, in yon path which store of straw'd flowers graceth,
The sober virgin paceth;
Except my sight faile, 'tis no other thing;
Weep not nor blush, here is no griefe nor shame,
To day put on perfection, and a woman's name.

Thy two-leaved gates, fair Temple, unfold,
And these two in thy sacred bosome hold,
Till, mystically joyn'd, but one they bee;
Then may thy leane and hungerstarved wombe
Long time expect their bodies and their tomb,
Long after their owne parents fatten thee.
All elder claimes, and all cold barrennesse,
All yielding to new loves bee far for ever,
Which might these two dissever,
All wayes all th' other may each one possess;
For, the best Bride, best worthy of praise and fame,
To day puts on perfection, and a womans name.

Oh winter daes bring much delight,
Not for themselves, but for they soon bring night;
Other sweets wait thee than these diverse meats,
Other disports than dancing jollities,
Other love tricks than glancing with the eyes,
But that the Sun still in our half Spheare sweats;
He flies in winter, but he now stands still,
Yet shadowes turn: Noone point he hath attain'd,
His steeds will be restrain'd,
But gallop lively downe the Western hill;
Thou shalt, when he hath run the worlds half frame,
To night put on perfection, and a womans name.

The amorous evening starre is rose,
Why then should not our amorous starre inclose
Herself in her wished bed? Release your strings
Musicians, and dancers take some truce
With these your pleasing labours, for great use
As much wearinessw as perfection brings;
You, and not only you, but all toy'd beasts
Rest duly; at night all their toyles are dispensed;
But in their beds commenced
Are other labours and more dainty feasts;
She goes a maid, who, lest she turne the same,
To night puts on perfection, and a womans name.

Thy virgin's girdle now untie,
And in thy nuptiall bed (love's altar) lye
A pleasing sacrifice; now dispossesse
Thee of these chains and robes which were put on
To adorn the day, not thee; for thou, alone,
Like vertue' and truth, art best in nakednesse;
This bed is only to virginity
A grave, but to a better state, a cradle;
Till now thou wast but able
To be what now thou art; then that by thee
No more be said, I may bee, but I am,
To night put on perfection, and a womans name.

Even like a faithfull man content
That this life for a better should be spent,

So she a mother's rich style doth prefer,
And at the Bridgegrooms wish'd approach doth lye
Like an appointed lambe, when tenderly
The priest comes on his knees t'embowell her;
Now sleep or watch with more joy; and O light
Of heaven, tomorrow rise thou hot and early;
This Sun will love so dearly
Her rest, that long, long we shall want her sight;
Wonders are wrought, for shee which had no maime,
To night puts on perfection, and a womans name.

—John Donne [of LI], 'Epithalamion made at Lincoln's Inn', ?1595.

Epithalamion is defined by the *OED* as 'a nuptial song or poem in praise of the bride and bridegroom'.

Some editors of Donne's writings had said that 'it is not known for whose marriage in the Inn this work was written'. However David Novarr, in *Review of English Studies, VII,* 1956, proposed that it was written not for a wedding but for performance at the Midsummer Revels of 1595 in the Inn. Donne was Master of the Revels in 1593, and chosen Steward of Christmas for 1594. This would also be consistent with seeing the *Epithalamion* as a parody of Edmund Spenser's eponymous work, published earlier in the same year. For this reason, the verses have been placed here under 'revel'.

Nearly two decades later, in February 1613/4, Donne wrote a more conventional epithalamion: *A Epithalamion, or marriage song, on the Lady Elizabeth and Count Palatine, being married on St Valentine's Day.* That marriage was followed by a masque at Whitehall, performed by members of the Middle Temple and Lincoln's Inn, the procession for which began at the Master of the Rolls' house, a literary record of which is noted in 2.3.3.i. above.

6.m.i. William Hogarth: Paul before Felix, 1748 [HSLI].
The scene is from *Acts of the Apostles*, 24: 24-25.

6.4. Hogarth's 'Paul before Felix': the painting and the prints

¶ The painting was commissioned by the Society, paid for by the gift of Lord Wyndham, LCI, and for most of the time since then has been on the walls of the Old Hall. It appears, therefore, in many of the old engravings of the interior. More than one distinguished visitor to the Inn in the C18th or C19th amongst whom Sir Joshua Reynolds, observed that Hogarth was not at home with Biblical scenes in the classical style. The comment in *London Interiors*, 1841—with which the present-day critic may be inclined to agree—was that 'this picture remains as a monument of the failure of an unrivalled artist in a department for which his very genius unfitted him'. The painting was adjusted in a number of details by Hogarth himself at the request of the benchers, when first displayed. It was later overpainted by another hand and was only restored to its original character in the late C20th.

Hogarth's choice of subject—an unjust judge—must surely have been a true expression of his opinions, and it is remarkable that the Society was content to leave such an image in the Old Hall, not least when it was in use as the High Court of Chancery.

Several scholars have written on the subject of this painting, amongst whom Clovis Whitfield and Ronald Paulson, each in essays for the *Burlington Magazine*, and Meg Weissmann in the LI Catalogue of Paintings.

6.m.ii. 'St Paul before Felix burlesqued: Designd & scratch'd in the true Dutch taste by Wm. Hogarth', 1751 [HSLI].
This engraving was first made to illustrate a subscription ticket for the commissioning and sale of accurate engravings of this painting and another. Later, with a slightly amended caption ('designd & etch'd in the rediculous manner of Rembrant…' [*sic*]) it was sold as a print in its own right. It is a satire on everyone, not least the lawyers, and shows Hogarth true to himself. Critics of Hogarth's work on the original painting seem often to have overlooked or not given credit for this version.

6.5. The Old Hall, in use as *the Lord Chancellor's, the Master of the Rolls'* and as *the Lords Justices'* Courts:

6.5.1. Its interior

¶ Although the Old Hall was built solely for the collegiate purposes of the Society, for almost two centuries it served also as a court of Chancery. This use began in the early 1700s, when the Rolls House in Chancery La., having become ruinous, was being rebuilt, and the Master of the Rolls in consequence needed suitable temporary accommodation nearby. Then, from 1733, the Lord Chancellors sat here out of law terms during which, until 1846, the Society required the Hall for dining.

Perhaps the most famous evocation of the Inn, these are the opening lines of the first chapter of Dickens' novel, a book which could have been entitled *Lincoln's Inn*:

'London. Michaelmas Term lately over, and the Lord Chancellor sitting in Lincoln's Inn Hall. Implacable November weather. As much mud in the streets, as if the waters had but newly retired from the face of the earth, and it would not be wonderful to meet a Megalosaurus, forty feet long or so, waddling like an elephantine lizard up Holborn Hill. Smoke lowering down from chimney pots, making a soft black drizzle, with flakes of soot in it as big as fullgrown snowflakes—gone into mourning, one might imagine, for the death of the sun. Dogs, undistinguishable in mire. Horses, scarcely better; splashed to their very blinkers. Foot passengers, jostling one another's umbrellas, in a general infection of ill temper, and losing their foothold at streetcorners, where tens of thousands of other foot passengers have been slipping and sliding since the day broke (if this day ever broke), adding new deposits to the crust upon crust of mud, sticking at those points tenaciously to the payment, and accumulating at compound interest. … Most of the shops lighted two hours before their time—as the gas seems to know, for it has a haggard and unwilling look.

The raw afternoon is rawest and the dense fog is densest, and the muddy streets are muddiest, near that leadenheaded old obstruction, appropriate ornament for the threshold of a leadenheaded old corporation: Temple Bar. And hard by Temple Bar, in Lincoln's Inn Hall, at the very heart of the fog, sits the Lord High Chancellor in his High Court of Chancery.

Never can there come fog too thick, never can there come mud and mire too deep, to assort with the groping and the floundering condition which this High Court of Chancery, most pestilent of hoary sinners, holds, this day, in the sight of heaven and earth.

On such an afternoon, if ever, the Lord High Chancellor ought to be sitting here—as here he is—with a foggy glory round his head, softly fenced in with crimson cloth and curtains, addressed by a large advocate with great whiskers, a little voice, and an interminable brief, and outwardly directing his contemplation to the lantern in the roof, where he can see nothing but fog.'

—Charles Dickens, from *Bleak House*, 1852.

The composer Geoffrey Bush (d. 1998) found a rather surprising inspiration in these words to set a few of them sparsely to music in a song, 'Fog'.

6.m.iii. William Hogarth (engraved by the artist from his own painting):
'St Paul before Felix', 1752 [HSLI].

This accomplished engraving is true to the spirit of the original painting, and at first sight accurate. But on close inspection, it differs in the minor figures and architectural background, but principally by omitting Drusilla, the Jewish wife of the Roman Governor, Felix, who in the original is sitting on her husband's l. hand. This omission is explained in Samuel Ireland, *op. cit.*, 1800, who, while not reproducing the engraving, observes that 'the pitiful critique that his (Paul's) hand was improperly placed before Drusilla… would never have entered the head of the most rigid caviller had it not been a most prevalent opinion, that Hogarth never could be serious on any subject whatever… it is however certain that in one of the prints from the picture, he totally expunged the figure of Drusilla'.

6.n. Thomas Rowlandson & Augustus Pugin: 'Court of Chancery' (w. view), in T Ackermann, *Microcosm of London*, 1808 [BM].

This may be compared with the later and well-known engraving by T H Shepherd, in *London Interiors*, 1841 (not reproduced here), which shows the Hall with the same general appearance but with small changes having been made: the canopy over the Lord Chancellor's head had become Victorian gothic; he was equipped with a desk; and the central stove had seemingly been removed. The view shown in this aquatint may therefore be taken to record the appearance of the Court at the period evoked by Dickens, which is believed to be in the 1820s.

In order to deaden the sense of smell, second-hand clothes-pegs will be used by the bench and the bar.

Lords Justices Bowen and Fry prepared to break the windows of the court, and relieve the asphyxiated bar.

OLD LAW COURT MEMORIES

6.o. 'Old Law Court Memories', *Punch*, *ca.* 1885 [LMA].

In 1852, the Old Hall was partitioned into two to create, in addition to the Lord Chancellor's Court, the court of the two Lord Justices of Appeal in Chancery who had been appointed in the preceding year. Then, in 1873, when the Court of Appeal was established by the Judicature Act, the partition was removed and the Hall served as the Court of Appeal's First Division until the RCJ were able to accommodate that Court. This cartoon imagines Bowen and Fry L JJ, attempting to break out of their unventilated courtroom in the Old Hall.

6.p. A W: 'Lincoln's Inn', *English Illustrated Magazine*, 1883 [LMA].

This is one of several robust and seemingly lifelike line drawings, illustrating an article by the distinguished legal historian, Frederic Maitland [of LI] (1850-1906), occasioned by the opening of the RCJ. Maitland was the co-author, with Sir Frederick Pollock [of LI] (1845-1937), of the *History of English Law*, 1895, the first great work on that subject in modern times.

6.5.2. Lord Eldon, LC

¶ Probably the most notorious judge to have sat in the Old Hall, and who is for ever associated in literature and history with it, was John Scott, first Earl of Eldon [of MT] (1751-1838). Eldon's delays and indecisions were the subject of widespread criticism in words and caricature. These words succinctly recorded the problem:

'He questions, makes the business slow, carries the papers home for consideration, gives another hearing to a cause, again carries the papers home, will hear again, and again carry back the papers. And something else having occupied his attention, this case will be added to heaps of other cases, and pass from his mind.'

—Joseph Farington, RA, from *Diaries*, 1793-1821.

'The school reputed to be the most significant is Lincoln's Inn. It is a huge edifice erected in the form of a quadrangle enclosing a garden. It houses students' and lawyers' accommodation, the latter frequently including offices for business purposes. It also includes a court room where the Lord Chancellor sometimes presides.

At the time of my visit such a trial was proceeding and it was the first time that I had seen Lord Eldon. He was sitting in the judge's chair, wearing a long red gown and wig, and his face stern and grave like that of a statue. In front of him, on a long table spread with a green cloth, were two considerable silver maces and two lawyers were arguing their cases at the bar. Lord Eldon is said to be the most able lawyer in the whole kingdom. He appeared to be approximately seventy years of age. He is tall, with an oval face and calm eyes and speaks in a quiet and slow fashion. I heard him admonish barristers who had wandered off the point, for the law tries to prohibit loss of time through vain discussions.'

—Krystyn Lach-Szyrma, from *Reminiscences of a Journey through England and Scotland, 1820-24* in *London Observed: A Polish Philosopher at Large…*, ed. Mona Kedslie McLeod, 2009.

> Translation: Malgorazata Machnice and Agnieska Kiersztejn.

To cause delay in Lincoln's Inn
Two different causes tend
His Lordship's[1] *judgments ne'er begin*
His Honour's[2] *never end.*

—Anon. epigram, *ca.* 1815.

[1] His Lordship: the Lord Chancellor, Lord Eldon.

[2] His Honour: the Vice-Chancellor, Sir Thomas Plumer [of LI].

> Sir Gerald Hurst KC [of LI], *A Short History of Lincoln's Inn*, 1946.

¶ A more literary response to Eldon's judgment, or specifically one of his judgments, was this:

Thy country's curse is on thee, darkest crest
Of that foul, knotted, many-headed worm
Which rends our Mother's bosom—Priestly Pest!
Masked Resurrection of a buried Form!

Thy country's curse is on thee! Justice sold,
Truth trampled, Nature's landmarks overthrown,
And heaps of fraud-accumulated gold,

Plead, loud as thunder, at Destruction's throne.
... Oh, let a father's curse be on thy soul,
And let a daughter's hope be on thy tomb;
Be both, on thy gray head, a leaden cowl
To weigh thee down to thine approaching doom!

I curse thee by a parent's outraged love,
By hopes long cherished and too lately lost,
By gentle feelings thou couldst never prove,
By griefs which thy stern nature never crossed.
... By all the days, under an hireling's care,
Of dull constraint and bitter heaviness,
O wretched ye if every any were,
Sadder than orpans, yet not fatherless!
... By thy most impious Hell, and all its terror;
By all the grief, the madness, and the guilt
Of thine impostures, which must be their error—
That sand on which thy crumbling power is built—

By thy complicity with lust and hate—
Thy thirst for tears—thy hunger after gold—
The ready frauds which ever on thee wait—
The servile arts in which thou hast grown old—
By thy most killing sneer, and by thy smile—
By all the arts and shares of thy black den,
And—for thou canst outweep the crocodile—
By thy false tears—those millstones braining men

Yes, the despair which bids a father groan,
And cry, 'My children are no longer mine—
The blood within those veins may be mine own,
But—Tyrant—their polluted souls are thine'—

I curse thee—though I hate thee not.—O slave!
If thou couldst quench the earth-consuming Hell
Of which thou art a daemon, on thy grave
This curse should be a blessing. Fare thee well!

—Percy Bysshe Shelley, from 'To The Lord Chancellor', 1816.

The verses from which those here are extracted were written as an invective—perhaps one of the most acerbic in the language—against Lord Eldon. In 1816, Shelley's first wife, Harriet, drowned herself, and immediately thereafter he married Mary (the author of *Frankenstein*), by then the mother of his third child, and began Chancery proceedings for the custody of the two children of his first marriage. In these, he failed, and the experience marked him deeply. He, in turn, died by drowning.

6.6. The passageways of the Old Hall

¶ Screen Passage is so named from the panelled screen at the s. end of the Hall on which traditionally notices were displayed (or 'screened'). This tradition continues, duly modified, in the notice-board on the wall of the Passage outside the Hall itself, which is used for social events, whereas professional or academic notices are pinned up outside the Treasury Office, or in the Library.

Although the term used in the Inn is 'screen passage', the generic architectural term is 'screens passage' and the term used for the construction separating one such from a hall is a 'spere'.

The passage outside the n. end of the Old Hall—and which has no specific name—was created when the Withdrawing Rooms were built above in 1928. It allows vehicular access to Gatehouse Court.

6.q. John Crowther: 'Lamp over Archway, no. 20 Old Sq., Lincoln's Inn', *ca.* 1880 [LMA].

This gas-lamp lit the way into Screen Passage, from the w.

6.r. M G Bailey: 17, Old Buildings, *ca.* 1920 (s.e. view) [Editor's coll. >> Francis Slingsby, solicitor].

This late afternoon view of 17, Old Buildings would have been taken just before the renovation of the Old Hall, when the doorway of 17 and the opening into Screen Passage (which runs through to Gatehouse Court) were transposed, thereby removing the need to climb an internal staircase to first floor level to gain access to these chambers.

6.s. Annabel Wilson: The Old Hall, 1993 (w. view) [coll. PHB] {the artist}.

The Chapel and the Old Hall were linked by an arch with rooms over (the Withdrawing Rooms) in 1928, giving to those buildings substantially their present-day appearance from this direction, as shown here.

The Withdrawing Rooms are now equipped as a kitchen, to serve the Old Hall.

6.t. Liam Martin: The Chapel road-way and Undercroft, 1991 (w. view) [LT].

Above, are the joists of the Withdrawing Rooms, and to the l., is the road-way, and to the r., the Undercroft. This drawing provides a glimpse of the brick-and-beam treatment of the link between the Chapel and the Old Hall, a distinctive vernacular style in the last decades of the C19th and first of the C20th, and the only example in the Inn.

7. THE CHAPEL, THE OLD HALL AND THE E. END OF LIBRARY ROW (AND LATTERLY THE E. SIDE OF THE WITHDRAWING ROOMS), FRAMING GATEHOUSE COURT ON ITS N. AND W. SIDES

7.a. Anon. English artist: Gatehouse Court, depicting: from w. to e., the Old Hall, the Chapel and the Gatehouse, *ca.* 1725 (n. view) [YCBA].

This is the earliest known painting of Gatehouse Court. Until it (and a related painting by the same artist of Paper Building, Temple) had been found in the course of research for this book, its existence and location were generally unknown in the Inns; and despite being catalogued at Yale, its historical significance not recognised there. The stationer's shop on the n. side of the Gatehouse can be seen, and also the sundial on the s. wall of the Chapel, the ordering of which is recorded in *The Black Books*, and of which this may be the only coloured image.

7.b. Anon. English artist: Preparatory sketch for the painting at Yale, *ca.* 1720 [SoAL].

This is one of a series of drawings, now in various hands, of all the Inns of Court and most of the Inns of Chancery—believed to be the first ever made. It is to be regretted that the artist of this endeavour is unknown.

7.c. Samuel Ireland: The Hall, e. end of Library Row and the Chapel, *ca.* 1799 (n.w. view) [YCBA].

This is the preparatory watercolour for the corresponding (and widely reproduced) engraving in his *Picturesque Views of the Inns of Court*. Making allowance for artistic inaccuracy, little seems to have changed in seventy-five years. But the sundial and the decorative urns on the Chapel buttresses seem to have gone, and the Old Hall has a very tall stove pipe.

7.d. T H Shepherd: Lincoln's Inn Hall, Chapel, and Chancery Court, *ca.* 1830 (n.w. view) [Editor's coll.].

The 'improvements' of 1817-9, which accompanied the building of the Vice-Chancellor's Court (on the other side of the Old Hall, not visible here), included the refronting with a battlemented parapet of Library Row (14-15, Old Buildings), between the n. end of the Hall, and the Chapel.

7.e. John Walton, RP: Gatehouse Court, 1980s (n.w. prospect, with the New Hall in the background) [HSLI].

This oil painting, by a distinguished portraitist and his gift to the Society, depicts an early afternoon in spring in the 1980s, and shows the green and leafy character of present-day Gatehouse Court, in marked contrast to its appearance in earlier centuries.

8. THE NEW OR GREAT HALL:

¶ In 1839, the Society identified the need for a new Hall and Library to accommodate the growth in the numbers of its members and books, and in its dignity. In 1842, they approved plans prepared by Philip Hardwick. The foundation stone was laid in 1843, and the buildings completed in 1846. The Old Hall continued in use for parts of the year as a law court. Thus this Inn became, and has remained, the only one of the four with two halls designed for its collegiate purposes.

8.1. The foundation of the Great Hall

¶ The inscription on the foundation stone of the New Hall, laid by the Society's Treasurer, Sir James Lewis Knight-Bruce, on 20th April 1843, reads:

Stet lapis arboris nudo defixus in horto
Fundamen pulchrae tempus in omne domus
Aula vetus lites et legum aenigmata servet
Ipsa nova exorior nobilitanda coquo

Sir George Rose [of IT], a Master in Chancery who was famous in his day for his gift of extempory versification, rendered the text very freely into English. Who, among the benchers, laboured on the original text with its Puckish pun, is not known:

The trees of yore
Are seen no more;
Unshaded now the garden lies
May the red bricks,
Which here we fix,
Be lasting as our equities
The olden dome
With musty tone
Of law and litigation suits
In this we look
For a better Cook[1]
Than he who wrote the Institutes.

—G W Bell, from *Sir George Rose, a Memoir,* publ. privately 1877 [BL].

[1] Sir Edward Coke [of IT], *Institutes of the Laws of England*, 1628-44.

8.2. The opening of the Great Hall by Queen Victoria

The Banquet ceased—the great ones pass'd away,
Yet still the scene look'd beautiful and gay;
For then the gallant Benchers, one and all,
The gallery sought, and to the splendid hall
The ladies brought, whose gentle forms were seen
To move and mingle in the festive scene.
The Bard beheld the decorated space,
And thus apostrophized the matchless place:—
'Majestic pile how well in thee appears
The blended glory of succeeding years.
Thy antique roof in modern lightness dress'd,
Thy antique screen to modern uses press'd,
Thy antique glass to modern brilliance brought,
Thy antique boards with modern comforts fraught;
Thy storehouse vast, where careful students find
Draughts for the fancysolids for the minds;
Thy gay saloons, intended to be lit
With Brougham's eloquence and Wakefield's wit…'

—Joseph Payne [of LI], from 'Lines written to commemorate the opening of Lincoln's Inn New Hall', 1845 [a monograph, HSLI].

These are but a few lines from a long poem, bound in leather, preserved in the Library. The author's preface to his slim volume is perhaps rightly modest as to the quality of his writing—but the lines have the great virtue of conveying what must have been the bursting pride and confidence of the membership of the Society on that day, fully corroborated by the sceptical observations of the French newspaper reporter in the next quotation.

'London's legal fraternity was in a state of emotion the day before yesterday. This was due to the presence of the Queen, who with some pomp and ceremony, went to participate in the opening of the new buildings, the new hall and library, of Lincoln's Inn.

What is more, on that day, clients would have been unwelcome, had they required the breed of consultants and pleaders to pursue their law suits for them.

In the sight of this royal procession at the heart of their sanctuary, the solicitors felt themselves grow by fifteen feet, the barristers gained immeasurably in majesty, and the ordinary pupils and students were prouder than ever in admiring the black gowns of their leaders and those more senior than them in their careers. For these young people, adept at the great art of turning black into white and *vice versa*, the judicial wig with its antique curls, received on this day a sheen which reflected gloriously upon the entire company.

8.a. The déjeuner in the Great Hall for Queen Victoria, 1845 (s. view) [HSLI].

But is Lincoln's Inn, therefore, a law court, some sort of seat of judgment, a place where chicanery sharpens the quill pen and makes more silver the tongue?… not in the least! Lincoln's Inn is to the tired and hungry soldiers of Themis, a good and comfortable hotel, and at the same time the headquarters of one of those great companies of lawyers of which Gray's Inn and Temple Bar [*sic*] complete the trilogy [*sic*]. In France the 'protectors of widows and orphans' are disunited and isolated, exercising a very limited power over their clients; the precision of the Codes, the hierarchy of jurisdictions, and more than that the provisions of certain regulations, sometimes restrain martyrs from procedures which are too outrageous. Here, where the texts are more numerous than the pine trees of Lithuania, here where the law provides an armoury from every century, from every munitions factory and a sword of every temper, the lawyer luxuriates in his power and his freedom. The team spirit of his Society adds further to his power, and woe betide a government or an individual who dares to attack the regiment of these lawyers' colleges.

Divided into three [*sic*] awesome battalions, who have pitched their tents at Temple Bar, Lincoln's Inn and Gray's Inn; rivals of one another, but united with a single idea—always the defender of widows and orphans—the men of law wield over a whole section of English society an influence from which none dares to escape. They take a man in his cradle and do not let him go even in his tomb; and during his life such are the ties which bind a man that without them it is scarcely possible to act in defence of interests, or liberty or fortune. Furthermore, the lawyers are the men who appear to be the most respected, but are in truth the most detested, in Britain.

Lincoln's Inn, one of their main lairs, has been in existence for more than 400 years. This hostelry served for a long time both as a lawyers' refectory and as the Lord Chancellor's court. But the number of law suits and consequently of benchers having considerably increased, the Society decided in 1842 to erect a new building with a dining room capable of accommodating 400 people, a library for 40,000 books, a council chamber, a drawing room, a vast kitchen and accommodation for indoor and outdoor staff. This is the edifice which was inaugurated today, and of which the architecture has above all the rare merit of being perfectly suited to its purpose.

The hall, whose style—if it were in a French law court, we would call the *salle des pieds perdus*—is 120 feet long and 45 wide with a ceiling of beautifully worked oak. But the purpose of the hall is not at all that it should be used for walking up and down; it is an immense refectory capable of receiving a hundred tables for the lawyers of different ranks who make up the Society, but above all for its students.

Those from overseas who read this will inevitably ask themselves the reason for this vast dining room, and what it possesses which could make students prefer it to the *cabarets,*[1] the *tables d'hôte*[2] and the restaurants of the neighbourhood. The answer reflects a custom which is to be found in no other country, a custom which certainly has its merits. In France, for example, in order to become an *avocat*, one must follow regularly the

8.b. T H Shepherd: The Library and New Hall, *ca.* 1845 (s.e. view) [LMA]. This is the w. elevation, seen from the Fields.

courses at the law faculty, and at predetermined points of time, obtain attendance records which attest as much to the punctiliousness as to the knowledge of the student. But how few among them attend regularly the law lecturers' classes! By contrast, how eagerly they would attend if the Ministry of Education allowed the restauranteur Flicoteaux, that supplier of manna to the Latin Quarter in past times, or old Lahire of the Café Procope, to set up their banners in the centre of the law faculty. Here, so far as is known, certificates of attendance at classes are not required, and to be certain that a young member has satisfactorily pursued matters at the bar, he is required, except during the vacations, to eat at the headquarters of a society of lawyers. A superintendent maintains an account, in duplicate or otherwise, of the meals taken by the students, and the certificate of admission is only issued after due attendance at a certain number of dinners.

It is scarcely surprising, therefore, that with such institutions as this, England should have so many big, fat and strong rascals!'

—from 'Nouvelles de Londres', in *Le Courier de l'Europe,*[3]
1st November 1845 [press cutting, HSLI].

---

1 *Cabarets*: establishments providing food, dancing and song. Although it is inconceivable that Holborn ever provided the sophistication of establishments in the Latin Quarter of Paris, the large and ornate Holborn Restaurant at 218, High Holborn (and its predecessors on the same site) provided at various dates from the mid-C19th on, a casino, and a restaurant with dancing shows.

2 *tables d'hôte*: left untranslated because it is a familiar restaurant expression at the present day. But at that date, its translation would have been 'ordinary' i.e. the fixed-price no-choices meal at a chop house, of which there were numerous in High Holborn, Fleet St. and the Strand.

3 This was a French-language newspaper published in London, read perhaps by, among others, the political refugees then living here who went to support the continental revolutions of 1848.

Editor's translation and notes.

8.3. The exterior of the Great Hall

8.c. R H Burden: New Hall and Library, 1847 (n.w. view): photograph R Todd White [coll. PHB].

The New Hall attracted widespread national interest, and in consequence was the subject of attention by several artists, and many versions exist of this view. Indeed, the passage of a century and a half suggests that this is one of the most successful buildings in the Victorian Tudor style in England. This watercolour by an architect (which has not been reproduced as an engraving, as several have) was made two years after the Hall was opened.

8.d. Lewis J Wood: 'The East Terrace, New Hall, Lincoln's Inn', *ca.* 1843 (design, n. view, e. side) [HSLI].

This very fine lithograph is one of a series of seven (of which several are reproduced in this book), published as building work was beginning. They are very close to, but not identical with, a series of six produced for the benchers before the project began, and of which a set was presented to Queen Victoria and is in Windsor Castle Library. The buildings, as erected, conformed closely to the general design, but differed in many details—presumably as a result of discussions with the benchers before, and during, building.

8.e. 'Time no object', *Punch*, 1884 [press cutting, HSLI].

Both the face and the escapement of the clock fitted to the s.e. tower of the Hall in 1884 were to the design of Lord Grimthorpe, QC [of LI], a distinguished amateur horologist and locksmith, responsible for the innovative design of the movement driving with great accuracy the clock in the Elizabeth Tower of the Houses of Parliament, which sounds the bell colloquially known as 'Big Ben'. As one of the first public clocks in London without numerals, the Inn's clockface provoked some derision.

8.4. The interior of the Great Hall; and the Watts fresco

¶ The distinguished portraitist G F Watts—in his day, one of the most famous and admired painters working in England—offered for no fee to paint a large fresco in the Hall, on which he worked between 1852 and 1859. It is thought to be the largest true fresco (using *tempera* in the Italian mode) in England. Its maintenance has been a continual problem. Indeed the verse-writer Basil Cottle (whose work is quoted above) neatly punned that it was 'temperamental'. The figures are great lawgivers of history, from the Medes and Persians onwards. Many are portraits of then living models, persons distinguished in the law, the arts and fashionable society.

'Watts's fresco carries the perspective of the Great Hall into an imaginery realm where the lawgivers of history meet in a 'hemicycle' or semicircle… the composition has particular effect here, where the circle is completed at dinner by the barristers and students of [the] Inn, the lawgivers of the future, who with their predecessors encircle the bench as lawgivers of the present.'

—Mark Ockelton [of LI], from Angela Holdsworth and others, *A Portrait of Lincoln's Inn*, 2007.

8.f. John Crowther: 'The New Hall, 1885' (s. view) [LMA].

The New Hall is, as noted in the Historical Essay, the largest in the four Inns, measuring 120' long, 45' wide, and 62' high.

8.g. John Crowther: The New Hall, showing the Watts fresco, 1884 (n. view) [LMA].

8.h. G F Watts: 'A Hemicycle of Lawgivers: Justice', from the reduced copy, commissioned by the Society, and now in the RCJ, painted by N M Lund, RA, 1905.

> J D Walker, *Short Notes on Lincoln's Inn*, 1906 [HSLI].

The reduced copy is used here, since it lends itself more conveniently to reproduction and deciphering of its detail. The original is shown in context in *8.g.* It is generally agreed, if not universally recognised, that the inspiration for both the concept and the disposition of figures in the fresco was Raphael's 'School of Athens' in the Apostolic Palace in the Vatican, painted in 1509-11: adjudged by some scholars to be his masterpiece. Watts, while clearly following Raphael, has gothicised or Tudorised the original to fit it into the architecture of the Great Hall. Philip Hardwick, its architect, had stated that his design was 'of the period towards the end of the sixteenth century before the admixture of Italian architecture'. 'The School of Athens', by contrast, has been called 'the perfect embodiment of the High Renaissance', and thus was the antithesis of the architect's vision. It might be generally considered that, at that period of history, England lagged behind Italy in its styles of art and architecture by more than a century.

8.i. Raphael: 'The School of Athens', 1509-11, from the Stanza della Segnatura, Vatican {Bridgeman}.

9. THE LIBRARY:

9.1. The exterior of the Library, as first built and as extended

9.a. Lewis J Wood: 'The east end of the new Library and Benchers' entrance', *ca.* 1843 (design, w. view) [HSLI].

This lithograph depicts the Library as originally proposed, and as built with some modifications, made in the course of construction. Originally, and as shown here, the Library did not extend e. beyond the width of the New Hall, and the porch over the Library stairs projected out from the building line.

9.b. Herbert Railton: The entrance to the Library, as enlarged, *ca.* 1890 (n.w. view), in W J Loftie, *op. cit.*, 1893.

An extension of three bays, to the east, was completed in 1872 to the designs of Sir George Gilbert Scott, closely following the design of Philip Hardwick for the original building.

9.c. and 9.d. Rick Mather Associates: proposed elevations of Library extension intended to be built on the site of the Under-Treasurer's house, 2015 (s.e. and n. views).

9.2. The interior of the Library

9.e. 'The Library, Presentation of the Address' (e. view), *Illustrated London News*, 1845 [press cutting, HSLI].

This small drawing shows the interior of the Library as first built.

9.f. Thomas Cowlishaw: The Library, *ca.* 1890 (e. view) [HSLI].

The interior of the Library, as extended to the e. in 1872.

9.3. *Fry J's Court* (now the Old Court Room), below the Library

¶ The Old Court Room, as it is now called, and used for meetings and receptions, was created below the Library for Sir Edward Fry, as an additional Chancery Court room, before the RCJ was fully available.

THE KITCHEN.

10.a. 'The Kitchen', *Illustrated London News*, 1846 [press cutting, HSLI].

10. THE KITCHENS:

10.1. The new Kitchens, and the old equipment

¶ The Kitchens, with their high vaults, are below the Great Hall, at its s. end.

LINCOLN'S INN

A CATALOGUE

OF THE SURPLUS

FIXTURES

AND FITTINGS-UP,

OF THE LATE

Kitchen of Lincoln's Inn,

SEVERAL COPPERS,

TWO LARGE WATER CISTERNS,

Lined with Lead,

LARGE SLATE CISTERN,

All the Iron Work of the Hot Plates and Stewing Stoves,

LARGE IRON RANGE & SMOKE JACK,

STEAM & GAS PIPING,

Large Stout Tables, quantity of Shelving and Presses and a variety of useful Stuff;

WHICH WILL BE SOLD BY AUCTION,

BY

MR. PRICE

ON THE PREMISES,

Old Square, Lincoln's Inn,

On TUESDAY, the 18th of AUGUST, 1846,

At Twelve for One o'Clock,

By Order of the Honourable Society of Lincoln's Inn.

May be viewed the Day prior and Catalogues had at

Mr. PRICE's Offices, 48, Chancery Lane.

Redford and Son, Printers, London Road, Southwark.

10.b. 'A Catalogue of the surplus Fixtures…of the late Kitchen of Lincoln's Inn', 1846 [HSLI].

10.2. The new Members' Common Room

¶ This new room was created in the first decade of the C21st, when the kitchens and their equipment were being comprehensively modernised.

A mezzanine floor was inserted, taking advantage of the high vaults of the kitchens. Those vaults have been preserved in the new Members' Common Room. The result is a very successful architectural *jeu d'esprit*, with the vaults springing from floor level and the chimney breast in the kitchens below protruding into the new room. The position of the new floor, at the point where the chimney breast begins its converging lines, can be pictured from the line drawing reproduced here of the kitchens as originally built. The space created must be unique in London, or almost so.

10.c. 'Fire-place in the Great Kitchen', *Pictorial Times*, 1846 [press cutting, HSLI].

D. THE CHAMBERS & OFFICES, GARDENS & WALKS OF THE INN; AND *COURT* *ROOMS, CHAMBERS & OFFICES OF CHANCERY & OF EXCHEQUER* WITHIN IT

11. GATEHOUSE COURT:

11.1. The chambers from the e. end of the Chapel to and in the n. tower of the Great Gatehouse: 15, Old Square and 1, Old Buildings, the site of *1-3, Old Buildings* (in *Chancery Lane Row*)

¶ The Hon William Murray's rooms.

William Murray, later first Earl of Mansfield, has been called the most powerful British jurist of the C18th: both one of the most eloquent advocates, and a judge whose judgments retain their value after more than two centuries. In Parliament he was regarded as the best speaker of his generation.

Thus far no building in the Inn has been named in his memory, nor has any set of chambers in the Inn adopted his name for its practice. This therefore is the one location in the Inn to which memory of him may be attached, apart from the Old Hall, if ever he appeared there as an advocate, out of term.

His first legal home in London was in rooms at 1, Old Square, adjacent to the Great Gatehouse, and to which he was introduced by William Hamilton [of LI], a friend who had sponsored him on joining the Society—reputedly the first Scots advocate to be called and practise at the English bar after the Union. On Murray's being called, and beginning practice, he took chambers in 5, King's Bench Walk, Inner Temple and from which he worked until elevated to the judicial bench. This panegyric was written by a friend and adviser whose executor he later became:

To Venus

Again? new tumults in my breast?
Ah, spare me, Venus! let me, let me rest!
I am not now, alas! the man
As in the gentle reign of my Queen Anne,
Nor circle sober fifty with thy charms.
Mother too fierce of dear desires!
Turn, turn to willing hearts your wanton fires:
To number five direct your doves,
There spread round Murray all your blooming Loves;
Noble and young, who strikes the heart
With ev'ry sprightly, ev'ry decent part;
Equal the injured to defend,
To charm the Mistress, or to fix the Friend.
He, with a hundred arts refin'd,
Shall stretch thy conquests over half the kind:
To him each rival shall submit,
Make but his Riches equal to his Wit.

—Alexander Pope, from 'The First Ode of the Fourth Book of Horace', 1738.

11.a.i. J P Emslie: 'No's 3, 2 & 1, Old Square, since pulled down', 1885 (n.e. view) [HSLI].

11.a.ii. J P Emslie: Back of Chancery Lane Row, from Chancery Lane, 1885 (s.w. view) [RCHM].

On the extreme r. (to the n.) may be seen a foot or two of the new 13, Old Square, just completed. The serrated edge of the bricks is ready to bond in with the next building to go up. 2, 3 & 4, Old Buildings are about to be demolished, and be replaced by John O Scott's buildings now numbered 14-15, Old Square. The view is taken from a point some yards s. of that in *13.c.*, and is clearly later. Not only has the demolition of Chancery La. Row progressed two windows further s., but more significantly, the Scott buildings have been put up.

¶ The most important early wall-painting (on plaster) to have been found in the Inn was in this range of chambers:

'Limited to their respective divisions, the subjects include figures, monsters, heads, amorini, birds, fruit, flowers, scrolls and the like—all well executed, though in somewhat crude colouring. The Cupid discharging his bow, the Pomona (or Ceres), the swinging boy, and the husbandman tilling the soil are very good. The style of the spade used by the lastnamed is in itself enough to mark the age of a curious mural decoration, for whose rescue some effort should be made. To the right is a capital composition of two dolphins, depicted in conventional guise, supporting a vase or fountain, whereon are two parrots, and above them a heart in flames.'

—from *The Builder*, 20th June 1885.

> Introduction to Vol. V, *The Black Books*.

11.b. J P Emslie: First-floor chamber in 3, Old Square before demolition, showing the location of the wall-painting, which had been hidden by wainscotting, 1885 [HSLI].

¶ Sir George Gilbert Scott was commissioned to prepare plans for the rebuilding of Old Square. He did so in a 'collegiate' style—thought fitting for institutions of learning—including plans for rebuilding the Gatehouse in conformity with the new buildings. Second thoughts by the benchers led to leaving the Gatehouse untouched. On Sir George's death, his son John assumed responsibility, but the superintendence of the construction of this particular block may well have been entrusted to Lord Grimthorpe [of LI]. It was finished in 1887.

11.c. J P Emslie: The detail of the wall painting in 3, Old Square, 1885 [HSLI].

The original wall-painting on plaster was removed and deposited at the V&A, but has since disintegrated.

11.d. ? Studio of Sir George Gilbert Scott: Proposed new set of chambers north of the Gatehouse (15, Old Square, as it now is), painted *ca.* 1872 [HSLI].

11.e. Waldo Sergeant: Old Buildings, 1883 (s.e. view): photograph R Todd White [Editor's coll.].

11.2. The chambers in the s. tower of the Great Gatehouse; and those on the e. and the s. of Gatehouse Court: 27, XXIV & 24-21, Old Buildings, formerly *21-26, Old Buildings (the Long Gallery)*:

11.2.1. Their front and rear elevations

¶ Two contrasting impressions, a century apart, of the same scene:

'We drove slowly through the dirtiest and darkest streets that ever were seen in the world (I thought), and in such a distracting state of confusion that I wondered how the people kept their senses, until we passed into sudden quietude under an old gateway, and drove on through a silent square until we came to an odd nook in a corner where there was an entrance up a steep, broad flight of stairs, like an entrance to a church. And there really was a churchyard, outside under some cloisters, for I saw the gravestones from the staircase window.

This was Kenge and Carboys.'

—Charles Dickens, from *Bleak House*, 1852.

'Lincoln's Inn was the first Inn I saw and has ever remained the most satisfying of them all. The astonishing shock of stepping out of the sombre commercial canyon of Chancery Lane into Old Buildings, with its lovely red brickwork, its Tudor lines of turret and castellation, its mullioned windowed hall with the trunk-and-hose arches on either side, was an unforgettable experience. The brilliant appositeness of that plaque of lawn and its rich-leafed tree gave the weathered brick a living glow. The blanched pile of Inigo Jones's chapel and the pillared shadows of the groined crypt pressed romantic mystery upon delight. To stand there on a summer evening in a London half light, while boys' voices sang in the chapel, was to take part in a moment few experiences can surpass, so deeply and enchantingly English is it.'

—Douglas Newton, from *London West of the Bars*, 1951 [GL].

11.f. ? J P Emslie: 'Panel over door of No. 25, Old Square: the zigzag pattern of cut bricks', 1880s [HSLI].

11.2.2. Their proximity to buildings in Baptist's Head Yard, outside the Inn

¶ For much of its length, the perimeter of the Inn has a wall to provide security, or the width of a street to afford privacy, from passers-by or the occupants of neighbouring buildings. Until the early C20th, however, the one place at which the outside world approached very close to the buildings of the Inn was at its s.e. corner.

At that period, a length of its boundary was formed by the back of 21-26, Old Buildings (standing where still they do after successive re-buildings) and which abutted directly onto a passageway then outside the Inn, latterly known as Baptist's Head Yard. A row of buildings enclosed that yard and separated it from the footpath of Bishop's Court, the present-day boundary, to the s. The yard was similar in length to the present-day yard, to which the name Hale (or Hale's) Court has attached itself, now separating 21-26, Old Buildings and Hardwicke Building.

A notable poet and playwright, with close connections to the Inn and the members of the Society, used the peculiarities of this cramped neighbourhood as a suitable setting for two scenes in one of his plays.

Extracts are quoted here:

'Act II scene II

Mrs Fitzdottrel: Oh! You'll anon prove his hired man, I fear.
What has he given you for this message? Sir,
Bid him put off his hopes of straw, and leave
To spread his nets in view, thus. Though they take
Master Fitzdottrel, I am no such foul
Nor fair one, tell him, will be had with stalking.
And wish him to forbear his acting to me
At the gentleman's chamber window in Lincoln's Inn there
That opens to my gallery; else, I swear
T'acquaint my husband with his folly, and leave him
To the just rage of his offended jealousy.
Or if your master's sense be not so quick

11.g. J P Emslie: 'View from Bishop's Court, Chancery Lane of backs of houses in Lincoln's Inn', 1899 (n. view of 21-23) [CLHL].

This view of the picturesque elevations of these C17th buildings was created for a short while by the demolition of the n. side of Bishop's Court for rebuilding—thereby opening up Baptist's Head Yard. The pale-coloured building in the l. foreground is a room with a door into the Kitchen Garden at the back of No. 21, protruding beyond the building line. It has since been demolished but its former site is still visible in the rendered and painted section of wall of Old Buildings. At the present day, this range of chambers, on the s. side of Old Buildings (now rebuilt, but to a similar, simpler, design without external chimneys), backs onto the narrow courtyard of Hale (or Hale's) Court, which separates it from Hardwicke Building.

To right me, tell him I shall find a friend
That will repair me. Say I will be quiet
In my own house! Pray you, in those words give it him.
Pug: This is some fool turned!

[*Exit Pug*]

Act II scene VI

How! Music? Then he may be there: and is, sure.
Pug: [Aside] Oh! Is it so? Is there the interview?
Have I drawn to you, at last, my cunning lady?
The devil is an ass! Fooled off! And beaten!
Nay, made an instrument! And could not scent it!
Well, since you have shown the malice of a woman,
No less than her true wit, and learning, mistress,
I'll try, if little *Pug* have the malignity
To recompense it, and so save his danger.
'Tis not the pain but the discredit of it.
The Devil should not keep a body entire.

'[*Manley's* chambers in Lincoln's Inn, and
Fitzdotterel's house opposite]

Enter *Witipol, Manly* above

Wittipol: This was a fortune, happy above thought,
That this should prove thy chamber, which I feared
Would be my greatest trouble. This must be
The very window, and that the room.
Manly: It is.
I now remember, I have often seen there
A woman, but I never marked her much.
Wittipol: Where was your soul, friend?
Manly: Faith, but now, and then,
Awake unto those objects.
Wittipol: You pretend so.
Let me not live if I am not in love
More with her wit, for this direction, now,
Than with her form though I ha' praised that prettily,
Since I saw her, and you, today. Read those.
[he gives him a paper, wherein is the copy of a song]
They'll go unto the air you love so well.
Try 'em unto the note, may be the music
Will call her sooner;

[Enter *Mistress Fitzdotterel* at a window]

'slight, she's here. Sing quickly.
Mrs Fitzdotterel: Either he understood him not: or else,
The fellow was not faithful in delivery,
Of what I bade. And, I am justly paid
That might have made my profit of his service,
But, by mistaking, have drawn on his envy,
And done the worse defeat upon myself.

[*Manly* sings, *Pug* enters [below], perceives it]

Wittipol: Away, fall back, she comes.
Manly: I'll leave you, sir.
The master of my chamber. I have business.

Wittipol: Mistress!
Mrs Fitzdotterel: You make me paint, sir.
Wittipol: They are fair colours,
Lady, and natural I did receive
Some commands from you, lately, gentle lady,
But so perplexed, and wrapped in the delivery,
As I may fear to have misinterpreted:
But must make suit still, to be near your grace.

[This scene is acted at two windows, as out of two contiguous buildings]

Mrs Fitzdotterel: Who is there with you, sir?
Witipol: None, but myself.
It falls out, lady, to be a dear friend's lodging.
Wherein there's some conspiracy of fortune
With your poor servant's blessed affections.
Mrs Fitzdotterel: Who was it sung?
Wittipol: He, lady, but he's gone,
Upon my entreaty of him, seeing you

11.h. The rebuilding of 24-26, Old Buildings, 1967 (e. view): photograph A' Court [RCHM]

The building work shown here was a continuation of the same project as the reconstruction of the Gatehouse, shown in the line drawing *3.f.*

Approach the window. Neither need you doubt him,
If he were here. He is too much a gentleman.'

—Ben Jonson, from *The Devil is an Ass*, 1616.

Fitzdottrel is a squire of Norfolk—a dottrel being a simple person, and by origin a plover, a bird which is easily taken.
Mistress Frances Fitzdottrel is his virtuous wife.
Wittipol is a young gallant, intent on seducing Mistress Frances.
Manly is his friend.
Pug is a minor devil, sent on Earth for a day by Satan.

11.2.3. Their reconstruction in the 1960s

¶ In the 1960s, the whole range of chambers enclosing the s.e. and the s. of Gatehouse Court was taken down and rebuilt. They were of great antiquity, and incapable of being adapted to the practice of a modern profession. The gables, the fenestration and the doorways were replicated, but the old external chimneys, which contributed everything to their character, were not.

11.i. One of two monochrome wall paintings on plaster of the second quarter of the C16th conserved and re-located in the corridor made in 21, Old Buildings: photograph G Rodrigues [LT].

11.2.4. Hale Court Passage

¶ As part of the rebuilding of Old Buildings, a new passageway was cut through 21, taking space from what had been chambers, to lead to the newly built chambers building originally called Hale Court and now Hardwicke Building.

11.3. *The temporary Courts for the junior Vice-Chancellors:* their exterior and interior

'To be prepared for the additional judges in Chancery, a new building is erecting in Lincoln's Inn Old Square, in the space between the hall and the old gateway leading into Chancery-lane. It occupies a very large portion of that space, proceeding along and near one side of the hall, towards the chapel; it then approaches the gateway, and one corner of it comes close to the path that previously existed between the archway from Chancery-lane to the well-known covered passage that leads to the hall, and onwards to the large open square. It is now about what may be termed one storey high. It makes no pretension to architectural beauty, being simply a square stock-brick building, without any ornament. It appears to be destined to have a species of piazza in front and near to the old footpath, similar to the sheltered accommodation of the Vice-Chancellor's court on the other side of Lincoln's Inn Hall; and, as the building then recedes, it further seems to be intended to secure light from the roof as well as from side windows. The works are being hurried forward, as the building will be required for the business of the sittings after next term. Its appearance by no means accords with any of the surrounding buildings, neither the stone and stucco of the hall, nor the black-red fronts of the neighbouring chambers.

……

11.k. 'A W': 'A Vice-Chancellor', in *English Illustrated Magazine,* 1883 [LMA].

These courts, designed for the Vice-Chancellors Wigram and Bruce, have in the short space of eight weeks been completed and rendered fit for immediate occupation. The exterior of the building is of brick, plain and unassuming, without the least attempt at architectural display. The entrances are of ample dimensions and well calculated to afford every facility of ingress and egress, and also to secure good internal communication between the courts. The interior appears commodious, light, and convenient, and the simple though neat, unostentatious decorations have a very pleasing effect. The tables, &c., are covered with deep crimson cloth, the curtains of drab moreen damask; though far from gaudy, the whole presents a grand appearance. On Sunday the Lord Chancellor, the Vice-Chancellors, and several friends, inspected the buildings, and were pleased to express their approbation of the excellence of their construction, as well as of the extraordinary expedition with which the builders had completed them. It is understood that sittings will take place there for the first time on or about the 2nd of December.'

—from *The Times*, 25th October and 25th November 1841 [press cuttings, HSLI].

11.j. Alan Stewart [of LI]: The Vice-Chancellors' Courts and the Chapel in 1880, painted 1904 (n.w. view) [HSLI].

An almost identical line drawing had been published in the *ILN*, which may have served as an exemplar for this watercolour. The image is rare in offerring a glimpse of a short section of the front (s.) of Garden Row, in the background.

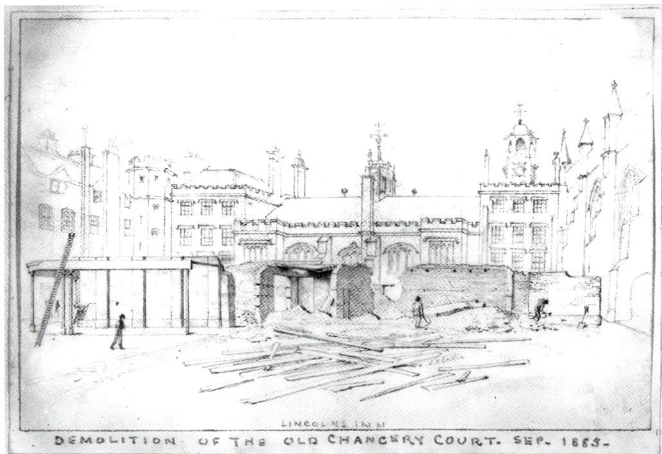

11.l. J P Emslie: 'Demolition of the old Chancery Court, Sept. 1883' (w. view) [CWA].

The demolition of the junior Vice-Chancellors' temporary courts became possible on those judges' being accommodated in the RCJ. They had become much derided as buildings (despite early commendation), and there was no thought of their being appropriated for the collegiate purposes of the Society.

11.m. Alan Stewart [of LI]: Clearing the site of the Vice-Chancellors' Courts, for landscaping and planting in 1883, painted 1904 (s. view) [HSLI].

This amateur artist executed a number of watercolours expressing the modest hope—which happily has been fulfilled—that they would constitute a record of the Inn 'in a hundred years' time'. That reproduced here was one of a cache previously unrecorded, and discovered in 2012, safely locked away in the Chief Porters' Lodge.

'The courts in which the Lord Chancellor, the Lords Justices of Appeal, and the three Vice-Chancellors sit, resembling externally—more than anything else I can remember—the sheds which one sees erected at steamboat wharves for the temporary reception of goods which are landed there. Internally the Courts at Lincoln's Inn present the appearance of a third-rate Dissenting Chapel in a fourth-rate provincial town. The advantage, however, in this last comparison lies, I am well aware, with the Dissenting Chapel, for the chances are that the ecclesiastical edifice in question would be clean and comfortable, whereas the buildings which are occupied by Her Majesty's High Court of Chancery are filthy and uncomfortable to a degree which it is impossible for me to describe in words. The atmosphere in them, moreover, is invariably humid with the moisture arising from the mass of sweltering humanity which daily throngs them.'

—from *Brief and Papers, Sketches of the Bar and the Press, by Two Idle Apprentices*, 1872.

> H H Paul Baker QC, 'Chancery Courts in Lincoln's Inn', in *LI Newsletter*, 1998/9.

11.4. *The proposed permanent* <u>*Courts*</u> *for the Vice-Chancellors:* their elevations

¶ In 1859, the Society offered to provide a site within the Inn and to construct, at its own cost, a new building to be designed by the distinguished architect Giles Gilbert Scott to accommodate Chambers for the Lord Chancellor, and Courts and Chambers for the three Vice-Chancellors with offices for their clerks. It would not, however, have provided Courts for the higher judiciary in the Court of Chancery. The Lord Chancellor's Court was contemplated as continuing to be accommodated in the Old Hall and the Master of the Rolls' in the Rolls House. The Lord Chancellor, Lord Chelmsford [of GI], introduced a Bill in the House of Lords to authorise the Crown to enter into arrangements with the Society. The proposal did not progress further, being overtaken by the move for a building to bring together all four higher courts—Equity, Common Law, Exchequer, Probate and Admiralty.

In Dublin the question of bringing together all the higher courts had been resolved some seventy-five years earlier, by the construction of the fine classical Four Courts built to the designs of James Gandon, on the banks of the Liffey. Those four Courts reflected the same division of jurisdiction as in London.

11.n. Giles Gilbert Scott: proposed Chancery Courts in Lincoln's Inn, 1859, *British Parliamentary Papers* [BL].

> David Brownlee: *The Law Courts: the architecture of George Edmund Street*, 1984.

12. OLD BUILDINGS, TO THE S. AND THE S.W. OF THE OLD HALL; AND 12-13, NEW SQUARE:

12.1. 16-20, Old Buildings (formerly *Field Gate Court or Kitchen Garden Court*)

'What I experienced at Lincoln's Inn must have been very much like what, as I imagine it, a new undergraduate might feel when he begins life in his college rooms (though in reality, undergraduates being seldom more than overgrown schoolboys, this must be very rare). It must have been like the experience of the novice entering religious life—but the comparison fails because few monasteries have any decency or dignity comparable to that of the old lawyers' Inns, and unless you were nearly blind, you would suffer unbearable offence from the fripperies of ecclesiastical worship. Nevertheless both these comparisons have justification. As in a college or monastery, we were bound by the rules and regulations of the house. The gates were shut at a certain hour every evening; boundary walls secluded us from the frivolities of the streets. There was a tacit agreement understood and accepted by all tenants of the Inn to conform to a certain unwritten but recognizable rule of dignity and decorum. It was in fact a community life and, as in all schools and colleges and religious houses, the rules were only irksome to those who didn't want to obey them. Edward Johnston was simply a tenant of the Inn and not a member, so of course we only lived there by courtesy. We usually went out to dinner in the evening—not for us to dine in hall with master and brethren—but we enjoyed the amenities of the collegiate life all the same…'

—Eric Gill,[1] from *Autobiography*, 1940 [BL].

[1] Gill, the distinguished carver, engraver, and typographer, shared for a while before his marriage the chambers in 16 rented from the Society by Edward Johnson, the then celebrated art teacher and calligrapher.

>> Michael Tooth [solicitor in LI].

12.2. *The old Kitchens*, in 17:

i. The standard of their food

¶ Sir Thomas More [of LI], having in 1532 just fallen from the King's grace and resigned as LC, spoke these poignant words on the Inn's food:

'"Then will I", said he, "show my poor mind unto you. I have been brought up", quoth he, "at Oxford, at an Inn of Chancery, at Lincoln's Inn and also in the King's Court, and so forth from the lowest degree to the highest, and yet have I in yearly revenues at this present left me little above an hundred pounds by the year, so that now must we hereafter, if we like to live together, be contented to become contributories together. But, by my counsel, it shall not be best for us to fall to the lowest fare first. We will not therefore descend to Oxford fare, nor to the fare of New Inn, but we will begin with Lincoln's Inn diet, where many right worshipful and of good years do live full well; which, if we find not ourselves the first year able to maintain, then will we the next year go one step down to New Inn[1] fare, wherewith many an honest man is well contented. If that exceed our ability too, then will we the next year after descend to Oxford fare, where many grave, learned and ancient fathers be continually conversant. Which if our power stretch not to maintain neither, then may we yet with bags and wallets, go a begging together, and hoping that for pity some good folk will give us their charity, at every man's door to sing *Salve Regina*, and so still keep company and be merry together."'

—William Roper, from *The Life of Sir Thomas More, ca.* 1535, publ. 1626.

[1] New Inn: More had attended New Inn, one of the Inns of Chancery, before progressing to Lincoln's.

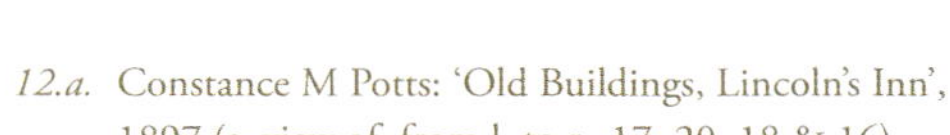

12.a. Constance M Potts: 'Old Buildings, Lincoln's Inn', 1897 (s. view of, from l. to r., 17, 20, 18 & 16) [V&A].

This is the second of two meticulous views of the Inn by this artist reproduced here. Views of the Inn by C19th women artists are not to be found in any quantity in the Society's or in public collections, despite the great number of such gifted artists, as this one. It may be speculated as to whether this was due to the Inns' being male preserves, into which self-respecting women—unless on legal business or in employment or invited and accompanied by a husband or father or son—were hesitant to venture.

ii. The buildings and its utensils

¶ For centuries, the kitchens had been immediately to the s. of the Old Hall, in 17.

'Naparye in the Buttrye at this accompte:
Inprimis, one diaper table clothe.
Item, 4 table clothes for the Benche.
Item, 19 table clothes for the Hall.
Item, one diaper towell.
Item, 24 diaper napkines.
Item, one olde dieper clothe.
Item, 6 dossen of diaper napkines.
Item, two hande-towells.
Item, 2 towells for shewers.[1]
Item, 4 latten[2] candlestickes.
Item, 4 wyne pottes, vz. on pottle pott,[3] ij quartes, and one pinte.
Item, a bason.
Item, 2 chippinge knives.
Item, 2 pewter saltes.
Item, one little trencher salte.

Kitchen stuff remayninge at this accompte:
Inprimis, 3 small brasse pannes of 4 gallons apece.
Item, 2 brasse pannes of xij gallondes apece.
Item, one brasse pott of 2 gallondes.
Item, 2 brasse pottes of 6 gallondes apece.
Item, 2 brasse pottes of 12 gallondes apece.
Item, 3 irone peeles, 6 longe spittes.
Item, 7 short spittes, and in dishes 9 dosson.
Item, 30 platters, and saucers 5 dosson.
Item, 6 trivettes, and one cowle to fetch water.
Item, one little brasse morter and one pestle.
Item, one clever and 2 choppinge knyves.
Item, 3 mynsinge knives, and 2 flaskettes.
Item, 2 olde chistes and v drippinge pannes.
Item, 4 gridiorns and one great fryinge panne.
Item, 2 smale fryinge pannes.
Item, 2 olde great fryinge pannes.
Item, one greate fyllinge ladle.
Item, one brassen ladle and an iron skomer.
Item, 2 slices and one brasen skommer.'

—from Vol. II, *The Black Books*, 1570.

[1] Shewers: ? sewers = servers.
[2] Latten: brass.
[3] Pottle pot: two-quart jug.

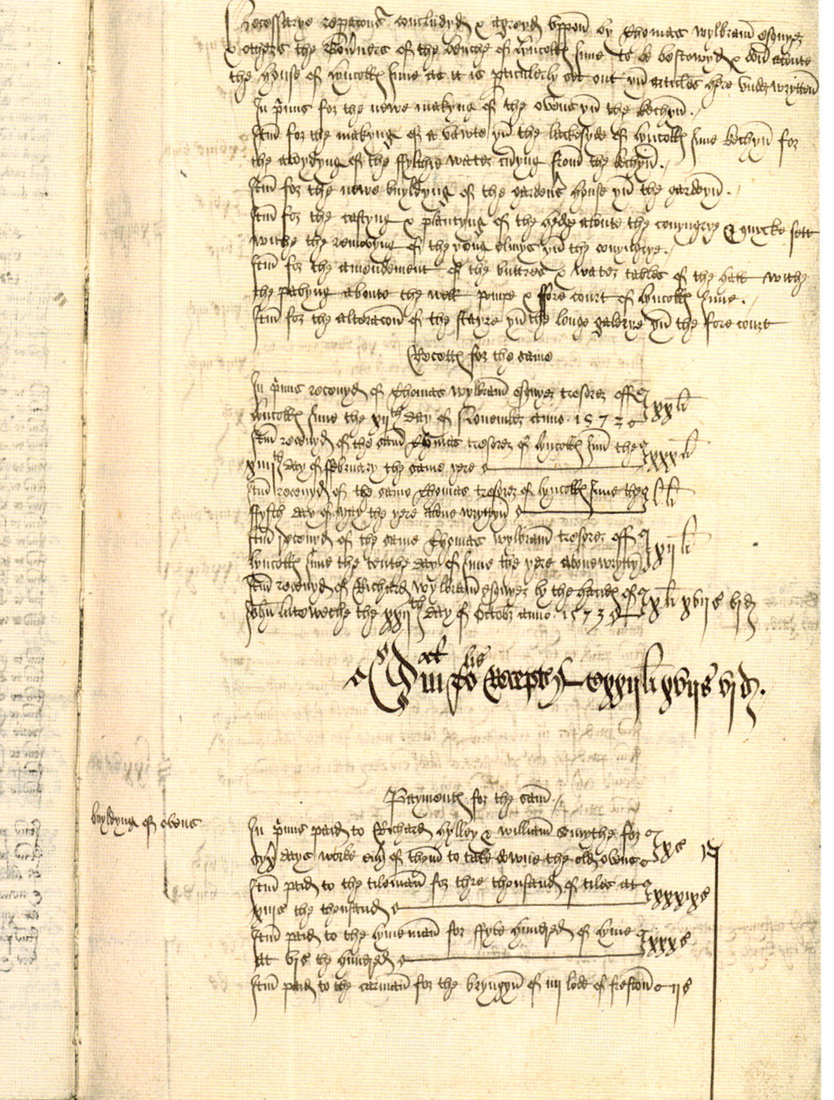

12.b. Accounts 1572-3. These accounts are *inter alia* for the newe makyng of the ovens yn the ketchyn and for the makyng of a vawte yn the backsyde of Lyncolles Inne ketchyn for the avoydyng of the Fylthie water runnyg from the ketchyn. The meticulous calligraphy—almost Islamic in beauty—is that of John Haydon, Associate Bencher. [HSLI archives, and *Lincoln's Inn Revealed* exhibition catalogue, 1990].

12.3. 12-13, New Square (formerly *Field Gate Row*)

'It was a house that was sure to attract the notice of the few sight-seers who ever strayed into these deep solitudes. Scarlet geraniums brightened the little bit of ground in front, and the branches of a fig-tree clung to the old wall, and framed the windows with broad green leaves.'

—Sarah Doudney, from *A Romance of Lincoln's Inn*, 1894 [BL].

'I have seen many lovely sights and buildings; but this little dark brown block of late seventeenth century work never fails to refresh me. Near the exquisite doors hangs a little vine which has never, at the least, produced ripe grapes but is yet a joy for ever.'

—E S P Haynes [solicitor in LI], from *The Lawyer, a conversation piece* (a posthumous collection, ed. Renée Haynes), 1951.

12.c. Charlotte Halliday: 13, New Square, 1980s (e.view) [coll. John Mowbray, QC [of LI]].

This charming building is also well shown in several older images in this book. At this date this doorway was marked '13', but with the integration of 12 and 13 into one set of chambers, the separate numbering of 13 has gone for professional purposes, but not for that of identification of the building.

12.d. T N Rooke: 'Lincoln's Inn', 1914 (s. view of 12-13, New Square) [coll. John Mowbray, QC [of LI]].

This painting, by a noted artist, has acquired the poignancy of depicting the Inn in the last summer before the war, and of showing the s.e. corner of the North Lawns—the exact spot soon to be occupied by the Society's War Memorial. In the 1980s, this corner was given the *ad hoc* name of Parker's Piece (familiar to Cambridge graduates) during Sir Roger Parker's tenure of office as Master of the Walks, and in recognition of his re-planting of shrubs here.

13. OLD SQUARE, TO THE N.E., THE N. AND THE N.W. OF THE CHAPEL:

13.1. Chambers to the n.e. and the n. of the Chapel: 14-13, Old Square, the site of *4-6, Old Buildings* (in *Chancery Lane Row*); and 12-11, Old Square, the site of 7-9, *Old Buildings* (*Garden Row in Garden Court*)

¶ In the wall of the original 8, Old Buildings was a stone memorial plaque to Mark Hilsly [of LI] (1630-93) which, on the demolition of those chambers in 1881, was re-set into one of the arch pillars supporting the Chapel, and where it remains. There are two lines of English and some twenty of Latin, rhyming *inhumator/satur/pater/ mater/frater/meatur/ datur/decorator/quater/beatur*. Some of the crudely chiselled text has been lost in the removal of the stone, and what remains is heavily abbreviated dog-Latin, not facilitating full transcription. Besides reference to his parents and brother, it seems to record that in life he was blessed with two wives and eight daughters. In death, his evident attachment to his chambers led to his being buried *in* the walls of his chambers, if the *ILN* note to that drawing is accurate, but if not then presumably *into* those walls under the adjacent paving: neither being consecrated ground, unless specially so on that occasion.

'I was offered chambers on the top floor of 13 Old Square. … It was a congenial setting, within walking distance of every civil amenity that London could offer. My workroom overlooked the solitary plane-tree in the small square beside Inigo Jones's chapel, and was thus comparatively quiet even during the day. I sat at my table, soothed by the shuffle-shuffle of lawyers' leather as the members of this close fraternity walked between chambers and the Courts, sometimes robed and bewigged.

…At six o'clock in the evening, and throughout the weekend, a strange, haunted silence fell over the City. The footsteps died away in New Square and Old Square, except for those occasional to a resident, or perhaps a reverent sightseer. The loud roar of traffic up and down Chancery Lane, below the east window of our long sitting-room, died to a trickle, finally to stop with the last bus late at night. The only sounds from midday on Saturday until Monday morning were the whirring of pigeons' wings and the gargling murmer from their throats.

Every quarter of an hour, a sprinkle of chimes fanned out from the clocks of the innumerable City churches, headed by that of St Paul's or Big Ben (as though Wren and Barry could never agree on the matter of procedure, and so submitted to vagary). The sound fell like flower petals over the dusty streets, to be lost in their emptiness, but not ineffectually, for it left, four times an hour, a faint perfume of history, a conjuration of memories, peopling the deserted city with ghosts.'

—Richard Church, describing the 1930s, from *The Voyage Home*, 1964 [BL].

13.a. John Crowther: 'Old Square, 1879' (e. view of 5 & 4, Chancery Lane Row, n. of the Chapel) [LMA].

The last days of Chancery Lane Row. Sir George Gilbert Scott's new chambers, 11 & 12, Old Square (at right angles, immediately to the l., and out of sight of this view) had just been completed. Demolition of this range began in 1879. The site is now occupied by 13-14, Old Square.

13.b. John Crowther: Chancery Lane, 1879 (n.w. view) [LMA].

The view is taken from the opposite side of the La. from the Gatehouse, and looking n., showing the chambers in the Gatehouse, the back of Chancery Lane Row and the former Six Clerks' Office.

13.c. 9, Old Buildings in Garden Row, with the new 12, Old Square behind (s.e. view): Anon. photographer [HSLI].

The w. facing sundial is that which was recreated on Stone Buildings, in memory of William Pitt.

13.d. Anon. artist: Demolition of Garden Row and 6, Chancery Lane Row, seen from Chancery Lane, early 1880s (s. view) [LMA].

The demolition is in progress, and a workman stands on the building, having removed its roof tiles.

'For some reason which I have never been able to discover, the large plane tree in the small square which is the part of the Inn that I and my companion inhabit when I can induce her to leave her activities in the country, has become known to the porters as *my* tree. It may be due to my habit of standing under it and looking up into its branches—in winter because it has no leaves on, and in summer because it has leaves on, a recurrent miracle to me. But there it is, a subtle piece of flattery which I humbly accept.'

—Richard Church, from *Green Tide*, 1945.

13.e. Charles Tunnicliffe, RA: The tree in Old Square, in *Green Tide*, 1945. [Editor's coll.] {Estate of artist}.

A new tree was planted in this spot in the first decade of the C21st, and the area surrounding it attractively re-paved.

¶ The front and rear elevations of the old Chancery La. Row are depicted in the watercolours and the drawings reproduced here. But Garden Row is the only range in the Inn for which no complete view of its front elevation has been found. A small section only of the front of No. 7 Garden Row is glimpsed at a distance in *11.j.* The rear was depicted as a background to the Walks, and is visible for that reason in several of the views reproduced in this book. It had the customary regular lines of gables with garret windows, but differed in having above each of them a second line of minuscule gable windows, presumably to light attics. There were two protruding ground floor rooms: one towards the e. with straight walls at right angles and the other towards the w., which was a round bay.

It did not have a jungle of chimneys on the external walls of the rear but may well have had on the front. It is probable that there were spiral staircases to the upper floors of the three chambers buildings.

13.2. *The Great Seal Patent Office*, in *4, Old Buildings*

¶ For a generation, at the beginning of the C19th, the Great Seal Patent Office, usually known as the Patent Office, was in chambers at 4, Old Buildings. Later, after a brief intermediate move nearby, the Office settled in chambers in the s. part of Staple Inn. It remained there until the last decade of the C20th, in greatly extended offices and with an imposing library.

The quotation below offers details of the legal procedure at that time for obtaining a patent, and evokes some of the to-ings and fro-ings of the Office in the Inn. Its halting style is intended to imitate that of an artisan who, having made a patentable invention, and experiencing the difficulties in obtaining a patent, sympathises with the Chartist cause for reform. The jurisdiction in respect of, and procedures for granting, patents were completely reformed by the Patent Law Amendment Act, 1852—a little time after this short story was written, and the Office had left the Inn.

'Thomas Joy delivered (from a book he had) that the first step to be took, in Patenting the invention, was to prepare a petition unto Queen Victoria. A declaration before a Master in Chancery was to be added to it. That, we likewise drew up. After a deal of trouble I found out a Master, in Southampton Buildings, Chancery Lane, nigh Temple Bar, where I made a declaration and petition to the Home Office, in Whitehall, where I left it to be signed by the Home Secretary (after I had found the office out), and where I paid two pound, two, and sixpence. In six days he signed it, and I was told to take it to the AttorneyGeneral's chambers, and leave it there for a report. I did so, and paid four pound, four. Note. Nobody all through, ever thankful for their money, but all uncivil.

The Attorney-General made what they called a Report-of-course (my invention being unopposed), and I was sent back with it to the Home Office. They made a Copy of it, which was called a Warrant. For this warrant, I paid seven pound, thirteen, and six. It was sent to the Queen, to sign. The Queen sent it back, signed. The Home Secretary signed it again. The gentleman throwed it at me when I called, and said, "Now take it to the Patent Office in Lincoln's Inn."

...At the Patent Office in Lincoln's Inn, they made "a draft of the Queen's bill," of my invention, and a "docket of the bill." I paid five pound, ten, and six, for this. They "engrossed two copies of the bill; one for the Signet Office, and one for the Privy-Seal Office."

I paid one pound, seven, and six for this. Stamp duty over and above, three pound. The Engrossing Clerk of the same office engrossed the Queen's bill for signature. I paid him one pound, one. Stamp duty, again, one pound, ten. I was next to take the Queen's bill to the Attorney-General again, and get it signed again. I took it, and paid five pound more. I fetched it away, and took it to the Home Secretary again. He sent it to the Queen again. She signed it again. I paid seven pound, thirteen, and six, more, for this... I was quite wore out, patience and pocket.

...But I hadn't nigh done yet. The Queen's bill was to be took to the Signet Office in Somerset House, Strand—where the stamp shop is. The Clerk of the Signet made "a Signet bill for the Lord Keeper of the Privy Seal." I paid him four pound, seven. The Clerk of the Lord Keeper of the Privy Seal made "a Privy-Seal bill for the Lord Chancellor." I paid him four pound, two. The Privy-Seal bill was handed over to the Clerk of the Patents, who engrossed the aforesaid. I paid him five pound, seventeen, and eight; at the same time, I paid Stamp-duty for the Patent, in one lump, thirty pound. I next paid for "boxes for the Patent," nine and sixpence. Note. Thomas Joy would have made the same at a profit for eighteenpence. I next paid "fees to the Deputy, the Lord Chancellor's Pursebearer," two pound, two. I next paid "fees to the Clerk of the Hanaper," seven pound, thirteen. I next paid "fees to the Deputy Clerk of the Hanaper," ten shillings. I next paid, to the Lord Chancellor again, one pound, eleven, and six. Last of all, I paid, "fees to the Deputy Sealer, and Deputy Chaffwax," ten shillings and sixpence. I had lodged at Thomas Joy's over six weeks, and the unopposed Patent for my invention, for England only, had cost me ninety-six pound, seven, and eightpence. If I had taken it out for the United Kingdom, it would have cost me more than three hundred pound.

...I will now conclude with Thomas Joy. Thomas said to me, when we parted, "John, if the laws of this country were as honest as they ought to be, you would have come to London—registered an exact description and drawing of your invention—paid half-a-crown or so for doing of it—and therein and thereby have got your Patent."

My opinion is the same as Thomas Joy. Further. In delivering "that the whole gang of Hanapers and Chaffwaxers must be done away with, and that England has been chaffed and waxed sufficient," I agree.'

—Charles Dickens, from 'A Poor Man's Tale of a Patent', 1850, in *Household Words;* and *Reprinted Pieces,* 1858.

As to various of the functionaries of the Court of Chancery, but not of the Patent Office, named here—some of whom were housed in the Inn—see also the caricature in *34.a.*

13.f. 'New Chambers, Lincoln's Inn—Sir G[eorge] G Scott, RA, Architect' (s.e. view) [LMA].

This drawing is of 8-10, Old Square. This block, which runs n.-s., extends from approximately the w. end of the former Garden Row to that of the former Dial Row. The elevation facing the gardens is shown. The entrances to the three Chambers buildings are on the s. and the e.

13.3. 10-8, Old Square: to the n.w. of the Chapel

¶ This building of 1872-6 was erected on a site where no chambers had previously stood. When built, it enclosed for the first time the area formerly called Garden Court, and now Old Square. Glimpses of corners of this building appear in some of the images in 14.

The consulting rooms in these chambers by the Scott family are built in, and some retain vestiges of furnishing and decoration of, the style which a distinguished commentator on domestic architectural taste labelled 'Anglican', and described generically in these words:

'There was one type of interior… the masculine apartment known as the study… of which many examples are still to be found in schools, colleges, and country vicarages differing hardly at all in furniture and decoration from those in which professors, divines and ecclesiologists laboured and reflected when the Gothic Revival was still young. It was never a style that one would find in every house; only in the homes of public-school men of a studious type. … it may perhaps be thought to represent, as does no other Victorian style, all that was best in that great age. The prevailing atmosphere of high thinking and plain living, of *mens sana in corpore sano*, may be a trifle oppressive, but it is balanced by an undeniable air of comfort. Today such isolated examples as exist represent… the final dying outposts of a vanished culture… they can still on occasion arouse a powerful nostalgia in the breasts of all but the most hard boiled.'

—Osbert Lancaster, from *Homes Sweet Homes*, fourth edn. 1963.

13.4. *The Incorporated Council of Law Reporting for England and Wales, in 10*

¶ The ICLR was founded in 1865 and incorporated in 1870 under the Companies Act 1862. It was registered as a charity in 1970 under the Charities Act 1960, following a successful appeal to the Chancery Division against rejection of registration by the Charity Commission.

The establishment of the Council was, of course, a response to the pre-existing situation of numerous law reports of notoriously varied quality, each published separately by individual reporters.

The Council had offices at several successive locations, until it settled in the late C20th at its present address at 119, Chancery La. At the turn of the C19th and C20th, it was accommodated at 10, Old Square. Hence its presence being noted in this paragraph.

The diverse character and reliability of the earlier law reports is briefly suggested here—exaggerated by humour—in these spontaneous lines of doggerel written by a Master in Chancery, when asked by a law reporter to deputise for him in a case part heard in the Old Hall:

Mr Leach made a speech,
Angry, neat and wrong;
Mr Hart, on the other part,
Was prosy, dull and long.

Mr Bell[1] *spoke very well,*
Though nobody knew what about;
Mr Trower[2] *talked for an hour,*
Sat down fatigued and hot.

Mr Parker made the case darker,
Which was dark enough without;
Mr Cook quoted his book,
And the Chancellor said, "I doubt".

—Sir George Rose [of IT], 'The History of a Case, shortly reported by a Master in Chancery', early C19th, in G W Bell, *Sir George Rose, a Memoir*, publ. privately 1877 [BL].

---

[1] Mr Bell: see *p2.*

[2] Mr Trower: a bar member of a legal family, numbering both bar and solicitors, long associated with the Inn, and with the firm of Trowers and Hamlins (formerly Trower Still and Keeling), who until the end of the last century were at 5, New Square, and are now in the City.

13.g. Annabel Wilson: 8-10, Old Square, with the doorway of No. 10 (n. view) [LT] {the artist}. On the r. is the corner of the Chapel extension, accommodating the stairs.

14. *DIAL* OR *CHAPEL COURT*, TO THE W. OF THE CHAPEL:

¶ Two Rows created an 'open jaw', which abutted on and extended w. from the Chapel, and almost enclosed a small courtyard between them. The Chapel was then accessible through an archway, the site of which is now part of that taken by the w. extension of the Chapel. No vestiges of these Rows, or the court enclosed by them, survive above ground.

14.1. *Dial* or *Chapel Row* (*10-13, Old Buildings*), to the n.w.

¶ This Row formed the n. perimeter of the court and comprised members' chambers. It took its name from the large s.-facing dial on No. 10, clearly shown in Samuel Scott's painting *15.b.* It was demolished to enable the Chapel to be extended to the w. (i.e. to the length it now is).

It was in 13 that John Thurloe (1616-68), secretary of the Council of State under Cromwell, latterly had chambers—and where he died. Behind a false ceiling were hidden, and in a later century found, his state correspondence—a collection which is now in the Bodleian, and constitutes what scholars regard as one of the most important primary sources for the history of the Commonwealth. Thurloe is the only member of the Society to be commemorated by a blue plaque in the Inn, which is on the Chancery La. front of 24, Old Buildings, where he had had chambers, in an earlier building on the same site. He has been colloquially described as 'Cromwell's master spy', and fulfilled a somewhat similar rôle to that played by Walsingham for Elizabeth I.

14.a. John Crowther: Chapel Court, with 12 and 13 in the foreground, Sir George G Scott's new w. range is to the l., and Stone Buildings in the distance, 1881 (n. view) [LMA].

These chambers had to be demolished, to permit the Chapel to be extended to the w. This watercolour is dated August 1881, the exact month in which the contract for those works was signed. Nos. 10 and 11 had been contiguous to the w. of 12, but by this date had been demolished to enable Scott's new 9 and 10 to be built. The idiosyncratic stepped corner seemingly was the consequence of 12 extending n. of 13, running e.-w., and of 13 extending n.-s. in front of the Chapel.

14.b. G B Lancaster Woodburne [of LI]: 'Old Buildings in Lincoln's-Inn now being demolished', *Illustrated London News*, 1881 (s.e. view) [*ILN*PL].

'We give an illustration of part of the old Buildings of Lincoln's Inn now being rapidly demolished. This may be added to preceding memorials of most of the picturesque buildings of Old London which the ruthless hand of the modern "improver" is so busy in sweeping away.'—*ILN.*

This is Dial Row, and is the other side of the chambers shown in *14.a.* The site is that now occupied by 8 & 9, Old Square.

14.c John Crowther: The n. side of Chapel Row and the Vice-Chancellor's Court (to the r.).

Facing is 13 Old Buildings, running across the full width of the Chapel, with the archway through to its Undercroft. Just shown on the l. is the s. end of Sir George G Scott's new chambers.

14.2. *Library Row* (*14-15, Old Buildings*), to the s.w.

¶ This Row formed the s. perimeter of the Court. It had always provided rooms for the collegiate purposes of the Society: the Council Chamber, the Benchers' Room, the Steward's Office, and the Preacher's Chambers. All of these functions were accommodated in rooms attached to the New Hall and Library, when built in 1845. No views of the interiors of these rooms have been found. None of their fittings, such as panelling or plasterwork or fireplaces, is known to have been saved and re-used elsewhere, when they were demolished in the 1880s. If any of the old rooms in the Inn were well fitted, then surely it would have been these. In 1819, this Row was extended by the construction of the Vice-Chancellor's Court, as noted in 14.2.2.

14.2.1. *The Council Chamber*; and *the old Library Building* and its books

¶ The first reference in the MS Black Books to a library (either the books or the room in which they were housed) is in 1475, when 30 shillings were paid to Roger Towneshend pro bibliotheca, and the first clear reference to a library as a room or building is in 1505. Prior to the construction of the present Library building, there had been libraries successively in rooms in 14, Old Buildings ('the Old Library Building') and, from the 1780s, in 2, Stone Buildings ('the Old Library').

14.d. Anon. artist: Chapel Court, with demolition of Dial Row in progress in the foreground, *ca.* 1882 (s.e. view) [LMA].

The building in the background, with the cupola above it, is Library Row.

'As a testimony of my honour and respect to the Society of Lincoln's Inn, where I had the greatest part of my education, I give and bequeath to that honourable Society the several manuscript books contained in a schedule annexed to my will. They are a treasure worth the having and keeping, which I have been near forty years gathering with very great industry and expense. My desire is that they be kept safe and all together in remembrance of me. They are fit to be bound in leather, and chained and kept in archives. I desire they may not be lent out or disposed of: only if I happen hereafter to have any of my posterity of that society that desires to transcribe any book, and gives very good security to restore it again within a prefixed time, such as the benchers of that society in council shall approve of, then, and not otherwise, only one book at one time may be lent out to them by the society; so that there be no more but one of those books abroad out of the library at any one time. They are a treasure not fit for every man's view, nor is every man capable of making use of them. Only I would have nothing of these books printed, but entirely preserved together for the use of the industrious and learned members of that worthy society.'

—Sir Matthew Hale [of LI], from his Will, 1676.

14.e. 'Phiz': 'The Little Old Lady', in *Bleak House*, 1852.

The Lord Chancellor had two withdrawing rooms, constituting his Chambers in the Inn, at 15, Old Buildings. In this picture, Esther Summerson, Richard Carstone and Miss Flite are standing at the foot of the steps of the Chambers. In the background, the distinctive gables of Old Buildings evoke a general impression of this corner of the Inn. The Lord Chancellor's carriage awaits him.

> Note XI in Vol. III, *The Black Books.*

14.2.2. A further <u>*Court*</u> and *Chambers of the High* <u>*Court*</u> *of Chancery*:

i. *The Lord Chancellor's Chambers*

'We conversed in a low tone, because a full-dressed gentleman in a bag wig frequently came in and out, and when he did so we could hear a drawling sound in the distance, which he said was one of the counsel in our case addressing the Lord Chancellor. He told Mr Kenge that the Lord Chancellor would be up in five minutes; and presently we heard a bustle, and a tread of feet, and Mr Kenge said the Court had risen, and his Lordship was in the next room.

The gentleman in the bag wig opened the door almost directly, and requested Mr Kenge to come in. Upon that, we all went into the next room… and there, plainly dressed in black, and sitting in an armchair at the table near the fire, was his Lordship, whose robe, trimmed with beautiful gold-lace, was thrown upon another chair. He gave us a searching look as we entered, but his manner was both courtly and kind.

The gentleman in the bag wig laid bundles of papers on his Lordship's table, and his Lordship silently selected one, and turned over the leaves.'

—Charles Dickens, from *Bleak House*, 1852.

14.f. Thomas Phillips RA, engr. Charles Turner: A composition of engraved cartouches of C19th Lord Chancellors associated with the Inn [Editor's coll.].

Four were members of the Society and the fifth, Eldon (noted in 6.5.2.), from his long tenure in office is uniquely identified with the Inn. All sat in Court in the Old Hall and in the Lord Chancellor's Chambers. The four members were:

Alexander Wedderburn, Lord Loughborough, and first Earl of Rosslyn, 1733-1805.

John Singleton Copley, first Baron Lyndhurst, 1772-1863.

Henry Brougham, first Baron Brougham and Vaux, 1778-1868.

Charles Christopher Pepys, first Earl of Cottenham, 1781-1851.

ii. *The Vice-Chancellor's* *Court*

¶ The office of Vice-Chancellor was created in 1813, the third judge of the Court of Chancery. A new court was erected for him in 1817-9, pursuant to an Act of 1816, at the w. end of 14, Old Buildings. Sir Thomas Plumer [of LI] was the first holder of the office. The prolixity of his judgments, once appointed, contrasted with the extreme sloth in the giving of any judgment by the Lord Chancellor (Eldon). Hence the first deficiency mentioned here. On Sir Thomas' elevation to MR, the Vice-Chancellorship went to Sir John Leach, to whom reference is also made. His manner in court was irascible and his giving of judgment over-hasty. Hence the second deficiency adverted here.

In Equity's high court there are
Two sad extremes, 'tis clear;
Excessive slowness strikes us there,
Excessive quickness here.
Their source 'twixt good and evil brings
A difficulty nice;
The first from Eldon's virtue springs,
The latter from his Vice.

—Anon. epigram, *ca.* 1820.

> Sir Robert Megarry [of LI], *Miscellany-at-Law*, 1955.

These lines make the same point as those in 6.5., but are placed here since they may post-date the building of a separate court for the Vice-Chancellor.

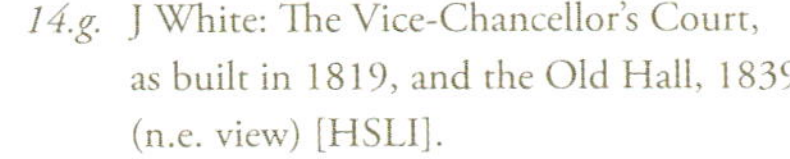

14.g. J White: The Vice-Chancellor's Court, as built in 1819, and the Old Hall, 1839 (n.e. view) [HSLI].

This watercolour depicts the court building as first constructed, and with the arcade linking it to the Old Hall.

14.h. John Crowther: The Vice-Chancellor's Court, 1883 (e. of n. view) [LMA].

This view shows the Vice-Chancellor's Court, and the chambers over it, as they were shortly before demolition, allowing the Chapel to be extended w., in 1883. The significant changes visible in comparison with the preceding illustration are probably those made in the 1840s, which accompanied the removal of the various collegiate rooms and offices of the Society to the New Hall and Library building.

¶ The Court of the Vice-Chancellor (or, as it later became, that of the Senior Vice-Chancellor) acquired the informal name of 'Vice-Chancellor Malins' Court', during that judge's years of tenure from 1866 to 1881, up to the time when the Chancery Courts were relocated from the Inn to the Royal Courts of Justice. The name was still used by senior members of the profession long after the Court was demolished. A distinguished novelist also gave the Court a family name: that of one of his characters, a long-serving counsel in practice there:

'Mr Wharton was and had for a great many years been a barrister practising in the Equity Courts, or rather in one Equity Court, for throughout a life's work, now extending to nearly fifty years, he had hardly ever gone out of the single Vice-Chancellor's Court which was much better known by Mr Wharton's name than by that of the less eminent judge who now sat there… In the Court no one ever contradicted him.'

—Anthony Trollope, from *The Prime Minister*, 1875.

> David Palfreyman, *London's Inns of Court*, 2011.

14.i. Lewis J. Wood: 'South End of the New Hall from the Vice-Chancellor of England's Court, 1843 (w. view) {HSLI].

15.a. J Maurer: Preparatory watercolour for his published engraving 'A Perspective View of Lincoln's Inn: Vüe de Lincolns Inn', *ca.* 1741 (n. view) [BM].

15. THE BUILDINGS OF 1-11, NEW SQUARE (ORIGINALLY *SERLE* OR *NEW COURT*):

15.1. The construction of chambers:

¶ The building of New Square (as it is now called) had a convoluted history. Henry Serle [of LI] claimed ownership of Fickett's Fields free of incumbrances, whereas the Society claimed certain rights over them. The disputes ensuing from Serle's wish to develop were compromised by an Agreement of 11th July 1682, prescribing in some detail the layout of the Square, and restricting the occupiers to members or former members of the Society. It was intended that the Agreement should be given greater force by a Court order or an Act of Parliament. All did not run according to plan, however, as the following extract from an Act passed to remedy the situation makes clear:

'Whereas Henry Serle was in his life seized [*sic*] in fee of some part of the fields heretofore called Ficketts and now of late called and known by the name of Little Lincoln's Inn Fields and was likewise possessed of the rest of the said fields for a long term of years yet to some upon which he did erect a great pyle of buildings which neither was nor could be of any profit to him without erecting another pyle of buildings adjoining to the former, which last buildings he had raised a great height but died before he had covered the same all which buildings and fields the said Henry Serle had mortgaged for a considerable sum of money… the said Henry Serle dying without issue or making a Will being much indebted besides the debts due on the said mortgages by a statute and bonds and otherwise his interest in the premises is descended upon and come unto Gilbert Serle an infant the eldest son of his only brother Robert Serle likewise deceased.

And Whereas the said Gilbert by reason of the tenderness of his years cannot nor any in behalf of the said infant will go on to finish the said buildings whereby the same is subject to the spoil of weather and the profit of what is finished will be lost and yet the interest runs upon the said mortgages whereby the said premises will in a short time be indebted upon the amount of the said mortgages to the value of the same if some course be not taken to prevent the same and the rest of his creditors will be thereby totally defeated of their debts.

Be it therefore enacted…'

—from the Preamble to the Serle's Estate Act, 1692.

15.b. Samuel Scott: 'Serle's Court, and the Walks, Lincoln's Inn', *ca.* 1740 (n. view) photograph R Greenly [Private collection, England].

The finest oil painting ever known to have been made of the Inn, this *veduta*, by the artist who has been called England's Canaletto, shows the Inn early on a summer's morning. Among the figures, a gentleman in the foreground is having his shoes polished; sedan-chair carriers are awaiting a client who is visiting No. 6; two serjeants (with their distinctive wigs) are walking in the middle distance. The buildings of the Square itself at first sight appear much as now, but the houses are their original height, without the additional storey now built on them, seen piecemeal in later images. The arched entrance (with an inscription over it) in No. 10, opening into Serle Street Passage is visible. On the r., beyond No. 1, is the flat-roofed one-storey building, latterly numbered 14, which accommodated a law stationer. Beyond it, is Field Gate Row (now numbered 12-13, New Square), looking, from this angle, unchanged to the present day; and beyond that, the ends of two further rows: Library Row and Dial Row, the demolition of both of which is recorded in 14, above. One further row, Garden Row, lying to the n. and enclosing Garden Court, is just out of sight, or deliberately omitted by artistic licence. The column and fountain are separately described in 16.4. The painter held a sinecure in the Stamp Office in 7 and 8, Serle's Court (as to which, see 15.5.). See *21.l.* for a related painting by the same artist.

15.c. W Herbert: 'Lincoln's Inn Great Square', 1804 (s.w. view) [*op. cit.*].

This view shows that the gradual accretion of an extra storey on the chambers had begun—seen clearly on Nos. 4 and 7. The column is somewhat misplaced towards the s.w.

15.1.1. Their internal fittings

¶ An C18th description of the disposition of rooms in, and the fixtures and fittings of, a C17th set of chambers:

'In the Study forwards:
Wainscoted, marble chimney piece and slipps and slabb firestone hearth and covings.

A chimney glass in a bolection frame the same of the room, five brass locks and keys, two sash windows inside shutts and turn buckles, two lockers with iron locks.

In the adjoining Closet:
One sash window with shutts and twenty five shelves and partitions for papers.

In the Passage out of the Stair Case:
A cloaths press and row of pins, a closett in the Jamb of the Door by the Passage and three shelves and Brass Turnbuckles.

In the Dining Room:
Wainscoted, marble chimney piece and slab, fire stone hearth and covings, a chimney glass in a bolection frame the same of the room, a landskip over the same in a bolection frame carved, two sash windows with inside shutts and turnbuckles, two lockers and iron locks. One brass lock and key to the door to the passage.

A cupboard and three shelves in the jamb of the doorcase and turnbuckles.

Bed Chamber backwards:
Wainscoted, wood chimney piece marble slabb firestone hearth and coving two sash windows inside shutts and turnbuckles, two lockers and iron locks.

A glass case with three shelves and a cupboard under the same with one shelf and an iron lock thereto. One brass lock and key to the door with a sash glazed with green glass over the same. One brass lock to the closet doors which are glazed in sashes of crown glass, over the same is a pannell of carved work consisting of fruits and flowers and leaves, in the spandrells are two cherubims heads. In the closet is one shelf and a row of pins, one iron lock with brass knobbs and a key to the door going into the passage.

In the Passage:
A door with an iron lock and key and brass knobs, an angle closet with two doors and brass turnbuckles and one shelf with ornaments and three cupboards with five shelves. One iron lock and key as two iron turns in the same. The passage wainscoted.

15.d. Annabel Wilson: Scene in New Square, 1993 (s.view) [coll. PHB] {the artist}.

This shows the rendered and painted upper storey of No. 6, a reminder of the addition of a top storey, to all but one of the chambers buildings in the Square, noted in *15.b.* and *c.* above.

In the Clerks Study:
Wainscoted, wood chimney piece, a shelf, a marble slabb, firestone hearth, a bed, two bolts, one brass turn, one press and row of pinns, an iron lock, three cupboards and three shelves, and four shelves and partitions for papers. A sash in the partitions glazed with crown glass.

Doors to stairs:
An iron spring latch to one, and an iron lock and key and two bolts and two iron doggs to the other, and an iron lock and key to the other.'

—Inventory scheduled to a Lease dated 19th June, 1745 of Chambers on the first floor left at 5, New Square [HSLI, Archive].

15.e. John Crowther: Interior of a room in No. 7, New Square, 1880s [LMA].

15.1.2. Their front elevations: the external 'areas', and the view from their windows

¶ The views from the windows of chambers:

'The most important transaction that has taken place in [my life] for a long time, and one which, for a very powerful reason, I ought to communicate to you, is that I have changed my chambers, and that your future letters are not to be addressed to Gray's Inn, but to Lincoln's Inn, no. 2 New Square. I have changed much for the better as a situation for business, but much for the worse as far as my own pleasure is concerned. Instead of having a very pleasant garden under my windows, I have nothing but houses before me, and I can't look any way without seeing barristers or attorneys. This is another sacrifice which I have made to a profession, which nothing but inevitable necessity forces me to submit to, which I every day feel more and more that I am unfit for, and which I dislike the more I meet with success in it.'

—Sir Samuel Romilly [of GI],[1] from Letter to Madame G—, from Lincoln's Inn, 6th December, 1791, in *Romilly's Memoirs, edited by his sons*, 1840 [HSLI].

[1] Romilly (1757-1815) had a practice chiefly in chancery matters—hence his removal to this Inn. His life was distinguished by his efforts to mitigate the harshness of the criminal law and to abolish slavery. He was an MP, and Solicitor-General.

> Sir Gerald Hurst, *A Short History of Lincoln's Inn*, 1946.

'…I see the noiseless hurrying to and fro
Of listless clerks bearing the tape-tied scroll.
I see a brougham[1] standing at the door
Of some great lawyer, where the Lady Strutt[2]
Is trying to persuade the master mind
That her aunt's will is fraudulent and void.
I see wigs passing. Some are old and dark
As are their owners' faces, both with years
And legal wisdom, then there passes one
Fresh curled and new; and under it a face
As fresh; but striving to look old and grave
And heavy with responsibility…'

—Addison M'Leod, from *A Window in Lincoln's Inn (And what was seen within and without)*, 1897 [BL].

[1] brougham: a one horse closed carriage designed by Lord Brougham QC [of LI]. Its design was in time transmuted into the London Hackney carriage.

[2] Lady Strutt: She would have been a member of the notable Essex family, of which Rayleigh is the title of honour, and who, it is thought, were at the time clients of a firm of solicitors in New Square.

15.f. CCM: 'New Square, 1936' (s.w. view from the North Lawns) [coll. PHB].

This watercolour shows No. 11 with its 1787 façade, rebuilt after the fire in that building, and with its mansard-attic top storey, as it was before bomb damage in the Second World War, and rebuilding (with the preservation of what survived) in 1951, to the design of A R F Anderson, with dormer windows.

No. 11 is the only building in the late C17th Square of which the walls have not been raised (in brick or plaster) to a full four storeys (above the half-basement) on the façade into the Square.

15.g. A E Pearce: 'Area in New Square', 1893 (w. view of s. side, towards No. 7) [in W J Loftie, *op.cit.*].

The 'areas' in front of the houses in the Square (and which afford air and light to the lower ground floors) are unusual by being continuous, and having bridges across them to give access to the front doors, both features distinguishing them from terraced family houses in n. or w. London.

15.h. Peter Morter: New Square, 1990 (n. view, of w. side, detail) [LT].
This detail shows the w. side of the Square, and its distinctive 'areas'.

¶ For a few years, in the mid-1950s, Margaret Thatcher was in practice in one of the Chambers then in 5, New Square. She had been called by Lincoln's Inn in 1953, and as an Oxford chemistry graduate, it was unsurprising for her to become a member of an intellectual property Set. The Society commissioned and now owns a formal portrait of her by the distinguished Australian artist, June Mendoza, the portraitist of royalty and of the great and the good of this country.

This book remembers her presence by a rather different image—a caricature of her, published on the first anniversary of her premiership.

15.i. Michael Leonard: 'Her first year', in the *Sunday Times*, 1980 [Michael Leonard].
Despite its being a caricature, this image achieves a remarkable likeness of the subject (whom it may be assumed had not sat for the artist). It is, of course, a parody of Ingres' iconic painting of Joan of Arc at the coronation of Charles VII. This imagery enabled the artist to portray eight recognisable members of her Cabinet as *putti* (was he suggesting that they were putty?), but possessed the remarkable foresight of portraying her as a war leader, as she became, only two years later, in the Falklands Campaign.

'For me Lincoln's Inn had personal associations. Years ago, when I returned from the Great War in France, it sheltered my body and ministered to what was left of my soul. For that I shall ever feel grateful. After experiences on the Somme, Passchendaele, the 5th Army retreat to Villers Brettonneux, and the final glorious advance over the Hindenberg Line, the change from war's alarms to the calm seclusion of Lincoln's Inn meant a good deal. High up in a corner of New Square, I could look out on a scene as peaceful as anyone might wish for—high trees and foliage, gracious buildings, barristers in wigs and gowns walking to and fro below… Clerks tripped along carrying those curious red or blue bags of antique, plushy look in which the law seems to carry its secrets about and into the Courts. Meanwhile the birds chirped merrily all through the spring and early summer days, pigeons squatted on my window sill—and pecked out the mortar!—the delicate film of leafage ripened to a rich green, and the shadows beneath grew longer. Of tragedies that might be in the making behind those dumb brick walls no hint obtruded…'

—Sydney R Jones, from *Thames Triumphant*, 1942.

>> Jan Maciag, RIBA.

Jones was an architect and master draughtsman, whose architectural views were published in several collections, and who also designed posters for London Transport.

15.1.3. Their rear elevations and view over Carey Street

15.j. J P Emslie: Carey Street, 1882 (n. view) [HSLI].

This view of the n. side of Carey St. is taken from the steps of the RCJ on the s. side. On the l. is a building (not then owned by the Society) on the corner with Serle St., demolished a few years later to build the Yemen coffee house. To its r. is the minuscule Seven Stars public house—one of the smallest in London—which still stands and which on its inn sign claims a foundation in 1602, some 80 years before New Square, which now backs onto it. Further r., Serle's Gate set back somewhat from the building line of Carey St., is visible with shops to either side of the carriage-way, and integral with the building. Then and now, there was or is a striking contrast between the one- or two-storey buildings in Carey St., and the backs of the houses of New Square, of four upper storeys above a half-basement. The shops visible here were occupied by law booksellers, law stationers, printers and law journal publishers.

15.1.4. A square with three sides

'Lincoln's Inn may reasonably boast of one of the neatest squares in town, and though it is imperfect on one side, yet that very defect produces a beauty, by giving a prospect to the gardens, which fill the space to abundently more advantage.'

—James Ralph, from *A Critical Review of the Public Buildings... in and about London and Westminster*, 1783 [BL].

'It is equally certain that the south side of New Square ought long ago to have been demolished, and thus there would be one of the finest open spaces of London, with the Law Courts at its southern end. The public spirit of the Hon Society of Lincoln's Inn will, we hope, one day effect this much desired improvement.'

—from *The Builder*, 3rd January, 1891.

> C W Heckethorn, *op. cit.*, 1896.

15.2. The flying freeholds in 1-10

¶ 'Flying freehold' is a colloquial term, for which there is no more formal equivalent, and which only in recent decades has found a place in law dictionaries. It is explained in Jowitt's *Dictionary of English Law*, 3rd edn., 2010. It describes a freehold interest in a building in which another proprietor has a similar interest, either above or below vertically. The curiosity of this to an English lawyer is that it flouts the principle expressed by the maxim *Cuius est solum eius est usque ad coelum et ad inferos*, by which the freeholder of a building in England is deemed at common law to have a corresponding interest in the ground below and the air space above (subject, of course, to any Act of Parliament to the contrary).

It was sometimes said that New Square was the only place in England to have flying freeholds, or, if not, that it has the oldest such. Those familiar with the higgledy-piggledy dividing walls of houses in C16th and C17th village streets will know that both these claims are untenable. What is, however, possible is that the Square at one time comprised the largest number in any one place (except for a short-lived fashion for creating freehold flats in the mid-C20th). It is remarkable that here, among the greatest concentration of consultant real property lawyers in England (referred to in 27.2.), the freeholds should have been created by accident, and one of legal documentation, not of building design. The top storeys of the buildings, which were added outside the scope of the terms of the 1682 Agreement, evidently—but not by accident—acquired the freehold status of the storey upon which they were superimposed.

It has been suggested that the freeholds arose in consequence of the Society's forgetting to collect rents for many years. This, as with some other legends in the Inn, is misconceived. The status appears to have arisen in consequence of the bankruptcy, in 1722, of the sole survivor in a partnership of goldsmiths which was then, by purchase, the freehold owner of the Square. The Court of Chancery ordered the sale of the freehold interest, and during 1723-5, chambers were sold off individually, in many cases to lessees in occupation, subject to the obligations under the 1682 Agreement, but imposing no new obligations—as should have been done—to reflect the multiple ownerships then being created.

By the 1850s, the problems of operating the provisions of the 1682 Agreement were such that the Society considered bringing Chancery proceedings to test their enforceability, but in the event promoted a private Act of Parliament.

'And whereas, from the frequent Change of Ownership, and the Variety of Interests of the several Proprietors of and in the said Chambers, it is in many Cases difficult for the said Masters of the Bench to ascertain who actually are the Proprietors, Successors in Title to the said *Henry Serle*, of the said Chambers respectively, and to enforce the Nomination of duly qualified Persons to be admitted, and Payment of the proper Admission Fines, Fees, and Dues in respect thereof, and the Employment of the said Chambers solely for the Purposes authorized by the said Articles of Agreement: And whereas, in order to settle such Disputes, and prevent Litigation, and also to provide hereafter for the proper Use and Employment of the said Chambers so erected by the said *Henry Serle* as aforesaid, and the future Government and Management of all other the Hereditaments and Premises comprised in the said Articles of Agreement, and the better lighting, paving, and watching of *New Square* aforesaid, it is expedient that… proper powers should be given to the said Society for enforcing Payment of such fixed annual Sums, and that proper Powers for the future Government and Regulation of *New Square, Lincoln's Inn*, aforesaid, should be granted; but the Purposes aforesaid cannot be effected without the Authority of Parliament: May it therefore please Your Majesty that it may be enacted; and be it enacted by the Queen's most Excellent Majesty, by and with the Advice and Consent of the Lords Spiritual and Temporal, and Commons, in this present Parliament assembled, and by the Authority of the same, as follows…'

—Preamble to the Lincoln's Inn Act, 1860.

15.3. *Serle's Coffee House*, in 3

¶ Surprisingly—given the care which had been taken to restrict the letting of chambers in New Square (Serle Court) to members of the Society—Serle's Coffee House was established for almost the entire century in the Square at No. 3, between the Prothonotary's Office and the Gate, moving out of the Inn into Serle St. in the 1790s. Coffee houses generally, and specifically those on the periphery of the Inn, outside its gates, are noted in 37.1. below.

'8th November, 1718. After dinner… about 3 o'clock went to Mr Horsmanden's chambers and from thence to the Temple where we looked upon some chambers which I liked very well. Then we went to Lincoln's Inn to the coffeehouse and from thence to the play, where was abundance of company.

11th. About twelve I went to Lincoln's Inn Coffeehouse and read the news and then saw the Chambers of Sir George Cooke and then went home and read several things from Virginia.

8th December. After dinner I put several things in order and about 4 o'clock went to the Temple with my cousin Horsmanden to discourse Sir George Cooke about his Chambers in Lincoln's Inn. Then I went to Will's[1] where I saw the Duke of Argyll.

19th. About 12 o'clock I went to the Virginia Coffee house and from thence to Mr Perry's and dined with the old gentleman and ate some roast beef. After dinner I received a hundred pounds and then went to visit Mrs Perry and drank tea with them and then to the playhouse in Lincoln's Inn and had a quarrel with several footmen about wearing their hats.

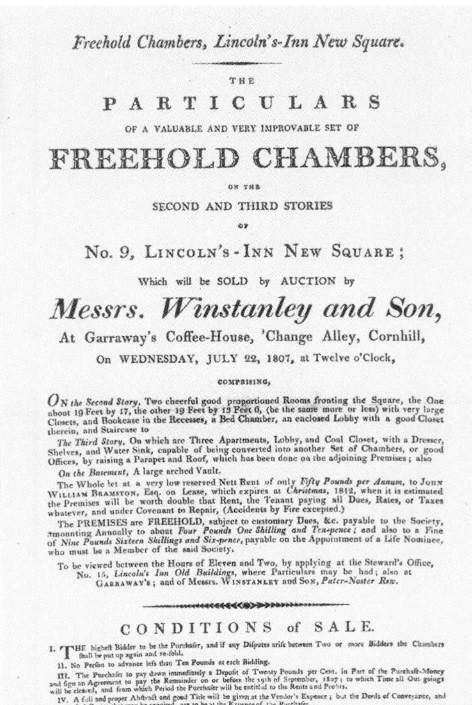

Freehold Chambers, Lincoln's-Inn New Square.

THE

PARTICULARS

OF A VALUABLE AND VERY IMPROVABLE SET OF

FREEHOLD CHAMBERS,

ON THE

SECOND AND THIRD STORIES

OF

No. 9, Lincoln's-Inn New Square;

Which will be SOLD by AUCTION by

Messrs. Winstanley and Son,

At Garraway's Coffee-House, 'Change Alley, Cornhill,

On WEDNESDAY, JULY 22, 1807, at Twelve o'Clock,

COMPRISING,

On *the Second Story*, Two cheerful good proportioned Rooms fronting the Square, the One about 19 Feet by 17, the other 19 Feet by 13 Feet 6, (be the same more or less) with very large Closets, and Bookcase in the Recesses, a Bed Chamber, an enclosed Lobby with a good Closet therein, and Staircase to

The Third Story, On which are Three Apartments, Lobby, and Coal Closet, with a Dresser, Shelves, and Water Sink, capable of being converted into another Set of Chambers, or good Offices, by raising a Parapet and Roof, which has been done on the adjoining Premises; also

On the Basement, A large arched Vault.

The Whole let at a very low reserved Nett Rent of only *Fifty Pounds per Annum*, to John William Bramston, Esq. on Lease, which expires at *Christmas*, 1812, when it is estimated the Premises will be worth double that Rent, the Tenant paying all Dues, Rates, or Taxes whatever, and under Covenant to Repair, (Accidents by Fire excepted.)

The PREMISES are FREEHOLD, subject to customary Dues, &c. payable to the Society, amounting Annually to about *Four Pounds One Shilling and Ten-pence*; and also to a Fine of *Nine Pounds Sixteen Shillings and Six-pence*, payable on the Appointment of a Life Nominee, who must be a Member of the said Society.

To be viewed between the Hours of Eleven and Two, by applying at the Steward's Office, No. 15, *Lincoln's Inn Old Buildings*, where Particulars may be had; also at Garraway's; and of Messrs. Winstanley and Son, *Pater-Noster Row*.

CONDITIONS of SALE.

I. THE highest Bidder to be the Purchaser, and if any Disputes arise between Two or more Bidders the Chambers shall be put up again and re-sold.

II. No Person to advance less than Ten Pounds at each Bidding.

III. The Purchaser to pay down immediately a Deposit of Twenty Pounds per Cent. in Part of the Purchase-Money and sign an Agreement to pay the Remainder on or before the 19th of September, 1807; to which Time all Out-goings will be cleared, and from which Period the Purchaser will be entitled to the Rents and Profits.

IV. A full and proper Abstract and good Title will be given at the Vendor's Expence; but the Deeds of Conveyance, and

15.k. Particulars of Sale of Freehold Chambers, 2nd & 3rd floors of 9, New Square, 1807 [coll. Messrs Hunters].

Despite the name, the Act extends only to the Square, and specifically only to the C17th houses in it, regulating the management by vesting powers in a Committee of Proprietors, constituted for that purpose, representing the Society and the other freeholders. The Square is believed to be the only place where an Honourable Society does not have title to all the land and buildings within the perimeter walls and gates of its Inn of Court.

A notice of auction of a freehold is reproduced here. Other freeholds in the Square were sold by auction or by private treaty in the last decade of the C20th and the first of the C21st.

An authoritative article by Dr Mary Vitoria QC [of LI] in *The Conveyancer and Property Lawyer*, 1977, traces the chain of title from Serle.

27th June 1719… Then I went to Mr Horsmanden's lodging and from thence we went to see the chambers at Lincoln's Inn and made Mr Md a visit.

3rd July 1719… I took a hundred pounds; then I walked to Mr Lindsay's and sat with him about an hour and then went home and read some English. Then I went to Mr Horsmanden's lodgings and he told me he had agreed about the chambers in Lincoln's Inn for nine hundred guineas. Then we went to walk in the park till we were tired, and then I went to Will's and from thence home about 11 o'clock and said my prayers.

9th. I went to the Virginia Coffehouse where I learned that twenty of the Virginia ships were arrived. Then I went to dine with old Mr Perry and got his note for five hundred pounds to purchase chambers in Lincoln's Inn.

10th. I rose about 6 o'clock and went at eight to Daniel Horsmanden's and from thence to Sir George Cooke's chambers to execute the Covenant and take possession of my chambers at Lincoln's Inn, which I did accordingly and about 10 o'clock walked home and read several letters from Virginia.

19th September… then came Daniel Horsmanden and we went to dine at the Blue Post in Oldbourne and ate some roast beef. After dinner we walked to my stone cutter and chose some marble for a chimney. Then we took a walk in Lincoln's Garden till five and then I walked home and wrote a letter till six and then walked to the playhouse in Drury Lane where I stayed the play and had the pleasure to see Mrs Drx there.'

—William Byrd, of Virginia [of LI], from *London Diary*, 1717-21, ed. Louis B Wright and Marion Tinling, 1958.

---

[1] Will's: The coffee-house adjacent to the Inn. There was a more famous and fashionable one of the same name in Covent Garden, but which clearly is not the one to which reference is made here.

'*Mrs Winifred*: Pray, Sir William, give me leave to ask you, where is the mighty matter, of interchanging civilities, between persons of a certain rank?—Lord Eustace spent, some months, at your house, in the country.

Sir William: Not by my invitation, sister, but yours—You know I was at my estate in Devonshire, the greatest part of the time he spent at Langwillan—I have, therefore, neither right, nor inclination, to accept of his house—Besides, it is extremely inconvenient to me, as I have so much business to transact, in Lincoln's Inn.

Mrs Winifred: You should have written to your broker, then, to provide you apartments, in some of the stoves, on t'other side Temple-Bar, Sir William;—but, as to my niece and me, we don't chuse to be suffocated, I must inform you…
Enter *Robert*.

Sir William: Send David for a Hackney-coach—take this key, and bring me a parcel of papers, which you will find tied up, in my strong box, Robert.

Robert: Yes, Sir.

Mrs Winifred: I hope, Sir William, you have your address written upon your cards, and that you have ordered your letters to be directed to Lord Eustace's House. As his Lordship honours me with his friendship, I think it necessary that our Acquaintance shou'd be informed, of his great politeness.

Sir William: (Aside) His lordship honours me with his friendship—how well the traffic is kept up, in that phrase, between vanity and vanity. I had ordered my letters to Serle's Coffeehouse, but since it is determined that I must stay here, I shall direct them to be sent to me.

Mrs Winifred: I must beg, Sir William, that you will order all the newspapers, and magazines, to be sent here, also. My mental faculties are quite at a stand—I have not had the least political information, these four days.'

—Elizabeth Griffiths, from *The School for Rakes*, 1769 [BL].

> H B Wheatley, *op. cit.*, 1891.

15.4. *The Society for Promoting Christian Knowledge: the SPCK*, in 6

¶ On 8th March 1699, five men under the inspiration of Dr Thomas Bray met in the chambers of Serjeant John Hooke (later CJ of Carmarthen) in Serle Court, and resolved to form themselves into The Society for Promoting Christian Knowledge.

The minutes of that first meeting indicate their then priorities, which may be summarised as: i. the teaching of the Catechism to children, ii.'the conversion of the Quakers… to… the belief of Christ', and iii. a scheme for promoting religion in the Plantations.

They continued to meet in those chambers for three years. Some years later they were meeting in other chambers in the Inn.

'With the Society for Promoting Christian Knowledge at their new

15.l. Thomas Rowlandson & Augustus Pugin: 'The Stamp Duty Office in Somerset House', 1808, in R Ackermann, *Microcosm of London*, 1808 [CWA].

This aquatint shows clearly the practical and mechanical arrangements for stamping documents, as they would have been in Serle's Court, albeit in a very different architectural setting. In the foreground, on the r., attorneys' clerks are handing in deeds to stamp clerks to assess the applicable duty, and for them then to pass to machine operators, on the l., who impress the stamps. The same process continued in Somerset House, or latterly in Bush House facing it across the Strand, until the last decades of the C20th.

apartments at Lincoln's Inn [6 in Serle Court]. After the business was over I looked at the curious and noble models of many churches proposed to be built; this pleasant room being that where the Commissioners[1] meet upon that account in the forenoons (as the Bishop of London, Mr Nelson, etc., did this day) and the Society in the afternoon.'

—Ralph Thoresby, from *Diary*, for 29th July 1714.

> H B Wheatley, *op. cit.*, 1891.

1 Commissioners: the Commissioners for the purposes of the Fifty Churches Act, 1711: charged with the building of that number of churches, to be in stone and to have spires. A dozen, but not fifty, fine baroque churches were built pursuant to the Act, which had been passed on the initiative of the Tory Government (in office after twenty-two years of Whig rule) with the motive of re-asserting the position of the Church of England. The nearest of these new churches to the Inn was and is St Mary-le-Strand.

The SPCK has survived from these small beginnings, to have become the oldest Anglican mission society in England. It is also the third-oldest established publisher (of any type) in this country. Its most visible manifestations were for many years, until the crisis in bookselling of the early C21st, its chain of over thirty bookshops in English cathedral cities and, abroad, its support in twice that number of countries, both within the Commonwealth and without, of religious publishing and bookselling.

15.5. *The Stamp Office*, in 7-8

¶ Stamp Duty, in the modern sense, was first imposed in England in 1694, by the Act quoted below, based on an idea brought from the Netherlands by William III. Intended to be temporary, it is still in force, though modified in concept and extended in scope, and no longer a mechanical operation. As appears above, the Commissioners were empowered to 'keep their Head Office in some convenient place within the cities of London or Westminster'. They found 7-8, Serle Court to be so—being then newly built and ready for occupation. The Royal Coat of Arms over the doorway of No. 8, indicating the Stamp Office, can be seen in Samuel Scott's painting of Serle Court. A century later, in 1787, the Office moved to occupy a part of the first purpose-built premises designed for more than one Government department at Somerset House, in the Strand, not far away. For some two hundred years, attorneys, solicitors and their clerks—and others, such as bankers and insurers—took their clients' deeds and documents, and their own cheques and policies, to these offices, and then in the C20th, to Bush House, opposite Somerset House, for duty to be assessed and stamps impressed.

'An Act for granting to Their Majesties several Duties upon Velum, and Parchment for Four Years, towards Carrying on the War against France.

We your Majesties most dutiful and loyal subjects, the Commons in Parliament assembled, having entered into a due and serious consideration of the extraordinary occasions which obliged your Majesties to a great and present expence for the necessary defence of

Richard Newſham, *of* Cloth-Fair, London, *Engineer*,

MAKES the moſt uſeful and convenient Engines for quenching FIRES, which carry a conſtant Stream with great Force, and yet, at Pleaſure, will water Gardens like ſmall Rain. All impartial Men of Art and Ingenuity will allow this, and the moſt Prejudic'd ceaſe objecting, when they ſee how compleatly the whole Contrivance is adapted to the Uſe intended. He hath play'd theſe Engines before His MAJESTY and the Nobility at St. *James*'s, with ſo general an Approbation, that the largeſt was inſtantly order'd to be left for the Uſe of the Royal Palace aforeſaid: And as a farther Encouragement, (to prevent others from making the like Sort, or any Imitation thereof) His MAJESTY has *ſince* been graciouſly pleas'd to grant him His Second Letters Patent, for the better ſecuring his Property in this, and ſeveral other Inventions for raiſing Water from any Depth, to any Height requir'd. The largeſt Size will go through any Paſſage one Yard wide, in compleat working Order, without taking off, or putting on, *any Thing*; which is not to be parallel'd by *any other Sort* whatſoever: One Man can quickly and eaſily move about the largeſt Size in as little Compaſs of Ground as it takes up to ſtand in, and it is work'd by Hands and Feet, or by Hands only. Thoſe by Suction feed themſelves from a Canal, Pond, or Well, *&c.* or out of their own Ciſterns, as Opportunity offers: They are far leſs liable to Diſorder, much more durable than any extant, and play off large Quantities of Water, at the Diſtances under-mention'd, either from the Engine, or a Leather Pipe, or Pipes, of any Length requir'd; (the Screws all fitting each other) *This* the **cumberſome Squirting-Engines**, which take up four times the Room, cannot perform; nor do they throw one 4th Part of their Water on the Fire, at the like Diſtances, but loſe it by the Way; neither can they uſe a Leather-Pipe with them to much Advantage, whatever Neceſſity may call for. The Four largeſt Sizes go upon Wheels, and the Two others are carried like a Chair. Their Performances are as follow, and their Prizes fix'd very reaſonable, (tho' ſome may think otherwiſe, becauſe his Inventions are ſecur'd to him by Letters Patent) he having a due Regard to the publick Good, as well as his own Profit, both in theſe, and divers other Inventions for ſeveral Purpoſes, which he has been the Inventor of, either for the Uſefulneſs, or Diverſion of Gentlemen.

Number of Sizes.	What Quantity of Water the Ciſterns hold in Gallons.	Quantity diſcharg'd per Minute in Gallons.	At what Number of Yards Diſtance.	Price without Suction.	Price with Suction.
1ſt.	30	30	26	18 *l.*	20 *l.*
2d.	36	36	28	20	23
3d.	65	65	33	30	35
4th.	90	90	36	35	40
5th.	120	120	40	45	50
6th.	170	170	40	60	70

Machina perfecta eſt, qua non præſtantior ulla
Aſſervare domos, & aquas haurire profundas.
Mutatam cernis naturam: ſurgit in altum
Artibus unda novis; dum flamma coacta recumbit.

15.m. Richard Newsham of Cloth-Fair: Advertisement for his fire engine, early C18th [LMA].

The Society owned one of these engines, made by the most celebrated manufacturer of the day, whose engines were even exported to the North American colonies.

your realms, and being desirous to raise such aids and supplies as may be proportionable to these occasions, do humbly present your Majesties with the free gift of the rates and duties hereinafter mentioned: and do beseech your Majesties, that it may be enacted… There shall be… raised, collected and paid unto their Majesties… during the term of four years and no longer, for the several and respective things hereinafter mentioned, which shall be written or ingrossed, during the term aforesaid… the several and respective rates, impositions, duties, charges and sums of money hereinafter expressed…
And be it further enacted by the authority aforeaid that for the better and more effectual levying, collecting and paying unto their Majesties it shall be and may be lawful for the Majesties… to nominate and appoint such persons as they shall think fit, to be commissioners or officers for the several purposes hereinafter mentioned; and that the commissioners so to be appointed, shall keep their Head Office in some convenient place within the cities of London or Westminster; and the said commissioners or the major part of them, are hereby impowered, under their hands and seals, to appoint such other inferior officers, for the marking or stamping of Velum, Parchment and Paper, or for the better collecting and levying the duties hereby granted to their Majesties, as they in their discretion shall think fit…'

—from the Preamble to the Stamp Act, 1694.

15.6. Fires and fire insurance

¶ The early history of fire insurance in this country has particular associations with the Square. Fire insurance is generally considered to have begun in England in the 1670s through the efforts of Nicholas Barbon—the developer behind the construction of Serle Court, and who was admitted to chambers in it—acting under stimulus of the Great Fire of London in 1666. For some time Barbon's company, the General Insurance Office (which obtained a Royal Charter), and a mutual Friendly Society were the only fire insurers. But then there was a flurry of activity in the 1690s and again in the 1720s. These decades saw the foundation of the Hand-in-Hand, Sun, Union, Westminster, London and Royal Exchange—and all of which businesses may be identified under those or amalgamated names, to the present day.

'Carey Street,

I've been much alarmed by the fire in Lincoln's Inn t'other night, though I think not much in danger; the account you have in the papers is pretty exact. The lives of Mr Chas. Yorke and four other gentlemen were probably saved by an old gentleman coming from the tavern, who found the porters breaking open Mr Wilbraham's door and with much difficulty stopt them till he had waked the gentlemen above stairs who had scarce got down stairs without their clothes when the fire burst through the door and set the whole staircase in flame at once.'

—Robert Ord, from Letter to Lord Carlisle, dated 30th June 1752.

'June 27. At about one in the morning broke out a terrible fire in Lincoln's Inn New Square, by which no. 10 and 11 were entirely consumed, particularly the Chambers of R Wilbraham, the Hon Edward Harley, Hon Charles York, E Hoskyns,—Cholmeley, Edmund

Sawyer, Master in Chancery and—Ansell, Esqs., all in no. 10 were the papers books, plate, furniture and wearing apparel were totally destroyed. The gentlemen in the next staircase, no. 11, viz. John Sharpe, solicitor to the Treasury, Edward Booth, Esq., Messrs Ambler, Fazakerly, Ferrers and Wilmot had just time to save most things of consequence. The loss and difficulties in which many families are involved, the titles to whose properties were lodged with the above gentlemen, are not to be computed. Mr Wilbraham had lately purchased an estate of great value, the title deeds of which, among other numberless deeds, mortgages, etc. were burnt. His clerk, Mr Pickering, lost a loan £1100 in money and bank notes of his own and others, and securities for £30,000 more, also all the title deeds of Lord Leigh's estate. When the fire was discovr'd most of the watch were asleep or drunk, and the wife of an upholder in Carey Street, whose husband left his bed to assist sufferers, hang'd herself in his absence.

July 1st. The Lord Chancellor suspended all proceedings in Chancery on account of the late fire in Lincoln's Inn Square.

August 1st. The rubbish in Lincoln's Inn Square having been sifted, most of the sufferers by the late fire have had the chief part of their properties in plate and cash restored to them, and Mr Pickering who lost bank notes to the amount of £1,000 has been so successful as to reestablish most of them.'

—from *The Gentleman's Magazine*, 1752.

> Note XXV, Vol. III, *The Black Books.*

In 1782, a serious fire broke out in Nos. 3 and 4. Its consequences are visible in the elegant stone staircase now serving No. 3. In 1849, a fire almost completely destroyed the interior of No. 2, the devastation being recorded in the watercolour reproduced here. The *Illustrated London News* also considered it worth recording the scene in a black-and-white drawing, not reproduced here.

15.n. Charlotte Halliday: 10, New Square, 2012 (n.w. view) [coll. Guy Green, solicitor in LI].

The effects of rebuilding of No. 10 are still visible in the different brickwork, slightly protruding building line and the pediment of the door-way of that building, eschewing the slightly baroque curved broken pediments of the other buildings in the Square. When rebuilt, stone stairs were incorporated as a precaution against, and as a means of escape from, fire.

15.o. J W Archer: 2, New Square, the morning after the fire, 1849 (s.e. view) [BM].

16. THE ENCLOSURE OF NEW SQUARE:

16.1. The parishes and the parish bounds

¶ The site of New Square lay within three parishes—Nos. 1-4, while being for ecclesiastical purposes in the Peculiar of the Liberty of the Rolls, were for certain civil purposes in the parish of St Dunstan-in-the-West; Nos. 5-10. and the s. half of No. 11 were in St Clement Danes; and the n. half of No. 11 was in St Giles-in-the-Fields. The original extent of the Inn lay within St Giles-in-the-Fields and St Andrew Holborn, but until the erection of the New Hall, the Society's collegiate buildings were confined to the latter parish. St Andrew's being now a Guild Church, no longer has a parish, and this part of its territory has accrued to that of S Alban—as that parish prefers to call itself. The following extract, from one of the important manuscript records relating to the Inn, quotes a description from the C16th of the ceremony of beating the bounds of the parishes, along the n. side of the land now occupied by the Square.

'...the tyme of Procession, which in ancient tyme was held usually upon the Tuisday in Gange-weeke[1] yerly. In which perambulation it was accustomed that the Churchmen of St Dunstan's Parrish did enter into this House.

The Soile of this House with the Parrish of Saint Dunstan begynneth at the Southend side of the Connygarth, or Cottrell Garden, and thence alonge into the Hall muche about the place where the nowe newe Skreene standeth and thence the Churchmen with their Procession issuenge fourth out of the Hall go [i]n di... to the Gate, and soe into Newstrete or Chancery Lane, and against the middle part of the Gatehouse they sange theire Gospell. Whereby it appeareth that [the Gatehouse] of Brick is erected within both Parishes, for, before the [Gatehouse] was erected, St Dunstan's Procession pacinge alonge out of the Hall... the old Gatehouse beinge then in the Corner did inviron the well, now st[opped up?]... thence, out of the same Gate into the Street or Lane aforesaid. And soe towards Holborne, till they came over againste the houses where the nowe new e[rected Gate] house of Brick standeth, and there the Gospell was chaunted.

Touchinge the like Procession in those daies made by the Churchmen of [St Andrew's] Parish in Gangweek, the same thus began. They cam in at the Ga[tehouse then in the] Corner, into the Court, and thence, passed alonge to the Chappell, where... was solempnlie songe, and that ended, they issued into the Hall... enterteynment, and decentilie satt down at the Tables there... them provided, Bread, Bere and Cheese, And that Refection en[ded, they] retourned out of the Hall, and thence paced directly into Cottrell Garden, or Connygarth, unto the dore thereof, beinge then made of Tymber, [in the] muddwall, at the northend of the said Connygarth. And soe pacing [about] that doore and certaine Houses there then built, issued thence ini... soe awaie. And this is the manner of that perambulation.'

—William Hakewill [of LI], 'The Extension of Lincoln's Inn being in three severall Parishes', from *The Middle Temple Manuscript, ca.* 1620-38, transcribed by W Paley Baildon FSA [of LI] [LI MS Misc. 720].

---

[1] Gangweek: Rogation week, the week ending on Ascension Day.

The gaps in the text reflect damage to the original MS., and the words in square brackets are those interpolated by W Paley Baildon.

16.a. Liam Martin: The parish boundary stones of St Clement Danes, 1693, and St Giles-in-the-Fields, 1787, in the wall of 11, New Square, 1991 [LT].

There are also stones marking the boundary of St Clement Danes and St Dunstan-in-the-West, in the wall of No. 5.

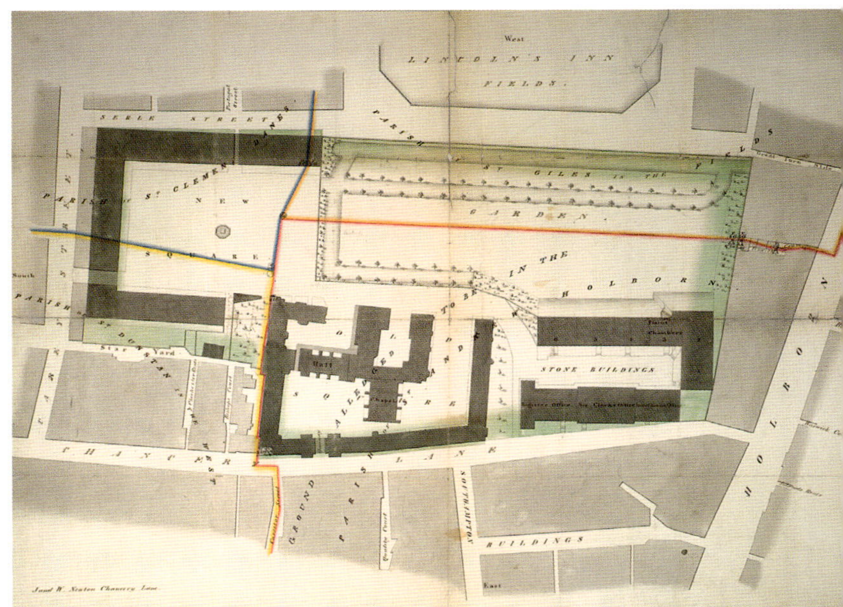

16.b. J & W Newton: Plan of the Inn, indicating parish boundaries, ? early C19th [HSLI].

This meticulous plan clearly indicates the boundaries of each parish, but pointedly delineates 'Ground alledged [*sic*] to be in the Parish of St Andrew Holborn'.

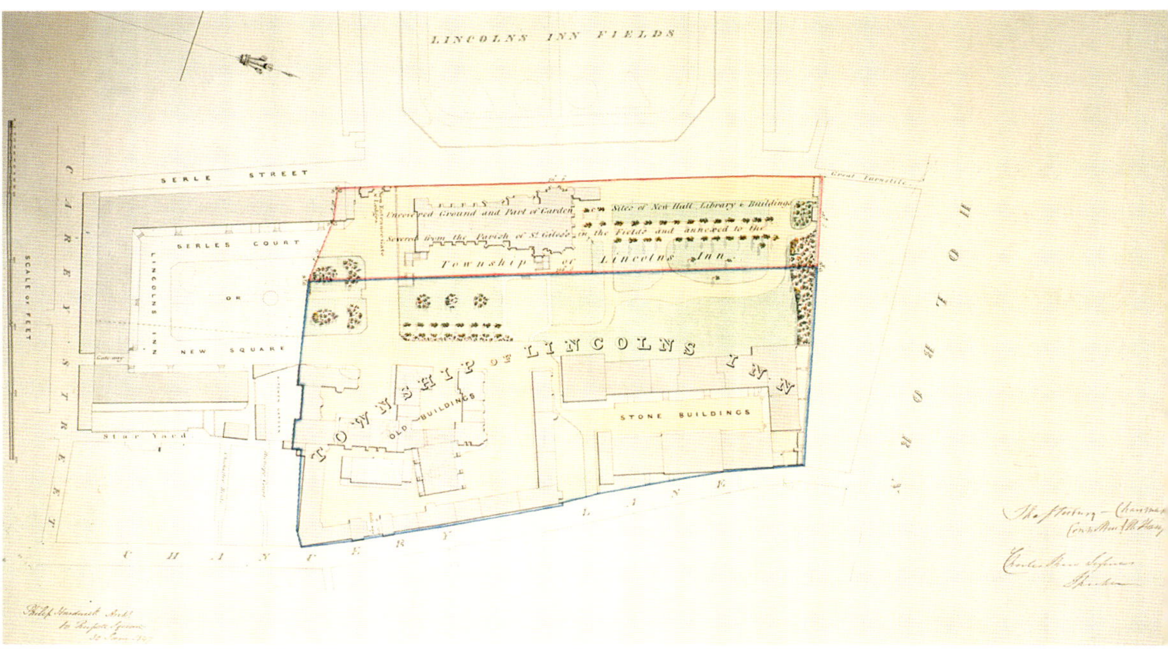

16.c. Philip Hardwick: Survey Plan of the Township of Lincoln's Inn, 1847 [HSLI].

The plan clearly delineates the boundary as it crosses New Square.

'As to the Bounds or Girt-Line of this Parish… it crosseth into Lincoln's Inn New Court, where the Parish Mark is set up in the Walls and to the Pump that stands by the Garden Pales: and from this Pump it runneth Northwards, in a direct line…'

—John Strype, *Survey*, 1720.

¶ In 1930, the *Illustrated London News* published photographs of the choristers of St Clement's preparing to beat the bounds in New Square of their parish, under the direction of their parish priest. They were in full dress of (hard) mortar-board, cassock and surplice, each equipped with a long willow wand. It may be surmised that this was an attempt, promoted by an historically minded bencher, to continue or to revive the practice evoked by *The Middle Temple Manuscript*, above.

16.2. The extra-parochiality of the Township of Lincoln's Inn

¶ The Society succeeded, over the centuries, in asserting and maintaining that the buildings in the original area of the Inn had extraparochial status (deriving from its former status as a bishop's town-house), leading to an exemption from liability to pay Poor Rates, and as to which see note 37, Historical Essay. Various attempts were made, both by the Society and by individual occupants of chambers, to assert that this privilege accrued, after it had been built, to New Square. These eventually failed, and the Overseers of the Liberty of the Rolls, and those of St Clement Danes, collected the rates respectively due to them. However, No. 11 was recognised as lying partly within and partly without the original boundaries of the Inn.

'The late Mr Sejeant Lens used to tell with great glee the following anecdote of his learned brother of the coif, Mr Serjeant Hill.[1] Having business to transact with him, he went to his chambers in New Square, Lincoln's Inn and found him with the bookcases, tables, chairs, and carpets on one side of the room… "Pray", said Mr Serjeant Lens, "what do you intend to do with all the furniture arranged in this strange fashion?" The learned Serjeant replied, that since half his chamber had been found to stand in the parish of St Clement Danes he formed his encampment on the side of the room belonging to Lincoln's Inn to prevent the officers from distraining his goods for the Poor Rates. At a future period Mr Serjeant Lens actually found the officers in the apartment, they having effected an entrance through the back windows, and his learned brother daring to touch his goods out of the parish… The Officers were so intimidated at the threats that they never again molested the learned Serjeant, who continued to reside in the chambers without paying any parochial dues. A case similar to this one occured only a few days since in the same parish.'

—'Division of Parishes', in *The Times*, 4th September 1840 [press cutting, HSLI].

[1] George Hill [of LI] (1716-1808): nicknamed 'Serjeant Labyrinth', on account of being lost in his own extensive learning.

Another learned and eccentric Chancery Counsel who practised in the Inn appears in *27.a.*

16.3. The boundaries of the Society's land and Henry Serle's

¶ On the front (i.e. the e.) wall of 11, New Square is a carved stone plaque in Latin, illustrated here, which announces to the passer-by that:

'The ground on which this building is erected belongs to this Society unbroken for 54 feet 1 inch northwards from the southern edge of this stone and also all that piece of ground eastward from this stone as far as the boundary of the old building nearest to the kitchen garden.'

As indicated above, the boundary of the Inn's land ran across the n. end what is now New Square towards what is now the n. wall of No. 1. On the side (i.e. the n.) wall of 1, New Square is a plaque, reproduced here, presumably seeking to pre-empt the then freehold owners' acquiring rights of light or 'ancient lights' over the Kitchen Garden. There is a window immediately above it, not forming part of the regular pattern of fenestration, and which seems to have been broken out after the building was put up. It may be surmised that the plaque was erected after the window was made.

16.4. *Cavendish Weedon's column and fountain*: 'lawyers were children once…'

¶ Cavendish Weedon [of IT and LI]—a great 'improver' and a noted musical impresario—moved into Serle Court in 1692 and was admitted also to membership of this Society. He set about vigorously improving, or proposing improvements to, the surroundings of his new chambers. At that date, chambers in Serle Court were probably the best as well as the most modern 'offices' in London. His name is associated with a fine project for the laying out of Lincoln's Inn Fields; proposals for embellishments to the Chapel; and a plan to re-house the Six Clerks' Office into the Inn (all then unsuccessful), and with the widening of the way, then called Jackanapes La., between Serle's Gate and Chancery La. (successful). It is, however, his successful proposal for the laying out of the grounds of the Court and the erection of a column and fountain in its centre, which—although now destroyed—has left a lasting record in words and pictures.

'In the midst of the Court is a curious Stone Pillar artificially wrought; on which is a Dyall Clock, with four Boys spouting out water out of Tritons Shells; and at the Bottom is a fountain that receiveth the said Streams of water falling down from the Shells: all encompassed with handsome Iron Bars.'

—John Strype, *Survey*, 1720.

'In the midst of this square, which is covered with gravel and neatly kept, is a fountain (as it is called), consisting of a small handsome column, of the Corinthian order, from a design of Inigo Jones: the top supported a sun-dial, and the four corners of the pedestal infant tritons holding shells, which formerly spouted water. This is in itself a handsome decoration; but if it was still kept playing, would preserve its name with more propriety, and give a greater pleasure than the basin of stag nant water, which at present scandalises the place.'

—W Herbert, from *Antiquities of the Inns of Court and Chancery*, 1804.

16.d. Liam Martin: The plaques set into the walls of 1 and 10, New Square, 1991 [LT].

16.e. Anon. artist: The column and fountain, ? mid-C18th [HSLI].

The column had a 'dyal' incorporated in the upper part, on the north-facing side which, remarkably, was a clock rather than a sundial.

'The artificial fountains of the metropolis are… fast vanishing. Most of them are dried up, or bricked over…

Four little winged marble boys used to play their virgin fancies, spouting out ever fresh streams from their innocent wanton lips, in the square of Lincoln's Inn, when I was no bigger than they were figured. They are gone, and the spring choked up. The fashion, they tell me, is gone by, and these things are esteemed childish. Why not then gratify children, by letting them stand? Lawyers, I suppose, were children once. They are awakening images to them at least. Why must everything smack of man, and mannish? Is the world all grown up? Is childhood dead? Or is there not in the bosoms of the wisest and the best some of the child's heart left, to respond to its earliest enchantments? The figures were grotesque. Are the stiffwigged living figures, that still flitter and chatter about that area, less gothic in appearance? or is the splutter of their hot rhetoric one half so refreshing and innocent as the little cool playful streams those exploded cherubs uttered?'

—Charles Lamb, from 'Old Benchers of the Inner Temple', in *Essays of Elia*, 1823.

This famous phrase—which clearly belongs to *this* Inn—has migrated to the Inner Temple, by being re-used as an inscription on the basin of a fountain of later date in the gardens of *that* Inn. Coffee mugs bearing this phrase under the glaze may be had in their Treasury Office.

It was also used as the epigraph to Harper Lee, *To Kill a Mockingbird*, 1960, and thus has reached every high school in the United States.

See also the quotation in 16.5.1. for the demolition of the fountain later in the C19th, and the aesthetic judgment on it at that time.

16.5. New Square garden:

16.5.1. The flora: trees and flowers

'Workmen are now busily employed in forwarding the alterations which are to take place in Lincoln's Inn. The whole of the unoccupied plot of ground in Newsquare is railed in preparatory to its being broken up and covered with grass; the unsightly basin in the centre of the square, which, from the uncouthness of its structure, and the stagnant water which it contained, was generally felt to be a nuisance, is already demolished, and in its place is to be erected a fine ornamental fountain. It is intended that the narrow passage[1] on the western side shall be blocked up… The middle of the square, which is intended to be enclosed with iron railings,[1] and round the outside of which there is to be a carriage drive, will thus be rendered a great ornament to the neighbourhood.'

—from *The Times*, April 1845 [press cutting, HSLI].

[1] passage: Serle St. Passage, in 10, New Square.

[2] iron railings: they stood until they were removed in the Second World War, to 'salvage' the iron for war use.

'We understand that the Benchers of Lincoln's-Inn will publish a gardening book in accordance with the complete revolution they have lately effected in the art of horticulture. They have been laying out New Square with trees, removed after forty years' growth, into a soil of stone, brick, and rubbish, thinly overlaid with mould to the depth of ten inches. The trees are said to be in full bearing; and if they will bear such treatment as this, they will undoubtedly bear anything. The operation of moving trees of forty years' standing has seldom been tried with success, but we understand that the Benchers of Lincoln's-Inn have caused writs of *certiorari* to be dug in all over the Square, because a *certiorari* will remove a case—and why not a tree?—in nearly all its branches.'

—'Legal Gardeners', in *Punch*, 1846 [press cutting, HSLI].

16.f. 'Legal gardeners', *Punch*, 1846 [press cutting, HSLI].

16.g. Thomas H Shepherd: 'Lincoln's Inn Great square', *ca.* 1846 [BM].

The gardens in New Square were created in the central area, which had previously been gravelled, in order to compensate the members of the Society for the loss of part of the Walks, caused by the construction of the New Hall and Library. The preparatory sketch (not reproduced here) is in the CWA, and entitled 'The New Plantations and Hall, Lincoln's Inn Great Square and splendid New Fountain &c.'. As indicated by its caption corroborating the news report in *The Times*, it differs by showing a fountain in the pond.

This piece, whimsical though it is, proved to be prophetic. Two tall *ailanthi* ('trees of heaven'), planted half a century later, and which are naturally shallow-rooted, were spectacularly blown down on the night of 16th October 1987, during the Great Gale, the worst for 250 years. They fell simultaneously, at about 3 a.m., falling n.e. and n.w. respectively, and causing no damage to buildings, people or vehicles. For some weeks they lay senescing in the Square.

16.h. John Crowther: New Square Gardens, 1879 (n.e. view) [LMA].

This watercolour depicts the high-Victorian bosky style of gardening, in contrast to the successive styles of laying out the Square in the mid- or late C20th. An intermediate 'municipal tulip beds' style of the early C20th is shown in the photograph *16.l.*

¶ At the n. end of the lawns stand two magnificent plane trees.[1] The lines quoted below, although not known to have been written in the Inn, have been borrowed to evoke them here. In describing a generic London scene, they specifically fit the topography of this corner of the Inn. The square referred to could be this one, and the garret—a term used in the Inn for rooms under the roofs or eaves in chambers—may be appropriated to No. 11 (which at that date had rooms in an English-style mansard roof) or Nos. 12-13. From a window there, the view is dominated by one or both of these trees.

Green is the plane tree in the square,
The other trees are brown;
They droop and pine for country air;
The plane tree loves the town.

Here, from my garret-pane, I mark
The plane-tree bud and blow,
Shed her recuperative bark,
And spread her shade below.

Among her branches, in and out,
The city breezes play;
The dun fog wraps her round about;
Above, the smoke curls grey.

Others the country take for choice,
And hold the town in scorn;
But she has listened to the voice
On city breezes born.

—Amy Levy, 'A London Plane Tree', 1889.

[1] plane trees (*platanus orientalis*): these are survivors of several planted in 1860 by Cornelius Temple, the Society's Head Gardener, under direction of the Garden Committee, to replace the elms mentioned elsewhere, because, as the Committee recorded, it appears that young elms will not flourish in the atmosphere which now surrounds Lincoln's Inn, and that plane trees, provided they are of the proper variety, are better adapted to and grow more vigorously in that atmosphere than any other tree.

Amy Levy, whose poetry was much admired, was reputedly the first Jewish woman to attend Cambridge University.

Thomas Hardy, 'To a Tree in London', 1920, evoked a similar theme, referable to Clement's Inn.

16.5.2. The fauna: water fowl and water nymphs

'The Inns of Court, as befits their great age and greater dignity, take particular pains about the character of those whom they allow to reside inside their gates; and as the Courts of Chancery claim a traditional preeminence over the Courts of Common Law as homes of the most austere rectitude, where rhetoric is never heard or is heard in tightlipped silence, so is no Inn more careful to maintain the standard of impeccability among its tenants than Lincoln's Inn. Common lawyers expect to jostle and mingle with all manner of men, but Chancery lawyers, who take neither pride nor pleasure in rough and tumble, are not to be offered any but the handpicked company of highly necessary solicitors, the more thoughtful and statistical kind of politician, and the staider sort of journalist. Into this company have now intruded individuals of a very different stamp, whose general air of insolvency, combined with an addiction to the pond and to matrimonial irregularities, suggests that they have mistaken the Inn for the neighbouring Courts of Bankruptcy or Probate, Admiralty, and Divorce. The Inn allows married couples, and smiles indulgently at the spectacle of children playing on its lawns. The law has always recognized marriage and its customary consequences as among the most valuable of the institutions which make the legal profession a necessity.

The litigation in Chancery is so peculiarly dependent on the family and the family quarrel that the noise of children quarrelling, so painful to many other men of affairs, is sweet prophetic music to the Chancery Silk. But the three drakes and two ducks who have started to live in New Square an unseemly life of indolence and pleasure, with an absence of reticence that a Hollywood publicity man might envy, are carrying things altogether too far. When a duck and a drake first appeared and settled in the pond in New Square and reared a family, every one wished them well and the only anxiety was how to retain so model a couple as an encouragement to every one else. They flew away; but another pair reappeared this year, and it looked as if the kindly offices of the Inn in making its pond comfortable had not been in vain, and that the lawyers were earning a good name among the better class of duck. But the correspondent who has followed events for this journal has had an increasingly disreputable tale to unfold. The drake brought a second duck openly to the pond, in full view of the King's Proctor, and the appearance of two more drakes has now given the pond an example of the type of promiscuous modern household which has sometimes been described in fiction but which respectable people have liked to think was exaggerated. It is only three days since this last development, but already the trouble which any experienced solicitor could have predicted seems to be breaking out, and the King's peace is endangered where it ought to be most secure. There is an excuse, and

16.i. Ken Howard, RA: The former fountain and pond in New Square, 1983, with 9, 10 & 11 in the background (w. view) (detail) [coll. PHB].

This watercolour depicts the fountain and fish pond as they were until the early years of the C21st, and would have been at the date of the article in *The Times*, save for a small adjustment to the statue in the fountain.

it is the excuse common in such entangling alliances—the excuse of unhappiness. Four out of the first wife's seven eggs were stolen, one by one, by rats, and the substitutes provided by the Inn have never seemed the same. If the feathered creation offends against the spirit of much of our legislation, at least it is guiltless of the kidnapping and rapine which make the name of rat enjoy so little favour.

But, though the guardians of the law must feel a little outraged that robbery can take place under their very noses like this, there is a certain consolation for legal men in the goings on by the pond. "That," the lawyer can exclaim, "is nature for you, in all her notorious disrepute." So ruminating he can turn away his gaze, and, thinking with pride what the policeman and the Judge have managed to make of human kind, and how seldom they steal each other's offspring, he can settle down with all the clearer conscience to the preparation of his bill of costs.'

—'Polygamy in Lincoln's Inn' in *The Times*, 1930 [press cutting, HSLI].

In Lincoln's Inn, 1930 was 'the Year of the Duck'. The then Under-Treasurer of the Society contributed a carefully written, if self-conscious, piece to *The Times*, published on 24th June, as 'from a correspondent' and entitled 'Wild Ducks in Lincoln's Inn: Story of a strange nesting place'. Following publication, this essay was ordered by Council to be inscribed in the MS Black Book, and is in consequence reprinted as Appendix 2 in Volume VI of *The Black Books*. There were two further news reports of events in the pond, also 'from a correspondent', published in August and September. This flurry of writing prompted that newspaper itself to a riposte and to publish the piece entitled 'Polygamy in Lincoln's Inn' which is reprinted here, but has not been so in *The Black Books*. Its irony supersedes the coyness of the first piece, and finds an anthropomorphic similarity between the ducks, and lawyers and their clients.

In April 1996, the duck then seised of the pond had fourteen ducklings.

Ducks no longer breed in the Square, nor do herons pause here on their long migrations, nor goldfish swim as once they did, since the construction in 2002 of the grassy knoll which now occupies the centre of the lawn in commemoration of HM The Queen's Diamond Jubilee.

16.j. Liam Martin: The water-pumps in New Square, 1993 [LT].

'Extreme measures have been taken to protect some of the country's finest legal minds, who were having to worry about significantly more than points of law on their way to work.

Hawks and falcons have been deployed at the Honourable Society of Lincoln's Inn in London, one of the four Inns of Court, to protect members from a flock of bombing seagulls.

The birds of prey arrived last month to "restore order" to the square in the heart of the society's estate and to ensure that the honourable members have a peaceful summer, the head falconer said.

Up until now, territorial seagulls have been attacking lawyers to viciously that the society's wardens were having to mop up the resulting bloody heads.

This year, members will be protected by two Harris hawks and a lanner falcon, who will stand guard on the rooftops.

Jake O'Neil, from Surrey Bird Control, who owns the birds, began guarding the society last year. During seagull nesting season, from about March until May, he and the birds will watch over the square for up to eight hours a day.

He said: "We arrive prior to the seagulls and provide a credible threat to stop them developing nests on the buildings. Normally you might use spikes or nets but because there's a lot of old architecture at Lincoln's Inn it's more efficient for us to use Harris hawks to make sure the honourable members have a nice, peaceful summer.

The hawks, Bob-Jack and Mischa, and the falcon, Shiva, who can fly at up to 150mph, are doing three shifts a week at Lincoln's Inn but will increase this to five days during the peak nesting season when the gulls are most dangerous.

Mr O'Neil said: "They swoop down out of the sky and aim themselves directly at someone's head so people are either injured by their beak or claws on contact or injured when they dive out of the way. In the past they've particularly attacked bald men and they've drawn blood."

The Harris hawks are trained not to attack people or kill seagulls, an endangered species. Instead, the swoop from building to building "concentrating on being a threat".

Mr O'Neil added: "Seagulls are very clever and they alert each other to the presence of a predator with the calls they make. When the hawks are around, seagulls all over central London know this isn't a safe place to nest. We're restoring order."

The society's wardens said the "powers that be" decided something needed to be done last year. As much as anything else they were "dropping all over the Range Rovers and Porsche Boxsters parked around the square", they said.

John Lancaster, a warden, said that the seagulls could be very aggressive.

He said: "I've treated people with bloody heads before who have been pecked or scraped by their beak or claws when they've swooped down. It's not been pretty".'

—Lucy Holden, 'It's raptors to the rescue as seagulls take aim at top legal minds' in *The Times*, 15th April 2015.

---

[1] wardens: porters

Eros is ill at ease in Lincoln's Inn,
Where blackgowned justice has her sober rule,
And no one plays the hero or the fool,
But such as I sit, staid and bald, within,
Adding provisos to a saving clause,
Taming adventurous pleadings with red ink,
Gelding too bullish statements with "I think",

16.k. 'Temporary Buildings in New-Square, Lincoln's-Inn, for exhibiting the Designs for the New Law-Courts', 1867 (view of interior), *Illustrated London News* [press cutting HSLI].

A matching drawing, showing the exterior of the exhibition galleries was published in the *ILN* (not reproduced here).

Making the cause in hand my only cause.
Yet may he seek revenge one summer eve
And lead a rout of satyrs through New Square,
To chase, a thing no Bencher would believe,
Young naked girls with vine leaves in their hair,
And treat the startled Judges with derision,
And make work for the Family Division.

—Michael Albery, QC [of LI], 'Eros in Lincoln's Inn', mid-C20th, in *Verses from Lincoln's Inn*, 1975.

16.5.3. Former and temporary constructions

¶ The design to be adopted for the proposed Royal Courts of Justice was a matter of great public interest. There were eleven competing architects. The winning design was that by George Edmund Street. There had been much debate which preceded this event as to where the Law Courts should be located: in Westminster near their then home or in the neighbourhood of the Inns whether in the open space of the Fields, or in the area to the s. of this Inn, and to the n. of the Temple. While this exhibition was taking place, demolition of the warren of court (-yard)s and alleys immediately s. of New Square was taking place in preparation for the new building. It was during the 1850s and 1860s that work was progressing on the numerous parts of the *Palais de Justice* in Paris, and during the 1850s to 1880s on the monstrously grand *Palais de Justice* in Brussels.

¶ The Inns of Court OTC had its own First World War Memorial, in the form of a captured German howitzer, mounted on a stone plinth

16.l. The Inns of Court OTC's War Memorial in New Square (e. view) between the Wars: Anon. photographer [HSLI].

16.m. Charlotte Halliday: The Ferris Wheel at the Fun Fair in New Square, 1997 [LT].

The Inns of Court Ball—which rotates intermittently among the four Inns—took place in the Inn in June of that year, of which this and dodg'ems were part.

16.n. Charlotte Halliday: The Brewster Gates, 1995 (s. view) [LT].

on New Square lawn, facing the Brewster Gates. The displaying of a gun as a war memorial was common in England after the First World War. The wish to use the metal for salvage led to the removal of this gun, and many others like it elsewhere in England, during the Second World War.

16.6. The Brewster Gates

¶ These decorative gates, of Belgian design, commemorate Colonel John Brewster [of LI], the first c.o. of the Inns of Court Volunteer Rifle Corps, who died in 1864. They were first erected in the Inn in 1872, and moved here in 1908.

16.o. Sir Arthur Underhill [of LI]: Snow in New Square (n. view) [HSLI].

16.p. Snow falling in New Square, 1987 (s. view of e. side): photograph Clive Berridge (s. view of e. side of the Square) [the photographer].

The scene is that of a week-day afternoon between 4 and 6 p.m. with the Square full of the parked cars of barristers and solicitors. The photographer was a member of staff of Wildy's, and published a book on London architecture, illustrated with his photographs.

16.q. New Square after a night's heavy snowfall: photograph Diana Froyland [solicitor formerly in LI], 2009.

16.7. Snow in the Square

¶ Snow does not, of course, fall only in New Square. However, more images of its falling or lying in the square to picturesque effect have come to hand in the compilation of this book than of other parts of the Inn.

17. THE S. ELEVATIONS OF 18-20, OLD BUILDINGS (FORMERLY *KITCHEN GARDEN ROW*); *THE KITCHEN GARDEN*; AND *THE COURTS* TO THE S.

17.1. *Kitchen Garden Row*, and the *Kitchen Garden*

¶ The Kitchen Garden was a feature of the Inn from its earliest days, and it was located adjacent to the old kitchens in 17, Old Buildings. There was a back door opening into it. For most of its existence after the construction of the Square, it would have been screened by a low building which may have dated from the construction of the Square, or a decade or two later. In 1928, it was demolished, thus opening up the view of the garden, after two centuries or more. There was something of the atmosphere of a fellows' garden in a university college to be experienced in walking into this garden, until that privacy was invaded by the construction of a through footpath in 1990, with the path steps being modified in 1996 with the renovation and alteration of the building called Hale Court, and then renamed Hardwicke Building.

17.b. John Crowther: The Kitchen Garden, with the back of Old Buildings (formerly known as Kitchen Garden Row), 1879 (n. view) [LMA].

17.a. C M Philips: 'Bishop's Court', *ca.* 1870 (e. view) [cutting, HSLI].

This sketch shows the door in the wall of the Kitchen Garden, which still exists but is not in use. The remaining length of the wall beyond that door is now occupied by the Garden House.

In 1996, a herb border—an allusion to one of the original functions of the garden, and an embellishment to it—was created between the footpath and Old Buildings, on the initiative of Sir John Balcombe. A small-white-on-black wall plaque records what was planted: winter savory, rue, green sage, Hidcote lavender, curry plant, cotton lavender, rosemary, black peppermint, pot marigold and thyme. By coincidence, the Royal Shakespeare Company first presented Peter Whelan's play *The Herbal Bed* at Stratford-on-Avon in the same year.

17.2. *The law stationer's shop*, and *the Volunteers' orderly room*

¶ This small, one-storeyed, flat-roofed building is clearly shown in Samuel Scott's *veduta* of the Square. It housed a law stationer's business and, on occasions, the office or orderly room of the Inn's Volunteers.

No description of its interior or its business has been found, and it is not to be expected that one exists. But Dickens furnishes a description of a law stationer's nearby, off Cursitor St., a few yards e. of Chancery La. The businesses in each location—an essential, if humble, element in the practice of the law, until the changes wrought by technology—would necessarily have been the same, and that description has therefore been borrowed to be placed here.

'…Mr Snagsby has dealt in all sorts of blank forms of legal process; in skins and rolls of parchment; in paper—foolscap,[1] brief,[2] draft, brown,

white, whitey-brown, and blotting; in stamps; in office-quills; pens, ink, India-rubber, pounce,[3] pins, pencils, sealing-wax, and wafers,[4] in red tape[5] and green ferret,[6] in pocket-books, almanacks, diaries, and law lists; in string boxes, rulers, inkstands—glass and leaden, penknives,[7] scissors, bodkins,[8] and other small office-cutlery; in short, in articles too numerous to mention…'

—Charles Dickens, from *Bleak House*, 1853.

17.c. J Ford Jones: The Kitchen Garden, 1922 (n.e. view) in *Souvenir of the 500th Anniversary of the Settlement of the HSLI, in its Present Abode* [HSLI].

This sketch shows the garden at a phase between its Victorian and modern appearance. It also shows the small two-storey rendered building projecting out from the rear of 21, Old Buildings, since demolished and depicted in *11.g.* in that process.

1 foolscap: a generic name for several 'imperial' sizes of paper, used for handwritten notes or opinions of Counsel: longer and narrower than A4. The name is a reference to a trade watermark of an early make, and does not imply a suitability for rolling into a dunce's cap. It was, however, well suited to boys' folding into aerodynamic darts.

2 brief: a larger size, used for briefs to counsel, when appearing in court.

3 pounce: powder for reducing the tendency of ink to run on vellum.

4 wafers: discs (large or small) of thick glazed red paper used as a substitute for sealing wax to take the impression of the seal of a company or represent the seal of an individual on a deed.

5 red tape: strong, loosely woven cotton or linen, dyed rose red, used for bundling papers for storage or for delivery to counsel. It has the virtue that, if tied in a bow or knot, it does not slip. Some Court or Government offices used a sage green version or one which was not dyed.

6 green ferret: narrow finely woven silk ribbon, dyed pea green, used for sewing together the pages of deeds or wills.

7 penknives: for cutting and sharpening quill pens.

8 bodkin: a sharp pointed instrument, with an eye in the point, on a wooden handle, used for sewing deeds and documents with ferret.

A related trade to that of a law stationer was that of a law-writer. The engrossing or copying of legal documents in a 'law hand' may have been done in the law stationer's premises or by outworkers in their own lodgings. From that trade evolved the skilled and responsible business of the law typewriter, or typist, some of whom, incorporated as a company, were still to be found in the lower ground-floor rooms of chambers in New Square adjacent to Serle's Gate in the second half of the C20th.

Editor's notes.

17.d. Charlotte Halliday: The Tomlin Gates, 1995 (e. view) [LT].

17.e. George Belcher: Lord Tomlin, *Punch*, 1929 [Editor's coll.].

17.3. The Tomlin Gates and Railings:

17.3.1. The ironwork

¶ These gates and railings were placed here in 1928 at the expense of Lord Tomlin [of LI] (1867-1935) and remember his son. They provide a boundary to the Kitchen Garden's frontage onto New Square, made necessary by the demolition of the law stationer's shop.

17.3.2. Lord Tomlin

¶ Lord Tomlin, as is indicated by the lines from *Punch*, became Lord of Appeal in 1929. He was a distinguished lawyer and was said by his contemporaries to have been an attractive personality. He dissented in *Donoghue v Stevenson* (1932) in the belief that an independent tort of negligence 'would have alarming consequences', and his judgment in *IRC v Duke of Westminster* (1936) has been much criticised for having regard in taxation matters solely to form and not to substance:

In legal matters only a very few men
Possess the new Law Lord's superb acumen
Nor does his capture of so steep a rise
Cause me, his messmate, any rude surprise,
Who knew his martial gifts that gave its tone
To no. 3 Platoon 'The Devil's Own'.[1]

—Mr Punch's Personalities, XC: Lord Tomlin, in *Punch*, 1929 [Editor's coll.].

[1] 'The Devil's Own': see 43.1.4.

17.4. *The Bog House* and its *Court*; *Base Court*, and *Lincoln's Inn Passage* (now New Square Passage)

¶ The name Base Court was given to the wedge-shaped area to the s. of the Bog House. It was hardly a court in either of the accepted senses—a quadrangle or a passageway. It was not as disparaging a term as might be imagined, being derived from the French *basse-court*. The term is defined by the *OED* as the lower or outer court of a castle or mansion occupied by the servants (as, for example, at Hampton Court) or the court in the rear of a farm-house, containing the outbuildings.

New Square Passage is the name of the footpath at the rear of No. 1, New Square, leading to the accommodation in the lower ground floor of No. 2—a passage formerly known as Lincoln's Inn Passage.

From peace with the French and war with the Dutch,
From a new mouth which will cost us as much,
And from councils of wits which advise us to such,
Libera nos, Domine.

From Pope and from priests which lead men astray,
From fools that by cheats will be so led away,
From saints that 'Go to the Devil' will pray,
Libera nos, Domine.

From Parliamentsellers elected for ale,
Who sell the weal public to get themselves bail,
And if e'er be dissol'd will die in a jail,
Libera nos, Domine.

—Anon., 'A Litany[1] wrote in a Lincoln's Inn Boghouse',[2] 1672.

> G de F Lord, *Poems on Affairs of State 1640-1714*, 1963.

[1] Litany: During the last quarter of the C17th, parodies upon the Litany of the Church of England were a popular mode for expression of disapproval or dissent: that quoted above being a good example of the genre. From 1670, Charles II pursued a policy of friendship with France, of encouraging Catholicism in England and of having as little as possible to do with Parliament. None of this was popular, and his relations with Louis XIV of France whose territorial ambitions many Englishmen thought should be checked, caused particular suspicion.

17.f. A W Brewer: Base Court (e. view), 1870s in *Pall Mall Magazine* [press cutting, HSLI].

The Bog House is on the l. and the works yard of the Inn on the r. The opening in the perimeter wall is the former Chichester Rents Gate. The tower in the distance is that of St Thomas' church on Breams Buildings, one of four churches in this quarter of London which have since vanished. Its churchyard survives, unmarked.

> Lord Baker of Dorking, *op. cit.*, 1988.

[2] Boghouse: the word is listed in the *OED* as a vulgar (but not an obscene) synonym for privy. The large-scale OS plan of the area published in the late C19th marks 'the Bogs'. There is no implied reference to the character of the adjacent land, as is sometimes mistakenly said in the Inn.

17.g. Jan Maciag: The Bog House, drawn from a photograph taken during the Second World War (n. view) [LT].

The Agreement between the Society and Henry Serle, 1682, stipulated for him to build a new bog house, which—repaired and presumably re-plumbed—is that shown here. The Bog House is the low building on the r., demolished in 1990. The signboard by its r. door reads 'Benchers Only'. There were doors for members, Tenants and Ladies. Across the Court, is the flank wall of the Garden House (see 20.2.).

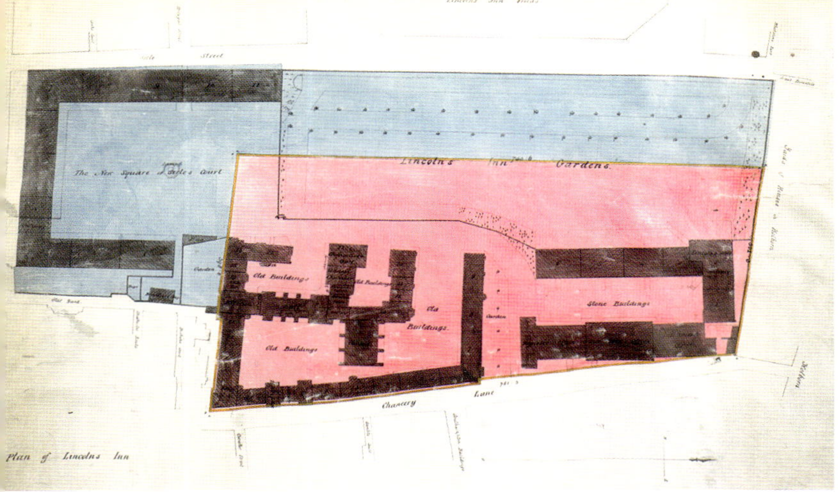

18.a. ? Thomas Clarke: Plan of the Inn, 1770 (detail) [HLSI Archives].
This shows the extent of Stone Buildings, as first built.

'This scene is rendered magnificently by the recently erected edifice, known [as] Stone Buildings: a handsome structure, which was designed by the late Sir Robert Taylor, and is faced with portland stone. It forms only a part of a more spacious design, one wing only at the north end being finished. This wing consists of six corinthian columns, with two pilasters at the angles, supporting a regular entablature and pediment. The basement consists of a rustic arcade[1], which is continued along the whole range of buildings…'

—Samuel Ireland, from *Picturesque Views of the Inns of Court*, 1800.

[1] arcade: this is a reference to the round-headed windows on the ground floor—the most distinctive feature of the façade. The basement storey is in plain brickwork, with rectangular windows. The ground floor is ill-described as rustic: the stonework, although of heavily bevelled blocks, is neither rusticated nor vermiculated. Whatever the detailing, however, its mass and length rank this as probably the most imposing of any chambers building in the four Inns.

18. STONE BUILDINGS (ORIGINALLY *STONE BUILDING COURT*):

18.1. The Stone Building: the Society's chambers for members, in 1-6, *the old Library*, in 2; and the *Plaint Office* in 4:

18.1.1. Their elevations

¶ In 1771, the Society embarked upon an ambitious plan for building new chambers for its members, in conjunction with the provision by the Court of Chancery of new accommodation for the officials of that Court on a strip of land abutting Chancery La., sold by the Society to the Crown. The Society's building programme was to be financed from the proceeds of sale of Thavies Inn (as to which, see 22.1.), as well as from the customary taking of premia on the granting of leases for lives. Robert Adam, James Payne, Matthew Brittingham and Robert (later Sir Robert) Taylor were invited to submit plans and elevations. The Society's choice fell upon Taylor, whose elevations were perhaps the most chaste and unadorned, and are depicted in several illustrations here, and both analysed and evoked in 19. below. Of the unsuccessful designs, Payne's and Brittingham's are preserved in the Library of the Inn, and those of Adam in the Soane Museum. Adam's, the elevations of whose buildings are not reproduced here, would have been the most decorative: the exteriors eminently worthy of a ducal seat in the shires.

18.b.i. Samuel Ireland: 'The Stone Buildings', watercolour *ca.* 1799 (n.e. view) [YCBA].
This is the preparatory watercolour for the corresponding etching in his *Picturesque Views of the Inns of Court*, 1800. The tree to the r. (that is to the s.w.) of the Buildings conceals the unfinished s. end. The Library was on the ground floor of No. 2, on the left, beneath the pediment. Between the trees, in the background—out of scale and mistakenly showing a pediment (instead of a balustrade)—is what is now named and numbered 9 & 8, Stone Buildings, and to the r. is the end of the former Garden Row.

18.b.ii. The façade of the RSA {RSA}.
Adam's inventions are not entirely lost to London. The distinctive Venetian window, set in the pedimented façade of the Royal Society of Arts (of which Adam was a member) still standing in John Adam St., reproduced here, is closely modelled on the Chancery La. frontage of the identical n. and s. pavilions of his proposed Court offices. Then, in 1775, John Crunden copied that design for the façade of Boodle's Club in St James's St., which also still stands.

18.c. F Nugent: Stone Buildings, watercolour (s.e. view), 1822 [MoL].

A corresponding view to that of Samuel Ireland. The gable-ends shown beyond Stone Buildings are those of Garden Row and Chapel Court.

'One of the best examples of Palladianism in a public building in London, built entirely of Portland stone, with a two-storey rusticated base, above which are two plain storeys topped by a cornice and open balustrade. The west front to Lincoln's Inn Gardens is impressively restrained, and the ends are articulated by projecting pedimented pavilions with giant Corinthian columns.'

—Edward Jones and Christopher Woodward, from *The Architecture of London*, 1983.

¶ The plans envisaged a much larger-scale rebuilding than occurred, extending s. to the Chapel. Had they been completed as designed, they would have borne favourable comparison with the slightly later King's Inns in Dublin. Taylor's designs included elements which would have been innovative in England for the construction of professional or Governmental buildings:

'…a set of chambers… which was to be of prodigious length with the lateral corridor running the full length of the buildings and linking all the chambers in each storey (unlike Chambers' contemporary offices at Somerset House which were largely conceived as a form of conventional terrace house plan). However, this ambitious scheme was not completed.'

—Dan Cruickshank, from *A Guide to the Georgian Buildings of Britain & Ireland*, 1985.

'In 1775, Taylor started to build Stone Buildings… The block towards the Benchers' garden is an unusual composition for a Palladian, consisting of a mass terminated by porticoed pavilions but with no central emphasis whatever. The explanation may be that a third portico was envisaged on a southward extension. On the other hand, Taylor favoured this composition elsewhere and there may be an association with Gabriel's recent palaces in the Place de la Nation at Paris. Taylor's last works include… Heveningham, Suffolk, where the pavilion theme of Stone Buildings reappears…'

—Sir John Summerson, from *The Pelican History of Art: Architecture in Britain 1530-1830*, 1991.

'In the design of Stone Buildings the medieval courtyard has been left behind, even more than with New Square. Viewed from between the two ranges of Stone Buildings it is a London street, but viewed from the garden it is somewhere between a Palladian country house and a government building such as Somerset House.'

—Robert Fookes [of LI] and Richard Wallington [of LI], from Angela Holdsworth and others, *A Portrait of Lincoln's Inn*, 2007.

18.d. Hanslip Fletcher: Stone Buildings Court (n. view) in his *Changing London*, 1925 [GL].

This drawing shows the full extent of what is now called, and numbered, Stone Buildings. As indicated above, 'the Stone Building' was the accurate name for the Society's premises to the w. (on the l.), and n. (at the end), of this courtyard. Those on the r. were separately named, as noted below, and erected with public funds for court offices. Now the name 'Stone Buildings' attaches to all of the chambers around this court, and the space within it.

18.1.2. The view from their chambers

'He had a large pleasant room in which to sit, looking out from the ground floor of Stone Buildings on to the gardens belonging to the Inn—and here in the centre of the metropolis, but in perfect quiet as far as the outside world was concerned, he had lived and still lived his life.'

—Anthony Trollope, from *The Prime Minister*, 1875.

> David Palfreyman, *op. cit.*, 2011.

'In the year's round, dusky mornings are the happiest to rise early in, when a south-west wind is driving river scents up the shelving Thames bank. The lamps in Stone Buildings court are making a pattern on my wall or may be just put out. I can step to the level of the balustrade and see St Paul's like an old woman in a shawl crouched dimly in the rain or humped against the breaking sky. There is about me the murmurous calm which passes for silence in a great city and can bear at that early hour certain sounds and still be silence: the swish of branches and birds awakening in the dim garden, doves roohooing about the chapel walls, the horn of a boat. As I wander from room to room the world takes form about me. Then I must be at the garden window again, spying out the ancient high walk through leafless trees, or in summer watching the shadows creep along the sward. At such moments I must always feel a debt unpayable to past and present in Lincoln's Inn.

According to their temper, people are attracted or repelled by the fortress-like enclosure of the Stone Buildings walls. I had chambers in an upper floor, and only after I had left that house for one in the square did I find from chance reading that my true address had been The Fourth Attic in the Stone Building. If ever a benevolent fate should redirect my steps thither, I shall have notepaper ready. At what date, by what error the Stone Building changed its name, adding a letter and losing a grace, I have not been able to find.

There is an aloofness to be felt in those balustraded chambers that dwellers in other parts of the Inn cannot know. The world is far away, down some eighty-eight steps. Light enters the broad rooms through a frieze of glass set high in the wall, so high that you must have a gallery built, and steps, to take you to the pane. It is a lodging for bookmen upon whose peace only the birds and the stars can spy. You may sport many an oak; there are two doors to each opening in the main walls, one on either face; whatever extreme of weather may assault one side of the house you are saved from it on the other by this barricade. If the Stone Building had been planned in an earlier century I might have suspected the Benchers of contriving a number of Little Eases for the young gentlemen of the Inn whose conduct at times was such as to be "utterly misliked".'

—Margaret Ashworth, from 'On living in Lincoln's Inn', in *Cornhill Magazine*, 1930 [an off-print, HSLI].

18.1.3. William Pitt, the younger, PM

¶ William Pitt, the younger [of LI], PM (1759-1806) had chambers in No. 4, Stone Buildings. He ranks as one of the nation's greatest war leaders, and was the King's chief minister almost continuously from 1784 (when he became the youngest such in English history) to the date of his death, having been broken by the burdens of office—the strain of dealing with the King, with his political colleagues and rivals, and of conducting the war against France. He survived to rejoice in the victory of Trafalgar, 1805, but was prostrated by the defeat at Austerlitz later in the same year.

Four of the verse panegyrics to him by some of the greatest writers of his age are quoted here:

Pitt is to Addington as London is to Paddington.

—George Canning [of LI], PM.

Henry Addington, first Viscount Sidmouth (1757-1844), succeeded Pitt as PM in 1801, and held office until, in 1804, Pitt returned.

18.e. Karl Anton Hickel: 'William Pitt addressing the House of Commons on the French declaration of war', 1793 [NPG].

Pitt was admitted in 1777, called in 1780 and practised in 1780-1, before entering Parliament and devoting himself exclusively to politics and government. He progressed through all of the offices of the Society, becoming Treasurer in 1794, and at Westminster became one of the greatest prime ministers, both as a parliamentarian and as a war leader against the forces of the French Revolution and Napoléon I. Other Lincoln's Inn men to be seen in this painting are George Canning, Thomas Erskine and Henry Addington.

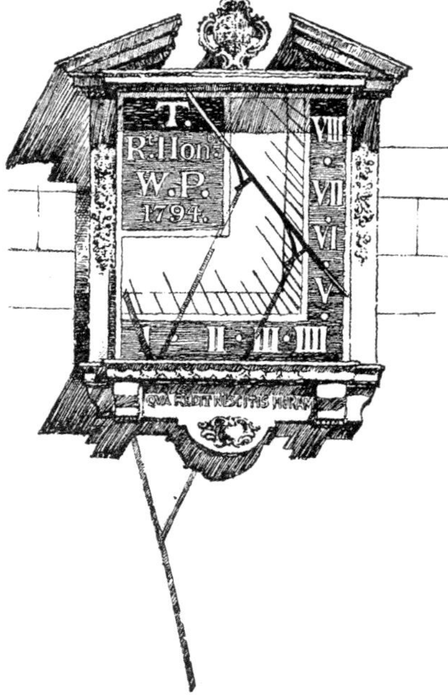

SUNDIAL, LINCOLN'S INN

18.f. E L Wratten: The 'William Pitt' sundial on Stone Buildings, in P H Ditchfield, *London Survivals*, 1914 [GL].

This is the only surviving sundial of several which once told the time in the Inn. Its origin is in 1757, when it was placed on the w. end of 9, Old Buildings (Garden Row). It was repainted in 1794, with the reference to Pitt, who was then Treasurer. When, as noted elsewhere, Garden Row was demolished in the early 1880s, the dial was moved to its present position, on the building where Pitt had had his chambers. The Latin ('You know not the hour when He returns') is a reference to *Luke* 12:40, but has been irreverently rendered as 'he is out to lunch, and it is not certain when he will be back'.

. . . the Pilot that weather'd the storm.

—George Canning [of LI], PM.

Now is the stately column broke
The beacon light is quenched in smoke
The trumpet's silver sound is still
The Warden silent on the hill.

—Sir Walter Scott.

Remember the man who in sorrow and danger,
When thy glory was set, and thy spirit was low,
When thy hopes were o'erturned by the arms of the stranger,
And thy banners displayed in the halls of the foe,

Stood forth in the tempest of doubt and disaster,
Unaided, and single, the danger to brave,
Asserted thy claims, and the rights of his master,
Preserved thee to conquer, and saved thee to save.

—Thomas, Lord Macaulay [of LI].

18.2. *Offices of the Courts* in *Stone Building Court*:

¶ The plan to construct Stone Buildings Court—and to do so on a more monumental scale than other chambers built before in any of the four Inns of Court—was significantly helped by the inclusion of offices of the Court of Chancery on the Chancery La. side, built at Government expense, on land which the Crown purchased from the Inn. There had long been thoughts of removing some or all of the offices of Chancery into the Inn. Two such earlier proposals may be mentioned:

Narcissus Luttrell's *Diary* for 1692 records that Nicholas Barbon (the developer associated with Serle Court) 'hath undertaken to pull down the Six Clerks' Office… and build a new one on arches in the new square adjoining Lincoln's Inn' (i.e. Serle's Court, now New Square).

Cavendish Weedon is reported in John Strype's *Survey*, 1720, as having proposed:

'the erection of a beautiful Range of Building, to be only one Story, without Chimneys, and to be covered flat with Lead, all along by the dead Wall, on the East side of Lincolns Inn Garden, upon the waste Ground between the said Wall and the Gravel Walk, for the use of some, or all the Offices of Chancery, viz. The Six Clerks, The Cursitors, The Masters of Chancery, The Examiners, The Petty Bag, The Registers, The Affidavit, The Hamper and the Subpoena.

The Reasons offered for this Erection, were, that the said Building would be much more secure and ornamental to the said Garden and all the Chambers in the same; defending them from Robbery, and the Dust and Noise of the next adjoining Street. And a Row of fine, regular Sash Windows would be a much pleasanter Sight on the Ground Rent to the Society. And these Offices would be most conveniently situated, almost in the Centre of the Inns of Court, and Chancery. And the same Offices being thus joined together would be of very great Ease to all the Officers: and also to all Attorneys, Solicitors and Practisers; as well as all other People that should have occasion to resort to the same. Whereby all the Officers might have a mutual Correspondency one with another. And the Situation being healthful, it might contribute not only to the great Ease, but the Health also of the several Officers and their Clerks: Especially those of the Six Clerks Office; who, the greatest Part of the Year, write by Candle Light in the Day time, annoyed with the Smoak and Smell of Candlegrease: and are so many and so near crowded up together in little Boxes.'

18.2.1. *The Record & Writ Office* and *the Register (or Registrar) & Report Office*, in 8-9

¶ These Offices were those through which all proceedings and pleadings in the Court of Chancery were processed, and replaced those of the Six Clerks (and the Sixty Clerks, under them), the Sworn Clerks and the Waiting Clerks.

18.g. T H Shepherd: The Record & Writ Office, *Pictorial Times*, 1846 [press cutting, John Johnson coll., Bodleian].

This office was seemingly on the ground floor.

18.h. T H Shepherd: 'The Registrar & Report Office, Court of Chancery', sketch for engraving (matching *18.g.*) in *Pictorial Times*, 1846 [CWA].

It would follow that this office was on the first floor. The figures in the drawing are named.

There were ten Registrars in the Court of Chancery. Their duties in the management of the processes of that Court complemented those of the Office just mentioned, being more concerned with the business in the Court itself. The buildings of both Offices were absorbed into the Inn in 1880, when the business conducted in them was transferred to the RCJ.

18.2.2. *The Office of the Corporation of the Six Clerks*, in 10

'The new Six Clerks Office is a very plain building neatly faced with stone. It has no pretence to praise, as containing no attempt to deserve it. On the Chancery-lane side we are offended at the door, which is not in the centre of the building, and for that reason destroys [its] regularity…'

—James Ralph, from *A Critical Review of the Public Buildings…in and about London and Westminster*, 1783 [BL].

¶ The Six Clerks' Office had previously been situated further down Chancery La., on the same side, the earlier building being noted and depicted in 34.1. Its architectural elevations and details are in harmony with those of the Stone Building, while differing from them, in particular by the one-and-a-half-storey round-headed windows, which once lit the office.

'The Six Clerks had a long run. Their origin is a little obscure, but in the twelfth year of the reign of King Richard II the "sworn officers of the Great Seal and of the Court of Chancery" were well established and their number had increased from three to six. They were "clerk" in the ecclesiastical sense, and an Act of Parliament was necessary to enable them to marry. The passing of the [Act] 14 & 15 Hen. VIII, c. 8, turned the celibate John Trevethan, Richard Welles, Oliver Leader, John Croke, William Jessen and John Lansey into happy husbands. During the Commonwealth an attack was made upon the Six Clerks from which they emerged triumphant. An Order in Council did away with them, substituting for the Six and their underlings three Chief Clerks and sixty "sworn clerks"; but the Commissioners of the Great Seal successfully resisted the Order on the ground that it abolished a freehold office without compensation. Their office having become ruinous, the existing handsome building was erected in the "ancient garden" of Lincoln's Inn, and the Six Clerks moved into it in 1776. The [Act] 28 Vict., c. 48, passed after their abolition, permitted the Benchers of Lincoln's Inn to repurchase the building upon repaying the money they had received for their land. The report of the Chancery Commissioners in 1826 was the undoing of the Six Clerks. One of them, Mr Francis Vesey, gave evidence which made it clear that their duties were inconsiderable and their emoluments more than sufficient. They had to see, said Mr Vesey, that bills, answers and records were fairly engrossed and properly stamped; they signed copies of the pleadings if they were wanted; one of them attended each day during the sittings of the Court of Chancery, except on the first day, when two presented themselves. The year was divided between them, each of the Six Clerks taking a period of two months; but if difficult questions of practice arose, it was their habit to meet together and discuss them. When invited to particularize the problems so discussed, Mr Vesey was unable to specify either the occasions or the subjects of debate. He was, however, satisfied that the office he held was one which should be filled by persons of a "certain rank and estimation in society." The [Act] 3 and 4 Will. IV, c. 94, enacted that future vacancies in the body should not be filled up, and by the [Act] 5 & 6 Vict., c. 103, the Six Clerks were finally abolished together with their assistants, the latter statute very properly providing that the Clerk of the Emoluments or his deputy, the Comptroller of the Hanaper, the Six Clerks, the Riding Clerk, the Sworn Clerk and the Waiting Clerk should receive "just and reasonable compensation." From Mr Vesey's evidence it appeared that the stipend of each of the Six Clerks was, in his day, about £750 a year. It had become more considerable in 1842 when the time for compensation arrived. Thereafter the Six Clerks' Office had fresh tenants. When Mr Street's Royal Courts of Justice were at last completed, its oak decorations and the accumulated records were removed to that building.'

—Theo. Mathew [of LI], from *For Lawyers and Others*, 1937.

18.2.3. *The Inrolment (or Enrolment) Office of Chancery,* and *the Accountant-General's Office*, in 11

¶ 'The office of the Accountant-General of the Court of Chancery was established in 1725, with an account at the Bank of England, in order *inter alia*, to handle cash and securities referable to suits in that Court, i.e. 'funds in court'. The office was abolished in 1872 and the functions absorbed into those of the Paymaster-General.

The extract below records the experience of a member of the public in visiting the Accountant-General's Office.

'I was hurried into action… & obliged to present myself… for the first time in my long life, in a Court of Law—the most imposing, in every way, in the kingdom, where to abide by what I heard, & to acquiesce in what I was bid do, sign, & pay, &… there to find myself, happy things were no worse, & thankful to get away… Just after my return from Twickenham… a letter came by the post… What was my surprise to read a summons from Messrs Clayton Scott & Clayton, to attend in person at Lincoln's Inn, to receive Mr Devayre's Legacy, before 2.00 o'clock on forfeiture of the same. It was now one—I had not a moment to ponder, or ask advice; I thought of Charles Parr & I knew your disaffection to Law & all its chicaneries: these Messrs also, had written me positive word that the demise of the acting executor without a Will rendered the Legacy null. What would this change mean?… Ordering a King's Chariot, I bid the postillion gallup with all speed to the Court of Chancery. I resolved, as I drove on, to ask frankly for the costs & should I find them such as Charles Parr represented, to withdraw, formally, our claim… And I set myself above the ridicule of not being conducted, as is usual, by a Lawyer, & made Ramsay, who had been there before, lead the way to Messrs Clayton. We alighted in Lincoln's Inn, & had to parade sundry courts, avenues, passages, archways & squares, most of them formed of stone structures of awful & gloomy grandeur, & wherein the desolate appearance of being nearly uninhabited, except by sundry busy clerks, & here & there some perambulating Advocates or Attorneys, with Briefs, parchments, velums & written Documents, hanging over their arms. But—as if all this was not enough to impress me, Ramsay presently called out "Oh look, ma'am There's the Lord Chancellor" &, crossing a small court to gain an open corridor, the Lord Chancellor, in his robes & enormous wig, was just before us. We then traversed various passages & staircases, till we met with a Clerk who pointed me the door of Messrs Clayton Scott & Clayton's Chambers. No one asked my name, nor offered to conduct me. I felt a little queer but would not be discouraged. My greatest difficulty was how I should make known who I was; & that, all at once showed me the propriety of a client's being accompanied by a lawyer. However, this occurred too late for any change, all my alarm being lest the Clock should strike 2 ere I was in presence. This fear helps me to exertion, &… I entered the inner & larger room, of which the door was open, & determined to behave like a man—being my first appearance in that character. A Gentleman in Black was looking over papers at a Desk, standing & with an air of arranging them for being gone; & a Clerk was writing at another Desk in a corner. He had very much the air of a gentleman, although he was so intently occupied, that he neither looked towards me, nor seem to perceive that anyone had appeared. This was rather awkward. I stood still a minute or two, & then, not willing to risk interrupting some calculation, yet

18.i. Drawing of the commemorative medal by John Kirk, issued by the Six Clerks to commemorate the completion of their Office (depicted on the reverse of the medal) in 1776, and in honour of the then Lord Chancellor Bathurst [of LI] (depicted on the obverse) [LMA].

OFFICE OF THE ACCOUNTANT-GENERAL, CHANCERY LANE.

18.j. Office of the Accountant-General, Chancery Lane, 1846 (n.w. view) *Illustrated London News* [*ILN*PL].

The office is at the n. end (to the r.) of the building with the round-headed windows. A line drawing (not reproduced here) by Emslie of the 1880s (when he was executing a number of views of the Inn), now in the CLHL, shows an intermediate stage, with an extra storey on 9, but not on 11.

The drawing of the office, published in the *ILN* was prompted by the fact that it had, in the words of the accompanying article, 'of late been the focus of considerable attention, from its being the receptacle of the millions of money as Railway deposits…'

not thoroughly satisfied with this mode of waiting his leisure, I quickly looked for the handsomest chair in the room, & composedly took possession of it. Upon this, he raised his Eyes. I then presented him my Letter, saying "Mr Clayton, I suppose?"—he bowed, took it, offered me another seat, proposed shutting the window if I feared the air, & gave me the pleasure of finding that I retain, what my dear father often loved to call it, An Honest Face; for he made no sort of enquiry, demanding no manner of identification, but went to his Documents, my letter in his hand, with as firm a conviction that I was I, as if he had known me all his life, & all my Parentage & kin… But while waiting until he should no longer seem too busy for interruption without impertinence, all on the sudden he darted to me, with a pen ready dipt in jet in his hand, and placing a paper on a Table before me, with a manner and look gravely polite, but in a voice that spoke to him accustomed to dispense with any reply, he gave me the Pen, and pointed to a spot on which he desired me to write my Name… My solicitor, clapping my paper into a small portfolio, which he grasped with his left hand, and clapping abruptly his hat upon his head, uttered these alarming words "Please to go with me, now, Ma'am, to the Accomptant General." The Accomptant General? thought I; what kind of a Badinage is this for a modicum of only five guineas without the partition? & then Taxes—Deductions—Fees. I hesitated whether I should comply; but he led the way, quitting the room with a quick pace even while speaking. If I go not, however, thought I, I may be fined for Contempt of Court—this suggestion forced me forward… I now hoped I should obtain an opportunity for my long intended harangue, by his entering into some conversation: but his politeness extended no further than in adopting my pace; for mouth he opened not. This was as new to me as all the rest, having never, that I remember, in my life, begun an attack; having always myself been addressed or remained silent; but I was Now upon Ground where, probably a Word and a Fee are one I did not, however, think of that till this moment; but soon finding I had nothing to gain by my taciturnity but it's reciprocity, I resolved to put in & to it. Which I did, by begging leave to enquire who was the Accomptant General? "Sir John Campbell," he answered. "Oh—I have not the pleasure to know him," quoth I. But not a syllable further uttered my Guide. This won't do thought I; I must come to the point more plumply. "Give me leave, sir," I said, "to ask whether my signature will be accepted, or hold good, for my absent sister, Mrs Burney, who resides at Bath, and could not, for such a trifle, be brought to town?" "Perfectly ma'am," he replied. "But I have written only for myself, sir, without naming her; and she is joint residuary legatee." "Your signature is all that is requisite, ma'am". Is this a hoax? thought I, or what does it mean? Total silence, however, ensued; till, seen, by numerous persons passing and re-passing into a handsome stone building that we were approaching our place of destination, I again assailed him, & more pointedly; growing really anxious to know whether there was not some error in the whole matter. "I have been seldom, sir," I said, "more surprised than by your letter, for I had received one, many months ago, to let me know that the Executor having died intestate, the legacy became null." "And such, madam," he now replied, "is the legal fact. The legacy is lapsed: but as it is for so small a Sum, no advantage has been taken of that accident, and I am directed to pay it to you." I now became a little comforted; but I was dying to ask by whom directed, as there appeared, in the all together of the affair, something mysterious. I had no sooner, however, answered, eagerly "That is very generous—and I feel very much obliged—and who ever complains of the Law and of Lawyers, I must stand forth to praise & laud them," than he quite unbent his Chancery Brow, & said, with a smile "Ma'am, your Legacy will now amount to £9. 11s., as interest upon interest has very nearly doubled it." A greater surprise, I think, never came upon me that this speech produced… However, we entered—mounted the stairs—and saw there the Accomptant General, seated at a immense Table, with clerks and writer under his command in great abundance, and several clients in waiting, and new ones entering every moment; it all so silent, so orderly, so awfully under subjection, that the Accomptant's voice alone was heard in that vast chamber, every reply being made in humble whispering. Mr Clayton went up to him; What passed no one could hear but the Accomptant: Mr Clayton, however, soon made me a motion to approach; I advanced: a paper again was placed before me to sign: after which, the Accomptant put into my hand a Draft on the East India House for £9. 11. 0.—Mr Clayton asked me whether I had four & sixpence. I said yes. "Give it to me, then, ma'am, & I will save you the trouble to call again to pay your costs. They amount to 4s. & 6d." I stared, really not believing my ears: but Mr Clayton abruptly disappeared. I looked at the Draft, and could not forbear ejaculating "I am very much surprised, indeed—and very much obliged—though I do not know to whom" The Accomptant turned quick round to look at me, with a pleased laugh; all the rest smiled… and I gracefully retired. Thus, my dear Esther, I have incurred you a debt of 2s. 3d. which I shall meanly deduct from your £4. 15s. 6d. in paying only £4. 13s. 3d. to your steward Edward.'

—Fanny Burney (Mme. d'Arblay), from Letter to Miss Esther Burney at Bath, 3rd September 1821 [Editor's transcription from the MS in the Berg Collection, NYCPL].

¶ This quotation offers the perspective of an office-holder:

'It was certainly a melancholy place, that signing-office, in which Mr John Vavasor was doomed to spend twelve hours a week, during every term time, of his existence. Whether any man could really pass an existence of work in such a workshop, and not have gone mad,—could have endured to work there for seven hours a day, every week-day of his life, I am not prepared to say. I doubt much whether any victims are so doomed. I have so often wandered through those gloomy passages without finding a sign of humanity there,—without hearing any slightest tick of the hammer of labour, that I am disposed to think that Lord Chancellors have been anxious to save their subordinates from suicide, and have mercifully decreed that the whole staff of labourers, down to the very message boys of the office, should be sent away to green fields or palatial clubs during, at any rate, a moiety of their existence…

The building in which Mr John Vavasor had a room and a desk… was called the Accountant-General's Record Office, and very probably, in the gloom of its dark cellars, may lie to this day the records of the expenditure of many a fair property which has gotten itself into Chancery, and has never gotten itself out again…

Up the stone stairs, from this hall, John Grey passed to Mr Vavasor's signing-room…

It was a large, dull room, which could not have been painted, I should think, within the memory of man, looking out backwards into some court. The black wall of another building seemed to stand up close to the window,—so close that no direct ray of the sun ever interrupted the signing-clerk at his work. In the middle of the room there was a large mahogany table, on which lay a pile of huge papers. Across the top of them there was placed a bit of blotting-paper, with a quill pen, the two only tools which were necessary to the performance of the signing-clerk's work. On the table there stood a row of official books, placed lengthways on their edges: the 'Post-Office Directory', the 'Court Circular', a 'Directory to the Inns of Court', a dusty volume of Acts of Parliament, which had reference to Chancery accounts,—a volume which Mr Vavasor never opened; and there were some others; but there was no book there in which any Christian man or woman could take delight, either for amusement or for recreation. There were three or four chairs round the wall, and there was the one arm-chair which the occupant of the chamber had dragged away from its sacred place to the hearth-rug. There was also an old Turkey carpet on the floor. Other furniture there was none.'

—Anthony Trollope, from *Can you forgive her?*, 1864.

18.2.4. *The Masters' Chambers* and *the Pleas Office of the Court of Exchequer*, in 7 (formerly in *8 & 9, Old Buildings*)

¶ What is now 7, Stone Buildings, the imposing s. end of the w. range of those buildings, was not included in the construction of the 1770s, through lack of funds. In 1845, Hardwick finished the building, with a pediment on its w. front, and a parapet on its e., to complete Taylor's classical design, and in striking contrast to his own Victorian-Tudor buildings which were going up at the same time. The Pleas Office of

18.k. T H Shepherd : 'New Chambers and Exchequer Court, Lincoln's Inn', *ca.* 1845 (n.e. view of 7, Stone Buildings) [HSLI].

the [Court of] Exchequer had been housed in 8 & 9, Old Buildings but, with the Masters of that Court, was provided with more modern and spacious accommodation here. These offices left the Inn, *ca.* 1880. This building now houses counsel's chambers. For some years in the late C20th, it accommodated a coffee bar for those studying or practising in the Inn to which the name 'Briefs' was given. An alternative suggestion had been 'Refreshers'.

18.3. *The Officers' Training Corps* (now the Inns of Court and City & Essex Yeomanry: the ICCEY), in 10 (the former *Six Clerks' Office*)

- See 43.1.5: the Volunteers in and after the First World War

18.m. Francis G Reeves: 'Stone Buildings and the Library', 1984 (w. view) {Robin Redsull, RIBA}.

An interesting juxtaposition of architectural styles by Philip Hardwick—the part of Stone Buildings shown being that constructed for the Court of Exchequer.

18.l. Thomas Cowlishaw: The Garden front of Stone Buildings (s.e. view), ? *ca.* 1890 [coll. PHB].

A watercolour with the rare view of the full length of the building, thus showing the two pedimented pavilions of which the s. was built, as noted here, in the 1840s.

19. DOORWAYS AND STAIRCASES, FIREPLACES AND CHIMNEYS, AND CURTAINS:

19.1. Some doorways and staircases

¶ Sets of chambers in the Inns of Court traditionally were built on the staircase model, in common with those in the colleges of Oxford and Cambridge. Each staircase had a pair of self-contained sets of rooms opening off it at each floor (unless a turret, containing a spiral staircase, where there would be one only). These tended, often if not always, to be called 'sets' at the universities, and 'chambers' in the Inns.

Customarily the staircase led, at ground or upper ground level, straight from the front doorway, which usually had no door. Each set of chambers, however, had its own front door in the form of an outer door (or 'oak', even if of pine) opening outwards onto the stairs, as well as a second door, opening inwards. This distinctive layout was well suited to the way of practising and living of the Bar in the times in which it was devised and developed. It is interesting to compare the very different internal design of, for example, Bedford Row houses and New Square chambers: both dating from the building boom after the Great Fire, put up through the influence of the same developer, Nicholas Barbon, and creating at first sight a not dissimilar effect as a street-scape. There is no ornamental plaster-work on Lincoln's Inn staircases (as there is in Bedford Row) nor are the doorcases within the Inn ornamented with carving as they were outside it. One of the most outstanding carved wooden door-hoods and -frames of C18th London, now preserved in the Victoria and Albert Museum, came from a Carey St. house just a few paces outside the Inn: it could not have come from *within*. The doorways and stairs of the Inn have attracted the interest of artists and architects, for the sake of their diversity, if not their ornamentation, and representations of a few of them appear here.

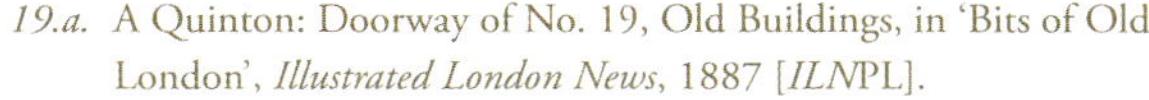

19.a. A Quinton: Doorway of No. 19, Old Buildings, in 'Bits of Old London', *Illustrated London News*, 1887 [*ILN*PL].

The small sketch serves to represent the spiral staircases of which there were once at least *eight* in Old Square and Old Buildings, both clockwise (as this one) and anti-clockwise in design. Indeed, there could have been a further *five*, set into the fronts of 4 and 5, Chancery La. Row and 7, 8, and 9, Garden Row.

19.b. Charlotte Halliday: 'New Square, Lincoln's Inn', 1996 [coll. PHB].

The doorway is of the typical New Square design, of the 1680s-90s, i.e. having a curved, broken pediment with a ball in the centre. This might be seen as baroque, in contrast to the triangular pediment, which might be seen as 'Georgian' and of which the later No.10 is an example.

19.c. Annabel Wilson: i. 6, Stone Buildings, ii. 13, Old Square, and iii. 22, Old Buildings, 1993 [coll. PHB] {the artist}.

'Each house, consisting of several sets of chambers, is ascended by a common staircase in the manner of the houses at Paris and Edinburgh; and each set of chambers usually occupies a floor…'

—W Herbert, *op. cit.*, 1804.

'…grubby mansions—as big and cheerless-looking as barracks—every one of them being destitute of doors, and having a string of names painted in stripes upon the door-posts, that reminds one of the lists displayed at an estate-agent's office.'

—Henry Mayhew and John Binney, *op. cit.*, 1862.

19.2. Some fireplaces and chimneys

¶ The chimneys of the former and surviving C16th-17th chambers in Old Buildings were or are idiosyncratic, being additions of contemporary or later date implanted on the fronts of the buildings, whether vertically ground-to-roof, or beginning above ground level and meandering over the external walls to avoid window openings. These features arose, it may be surmised, from a combination of circumstances: the absence or insufficiency of fireplaces installed when the chambers were built; the unavailability of the enclosed heating stoves of northern continental Europe; the legal framework of long 'leases for lives' by which many chambers were occupied, which perhaps encouraged individual projects of improvement; and there being no back yard to many of the chambers in which a chimney of later date could have been hidden from view. Several of the watercolours and drawings reproduced in this book show also the elongated chimney pots, cowls and weather-vanes needed to make these chimneys serviceable, and an iron rod embedded into the chimney stack, to hold it steady.

The chimneys in other parts of the Inn were not idiosyncratic in the same way, but nonetheless were vulnerable to the elements.

The repair and rebuilding of chimneys of chambers in the Inn will have been a constant labour over the centuries, testified by numerous references in *The Black Books*. The pieces which follow are reminders of the recurring conflict with the weather.

'In this Mausoleum lieth the body of Robert Michell late of Lincolns Inn and Savile Street London, and also of this parish… And who was most miraculously preserv'd by the providence of Almighty God from

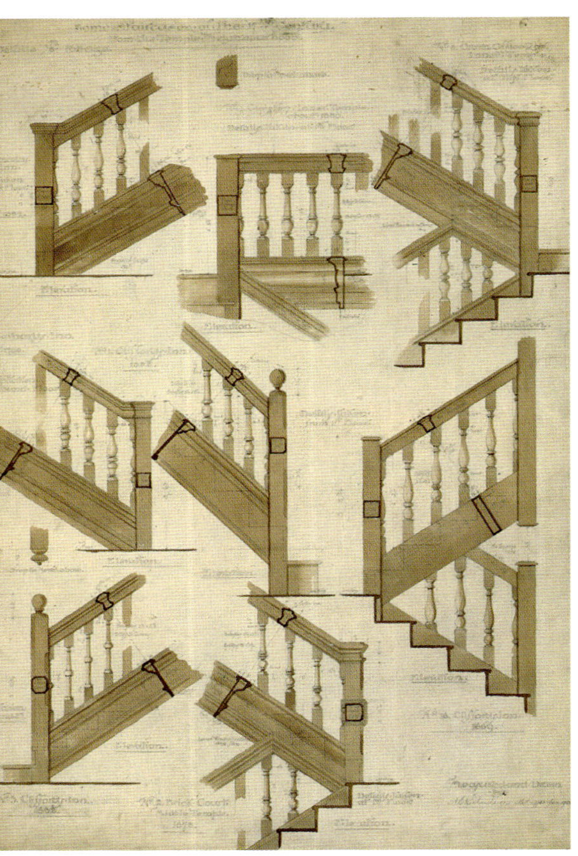

19.e. John Crowther: Jacobean chimney-piece, in 13, New Square, 1881 [LMA].

This elaborate chimney-piece still exists, but with the Victorian 'register plate' fireplace altered.

19.d. Sir Albert Richardson, PPRIBA: 'Some staircases of the C17th from The Temple & Neighbourhood', *ca.* 1895 [V&A].

This fine piece of draftsmanship illustrates the varied detailing in the joinery of oak staircases built in three of the Inns, during the major building programme there, in the thirty years after the Great Fire. Sketch 7 is of New Square. Richardson, a distinguished late Victorian architect, had a studio in New Square—as did others of note: C F A Voysey and Sir Charles Nicholson.

19.f. Rococo plasterwork in the overmantle to a fireplace in 1, New Square: photograph G Rodrigues [LT].

The style suggests an embellishment of *ca.* 1750 to a fireplace of *ca.* 1690.

great peril and danger of his life to which he was exposed, by the fall of a stack of ten chimneys into his chamber in his Inn, and on his bed, when in it, in the late violent storm of wind which happened about six o'clock in the morning on Fryday the 2d of December 1763, and departed this life the 17th day of March in the 65 year of his age 1779.'

—Monumental inscription in the parish church of All Saints, Chitterne, Wiltshire.

> David Long [solicitor formerly in LI].

'23rd December. Between four and five o'clock in the morning, a violent storm blew from the south-west, attended with successive flashes of lightning, and continued rolls of loud thunder, succeeded by heavy showers of hail and rain. Part of the copper roofing of the new stone buildings in Lincoln's-inn was blown over the six clerks' office into Chancery-lane, and some part of it over the roofs of the opposite houses in the land, into a yard, and part passed through a garret window of one of those houses, inhabited by Mr White; so that it must have been raised near a hundred feet into the air. Thirteen trees were blown down in Lincoln's-inn gardens. A maid servant of counsellor Graham's was killed in her bed, by the falling of a stack of chimnies, at his chambers on the south side of Lincoln's-inn New-square: his man-servant fortunately escaped, by quitting his bed on the first alarm.'

—from *The Annual Register*, 1790.

> Vol. IV, *The Black Books*.

19.g. C F A Voysey: drawing of iron fireplace of the same design (with the distinctive heart and bird *motif*) as that fitted in his studio in 10, New Square, early C20th, in Wendy Hitchmough, *CFA Voysey*, 1995.

19.h. J P Emslie: The chimneys of 19, Old Buildings being rebuilt, 1880s [CLHL].

One of the two tall, unsupported chimneys visible in Constance Potts' view of 1897 has been taken down to be rebuilt.

19.i. Dorothy Thomas: The chimneys of Old Square, 1990 (w. view of 11, 12 & 13, with 8 & 9 in background) {the artist}.

The exuberance and fine detailing of the Victorian-Tudor chimneys (designed to extract coal smoke, and perhaps also a little hot air) on the Scott buildings cannot be fully appreciated from the ground. The design is modelled on Hampton Court. Dr John Goodall, in his *The English Castle*, 2011, observed that ornate chimneys such as these are a particularly English style of building. This view is taken from an upper floor of a building, not part of the Inn, on the e. side of Chancery La.

19.3. Some curtains and textiles in chambers, five centuries apart

¶ An extract from a letter addressed to Lady Lisle, dated 27th January 1534/5, from her agent, John Husee, concerning one of her kinsmen, John Bassett, admitted as a student of the Inn, at the age of seventeen, on 6th February, 1534/5:

'My humble duty premised unto your good Ladyship…

Madam, Mr Basset came hither the xxvjth of this month, who shall continue here till the morrow after Candlemas Day. And then, God willing, he shall enter his chamber at Lincoln's Inn… More he hath brought with him a feather bed, bolster, blankets, counterpoint[1] and ij pair of sheets. He must have another bed furnished with a pillow, tester, saye[2] or other, with curtains.

If your ladyship may send me iij or iiij more with the next it would ease well to pay for much of the premised, which will cost xx mark at the least. I shall, as much as in me lieth, see him ordered accordingly, and see also that he lack nothing, with the best service that I can do him, as I am bound to do for your ladyship and all yours. Trusting to have your answer shortly… I would gladly know your ladyship's pleasure in the premises speedily, as God knoweth, who preserve your ladyship in long life with honour to your most heart's aggradation.

From London, the xxviijth in January,

To your ladyship most bounden,

John Husee'

¶ An extract from a further such letter, dated 7th February 1534/5:

'My humble duty to your good ladyship premised… where your good ladyship wrote that you sent ij pieces of red say and green, those pieces which was packed with the other stuff are yellow and green; and as far as I can perceive iij pieces more will scant trim up Mr Basset's chamber, for it is very large; and it shall be necessary your ladyship send the said say with speed, for till it come his chamber cannot well be trimmed. Also it shall be necessary your ladyship send a coffer to keep his apparel, and another for his sheets and linen.

At London the vijth day of February,

By him that is wholly your ladyship's during life, John Husee'

---

1 counterpoint: counterpane.

2 saye: a fine twill woollen cloth, from the s.w. of England.

> Muriel St Clair Byrne, *The Lisle Letters*, 1981.

¶ For a few years, during the First World War, the distinguished architect and designer C F A Voysey (1857-1941) had his drawing-office and studio in a set of chambers on the third floor of 10, New Square.

His creativity in design ranged from architecture and architectural fittings to textiles and wall-papers. Some of his textile designs could be taken to be the work of William Morris (born twenty-three years earlier) but there is a diversity and originality in many of Voysey's designs which are distinctively his.

The designs for textiles would have been intended for curtains and furnishing, to be printed on linen or cotton, or woven for woollen carpets.

One example of his work executed while he was in New Square is shown here, and was signed and dated 1916, and giving the Lincoln's Inn address in the lower right-hand corner. Another such, not reproduced here, was—appropriately for the times—a patriotic design of roses, thistles and shamrocks.

19.j. C F A Voysey: Textile design made at 10, New Square, 1916 [RIBA Architectural Library, V&A].
The date and address are shown in the corner.

20. OTHER CHAMBERS, *OFFICES* AND *SHOPS* IN THE INN, OR OF THE SOCIETY OUTSIDE, OF THE C19TH TO THE C21ST:

20.1. More House (*the Yemen Coffee House*, before incorporation into the Inn), on Carey Street and Serle Street:

20.1.1. The building

¶ This small building is (at the present date) one of the last contiguous freehold expansions of the Inn, having been purchased by the Society in 1924, and now constituting the extreme s.w. corner of the Inn. Since its construction, it has served a diversity of purposes: a coffee house, the Women's Press Club, solicitors' offices and counsel's chambers.

It was evidently designed as, and has served the purpose of, a statement in what might be termed the movement for 'political rehabilitation' in England of More, and in the Cause for his canonisation by Rome. While, at the present day, he enjoys widespread admiration, in past centuries in England (by contrast to the United States) it was otherwise.

The statue, with '*Sir* Thomas More, Lord Chancellor and *Martyr*' incised below it, pre-dates the acquisition by the Society itself of an image of him, in the form of a portrait in oils, a copy of the celebrated one by Holbein in the Frick. The building was commissioned by a solicitor, George Arnold, who was a Roman Catholic. The major public statue of More in London, outside Chelsea (Old) Parish Church, dates only from 1969. This is the sole outdoor statute of a member of the Society in the Inn—and that accidentally for the reason just given. The first of the modern biographies of More by the Rev T E Bridgett—a significant step in the Cause—was published three years after the completion of this building. There is no suggestion (as is sometimes mistakenly said) that More ever lived in a house or in chambers on this site.

'Here we have certain restrictive conditions as regards the site and its surroundings, which have given Mr Sherrin, the architect, his opportunity. That he has made the most of it we think all will agree.

Though almost the most diminutive building in Carey Street, "The Yemen Coffee-House" is at the same time one of the most conspicuous. Surrounded on two of its sides by the commonest of common types of tall red brick houses, it has for near neighbours Mr Street's Law Courts (facing the front elevation), and Mr Waterhouse's big red terra-cotta business premises[1] (facing the end elevation). Yet such is the robust vigour and character of Mr Sherrin's design that the diminutive coffee house loses nothing by contrast with its imposing neighbours, whilst the background of grimy brick dwellings serves but to emphasize its architectural quality.

The restriction as to height has been made to serve the purpose of still more clearly individualizing the general character of the building, and it has been treated with a sturdy breadth, which makes it a distinctive and attractive design, even alongside the adjoining larger works of Street and Waterhouse. Our view of the exterior pretty well describes what we see from the street. The ground floor front is built of Portland stone, well enriched with carving, which by the way, is particularly good of its kind. The first and second floor fronts are of red brick...'

—from 'Street Architecture' in *The British Architect*, 13th September, 1889.

---

[1] New Court, Lincoln's Inn, as to which see 24.

For views of More House, see *3.aa.* (front) and *34.t.* (side).

20.1.2. Sir Thomas More, LC

¶ Margaret Roper's farewell to her father, as recorded by her husband, has been called one of the most poignant scenes in English biography:

'When Sir Thomas More came from Westminster to the Towerward again, his daughter, my wife, desirous to see her father, whom she thought she should never see in this world after, and also to have his final blessing, gave attendance about the Tower wharf, where she knew he would pass by, before he could enter into the Tower, there tarrying for his coming home. As soon as she saw him, after his blessing on her knees reverently received, she hasting towards him, and without consideration or care of herself, pressing in among the middest of the throng and company of the guard that with halberds and bills went

20.a. W F Yeames: preparatory oil sketch for the painting 'Thomas More with his daughter at the Tower after his sentence of death', *ca.* 1863. [coll. Jacqueline Brown [of MT]].

The finished oil painting is now in the Constable's apartments in the Tower of London.

round about him, hastily ran to him, and there openly, in the sight of all, embraced him took him about the neck and kissed him. Who, well liking her most natural and dear daughterly affection towards him, gave her his fatherly blessing and many godly words of comfort besides. From whom after she was departed, she, not satisfied with the former sight of him, and like one that had forgotten herself, being all ravished with the entire love of her dear father, having respect neither to herself nor to the press of the people and multitude that were there about him, suddenly turned back again, ran to him as before, took him about the neck, and divers times together most lovingly kissed him, and at last, with a full heavy heart, was fain to depart from him. The beholding whereof was to many of them that were present thereat so lamentable that it made them for very sorrow thereof to mourn and weep.'

—William Roper, from *The Life of Sir Thomas More*, *ca*. 1535, publ. 1626 [BL].

20.2. The Garden House: 14-15, New Square (originally *the new law stationer's shop*)

¶ The Garden House is of 1927, by Sir John Simpson, the architect who had restored the Old Hall. Its elevations, with their sash windows, show deference to the C17th buildings of the Square, but with fewer storeys and projecting eaves, are domestic rather than collegiate.

20.b. Sarah Cooke: The Garden House, 1980s (s.e. view) (detail) [Messrs. Minet Pering] {the artist}.

20.3. Hardwicke Building (originally *Hale Court chambers* and *the Lincoln's Inn Post Office*):

20.3.1. The building

¶ This building of 1966-9 by K A Williams was part of the project which included the rebuilding of the adjacent corner of Old Buildings. The site had been occupied by 1-4, Bishop's Court.

The Rev Sir Hugh Barrett-Lennard, Bt., a Roman Catholic priest who had been born in Old Buildings, averred that when demolitions were in hand in preparation for erecting this building, a doorway was found marked with a red cross and the words 'Lord have mercy on us'—a survival of the Great Plague of 1665.

The building, when erected, was named Hale Court after Sir Matthew Hale [of LI] (1609-76). In 1996, the name Hardwicke Building was brought with them by the chambers which had occupied the adjacent building.

The name Hale (or Hale's) Court has accrued to the yard on the n. of these Chambers.

The Lincoln's Inn (or Chancery La.) Post Office, which had been 78, Chancery La., was incorporated in this building with an entrance on the corner of Bishop's Court and Chancery La. The Post Office was closed in 1993, and its Chancery La. street frontage replaced

20.c. Dorothy Thomas: Hale Court (as it was then called), and the Garden House, *ca.* 1988 (n.e. view) {the artist}.

by a shop, during the remodelling of this building in 1996, which included the adding of further windows in the façade facing New Square.

20.3.2. Sir Matthew Hale, CJ

Such was thy wisdom… *…in whom*
Our British Themis[1] *gloried with just cause,*
Immortal Hale! for deep discernment praised,
And sound integrity, not more than famed
For sanctity of manners undefiled.

—William Cowper [of IT], from *The Task*, 1785.

[1] Themis: the Greek goddess of Justice.

Hale (1609-76) was CJ of the King's Bench and CB of the Exchequer. He succeeded in navigating his way through the Civil War, the Commonwealth and the Restoration, retaining a reputation for judicial integrity, if not for political commitment. His greatest reputation is as a jurist, notably his *History of the Pleas of the Crown*. His important library, bequeathed to the Society, is noted in 14.2.1.

20.4. 16, New Square (originally *Hardwicke Building*):

20.4.1 The building

¶ This chambers building of 1991—middle distance, r.—designed to fit into a narrow, wedge-shaped site, has elements of design from two firms of architects and the Society's then estates manager. Its diapered brickwork pays tribute to Philip Hardwick's New Hall, while being unmistakably a building of the late C20th. A wall plaque records the earlier use as the Boghouse of part of the site. On the l. is the Garden House; on the near r., the flank of No. 1, New Square. Centre, outside the newly rebuilt diapered perimeter wall of the Inn, rises the 'dome and dormer' (or 'minaret and mansard') development of 1991 on Bishop's Court, the roof of which has been reconfigured in 2015.

The building, when erected, was called Hardwicke Building, in tribute to Philip Yorke, first Earl of Hardwicke [of LI], LC (1690-1764).

20.d. Liam Martin: Hardwicke Building (as it then was called), 1991 (e. view) [LT].

On the l. is the side of the Garden House, and ahead (outside the walls of the Inn) the commercial building on Chichester Rents, partly demolished and rebuilt in 2014–15. The most visible change in its appearance from within the Inn is to the windows on the roof.

20.4.2. The first Earl of Hardwicke, LC

¶ Lord Campbell, in his *Lives of the Lord Chancellors*, said of him that 'he was the most consummate judge who ever sat in the Court of Chancery' and that he was responsible for 'perfecting English equity into a systematic science'.

20.e. Ken Price, RIBA: 'Elevations of proposed new building on the North Lawns', 1989 (detail) (e. view) {Casson Conder Partnership}.

The architect's drawing of the elevations and plan of the proposed Erskine Chambers (building) was adjudged by the Royal Academy as worthy of inclusion in the architectural section of the Summer Exhibition in 1990. The building was added to in 1998. The elevations were inspired by Sir John Soane's 'pared down' classicism.

20.5. 30, Lincoln's Inn Fields (originally *Erskine Chambers*), on Newman's Row

20.5.1. The building

¶ This set of chambers, built in 1990 on the extreme n.w. corner of the Gardens (where no building stood before) was given the name Erskine Chambers in honour of Thomas Erskine, first Baron Erskine [of LI]. That name was adopted by the chambers who first occupied it, and taken by them when they removed to larger premises in Chancery La. Hence, it is now known as 30, Lincoln's Inn Fields.

20.5.2. Lord Erskine, LC

¶ Samuel Taylor Coleridge wrote this rather grandiloquent eulogy in 1794 (later revised) before Erskine had become LC and been raised to the peerage. It was inspired by his courageous legal defences of several political figures, notably Tom Paine and Horne Tooke, which he undertook regardless of personal cost. His successful defence of Lord George Gordon was remarkable. He has a lasting reputation as one of the most brilliant advocates in English legal history.

When British Freedom for a happier land
Spread her broad wings, that flutter'd with affright,
Erskine! thy voice she heard, and paus'd her flight
Sublime of hope! For dreadless thou didst stand
(Thy censer glowing with the hallow'd flame)
An hireless Priest before th' insulted shrine,
And at her altar pour'd'st the stream divine
Of unmatch'd eloquence. There thy name
Her sons shall venerate, and cheer thy breast
With blessings heaven-ward breath'd. And when the doom
Of Nature bids thee die, beyond the tomb
Thy light shall shine: as sunk beneath the West
Tho' the great Summer Sun eludes our gaze,
Still burns wide Heaven with his distended blaze.

—Samuel Taylor Coleridge, 'To the Honourable Mr Erskine', 1794.

A different perspective is, however, expressed in these lines:

Crazy Lord Erskine is an Ass
ortment of all follies:
He was the first to slur the Queen;
But since his trip to Gretna Green,
He's wondrous kind to dollies

—Theodore Hook, from *Ass-Ass-Ination*, 1809.

These unkind, but factually based, verses refer to Erskine's acting as counsel to the King in the Trial of Queen Caroline, and to his second marriage in 1820 at Gretna Green to the mother of his illegitimate second family, in the face of the opposition of his eldest (legitimate) son.

> Lord Baker of Dorking, *op. cit.*, 1988.

Erskine's forensic skill is symbolised by the representation of him in a Roman toga, as Cicero, in Westmacott's statue now standing in the Library. Westmacott carved a toga'd statue of another eloquent member of the Society, the Parliamentary orator and Prime Minister George Canning, now on Canning Green at the side of Parliament Square, adjacent to the Supreme Court of the UK. Joseph Farington, *Diaries*, 1793-1821, records that in 1814 Nollekins was making busts of Erskine, priced at 150 guineas if in marble, and at half price if in plaster.

20.6. 76A, Chancery Lane, and *its python*

¶ This unprepossessing small building was put up in the 1890s by a developer, and occupies the extreme n.e. corner of the Society's land. It has since been let intermittently as an antiquarian bookshop, or offices and latterly—at lower ground level—as an extension to counsel's chambers. There are two lock-up shops at street level. It obliterates what was a fine view of the e. pediment of 1, Stone Buildings, but thereby creates the pleasurable surprise of seeing it, as evoked in 3.2.

20.7. 33, Chancery Lane (*Law Courts Chambers*, before incorporation into the Inn)

¶ This building, in early French Gothic style, is of 1873-4. It was a commercially built speculation, and destined for letting to lawyers as chambers or offices. The original name was evidently a reference to the Chancery Courts then nearby in the Inn. It was purchased in the early C21st by the Society for use as additional collegiate rooms, and for letting to counsel's chambers.

The editors of *Pevsner* attribute the architecture to Giles & Gough, but say that a contemporary edition of *Building News* gave credit to A Bridgman.

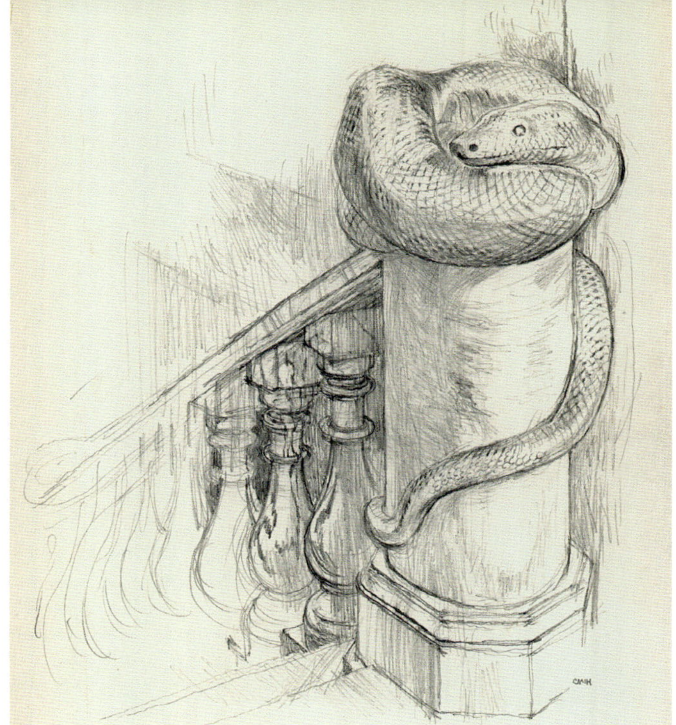

20.f. Charlotte Halliday: The entrance to the lower floor of 76A, Chancery Lane, 1995 [LT].

This marble staircase was, incongruously, the most opulent of any building in the Inn, and its hand-rail and balustrade embellished—for no known reason—with a carved python, as shown here. This staircase was dismantled in the last decade of the C20th, when the adjacent chambers in Stone Buildings were extended below street level.

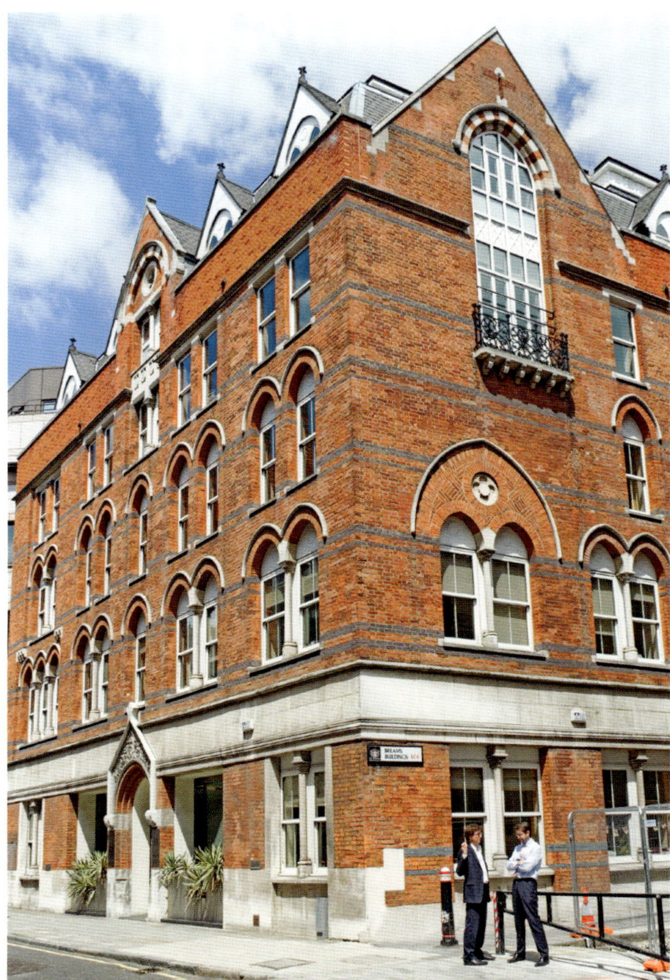

20.g. 33, Chancery La. (n.e. view), photograph G Rodrigues [LT].

21. *THE WALKS* (NOW THE CHERRY TREE WALK, THE NORTH LAWNS, THE BENCHERS' BORDER AND PARKER'S PIECE)

21.1. The flora: trees, blossom and flowers

'...the walks of Lincoln's Inn
Under the elms[1]...'

—Ben Jonson, from Act I, scene vi, *The Devil is an Ass*, 1616.

[1] The elms are no more, having been replaced principally by planes, chestnuts and ornamental cherries. 'The Walks' under the trees in the Coneygarth were of C16th construction, the precursors to the Gardens and Lawns. It was in 1608 that work began on the Gardens. Their successive arrangements are shown in Lawrence Baker's Plans in the Appendices.

'And so to Lyncoln's Inne, and there walked up and down to see the new garden which they are making and will be very pretty.'

—Samuel Pepys, from *Diary* for 27th June 1663.

> both: H B Wheatley, *op. cit.*, 1891.

21.a. François Gasselin: 'Le coin qui entre en Oborne du jardin des avoscat[s]', late C17th (e. view) [BM].

This may well be the second-earliest view specifically of the Inn. The dome of St Paul's is prominent in the background.

21.b. J Maurer: 'A view of Lincoln's Inn Garden from the Terrass: Vüe du Jardin du Lincoln's Inn du Terrase', *ca.* 1740 (e. view) [Editor's coll.].

This is one of a pair of engravings by the same artist, and with the caption in English and in French. As shown in engravings of the Inn by other artists, there were statues (presumably of classical figures) on plinths in each segment of the Walks. There is a screen of trelliswork along the length of the chambers in Garden Row. The two distinctive bays—one round and one straight-sided—are shown.

'...the Gardens... are now exceedingly improved with curious Walks, Grass Plots, fine Rows of Shady Trees to walk under, and a Tarras Walk or Mount, which gives the Prospect of Lincoln's Inn Fields.'

—John Strype, *Survey*, 1720.

Gray's Inn for walls,
Lincoln's for a walk,
The Inner Temple for a garden,
And the Middle Temple for a hall.

—Anon. dogerell, of unknown date.

> H H L Bellot, *The Inner and Middle Temple*, 1902.

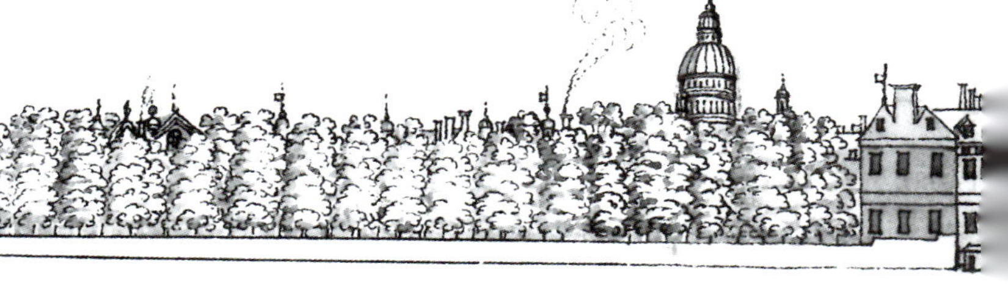

21.c. Sir Arthur Underhill [of LI]: The lawns abutting the New Hall, 1900 (w. view) [HSLI].

21.d. Lady Victoria Manners: 'Lincoln's Inn, 1906', in Alicia Cecil, *London Parks and Gardens*, 1907 (s. view) [GL].

This is the upper walk or 'Cherry Tree Walk', looking s., with the border abutting and retained by the Wall on the r. At the end of the Walk is the then Under-Treasurer's house. *44.i.* shows the far end of the walk from the s.

'You can see the months and their mother heralded and lamented in the long flower-bed under the wall, out of the weather that can drive so bitterly across the Fields. There is no need to ask is February here, or May, when you pace that solitary walk: few more solitary in London. Now and again on a week-day a decorous figure comes out of the new Hall archway and advances along the gravel stretch, looking at the flowers yard by yard. Perhaps he is a Bencher and has a right to dictate what shall be planted there, lily or rose. The garden was the last outpost of the private rights of the Inn; residents who were not members of the Society understood that they might pass through, but not loiter there. It is in my memory that the Masters of the Bench pulled up their imaginary stakes and said "Enter; you are welcome".

For many a generation the Benchers have peered among their flowers and paced beneath the trees. They have mourned the passing of great elms their grandfathers told them of, have watched jealously the leafing of slips that then were tender and now are stalwart trees or have come to be numbered with the fallen. I can see them cloaked and spurred, with generous hats over their long hair wigged, shrunken in apparel, ever changing and ever the same. They grieved to see the tree trunks so black, and mused on what London must have been before the ships carrying seacoal berthed in the Flete river. They have told out on a deliberate finger the plants most loved. I can count those plants as if it were only a long yesterday that saw them rooted there: pansies, columbines, sweet William, marigold, larkspurs and monkshood, snapdragon and bergamot, the Rose of Sharon and the Marvel of Peru, seathrift in patches and Canterbury bells; and one tawny lily looking earnestly at the sky. I know that dahlias will come out as the others fade. When autumn leaves are drifting sideways down, and the faire walke is rusty, there are always Michaelmas daisies left to brighten the meagre noon.

It is not for nothing that the Benchers clung so long to their high garden. The weight and tenure of the past, bodiless and unbreakable, is most felt here.'

—Margaret Ashworth, from 'On Living in Lincoln's Inn', in *Cornhill Magazine*, 1930 [an off-print, HSLI].

21.e. Audrey Sant, ARCA: The Benchers' Border, 1980s (s.w. view) [LT].

This drawing in chalks shows this herbaceous border at the height of its then summer splendour. It was replanted in 1994 in a deliberately less colourful style, in accord with changing fashions in garden planting, and as fully explained at the time in the Society's *Newsletter*. What may seem in this picture to be a carefully contrived composition of the trees and plants of the Inn in the foreground, and the headquarters building of the then HM Land Registry (now a building of the LSE) in the background just outside the Inn, was in fact accurate and scarcely improved by art. This artist, under her maiden name of Lewis, was a fashion illustrator and on the staff of *Vogue*. Under her married name, she established a reputation as an artist of buildings and landscapes and as a portraitist.

Spring comes as a surprise to Lincoln's Inn.
The early crocuses beyond Old Square
Strike through the winter grasses unperused.
A solitary snowdrop swells and dies
Unnoticed. Men in labyrinthine wills
And glabrous deeds engrossed to all the flounce
And affidavit of the daffodils
Are blind. The branches of the plane begin
To thrust a closer lattice to the skies,
To bud umbrellas, filmy green and furled
Against the inattention of the world;
And still practitioners are not aware.
And then one day the crimson buds are there
Along the cherry branches tense but faint
As if they suffered under some restraint
Against anticipation; and the next
Incomparable April, pointilliste
Supreme, has turned impressionist and pink
And pale, has daubed with blossom every least
Inconsequential twig, and all aver,
Equity draftsman and conveyancer,
That Spring is very sudden, never used
To burst in so upon one as it were
Between hereinbefore and hereinafter.
Then staid trustees grow jaunty and perspire
About their wise appointments, and desire
Returns to darken counsel at his text
And cold solicitors can scarcely think,
Whose clerks for joy their articles renounce,
And round Stone Buildings echoes musty laughter.

—Nathaniel Micklem (HH Judge Micklem) [of LI], 'Spring in Lincoln's Inn', 1958, in *Verses from Lincoln's Inn*, 1975.

21.f. Liam Martin: Lead cistern of 1685, now used for flowers, 1991 [LT].

21.2. The fauna: promenaders, men seeking women, litigants, garden-party goers and dogs

¶ In 1597, the Walks of Gray's Inn were laid out to the designs of Sir Francis Bacon, the poet, philosopher and judge, and author of the essay 'Of Gardens'. It is appropriate that one of Gray's masques in the early C17th was *The Masque of Flowers*. During that century those of Gray's became the most fashionable of the Walks in the Inns: a place for gentlefolk to promenade, and to be seen. There is thus a more extensive C17th literature in poetry and prose on that Inn's Walks than on those of the other three, in which are to be found several contemporary observers' accounts of the appeal of a visit there. One such is accordingly quoted here, followed by a few lines by a member of Lincoln's, evoking the similarity between the Walks of the two Inns.

Here Damsel sits disconsolate,
Cursing the Rigor of her Fate,
Till Squire Insipid having spy'd her,
Takes Heart of Grace, and squats beside her.
He thus accosts,—Madam, by God
You are at once both fair and sad.
She innocently does submit
To all the Tyrants of his wit.
The Bargain's made, she first is led
To the Three Tuns, and so to Bed.

But yonder comes a graver Fop,
With heavy Shoe, and Boot-hose-top;
To him repairs a virtuous Sir,
Whose question is, What News does stir?
With Face askrew, he then declares
The probability of wars:
And gives an ample satisfaction
Of English, French and Dutch Transaction
Thus chattering out three houres Tale,
They tread to th'Mag-pye, to drink Ale.

—Alexander Radcliffe [of GI], 'Wrote in the Banquetting-House in Grayes-Inn-Walkes', 1682.

> Harold Love, *The Penguin Book of Restoration Verse*, 1968.

Could Grays Inn Walks, or those of Lincolns Inn,
(Places where women teach their minds to sin,)
Or Park,[1] *or either Play-House*[2] *but relate,*
What fine Discourse, what pretty am'rous Chat
Between the Gallant and the Wife is made.

—Richard Ames [of LI], from *The Folly of Love, or an Essay… Against Woman,* 1691 [BL].

---

1 Park: St James's Park.
2 either Play-House: The Theatre Royal Drury Lane and the Lincoln's Inn Fields Theatre, the only ones in London authorised by Royal Patent at the time.

¶ An amorous encounter—or an attempt at one—at the other end of the social scale, in a later generation, and after the gardens had been replanned:

O Monstrous Love! disastrous Fate,
No Tongue or Pen did e'er relate
A Parallel to my sad Song,
E'er since the Date of Right and Wrong:
But cutting here Reflection's Thread
To present Purpose I proceed.

Young Corydon,[1] *who'd long in vain*
By Dress and Address strove to gain

His Phillis; by each subtle Art
Skill cou'd invent to win her Heart,
Us'd various Whims to mend his Face,
But Art to Nature must give place.
Obdurate she, deaf to his Prayers,
Smiles at his Sighs, laughs at his Tears:
Abandoned thus to raving Fits,
The cause well known confounds his Wits;
For Stratagem he casts about,
Calls Impudence to help him out;
Quoth he—If I mistake not much,
Tho' Phiz be rough, my Parts—are such,
That where well shewn may fairly pass,
And rank with those, o'th' upper Class;
Then why shall I my Suit give up?
I'll not—to try to make her stoop.

Phillis, thus coy, and cold 'tis said
Had Charms (tho' but a Chambermaid)
To urge poor Corydon to prove,
The Heat of odd romantick Love.
The fair One dwelt in House that fac'd
A Garden oft' with Beauties grac'd
Hight Lincoln's Inn—'twas there he chose
To win the Day, or Life to lose;
His last Effort, (minutely weigh'd)
Approv'd,—determines shall be try'd.

Clad in Blue Grey, his Buttons Gold,
With Hat on cap, the Morning cold,
(shall Love by Frost be e'er control'd?)
He sally'd forth; Sunday it was
(Alack too near sad Childermass[2]*)*
Cupid conducts him to the Grove,
Devote to Secrecy and Love;
Secure, unseen, in Thought possess'd
Of all can make a Lover bless'd,
Let him but catch her once appear
His Project traps her in his snare.

Thus freed from Doubt, as light as Air,
Her Window's now his only care;
Three Stories high, the Nymph must fall,
(As raptur'd Birds to Serpent's Call)
So certain is poor Phillis Fate,
On first Appearance at the Grate.

Thus he concludes—but mark the Trick,
Cupid quite baffled by Old Nick,
Deserts his Charge, resigns his Post,
Poor Corydon's Designs are cross'd.

Phillis had scarce her Garters ty'd,
When from her Window she espy'd
Somewhat—but what, she cou'd not tell
For Cory' had contriv'd so well,
That at the Instant she appear'd,
Down went his Trousers, up he rear'd
The beastly End of senseless Shame,
Almost as fit to show as name.

Unhappy Chance! Just as he turned
To ask if Phillis froze or burn'd
An Imp in ambush, plac'd by Hell
And Envy, took his Aim so well,
Lodg'd such a Load in Cory's Bum,
And in his—lack a Day—but mum,
As ruin'd all his Hopes to come.
Strait off, like wounded Duck he waddled,
Or three legg'd Ass, uncouthly saddled,
To Barthol'mew's to find a Friend
To dig out shot from nether End,
So shatter'd, in such rueful case,
Nothing so like it, as his Face.

Judge Damsels, will he e'er again,
This Way make known his am'rous Pain,
Or rather from this smart Rebuff,
Will he not gather such Reproof
As may produce these signs of Grace,
No more to shew or—Ase or Face.

—Anon., 'The Fair Shoot at a Foul Mark, or a New Way of Wooing', 1741 [Crace Collection, BM].

21.g. Wilfrid F Waite, QC [of LI]: 'The Woman that stole the dial', in his *Old Clocks and Sundials of Lincoln's Inn*, unpubl. MS, 1942 [HSLI].

The Black Books record that, in 1736, a woman stole a dial from the gardens—seemingly a pedestal sundial. The woman was never caught. Two centuries later, however, the scene was captured by this bencher, and included in his scholarly monograph. Its title does not do justice to the extent of information it contains on the Inn's demolished buildings.

21.h. Engraving: Benjamin Cole, verses: Anon: 'The Fair Shoot at a Foul Mark, or a New Way of Wooing' (s. view), 1741 [BM].

This rare print is relatively unusual for providing a s. prospect of the Inn—essential in this context to show the Gardens and clearly to locate them as appurtenant to the Inn. No version without the verses has been found, and there seems every reason to imagine that it records or was inspired by a true incident, dressed (or otherwise!) in classical garb. It may be imagined as having been published as a scandal sheet.

In the left background is the n. elevation of Garden Row in Garden Court, with its two distinctive bays, one with curved and one with straight walls. On the l. (the e.) is the terrace of houses on the e. side of Chancery La., there being no chambers in the Gardens until the construction of the Stone Building in the 1770s. Of this terrace, Strype said that it 'hath the best buildings, and best inhabited... especially that Part... that hath the prospect of Lincoln's Inn Gardens...' On the r. (the w.) is the carriage-way in the Fields abutting Lincoln's Inn Wall. The chambermaid and the Inn porter mentioned in the text are shown.

21.i. Anon. artist: A summer garden party on the North Lawns, 1980s (n.e. view) {Dennis Gordon, Holborn and Westminster Law Society}.

This drawing evokes the garden parties which are now held every summer in the Inn, this one being held in June for the benefit of the legal professions' charities.

1 Corydon and Phyllis: mythological lovers, shepherds pursuing shepherdesses in an Arcadian landscape, ultimately from the bucolic poetry of Theocritus and Virgil, and more immediately from Alexander Pope, *The Pastorals*, 1707.

2 Childermas: the Festival of the Holy Innocents, 28th December.

3 Bartholomew's: St Bartholomew's Hospital in Smithfield, then, and for most of its history, the nearest to the Inn. At a much later date, King's College Hospital was established in Portugal St., before migrating to Camberwell.

¶ Two examples of Sir Richard Steele's polished irony:

'Much hurry and business had today perplexed me into a mood too thoughtful for going into company; for which reason, instead of the tavern, I went into Lincoln's Inn Walks; and having taken a round or two, I sat down, according to the allowed familiarity of these places, on a bench, at the other end of which sat a venerable gentleman, who speaking with a very affable air, "Mr Bickerstaffe," said he, "I take it for a very great piece of good fortune, that you have found me out." "Sir," said I, "I had never, that I know of, the honour of seeing you before." "That," replied he, "is what I have often lamented..."'

—Sir Richard Steele, from *The Tatler* (no. 13), 10th May 1709.

'My man Humphrey, who has lived with me for many years... He is a diligent, careful, sensible man, and has had a right in all that comes off my person these forty years; for so long he has been my *Valet de chambre*, or Gentleman as they call it, I cannot accuse him but of one ungentlemanly thing during all our whole time together; and that was, he brought a Taylor to see me as I walked in Lincoln's Inn Garden, and sold him the coat I had then on my back, while I was musing concerning the course of human affairs in the upper walk. This I cannot call an injustice; for I had given him the suit, and he put me in it because it was warm, the day after I gave it him being cold. However, I may call it an unpoliteness, and an indecorum, because his master had it on while he was making the bargain.'

—Sir Richard Steele, in *The Theatre* (no. 3), January 1720/1.

> both, H B Wheatley, *op. cit.*, 1891.

¶ The demented Miss Flite passes the time awaiting the re-opening of the Lord Chancellor's Court in Lincoln's Inn, and the possibility that one day her case may be called:

'"Ha" said the old lady. "She does not expect a judgment? She will still grow old. But not so old. O dear, no. This is the garden of Lincoln's Inn. I call it my garden. It is quite a bower in the summertime. Where the birds sing melodiously. I pass the greater part of the long vacation here. In contemplation… When the leaves are falling from the trees, and there are no more flowers in bloom to make up into nosegays for the Lord Chancellor's court," said the old lady "the vacation is fulfilled; and the sixth seal mentioned in the *Revelations,* again prevails."'

—Charles Dickens, from *Bleak House*, 1852.

From a tree in the garden our Benchers have hung
A notice 'DOGS only admitted if led'.
May an equity draftsman respectfully ask
Whether what they intended is what they have said?

'Dogs only'? Not men, women, children and cats?
Or 'only admitted'? Not fondled or fed?
These are doubts which may well be expected to be
Overcome by a junior only if led.

English owns less precision than Latin or Greek,
In the classics our Benchers have nothing to learn.
But why do they place this poor 'only' between
The only two words which it does not concern?

—Arthur Cole [of LI], 'Dogs Only', mid-C20th,
in *Verses from Lincoln's Inn*, 1975.

21.3. *The Jakes*

¶ The Inn's communal privy, built in the middle of the Walks, had claims to have been the earliest in England with a flushing mechanism, and seems in consequence to have gained a certain notoriety. This is how it was built:

'Another way, is either upon close or open vaults, so to place the sieges or seats as behind them may rise tunnes[1] of chimneys, to draw all the ill aires upwards: of which kind I may be bold to say, that our house of Lincolnes Inne, putteth downe all that have bene made afore it, and is indeed both in reason and experience, a meanes to avoid much of the annoyance that is wont to come of them, and keepeth the place all about much the sweeter. But yet to speake truly, this is not safe from all infection or annoyance while one is there, as my sense hath told me for… And further, when the weather is not calme, the wind is so *Sensus non fallitur in proprio objecto* unruly, that it will force the ill aires downe the chimneys, and not draw up, as we see it doth in chimneys where fire is made, force downe the smoke, notwithstanding that the verie nature of fire helpeth to enforce it upward, whereas these moist vapours are apt (even of their owne nature) to spreade abrode, & hang like a deaw about every thing. Wherfore though I am but a punie[2] of Lincolnes Inne, and the builder hereof was a grave bencher, yet I will under reformation, preferre my deevise afore his, either because it is better, or else out of the common fault of young men in this age, that we thinke our devises wiser then our elders. Yet by the way, I hope all the Innes of court will gratulate the present flourishing estate of our Lincolnes Inne: not so much for furnishing the realme with most honourable, upright and wel learned magistrates, great sergeants, grave counsellors, towardly barresters, yong gallants of worth and spirit *sans nombre*, but also (that I may now deale with mine equals, & not with my auncients) with two such rare enginers, me for this one devise, & Maister Plat[3] for verie many…'

—Sir John Harington [of LI],[4] from *The Metamorphosed A Jax*,[5] 1596 [BL].

>> Sir George Engle [of LI].

1 tunnes: barrels or pipes.

2 punie: a junior member.

3 Sir Hugh Plat [of LI], called 1581, produced 'sundry new and rare inventions', in a wide variety of scientific and technical fields. His books of them survive.

4 Harington (1561-1612), poet and courtier, was a godson of Elizabeth I. This extract is taken from his trilogy on this subject, containing the first description in the English language of, and first published design for, a water closet. At this time, the Inn's house of office ('the Red House') was in the Gardens at what is now the centre of the North Lawns. Its location is shown in the Hollar prospect in 1.3., and in the plans in the Appendices. *The Black Books* refer to its savours.

5 A Jax: a pun, common at the time, on 'jakes', itself a C16th colloquialism, of uncertain etymology, for privy. Variations on the word survive in English regional dialect to this day.

Editor's notes.

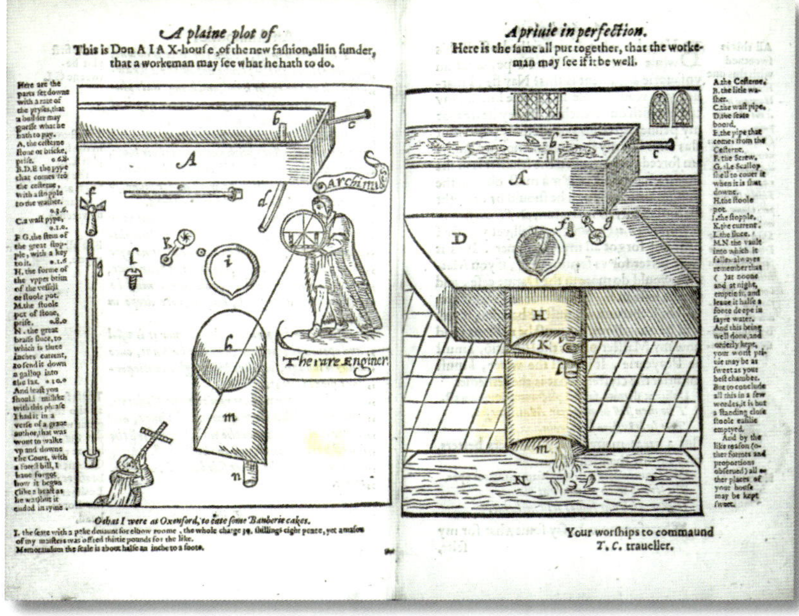

21.j. 'This is Don AJAX-house, of the new fasion, all in sunder, that a workman may see what he hath to do. Here are the parts set downe with a rate of the pryses, that a builder may guesse what he hath to pay.

	£. s. d.
A. the cesterne stone or bricke, price:	0. 6.0½
B.,D.,E. the pype that comes from the cesterne, with a stopple to the weather:	0. 3.6
C. 2 waste pype:	0. 1.0
F.,G. the stem of the great stopple, with a key to it:	0. 1.6
H. the forme of the upper brim of the vessell or stoole pot:	
M. the stoole pot of stone, prise:	0. 8.0
N. the great brasse sluce, to which is three inches current, to send it down a gallop into the Jax:	0.10.0
I. the seate with a peke devaunt for elbow roome, the whole charge:	0. 3.8

yet a mason of my masters was offered thirtie pounds for the like.

Memorandum, the scale is about halfe an inche to a foote.

A privie in perfection—

Here is the same put together, that the workman may see if it be well.

A. the cesterne
B. the litle washer
C. the waste pipe
D. the seate board
E. the pipe that comes from the cestern
F. the screw
G. the scallop shell to cover it is shut downe
H. the stoole pot
I. the stopple
K. the current
L. the sluce
M.N. the vault into which it falles always remember that at noone and at night emptie it, and leave it halfe a foote deepe in fayre water. And this being well done and orderly kept, your worst privie may be as sweet as your best chamber. But to conclude all this in a few wordes, it is but a standing close stoole easilie emptyed. And by the like reason (other formes and proportions observed) all other places of your house may be kept sweet.'

—Sir John Harington, 'A plaine plot of a privie in perfection' from *The Metamorphosed A Jax*, 1596 [BL].

¶ This indicates the impression which it created:

'…the glorious A-jax of Lincoln's Inn survey'd with wonder by me when I lay factor in London…'

—John Marston, *What you will*, 1607 [BL].

> E H Sugden, *A topographical dictionary to the works of Shakespeare and his fellow dramatists*, 1925.

21.4. The Terrace wall (formerly *Lincoln's Inn Wall*); and *the Terrace* (now the Cherry Tree Walk) and its prospect over the Fields

¶ 'Lincoln's Inn Wall' is the name given to the wall extending for about a hundred and fifty yards, to the w. of the Walks, enclosing and retaining them. It is thus named on some old plans. The n. part, down to the Garden Gate, is of C17th-C18th workmanship, much patched and repointed. The s. part from there to the Lincoln's Inn Fields Gate is contemporary with the New Hall, in the same red-and-blue diapered brickwork. The noteworthiness of the wall, as it once was, is recorded by these lines:

Gray's Inn for Walks[1]
Lincoln's Inn for Wall
The Inner Temple for a garden
and the Middle for a hall.[2]

—Anon. doggerel, written before 1658.

> R J Blackham, *The Story of the Temple, Gray's and Lincoln's Inn,* 1932.

1 Walks: see 21.2.
2 hall: see Historical Essay (note 59).

¶ A stone plaque bedecked with a carved garland of fruit and flowers, set into the n. wall of 11, New Square at second-floor level records that:

This Terrace Wall Was
Finished and completed
In the Year of our Lord 1694
Edward Byde Esq.
Treasurer

This indicates the former s. extent of the Walks and Gardens, which were agreed between the benchers and Nicholas Barbon, the developer who completed the Square. The terrace was curtailed by the construction of the Fields Gate and the New Hall. It is one of three plaques on No. 11, each for a different purpose, the other two of which having already been noted here. The RCHM's volume *Monuments of West London*, 1925, considered the plaques of New Square of sufficient interest to allocate a full page to photographs of them.

'The terrace walk… forms an uncommonly fine promenade, and is always open in summer to the public. … From the terrace walk we have a prospect of one of the largest and most beautiful squares in Europe, originally laid out by the masterly hand of Inigo Jones, and intended to have been built all in the same style and taste, but unfortunately not finished agreeable to the design of that great architect, "because the inhabitants had not taste enough to be of the same mind, or to unite their sentiments for the public ornament and reputation."'

—W Herbert, from *Antiquities of the Inns of Court and Chancery*, 1804, largely reiterating James Ralph, *op. cit.*, 1783.

21.5. The spirituality of the Gardens

'I was last week taking a solitary walk in the garden of Lincoln's-Inn (a favour that is indulged me by several of the benchers, who are my intimate friends, and grown old with me in this neighbourhood) when, according to the nature of men in years, who have made but little progress in the advancement of their fortune or their fame, I was repining at the sudden rise of many persons who are my juniors, and indeed, at the unequal distribution of wealth, honour, and all other blessings of life. I was lost in this thought, when the night came upon me, and drew my mind into a far more agreeable contemplation. The heaven above me appeared in all its glories, and presented me with such a hemisphere of stars as made the most agreeable prospect imaginable to one who delights in the study of nature. It happened to be a freezing night, which had purified the whole body of air into such a bright transparent aether, as made every constellation visible; and, at the same time, gave such

21.k. The texture of a section of the Wall, heavily repointed (n. view): photograph G Rodrigues, 2011 [LT].

a particular glowing to the stars, that I thought it the richest sky I had ever seen. I could not behold a scene so wonderfully adorned and lighted up, if I may be allowed that expression, without suitable meditations on the author of such illustrious and amazing objects: for, on these occasions, philosophy suggests motives to religion, and religion adds pleasure to philosophy.'

—Joseph Addison, from *The Tatler* (no. 100), 29th November 1709.

> H B Wheatley, *op. cit.*, 1891.

21.6. Gentlemen gardeners of the Society, and their philosophies

¶ The Society's most celebrated (gentlemen-) gardeners of past centuries were probably Edmund Waller (1606-87), who created a famous early garden in the classical French style at his seat of Hall Barn at Beaconsfield in Buckinghamshire, and Horace Walpole (1717-97), who laid out one in the English landscape style, surrounding his fashion-setting 'gothick' house at Strawberry Hill at Twickenham, in Middlesex. Being *litterati* rather than practising barristers, both wrote on these subjects. Waller's poems, inspired by gardens and parks, are to be found in many modern anthologies. Walpole wrote an influential essay, 'The History of the Modern Taste in Gardening', 1780, and coined the word 'gardenist', to encompass both those who conceive the designs and those who do the spade-work. However, among the Society's membership it is perhaps George Wither (1588-1667), whose writing expressed most forcefully the virtues of planting for the future. Although, as a man of his time, he wrote implicitly of planting trees on an estate, the message is the same as that in the modern vogue words—ecology and renewable resources—and could hardly be bettered as a credo for the modern conservation movement. This is what he had to say:

21.l. Samuel Scott: Lincoln's Inn Fields from Lincoln's Inn Wall, *ca.* 1740 (w. prospect) [coll. the Earl of Pembroke, Wilton House, Wilts.] {Bridgeman}.
This *veduta* depicts the scene visible from a mid-point on the wall. The Fields are still un-enclosed and are not planted, but are grassed.

When I behold the havoc and the spoil
Which, even within the compass of my days,
Is made through every quarter of this isle,
In woods and groves, which were this kingdom's praise;
And when I mind with how much greediness
We seek the present gain in everything,
Not caring (so our lust we may posses)
What damage to posterity we bring:
They do, methinks, as if they did foresee
That some of those whom they have cause to hate
Should come in future times, their heirs to be;
Or else why should they such things perpetrate?
For if they think their children shall succeed,
Or can believe that they begot their heirs,
They could not, surely, do so foul a deed.

As to deface the land that should be theirs.
What our forefathers planted, we destroy:
Nay, all men's labours, living heretofore,
And all our own, we lavishly employ
To serve our present lusts, and for no more.

But let these careless wasters learn to know
That, as vain spoil is open injury,
So planting is a debt they truly owe
And ought to pay to their posterity.
Self love, for none but for itself, doth care,
And only for the present taketh pain;
But charity for others doth prepare,
And joys in that which future time shall gain.
If after ages may my labours bless,
I care not, much, how little I possess.

—George Wither [of LI], 'Planting' from *A Collection of Emblems*, 1635.

> Alastair Fowler, *The New Oxford Book of Seventeenth Century Verse*, 1991.

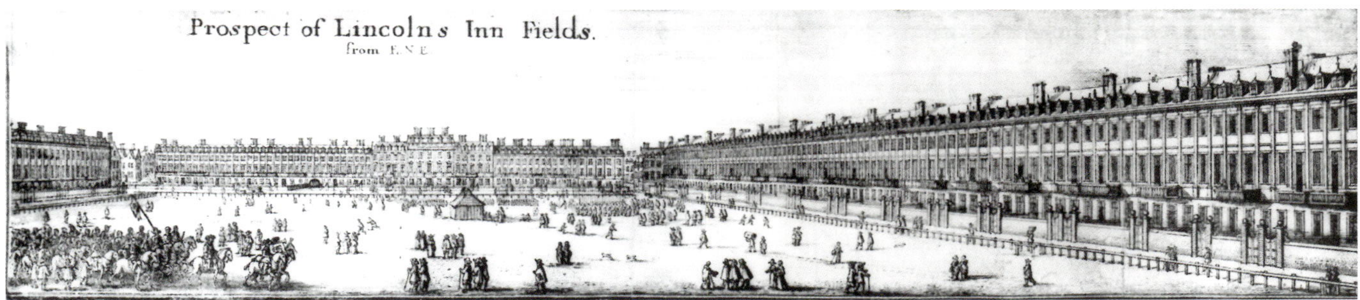

21.m. Wenceslas Hollar: 'Prospect of Lincoln's Inn Fields from E.N.E.', *ca.* 1660 (w. prospect) [BM].
This painting is contemporary with Hollar's aerial prospect of central London, centred on the Fields, in *1.b.* Given that scholars have debated whether that prospect included an element of what was planned as well as what existed, the same question could be asked of this prospect.

22. THE SOCIETY'S *INNS OF CHANCERY*:

¶ For most of their history, each of the Inns of Court had one, two or three Inns of Chancery dependent on them. Lincoln's had two: Thavies and Furnival's. Originally, they served as 'preparatory schools' to the Inns of Court—although there was by no means a need to progress from daughter to mother Inn—and latterly, when the usual progression was direct from university to Inn of Court, they served also as educational establishments for, or dining clubs of, attorneys and solicitors, and provided chambers for them. Each Inn of Chancery had comparable facilities and architecture to an Inn of Court, but differed significantly in that none save one had a chapel (pews usually being reserved in the adjacent parish church). At least two had modest libraries, but not necessarily all.

'The Chancellor: But, Prince, in order that the form and arrangement of this academy may be clear to you, I will now describe it as far as I can. For there are in this academy ten lesser inns, and sometimes more, which are called Inns of Chancery. To each of them at least a hundred students belong, and to some of them a much greater number, though they do not always gather in them all at the same time. These students are, indeed, for the most part, young men, learning the origin and something of the elements of law, who, becoming proficient therein as they mature, are absorbed into the greater inns of the academy, which are called the Inns of Court. Of these greater inns there are four in number…'

—Sir John Fortescue [of LI], from 'Here he shows the general organisation of the academy of the laws of England', Chapter XLIX of *De laudibus legum Anglie,*[1] *ca.* 1470, English translation by Sidney Chrimes, 1941.

---

[1] *De laudibus…*: 'In praise of the Laws of England'. *Anglie* is the medieval spelling of *Angliae*. This beautifully written work, an apologia in benign terms for the profession and the Inns, was addressed to Prince Edward of Westminster, heir to the throne, killed in combat or murdered on the field of battle before being able to succeed his father to the throne.

The generally accepted list of Inns of Chancery for much of the C17th and C18th is: Thavies and Furnival's (LI); Staple and Barnard's (GI); Clifford's, Clement's (otherwise Dane's) and Lyons (IT); and New (MT). Before then, two had gone: St George's (on the e. bank of the Fleet) and Strand (on part of the site now occupied by Somerset House). Sir John Baker has written that he believes that a further Inn of Chancery—the Outer Temple—(probably dependent on MT) had a brief life, but had gone before the beginning of the C17th.

22.a. Map of Farringdon Ward Without (detail), from John Strype, *Survey*, 1720 [LMA]

This is probably the clearest map to include the first Thavies Inn; no plan specific to that Inn and no prospect is known to exist.

'...the Inns of Chancery being, as it were, provinces, severally subjected to the Inns of Court, be chiefly furnished with officers, attorneys, solicitors and clerks, that follow the courts of King's Bench or Common Pleas; and yet there want not some other being young students, that come thither sometimes from one of the Universities, and sometimes from grammar schools; and these having spent some time in studying upon the first elements and grounds of the law, as having performed the exercise of their own houses, they proceed to be admitted, and become students in some of these four houses or inns of Court...'

—John Stowe, *Survey*, second edn., 1603.

22.1. *Thavies Inn*, and its associations with St Andrew's church

¶ This Inn was the older and is usually listed first of the Society's two Inns of Chancery, although certainly smaller and perhaps of lesser standing. Conventionally, the name is spelt without an apostrophe.

John Thavie had died in 1348. He left property from which to assist in maintaining St Andrew's church—which, after more than 650 years, it still does. His house became a hostel for law students at some time in the C14th—it was a dependency of the Inn before the MS Black Books began in 1422. The Society purchased the freehold in 1549. Strype, in 1720, had said that it was 'chiefly taken by the Welsh attorneys'.

The Inn was located behind Holborn and off Shoe La., with pedestrian access from each, and had a small formal garden which adjoined both that of the Bishop of Bangor's Inn, and the church-yard of St Andrew's. St Andrew's was the largest City parish church as rebuilt by Wren after the Great Fire, and included part of the land and buildings of Lincoln's Inn within its parish.

St Andrews had side chapels for each of the four Inns of Chancery on Holborn, and reserved pews for the members of Thavies, its nearest legal neighbour, and perhaps also for each of the other three.

'I must and will begin with Thavis [*sic*] Inn, for besides that at my first coming to London I was admitted for probation into that good house, I take it to be the oldest Inn of Chancery, at the least in Holborn. It was before the dwelling of an honest citizen called John Thavie an armorer, and was rented of him in the time of King Edward the III by the chief Professors then of the Law, viz., yet extant in a record in the Hustings, and whereof my Lord Cooke showed to me the transcript, but since that time it was purchased for the students and other professors of the Law of Chancery by the Benchers of Lincoln's Inn, about the reign of King Henry the Seventh and retaineth the name of the old Landlord or owner Thavie.'

—Sir George Buc, from 'England's Third University', in John Stowe, *Chronicle of England*, 1615.

> H B Wheatley, *op. cit.*, 1891.

62

22.b. Unidentified artist: St Andrew's church, Holborn Hill (n. view), *ca.* 1838 [LMA].

22.c. John Carter: 'View of Thaves [*sic*] Inn, taken from the avenue leading out of Holborn, previous to its being pulled down', 1771 [LMA].

This is the only known view of or into the original Inn. It is complemented by Hogarth's satirical engraving (not reproduced here), *The Second Stage of Cruelty*, 1751. That engraving shows the s. side of Holborn, in which may be seen the Thavies Inn Coffee House, standing next to the doorway onto the street at the end of the passage from Holborn into the Inn—the door being closed in that image, and showing nothing of the Inn.

View of Thaves Inn, taken from the
avenue leading out out of Holborn, previous
to its being pulled down. [by moon light.] 1771

22.2. Furnival's Inn:

22.2.1. The buildings

¶ The second of the Society's two Inns of Chancery was Furnival's. Evidence of occupation by students dates from 1385, two years after the death of William, 4th Lord Furnival. Lincoln's Inn acquired the freehold in 1547. The Inn was situated on the n. side of Holborn, immediately to the e. of Holborn Bars.

'This inn of chancery is situated in Holborn between Brook Street and Leather Lane: it occupies a very considerable plot of ground, and is divided into two squares or courts. The first towards Holborn is of a good width, but shallow, and built round on the four sides. The second or inner court extends the depth of a great part of Brook Street, and has chambers on one side only: the buildings of both are in a sad state of decay, and appear to be very much neglected.

The date of this inn, that is to say, of the buildings, is not very ancient, though it has greater claims in point of age than most of the other inns of chancery: but whatever it may gain in this respect, it most certainly loses in neatness and convenience; for it is, without exception, the most dirty and desolate in its appearance of the whole.

The street front is an uncommonly fine specimen of brickwork, being adorned with pilasters, mouldings, and various other ornaments, and extends a considerable length. It contains a range of very good chambers, and beneath a handsome arched gateway leading to the interior parts of the inn. It appears to have been erected about the time of Charles II.

22.d. Sutton Nicholls: 'Furnival's Inn in Holbourn', 1754 (n. prospect) [BM].

This prospect, one of the finest of any Inn of Court or Chancery, shows the full extent of this grand Inn, which could have been mistaken for an Inn of Court, were it not for the lack of a chapel. It had the most imposing street frontage of any Inn of Court or Chancery, then or since, reputedly designed by Inigo Jones, erected in 1638.

22.e. S Ireland: Furnival's Inn, *ca.* 1799 (n.e. view) [YCBA].

This is the original watercolour from which the engraving in his *Picturesque Views of the Inns of Court*, 1800, was drawn. The architectural embellishments are more clearly shown. The watchman's shelter standing on the pavement is preserved at the MoL.

The hall is seen on entering the gateway; but its aspect is by no means calculated to make a favourable impression on the spectator. It is a low plain brick building, with a small turret, and two large projecting bow windows at the west end, and is, like the rest of the inn, in a most neglected state. The north side of it, on passing through the passage or entrance to the inner court, with a small range of old chambers that adjoins, and whose fronts are plastered in the cottage style, have a singularly rustic appearance, and bear a much greater resemblance to a country village than a London inn of chancery.

The interior of this hall is the best; and, if not handsome, has at least some pretensions to antiquity; a circumstance which, combined with the probability of its being soon destroyed, has made it thought worth preserving by a plate. Its dimensions are 40 feet by 24. The roof is of timber, arched, and divided into pannels [*sic*] by ribs springing from the sides; but it is very plain and poor, compared with others of a similar kind. The floor at the upper end of the hall is raised a step for the principals, as at the Middle Temple, &c. It has in like manner a fireplace in the midst, and the same disposition of tables and benches; but they have no appearance, nor the hall itself, of being often used.'

—W Herbert, from *Antiquities of the Inns of Court and Chancery*, 1804.

22.2.2. The students

¶ This extract evokes the years in the C16th when the City gates were still locked at night. The students of Furnival's, after an evening's recreation of eating, drinking and perhaps wenching in the City,

22.f. W Herbert: 'Furnival's Inn, from the Inner Square' (s.w. view), *op. cit.*, 1804 [HSLI].

This view is that from the walks abutting the railed gardens at the n. of the Inn (top of the prospect in *22.e.*). It shows the country village character of this part of the Inn—probably unique among the Inns of Chancery.

would have needed to pass through Newgate, down Snow Hill, across the Fleet Ditch and up Holborn Hill, to the outpost of the City at Holborn Bars, on returning to their Inn:

'Watchwordes for divers yeres for Gentlemen passinge throughe Newgate *in tempore nocturno*, for which the porter had yerely at Christmas a reward, as is before remembered. I recite a fewe.

Anno nono H.7, watchword, Greneginger.
Anno 10 H.7, Peper is black.
Anno 11 H.7, Sweete meate, sowre sawce.
Anno 12 H.7, Newtidinges.
Anno 14 H.7, Wellfare the Furnyvall.
Anno 1 Eliz., watchword, Nothing has no smell.'

—? William Hakewill [of LI], from *The Middle Temple Manuscript*, *ca.* 1620-38, transcribed by W Paley Baildon FSA [of LI] [LI MS Misc. 720].

> D S Bland, 'Proverbs as Passwords', *NQ*, cxcii (1949), cxcvi (1951).

Beware of tailors' curious cuts for they will sake your bags;
The merry mean I hold for best 'tween roist'ring silks and rags.
The tippling tavern, and such like, to haunt have small desire;
Of all reports it is the worst to be a drunken squire... Out of the merchants' journals keep, buy seldom ware on trust;
Such usury bites above the rest, do try whoso lust... When wedlock life doth like your mind, match with a virtuous maid;
The mischief of the contrary a plague next hell is said.
And married well, the city leave, sing then Piers Plowman's song;
For women used to London once will ever thither long.

—George Whetstone, from 'Fifty Apples of Admonition, Bestowed on... Gentlemen of Furnivall's Inn', in *The Orchard of Repentence*, 1576.

> Lawrence Manley, *London in the Age of Shakespeare*, 1986.

'The gentlemen of Furnivall's Inn lie a-bed while their hose are a-mending.'

—Giovanni Torriano, from *A Commonplace of Italian Proverbs and Phrases*, 1666 [BL].

¶ Feasts in Furnival's Inn in the C16th:

'A Banquett ordayned, for Thavis Inn and some invited Guestes of the Innes of Court, and other Houses of Chauncerie, mention is made here of stoare of venison and daintie viands, liberally and amplie provided, as Jellies, Succade, Doulcetts, Compfites, Creame, Almonds, Blanchpowder, Suger, Wine, Apples, Peares, Tardburgoine (a bancketinge dishe wee have not hearde of in theis daies), Torches, Candleperchors, etc. The chardges not expressed.

At Candlemas feast this yere, Music, Capons, hennes, wyne, and so great a supplie of venison that they had so much unexpended, that to preserve the same, sweete divers peices were by the Cook commyted to the powderinge to be preservid.

Christmas Daie, *Anno* 19 H.7, *Dies Lunae*.

A Banckett ordayned at this feastivall tyme for Thavis Inn and others invited Guestes of Innes of Court, whereat was much dancinge and revellinge, and for that purpose, the minstralsey of the Ladie Princes and her Servantes were heare, with the waites of London, the harpur and other musicall instrumentes.

Venison, Jellies, Succad, panpuffes (*id est* fruters) Langeretes, Tartes, wardens, wyne, etc., great plenty, Torches, etc.'

—? William Hakewill [of LI], from *The Middle Temple Manuscript*, 1620-38, transcribed by W Paley Baildon FSA [of LI] [LI MS Misc. 720].

> D S Bland, from *Review of English Studies*, iii (n.s.), 1952.

23. THE DEMISE OF THE SOCIETY'S *INNS OF CHANCERY*:

23.1. Their physical decay

¶ The appearance and atmosphere of decay of the Society's two Inns of Chancery (in their original state), seems not to have inspired any poet or novelist, but the theme clearly emerges from Herbert's topographical description of Furnival's, above. There are, however, several literary evocations of other Inns of Chancery, while they were still just functioning as such, and before their second 'half-lives'. It may be imagined that the scene scarcely differed between them. The following quotation is the earliest and perhaps the best, and may be taken as generic.

'Bred up, like a bailiff or a shabby attorney, about the purlieus of the Inns of Court, Shepherd's Inn[1] is always to be found in the close neighbourhood of Lincoln's Inn Fields, and the Temple. Somewhere behind the black gables and smutty chimneystacks of Wych Street, Holywell Street, Chancery Lane, the quadrangle lies, hidden from the outer world; and it is approached by curious passages and ambiguous smoky alleys, on which the sun has forgotten to shine. Slop-sellers, brandy-ball and hardbake vendors, purveyors of theatrical prints for youth, dealers in dingy furniture, and bedding suggestive of anything but sleep, line the narrow walls and dark casements with their wares. The doors are many-belled: and crowds of dirty children form endless groups about the steps: or around the shell-fish dealers' trays in these courts; whereof the damp pavements resound with pattens, and are drabbled with a never-failing mud. Ballad-singers come and chant here, in deadly guttural tones, satirical songs against the Whig administration, against the bishops and dignified clergy, against the German relatives of an august royal family: Punch sets up his theatre, sure of an audience, and occasionally of a halfpenny, from the swarming occupants of the houses: women scream after their children for loitering in the gutter, or, worse still, against the husband who comes reeling from the gin-shop;—there is a ceaseless din and life in these courts, out of which you pass into the tranquil, old fashioned quadrangle of Shepherd's Inn. In a mangy little grass-plat in the centre rises up the statue of Shepherd, defended by iron railings from the assaults of boys. The Hall of the Inn, on which the founder's arms are painted, occupies one side of the square, the tall and ancient chambers are carried round the other two sides, and over the central archway, which leads into Oldcastle Street, and so into the great London thoroughfare.'

—William Makepeace Thackeray, from *The History of Pendennis*, 1850.

---

[1] Shepherd's: The invented name is seemingly inspired by that of Staple Inn, facing across Holborn from the site of Furnival's. One of the explanations for its name is that of a wool staple. The street references, however, point to Clement's, Lyons or New Inns, which lay close together to the s.w. of Lincoln's, forming between them another legal enclave. It may therefore be adopted here as an archetype of an Inn of Chancery. This picture of the decay of specific Inns of Chancery is echoed in: Dickens, *Great Expectations*, 1860 (Barnard's); and in Samuel (*Erewhon*) Butler, *Notebooks*, publ. posth., 1912 (Clifford's).

23.2. The rebuilding after damage by fire, and the final destruction by bombing, of *the second Thavies Inn*

¶ The end of Thavies as an Inn of Chancery came in 1769 when Lincoln's Inn declined to renew its lease. This decision may have been prompted by the declining relevance of Inns of Chancery as preparatory schools to the Inns of Court—or alternatively by the prospect of the value to be realised by the sale of the site. The Inn was, after due advertisement, sold to a member of Lincoln's and the proceeds of sale were used towards the construction of the Stone Building in Lincoln's Inn.

¶ The watercolour by T H Shepherd of 1838, and the line drawing by Arthur Moreland of 1928, are two of the few known views of the Inn after rebuilding, following destruction by fire in 1804. It was rebuilt as a courtyard of terraced houses (not chambers) such as were classified as 'third rate'—not a pejorative term—under the London Building Act 1774. Within a few decades, those buildings may well have been mistaken by most visitors to be the vestiges of the old Inn. Then, on the publication of *Bleak House* in the 1850s, the second Inn acquired a literary existence in which it was given a new association with Lincoln's Inn and the law, thereby acquiring a modest name throughout the English-speaking world.

¶ The way from Lincoln's to Thavies Inn, described a century after the demise of the original Inn of Chancery, and at a time when it survived in its rebuilt form. The route was the same as ever it had been:

'"Where is 'there', Mr Guppy?" said Richard, as we went down-stairs. "No distance, round in Thavies Inn…" "Only round the corner… we just twist up Chancery Lane, and cut along Holborn, and there we are in four minutes' time, as near as a toucher."[1]
…We turned up under an archway to our destination: a narrow street of high houses, like an oblong cistern, to hold the fog.'

—Charles Dickens, from *Bleak House*, 1852.

---

[1] toucher: one thing which touches another, especially as in bowls—*OED*.

¶ The external appearance of the second Inn remained largely unchanged until its sudden and complete destruction. Arthur Moreland had written in 1928 that: 'Thavies Inn has been left a backwater while everything round it has been transformed beyond recognition.'

A bombing raid in 1941 destroyed the Inn and its surroundings. Holborn was one of the most intensively bombed neighbourhoods in central London. One centre of devastation extended from Smithfield to Holborn Circus and Thavies Inn, then half-way down Great New St. and Fetter La., and was graphically recorded in two paintings by the notable artist, Carel Weight, RA, of which one is reproduced here.

23.a. T H Shepherd: Thavies Inn, 1838 (s. view) [BM].

This view accords with the description of the Inn in *Bleak House,* when rebuilt as houses—some of which might have been informally divided horizontally into separate apartments.

23.b. Arthur Moreland: Thavies Inn, 1928 (s.e. view), in his *Dickens Landmarks in London*, 1928 [GL].

23.c. Carel Weight, RA: 'Holborn, '47' {Estate of the artist}.

The view of part of the bombed area of Holborn as it still was some six years after the bombs fell. The view is to the e. The white stone building of the Midland Bank was contiguous with and overlooked on its s. side (to the r., in this painting) Thavies Inn, which was entirely destroyed. An office building put up after that war perpetuates the name, and with a stone archway, brick elevations, sash windows and some neo-Georgian detailing was seemingly intended to pay tribute to the former buildings of the first Inn, being more collegiate and less domestic than the second. But the associations with the legal profession and the sense—or illusion—of continuity have gone. There is not even a blue plaque in the wall, as there is for Furnival's.

>> Professor Alan Williams of Auckland, NZ.

23.d. Robert Schnebbelie: 'Interior of the Hall of Furnival's Inn', (e. view) 1820 [MoL].

The scene depicted is evidently that of the early stage of the dismantling of the Hall, with the workmen removing the panelling. This, and the following watercolour by the same artist, are related to but slightly different from the engravings in Wilkinson, *op. cit.* The date of this and the other watercolours of the old Inn is evidently a few years after they were first sketched.

23.3. The dismantling of *Furnival's Inn* for rebuilding

¶ Furnival Inn's collegiate existence ended in 1817, when Lincoln's declined to renew its lease. The lesser Society was dissolved, and Lincoln's granted a ninety-nine-year building lease of the site to Henry Peto, a builder-developer who was responsible for other buildings in this quarter of London.

He proceeded to clear the site of the old Inn for rebuilding. One of the outstanding topographical artists of the day meticulously recorded the process of dismantling the Hall of the Inn, and of the building of the new Inn, in the three watercolours shown here. In so doing, he produced some of the best views of the Inn, including the only known surviving watercolour of the interior of the Hall, a building of 1588.

23.4. *The second Furnival's Inn*, and its demolition for redevelopment

¶ On the site, a substantial building—Italianate in style—was erected, having the same name, and providing chambers for lawyers and non-lawyers, as well as a hotel. Dickens had his first matrimonial home here. Since it provided chambers, and yet was not built as an Inn of Chancery, it might be speculated as to whether this may have been the first purpose-built apartment house in London. Historians of London architecture have usually credited buildings on and off Victoria St in Westminster with that distinction, but they were built some decades later. Albany, off Piccadilly, was adapted to apartments or chambers a few years earlier—but seems always to have been seen as *sui generis*.

23.e. Robert Schnebbelie: 'West View of the Interior of Furnival's Inn', 1820 [MoL].

The main (s.) square under demolition.

'There is little enough to see in Furnival's Inn. It is a shady, quiet place, echoing to the footsteps of the stragglers who have business there; and rather monotonous and gloomy on summer evenings.'

—Charles Dickens, from *Martin Chuzzlewit*, 1844.

The Inn in its rebuilt form came to an end in 1888-97, when on the former date, the Prudential Assurance Company bought the freehold of the site and building from the Society (and presumably bought out the lease then or shortly thereafter) and on the latter date, that company demolished the Peto buildings to extend westwards its Alfred Waterhouse red-brick headquarters building of 1879. The Prudential, in its turn, largely relocated its administration in the late 1980s and adapted the building for letting to third parties as offices. A blue plaque in the street wall records the former Inn of Chancery.

23.f. Robert Schnebbelie: 'The present Furnival's Inn, erected 1818', 1819 [LT].

This watercolour appears clearly to be part of a series with the preceding two, albeit not reproduced in Wilkinson, *op. cit.*, nor for long in the same custody. Having been found in the course of research for this book, it has been donated to the MoL, to join the others. Its appendage is of the inscription on the cornerstone of the entrance arch. No other known image shows this. It proclaims Lincoln's ownership and the initials of its Treasurer, Nathaniel Clarke, KC (in contrast to the 'P' which would have been incised in such a place in former times above the initials of the Principal of the Inn of Chancery, when it was functioning as such). The Crace Collection, BM, has an 1830 watercolour of the Inn by T H Shepherd, which was reproduced and widely circulated as an engraving (neither being reprinted here); but this façade appears in the street-scenes of Holborn, reproduced in this book.

24. *NEW COURT* (ORIGINALLY *COURT CHAMBERS*), *LINCOLN'S INN*: THE BUILDING AND ITS TENANTS

¶ This building was erected by a property company, anticipating a demand to be generated by the construction of the RCJ. The design included a bank and a restaurant. The demand from lawyers proved to be less than expected, and other tenants also moved in, attracted by the small sets of chambers and seclusion, well suited for studios. Thus it became a part-legal, part-bohemian adjunct of the Inn, possessed of great architectural and human character. More than one distinguished set of Chancery chambers and firm of City solicitors have their origins there. Regrettably, it was never absorbed into the Society's ownership. Although their history and status were different, there was perhaps in New Court and new Furnival's Inn a comparable character. Its demolition in the 1960s, just before high Victorian buildings such as this were appreciated and listed, constituted a loss not only to the architecture of London, but to the perimeters of legal London and to the accommodation now available to the practising Bar.

'The Serle Street and Cook's Court Improvement Company was incorporated in 1872 by a Special Act of Parliament, with a capital of £300,000 for the purpose of acquiring and rebuilding, chiefly as chambers for the legal profession, a block of property covering more than an acre of ground, and immediately facing the northern façade of the New Royal Courts of Justice.

The new buildings of the Company, to be called "Court Chambers", will be erected round four sides of a square (134 by 101 feet), approached by an entrance archway, with porter's lodge at the junction of Serle Street and Carey Street, immediately opposite the principal entrance to the New Courts on the north.

Court Chambers will thus be in the closest possible juxtaposition with the Courts themselves, the entrance to the Company's block being only twenty yards from the Serle Street entrance to the New Courts, which will be the most convenient one for the Profession.

It is intended that Court Chambers shall consist of thirteen distinct houses, which will all be entered from the interior of the square. Each house will have its separate staircase, as in other squares appropriated to legal chambers in Lincoln's Inn and the Temple, this arrangement being found conducive both to privacy and quiet, and to safety against fire.'

—from the Company's Prospectus, 1874.

> J Diprose, *The Parish of St Clement Danes*, 1876.

¶ Arnold Bennett, the novelist and journalist, on his arrival in London from the 'Five Towns'—the centre of the pottery industry of Staffordshire—first worked in a solicitor's office in New Court, to which he gave the name of New Serjeants' Court (an invention referring to the Order of Serjeants, mentioned in 34.9.):

'New Serjeants' Court was a large modern building of very red brick with terra-cotta facings, eight storeys high; but in spite of its faults of colour and its excessive height, ample wall spaces and temperate ornamentation gave it a dignity and comeliness sufficient to distinguish it from other buildings in the locality. In the centre of the Court was an oval patch of brown earth, with a few trees whose pale leaved tops, struggling towards sunlight, reached to the middle of the third storey. Round this plantation ran an immaculate roadway of wooden blocks, flanked by an equally immaculate asphalt footpath. The Court possessed its own private lamp posts and these were wrought of iron in an antique design.

Men and boys, grave and unconsciously oppressed by the burden of the coming day, were continually appearing out of the gloom of the long tunnelled entrance and vanishing into one or other of the twelve doorways.'

—Arnold Bennett, from *A Man from the North*, 1898 [BL].

24.a. Alfred Waterhouse: elevations of New Court (n.w. corner view), 1870s: photograph G Rodrigues [coll. fieldfisher, formerly Messrs Field Fisher Waterhouse].

24.b. Alfred Waterhouse: e. view in the internal square of New Court, 1870s [*loc. cit.*].

In Carey Street did Waterhouse a stately pleasuredrome decree
Not rose-red, half as old as time, more neo-Gothic-brick-sublime;
Here was our fons and origo *in eighteen eighty three.*
(The fons *was bronze 'after Verocchio')...*

—Nathaniel Micklem (HH Judge Micklem) [of LI],
from 'Homage to Chambers', 1983.

>> Andrew Francis [of LI].

The evocative lines quoted above open a centenary celebration in verse of a notable set of Chancery chambers, which began its existence in New Court. They are framed and displayed in 11, New Square. The lines do, of course, parody S T Coleridge's *Kubla Khan*, 1816, and J W Burgon's *Petra*, 1845.

¶ Arthur Rackham, the distinguished watercolourist, book illustrator and portraitist, was for a brief time a typical non-lawyer occupant of New Court. It seems likely that, as a skilled topographical artist, he would have executed a watercolour of this, his first proper studio: but none has been located in the compilation of this book.

'New Court, a red-brick block of chambers designed by Alfred Waterhouse RA around a central courtyard and completed in 1884... was densely inhabited by a curious mix of barristers and artists, as well as architects, trade wood-engravers and legal shorthand writers. Rackham's section, number 12, had nineteen residences alone, and he shared the busy staircase with an architect, Henry Leonard Hill, wood-engravers Iago and Crossfield, artists Kate Banning, Lindsay Butterfield and Reginald Dick, nine Barristers, a Queen's Counsel, and three firms of Solicitors. The Attorney-General, Sir Charles Russell, QC, MP, kept rooms nearby at number 10.'

—James Hamilton, from *Arthur Rackham, A Life with Illustration*, 1990.

25. THE NEWLY CALLED BARRISTER OF THE SOCIETY:

25.1. His manner of speech

… time… Hath made a Lawyer, which was (alas) of late
But a scarce Poët; jollier of this state,
Then are new benefic'd ministers, he throwes
Like nets, or limetwigs, wheresoever he goes,
His title of Barrister, on every wench,
And wooes in language of the Pleas, and Bench
A motion, Lady; Speake Coscus; I have beene
In love, ever since tricesimo of the Queene,
Continuall claimes I have made, injunctions got
To stay my rivals suit, that hee should not
Proceed; spare mee; In Hillary terme I went,
You said, If I return'd next size in Lent,
I should be in remitter of your grace;
In th'interim my letters should take place
Of affidavits:

—John Donne [of LI], from *Second Satire* ('On Lawyers'), ? 1594.

25.2. His choices of career

¶ By no means all—indeed a minority of—barristers of the Society, having been called, chose practice at the Bar from chambers in this Inn (or in the streets nearby) as their calling or only occupation. Practice as a Government lawyer in England and Wales or overseas, or part-time practice at the Bar in tandem with being a member of Parliament, were and are well-recognised and respected choices:

'The ways about Pall Mall and across the Park to Parliament Street, or to the Treasury, were much pleasanter, and the new offices in Downing Street, already half built, absorbed all that interest which he had hitherto been able to take in the suggested but uncommenced erection of new Law Courts in the neighbourhood of Lincoln's Inn. As he made his way to the porter's lodge under the great gateway of Lincoln's Inn, he told himself that he was glad that he had escaped, at any rate for a while, from a life so dull and dreary. If he could only sit in the chambers at the Treasury instead of chambers in that old court, how much pleasanter it would be! After all, as regarded the question of income, it might well be that the Treasury chambers should be the more remunerative, and the more quickly remunerative, of the two. And, as he thought, Lady Laura might be compatible with the Treasury chambers and Parliament, but could not possibly be made compatible with Old Square, Lincoln's Inn.'

—Anthony Trollope, from *Phineas Finn*, 1868.

25.a. Anon. artist: 'A limb of the law', 1802 [BM *Catalogue of Satire* 9935].

The learned editor of the *Catalogue* poses the question as to whether this is a barrister's clerk, but the answer must be that the clothes worn and the blue bag (to hold wig and gown) are clearly indicative of a young barrister, newly called (who has not yet earned the accolade of a red bag), from one of the four Inns.

THE ILLUSTRATED LONDON NEWS

25.b. S Begg: 'Called to the Bar by the Prince of Wales', *Illustrated London News*, 1904 [HSLI].

It is rare for call to the Bar to merit being recorded by an artist. But it is correspondingly rare for a royal bencher to perform the task. It is noteworthy that this is the second record of events in the Inn over the same decade which made the front page of the *ILN*.

26. COUNSEL'S CHAMBERS

'"Aha!" said the old man, "Aha! who was talking about the Inns?"

"I was, sir" replied Mr Pickwick; "I was observing what singular old places they are."

"You!" said the old man, contemptuously, "What do you know of the time when young men shut themselves up in those lonely rooms, and read and read, hour after hour, and night after night, till their reason wandered beneath their midnight studies; till their mental powers were exhausted; till morning's light brought no freshness or health to them; and they sank beneath the unnatural devotion of their youthful energies to their dry old books? Coming down to a later time, and a very different day, what do you know of the gradual sinking beneath consumption, or the quick wasting of fever—the grand results of 'life' and dissipation—which men have undergone in these same rooms? They are no ordinary houses, those. There is not a panel in the old wainscotting, but what, if it were endowed with the powers of speech and memory, could start from the wall, and tell its tale of horror—the romance of life, sir, the romance of life. Commonplace as they may seem now, I tell you they are strange old places, and I would rather hear many a legend with a terrific sounding name, than the true history of one old set of chambers."
... "Talk of your German universities,"... "Pooh, pooh! there's romance enough at home without going half a mile for it; only people never think of it."'

—Charles Dickens, from *The Pickwick Papers*, 1837.

'It is to be remarked of chambers in general, that they must have been built for chambers, to have the right kind of loneliness. You may make a great dwellinghouse very lonely by isolating suites of rooms, and calling them chambers, but you cannot make the true kind of loneliness. In dwellinghouses there have been family festivals; children have grown in them, girls have bloomed into women in them, courtships and marriages have taken place in them. True chambers never were young, childish, maidenly; never had dolls in them, or rockinghorses, or christenings, or betrothals, or little coffins. Let Gray's Inn identify the child who first touched hands and hearts with Robinson Crusoe in any one of its many "sets," and that child's little statute, in white marble with a golden inscription, shall be at its service, at my cost and charge, as a drinking fountain for the spirit to freshen its thirsty square. Let Lincoln's produce, from all its houses, a twentieth of the procession derivable from any dwellinghouse one twentieth of its age, of fair young brides who married for love and hope, not settlements, and all the Vice-Chancellors shall thenceforward be kept in nosegays for nothing, on application to the writer hereof. It is not denied that on the terrace of the Adelphi, or in any of the streets of that subterranean-stable-haunted spot, or about Bedford Row, or James Street of that ilk (a gruesome place), or anywhere among the neighbourhoods that have done flowering and have run to seed, you may find chambers replete with the accommodations of Solitude, Closeness, and Darkness, where you may be as lowspirited as in the genuine article, and might be as easily murdered, with the placid reputation of having merely gone down to the seaside. But, the many waters of life did run musical in those dry channels once;—among the Inns, never.'

—Charles Dickens, from *Chambers,* in *The Uncommercial Traveller*, 1860.

---

27. COUNSEL IN AND OUT OF THEIR CHAMBERS:

27.1. In practice in chambers

'"Where does Serjeant Snubbin live?"
"In Lincoln's Inn Old Square," replied Perker.
"I should like to see him," said Mr Pickwick.
"See Serjeant Snubbin, my dear sir" rejoined Perker, in utter amazement.
"Pooh, pooh, impossible. See Serjeant Snubbin. Bless you, my dear sir, such a thing was never heard of, without a consultation fee being previously paid, and a consultation fixed. It couldn't be done, my dear sir; it couldn't be done."

Mr Pickwick, however, had made up his mind not only that it could be done, but that it should be done; and the consequence was, that within ten minutes after he had received the assurance that the thing was impossible, he was conducted by his solicitor into the outer office of the great Serjeant Snubbin himself.

It was an uncarpeted room of tolerable dimensions, with a large writing-table drawn up near the fire: the baize top of which had long since lost all claim to its original hue of green, and had gradually grown grey with dust and age, except where all traces of its natural colour were obliterated by inkstains. Upon the table were numerous little bundles of papers tied with red tape; and behind it, sat an elderly clerk, whose sleek appearance, and heavy gold watch chain, presented imposing indications of the extensive and lucrative practice of Mr Serjeant Snubbin...

Mr Serjeant Snubbin was a lantern-faced, sallow complexioned man, of about five-and-forty, or—as the novels say—he might be fifty. He had that dull-looking boiled eye which is often to be seen in the heads of people who have applied themselves doing many hours to a weary and laborious course of study; and which would have been sufficient, without the additional eyeglass which dangled from a broad black riband round his neck, to warn a stranger that he was very near-sighted. His hair was thin and weak, which was partly attributable to his having never devoted much time to its arrangement, and partly to his having worn for five-and-twenty years the forensic wig which hung on a block beside him. The marks of hairpowder on his coat-collar, and the ill-washed and worse tied white neckerchief round his throat, showed that he had not found leisure since he left the court to make any alteration in his dress: while the slovenly style of the remainder of his costume warranted the inference that his personal appearance would not have been very much improved if he had. Books of practice, heaps of papers, and opened letters, were scattered over the table, without any attempt at order or arrangement; the furniture of the room was old and ricketty; the doors of the book-case were rotting on their hinges; the dust flew out from the carpet in little clouds at every step; the blinds were yellow with age and dirt; the state of everything in the room showed, with a clearness not to be mistaken, that Mr Serjeant Snubbin was far too much occupied with his professional pursuits to take any great heed or regard of his personal comforts.'

—Charles Dickens, from *The Pickwick Papers*, 1837.

The character of Snubbin is generally taken to have been based on the historical figure of Serjeant Arabin, an eccentric who is the subject of Sir Robert Megarry's monograph *Arabinesque-at-Law*.

'Mr Furnival's chambers were on the first floor in a very dingy edifice in Old Square, Lincoln's Inn. This square was always dingy, even when it was comparatively open and served as the approach from Chancery Lane to the Lord Chancellor's Court: but now it has been built up with new shops for the Vice-Chancellor,[1] and to my eyes it seems more dingy than ever.

He there occupied three rooms, all of them sufficiently spacious for the purposes required, but which were made oppressive by their general dinginess and by a smell of old leather which pervaded them. In one of them sat at his desk Mr Crabwitz... The door opening into the room of Mr Crabwitz was in the corner fronting you on the left-hand side as you entered the chambers. Immediately on your left was a large waiting-room, in which an additional clerk usually sat at an ordinary table. This waiting-room was very dingy, much more so than the clerk's room, and boasted of no furniture but eight old leathern chairs and two old tables. It was surrounded by shelves which were laded with books and dust, which by no chance were ever disturbed. But to my ideas the most dingy of the three rooms was that large one in which the great man himself sat; the door of which directly fronted you as you entered. The furniture was probably better than that in the other chambers, and the place had certainly the appearance of warmth and life which comes from frequent use; but nevertheless, of all the rooms in which I ever sat I think it was the most gloomy. There were heavy curtains to the windows, which had once been ruby but were now brown; and the ceiling was brown, and the thick carpet was brown, and the books which covered every portion of the wall were brown, and the painted wood-work of the doors and windows was of a dark brown.'

—Anthony Trollope, from *Orley Farm*, 1862.

---

[1] To be precise—for the junior Vice-Chancellors, described in 11.3. This serjeant's chambers were thus evidently in Old Buildings (in the modern nomenclature). The (senior) Vice-Chancellor was accommodated to the w. of the Old Hall, as noted in 14.2.2.ii.

'There was nothing to forewarn me, on my arrival in the capital, of the dark and sinister events in which I was shortly to become embroiled. The sun was shining on Lincoln's Inn Fields; the azaleas were blooming in the gardens at the edge of New Square; the barristers hurrying in wigs and gowns across Carey Street were exchanging seasonable gossip about who was going to get Silk—it is on Maundy Thursday,[1] as my readers are doubtless aware, that the Lord Chancellor announces which members of the Junior Bar are to be elevated to the eminent and lucrative rank of Queen's Counsel.

My young friends in 62 New Square, when not engaged in deploring the inadequate remuneration negotiated on their behalf... were innocently employed in activities befitting to the Chancery Bar: Selena Jardine, if my memory serves me, in a lengthy and acrimonious piece of litigation relating to the rights of the debenture-holders in a public company; Desmond Ragwort in advising on the construction of documents affecting the title to certain land in the West Country; Michael Cantrip in sundry possession actions in various county courts. In the Revenue chambers next door, Julia Larwood was peacefully studying the latest Finance Bill.

Everything, in short, was proceeding in a manner appropriate to its nature and the season, with no such departure from the natural order of things as might be expected to be the portent of hidden danger and mysterious death. Or so, at any rate, it seemed to me; I did not realize, of course, how odd it was for Cantrip to be sent to the Channel Islands...'

—'Sarah Caudwell' (Sarah Cockburn [of LI]), from *The Sirens Sang of Murder*, 1989.

>> Max Hudson [solicitor in LI].

[1] Maundy Thursday: it was traditional for the names of those who had been elevated to the rank of Queen's (King's) Counsel to be published (in *The Times*, and in the Inns) on the last Thursday before Easter. See also Glossary: Queen's Counsel.

27.a. George Cruikshank: 'The celebrated Bell of Lincoln's Inn', *ca.* 1825 [HSLI].

This caricature shows r., the w. end of the Vice-Chancellor's Court arcade. John Bell [of GI] (1764-1836) practised on the equity side of the Bar, from chambers in Lincoln's Inn. His appearance was short and stout. He was lame, and he spoke with a broad Westmoreland accent, the effect of which was accentuated by a stammer, and he wrote in handwriting which was never more than barely legible. This caused Lord Eldon, overheard in conversation with the Prince Regent, to describe Bell as the best lawyer in the land, although 'he can neither read, write, walk or talk'. Bell himself said that he wrote in three hands: one which he could read, one which his Clerk could read, and one which neither he nor his Clerk could read—*ODNB*.

27.2. The concentration of conveyancing counsel and equity draftsmen in the Inn

The Inner for a Rich Man
The Middle for a Poor
Lincoln's for a Parchmenter
and Gray's for the Law [or *a Boor*].

—Anon. doggerell, of unknown date.

> W Ball, *Lincoln's Inn*, 1947.

'...there is a certain sort of legal person, in bowler hat, black jacket a little dusty, striped trousers concertina-ing at the ankles and over wrinkled shoes, and a general expression of pinched antique gleam, that I seem only to see in Lincoln's Inn.'

—David Piper, from *The Companion Guide to London*, seventh edn., 1992.

This description was apt to members of a generation of very learned Chancery silks, who could have been named, and of whom some have retired or died since the date of this book's publication.

Who wyll be ware in purchasynge
consider the points here folowyng
Furst see that the lond be
clere in tytle of the sellere
See that he out of prison be
and that of good mynde he be
And that it stand in no daunger
of no woman's dower
See whether the tenour be bond or free
and see release of every feoffe
See that the seller be of age
and that it ly in no mortgage
Looke whether a tale thereof be found
and yf it stand of stat[ute] bound
Consider what service longe therto
and what quite rent therout must go
And iff it move of wedded woman
thinke on covert de baron than
And iff thee may in any wise
make ye charter with warantise
To thin heirs and assigns also.
This schall a wise purchasour doo
In xv yeres iff thee wise be thou
schalt agane the monay see.

—Sir John Fortescue [of LI], 'Who wyll be ware', mid-C15th.

>> Professor Paul Brand.

These lines summarise admirably the investigation of title which a prudent conveyancer would have needed to make in order to ensure that his client acquired good title to land, or had good security for the lending of money on mortgage. The check-list would have remained largely unaltered until the major property law reforms of 1922-5. A few of the points remain relevant, and the prudence entirely so, half a millennium later.

'It is night in Lincoln's Inn—perplexed and troublous valley of the shadow of the law, where suitors generally find but little day—and fat candles are snuffed out in offices, and clerks have rattled down the crazy wooden stairs, and dispersed. The bell that rings at nine o'clock, has ceased its doleful clangour about nothing; the gates are shut; and the night porter, a solemn warder with a mighty power of sleep, keeps guard in his lodge. From tiers of staircase windows, clogged lamps like the eyes of Equity, bleared Argus with a fathomless pocket for every eye and an eye upon it, dimly blink at the stars. In dirty upper casements, here and there, hazy little patches of candlelight reveal where some wise draughtsman and conveyancer yet toils for the entanglement of real estate in meshes of sheepskin, in the average ratio of about a dozen of sheep to an acre of land. Over which beelike industry, these benefactors of their species linger yet, though officehours be past; that they may give, for every day, some good account at last.'

—Charles Dickens, from *Bleak House*, 1852.

In the attic rooms of Lincoln's Inn there dwell
A race of lawyers, who, I've heard men tell,
Can almost anything on earth convey—
Except the meaning of the things they say.
Far from the Courts, far from the dust of strife,
The dust of documents o'erlays their life—
If life there be for dusty creatures who
Know only deeds you execute, not do.
Your blood is red, from all the wine you drink.
If theirs is blue, it's only blue with ink.
A well drawn settlement's their one true joy.
Wine, women, song serve only to annoy.

The mysteries of life? 'Tis plain to see
That Elphinstone[1] *for them could find no Key*[1]
And yet—three times a year these wretches meet,
Make bawdy jokes, drink far too much, and eat,
And laugh, and shout and make a mighty din,
Which wakes the dead in quiet Lincoln's Inn.
Then men turn pale and virgins in a fright
Cry 'May the Lord be kind to us tonight!'
For pure conveyancers have ill repute,
When they've been dining at their Institute.[2]

—Thomas Shelford [of LI], 'Conveyancers', mid-C20th, in *Verses from Lincoln's Inn*, 1975.

[1] Key and Elphinstone, *A Compendium of Precedents in Conveyancing*, first edn. 1875.

[2] The Institute: the name of an association open to distinguished junior chancery counsel, with a membership *numerus clausus* of forty, and who generally are in practice in the Inn. It was founded by twelve men, meeting at the Freemasons' Tavern, in 1815.

The law the lawyers know about
Is property and land;
But why the leaves are on the trees,
And why the waves disturb the seas,
Why honey is the food of bees,
Why horses have such tender knees,
Why winters come when rivers freeze,
Why Faith is more than what one sees,
And Hope survives the worst disease,
And Charity is more than these,
They do not understand.

—Hilary Pepler, from 'The Devil's Devices', 1915.

These lines have been much quoted in anthologies, both legal and general. None, however, has suggested a connection with Lincoln's Inn. It seems very probable that—for better or worse—they were inspired by Pepler's visits to the Inn. He was a friend of Edward Johnston, the art teacher and calligrapher in whose Old Buildings chambers Eric Gill, the sculptor and typographer, lodged for some years. Gill's sensibility to that experience is quoted elsewhere. Pepler and Gill became related by marriage: Pepler's son married Gill's daughter. They lived and worked in a circle of notable artists, writers and craftsmen in suburban London and rural Sussex, and these residential chambers in the Inn were their only known immersion in the legal world.

¶ The author of these lines spoke them at the Memorial Service in Temple Church for her grandfather, Ted Nugee, in February 2015. Edward Nugee QC [of IT] had long been respected in the legal profession as the doyen of the Chancery Bar, having practised from chambers in New Square for some sixty years:

I do not know, but I presume,
There will be walks in which I miss
The smiling shuffle, and the room
Where on your chair you sank content
Ensconced by books, wrapped round with
Memories, tea-scented, kindly lent.

I shall never possess what you
Bequeathed. I have not got the space
To store your antique worn-copper words,
To remember exactly who married whom,
And in which place.

The chronology of ancient battles, the fleets
Which glitter gold in your flecked lids
Shall dullen when they close. The streets'
Original names shall fade once more,
Erased as the brick-work topples.

The obscure, to its obscurity
Once more shall fall. But through the leaves
Of certain knowledge I shall still trace,
Though you not there to help,
From the easy chair, in the easy place,
The marks left by a guiding finger, facts which lace
back together
The chuckle, the shuffle, the smile, and the familiar face.

—Rose Nugee, 'I do not know', 2015 [the author].

27.3. Draftsmen of constitutions and codes

¶ Knowledge, values and skills acquired within the Inn have been widely applied beyond these shores.

A paradox of British constitutional history is that a nation which proclaims with pride that it has an unwritten constitution should have produced lawyers who have drafted (or assisted in drafting) written constitutions for many other territories; and a corresponding paradox of English legal history is that a system which shuns the codes of the Civil Law should be served by a legal profession whose members have drafted codes for other jurisdictions. The explanations are, of course, to be found in the needs of the British settlements and colonies, and in later times the dominions, states and republics of British origin.

Prime examples of a constitution and of a code are quoted below. They were not drafted in the Inn, but they were drafted by members of the Society, and it would be pleasurable to imagine that they had acquired something of their skills in the Inn.

¶ William Penn (1644-1718) [of LI], the founder of Pennsylvania, promulgated an early and idealistic constitution for his chartered colony. It was influential on the Founding Fathers when they came to draft the Constitution of the USA, a century later. Extracts are quoted here:

'To all Persons to whom these presents may come:

Whereas King George the Second by his letters Pattents under the Great Seal of England, bearing date the Fourth day of March, in the thirty third year of the King, for divers good causes and considerations therein mentioned, hath been graciously pleased to give and grant unto me, William Penn… son and heir of Sir William Penn deceased, and to my heirs and assigns forever, all that tract of land or Province of Pennsilvania in America… And whereas the Kings dearest brother James Duke of York and Albany, etc. by his Deeds of Feoffment under his hand and seal, duly perfected, bearing date the 24th day of August

1682, of all that tract of land, lying and being from twelve miles northward of Newcastle upon Delaware River, in America, to Cape Henlopen upon the said river and Bay of Delaware.

Now know ye, That for the well-being and good Government of the said Province and territories thereunto annexed, and for the encouragement of all the free-men and planters that may be therein concerned, in pursuance of the rights and powers aforementioned, I the said William Penn… do declare, grant and confirm unto all the free-men, planters, and adventurers of, in and to the said province and territories thereof, these liberties…

Imprimis: That the Government of this Province and Territories thereof, shall from time… consist of the proprietary and Governour, and the free-men of the said Province and Territories thereof in the form of a Provincial Council and assembly, which Provincial Council shall consist of eighteen persons, being three out of each County, and which Assembly shall consist of thirty six persons, being six out of each County, men of most note, for their virtue, wisdom, and ability, by whom all laws shall be made, and publick affairs transacted, as is hereafter limited and declared.

……

4thly. That the Provincial Council in all cases and matters of moment, as their arguing upon bills to be past into laws, or proceedings about erecting of Courts of Justice, sitting in judgment upon criminals impeached, and choice of officers in such manner as is hereinafter expressed, not less than two thirds of the whole, shall make a quorum, and that the consent and approbation of two thirds of that quorum shall be had in all such cases or matters of moment. And that in all cases and matters of lesser moment, one third of the whole shall make a quorum, the majority of which shall and may always determine in such cases and causes of lesser moment.

5thly. That the Governour and Provincial Council shall have the power of preparing and proposing to the assembly hereafter mentioned, all bills which they shall see needful, and that shall at any time being past into laws within the Province and Territories thereof, which bills shall be published, and affixed to the most noted place in every County of this Province and Territories thereof twenty days before the meeting of the assembly, in order to passing them into laws.

6thly. That the Governour and Provincial Council shall take care that all laws, statutes and ordinances which shall at any time be made within the said Province and Territories, be duly and diligently executed.

7thly. That the Governour and Provincial Council shall at all times have the care of the peace and safety of this Province, and Territories thereof; and that nothing be by any person attempted to the subversion of this frame of Government.

……

11thly. That one third of the Provincial Council residing with the Governour, shall with the Governour from time to time have the care of the management of all publick affairs, relating to the peace, justice, treasury and improvement of the Province and Territories, and to the good Education of youth, and sobriety of the manners of the inhabitants therein, as aforesaid.

……

In Witness whereof, I the said William Penn at Philadelphia in Pennsilvania, have unto this present Charter of Liberties set my hand and broad seal this Second day of the Second Month, in the Year our Lord 1683, being the thirty fifth year of the King, and the third year of my Government.

William Penn.

This within Charter which we have distinctly heard read, and thankfully received, shall be by us inviolably kept, at Philadelphia, the 2d of the 2d Month, 1683.

The Members of the Provincial Council present…
The Members of the Assembly present… Some of the inhabitants of Philadelphia then present…'

—from *The Frame of Government of the Province of Pennsilvania and Territories thereunto annexed, in America*, 1683 (printed edn. 1689) [SoFP].

¶ This is a later view of those laws:

'I took a trip once with Penn to his colony of Pennsylvania. The laws there are contained in a small volume and are so extremely good that there has been no alteration in them ever since Sir William made them. 'Tis a fine country, and the people are neither oppressed by poor rates, tithes nor taxes.'

—Lord Peterborough, quoted in Rev Joseph Spence, *Observations, Anecdotes and Characters*, 1830.

> James Sutherland, *Oxford Book of Literary Anecdotes*, 1975.

¶ Among those members of the Society who have drafted codes of law may be taken, as a prime example, Thomas, Lord Macaulay (1800-59), the historian, whose views on kings and queens and on England were widely influential for half a century after his death. Those views and his of colonial administration are now out of fashion and seem unlikely ever to regain general acceptance.

However, Macaulay's efforts in law-making have had a lasting, if not fully acknowledged, influence. He finished drafting, almost single-handed, the Indian Penal Code in 1857, which was enacted in 1860 and brought into force in 1862. It was a remarkable achievement of lucidity and logic; its form was followed in other Indian codifications, and its content was widely emulated in other territories throughout the Empire. Under various names, and with amendments or repeals, it is still part of the law in several independent jurisdictions of the world at the present day.

The following are the opening sections of The Indian Penal Code, 1860:

'WHEREAS it is expedient to provide a General Penal Code for British India; It is enacted as follows:–

1. This Act shall be called THE INDIAN PENAL CODE, and shall take effect on and from the 1st day of May, 1861, throughout the whole of the Territories which are or may become vested in Her Majesty by the Statute 21 and 22 Victoria, chapter 106, entitled "An Act for the better Government of India" except the Settlement of Prince of Wales' Island, Singapore and Malacca.

2. Every person shall be liable to punishment under this Code and not otherwise for every act or omission contrary to the provisions thereof, of which he shall be guilty within the said Territories on or after the said 1st day of May, 1861.

3. Any person liable, by any law passed by the Governor General of India in Council, to be tried for an offence committed beyond the limits of the said Territories, shall be dealt with according to the provisions of this Code for any act committed beyond the said Territories, in the same manner as if such act had been committed within the said Territories.

4. Every servant of the Queen shall be subject to punishment under this Code for every act or omission contrary to the provisions thereof, of which he, whilst in such service, shall be guilty on or after the said 1st day of May, 1861, within the dominions of any Prince or State in alliance with the Queen, by virtue of any treaty or engagement heretofore entered into with the East India Company or which may have been or may hereafter be made in the name of the Queen by any Government of India.

5. Nothing in this Act is intended to repeal, vary, suspend, or affect any of the provisions of the Statute 3 and 4 William IV. chapter 85, or of any Act of Parliament passed after that Statute in any wise affecting the East India Company, or any of the provisions of any Act for punishing mutiny and desertion of Officers and Soldiers, in the service of Her Majesty or of the East India Company, or of any Act for the Government of the Indian Navy, or of any special or local law.'

A. ATTORNEYS AND SOLICITORS

28. ATTORNEYS AND SOLICITORS IN THE INN:

¶ It is widely believed that the Inns are places in which only barristers are to be found at work. It was not so in past centuries, and while it has now become substantially true in the two Temples, in the present generation Lincoln's and Gray's retain a mix of counsel's chambers and solicitors' offices. In Lincoln's, the firms of solicitors in (or until recent decades in) New Square include some which established themselves or moved in there in the first half of the C18th.

This Society was the first of the four to pass a regulation excluding practising attorneys from being called to the Bar, in 1556.

In the past, attorneys were by no means the only tenants in the Inn who were not members of the Society, there being a tradition of architects' studios and surveyors' drawing-offices, as well as a policy of letting surplus residential chambers to members of the artistic or literary world. A very few such tenancies continued in Gray's and Lincoln's into the latter half of the last century.

28.1. Four attorneys and their respective clients

¶ Successive generations of attorneys and solicitors have conducted their practices in the Inn for several centuries, and in consequence a good number of C19th and C20th novels and plays evoke them in imagination, of which a few are quoted in the following section. But attorneys or solicitors in practice as such in the Inn have rarely if ever been named in books on the Inn and its history. Accordingly, a handful of such practitioners of the C18th and C19th are so here. They are men of whom a lasting record survives of themselves, their abilities and success, but are not untypical of many others.

i. The brothers, Sir James Graham, Bt., MP and Thomas Graham, FSA

'Thomas and James Graham were at the age of 16 sent to their mother's brother, James Coulthard, of Lincoln's Inn an eminent and able solicitor, attorney and conveyancer (his wife during their early years being a foster parent to them) who brought them up in his profession and took them into partnership. On his death they succeeded to his business, which they conducted for 30 years; during which period they had the superintendence of the affairs of several of the nobility and gentry in the kingdom, as their confidential professional advisers, and by their zeal, ability, integrity and indefatigable industry, restored many families of distinction to their estates, and to wealth, ease and comfort, by the judicious arrangement of their affairs. They were consequently honoured with the warmest friendship of the greater part of their respectable clients; and

28.a.i. C S Taylor after J Opie: Sir James Graham, Bt., MP [Editor's coll.].

several of the most able men on the bench, at the bar, and in high public situations, have received the first part of their legal education in their office. They were never known to recommend or promote a law suit; on the contrary, by their liberal, judicious, and conciliating manners, they have accommodated and prevented numberless family and other disputes; but, when legal proceedings have been inevitable, or deemed necessary by the advice of their superiors, they have prosecuted such causes, with that determined spirit and exertion, which received the constant approbation of their employers. We sincerely wish that many individuals of the legal profession would imitate such conduct.'

—William Playfair, from *British Family Antiquity*, 1809-11 [BL].

From the solicitors named here is descended the firm, as part of Wragge Lawrence Graham, formerly known as Lawrence Graham, who for long were at 6, New Square, and are now in modern offices at More London on the s. bank of the Thames. The reference to members of the bench and bar having spent time in their offices is significant. This was a recognised way of obtaining a part of a legal training for members of the Bar.

ii. Thomas Wildman, MP

¶ Wildman was among the most colourful, fashionable and successful of late C18th attorneys, equalling if not excelling William Hickey, whose name is more widely known at the present day on account of his *Diaries*.

He acted for a number of great landowning families. Of those, a client of his who—for better *and* for worse—has an enduring name was William Beckford (1760-1844). Wildman was one of those entrusted with the management of the notorious fortune founded on the Jamaica sugar plantations, which Beckford inherited in infancy on the death of his father Alderman Beckford, Lord Mayor of London. Wildman continued as Beckford's attorney and *homme d'affaires* on the latter's attaining his majority, assisted in the management of the client's landed property in England and the West Indies by two of his brothers. Besides his personal life of exceptional eccentricity and scandal, Beckford is remembered as the builder of one of the first and greatest 'gothick' follies in England—Fonthill Abbey in Wiltshire (around the park of which he built a wall to keep out the local hunt)—and of the classical Greek-inspired tower on Lansdown Hill in Bath, and lastly as the owner of the palace of Monserrat in the hill town of Sintra above Lisbon. Wildman sat in Parliament as MP for Hindon in Wiltshire, a rotten borough owned by his client, and thereby to represent in the Commons his client alone. He was admitted to Lincoln's Inn, but not called.

'The late Mr T Wildman was an eminent solicitor, and partner with, but not in any way related to the late Mr Coulthard of Lincoln's Inn. As a practitioner in the law, he was a man of intelligence, endowed with a mind active and ever fervid for the good of his client, whose

28.a.ii. George Romney: A member of the Wildman family, believed to be Thomas Wildman, 1780s, photograph R Todd-White [coll. PHB].

The documentation referable to this portrait suggests that Wildman commissioned Romney to paint his portrait, and that an exact copy by Romney was commissioned by the landowner of an estate in the Dukeries of Nottinghamshire on the death of Wildman. It may be speculated that perhaps a grateful client wished to remember the attorney who had saved his fortune.

cause he seemed to make his own, and in the close of which he was seldom unsuccessful… the ardour of his zealous endeavours, added to the natural warmth of his mind, has more than once introduced Mr Wildman among the squibs of the day, in some strokes of wit, probably from the pen of an unfortunate opponent, who has too late known that a firm and active solicitor could make the worse a better case.'

—from *Gentleman's Magazine*, March 1796.

From Wildman is descended the firm of Payne Hicks Beach, which practises at 10 New Square, as did he, and in five other chambers buildings in the Inn.

iii. John Allan Powell

¶ Powell is believed to have begun his professional career in Dublin, as attorney to Lord Blessington, but the days of his prominence were spent in 9, New Square, Lincoln's Inn, in the then firm of Powell, Broderick and Wilde.

He played a significant rôle both in the most celebrated contentious lawsuit and in one of the more notable pieces of a solicitor's non-contentious legal business of his age, each of which is evoked in the sub-paragraphs which follow. Outside the usual world of legal practice he was, remarkably, a member of a British diplomatic mission sent to Italy to negotiate an international treaty.

There is a portrait of him by Alfred, Count d'Orsay in the NPG.

28.b. Sir Geo. Hayter: 'The Trial of Queen Caroline in 1820', 1823 [NPG].

The scene is in the old House of Lords. Powell is standing on the extreme l. of the picture. His professional opponent, the solicitor for the Queen, was William Vizard, who is in the centre foreground, sitting on the floor by a rail. Counsel instructed by Powell are Sir Robert Gifford, A-G., and Sir John Copley, Solicitor-General, standing together, bewigged, a little way in front of him. Lincoln's Inn luminaries dominate the scene. Those to be seen are (alphabetically):

Henry Brougham, later Baron Brougham and Vaux, later LC (Counsel to the Queen).

John Scott, Earl of Eldon, LC at that date

Thomas Erskine, Baron Erskine, formerly LC

John Singleton Copley, later Baron Lyndhurst, later LC

William Lamb, later Viscount Melbourne, later PM

Henry Addington, Viscount Sidmouth, formerly PM

William Van Mildert, sometime Preacher to the Society and later Bishop of Durham, the last of the earl-bishops of that county palatine.

• George IV, and his divorce suit against Queen Caroline

¶ Caroline of Brunswick married George, Prince of Wales, in 1795, and they parted in the following year, she returning to Germany. On his succeeding to the throne in 1820, she returned to England and resolved to be crowned Queen, and he determined to divorce her. There being no civil divorce procedure in England, an Act of Parliament was necessary, and a Bill of Pains and Penalties was introduced by the Government in the Lords. The proceedings became a trial of the Queen's honour, and were eventually abandoned. The case was the *cause célèbre* and scandal of its age. The solicitor to the Crown—the man instructed to orchestrate this attempt to obtain a royal divorce—was John Allan Powell.

• The probate of Napoléon Bonaparte

¶ Napoléon died on the 5th May 1821, at St Helena.

The extract printed below is taken from the engrossment of the official translation of his will, now in the PRO, followed by the grant of probate to his English and colonial estate. Interpolations have been made here, where that translation is misleading, but otherwise its infelicities have been left unchanged.

Although the calendar at the PRO does not show it, this will was first promulgated (by *acte de notariété*) in Paris. Its provisions provoked a

28.c. Carl Teuben: Napoléon dictating a draft of his will to Général Marchand, 1821 [Bibliothèque Paul Marmottan, Paris].

number of legal issues in France. It was on the advice of Jean-Jacques-Régis de Cambacérès (1753-1824) of Montpellier, the chairman of the commission which had drafted the *Code Civil* of 1804, that Montholon later applied to prove the will in England.

Powell would probably have taken responsibility as an *homme d'affaires* for superintending the general administration of the estate and its payment or transfer to France, instructing William Fox as a proctor to extract the grant of probate from the Prerogative Will Office, adjacent to Doctors' Commons, in Knightrider St., s. of St Paul's. This Office—the precursor of the present-day Principal Registry (Probate) of the Family Division—was under the legal superintendence of the Archbishop of Canterbury's Surrogate (an advocate from Doctors' Commons), and had probate jurisdiction over estates comprising assets located in more than one diocese of the Church of England, and estates of persons dying domiciled outside England and Wales but with assets within, or dying domiciled here but leaving an estate partly situated abroad. William Fox's other legal profession, that of notary public, also depended (as, in London within the jurisdiction of the Scriveners' Company, it still does) upon the Archbishop of Canterbury.

The grant is interesting at a technical level: it admits a will written in a foreign language by means of an English translation; it overcomes the absence of an attestation clause and the signatures of witnesses on the will by means of an affidavit of due execution by one or more of those who were present at the time when Napoléon signed his will; and it grants probate to one executor alone, with power reserved to the other two to apply at a later date. Thus the requirements of English law and practice were found to have been satisfied by a testator whose intent was manifestly to make a will in accordance with the law of France, and the *Code* which bears his name, and having no regard to the laws of England.

'15 April 1821 at Longwood,
Island of St Helena

This is my Testament
or Act of my Last Will

1: I die in the apostolic and Roman religion in the bosom of which I was born above fifty years since.

2: I desire that my ashes may repose upon the banks of the Seine in the midst of that French people whom I have so much loved.

3: I have always had reason to be perfectly satisfied with my dearest wife Marie Louise. I retain for her to my last moment the tenderest sentiments—I pray her to watch over my son in order to preserve him from the snares which still surround his infancy.

4: I recommend my son never to forget that he was from birth a French prince and never to allow himself to become an instrument in the hands of the Triumvirs who oppress the people of Europe. He ought never to combat against nor in any manner injure France. Let him adopt my motto *Tout pour le peuple François*[1].

5: I die prematurely, assassinated by the English oligarchy and their hired assassin — [2]. The English people will not be slow in avenging me.

6: The two unfortunate results of the invasions of France, when she still had so many resources, are to be attributed to the treason of Marmont, Angereau, Talleyrand, and La Fayette. I forgive them—may the posterity of France forgive them like me!

......

[The main dispositive parts of the Will, omitted here, contain very numerous legacies and gifts of shares of residue, which were the cause of the legal issues in France referred to above.]

......

I appoint Count Montholon Bertrand and Marchand my testamentary executors.

This present testament wholly written with my own hand is signed and sealed with my arms.
Napoléon.

The paper writings hereto annexed contain a true and faithful translation of the original last Will and Testament and seven Codicils thereto of Napoléon Bonaparte late of the Island of St Helena deceased, in the French language also hereto annexed made by us this 21st day of July One thousand eight hundred and twenty four: as witness our hands and seals:

Wm. Fox, not: pub: (L.S.)

John A. Powell, Lincoln's Inn (L.S.)

Proved at London (with seven Codicils) 5th August, 1824 before the Worshipful Stephen Lushington, Doctor of Laws and Surrogate, by the oath of Charles Tristan Comte de Montholon the first named executor to whom administration was granted being first sworn duly to administer power reserved of making the like grant to Henry Gratian Comte Bertrand and Louis Marchand the other executors named in the Will when they or either or them shall apply for the same.

Extracted by: William Fox, Proctor, Doctors' Commons.'

>> Napoléon connection: Martyn Gowar (solicitor formerly in LI).

1 *françois*: the old spelling of *français*.

2 hired assassin: a reference to the Governor of St Helena, Hudson Lowe, whose régime Napoléon bitterly resented. He had also said, a few days before his death, that he laid 'the horror and approbium of my death at the feet of the ruling family of England'.

It may be remarked that Napoléon, in his bitterness, chose to forget the beauty, fecundity and language which he had chosen to leave behind in Elba.

28.2. Solicitors' partnerships

'On the appointed day the Minister, wearing a clean linen surplice, and accompanied by Mrs Pennington Bickford shall call at 9, New Square, Lincoln's Inn, and shall say in an audible voice the words here following:—

COLLECT:

> O Lord, for as much as it pleased Thee in times past to join together these Thy servants, Robert Lewin Hunter & Edmund Sidney Pollock Haynes, in a remarkable manner, let it now please Thee to put them lawfully and irremediably asunder, that forsaking one another they may simultaneously and severally work for their own advancement, and as their union has been singularly fruitless grant that their disconnexion may be rich with increase, and let them avoid all recrimination, neither turning to other (except in certified sickness) so long as they both shall live, according to the promises distinctly conveyed to our forefathers Abraham and Lot in the Holy Scriptures. AMEN.

HYMN:
(by Louie Pennington-Bickford; music by the Reverend W Pennington-Bickford)

mf *Children of Saint Clement Danes*
ff *Pray for Hunter* dim *pray for Haynes*
cr *Doubt of what may be in store*
mf *Makes us pray for Haynes the more.*
And as nothing else will rhyme
f *Pray for Hunter* ff *all the time.*

Haynes and Hunter in the past
Made a pact that could not last;
In the ordinary course
p *Hunter claims a quick divorce;*
All's arranged behind the scenes.
f *No King's Proctor* ff *intervenes.*

Orange sweet and lemon sour
Lay before them in this hour,
Wherein symbolised we see
f *Incompatibility.*
Lest this prove a time of loss
p *Grant them, Master, thy divorce. Amen.*

At this point oranges and/or lemons[1] will be distributed among the clerks of the dissolving partners. Hunter & Haynes will then be taken to the Old Roman Bath[2] in Strand Lane and partially immersed.

A Collection will then be made.

Hunter & Haynes will be dried and conducted to their several offices where they will proceed to DISSOLVE.'

—Charles Scott-Moncrieff, 'Order of Service authorised to be said on the dissolution of Messrs Hunter & Haynes', *ca.* 1922.

> E S P Haynes [solicitor in LI], *The Lawyer, a conversation piece*, 1951 (a posthumous collection, ed. Renée Haynes).

This imagined order of service was inspired by the fact of an acrimonious dissolution of the partnership between two prominent solicitors practising at 9, New Square, and whose names are correctly recorded in this piece. One was a figure in the London literary world, and the author of several books (one of which is briefly quoted elsewhere in this book), and the other's name is remembered in the distinguished firm of Hunters who still practise at that same address. The footnotes which follow are included for a reader not familiar with the topography of this corner of London.

1 oranges and lemons: a reference to the nursery rhyme beginning thus and to St Clement Danes, the church in the Strand in whose parish the offices lay.

2 Roman Bath: there are remains of a bath just s.w. of the Inn, adjacent to King's College, supposedly Roman but probably Georgian.

28.3. Their character, their offices and their practices

'The office of Voysey and Son is in the best part of Lincoln's Inn. Its panelled rooms give out a sense of grandmotherly comfort and security, very grateful at first to the hesitating investor, the dubious litigant. Mr Voysey's own room into which he walks about twenty past ten of a morning radiates enterprise besides. There is polish on everything; on the windows, on the mahogany of the tidily packed writing table that stands between them, on the brasswork of the fireplace in the other wall, on the glass of the firescreen which preserves only the pleasantness of a sparkling fire, even on Mr Voysey's hat as he takes it off to place it on the little red curtained shelf behind the door. Mr Voysey is sixty or more and masterful; would obviously be master anywhere from his own home outwards, or wreck the situation in his attempt. Indeed there is a buccaneering air sometimes in the twist of his glance, not altogether suitable to a family solicitor. On this bright October morning, Peacey, the head clerk, follows just too late to help him off with his coat, but in time to take it and hang it up with a quite unnecessary subservience. Mr Voysey is evidently not capable enough to like capable men about him. Peacey, not quite removed from Nature, has made some attempts to acquire protective colouring. A very drunken client might mistake him for his master. His voice very easily became a toneless echo of Mr Voysey's; later his features caught a line or two from that mirror of all the necessary virtues into which he was so constantly gazing; but how his clothes even when new contrive to look like old ones of Mr Voysey's is a mystery, and to his tailor a most annoying one. And Peacey is just a respectful number of years his master's junior. Relieved of his coat, Mr Voysey carries to his table the bunch of beautiful roses he is accustomed to bring to the office three times a week and places them for a moment only near the bowl of water there ready to receive them while he takes up his letters. These lie ready too, opened mostly, one or two private ones left closed and discreetly separate. By this time the usual salutations have passed, Peacey's "Good morning, sir;" Mr Voysey's "Morning, Peacey." Then as he gets to his letters Mr Voysey starts his day's work.'

—Harley Granville-Barker, Stage Directions for Act I, scene vi, *The Voysey Inheritance*, 1903.

>> Michael Rugman, FCA.

'Mr Giles was a leading partner in the firm of Roundells, Giles and Roundell, among the most eminent solicitors of Lincoln's Inn. He, in these days of prolonged maturity, might be described as still a young man. He had inherited from his father not only a large share in a first rate business, but no inconsiderable fortune; and though he had, in her circles, a celebrated wife, he had no children. He was opulent and prosperous, with no cares and anxieties of his own, and loved his profession, for which he was peculiarly qualified, being a man of uncommon sagacity, very difficult to deceive, and yet one who sympathised with his clients, who were all personally attached to him, and many of whom were among the distinguished personages of the realm.'

—Benjamin Disraeli, from *Lothair*, 1870.

Disraeli was enrolled as a student of the Society, but never called. He spent some time reading in the chambers in the Inn of his kinsman Nathaniel Basevi.

'"Horniman, Birley and Craine," said John, "is not one firm but four firms. It is the Gordon Selfridge of solicitors, different departments to suit all tastes and purses. For the humble but well-meaning citizens of Streatham or Brixton, Mr Brown and Mr Baxter labour unceasingly, resting not day nor night. For the hardfaced, sternbrowed moguls of commerce and industry, our City offices are ever open, and the warm

28.d. W Dendy Sadler: 'The New Will (Everything to my Wife absolutely)', publ. *ca.* 1890 [coll. PHB].

This engraving of a mid-C19th solicitor in his office, being consulted by clients, is based on a scene witnessed by the artist in a solicitor's office in a country town. Although not set in the Inn, it nevertheless depicts in perfect detail a room identical in all material respects to those which face into New Square, rebuilt or refurbished in the mid-C18th, whether after fire damage or otherwise. No drawing of the interior of an Inn solicitor's office has been found in the research for this book. Many items of equipment or furniture would have remained unchanged within such rooms in the Inn into the early 1960s, with the only significant intrusions being a telephone and a fountain or ball-point pen. These include japanned black boxes for storing the parchment deeds of individual clients, and box-cupboards which served as filing cabinets for bundles of correspondence (individually tied with red tape). Rooms in the Square such as this often have a large walk-in cupboard in which was kept, among other items, a commode or a chamber-pot, until the general installation of WCs, which in some chambers was only after the Second World War.

hearts and subtle brains of Mr Bourlass, Mr Bridewell and Mr Burt beat in a mighty diapason, and their cunning fingers are never still—here underwriting a charter party, there endorsing a bill of exchange, *sans recours*; and if all else palls, why bless me, they can always fill in the time between lunch and tea by forming a limited company. In Piccadilly, those gilded darlings of fortune, Osric Rasmussen and Emmanuel Oakshott, pin carnations to the palpitating bosoms of a horde of comely divorcees and spend their time, or such time as they can spare from race meetings and first nights, in drawing fantastic leases of flats in Half Moon Street and shops in the Burlington Arcade—"

"Two more whiskies," said Henry, "What do we do in Lincoln's Inn?"

"I've never really found out," said John, "but it's all most terribly gentlemanly. Our books of reference are *Burke* and *Debrett* and we're almost the last firm in London that draws up strict marriage settlements and calls the heir up on his twenty-first birthday to execute a disentailing deed and drink a glass of pre-1914 sherry."

"I thought that the peerage were all broke these days."

"So they are," said John regretfully. "So they are. I expect that's why we bought up the other offices. All the real money's in Streatham."'

—Michael Gilbert CBE [solicitor in LI],
from *Smallbone Deceased*, 1950.

Gilbert was a prolific writer of crime novels, much appreciated both in England and the USA. For thirty years he was a partner in the firm of Trower, Still & Keeling, then at 5, New Square.

28.4. Their taking the opinion of counsel in the Inn

'Mr Thomas Dove, familiarly known among clubmen, attorneys' clerks, and, perhaps, even among judges when very far from their seats of judgment, as Turtle Dove, was a counsel learned in the law. He was a counsel so learned in the law, that there was no question within the limits of an attorney's capability of putting to him, that he could not answer with the aid of his books. And when he had once given an opinion, all Westminster could not move him from it—nor could Chancery Lane and Lincoln's Inn and the Temple added to Westminster. When Mr Dove had once been positive, no man on earth was more positive and though, whether wrong or right, he was equally stubborn, it must be acknowledged that he was seldom proved to be wrong. Consequently the attorneys believed in him, and he prospered. He was a thin man, over fifty years of age, very full of scorn and wrath, impatient of a fool, and thinking most men to be fools; afraid of nothing on earth—and, so his enemies said, of nothing elsewhere; eaten up by conceit; fond of law, but fonder, perhaps of dominion, soft as milk to those who acknowledged his power, but a tyrant to all who contested it; conscientious, thoughtful, sarcastic, bright-witted, and laborious. He was a man who never spared himself. If he had a case in hand, though the interest to himself in it was almost nothing, he would rob himself of rest for a week, should a point arise which required such labour. It was the theory of Mr Dove's life that he would never be beaten. Perhaps it was some fear in this respect that had kept him from Parliament and confined him to the courts and the company of attorneys...

At the present moment Mr Dove is interesting to us solely as being the learned counsel in whom Mr Camperdown trusted—to whom Mr Camperdown was willing to trust for an opinion in so grave a matter as that of the Eustace diamonds. A case was made out and submitted to Mr Dove immediately after that scene on the pavement in Mount Street, at which Mr Camperdown had endeavoured to induce Lizzie to give up the necklace; and the following is the opinion which Mr Dove gave...

When Mr Camperdown had thrice read this opinion, he sat in his chair an unhappy old man.

...A better attorney, for the purposes to which his life was devoted, did not exist in London than Mr Camperdown. To say that he was honest, is nothing. To describe him simply as zealous, would be to fall very short of his merits. The interests of his clients were his own interests, and the legal rights of the properties of which he had the legal charge, were as dear to him as his own blood. But it could not be said of him that he was a learned lawyer. Perhaps in that branch of a solicitor's profession in which he had been called upon to work, experience goes further than learning. It may be doubted, indeed, whether it is not so in every branch of every profession. But it might, perhaps, have been better for Mr Camperdown had he devoted more hours of his youth to reading books on conveyancing. He was now too old for such studies, and could trust only to the reading of other people. The reading, however, of other people was always at his command, and his clients were rich men who did not mind paying for an opinion. To have an opinion from Mr Dove, or some other learned gentleman, was the everyday practice of his life; and when he obtained, as he often did, little coigns of legal vantage and subtle definitions as to property which were comfortable to him, he would rejoice to think that he could always have a Dove at his hand to tell him exactly how far he was justified in going in defence of his clients' interests...

He and Mr Camperdown had known each other intimately for many years, and though the rank of the two men in their profession differed much, they were able to discuss questions of law without any appreciation of that difference among themselves. The one man knew much, and the other little; the one was not only learned, but possessed also of great gifts; while the other was simply an ordinary clearheaded man of business; but they had sympathies in common which made them friends; they were both honest and unwilling to sell their services to dishonest customers; and they equally entertained a deeprooted contempt for that portion of mankind who thought that property could be managed and protected without the intervention of lawyers. The outside world to them was a world of pretty, laughing, ignorant children; and lawyers were the parents, guardians, pastors and masters by whom the children should be protected from the evils incident to their childishness.'

—Anthony Trollope, from *The Eustace Diamonds*, 1872.

>> Gordon Exall [of LI].

28.5. London agency

'As a country lawyer grows more successful and more senior he tends to retreat from the law's ferocities, from confrontations in the local courts, from days on end waiting around the High Court and from the inevitable conferences with Counsel with which these days are linked. The senior solicitor will contentedly become increasingly involved in the problems of his local clients. Some never make this change and one sees them daily in the law courts, balding men sitting behind Counsel, passing notes and copy letters, insiders all, knowing exactly where Court C 49 is, where a quick snack can be found and where spontaneous conferences can be held.

Until customs change, someone has to do it. The first step is to hire an assistant solicitor with a view to eventual partnership in your progressive, long established and witty firm. I became, soon after the war, a frail addition to these ranks.

At that time solicitors in the country thrived and kept themselves afloat on the backs of their London Agents. We did not know how to do without them. We did our divorces, in the main, in the Law Courts and let our Agents do all our Registry work. Nowadays, though we still have London Agents, we rarely have to bother them; we have tardily acquired much of the knowhow under our own roof. In 1946 there was nothing like it.

Very soon, therefore, I was starting to call, almost weekly, on Rider Heaton Meredith and Mills, at their offices at New Square in Lincoln's Inn. I could never get over their rhythmic title. I spent too much time for my own good travelling third class in the unheated Fenman, making up doggerel, the last triumphant line of which was the firm's name. I should, of course, have been relearning the law.

From Liverpool Street I would catch a tube to Holborn and walk through to New Square via a number of tennis courts on which, it seemed to me, the more nubile members of the Palladium chorus were playing patball. Eyes averted, I walked to New Square and down the steps into the dungeon part of the property where our London Agents dealt with their country clients. All the property in this area, offices, chambers and courts, were suffering from the effects of "Don't you know there's a war on?" It was a licence to permit disrepair, everything dingy, unpainted and dimly lit.

In this Victorian ambience (you could see, through the upper windows, the feet and ankles of people walking round New Square) Herbert Hudson, black coat and striped trousers, cockney to his shoelaces, held sway. There was nothing and no one that he didn't know. No question of procedure—or even of law—caused him any difficulty. He was a complete master of his craft. The firm had, I am sure, numerous partners, but I homed in on Herbert, convinced that no one could improve on the service he gave.

He was on best-friend terms with a widespread group of Counsel's Clerks. He was welcomed to their Chambers like visiting minor royalty. The solicitor in tow, wearing (in my case) his ill-fitting demob suit, pre-war shoes and tie, shared some of the glory. The barristers, too, treated him, if not with subservience, at least as a respected nearly equal. He had, naturally, his current favourite Counsel. I would never have dreamed—however awful some of them turned out to be—of making any criticism.

With hindsight I have realised why our divorce petitions were heard in London. He had a particularly close connection with an elderly barrister who specialised in undefended divorces and never moved out of London. He was a meticulous old man, pale from too many hours spent in the half-light of his Chambers and of the Law Courts. I wondered, sometimes, how he would have coped if anything had gone wrong. In all his cases we had what Herbert called a con., and con. it sometimes was. Having brought the bemused client up from Wisbech (or is it down?) I listened, more than once, with apprehension as the old gentleman took him, paragraph by paragraph, through someone else's petition.

In some ways Herbert was like the ambitious manager of a football team. He was forever on the lookout for fresh and talented Counsel; like all the best managers he made some wrong judgements. "I'm having the papers" he would say "sent over to Mr DoubleBarrelled. He's a very promising young man. Everyone thinks he will go far. It won't last long of course, but his clerk is marking his briefs very reasonably indeed." Not long afterwards we saw the up and coming young man on his feet in court, so covered with confusion that even a kindly judge failed to extract much sense from him. We could understand why the fee was on the small side. "Pity about Mr Double-Barrelled" remarked Herbert, not a bit abashed. "Fortunately I've just come across a real tiger—even the judges dread him."

Barristers in those days were generally not so down to earth and comradely as they have become. There were all kinds of shibboleths that I never understood—to do with shaking hands and the use of surnames. I just limped along my own furrow, aiming at treating them as people. It was sometimes, with Chancery barristers in particular, not too easy. Their faces would go scarlet and their eyebrows would lift. They would say to my bemused client "Surely you must realise that what you are suggesting would be a clog on the equity?"—or worse still, on one occasion,

"I can't believe that those advising you have not warned you of the dire consequences of ignoring a restraint on anticipation." The strange thing was that they were brilliant men, with double firsts, unable to understand a different outlook. Back in the Fenman, hastening home, I found it hard to explain what the fuss was about.

Herbert had many successes in his search for talent. One particular goose turned into an unmistakeable swan. A slight, affable, amusing and ingenious young man he was, a common lawyer, younger even than I. The advice he gleefully gave was invariably going to set the opposition back on its heels. He was effortlessly good in court. This star soon shot out of our reach—and now he is a Lord Justice of Appeal. Judging by a newspaper photograph—unless there was some hideous mistake—he looks as though success has turned him into a ferocious and elderly old man.'

—David Barr [solicitor in Wisbech], describing the 1950s, from 'A Country Solicitor visits his London Agents', unpubl. essay, 1989 [LT].

David Barr was the author of several published books on the life of a country solicitor. He served as a coroner, and was for many years the fishing correspondent of *Country Life*.

28.6. Their professional associations, and their buildings:

i. The Law Society and its Hall

¶ It may confidently be assumed that some, at least, of the attorneys and solicitors with offices in the Inn will have been members of the earliest gatherings of those in practice in this quarter of London. Those were, as noted elsewhere, the Inns of Chancery (as they ceased to function as preparatory colleges for the Inns of Court), then from 1739 'The Society of Gentlemen Practisers in the Courts of Law and Equity' (the old Law Society).

In 1825 was formed 'The Society of Attorneys, Solicitors, Proctors and others not being barristers, practising in the Courts of Law and Equity in the United Kingdom'. This latter society was generally known as The Law Institution—then from 1831, when it received a royal Charter, The Incorporated Law Society, and finally on the grant of a new Charter in 1903, The Law Society.

Thus, the cohesiveness of the profession—and with it the ability to educate and discipline its members—came centuries later than for the Bar. But a more relevant comparison is with the establishment of, and the grant of royal charters of incorporation to, the other leading modern professions: the Architects (1834, 1837), the Chartered Actuaries (1848, 1884), the Chartered Surveyors (1868, 1881) and the Chartered Accountants (1870, 1880).

Few if any of the leading attorneys or solicitors in the movements for professional standards or law reform in the C18th or C19th appear to have been from Lincoln's Inn. Perhaps they were all too busy attending to their distinguished clients' affairs to concern themselves with the professional standards of education or discipline of their lesser brethren outside the Inn! Several Presidents of the Law Society have, however, been in practice in the Inn and soon made good any early omissions. Those during the first 175 years of the Society's existence were:

1835	George Frere: 6 New Square
1841	Thomas Metcalfe: 5 New Square
1845	Michael Clayton: 6 New Square
1846	Edward R Pickering: 4 Stone Buildings
1853	George H Kinderley: 6 New Square
1860	W Strickland Cookson: 6 New Square
1868	John Henry Bolton: 1 New Square
1876	Henry Thomas Young: 9 New Square
1879	Nathaniel T Lawrence: 6 New Square
1888	Benjamin G Lake: 10 New Square
1891	W Melmoth Walters: 9 New Square

28.e. ? I Dodd: The façade of the Law Institution, 1832.

The architect responsible for the original building was Lewis Vulliamy. Vulliamy's design was pure Grecian, in the Ionic order, different from anything in the Inns of Court or Chancery and bearing comparison with the medical Royal Colleges. The original portico (since remodelled) of the Surgeons' in Lincoln's Inn Fields of 1805-13 and of the Physicians' in Trafalgar Square of 1824-7 (now Canada House) were Ionic and thus probably set the style. The house was extended to designs by Philip Hardwick (who had worked extensively in Lincoln's Inn) and Charles Holden (later noted for his Senate House, London Transport headquarters and London Underground stations).

The austere elegance of the façade is easily missed in the narrowness of Chancery La., and seems undervalued. Neither Dickens nor Trollope set a scene of one of his novels there. There is more printed in the books on or guides to Legal London as to the devolution of title to the site on which it is built, or on the heraldry of its grant of arms than on the building itself. *Legal London*, 1971, sedulously omits it.

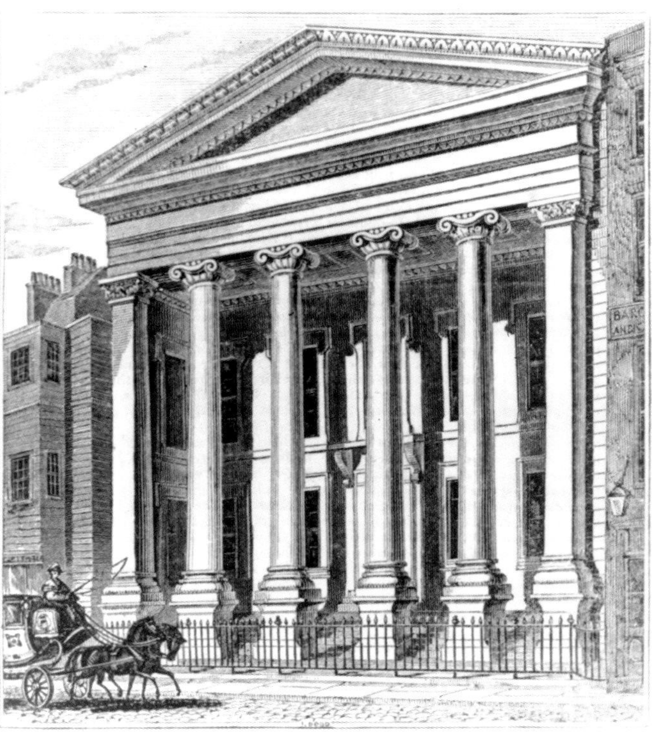

28.f. Dorothy Thomas: 'The House of the President of the Law Society', 1989 [coll. Sir Richard Gaskell, PPLS] {the artist}.

To the r. (e.) of the House, Star Yard runs n. from Carey St. To the l. of this view is the rear of 3, New Square, and the railings are at the corner of the RCJ.

1894	John Hunter: 9 New Square
1909	Sir William Winterbotham: 1 New Square
1913	Sir Walter Trower: 5 New Square
1935	Sir Harry Pritchard: 12 New Court
1952	Sir Dingwall Bateson: 9 New Square
1979	Sir John Stebbings: 10 New Square
2003	Peter Williamson: 2 New Square

>> List: Florence Sandberg.

Of these Presidents, two came from the same firm which still practises in the Inn, and at the same address, and one from another such. The others were from firms which (or the successors to which) have since moved out. The names of several of those are preserved in the current names of firms, of which one is in practice in the Inn and three or four of which are so outside.

ii. The President of the Law Society's House

¶ This house—60, Carey St.—has served since 1929 as the residence during his or her year of office, of the President of the Law Society. It lies within one of the few small incursions into the straight lines of the Inn's boundaries, and was built in 1731-2 for Richard Foley, MP, a bencher of the Society. The positioning of the central windows seems to suggest that it was intended to look as though it were a pair of houses, or perhaps that it once was. The front door is later than the house itself. If so, then this dwelling would have been more in proportion to the other gentlemen's houses of the early C18th once standing in Chancery La. (facing the N. Lawns), and parts of Serle St (facing the side of New Square). As has been remarked upon elsewhere, the quality of the interiors of C17th and C18th gentlemen's houses on the periphery of the Inn was much higher than those of chambers in the Inn (or any of the Inns). This house is embellished with pine panelling, carved marble fireplaces, mahogany doors and stairs, and rococo decoration in plaster or *papier mâché*, the last of these being comparable to that in No. 1, New Square. There are painted ceilings after the style of Sir James Thornhill.

B. COUNSEL'S, AND ATTORNEYS' & SOLICITORS' CLERKS

29. COUNSEL'S CLERKS

'Mr Bowker, or Bill Bowker, as he was generally called, was a stout, square-built, ruddy-complexioned, yellow-haired, bustling, middle-aged man, with a great taste for flash clothes and jewellery. On the present occasion, he sported a smart nut-brown coat, with a velvet collar; a sky-blue satin stock, secured by numerous pins and brooches; a double-breasted red tartan waistcoat, well laid back; with brownish drab stockingette pantaloons, and Hessian boots. A great bunch of Mosaic seals dangled from a massive chain of the same material; and a cut steel guard, one passing over his waistcoat, secured a pair of mother-of-pearl-cased eye-glasses, though Bill was not in the least short-sighted.

"You're early" said Bowker, as Charles deposited a dripping umbrella in the stand. "You don't look like a sap either," added he, eyeing Charles in a free and easy sort of way, for Bill was a real impudent fellow.

"What is the right hour?" inquired Charles, with a schoolboy sort of air.

"Right hour?" exclaimed Bill, "any time you like—saps come at opening, others at noon, the Honourable not till afternoon. There are two chaps copying precedents now, that the laundress left here at ten last night—(tinkle, tinkle, tinkle, went a little hand-bell). There's the old file himself," observed Bill, bundling off, adding, as he went, "be back to you directly."...
The Hon Henry Lollington, the ninth son of an Earl, was quite a used-up West-end man. He was a tall, drawling, dancing sort of a man, in great request at balls, and had a perfect abhorrence of anything coarse or commonplace. He was a mortal enemy to Mr Bowker, whom he kept at arm's length, instead of treating as an equal, as some of the pupils did.

"Mr Bowker," drawled he, as he encountered that worthy in the passage, "bring me a piece of paper, and let me give you orders about my letters—I'm going to Bath."

"Yes, my LUD," responded Bill, in a loud tone, to let Charles hear what a great man they had among them.

"Dem you, Mr Bowker, 'm not a Lord," responded the Hon Mr Lollington. "Beg pardon, my Lud," replied the imperturbable Bill, bustling out.'

—R S Surtees, from *Handley Cross, or Mr Jorrocks's Hunt*, 1843.

'...Mr Crabwitz, a gentleman who had now been with Mr Furnival for the last fifteen years, and who considered that no inconsiderable portion of the barrister's success had been attributable to his own energy and genius. Mr Crabwitz was a genteel-looking man, somewhat over forty years of age, very careful as to his gloves, hat, and umbrella, and not a little particular as to his associates. As he was unmarried, fond of ladies' society, and presumed to be a warm man in money matters, he had his social successes, and looked down from a considerable altitude on some men who from their professional rank might have been considered as his superiors. He had a small bachelor's box down at Barnes, and not unfrequently went abroad in the vacations.'

—Anthony Trollope, from *Orley Farm*, 1862.

'From references which will from time to time be made to him some of my readers, unfamiliar with the system, may infer that Selina and the rest are employed by Henry under a contract more or less equivalent to one of personal servitude. I should explain that this is not the case: they employ Henry. It is Henry's function, in exchange for ten per cent of their earnings, to deal on their behalf with the outside world: to administer, manage and negotiate; to extol their merits, gloss over their failings, justify their fees and extenuate their delays...'

—'Sarah Caudwell' (Sarah Cockburn) [of LI],
from *Thus Was Adonis Murdered*, 1981.

> D Palfreyman, *London's Inns of Court*, 2011.

---

30. ATTORNEYS' AND SOLICITORS' ARTICLED CLERKS AND MANAGING CLERKS

'A very little world and a very dull one.'

—Charles Dickens, from a Letter, believed to describe the offices of Charles Molloy of Symond's Inn, Chancery La. and 8, New Square, Lincoln's Inn (in whose practice he worked as a clerk, before becoming a reporter).

'Scattered about are certain dark and dirty chambers, in and out of which, all the morning in Vacation, and half the evening too in Term time, there may be seen constantly hurrying with bundles of papers under their arms, and protruding from their pockets, an almost uninterrupted succession of Lawyers' Clerks. There are several grades of Lawyers' Clerks. There is the Articled Clerk, who has paid a premium, and is an attorney in perspective, who runs a tailor's bill, receives invitations to parties, knows a family in Gower Street, and another in Tavistock Square: who goes out of town every Long Vacation to see his father, who keeps live horses innumerable; and who is, in short, the very aristocrat of clerks. There is the salaried clerk—out of door, or in door, as the case may be—who devotes the major part of his thirty shillings a week to his personal pleasure and adornment, repairs half-price to the Adelphi Theatre at least three times a week, dissipates majestically at the cider cellars afterwards, and is a dirty caricature of the fashion which expired six months ago. There is the middle-aged copying clerk, with a large family, who is always shabby, and often drunk. And there are the office lads in their first surtouts, who feel a betting contempt for boys at day-schools: club as they go home at night, for saveloys and porter: and think there's nothing like "life". There are varieties of the genus, too numerous to recapitulate, but however numerous they may be, they are all to be seen, at certain regulated business hours, hurrying to and from the places we have just mentioned.'

—Charles Dickens, from *The Pickwick Papers*, 1837.

This passage in context describes clerks in the Temple. It may be imagined, however, that the scene would have been indistinguishable between the four Inns.

30.a. 'Phiz': 'Lawyers' Clerks', *Punch*, *ca.* 1842 [press cutting LMA].

This cartoon illustrated an article in the same series as that in which the Ticket Porter (see 32.2.) appeared, with a similar sample of conversation, and some verses (not reproduced here). The clerks were probably from the Inns, but could have been in the City.

'The most important people in a lawyer's office, apart from the senior partner, were the managing clerk—and the office-boy. The former, like the barrister's clerk in chambers, acquired over the years a profound knowledge of the practice of the law, from the preliminary procedures to the foibles of a judge. Devoted to the senior partner, or head of the chambers, whose successes and failures they had shared for many years, these men worked until they "dropped" for there was no retiring age and physical disability was not regarded as a handicap to an experienced man. The office-boy performed many functions especially before the telephone came into general use. Storekeeper, messenger, with a detailed knowledge of the city streets and alleys, he worked the letter press, kept the post book, "licked the stamps", and posted the letters and, as he became more knowledgeable, performed the duties of a junior or copy clerk. Sometimes this work was done by much older men who from lack of ambition or capacity did not want further responsibility. In one such office in Lincoln's Inn the managing clerk when I was a boy was a dignified old gentleman with a pointed white beard who finally gave up work after breaking his leg at the age of eighty-three. His son, a junior clerk in the same office, was badly wounded in the head in the First World War with the resulting loss of concentration and a curious jerky gait. He returned to work in the same office as, in effect, office boy where he stayed quite happily and was extremely useful for he had an encyclopaedic memory, and clerks in other offices in doubt about the procedure would be told to ask "old so-and-so". Many years later, when I was coming out of the College of Surgeons, I was astonished to see his angular jerky figure hurrying from the same office, with the same intent air, to catch the evening post. It was rather like seeing a ghost, for he must by then have been over eighty.'

—Professor A Leslie Banks, describing the early C20th, from *Lincoln's Inn Fields*, unpubl. memoirs, 1980 [the author].

C. CRAFTSMEN, SERVANTS AND TRADESMEN

31. CRAFTSMEN AND SERVANTS OF AND IN THE INN:

31.1. Two bricklayers

i. Ben Jonson
'His mother, after his father's death, married a bricklayer; and 'tis generally said that he wrought some time with his fatherinlaw (and particularly on the garden wall of Lincoln's Inn next to Chancery Lane)… and that a knight, a bencher, walking through and hearing him repeat some Greek verses out of Homer, discoursing with him, and finding him to have wit extraordinary, gave him some exhibition to maintain him at Trinity College in Cambridge.'

—John Aubrey [of MT], from *Brief Lives*, 1679-80.

¶ An example of Jonson's juvenile wit, while working as a bricklayer, was furnished by this reputed encounter:

'Lady : "With line and rule
Works man, a fool:
Good morrow, mason."

Jonson : "In silk and scarlet
Goes many a harlot:
Good morrow, madam."'

—R Pearce [of GI], *A History of the Inns of Court…*, 1848.

---

ii. Venteris Mandey
'Beneath this place lyes interred the Body of Venterus Mandey of the Parish of St Giles in the Fields in the County of Middx. Bricklayer, son of Michael Mandey Bricklayer and Grandson to Venterus Mandey of this Parish Bricklayer, who had ye honour of being Bricklayer to the Honble. Society of Lincolns-Inn from the year of our Lord 1667 to the day of his Death. He was studious in the Mathematicks and wrote and Published three Books for Publick good one Entitled *Mellificium Mensionis* or ye Marrow of Measuring. Another of Mechanic powers, or the Mystery of nature & Art unvayled. The Third An universal Mathematical Synopsis. He also Translated into English *Directorum generale Vranometricum* And *Trigonometria Plana & Sphaerica, Linearis & Logarithmica*, Auctore Fr. Bonaventura Cavalerio Mediolanensi & some other tracts which he designed to have Printed if Death had not prevented him. He Dyed the 26th day of July Anno Domini 1701, Aged 56 Years & upwards. He also Gave Five Pounds to the Poor of this Parish.'

—Monumental inscription in the north aisle of St Peter's Church, Iver, Buckinghamshire.

> Howard Colvin, *Biographical Dictionary of British Architects, 1600-1840*, 1978.
>> Mrs Robin Purchas.

¶ Minutes of Council for 4th May 1675 in *The Black Books* record that Mr Maundy, the Society's bricklayer, was to attend the next Council, to answer for his unhandsome carriage towards one of the Masters of the Bench. Those for 12th May 1675 record that Mr Maundy, the bricklayer, shall not be any more employed on the work of this House, until he apologise to Mr Thomas Strode, a Bencher.

31.a. Engraving: R White: 'Vera Effigies Venteri Mandey, Etatis Suae 37, Anno 1682', in *Mellificium Mensionis*, 1717 [BL].
This is a fine book, illustrated with engraved line drawings of high quality.

31.b. Anon. artist: Two porters resting, with the column and fountain behind them, early-mid-C18th (n.w. view of Serle's Court towards Old Buildings) [HSLI].

This charming watercolour is unusual for its period—indeed for any period—in its prominent depiction of Inn servants.

Perhaps the bricklayer had corrected the bencher on a point of Latin grammar or the mathematicks!

Relationships were repaired sufficiently for him to dedicate his *Synopsis Mathematica Universalis* to the benchers in 1701 and for them to make a gift to him of £8.

31.2. Porters

Here lyes entered with in this cave
Not Charls ye great but Charls ye grave
And sure yt worthy could not bee
More constant to his sword yn [=than] *hee*
Before, behind, soe equall was its waight
I think it keept his aged body straight
But Bevis[1] *dead what could his Morglay*[2] *doe*
Nor can this sword to any else be true
Though with a sword a sergeants ear[3] *didst lope*
He with a sword could fliing bullits stope
That on each hand 2 dying might be seene
And hee as freind yet victor stand betwene
Oh yf wee could exchange with fate
For him, ye keys or Pillers of our gate
We all doe know, if hee the doors did keepe
The house were safe through all overcome with sleepe
Pomanders, corncutts, or those early cryes
Or that prodigious note, hot pudding pys[4]
Could not molest our ears, but hee with speed
Would make them packe, or pats must bleed
Now for his place soe well performd below
Heaven sure on him a better will bestow
At whose bright gats if gownmen chance to knocke
They need not feere but Charls wil soon unloke

—Henry Anderson [of LI], later Sir Henry, first baronet:
'On Charls the Porter of Lincons Inn, 1631'
[MS. Eng. poet. e.14, *fo.*1 *r.* & *v.*, Bodleian].

[1] Sir Bevis: the hero of a popular English medieval romance.

[2] Morglay: a generic name given to an unbreakable, supernatural, sword—as was Arthur's Excalibur.

[3] The 'sergeants ear' would, of course, previously have been attached to the side of the head of a serjeant-at-law, as to which manner of men, see 35.8.

[4] The cries of the street-vendors of Chancery La.

> Transcription: Dr Elizabeth Kreager.

Charles died in 1631 and was buried at the expense of the Society. See Glossary: livery (b). The author's claim to memory in the Society is that of being one of the group of its young members, who in 1629 'pumpt… and shaved… and disgracefully used…' a royal messenger seeking to serve a warrant in Lincoln's Inn Walks—the incident being mentioned in *State Papers, Domestic, Charles I*, and the subsequent disciplinary proceedings recorded in *The Black Books*.

¶ The Bodleian MS reprinted above does not appear previously to have been transcribed or printed. By chance, the terms of appointment of Charles survive, and *have* been printed and published. They are reprinted here in full. A modern-day service contract could hardly be more precise or exacting:

'First, that hee shall not suffer any wandringe or idle persons, rogues, vagabondes, or beggers, to walke or wander up and downe in any parte of the Howse, or to lurke or abide about the Gate, but that hee ridde the House of them; and if they shall make resistance, to carry them to the constable, to bee further proceeded against accordinge to the lawe.

Item, like care and course to bee had and used in the night for night walkers in and about the Howse, and for such as sculke and lurke in corners or entryes of the House, likelie to steale or pilfer in chambers or otherwise.

Item, that hee been circumspect and diligent in lookinge to such nusances as shall happen in the House by the sluttishnes of laundresses and others, and that hee shall give notice and warninge of the same to the gentlemen of such chambers from w[hi]ch such nusances come; and if after such warninge and notice there bee againe anye such faultes committed, the gentlemen of those chambers to bee questioned for the same before the Masters of the Bench.

Item, hee is injoyned, in case hee finde any such nusance in the Garden or Backside, to admonishe the Panierman and Gardiner respectivelie thereof; and if the same bee not ridd and removed, then, if it appeare that noe warninge were given, the Porter to bee punished by the Masters of the Bench by beeinge put out of commons or otherwise; or, if notice bee by him thereof given, then the Gardiner or Panierman to be punished for the same as shalbee thought meete.

Item, that in the day tyme hee shall dilligently attende aboute the Gate, unlesse at such tymes as hee shalbee imployed in the businesses aforesaid; and that hee shutt and locke up the Great Gate at eleaven of the clocke in the night in sommer, and at tenn of the clocke in wynter.

Item, for preventinge such trouble and annoyans as are done by coaches w[i]thin the House, that he contynuallie in the daye tyme keepe the one leafe of the Gate shutt, w[i]th the barr of yron soe extended towardes the other leafe of the Gate that noe coaches maye come in, onely while the Lord Cheife Justice of the Common Pleas lodgeth in the Howse, hee shalbee ready to open the Gate for the comming in or goinge out of his Lo[rdshi]pp's coach, and not otherwise.

Item, in regard of his paynes about his saide office, wee thinke it fitt that hee shall have his dyett w[i]th the officers of the Howse, and that once in two yeares hee shall have a liverye cloake at the charge of the Howse, and shall also for his wages have every yeare fower poundes, the same to be paid by the Pentioner every terme by equall porcions.'

—Minutes of Council on 29th November 1613,
in Vol. II, *The Black Books.*

31.3. Gardeners

God of gardeners, accept this coil
Of acrid smoke from nettle and weed,
This left-hand mound of sinful soil
That I have sifted from the seed.

With hoe and mattock, spade and rake,
From morning dew to evening grace,
My back has bended for Thy sake,
To bring sweet order to this place.

31.c. Lewis J Wood: The Library (detail from design) (s.w. view), 1842 [HSLI].

The gardeners in the foreground, whose duties remain substantially the same to this day, seem here, on account of their clothes and implements, almost to be in a harvest field.

Thy fruits and tubers basketed,
Thy flowers lit from setting sun,
With fragrant heart and reverent head
I tend this altar gleaming red,
As my forefathers must have done.

—Richard Church, 'The Bonfire', in *Twelve Noon*, 1936.

The author of these verses was not a member of the Society but, at the time of writing them, had a *pied-à-terre* in a top-floor set of chambers in 13, Old Square. His prose, some of which is quoted elsewhere in this book, is testimony to his treasuring memories of the experience. Were therefore the Inn's gardeners, at work one autumn, a source of inspiration for these verses?

31.4. Laundresses:

¶ A laundress is defined in the *OED* as 'a caretaker of chambers in the Inns of Court'. Analogies may be made with 'scout' or 'bedder' in some universities.

i. Between the ages of 12 and 40

The classification adopted here is that of the Society itself:

> Ordered that no woman, except under th' age of xij yeres or above th' age of fourtie yeres, shall resort or hawnt to any chamber in this Howse as a laundres or maker of beddes, or otherwise for service…

—Minutes of Council on 26th November 1565,
in Vol. I, *The Black Books.*

31.d. Annabel Wilson: 'The Gardeners' Castle', 1993 [LT] {the artist}.

This charming piece of rustic Victorian-Tudor architecture was designed by Sir Giles Gilbert Scott. It has been debated as to whether it was intended as a folly, or as a gardeners' hut and store, or as a seat for ostlers attending to the horses of members and visitors coming to the New Hall.

The Lavvyers Plea,
In the behalf of Young
TOM of LINCOLN.
Being an Anſwer to a late Scandalous Ballad, Entituled,
Merry News from Lincolns-Inn.
Adreſt to the Author of the ſaid Ballad, by *Tom of Lincoln.*
To the Tune of, *Help Lords and Commons, &c.*

LOrd help us all! what Story's this,
that makes ſo great a ſtir?
Forſooth who ever keeps a Miſs,
muſt fear this barking Cur;
As if no place but *Lincolns-Inn*,
did harbour ſhe deſtroyers,
With Puritans he might begin,
they wench as well as Lawyers:
You Nonconformiſt-*crop-ears, peace,*
and rail not againſt Wenchers,
VVith you, Fanatick *Babes encreaſe,*
far more than with the Benchers.

Thou who want'ſt judgement talk'ſt of it,
like a vile canting Varlet,
And exerciſeſt thy No-wit
againſt an honeſt Harlot,
Out of our houſe ſhould ſhe depart,
ſhe'l learn to be more fickle,
Lifting up whoriſh eyes with Art,
at zealous Conventicle.
You, &c.

She went up ſtairs thou ſayeſt at ten,
and what of that you Tony,
At twelve the learned'ſt of your men
tip'd over the Balcony:
To this ſo ſtrange a ſight there came
a hundred pious ſticklers,
But all went off again with ſhame,
like crop-ear'd Conventiclers:
You, &c.

It ſeems he call'd himſelf a Cat,
and would have been a gibing,
Her husband underſtanding that,
came in and ſpoil'd his nibing:
Says he, Cats fall upon their feet,
when downwards they are tumbled,
So down he threw him in the ſtreet,
till his proud fleſh was humbled:
You, &c.

But for the wench and Laundreſs *Ruth*,
I muſt confeſs the ſtory,
That there was ſomething in't of truth,
but all is for our glory:
We keep the Child we have begot,
and able are to bear it,
Whilſt others, do, or do it not,
are ready to forſwear it:
You, &c.

Is not this better than to go
at night to the Peatches,
Reeling and rambling to and fro,
in danger of the VVatches:
And meet at laſt a drab or ſo,
with Petticoats bedagled,
Or with a pocky Barren-doe,
that from the Park has ſtragled:
You, &c.

VVoe and alas! your Rudder's ſpoil'd,
I pitty your miſhap,
And though you get not her with child,
you get your ſelf with clap:
Then you go home and curſe the whore,
with all her Art-full dry-blows,
Finding one pox to coſt you more,
than keeping twenty by-blows:
You Nonconformiſt-*crop-ears, peace,*
and rail not againſt VVenchers,
VVith you, Fanatick *Babes encreaſe,*
far more than with the Benchers.

Thus you abroad with hazard roam,
to find out Harlots fulſome,
VVhile we more ſafely prey at home,
upon a Girl that's wholſome:
Look to your ſelves, your caſe is worſe,
dry up your ſlubbring Ink-horn,
I'le warrant you we'l find a Nurſe,
for our young *Tom-a-Lincoln*;
You, &c.

A Bencher's Grand-child! you miſtake,
you ſilly Rogue, I ſcorn ye,
If a Lawyers Son a Lawyer makes,
his Baſtard's an Attourney:
And thus our *Tom* in little time,
ſhall grow to be our Brother,
As a Bawds Daughter whores betime,
t'enrich her greaſie Mother;
You, &c.

As for the woman, I confeſs
we wrapt her in a Gown,
And whoſoever had done leſs,
had been an arrant Clown;
For being to be call'd to' th bar,
and turn a female pleader,
'Twas reaſon we ſhould have a care,
ſhe ſhould not ſhame our Reader;
You, &c.

Long may ſhe live a merry crack,
brisk, airy, gay, and fruitful,
She never any thing ſhall lack,
ſo long as ſhe is youthful:
Grown old, her Daughters ſhall turn up,
to pleaſe our youthful VVenchers,
As when we've eat our Commons up,
we fall upon our Trenchers;
You, &c.

As for young *Tom* I doubt it not,
he'l make ſome Learned ſpark,
More wit he has already got,
then an Attourneys Clerk;
Before that ever he could ſpeak,
he ſu'd for Alimony,
Inſtead of Mothers-milk, he'd take
no Liquor but Stipony;
You, &c.

Then blame not us of *Lincolns-Inn*,
for what has hapned to us,
Such wenching is a gainful ſin,
that never will undoe us;
For we ſhall keep the bantling cheap,
among ſo many purſes,
Like Citizens that take a leap
amongſt their Country Nurſes;

God bleſs the King and Queen, likewiſe
the Houſe of Lords and Commons,
But truly we ſhall ne'r deſpiſe
ſome thing that is a woman;
For ſhould the Laws cart every one,
that loves a little cracking,
The City would be quite undone,
their VVives muſt all be packing.

FINIS.

31.e. The Lawyers Plea, in the behalf of Young Tom of Lincoln, being an Answer to a late Scandalous Ballad, Entitled Merry News from Lincoln's Inn, ca. 1674 [BL].

31.f. Charles Flower: Old Buildings, with a laundress drawing water from a pump, late C19th (detail) [Raphael Tuck].

ii. Under the age of 12 or over the age of 40

'The genuine laundress is an institution not to be had in its entirety out of and away from the genuine Chambers. Again, it is not denied that you may be robbed elsewhere. Elsewhere you may have—for money—dishonesty, drunkenness, dirt, laziness, and profound incapacity. But the veritable shining-red-faced shameless laundress; the true Mrs Sweeney—in figure, colour, texture, and smell, like the old damp family umbrella; the tiptop complicated abomination of stocking, spirits, bonnet, limpness, looseness, and larceny; is only to be drawn at the fountainhead. Mrs Sweeney is beyond the reach of individual art. It requires the united efforts of several men to ensure that great result, and it is only developed in perfection under an Honourable Society and in an Inn of Court.'

—Charles Dickens, from 'Chambers',
in *The Uncommercial Traveller*, 1860.

¶ The scandal-mongering—and doubtless money-making—broadside reproduced here concerns a laundress, Ruth, who gave birth in chambers in the Inn, the father being a member of the Society, Thomas Middleton, the son of a bencher. The specialist reader will be able, if he wishes, to work through the double 'v's and long 's's to decipher its mildly lewd message.

Minutes of the Council in *The Black Books* record that he must attend at the first Council next term to answer such things as shall then be objected against him. A marginal note in the MS Black Books (reproduced in the printed edition) records: Tom of Lincoln. A bastarde child born in his chamber, and ballads of it. There seems to be no copy in the Society's archives, nor is the survival of this copy mentioned in the footnotes to *The Black Books*. 'Tom of Lincoln' is the name of the great bell of Lincoln Cathedral.

It should not be imagined from this that the members of the Society were uniquely sinful. The Houghton Library at Harvard holds a broadside of 1695 which, like this, was expressed to be a riposte to an earlier one such, and which concerned the birth of twins in chambers in the Temple: but in that instance to a prostitute and not a laundress—the distinction which is drawn in this broadside.

A Case of Self-Sacrifice.—*Mrs. Grimes.* "No, sir, Mr. Smith ain't a-bin in 'is chambers not for a week, sir." *Mr. Brown.* "Oh! You're sure now you know the gentleman I mean—Mr. Meldon Smith?" *Mrs. Grimes.* "*Hi* knows 'im right enough. Wy, I does all 'is washin' and mendin' for 'im!"

31.g. 'A Case of Self-Sacrifice', *Punch*, *ca.* 1880.

It seems unlikely that this cartoon, with its weak play on words has an innuendo of the biblical usage of 'know' and which might have been pertinent to the forbidden category of laundresses in i. above. Probably it simply implies that the laundress knew her employer better than the two very elegantly dressed gentlemen—'no man is a hero to his valet', as Montaigne observed. It had been said, by an unknown English wit, that what laundresses and barristers had in common was their duty to press the suits of their clients.

32. SERVICES AND TRADES IN, AND AT THE GATES OF, THE INN:

32.1. Postmen

'...here is brightness and whiteness and a glow from the red grate. I have just heard the postman slam the door of the pillar-box below, and then the gate into "The Fields" shutting after him.'

—Edward Johnson, the art teacher, from Letter written from 16, Old Buildings, 1902, quoted in Priscilla Johnson, *Edward Johnson*, 1959.

32.a. Charlotte Halliday: The pillar box in New Square, 1995 [LT].

A Royal Mail van normally makes daily collections from the letter box, and also deliveries to and a collection from chambers and offices, in the Inn. Since the closure in the early 1990s of the Inn's PO, the only publicly accessible Royal Mail installation in the Inn is this letter box on the n.e. corner of New Square. The large direction sign on top of the box (which is the one referred to in the quotation above) pointed towards the former PO, and now towards the sub-PO in High Holborn. The box is of Edward VII's reign and of the 1889 'town and country' design—and may also serve the unpremeditated purpose of the Inn's memorial to the novelist Anthony Trollope, who (as noted elsewhere) was born in the Inn. Trollope is credited, while working as surveyor to the Post Office, with introducing in 1852 street pillar boxes (which had been in use at an earlier date in Paris) first to the Channel Islands, and then to London.

32.2. Messengers

'Here have I been all this blessed day, and not had a job. I suppose customers are out of town; and I'm not a ticketporter if I'm not out of luck, and what's worse I can't persuade myself I'm not hungry. Drat it, if I couldn't eat the hind leg of a cab-horse.'

Anxious an honest bob to win,
Oft have we seen thee take thy station,
At Temple, Gray's, or Lincoln's inn,
Still wide awake in thy vocation.

Active and diligent thou art,
And of fatigue a thorough scorner;
Still ready like a shot to start
For Mile-end-road or Hyde-park-corner.

Most multifarious are thy works
For all domestic duties able—
Carpets to beat, clean knives and forks
Decanter wine, and wait at table.

We mark the still on the alert
The inclination never lacking
To brush from clothes the dust and dirt
Or polish boots with Warren's blacking.

Of ticket and of badge a star
With thee each hour in duty passes
We hail thee a 'Particular,'
And one of the industrious classes.

'Sir vot you says mayhap is right
To do a job I'm always willing
But here I've stood from morn till night
And hang me if I've yarn'd a shilling.

'Business I'm sure I never shirk
And none I knows can do it quicker;
Now Sir if you can't give me vork
Mayhap you'll stand a drap of liquor.

'I would—for I am wery dry—
Drink your good health with satisfaction—
and vet's the use of hindustry
If you can't bring it into haction?'

—'The Ticket Porter', in *Punch*, 1842.

THE TICKET PORTER.

"Here have I been all this blessed day, and not had a job. I suppose customers are out of town; and I'm not a ticket-porter if I'm not out of luck, and what's worse I can't persuade myself I'm not hungry. Drat it, if I couldn't eat the hind leg of a cab-horse.

Anxious an honest bob to win,
Oft have we seen thee take thy station,
At Temple, Gray's, or Lincoln's-inn,
Still wide awake in thy vocation.
Active and diligent thou art,
And of fatigue a thorough scorner;
Still ready like a shot to start
For Mile-end-road or Hyde-park-corner.
Most multifarious are thy works,
For all domestic duties able—
Carpets to beat, clean knives and forks,
Decanter wine, and wait at table.
We mark the still on the alert,
The inclination never lacking,
To brush from clothes the dust and dirt,
Or polish boots with Warren's blacking.
Of ticket and of badge a star,
With thee each hour in duty passes,
We hail thee a "Particular,"
And one of the industrious classes.
"Sir, vot you says mayhap is right,
To do a job I'm always willing,
But here I've stood from morn till night,
And hang me if I've yarn'd a shilling.
"Business I'm sure I never shirk,
And none I knows can do it quicker;
Now, Sir, if you can't give me vork,
Mayhap you'll stand a drap of liquor.
"I would—for I am wery dry—
Drink your good health with satisfaction—
And vot's the use of hindustry
If you can't bring it into haction?"

32.b. ? 'Phiz': 'The Ticket Porter', 1842 [press cutting, LMA].

Ticket porters are also mentioned in passing in Charles Dickens, *Bleak House*, 1852.

¶ Three definitions of 'Lincoln's Inn', in the parlance which might well have been used by the messengers in the Inns:

'i. A £5 note: racing rhyming slang on synonym (originally underworld) 'finn' from 'finnif'… often heard in low racing slang, ex German *fünf*, via Yiddish.

ii. A hand: rhyming slang on 'fin'—an arm or hand.

iii. gin (the drink): rhyming slang.'

—Eric Partridge, from *A Dictionary of Slang and Unconventional English*, 8th edn., by Paul Beal, 1984.

A definition of 'Chancery', which might have been in the same vocabulary:

'Pugilism (from the control of the Court of Chancery, and the certainty of cost and loss to property "in Chancery"). The position of the head when held under the opponent's left arm to be pommelled; hence figuratively an awkward predicament, 1832'.—*OED*.

32.3. Purveyors of food: costerwives, roast chestnut vendors and hot pudding-pie men

'There is no more familiar object to the frequenters of Chancery Lane than the apple stall at the antique entrance of Lincoln's Inn in that thoroughfare. The stall can in truth claim to be historic, for it has been carried-on on that spot for about 100 years by members of the same family. Mrs Haley, of whom we give a portrait, has managed the stall for some sixty odd years, and was only constrained to surrender it to her daughter last summer by the pressure of ill-health. She suffers much from rheumatism, no doubt largely brought on by exposure to all weathers. And though fortunate in the possession of the old age pension she is very attached to the stall and would gladly sit at it still.

"It was my mother who had the stall first," she explained to a *Lloyd's News* representative, "and I went there in the beginning to help her; I think I was about fifteen at the time. I suppose I have worked at the stall for more than sixty years or thereabouts; I am 77 now."

"It used to be a pretty good business," went on Mrs Haley, "that was when the courts were held in Lincoln's Inn Hall. There would be crowds of people then—witnesses and lots of countryfolk come to see what was going on; it made a great difference when the new law courts were built in the Strand. I used to know all the gentlemen in the Inn, but most that I knew are dead now. Still, people often used to come and buy for the sake of old times. I have had elderly gentlemen come and buy something because they said years ago when they were boys they used to buy apples at my stall."

Of course, during her sixty years' acquaintance with Chancery Lane, Mrs Haley has seen a great many changes.

"There usen't to be anything like the traffic that there is now," she said. "No motor 'buses, of course, and only the old horse 'buses, with the two seats on top, facing either way. Then the other side of the street to the Inn—that has quite been altered. It used to be nice, gentlemen's private houses, with flights of five steps up to the front doors; I remember where there used to be three separate houses there is now one big block."

Keeping a stall may seem at first sight rather an easy business, but the hours are long, and the exposure to the weather very great. Mrs Haley explained that in summer she was generally at her stall from between 8.00 and 9.00

32.c. 'The Old Apple Stall at Lincoln's Inn' (w. view of Gate), *Lloyd's News*, 1912 [LMA].

32.d. Charles Flower: Lincoln's Inn Gate with a stallholder (w. view, through Gate), ? 1902 [Raphael Tuck].

There is a brazier from which presumably in the winter and spring, muffins or chestnuts were sold outside the Gatehouse. A woman enigmatically sitting at the first-floor window on the r. of the Gatehouse is perhaps a laundress at her sewing, needing as much light as possible.

32.e. 'Luke Limner' (John Leighton): 'Knives and Scissors to Grind, Buy a Mat, a Rope- or Parlour-Mat' (n. view of New Square, through Serle's Gate), 1848 [BL].

in the morning 'til nearly 6.00 in the evening; of course, in winter the hours were a good deal shorter and business a good deal less brisk. Then the day always began with an early visit to Covent Garden to buy stock.

"It was when mother got too weak to go to the market that I first began to help with the stall," said Mrs Wise (Mrs Haley's daughter), "but I have always done a good deal of selling with flowers; it really seemed as if I had to take to that kind of work. It was just bred in the bone with me; I always wanted to be a seller. I think I began when I was about ten years old." However, she pursued, cheerfully, "I might have chosen worse; there's ups and downs in everything, and it really seems at times that there is nothing very good in any trade."

So the apple stall is likely to remain in the family, though in very bad weather Mrs Wise prefers to keep up her flower round, which is a more profitable concern then.

"People won't stand to buy in wet weather," she said; "and, with four little ones at home, and my husband not in regular work and my mother here, it's sometimes a hard matter to keep things going." '

—'The Old Apple Stall at Lincoln's Inn', in *Lloyd's News*, 1912.

¶ A roast chestnut vendor is illustrated in *32.d.*

Hot pudding-pie men outside the gates of the Inn are mentioned in 31.2. An idiosyncrasy of selling which was traditionally used by pie-men was to invite prospective purchasers to call 'heads' or 'tails' to a tossed coin. If the guess were right, the pie was free.

32.4. Pedlars

'Knives To Grind!—Scissors to Grind!

'We here have a grinder executing a job under the entrance gateway to New Square, Lincoln's Inn; who, if we may judge from the smile of satisfaction playing on his countenance, has had merry work amongst the cleavers of Clare Market, adjacent. Hoping he may find the like success with the penknives of the lawyers of Lincoln's Inn, we wish him "Good day!"

Buy a Mat!—Buy a Door or Parlour Mat!

They are manufactured of different materials: rope and rush mats for halldoors. Parlour and carriage mats are made of sheepskins, with the wool on, dyed of various hues.'

—'Luke Limner' (John Leighton), from *The Cries of London*, 1851 [BL].

D. CHILDREN

33. CHILDREN OF THE NEIGHBOURHOOD IN THE INN:

i. Their playtimes

'It is five post-meridian, and the sun still shines over Lincoln's-inn-fields. A very muggy sun, it is true, with an indifferent sunshine, being adulterated with London smoke, which is itself a low-class smoke. Lincoln's-inn is certainly a highly respectable quarter, but it is surrounded by some of the lowest rookeries that are to be found in all London. However, as this is a neighbourhood where sugar is sanded, where wheel-grease is called butter, and things are not exactly what they seem, it is not surprising that sunbeams are mixed with foreign substances such as blacks and coaly vapour. And it is the thousands of low-class fires in these very low-class rookeries which give such a muggy look to the sun's countenance this afternoon. Five strikes, and every one of those narrow courts and fetid alleys swarms with children. If you happen to be passing through one of these melancholy passages, you may notice that many of the children are making their way into the great square of Lincoln's-inn, as if bent on reaching some particular rendezvous. Some walk, some run, some even turn a cartwheel, some go in perambulators, some are in arms, and one by one they disappear through a narrow gateway which admits you into a fine old garden cut off from the great square by a high wall. Rows of leafy plane trees afford a pleasant shade from the heat, and the closely-shorn grass, smooth and even, is delightfully cool and refreshing for weary eyes to rest upon. The sun cheers up a little; a puff of wind drives the sluggish heat mists along, and the slanting beams, divided by the trees, fall in patterns of rich golden green on the lawn. Every minute the children come trooping in through the open doorway. Most of them are in rags; most of them look as if they would be the better in every respect if a steam fire-engine could play a few hundred gallons of water upon them. But dirt is such an old acquaintance that I really think they would miss it. Suddenly the wild skirling of the pipes is heard, and at least three hundred pairs of remarkable little legs begin to go like galvanized monkeys. The music has got into their legs, and their arms, and their heads, and their eyes. The piper marches sedately down the gravel walk, cheeks distended, chest well out, head up, white-bearded. Under the skilful fingers of the old piper that mysterious bag full of air acts upon the children like a reservoir of laughing-gas. The dull, slum-sodden little faces light up; the thick coats of dirt crack with laughter. Some turn somersaults; some form a circle and squat on the grass round the piper, gazing up at him with awe-stricken faces. A little girl of six, clad in a greasy petticoat, with a pair of black stockings, takes her shoes off, and dances through two holes in the heels of her stockings. Another little girl faces her. Arms akimbo, hats off, they go at it. They dance the stockings down; they dance the hair down; they dance the buttons off. Neither yields; the piper takes pity on them, stops and the reel dies off in a gasping wail, as is the custom of the pipes. The pipes, I dare swear, take the old piper far away from the roar of London to his native glens. But the children are thinking of other things.

33.a. 'The Children of the Slums: the Evening Playtime…' (e. view, in the background, of Stone Buildings), *The Daily Graphic*, 1891 [LMA].

"Oh! Molly Down-at-heel, you'll catch it," says one little girl.

"Who are you a-talking to?" says number two.

"You'll catch it."

"Why shall I catch it?"

"Becos you've danced a hole in mother's Sunday stockings."

"In for a penny, in for a pound," replies Miss Down-at-heel, or that is what she would have said, only she had never seen a gold piece in her life. "Fardens" was her currency. At any rate she began again with the piper, until she blew like a porpoise in a gale, and nearly bit her tongue off—low little girls having a bad habit of allowing their tongues to loll out for an airing. Then the piper begins an inspiring march, to which he steps out, taking short, measured strides. A piper takes his music seriously. We give a sketch[1] of this curious scene, which will serve better than columns of description.

The piper is Mr John Mackenzie, a champion piper, once in the Scots Guards, and now garden porter to the Benchers of Lincoln's-inn. He plays to the children every night for half an hour, and enjoys the music as much as they do.'

—'The Piper and the Poor Children, a Sketch in Lincoln's Inn Gardens', in *The Pall Mall Budget*, 1891 [LMA].

---

[1] Not reproduced here—a more accomplished sketch, from another journal reporting the same event, is.

At the date of this report, and the one following, the Fields had not yet been opened to the public, and children from tenements in the neighbourhood of the Inn would have had no grass on which to play.

---

ii. Their treats

¶ The Society arranged a Poor Children's Treat each summer, for a number of years, at this period. This is the official report for one such event:

'The Committee beg to report that the treat to the poor Children of the neighbourhood ordered at the Council held on the 13th day of June, and for which a sum of £60 was authorised to be spent, was given on Wednesday last to 600 poor Children attending Schools of all denominations.

Owing to circumstances beyond the control of your Committee the cost of tending was heavier than in 1887, so that the sum authorised to be spent has been exceeded.

In addition to the entertainment of 600 Children authorised by the Bench, the Committee, on finding that the poor Children who are the ordinary visitors to the gardens of the Society had not been reached by the distribution at the Schools, authorised the admission of 250 more Children, and all the poor Children of suitable age who had collected round the Gates were admitted whilst the 600 were at tea. The amount authorised to be spent has been further exceeded by £10 in respect of these 250 Children.

The total cost of the Treat is as under:

Mr Elliott for tending tea, bread and butter,

Jam, Cake, and fruit for 850 Children,

Tea etc. for 100 teachers,
Meat tea for Band (26 performers),
Milk etc. and buns and toys for 850 Children,

Mr Elliott as agreed, being the difference in the amounts paid by him for tending in 1887 and now
For Punch and Judy
For Marionettes
Travelling expenses
To the Band Master and Band
Payments for services, Piper, Porters etc
Printing

£ 60. 0. 0.

9. 0. 0.
1.17. 6.
1.11. 6.
6. 0.
2. 7. 0.
1.15. 0.
11. 3.

£ 77. 7. 3.

The Committee are able to assure the Bench of the success of the entertainment and the thorough enjoyment of the poor Children.

Excess of expenditure allowed.'

—Report of the Poor Children's Treat Committee, 28th July 1893, from Vol. V, *The Black Books*.

---

34. *COURTS*, *CHAMBERS* AND *COURT OFFICES* ON THE PERIPHERY OF THE INN, AND SOME OF THEIR PERSONNEL:

• The High Court of Chancery

¶ As evoked by quotations in the early part of this book, Chancery La. was the artery of legal London, and a large number of law courts and their related chambers and offices were to be found on or just off it, and thus within a few yards of the Inn. Most have vanished—and left scarcely a trace of their presence there. The Rolls Building, lying just off Chancery Lane and Fetter Lane, does, however, represent continuity as well as change. A Royal Commission of 1860 had reported that there were fourteen distinct buildings which housed the courts, chambers and offices of Chancery on the periphery of the Inn.

The former courts of jurisdictions other than Chancery in the streets immediately to the w. and s.w. of the Inn have similarly disappeared, leaving few images of their former existence.

A few of these many courts and offices are remembered here: the selection being made from among those of which an image of the building or of its approaches, or a description of it or of business in it, has been found.

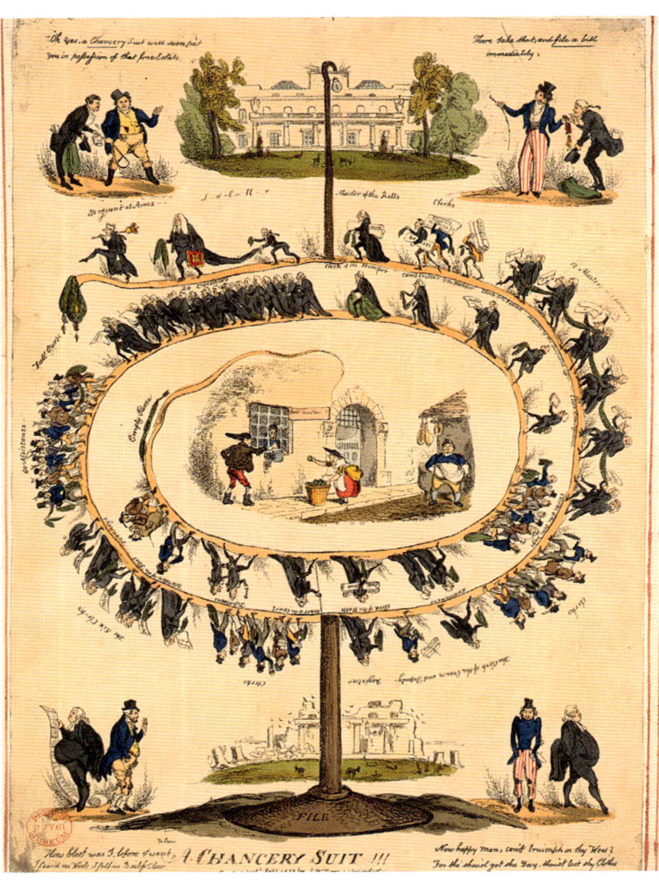

34.1. *The Office of the Corporation of the Six Clerks*, and *the Inrolment* (or *Enrolment*) *Office of Chancery*, in Chancery Lane

¶ The Six Clerks and their function have already been looked at in this book, in the section on their later purpose-built home within the Inn, in Stone Buildings.

The Six Clerks (and their sixty under-clerks) had from the 1540s been housed in the former town-house of a cleric—yet another man from Lincolnshire—the Prior of Nocton Park, from whom it had been expropriated on the Dissolution. It stood on the w. side of Chancery La., s. of its intersection with Jackanapes La. Its location is shown in *3.r.*: 'A plot for all Thickett Field', of 1592.

Samuel Pepys recorded a visit to the office:

'But he not having the time to get [my patent engrossed] in chancery-hand, I was forced to run all up and down Chancery-lane and the Six Clerks' Office, but could find none that could write that hand that were at leisure: and so in despair went to the Admiralty…'

—from *Diary* for 12th July 1660.

'The Clerks at their own proper cost and charges (to the value of about £3,000 or £4,000) in a year's time substantially and very commodiously new built the Six Clerks House and Office from the ground, all of brick (which before was of combustible timber) with several rooms and separate lodgings and conveniences for each of the Six Clerks and several rooms therein vaulted over with brick for the safe keeping of the King's and Subjects' records in the Inrolment Office and preserving them from the like danger for the future for the general good and benefit of future ages as well as the cohabitation of themselves and their successors the future Clerks.'

—Nathaniel Bladen, 1701.

34.a. Anon.: 'A Chancery Suit!!!', 1828 [BM *Catalogue of Satire* 15517].

This is one of many caricatures of Chancery suits, but of exceptional value for detailing almost all the personnel of the Chancery. This caricature depicts the ruin of two country estates by the delays and expense of that Court. The procession consists of most of the categories of the personnel of Chancery at that date—several of whom appear fleetingly in this book, on account of their having had a presence in the Inn. They are: the Serjeant at Arms; the Lord Chancellor; his trainbearer; the Master of the Rolls; three Clerks; 12 Masters in Chancery; 6 Clerks; the Clerk of the Crown and Deputy; the Register/rar; more clerks; The Six Clerks, 60 assistants (to the Six Clerks); 24 Cursitors; the Clerk of the Hamper [=Hanaper]; the Comptroller of the Hamper [=ditto]; Clerk of the Patents; the Master of the Suppoena [=Subpoena] Office; the Clerk of the Affidavits, 8 Clerks of the Petty Bags; 2 Examiners; the Clerk of the Rolls; the Usher of the Court; 2 Tipstaves; the Warden of the Fleet (Prison); and 2 Turnkeys. The Vice-Chancellor, whose office dated from 1813, is omitted: the explanation offered by the learned editor of the *Catalogue* being that the engraving (or its preparatory cartoon) was perhaps made some years earlier than its date of publication.

> Note from *Catalogue*.

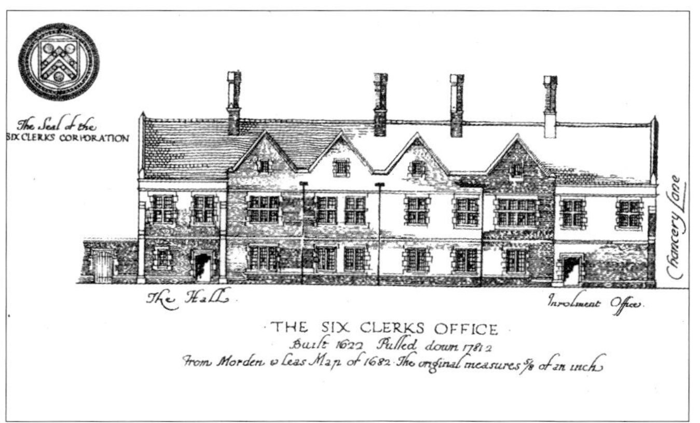

34.c. Matthew Paris: The Rolls Chapel in *Chronica Majora*, *ca.* 1260 [CCC].

This image, in the text of a manuscript on vellum, shows the Chapel as it would have been at the date of *London Lickpenny*.

34.b. Anon. draftsman: The Six Clerks' Office of 1622 [LMA].

Their fine new office in the Oxford collegiate style is clearly shown in Morden & Lea's map of 1682, of which this is a re-drawing. It was demolished in 1781/2, after the Office had moved to Lincoln's Inn.

34.2. *The Master of the Rolls' Court, in the Rolls House*, in Chancery Lane

¶ The Rolls was situated just n. of (the Chancery La.) Serjeants' Inn and of Clifford's Inn and was the centre of its own ecclesiastical jurisdiction or 'liberty', which extended outside its perimeter walls to include part of Lincoln's Inn.

This house was first the property of John Herlizan, a Jew, and became in 1233 the *Domus Conversorum*: the hostel (or voluntary semi-ghetto) of the small community of converted Jews. On the Expulsion of 1290, the trickle of new converts necessarily ceased, but the functions of the hostel and of the school for this community continued. Accounts survive of allowances granted to the descendants of converts for a further three centuries. The keeper of the house was customarily the Master of the Rolls, and from the late C14th it was formally granted to the holder of that office, and in consequence also held the Chancery rolls. The chapel of the *Domus* survived in appearance as a medieval building, despite rebuilding by Inigo Jones in 1617—the year before he was asked to make a 'modull' for the Inn's intended new chapel. This chapel was demolished in 1895. The house of the Rolls was successively rebuilt as a classical building of some importance, first by Inigo Jones in 1617 and then more substantially and in the Palladian style by Colen Campbell in 1717-24. It was during the period of rebuilding of the Rolls House that Lincoln's Inn offered the Master the use of the Old Hall as a court-room.
The Rolls House and its chapel fulfilled a variety of legal functions over the centuries, the former notably that of the Court of the Master of the Rolls, the second judge in the Court of Chancery, and the latter (besides its religious function) of a record repository. Its papers were moved into the Public Record Office, built in stages at the n. end of the Rolls land, between 1851 and 1896.

34.d. Colen Campbell: The Rolls, 1718 (w. front, e. view) [BM].

This fine archetypal Palladian building, by the distinguished architect Colen Campbell, housed the Master of the Rolls' Court and his private apartments, to which was attached on the s., the Rolls Chapel. For centuries, the Lord Chancellor and the Master of the Rolls were the only judges of the Court of Chancery, and indeed it was only from 1833 that the MR sat continuously as a Chancery judge. The Lord Chancellor's equivalent domain comprised his apartments in the House of Lords, and his court in a partitioned area of Westminster Hall. The Rolls Court House (by then housing one of the Courts of the Chancery Division) became redundant on the construction of the RCJ, and the various buildings of the Rolls were demolished as the Public Record Office gradually encroached on them. The PRO's claim upon the site was that it was the embodiment of the other branch of the Master's historic responsibilities—the custody of legal (and some State) archives. It, in turn, moved away in 1996, when all of its records were concentrated at Kew. It is now the Maughan Library of King's College, University of London.

34.e. J P Emslie: Court room in the Rolls Court, 1892 [LMA].

34.f.i. John Crowther: Interior of the Rolls Chapel, 1886 (e. view) [LMA].

¶ The lines quoted here are the opening and closing stanzas and one other such of a long set of verses evoking the successive rebuffs experienced by a countryman when visiting London: first at the hands of a series of shopkeepers in the City and then in a sequence of law courts, of which one was the Rolls. It exists in several variants, one being 'Lackpenny'—either title being apt:

In London there I was bent,
I saw my-selfe, where trouthe shuld be ateynte;
Fast to Westminstar-ward I went
To a man of lawe, to make my complaynt.
I sayd, 'For Marys love, that holy seynt,
Have pity on the powre, that would procede.[1]
I would gyve sylvar, but my purs is faynt. For lacke of money, I may not spede.
… Then I went me unto the Rollis
Before the clerks of the Chauncerie.
There were many qui tollis,[2]
But I herd no man speke of me.
Before them I knelyd upon my kne,
Shewyd them myne evidence and they began to reade.
They seyde trewer things might there nevar be,
But for lacke of money I may not spede.
… Then I conveyed me into Kent,
For of the law would I medle not more;
By-caus no man to me would take entent,
I dight me to the plowe, even as I ded before.[3]
Jhesus save London, that in Bethelem was bore,
And every trew man of law, God graunt hym souls med;[4]
And they that be other, God theyr state restore:
For he that lackethe money, with them he shall not spede!

—? John Lydgate, from *London Lickpenny*, C14th,
MS Harley 542, *fos.* 102*r*-104*r* [BL].

---

[1] procede: bring proceedings.

[2] *qui tollis peccata mundi* (who takes away the sins of the world: from the Mass).

[3] dight me: set myself.

[4] med: reward or recompense.

34.f.ii. Roland W Paul: The Rolls House and Chapel, 1893 (s.e. view) [LMA].

34.g. Hanslip Fletcher: Entrance Gate, Rolls Yard, in *London Passed and Passing*, 1909 (e. view) [GL].

The front door of the Rolls Chapel is visible through the Gate.

¶ Samuel Pepys also had business here, some three centuries later:

'After that, he went to his [Mr Chetwind's] office in Chancery-lane, calling at the Rolles, where I saw the lawyers pleading; then to his office, where I sat in his study singing [*sic*] while he was with his man (Mr Powells son) looking after his business.'

—from *Diary* for 11th February 1660.

'In my way home, I went to the Chapell in Chancery Lane to bespeak paper of all sorts and other things belong to writing, against my voiage.'

—from *Diary* for 16th March 1660.

'Up, and by water… to the Temple; and thence to the Chapel of Rolles, where I made enquiry for several Rolles and was soon informed in the manner of it… I hired a clerk there to read to me about twelve or more rolls which I did call for: and it was a great pleasure to me to see the method in which the Rolles are kept.'

—from *Diary* for 11th February and 15th March 1669.

34.3. *The Examiners' Office* and *the Petty Bag Office*, in *the Rolls Yard*

¶ The function of the Examiners' Office was to assist the Master of the Rolls in taking evidence. That of the Petty Bag Office was to handle specific suits in Chancery and particularly those against attorneys and officers of the Court, and to regulate members of those professions.

34.4. *The Register* (or *Registrar*) and other *Court Offices* in *Symond's Inn*, in Chancery Lane

¶ Symond's Inn was a small group of buildings with a courtyard, no image of which has been found—although its footprint is clearly visible on C18th and C19th maps. It was set back a short distance from Chancery La. on the e. side, to the n. of the Rolls and contiguous with it, on the rear half of the site now occupied by the office building 22, Chancery La. It is believed that no records have been found to evidence that it was ever an Inn of Chancery, and there is no suggestion that it possessed a hall. Some C19th topographical guides, however, listed it as though it were one such. But the better view is that Dickens and Trollope were right in evoking an individual owner or developer.

John Strype remarked that in 1720 it was 'lately new built, and now a pretty handsome Place, in which several offices are kept, as the Registers Office, etc.'

It housed a number of lesser offices of the Courts of Chancery, King's Bench and Common Pleas, in the manner of the Inns of Court and of Chancery. The Chancery offices were re-housed in Stone Building Court, when that was constructed in the 1770s. The so-called Inn was demolished in 1873.

'…Symond's Inn, Chancery Lane: a little, pale, wall-eyed, woe-begone inn, like a large dust-bin of two compartments and a sifter. It looks as if Symond were a sparing man in his way, and constructed his inn of old building materials, which took kindly to the dry rot and to dirt and all things decaying and dismal, and perpetuated Symond's memory with congenial shabbiness.'

—Charles Dickens, from *Bleak House*, 1853.

'Opening off from Chancery Lane are various small lanes, quiet dingy nooks, some of them in the guise of streets going no whither, some being thoroughfares to other dingy streets beyond, in which sponging-houses[1] abound, and others existing as the entrances to so-called Inns of Court—inns of which all knowledge has for years been lost to the outer world of the laity, and, as I believe, lost almost equally to the inner world of the legal profession. Who has ever heard of Symonds' Inn? But an ancestral Symonds, celebrated, no doubt, in his time, did found an inn, and there is it to this day.'

—Anthony Trollope, from *Can you forgive her?*, 1864.

1 sponging-houses: privately owned houses of preliminary detention of accused debtors, one stage before their reaching an accommodation with creditors or being sent to a debtors' prison. They appear frequently in the literature of the period.

34.h.i Herbert Railton: 'Staple Inn from Southampton Buildings', in *Loftie, op. cit.*, 1895.

This is the approach from Chancery La. to the n. entrance of the former Masters' Office. The prosperous and self-important gentleman in the foreground walking towards the lane may perhaps be a patent agent or the client of one. He could not, at this date, be a Master. A woman street-vendor, holding a tray, on the other side of the street, stands there to sell to those who, at that date, had business in the Patent Office.

34.5. *The Office of the Corporation of Cursitors of Chancery*, on Chancery Lane and Cursitor *Alley* (now Street)

¶ The Cursitors were also a part of the Court of Chancery, and originated with twenty-four men first appointed in 1566 and incorporated in 1573 by Sir Nicholas Bacon, Lord Keeper, to make out and issue writs for that Court. They were assisted by the same number of holders of secondaryships. Their office was purpose-built for them by Bacon sometime after they were incorporated, and was vacated in 1813, when they removed to a building belonging to the Petty Bag Office in the Rolls Yard. No illustration of the elevations of either office has been found. John Strype recorded that it was 'a fair building, all of brick and timber', and that the Cursitors' Office was 'above stairs'. It stood on the n. corner of Chancery La. and Cursitor Alley.

34.6. *The Office of the Masters in Ordinary in Chancery*, on Southampton Buildings and Quality Court (accommodated with *the Offices of the Secretaries of Bankrupts* and *of Lunatics*)

¶ An Act of Parliament which authorised the deposit at interest of suitors' funds in Chancery had also authorised the application of the then accumulated funds for the building of these offices. The first wing of the offices had been built in 1797.

The building which housed the Masters' offices was built on and between Southampton Bldgs. (facing Staple Inn) and Quality Court. John Strype, in 1720, had described Quality Court as 'a very handsome large and airy court, lately built.' The Masters' Office here seemingly replaced earlier accommodation in Symond's Inn. The existence of front and back doors—each accessible to lawyers and litigants—explains why the same offices are given the address of Quality Court in two of the pieces here, and Southampton Buildings in the third.

The design has been attributed to Sir Robert Taylor, later responsible for Stone Buildings, or to the Studio of Sir William Chambers, the architect of Somerset House. The n. and s. façades were in a strictly classical style, in harmony with one another—that on the n. having a balustraded roof-line, and that on the s. a pediment, each with heavy fluted columns.

An unidentified visitor described the internal arrangements thus:

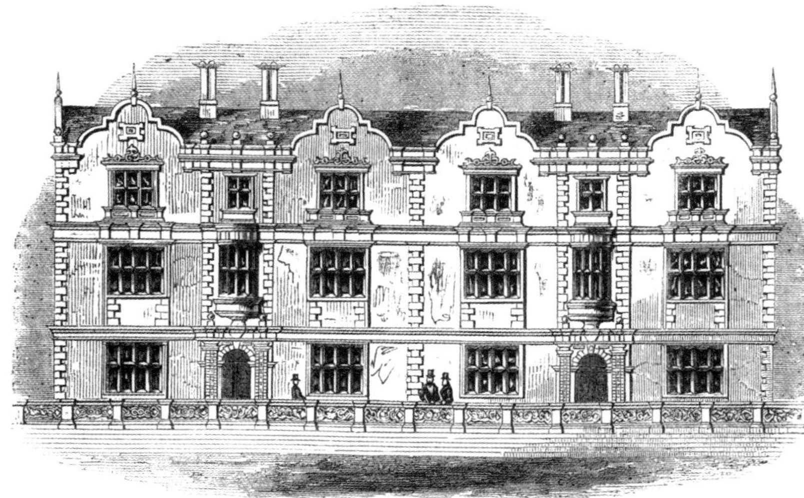

34.h.ii. Anon. artist and engraver: 'Staple Inn, New Chambers' (s. view), 1844 [BM].

This is the extension and new n. frontage of the Masters' Office. It replaced the classical, balustraded façade, as first built. It would seem that the r. (w.) end accommodated the Taxing Masters, and the l. (e.) the Masters in Chancery. This building became known as 'Staple Inn Buildings'.

34.i. Sir Albert Richardson, PPRIBA: 'The Old Patent Office, Quality Court', in his *Monumental Classic Architecture in Great Britain and Ireland*, 1914.
As explained here, this is the building designed and built for the Masters in Ordinary in Chancery.

>> Jan Maciag, RIBA.

34.j. Hanslip Fletcher: Quality Court, in the *Sunday Times*, 1928 [LMA].
This drawing shows the approach from Chancery La. to the s. entrance of the Masters' Office. The C18th frontage and entrance had been at the far end, on the l. (n.). At this date, Quality Court was destined for rebuilding.

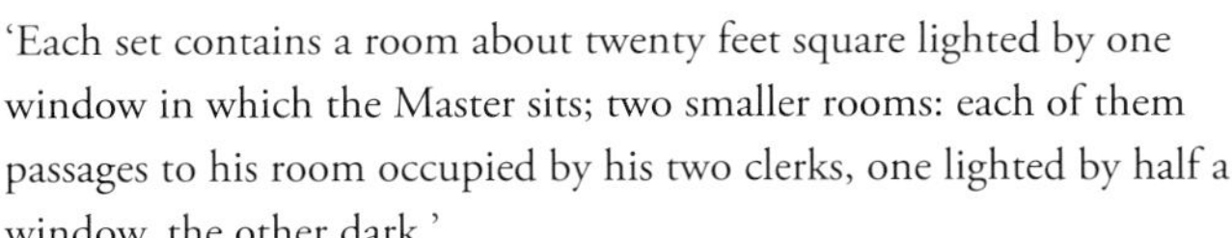

'Each set contains a room about twenty feet square lighted by one window in which the Master sits; two smaller rooms: each of them passages to his room occupied by his two clerks, one lighted by half a window, the other dark.'

In 1842-3, the front of the Office (and doubtless some of the rooms behind it) was demolished to allow for an extension in the Jacobean style—the building then being named 'Staple Inn Buildings'.

> quotation: John Hewish, *Rooms near Chancery Lane*, 2000.

'"More Wiglomeration", said he. "It's the only name I know for the thing… Master Somebody—a sort of ridiculous Sexton, digging graves for the merits of causes in a back room at the end of Quality Court, will have something to say about it…"'

—Charles Dickens, from *Bleak House*, 1853.

'… it must be confessed that the back of the Patent Office[1] (in Quality Court) is somewhat disappointing after its front view;[2] it resembles, with its old blackened pillars, a disused dissenting chapel; and Quality Court itself seems, like so many of the purlieus of the smaller Inns, mainly redolent of charwomen, cats and orange peel.

34.k. Lewis J Wood: Taxing Masters' Office, *ca.* 1840 (e. view) [BM].

Nevertheless, even in dingy Quality Court there are some respectable houses with quaint old doorways, as well as some good iron-work in the upper balconies.'

—Mrs E T Cook, from *Highways and Byways in London*, 1902 [GL].

---

1 The Patent Office: this name is explained by the fact that the institution of the Great Seal Patent Office under the responsibility of Commissioners, independent of the High Court of Chancery, coincided with the abolition of the Masters in Ordinary in Chancery. There was no causal connection. The Patent Office was therefore allocated accommodation in the building which had been designed for the Masters, and occupied by them until the 1850s. Over the following 150 years, the Patent Office expanded to extend also onto Took's Court and Furnival St. At the date of Mrs Cook's writing, the back of the Patent Office remained as built for the Masters, but not long after was demolished and rebuilt in the constant expansion of the Patent Office.

2 front view: Mrs Cook evidently preferred the neo-Jacobean architecture of the front extension to the classical of the rear. The new building would have been exposed to London soot for half the time as the old.

The writing clearly apes Dickens', but it serves to capture the moment in time just before the old building vanished.

'"All hope abandon, ye that enter here." should have been the sentence inscribed over the gateway of the Masters' Office in Southampton Buildings. Which of us ancient lawyers now living does not remember, and remember with horror, that sepulchral tenement, recalling also the drowsy divinities who presided over it? Roupell, Martin, Dowdeswell, Griffin Wilson, Wingfield, Henley, and some four or five others of their colleagues? Each of the masters had his suite of three rooms—the outer or clerk's room, entered by a door leading out of a long, dark, narrow corridor, which was the public thoroughfare; an inner room, in which sat the chief clerk; and the third room, which enshrined the master himself, when it was convenient for him to be present.

All business in the Masters' Office was conducted by appointments, which took the name of warrants, being printed forms, filled up by the outer clerk, handed to the solicitor having the conduct of the proceeding, and by him served on the other parties, who then attended the appointment accordingly, or, as often as not, failed to attend it. Thus, the first warrant would probably be one to consider the offer. Then, at an interval of a fortnight or more, another warrant on leaving—we will suppose, for example, the charge against an accounting trustee or executor; then warrants at further long intervals, to proceed on the charge, and so on with the discharge—supported possibly, if the cause were a hostile one, by affidavits and counter-affidavits and documentary proofs, copies of these being, in all cases supplied by the office to the opposing parties at the extreme cost to the suitor; only in this case the money was paid to the officials, not for their individual benefit, but on account of the suitors' fee fund.

These appointments were not few, but they were certainly far between, depending on the block of other business or on the convenience of the master; for he gave out his own days for work, and reserved what he pleased for holidays. The bugbear of the Parliamentary return of his official work being ever required from him stood not within the prospect of belief. And so the reference dragged on, two or three long vacations probably intervening, till it issued in the report, which was again the subject of protracted discussion, warrants to settle the report being innumerable. The report being at length settled and signed, it was open to any of the parties to take exceptions to it; when the cause was again shunted on to a siding to be heard on the exceptions; and if it escaped being referred back to the master, as not unfrequently happened, it was set down to be heard in its turn on "further directions," when a final decree was pronounced, final only in the event of there being no rehearing or no appeal; and the suitors, if they did not always get the bare shell, were certainly not rewarded with the full oyster, for even the victorious combatant was heavily mulcted in costs. As with the six clerks so with the masters. The voice of public opinion at length terminated the official existence of the denizens in Southampton Buildings, and in 1853 the masters were themselves abolished with, as usual, compensation in the form of their full salaries for the rest of their lives.'

—Sir John Hollams[1], from *Jottings of an Old Solicitor*, 1906 [LS].

---

[1] Hollams was a distinguished City of London solicitor who had served as President of the Law Society, and whose retirement from practice was marked, most exceptionally, by a dinner in his honour attended by many of the higher judiciary. His family firm in time became Coward Chance, one of the two firms which amalgamated in the 1980s to become Clifford Chance.

34.7. *The Office of the Taxing Masters in Chancery,* in Staple Inn

¶ The Taxing Masters in Chancery—responsible for assessing the reasonable legal costs and disbursements of a successful litigant when to be paid by the unsuccessful, or by the estate or fund over which litigation had taken place—were housed for nearly half a century in Staple Inn Buildings, built in 1842-3, on the s. of Staple Inn, and adjoining the Masters in Ordinary in Chancery, and their successors in the same premises, the Great Seal Patent Office.

• The Courts of Common Law

34.8. *The Fire Court* in *Clifford's Inn,* off Chancery Lane, Fleet Street and Fetter Lane

¶ Clifford's Inn is considered by legal historians as the first of the Inns of Chancery to be founded (in 1310) and it is known to have been the last to be disbanded (in 1903). It was the only Inn of Chancery accessible from Chancery La. Its historic buildings were demolished in 1934, with the exception of the small early C19th gatehouse at the end of its passage onto Fleet St., which still stands.

34.1. T H Shepherd: The hall of Clifford's Inn (s. view), 1840 [BM].

The Inn underwent extensive rebuilding in 1767, which accords with the date on the clock face on the flank wall of the hall. The windows of the hall look late medieval, and neither 'gothick' nor classical, either of which they could have been at this date. It may be imagined therefore that the rebuilding of the hall was in the same style and on the same site (as with the rebuilding of the Old Hall of Lincoln's Inn), and that accordingly this was in that sense the same hall as that in which the Fire Judges sat.

As with several of the other legal Inns, from time to time it housed various offices and chambers of the Courts. For some decades in the C19th it accommodated in its hall the Court of Exchequer. But its unique curial connection was to accommodate the Fire Court, constituted under the Fire of London Disputes Act, 1666. That statute constituted a bench of judges drawn from the King's Bench, Common Pleas and Exchequer who were charged with determining the property boundaries and the respective rights of landlords and tenants in those parts of the City destroyed by the Great Fire of London. The fire had reached within a few yards of this Inn.

Twenty-two judges served in rotation, sitting at a round and gate-legged table, which is conserved in the Museum of London. Such was the gratitude of the City that full-length portraits of each of them were commissioned, those surviving being now distributed between the Guildhall, Lincoln's Inn and Inner Temple.

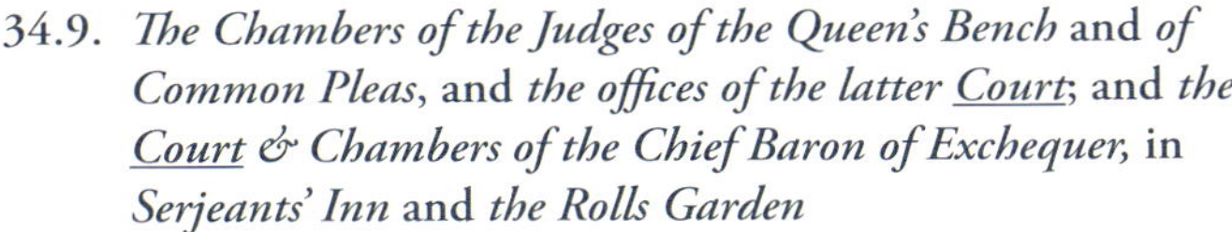

34.9. *The Chambers of the Judges of the Queen's Bench* and *of Common Pleas*, and *the offices of the latter Court*; and *the Court & Chambers of the Chief Baron of Exchequer*, in *Serjeants' Inn* and *the Rolls Garden*

¶ The Serjeants were the ancient higher rank of barrister, and for centuries had their own Inns. Three Serjeants' Inns have existed in London: Scrope's on Holborn opposite St Andrew's (which ceased to function *ca.* 1498), Serjeants' Inn Fleet St., on the s. side opposite Fetter La. (which ceased to function in 1733), and Serjeants' Inn Chancery La., at the s. end on the e. side. The last of these formed part of a legal enclave contiguous with the Rolls, Symond's Inn and Clifford's Inn. It ceased to function in 1876, at which time all serjeants (whether judicial or otherwise) returned to the Inns of Court whence they had come. Serjeants' Inn in Chancery La. possessed a chapel, hall, library, kitchen and chambers, as with an Inn of Court. As with other Inns, space was found for the administration of the law in existing Inn buildings, or purpose-built rooms erected in its courtyards or gardens.

34.o. Samuel Ireland: Serjeants' Inn, Chancery La., *ca.* 1795 [LMA].
This is the principal hall of the Inn, facing Chancery La. across its courtyard.

34.m. John Crowther: Clifford's Inn and the judges' chambers (n. view), 1880 [LMA].

The tower is that of the Public Record office.

34.n. Sir Alfred East, RA: Clifford's Inn (s. view), late C19th [Hargreave Fine Art, Northants.].

The tower is that of St Dunstan-in-the-West.

This Inn is described by Dickens as housing the chambers of the judges of two of the common law courts:

'…they reached the low archway which forms the entrance to the Inn…

There were two judges in attendance at Serjeants' Inn—one King's Bench and one Common Pleas—and a great deal of business appeared to be transacting before them, if the number of lawyer's clerks who were hurrying in and out with bundles of papers, afforded any test…

This was a room of specially dirty appearance, with a very low ceiling and old panelled walls; and so badly lighted, that although it was broad day outside, great tallow candles were burning on the desks. At one end, was a door leading to the judge's private apartment, round which were congregated a crowd of attorneys and managing clerks, who were called in, in the order in which their respective appointments stood upon the file. Every time this door was opened to let a party out, the next party made a violent rush to get in; and, as in addition to the numerous dialogues which passed between the gentlemen who were waiting to see the judge, a variety of personal squabbles ensued between the greater part of those who had seen him, there was as much noise as could well be raised in an apartment of such confined dimensions…

Standing on a box behind a wooden bar at another end of the room was a clerk in spectacles who was 'taking the affidavits'; large batches of which were, from time to time, carried into the private room by another clerk for the judge's signature. There were a large number of attorneys' clerks to be sworn, and it being a moral impossibility to swear them all at once, the struggles of these gentlemen to reach the clerk in spectacles, were like those of a crowd to get in at the pit door of a theatre when Gracious Majesty honours it with its presence. Another functionary, from time to time, exercised his lungs in calling over the names of those who had been sworn, for the purpose of restoring to them their affidavits after they had been signed by the judge, which gave rise to a few more scuffles; and all these things going on at the same time, occasioned as much bustle as the most active and excitable person could desire to behold. There were yet another class of persons—those who were waiting to attend summonses their employers had taken out, which it was optional to the attorney on the opposite side to attend or not—and whose business it was, from time to time, to cry out the opposite attorney's name; to make certain he was not in attendance without their knowledge.

…All this time the man in spectacles was hard at work, swearing the clerks: the oath being invariably administered, without any effort at punctuation, and usually in the following terms:

"Take the book in your right hand this is your name and handwriting you swear that the contents of this your affidavit are true so help you God a shilling you must get change I haven't got it."'

—Charles Dickens, from *Pickwick Papers*, 1837.

34.p. Anon. artist: 'View of the archway into Serjeants' Inn looking from Chancery Lane' (e. view), in *The Graphic*, 1877 [LMA].

¶ Very shortly after the above description was written, those two judges and also the head of the Court of Exchequer had their judicial chambers in a long building built for the purpose nearby in the garden of the Rolls, abutting also that of Clifford's Inn, which in turn joined Serjeants' Inn. No image of those chambers has been found. Sir Robert Smirke was the architect in charge of the building and rebuilding in Serjeants' Inn and the Rolls Garden.

'These chambers have been recently altogether rebuilt.

The building containing the judges' chambers stands separated from the rest, upon a part of the Roll's-garden. It is 125 feet long, and contains apartments for each of the three chief justices, and others also for puisne judges of each of the three courts, who sit in them during term and at other periods, engaged upon duties connected with their several courts.

There are three public halls of large dimensions in this building, in which the attornies and clerks, having business in three courts (Common Pleas, Exchequer, and Queen's Bench), assemble; and, adjoining each of these halls, is the office of the judge's clerk and the chamber of the judge.'

34.q. Anon. artist: the former Chapel of Serjeants' Inn, latterly used as a court room, in *The Graphic*, 1877 [LMA].

To one side of the principal hall, at 90°, the former chapel was used as a subsidiary dining hall, and which apparently was pressed to service as a court-room. The room was of the reign of Charles II, with a fine marble fire place, and inappropriately 'restored' in 1837 with a Jacobean ceiling.

'The old dining-hall of the society has been fitted-up as a court for hearing equity causes of the Exchequer, instead of the hall at Gray's-inn, hitherto used as a temporary court for that purpose. On the north side of it, rooms have been built for the judge, masters, and counsel attending the court; and on the south side is a large dining-hall, now used by the judges and serjeants during the term.

A room for solicitors, having business in the court, is also provided on the south side of it.'

'A range of buildings, next Chancery-lane, about 130 feet long, has been erected, upon the ground-floor of which are all the public offices of the Court of Common Pleas. The principal entrance to these offices is in Chancery-lane; but there are also additional entrances, for the convenience of the attornies and others having business in these offices, from the court-yard on the east side of the building.

There are two stories above, which contain chambers for eight of the serjeants-at-law; and chambers for six more are provided in an adjoining building, the east front of which looks on the gardens of Clifford's-inn. Each set of chambers consists of three (and some of four) rooms, with every convenience necessary for their occupation attached to them.'

—all from *The Mirror of Literature, Amusement and Instruction*, December, 1838 [LMA].

34.r. Anon. artist: The Judges' and Serjeants' Chambers, Chancery La., in *The Mirror*..., (s. view) 1838 [LMA].

The stone-faced or rendered, sash-windowed chambers here seem to correspond closely with those in *34.m.* in Clifford's Inn.

34.10. *The Insolvent Debtors' Court*, in Portugal Street

¶ The streets surrounding the Inn had a long history of the processing of debtors. In the streets on the e. side of Chancery La. were sponging houses (noted above in 34.4.). To the w. of the Inn was erected the Insolvent Debtors' Court, pursuant to an Act of 1813, at a time when debtors who were not tradesmen could be declared insolvent, but could not purge their sins by becoming bankrupt. It stood in Portugal St., just outside the former Serle St. Passage leading out of the Inn, housed in an austere court house designed by Sir John Soane in his distinctive 'pared-down' classical style. The court became redundant on the reform of the bankruptcy laws in 1861, and the building was demolished to allow for the construction of HM Land Registry on the corner of Lincoln's Inn Fields and Serle St.

34.s. Sir John Soane: Elevations for the proposed Insolvent Debtors' Court, 1824: photograph Geremy Butler [SM].

34.t. Ken Howard, RA: Carey Street, 1984 (e. view) [coll. PHB].

To the l. of Thomas More Chambers, and attached to it, is the back of New Square. In the foreground, l., is the corner of a balcony on Richard Seifert's New Court (since demolished), and to the r., the several back entrances (including the Judges') to Street's RCJ. Beyond the RCJ, the white-painted elevations of the n. extension by Charles Holden to the Law Society's Hall by Lewis Vulliamy in Chancery La. It is a sunny late afternoon in term: barristers and solicitors and their clients are coming out of the Courts, crossing Carey St., and returning to chambers in the Inn. The Rolls Royce or Bentley of a judge or, more probably, a litigant awaits. This watercolour conveniently illustrates the proximity of the RCJ to the Inn. Views of the elevations of the Carey St. side of the RCJ are, perhaps predictably, few—given that the Strand front was intended to create an impression, tell a story and form a streetscape. There was, however, a meticulous steel engraving of this elevation (not reproduced here) which illustrated the report in the *ILN*, reprinted here.

'In a lofty room, ill-lighted and worse ventilated, situated in Portugal Street, Lincoln's Inn Fields, there sit nearly the whole year round, one, two, three, or four gentlemen in wigs, as the case may be, with little writing-desks before them, constructed after the fashion of those used by the judges of the land, barring the French polish. There is a box of barristers on their right hand; there is an enclosure of insolvent debtors on their left; and there is an inclined plane of most especially dirty faces in their front. These gentlemen are the Commissioners of the Insolvent Court, and the place in which they sit, is the Insolvent Court itself.

It is, and has been, time out of mind, the remarkable fate of this court to be, somehow or other, held and understood, by the general consent of all the destitute shabby-genteel people in London, as their common resort, and place of daily refuge. It is always full. The steams of beer and spirits perpetually ascend to the ceiling, and, being condensed by the heat, roll down the walls like rain; there are more old suits of clothes in it at one time, than will be offered for sale in all Houndsditch in a twelvemonth; more unwashed skins and grizzly beards than all the pumps and shaving-shops between Tyburn and Whitechapel could render decent, between sunrise and sunset.

… Some of them sleep during the greater part of the sitting; others carry small portable dinners wrapped in pocket-handkerchiefs or sticking out of their worn-out pockets, and munch and listen with equal relish; but no one among them was ever known to have the slightest personal interest in any case that was ever brought forward. Whatever they do, there they sit from the first moment to the last. When it is heavy, rainy weather, they all come in, wet through; and at such times the vapours of the court are like those of a fungus-pit.

A casual visitor might suppose this place to be a temple dedicated to the Genius of Seediness. There is not a messenger or process-server attached to it, who wears a coat that was made for him; not a tolerably fresh, or wholesome-looking man in the whole establishment, except a little white-headed apple-faced tipstaff, and even he, like an ill-conditioned cherry preserved in brandy, seems to have artificially dried and withered up into a state of preservation to which he can lay no natural claim. The very barristers' wigs are ill-powdered, and their curls lack crispness.'

—Charles Dickens, from *Pickwick Papers*, 1837.

• **The Supreme Court of Judicature** ***(now the Senior Courts)*****:**

34.11. *The Royal Courts of Justice*, between Carey St. and the Strand

¶ The rear elevations of the RCJ back onto Lincoln's Inn across Carey St., extending slightly further to the w. The front is on the Strand, at its easternmost limit, abutting the City boundary. They were designed by George Edmund Street, the eminent Gothic architect, and were opened by Queen Victoria in 1882.

'The north front, in Carey-street, has a stately but agreeable appearance, showing more of the distribution of the main blocks of

34.v. Jan Maciag, RIBA: The Bankruptcy Courts, as they were *ca*. 1900-40 (n.w. view) drawn from photographs [LT].

building, with regard to the accommodation of the different Courts and their offices. We consider the central portion of the north front, opposite Serle-street, to be really beautiful in itself; but the intelligibility of this entire front is a practical merit. The entrance on this side will be much frequented by professional men from their chambers in and about Lincoln's-Inn...

34.u. Charles Paul Renouard: Barristers in the rain, *Illustrated London News*, 1886 (s. view of Serle St.) [*ILN* PL/Mary Evans].

This sketch, by a noted French artist, captures a quintessential Inns of Court scene. The leading and junior Counsel are walking along Serle St. towards the lawyers' and clients' entrance into the RCJ, at the corner of that street and Carey St. The rear of No. 7, New Square and its London railings is to the l. of the nearest QC.

The eastern block or wing, on the Carey-street side, is not the principal seat of any Court or judicial tribunal, but consists entirely of chambers for officers of the Courts, Masters in Chancery, Chief Clerks, Registrars, Accountants, and a Branch Bank of England; with those to whom solicitors have to apply for all manner of legal formalities in the conduct of a suit at common law or equity, filing documents, sealing writs, entering an appearance, amending pleas, obtaining leave or order for this, that, and the other; even for procuring stamped paper. These offices have been carried on in the new building for two years past, and the dark corridors and the convenient waiting-rooms have been daily visited by hundreds of clerks of London solicitors, intent on such details of business, which neither the clients who pay their costs, nor anybody out of the profession, can possibly understand...

The Strand front is a complex and elaborate architectural composition of manifold Gothic features, partaking of the ecclesiastical, the baronial, and the palatial characteristics. Here of the Plantagenet, there of the Tudor or the Elizabethan period, as though it were intended to symbolise the different ages of English history, from the time of Magna Charta to the sixteenth century, which have witnessed successive phases in the development of the monarchy, the consolidation of legal authority, overruling the excesses of feudalism, vindicating the prerogative of the Crown, repressing the interference of the Papacy, assuring the independence of this realm. All this is what the thoughtful historical student can see in Mr Street's most instructive and interesting design, which is a significant commentary, if stone walls can speak, upon the reigns of the Kings and Queens of England, and upon the political and social progress of the English nation, let us say, during the times so dramatically revived for us by Shakespeare's series of historical plays. From a still earlier date, from the thirteenth century onward, the stamps of the times of our Henrys and Edwards, in their regal stateliness; with the great Earls, Dukes, Regents, and King-makers, warlike vassals; and with the great political prelates, who were also great lawyers and statesmen, the Bishops, Archbishops, and Cardinals who were Lord Chancellors (see the cathedral-like window); and with the King's Justices of different Courts, originally belonging to the Royal Household; and with the strong infusion of foreign Court influences, from France or Anjou, denoted by some of the forms of those baronial towers, by their conical roofs and their jutting circular turrets, may be seen in the mingled configuration of this new Palace of English Laws.'

—from 'The Royal Courts of Justice', in *The Illustrated London News*, 9 December 1882 [*ILN*PL/Mary Evans].

34.12. *The Bankruptcy Courts*, on Carey Street and Grange Court

¶ The Bankruptcy Courts were housed in grandiose, ornate buildings erected in the 1890s to the design of Sir John Taylor, marching with the boundary of the West Green of the RCJ and abutting Grange Court and Clement's Inn. Their presence off this street gave rise to the former phrase 'in Carey Street', a circumlocution for being in financial straits. The s. end was destroyed and the n. end damaged by bombing in the Second World War; and, with no regrets on the part of lawyers or clients, the whole building was in time entirely demolished—the site now being occupied by one of the buildings of the LSE. The Queen's and the Thomas More Buildings of the RCJ continue the jurisdiction, among others, in adjacent locations.

'At the western end of Carey Street has been erected the new Bankruptcy Court… The splendid building, occupying a commanding position, its grand front facing the open lawns to the west of the Law Courts, must, we fancy, appear as the mockery of Fate to the unfortunate individuals for whose special accommodation it has been erected. Architectural experts of course carp at it, and do not know whether it is in the Italian Renaissance style, or in some other style. It is constructed of brown Portland stone…'

—C W Heckethorn, *op cit.*, 1896.

'…the original bankruptcy complex in Carey Street… consisted of a large, lengthy building stretching down towards the Strand.

…The entrance to the building was up a few steps. On the right hand side, on the ground floor, there was a large rectangular court specially designed for hearings in open court including public examinations and discharge applications. There were sections for the Official Receiver, members of the bar and also for the press.

In the Carey Street buildings on the left hand side were two rooms where the Registrars sat in chambers. For several years I used to appear frequently in front of each of them, mainly Mr Registrar Cunliffe, Mr Registrar Bowyer, and Mr Registrar Berkeley. Each of them helped me to understand the finer points of insolvency procedure; I have fond memories of the three, but particularly Morris Berkeley who was a great cricket fan…

The upper floors of the building were occupied by the Official Receivers' department. A newly declared bankrupt was obliged to go to be interviewed by one of them at once on a preliminary basis. Several articles appeared in magazines, such as the *New Statesmen*, during the 1960s describing the experience of well known bankrupts in this gloomy old building. I seem to recollect that counsel's robing room was non-existent and we were helped by a friendly usher keeping our belongings in what was probably a broom cupboard. Chambers were, I think, still heated by coal fires.'

—Professor David Graham, QC [of MT], from *Bankruptcy, Insolvency and Corporate Rescue*, 2009 [a web publication].

Some folks may wish to be very big fish
In the blocks that front Whitehall,
While others may thrill to exhibit their skill
With racket and rod and ball,
And some may sigh for a starry sky
And romantic islands far,
But my ambition's the proud position
Of Bankruptcy Registrar.

Oh! a friend in need is a friend indeed,
So pass me a fat cigar:
For you yet may greet in Carey Street
A Bankruptcy Registrar.
Ha! Ha! A Bankruptcy Registrar.

To be much in the red is nothing to dread
With me for a friend at court.
For you need not despair, however severe
The Official Receiver's report.
You will soon be at large with a quick discharge,
While your wife keeps her Bentley car
Without any reference to fraudulent preference
From the Bankruptcy Registrar.

So in case we meet in Carey Street
You may take me into the bar;
For the chaps I've met, I don't forget
When Bankruptcy Registrar---
Hurrah for the Bankruptcy Registrar!

—Michael Albery, QC [of LI], 'The Registrar in Bankruptcy', mid-C20th, in *Verses from Lincoln's Inn*, 1975.

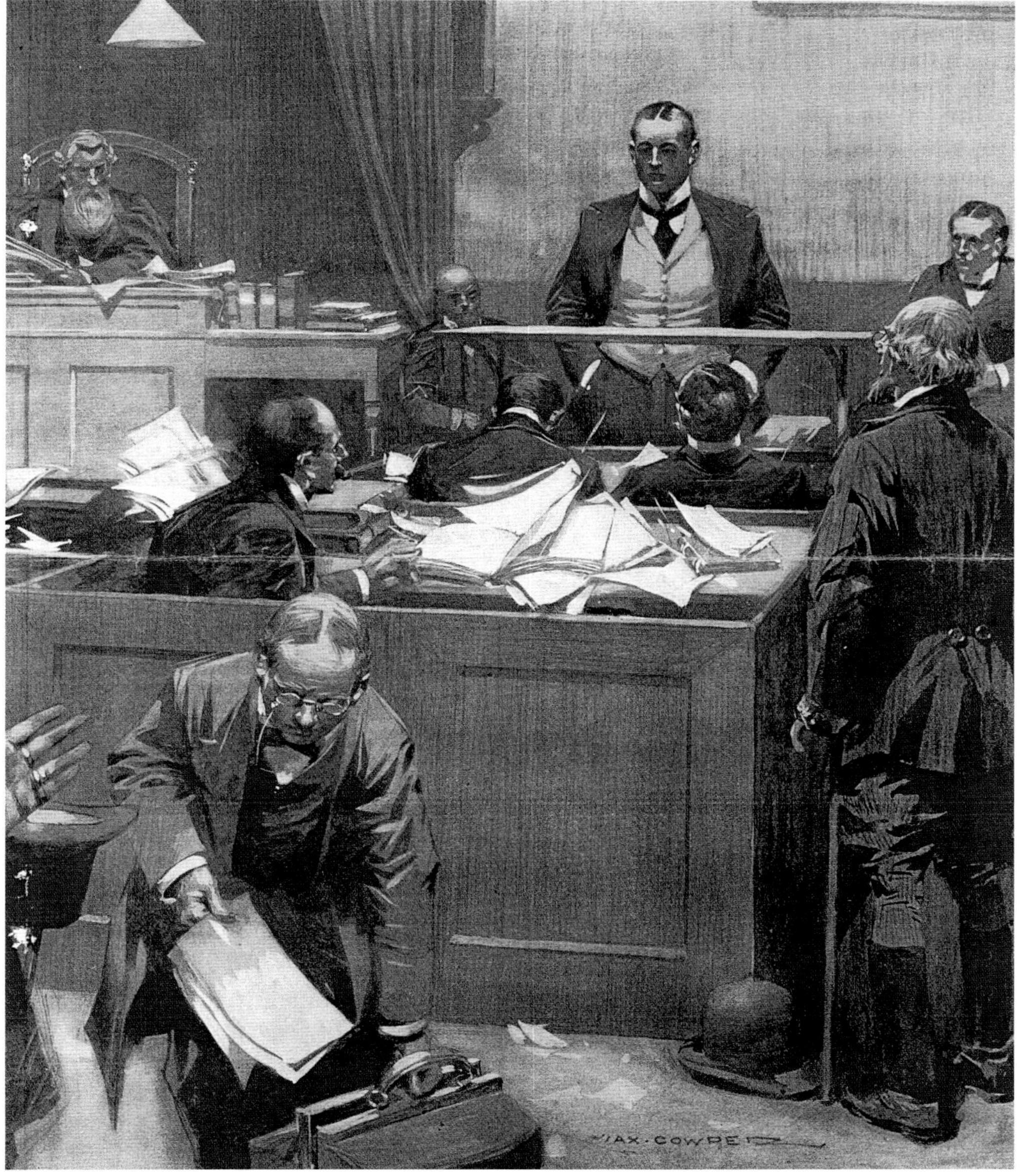

34.w. Max Cowper: 'Life's Real Tragedies No. III—A Young Spendthrift in the Bankruptcy Court: Ruined on the threshold of Life' (detail), *Illustrated London News*, 1907 [*ILN*PL/Mary Evans].

The caption read: 'The Bankruptcy Court is one of the saddest places in London. There is played daily the last act of many real tragedies. The debtors, who are the victims of misfortune or their own folly, are of every kind. The once-prosperous merchant, the too-sanguine speculator, the gambler, and the young man who has wasted a fortune pass before the Registrar and give an account of their liabilities. The debtor who is suspected of fraud is examined with the rigour of the Inquisition. For merely unfortunate debtors their position is made as easy as possible.'

35. THE DISTRACTIONS TO BAR STUDENTS AROUND THE INN:

35.1. Their multiplicity

¶ This section of the book evokes the distractions from the study of law which lay around the Inn, in a variety of buildings some of which are named here.

The poem from which the following lines are drawn is a mock will, bequeathing to London all which it already possessed. It was customary in England until the C19th to begin a will with a recital (of which this includes a pleasing parody) as to either the testator's physical health or weakness but invariably his or her full mental health, followed by a first bequest of the soul to the Almighty.

Each of the elements of a student's authorised or unauthorised curriculum referred to in the verses appears in this book in greater detail: law and other books, tennis courts, dancing, fencing and playhouses:

I, whole in body and in mind
but very weak in purse,
Do make and write my testament
for fear it will be worse
… At the Inns of Court, I lawyers leave
to take their cause in hand;
And also leave I, at each Inn
of Court or Chancery,
of gentlemen a youthful rout
full of activity.
For whom I store of books have left
at each bookbinder's stall.
And part of all that London hath
to furnish them with all;
And when they are with study cloyed
to recreate their mind
Of tennis courts, of dancing schools,
And fence, they store shall find
And every Sunday at the least
I leave, to make them sport,
In divers places players that
of wonders shall report…

—Isabella Whitney,[1] from 'The Manner of Her Will and What She Left to London and to All Those in It at Her Departing', in *A Sweet Nosegay…*, 1573.

[1] Isabella Whitney: *fl.* 1567-73, the sister of a barrister, who himself wrote a collection of poetry. *A Sweet Nosegay…* is the earliest published volume of poems by an Englishwoman.

A century later than Fortescue's benign description of the studiousness of those reading for the Bar in the Inns, it is thought to be one of the earlier literary evocations of the full scope of students' lives, a theme which provoked much literature in the C17th.

> Sandra Gilbert and Susan Gubar, *The Norton Anthology of Literature by Women*, second edn., 1996. Modernised English by Mary Moore.

¶ These verses, written some fifty years later, expand on what was evoked by Isabella Whitney but from the perspective of a participator:

… his Parents… therefore send him to the Inns of Court,
To study laws, and never to surcease,
Till he be made a Justice for the Peace.
Now here the ruin of the Youth begins,
For when the Country cannot find out sins
To fit his humour, London doth invent
Millions of vices, that are incident
To his aspiring mind; for now one year
Doth elevate him to a higher sphere;
And makes him think he hath achieved more
Than all his father's ancestors before.
Now thinks his father, here's a goodly son,
That hath approached unto Littleton,[1]
But never looked on't; for instead of that
Perhaps he's playing of a game at Cat.
No, no, good man, he reads not Littleton,
But Don Quixote,[2] *or else* The Knight o' the Sun;[3]
And if you chance unto him put a case,
He'll say perhaps you offer him disgrace,
Or else upon a little further pause,
Will swear he never could abide the laws:
That they are harsh, confused: and to be plain,
Transcend the limits of his shallow brain.
Instead of Perkins[4] *pedlars French, he says*
He better loves Ben Jonson's book of plays,
But that therein of wit he finds such plenty,
That he scarce understands a jest of twenty;
Nay keep him there until the day of doome,
He'll ne'er read out Natura Brevium;[5]
But Ovidlike against his father's mind,
Find pleasant studies of another kind… Now twice the Sun his annual course hath flitted
Since first this goodly Gallant was admitted,
And now as he approacheth towards the Bar,
His friends, and parents, very jocund are;
And to encourage him in the Law's lore,
He spends much money, and they send him more.
… His parents him supply to buy him books,

As he pretends: but instead of Coke's Reports,[6]
He's fencing, dancing, or at other sports.
Thus he affects himself in these fond ways,
To gain an outward superficial praise
Amongst a crew, of sense so much bereft,
They scarcely know the right hand from the left.
His dancing master he supposeth can
Make him a right accomplished gentleman,
Although his birth abridged it, there he
Now learns the postures of the cap and knee
Carrying his body in as curious sort,
As any reveller in the Inns of Court…

—Francis Lenton [of LI], from
The Young Gallant's Whirligigg, 1629 [BL].

---

1 Sir Thomas Littleton's *Tenures*, published in law French, in 1481, for long the main authority on real property law.

2 Cervantes' *Don Quixote*, publ. 1605 and a second part 1615, translated into English in 1616.

3 *The Knight of the Sun*: another character in *Don Quixote*.

4 John Perkins' *Perutilis Tractatus*, a popular students' book, published in law French in 1530, and in English translation (too late for the young gallant in these verses) in 1642.

5 *Natura Brevium*: A treatise in law French by Richard Pynson, published in 1510.

6 Sir Edward Coke's *Reports*, the first parts of which were published in 1600-15.

Editor's notes.

35.2. Seeking to resist them

Away thou fondling motley humourist,
Leave mee, and in this standing woodden chest,[1]
Consorted with these few bookes, let me lye
In prison, and here be coffin'd, when I dye;
Here are Gods conduits, grave Divines; and here
Natures Secretary, the Philosopher;
And jolly Statesmen, which teach how to tie
The sinewes of a cities mistique bodie;
Here gathering Chroniclers, and by them stand
Giddie fantastique Poëts of each land.
Shall I leave all this constant company,
And follow headlong, wild uncertaine thee?

—John Donne [of LI], from the *First Satire*
('On London Society'), ? 1593.

---

1 standing woodden chest: a study carrell.

36. THE ATTRACTIONS OF *PLAYHOUSE STREET*:

36.1. The real tennis court

¶ One of the small number of (real) tennis courts in London in the C17th outside the royal palaces was to be found some yards w. of the Inn. It is recorded in Hollar's prospect of 1658 (*1.b.*), in which the distinctive design of a tennis court is clearly visible. The tennis court prompted several references in *The Black Books* on account of the fears of the Council of the Society as to its encroachment on the Fields. The court must surely have provided facilities for one of the principal structured athletic recreations of the students or younger barristers of the Inn.

Intermittently, the tennis court was converted into a theatre, only to revert once more to its original purpose. These lines, written for a theatrical production there, evoke the original function of the building as a tennis court:

Sure Providence at first designed this place
To be the player's refuge in distress;
For still in every storm they all run hither,
As to a shed that shields 'em from the weather.

And thus, our audience, which did once resort
To shining theatres to see our sport,
Now find us tossed into a tenniscourt.
These walls but t'other day were filled with noise
Of roaring gamesters, and your damn me boys;
Then bounding balls and rackets they encompast,
And now they're filled with jests, and flights, and bombast

I vow, I don't much like this transmigration,
Strolling from place to place by circulation;
Grant, Heaven, we don't return to our first station
I know not what these think, but, for my part,
I can't reflect without an aching heart,
How we should end in our original, a cart.
But we can't fear, since you're so good to save us
That you have only set us up,—to leave us.
Thus from the past, we hope for future grace
I beg it—
And some here know I have a begging face.
Then pray continue this your kind behaviour,
For a clear stage won't do, without your favour.

—William Congreve, *Love for Love*, from the *Prologue, spoken at the opening of the New House, by Mrs Bracegirdle*, 1695.

36.a. William Hogarth: 'The first night of *The Beggar's Opera*, Act III, scene xi, 1728' [YCBA].

Five versions (of which this is the last) exist of this famous painting, the artist having been persuaded to repaint his original version so as to include some of the aristocratic audience present on the first night. On stage, the leading lady, Lavinia Fenton, is looking at the character of her father and, in the front row of the audience, at her real-life lover and later her husband, the Duke of Bolton.

36.b. Unidentified artist: Lincoln's Inn Fields Theatre, 1801 (n. view) [LMA].

By this date the theatre had been reduced to being 'The Salopian China Warehouse', but the façade onto Playhouse (or Portugal) St. appears to be unaltered from when the building was functioning as a theatre.

36.2. *The Lincoln's Inn Fields Theatre*, and David Garrick's performances

¶ The w. gate out of Serle Court, Serle St. Passage, faced directly into the Playhouse St. Thus the sight may be imagined of students and barristers, after a day's study or practice, making their way from chambers in the Inn or from the Old Hall and through the Passage, for an evening at the Playhouse. The conversation in the Inn must, if not of law, often have turned to the latest production at the Lincoln's Inn Fields Theatre, close by.

'Another numberless branch of the peaceable lawyers are those young men, who, being placed at the Inns of Court in order to study the laws of their country, frequent the playhouse more than Westminster Hall...'

—Joseph Addison, from 'The Overcrowding of the learned professions', in *The Spectator* (no. 21), 24th March 1711.

The score or more of playhouses in London had been closed, and the companies of players disbanded, in the Commonwealth. Charles II immediately after his Restoration in 1660 granted Patents to two theatres and their companies: in central London, in contrast to the peripheral sites in Southwark or Moorfields where usually the playhouses had been found in Elizabethan and Jacobean England. They were the Theatre Royal Drury Lane, founded by Thomas Killigrew, and the Lincoln's Inn Fields Theatre (or Duke's Theatre), founded by Sir William Davenant. These two Patent Theatres maintained the monopoly of 'legitimate' theatre in London until 1843. The Letters Patent for the Lincoln's Inn Fields Theatre have survived to the present day (via a migration to and from Dorset Gardens Theatre) and now attach to the Royal Opera House, Covent Garden.

Three houses successively stood on the site. The first was that of Sir William Davenant, of 1661: the first in England to have a proscenium arch, a theatre frequently mentioned by Pepys. The second, of 1695, was opened by William Congreve, and the third, of 1714, was re-opened by John Rich—notable particularly for first playing John Gay's *The Beggar's Opera* on 29th January 1727/8. The theatre also provided—to some popular derision—the first home in England for harlequinades and pantomimes, of Italian and French origins. In 1733, Rich moved to his new theatre in Bow Street, Covent Garden, and thereafter until it was pulled down in 1848, the Lincoln's Inn Fields Theatre functioned intermittently as a theatre, a ballroom, a concert hall, and finally became a china depository.

¶ Garrick was enrolled as a student of the Society in 1737, but in the following year changed career to become a wine merchant, and three years later found his true *métier* on the stage, developing into the greatest actor of his generation. Whether, in the years of his fame, he or the Society chose to remember or to forget that acquaintance has been ascertained in the compilation of this book. Certainly, he appeared at the Lincoln's Inn Fields Theatre, where his performances were greatly admired, and—as noted above—the membership of the Society much in evidence in the audience.

The following lines explore his gifts and his failings:

Here lies David Garrick, describe me who can,
An abridgement of all that was pleasant in man;
As an actor, confessed without rival to shine,
As a wit, if not first, in the very first line;
Yet with talents like these and an excellent heart,
The man had his failings, a dupe to his art.
Like an ill-judging beauty his colours he spread,
And beplastered with rouge his own natural red.
On the stage he was natural, simple, affecting:
'Twas only that, when he was off, he was acting.
With no reason on earth to go out of his way,
He turned and he varied full ten times a day.
Though secure of our hearts, yet confoundedly sick
If they were not his own by finessing and trick,
He cast off his friends, as a huntsman his pack,
For he knew when he pleased he could whistle them back.
Of praise a mere glutton, he swallowed what came,
And the puff of a dunce, he mistook it for fame;
Till his relish grown callous, almost to disease,
Who peppered the highest was surest to please.
But let us be candid and speak our mind:
If dunces applauded, he paid them in kind…

—Oliver Goldsmith, from 'Retaliation', 1774.

37. *COFFEE-HOUSES* AND *CLUBS*:

37.1. *Coffee-houses adjacent to the Inns of Court and Chancery*

¶ The first coffee-house in England is believed to be that established in Oxford, in 1640 by Jacob, a Jew from the Ottoman Empire, who removed later to London, and set up shop in Southampton Buildings, mid-way between Gray's and Lincoln's and adjacent to Staple Inn. The second was that established in the City by Pasqua Rosée (another subject of the Turks, who had been born in Ragusa), and the third by Inner Temple Gate. By the end of the C17th, there were coffee-houses throughout London, and a profound change had been made to the social habits of the middle and upper classes. From these early coffee-houses and chocolate-houses may be traced the origins of City institutions such as the Stock Exchange, and Lloyd's of London (to the e. of the Inns), and the foundations of the gentlemen's clubs of St James's (to the w. of the Inns). The popularity of coffee-houses among the members of the Inns of Court was particularly noted in the late C17th and in the C18th. No indigenous legacy from them seems to endure in this part of mid-town London, probably on account of the pre-existence of the Inns. However, the oldest tea retailer's shop in London, Twining's, has traded since 1706 (in premises which were before a coffee house) on the Strand, just outside Middle Temple. The two coffee houses of the C18th which are most associated with Lincoln's Inn were Serle's and Will's. Serle's, as noted above, was first established *in* New Square. This section looks at coffee houses *outside* the Inn. Will's was established in Serle St., just opposite the passage of that name into New Square. The only contemporary illustration which has been found of the outside of a coffee-house associated with Lincoln's or its Inns of Chancery is that of the narrow street front of Thavies, on Holborn, in William Hogarth's satirical engraving 'The Second Stage of Cruelty', 1751 (not reproduced here).

'Our coffee house is near one of the Inns of Court, and Beaver has the audience and admiration of his neighbours from six till within a quarter to eight, when he is interrupted by the students of the house, some of whom are ready dressed for Westminster at eight in the morning with faces as busy as if they were retained in every cause there, and others come in their nightgowns to saunter away their time as if they never designed to go thither. I do not know that I meet on any of my walks objects which move both my spleen and laughter so effectually as those young fellows at the Grecian, Squire's, Serle's[1] and all other coffee houses adjacent to the law who rise early for no other purpose but to publish their laziness. One would think these young virtuosos take a gay cap and slippers, with a scarf and party coloured gown, to be ensigns of dignity; for the vain things approach each other with an air, which shews they regard one another for their vestments. I have observed that the superiority among these proceeds form an opinion of gallantry and fashion. The gentleman in the strawberry sash, who presides so much over the rest, has, it seems, subscribed to every opera this last winter, and is supposed to receive favours from one of the actresses.'

—Sir Richard Steele, from 'The Coffee House',
in *The Spectator* (no. 49), 26th April 1711.

1 Grecian and Squire's were the coffee houses respectively *outside* Middle Temple and Gray's Inn, and as noted above Serle's was at this date *in* Serle Court, Lincoln's Inn.

'All the beaux that used to breakfast in the coffee-houses and taverns appendant to the Inns of Court, struck their morning strokes in an elegant *déshabille*, which was carelessly confined by a sash of yellow, red, blue, green, etc. according to the taste of the wearer, and were of the celebrated Doiley manufacture. The idle fashion was not quite worn out in 1765. We can remember having seen some of those early loungers in their nightgowns, caps, etc. at Will's, Lincoln's Inn Gate, Serle Street, about that period.'

—Joseph Moser, 'Vestiges' in
The European Magazine and London Review, 1803.

> C W Heckethorn, *op. cit.*, 1896

37.a. Anon. artist: The interior of a London coffee-house, *ca.* 1705 [BM].

This widely reproduced watercolour—contemporary with Steele's writing—doubtless captures the spirit of the top of the market, but is consistent with Steele's and Moser's descriptions. Other extant images in public collections depict more soberly dressed men in brown and black.

¶ One of the earliest known printed references to the use in England of an umbrella in the rain (rather than, as the word suggests, for shade) is a newspaper advertisement of 1707 by W*a*ll's Coffee House (seemingly a misprint for W*i*ll's, the coffee-house in Serle St.) asking for the return of its umbrella, taken during a shower of rain by some 'young gentlemen of Lincoln's Inn'. It became customary at that period for coffee-houses to provide a large umbrella for their customers' use, when alighting from or mounting into their carriage or chair—although Jonas Hanway is usually given the credit for the introduction of umbrellas as items of gentlemen's accoutrement, some decades later, in 1756.

The verses quoted below evoke another Inns of Court or Chancery man on a rainy day, three years later, in a vicinity at the e. end of (the street named) Holborn, adjacent to Thavies Inn, and conceivably in its eponymous coffee-house. Their reference to an umbrella is thought to be one of the next such in print to have survived, after the incident at Will's.

Careful observers may foretell the hour
(By sure prognostics) when to dread a show'r:

If you be wise, then go not far to dine,
You'll spend in coachhire more than save in wine.
A coming show'r your shooting corns presage,
Old aches throb, your hollow tooth will rage.
Saunt'ring in coffeehouse is Dulman seen;
He damns the climate, and complains of spleen.

Now in contiguous drops the flood comes down,
Threat'ning with deluge this devoted town.
To shops in crowds the daggled females fly,
Pretend to cheapen goods, but nothing buy.
The Templer[1] *spruce, while ev'ry spout's abroach,*
Stays till 'tis fair, yet seems to call a coach.
The tuckedup sempstress walks with hasty strides,
While streams run down her oil'd umbrella's sides.
Here various kinds, by various fortunes led,
Commence acquaintaince underneath a shed.
Triumphant Tories and desponding Whigs
Forget their feuds, and join to save their wigs.
Boxed in a chair the beau impatient sits,
While spouts run clatt'ring o'er the roof by fits;
And ever and anon with frightful din
The leather sounds, he trembles from within.

Now from all parts the swelling kennels flow,
And bear their trophies with them as they go:
Filth of all hues and odours seem to tell
What streets they sailed from, by their sight and smell.
They, as each torrent drives, with rapid force
From Smithfield or St Pulchre's shape their course,
And in huge confluent join'd at Snow Hill Ridge,
Fall from the Conduit[2] *prone to Holborn Bridge.*[3]

Sweepings from butchers' stalls, dung, guts and blood,
Drown'd puppies, stinking sprats, all drench'd in mud,
Dead cats and turniptops come tumbling down the flood.

—Jonathan Swift, from 'Description of a City Shower', 1710.

---

[1] Templer (or Templar): colloquially the name was given not only to members of the Inner and Middle Temples, but also generally to students or practising members of any of the Inns of Court or Chancery, amongst whom especially those to be found in the taverns, coffeehouses, playhouses and bagnios in the neighbourhood of the legal Inns.

[2] Conduit: of the river Fleet.

[3] Holborn Bridge: over the river Fleet, from the w. bridge-foot of which Holborn Hill, running into Holborn, began. The Inn's parish church, St Andrew's, and one of its Inns of Chancery, Thavies, and the coffee house of the same name (shown in an engraving by Hogarth noted above) were adjacent. Holborn Viaduct now spans the valley of the Fleet, eliminating the need for travellers e.-w. or w.-e. to descend into it.

37.2. *Clubs and literary taverns* in the neighbourhood of the Inn

¶ Clubs—in the sense of informal groups of friends meeting in a fixed place—have over the centuries been established, flourished and vanished on the periphery of the Inn, being by nature more ephemeral than the taverns in which usually they chose to meet.

The verses written in praise of the taverns of Fleet St. are among the most memorable of that genre in English literature—comparable to the famous lines by Francis Beaumont remembering, and John Keats evoking, the fame of The Mermaid in Bread St., Cheapside. That City tavern had been a centre of literary life at the turn of the C16th and C17th, which included among its participants Shakespeare and other leading dramatists and poets, and some lawyers. Those of Fleet St., at various periods from the C16th to the early C20th, similarly attracted a number of notable literary figures and lawyers.

---

i. The Apollo Club

¶ The Apollo Club met at the Devil Tavern, which lay at the w. extremity of Fleet St., on its s. side, facing Shire La., which ran n. to the Inn. Its site is now marked by a blue plaque. It was a favourite meeting place in the C17th for professional writers who were members of the Inns or associated with their intellectual and social life, and for professional lawyers who were amateur writers.

Let none but guests or clubbers hither come;
Let dunces, fools, sad, sordid men keep home;
Let learned, civil, merry men be invited,
And modest, too; nor the choice ladies slighted.
Let nothing in the treat offend the guests;
More for delight than cost prepare the feasts;
The cook and purveyor must our palates know;
And none contend who shall sit high or low.
Our waiters must quicksighted be, and dumb;
And let the drawers quickly hear and come.
Let not our wine be mixed, but brisk and neat,
Or else the drinkers may the vintners beat.
And let our only emulation be
Not drinking much, but talking wittily.
Let it be voted lawful to stir up
Each other with a moderate chirping cup;
Let none of us be mute, or talk too much;
On serious things or sacred let's not touch
With sated heads and bellies. Neither may
Fiddlers, unasked, obtrude themselves to play.
With laughing, leaping, dancing, jests, and songs
And whate'er else to grateful mirth belongs
Let's celebrate our feasts. And let us see
That all our jests without reflection be;
Insipid poems let no man rehearse,
Nor any be compelled to write a verse.
All noise of vain disputes must be forborne,
And let no lover in a corner mourn.
To fight and brawl like Hectors let none dare,
Glasses or windows break, or hangings tear.
Whoe'er shall publish what's here done or said
From our society must be banished.
Let none by drinking do or suffer harm,
And while we stay let us be always warm.

—Ben Jonson, *Leges Convivales, Sociable Rules for the Apollo*, *ca.* 1619, translated from the Latin by the attorney, Alexander Brome.

---

ii. The Kit-Cat Club

¶ The club which, in this neighbourhood, has secured the most lasting celebrity—and to which is attributed the greatest lasting influence—in contributing to the creation of the gentlemen's clubs of St James's was the Kit-Cat Club, formed probably at the end of the C17th. It met at *The Trumpet* in Shire La., a few yards s. of Serle's Gate. This numbered among its members aristocrats, politicians (notably Sir Robert Walpole [of LI] PM) and distinguished men in the arts and lawyers, and was a group of men dedicated to the Protestant succession.

A collection of their distinctive portraits is now in the NPG, and there given the sub-title 'Whigs in wigs'. A 'Kit-Cat' is a recognised term for a shorter portrait than is customary for head, shoulders and hands.

The Club was famous in its day for its toasts, and for its toasting glasses engraved with verses in praise of the 'reigning beauties' of the day. On this account, it was sometimes known as 'The Order of the Toast'. The origin of the name was much debated at the time, but the name of Christopher Catling, the keeper of a pie house in Shire La., seems almost certainly to have been the inspiration.

Whence deathless Kit-Kat took his name
Few critics can unriddle
Some say from pastry cook it came
And some from Cat and Fiddle

From no trim beaus its name it boasts
Grey statesmen or green wits
But from the pell-mell pack of toasts
Of old Cats and young Kits

—Dr John Arbuthnot, 'The Kit Cat Club', early C18th.

One Night in Seven, at this Convenient Seat,
Indulgent Bocaj[1] *did the Muses treat,*
Their Drink was gen'rous Wine, and Kit-Cat's Pyes their Meat,
Here he assembled his Poetic Tribe,
Past Labours to Reward, and new ones to prescribe,
Hence did th'Assembly's Title first arise,
And Kit-Cat Wits sprung first from Kit-Cat's Pyes
Bocaj the mighty Founder of the State
Led by his Wisdom, or his happy Fate,
Chose proper Pillars to support its Weight,
All the first Members for their Place were fit,
Tho'not of Title, men of Sense and Wit...

—Sir Richard Blackmore, from 'The Kit-Cats', 1708.

---

[1] Bocaj: Jacob Tonson, the publisher and bookseller of Chancery La., the Secretary of the Kit-Cat Club.

The name was given a new association and notoriety in the last hundred years by having been appropriated by a famous jazz club in London in the 1920s, and misappropriated—with no historical justification—in the 1972 film, *Cabaret*, about the louche life of Berlin under the Weimar republic.

>> C20th: Ophelia Field, *The Kit-Cat Club*, 2008.

Other clubs worth noting which once met on the perimeter of the Inn were those grouped around William Hazlitt in Southampton Bldgs., and John Sterling in Serle St.—both predominantly literary, with some legal membership.

38. FREEMASONS' LODGES IN THE VICINITY OF AND IN THE INN

¶ It might be expected that the neighbourhoods surrounding the Inns of Court, being situated at the axis of the nation's metropolis and close to the centre of its social life, should have links with freemasonry.

The origins of what is termed 'speculative' masons (i.e. freemasons)—as distinct from 'operative' masons (i.e. stone-masons)—are surprisingly obscure even apparently to initiates. Whatever their origins in earlier times, in medieval guilds or with the Knights Templar, or even in Ancient Egypt, in their present form and character their beginnings are generally taken to be in the mid-C17th England, in the Midlands or North.

The antiquary and freemason Elias Ashmole (1617-92) lived just s. of the Inn in Shire La. He, in his *Diaries*, recorded his admission to a lodge in Cheshire in 1646—the first such known or surviving record—and his subsequent attendance at a lodge meeting in London, under the aegis of the City livery company, the Worshipful Company of Masons. W. of the Inn, in Great Queen St. (a street which until the cutting through it of Kingsway at the end of the C19th was always known as 'Great Queen Street, Lincoln's Inn Fields') is the Hall of the United Grand Lodge of England, first built in 1776. The Freemasons' Tavern, which occupied the street frontage of the original hall, served as a notable venue for concerts, etc., in the London season. The Holborn Restaurant at 218, High Holborn, just n.w. of the Inn, and demolished after the Second World War, accommodated several masonic temples.

With a history of masonic activity around the Inns it might be surprising if there were no masonic life within them. Lincoln's and Gray's are themselves meeting places of freemasons' lodges, which are thereby associated with each Inn, or some members of its Society, but no part of its hierarchy. In the case of this Inn, they are the Chancery Bar Lodge (no. 2456), founded here, and the Lodge of Comity (no. 5649), founded elsewhere but including among its founding members the first Viscount Hailsham, LC [of LI]. A further legal lodge, the Templars' (no. 4302), which meets outside the Inn, had as its founding members a judge, barristers, solicitors, and clerks to barristers and solicitors. The foundation of the first-named of these lodges took place on 28th November 1893 at an elaborate ceremony of 'consecration' of the lodge, in the presence of the Prince of Wales, held in the Library followed by dinner in the Great Hall. At this period, masonic ceremonies and processions played a visible rôle in the public life of the nation, and the former were witnessed by invited representatives of the Press and widely reported.

THE ILLUSTRATED LONDON NEWS

REGISTERED AT THE GENERAL POST OFFICE FOR TRANSMISSION ABROAD.

No. 2851.—VOL. CIII. SATURDAY, DECEMBER 9, 1893. With Extra Supplement: The Late Professor Tyndall | SIXPENCE. By Post, 6½d.

38.a. R Potter, from sketch by W Simpson: The constitution of the Chancery Bar Lodge, *Illustrated London News*, 1893 [a cutting, HSLI].

It is evidence of the public importance attached at the time to a masonic event such as this, and doubtless to the presence of the Prince, that the *ILN* should have devoted its front cover to an image of the ceremony. The Earl of Lathom is on the Prince's left and the Earl of Mount Edgcumbe on his right, both peers being officers of the Grand Lodge, but not members of the legal professions. More interesting therefore, for its legal significance, is the presence of the Lord Chancellor, the Earl of Halsbury. Sir Arthur Underhill [of LI] (some of whose artist's records of scenes in the Inn are reproduced in this book) joined the lodge shortly afterwards.

39.a. Anon. artist (? Ned Ward): 'Sots rampant, dormant, and couchant', in *A Vade Mecum*…, 1712 [BL].

Ned Ward has gained immortality for his gossipy *The London Spy*, a title which has been reused by others from time to time. He kept an ale-house in one of the alleys leading into Gray's Inn, and wrote extensively about the hostelries of the neighbourhood of the Inns, and their clients, many of whom necessarily were lawyers or their clerks.

39. *DRINKING-HOUSES* AND *CHOP-HOUSES* CLOSE TO THE INN:

39.1. Their premises, proprietors and personnel

i. Newman's Tipple House

The Muse would inexcusably do Wrong,
Should Newman's[1] *Tipple House remain unsung;*
Where there is not a Pot or Tankard brought,
That argues not a quick and sprightly Draught,
And shuts out every Cause of finding Fault.
Here in the Evening, after Six, are seen,
Loit'rers, 'till then, from Five, in Lincoln's Inn;
Gentry, that walking upon Stone Parade,
Consult to get this House a swimming Trade;
And when got Sappy[2] *in conjuncture nice,*
To swallow each a gallon for a Sice.[3]
Since it has been, from just Observance found,
A three Pint Tankard goes but half way round,
And every Health with two of them is
crown'd...

---

ii. The Gin House,* in *Lincoln's Inn Back Side

As in our First Part we a Tavern chose,
With which we did our livesome Journey close;
So now, fatigu'd with drinking common Bub,[5]
Pass we to the red hot Geneva[6] *Club,*
Assembled, as on Purpose, not by Chance,
Where Youths are taught to Read, and Write, and Dance:
Since, when Two Peny's worth of it is guzzled down,
Learning of all kinds gets within the Crown.
This Simon Pen, with virtuous Mrs Jude
His Wife, that's neither a Coquet or Prude;
Both Servants to the fam'd Sir Edward Northey,
And of all Sots good Words for every worthy,
Know to be true, when they fresh Quarterns[7] *draw,*
To quench the Thirst of Hackneys[8] *of the Law...*

—Ned Ward, from *A Vade Mecum for Malt-Worms*, 1712 [BL].

39.b. William Hogarth: 'A Midnight Modern Conversation', 1733 [LMA].

---

1 Newman's Row is the name now given to the pavement at the n.w. corner of the Inn, between the Fields and Great Turnstile, and onto which now face the Inn's chambers at 30, Lincoln's Inn Fields. Formerly the name attached to the whole of the n. side of the Fields.

2 sappy: foolish.

3 sice: sixpence.

4 Lincoln's Inn Back Side is the alley now known as Star Yard, noted in 3.4.2.

5 bub: strong beer.

6 geneva: the original word in England for the gin imported from Holland, flavoured with juniper berry.

7 quarterns: quarter-pints.

8 hackneys: hacks.

---

iii. St John's Coffee House

¶ This establishment is included as perhaps representative of the dozen or more coffee houses and taverns which lined the short length of Shire La., the usual pedestrian approach from the s. to Serle's Gate. At the period of history—or perhaps the time of day—depicted, it is clear that the sale of roasted beverages had been supplemented by those of which the ingredients had been fermented or distilled.

Hogarth's caption does not assert that any of those men depicted was a lawyer from the Inn, and it is earnestly to be hoped that none was!

---

iv. The Cock

¶ A tavern which, in the C19th, attracted a coterie of writers and of lawyers from the four Inns was The Cock, on the s. side of Fleet St., between Chancery La. and Fetter La. A succession of taverns or coffee-houses of the same name claiming continuity with one another existed before and since on the same or neighbouring sites, and one is there still. A Poet Laureate praised it in a poem, three verses of which are quoted here, the original being some ten times longer:

O plump headwaiter at The Cock,
To which I most resort,
How goes the time? 'Tis five o'clock.

39.c. John Crowther: Interior of The Cock Tavern, 1881 [LMA].

The room is depicted a generation later than that of Tennyson's poem—but it may be imagined that there would have been no particular call on the part of its clientèle to change it.

Go fetch a pint of port:
But let it not be such as that
You set before chancecomers,
But such whose fathergrape grew fat
On Lusitanian summers.
… Head-waiter, honoured by the guest
Half-mused, or reeling ripe,
The pint, you brought me, was the best
That ever came from pipe.
But though the port surpasses praise,
My nerves have dealt with stiffer.
Is there some magic in the place?
Or do my peptics differ?
… For since I came to live and learn,
No pint of white or red
Had ever half the power to turn
This wheel within my head,
Which bears a seasoned brain about,
Unsubject to confusion,
Though soaked and saturate, out and out,
Through every convolution.

—Alfred, Lord Tennyson, from 'Will Waterproof's Lyrical Monologue, Made at "The Cock",' 1842.

As to the friendship between Tennyson's family and a Chaplain of Lincoln's Inn, the Rev J F D Maurice, see 42.1.

39.2. Their Inn clientèle

Dost thou endeavour, Frank, to leave thy drink
That made thee such high raptures write and think?
Or art a'weary of the Muses? For
What else would make thee Phoebus' sack[1] *abhor?*
It is our grief, our mourning, and thy shame
That the Queen's poet[2] *and a man of name*
Should drive Apollo from his breast with a
Fine glass of six shillings or a glass of whey[3]
Redress our sorrows and return again
To wine and make thy head like Charles his wain.[4]

—Sir Aston Cockayne, 'On Mr Francis Lenton[5] refusing wine', in *Small Poems*, 1658 [BL].

[1] sack: dry white wine, from Spain or the Canaries. Phoebus or Apollo are presumably references to the sun on the vineyards whence the wine came.

[2] Queen's poet: a title analogous to, but of lower status than, Poet Laureate.

[3] whey: ? wine whey.

[4] Charles his wain: 'Charles' wain' is the constellation of the Great Bear or the Plough, hence presumably 'to see stars'.

[5] Francis Lenton [of LI] *fl.* 1630-40, d. 1642, a member of a literary circle of courtiers and Inns of Court men, who frequented The Fleece, in Covent Garden, some ¾ mile w. of the Inn.

¶ A precursor, perhaps, to the modern colloquial word association between drinking and plastering:

'He[1] was generally temperate as to drinking; but one time when he was a student of Lincoln's Inn, having been merry at the tavern with his comrades, late at night, a frolic came into his head, to get a plasterer's brush and a pot of ink, and blot out all the signs between Temple Bar and Charing Cross,[2] which made a strange confusion the next day, and it was in term time. But it happened that they were discovered and it cost them and him some moneys. This I had from R. Estcott, Esquire, that carried the inkpot.'

—John Aubrey [of MT] from *Brief Lives*, 1680.

[1] He: Sir John Denham [of LI] (1615-69).

[2] Temple Bar and Charing Cross: the length of the Strand, running from the end of Fleet St., due s. of the Inn, w. to Whitehall.

40. *MUSIC HALLS*

¶ During the decades after the 1850s from the passing of the Theatres Act, 1843, until this form of entertainment faded away between the two world wars, High Holborn was a noted centre for the music halls. While it may be difficult now to imagine members of the Bar of, or solicitors in, the Inn forming a significant proportion of their audience, it is a fact that shareholders in the music hall mentioned here included lawyers in practice in the vicinity, and who are likely to have been devotees as well as investors. It is, perhaps, less difficult to imagine law students and lawyers' clerks there. Established in 1857, one of the earliest and most successful music halls in central London was that at 242/3, High Holborn, known successively under different owners, rebuilt and extended over the years, as Weston's Music Hall, the Royal Music Hall, the Royal Holborn Theatre of Varieties and finally the Holborn Empire. It stood, set at some distance back from the road, adjacent to Little Turnstile, and backing onto Whetstone Park, at the n.w. corner of Lincoln's Inn Fields. It was destroyed by bombing in May 1941.

Another music hall, the Embassy Theatre, stood nearby on High Holborn, 100 yards to the w. The music hall song of which a brief extract is quoted here must surely have been performed in one or both of these theatres on numerous occasions.

The sheet music and its accompanying text quoted here has, as was customary, a full-colour lithographic front cover—in this instance of a slimy-looking barrister, fully robed as though in Court. It was claimed to have been 'sung throughout the United Kingdom with immense success by A G Vance'.

Ahem! ahem! how d'you do?
Gentlemen and ladies too,
There's not a doubt that known to you
Is Sergeant Sharp of Lincoln's Inn.
Everybody knows my name,
Everyone has heard the fame,
In town or circuit it's the same,
Of Sergeant Sharp of Lincoln's Inn.

'Spoken: Yes, gentlemen (if I may be allowed the expression) when I look around me and see so many bright intelligent faces, when I behold the beautiful and bright flashing bloom of Bass and Allsopp[1] radiating in a glorious halo around your Grecian straits and Roman bumps, I say, gentlemen (if I may be allowed the expression), that when I observe those unmistakable marks of intelligence, I have no doubt, I cannot doubt but that you have all heard of…'

Chorus: *Sergeant Sharp of Lincoln's Inn,*
Lincoln's Inn, Lincoln's Inn,
There's none can pitch the blarney in,
Like Sergeant Sharp of Lincoln's Inn.

I think at once I'd better state,
Perhaps before it is too late,
There's nothing at all like six and eight[2]
About Sergeant Sharp of Lincoln's Inn.
That figure ne'er would do for me.
I never less than guineas see,
From five to fifty is the fee,
For Sergeant Sharp of Lincoln's Inn.

—Walter Greenaway and Alfred Lee,
from *Sergeant Sharp of Lincoln's Inn*, 1872 [BL].

---

1 Bass and Allsopp: at various times in the mid-C19th Bass and Allsopp were the two largest brewers in Burton-on-Trent. Their respective heads of family, on being enobled as Baron Burton and Baron Hindlip, were irreverently called 'the beerage'.

2 six and eight: eighty pence—historically half-a-mark.

41. *BAWDY-HOUSES* IN PROXIMITY TO THE INN

'Meds' ain't good for much; they're larky young blokes, but they've never much money, and they're fond of dollymopping.[1] But talk of dollymopping—lawyers are the fellows for that. Those chambers in the Inns of Court are the ruin of many a girl. And they are so convenient for bilking,[2] you've no idea. There isn't a good woman in London who'd go with a man to the Temple, not one. You go to Kate's, and take a woman out, put her in a cab, and say you were going to take her to either of the Temples, which are respectable and decent places when compared to the other inns which are not properly Inns of Court, except Gray's Inn and Lincoln's Inn, and she'd cry off directly. I mean Barnard's Inn, and Thavies' Inn, and New Inn, and Clement's Inn, and all those.'

—Henry Mayhew, 'The Dress Lodger Follower',[3] *op. cit.*, 1851.

---

1 dollymopping: visiting bawdy-houses.

2 bilking: within the wide range of possible meanings, probably 'making money by profiting from well-to-do clients'.

3 dress-lodger: a prostitute, inhabiting a dress-house.

It is interesting to note the girl's awareness of the difference between Inns of Court and Inns or former Inns of Chancery.

¶ Whetstone Park is a narrow lane running w. from the n.-w. corner of the gardens of the Inn, opening off Great Turnstile opposite the site now occupied by 30, Lincoln's Inn Fields (originally Erskine Chambers). In the C17th it was famous for its bawdy-houses, and there are corresponding references in Pepys' *Diary* and many plays of the period. It may be surmised that its character was set by its being comprised of modest buildings lying in close proximity to High Holborn—one of the busiest thoroughfares and concentrations of coaching inns and livery stables in London (as noted in 2.2.ii. above)—but also by being just outside the jurisdiction of the City, the w. extent of which was marked by Holborn Bars.

In February 1670/1, a party of royal and aristocratic gentlemen visited Whetstone Park and, being reproached for their rowdiness by the parish beadle, drew their swords and murdered him. The Dukes of Monmouth and of Albemarle, and Viscount Dunbar were known to have been there and the Duke of Somerset was suspected. It is likely that the party were concluding an evening's entertainment in this quarter of London—some distance from their usual haunts—which might have begun at the Lincoln's Inn Fields Theatre or with revels in any one of the Inns of Court.

The lines quoted below—one of two such forthright protests printed and circulating in London at the time—advocate the execution of the dukes for what they were believed to have done. The King reluctantly pardoned the suspects:

Near Holborn lies a Park[1] *of great renown*
The place, I do suppose, is not unknown
For brevity's sake the name I shall not tell,
Because most gentle readers know it well.
(Since Middle Park[2] *near Charing Cross was made,*
They say there is a great decay of trade.)
'Twas here a gleek[3] *of dukes, by fury brought,*
With bloody mind a sickly damsel sought
And against law her castle did invade
To take from her her instrument of trade.
'Tis strange (but sure they thought not on't before)
Three bastard dukes should go t'undo a whore.
Murder was cri'd (truth is, her case was sad,
When she was like to lose e'en all she had);
In came the watch, disturb'd from sleep and ale
By the shrill noise, but they could not prevail
T'appease their Graces; straight rose mortal jars[4]
Between the night's Black guard and silver stars.[5]
Then fell the beadle by a ducal hand
For daring to pronounce the saucy stand!
(The way in blood certain renown to win
Is first with bloody noses to begin.)
The high-born youths their hasty errand tell,
'Damn you, you rogue, we'll send your soul to Hell!'
They need not send a messenger before—
They're too well known there to stand long at door.
See what mishaps dare e'en invade Whitehall!
This silly fellow's death puts off the ball[6]
And disappoints the Queen, poor little chuck[7]
(I warrant would have danc'd like any duck):
The fiddlers, voices, entries, all the sport,
And the gay show put off, were the brisk Court
Anticipates in rich subsidy-coats[8]
All that is got by mercenary votes.
Yet shall Whitehall, the innocent, the good,
See these men dance, all daub'd with lace and blood.
Near t'other Park[9] *there stands an aged tree,*[10]
As fit as if't were made o'the nonce for three,
Where, that no ceremony may be lost,
Each duke for state may have a several post.
What storms may rise out of so black a cause,
If such turd-flies shall break through cobweb laws!

—Anon., 'On the Three Dukes Killing the Beadle On Sunday Morning, Feb. The 26th, 1670' [=1670/1] in *Poems on Affairs of State*, 1697.

---

1 a Park: Whetstone Park.

2 Middle Park: St James's Park.

3 gleek: a set of court cards, three in the same hand.

4 jars: harsh sounds.

5 stars: the stars of the Order of the Garter.

6 ball: it seems that one of the masked balls at Westminster was cancelled, by royal command, because of this scandal.

7 chuck: chunk.

8 subsidy-coats: coats purchased from (or received as) bribes for passing State subsidies.

9 t'other Park: Hyde Park.

10 tree… three: the triple gallows at Tyburn.

> Notes from George de F Lord.

King Charles II visited Lincoln's Inn on several occasions in 1670 to 1672, both openly and supposedly incognito, but always accompanied by a party of courtiers. The name of at least one of the suspected murderers is inscribed in the Inn's Royal Admission Book.

In February 1671/2, the Duke of Monmouth returned to the neighbourhood, as a member of the King's party which dined in Lincoln's Inn. Did the benchers remember, as they revelled with him that night, the murder in which he had reputedly been involved just outside the gates of the Inn almost exactly a year before, and the malleability in the hands of the King of the criminal law (of which some of them were by profession its custodians) towards him? But Monmouth was eventually put to death, for treason, after Sedgemoor in 1685.

Editor's note.

42. THE EXODUS FROM THE INN IN THE LONG VACATION:

42.1. The law terms

¶ From early times, the calendar of law terms evolved. During these periods, the courts sat and procedural steps in litigation could be taken. The terms were fixed so as to avoid the feasts and fasts of the medieval Church, and certain periods of the agricultural year, notably harvest, rent collection and accounting at Michaelmas. Until 1830, the terms were still calculated by reference to the ecclesiastical calendar—having passed imperceptibly from that of the Roman Catholic Church to that of the Church of England. These lines evoke the four terms:

London hath likewise four terms of law most fit,
The fourfold year in equal parts divide,
In which the judges of the law do sit,
Depending matters justly to decide—
The poor man's plaint, and eke the rich man's cause,
And sentence given by justly dooming laws.

First of the four fresh spring doth entertain,
The second is in sweating summer placed,
The third with windy harvest doth remain,
And freezing winter doth delight the last:
When these times come, and courts of law unlock,
'Tis strange to mark how men to London flock.

—Richard Johnson, from 'London's Description',
in *The Pleasant Walks of Moorfields,* 1607.

> Lawrence Manley, *op. cit.,* 1986.

The ebb and flow of the terms gave rise to the noun 'termer' for a student, barrister or client who resorted to London in term-time.

In 1831, the dates were fixed by reference to the civil calendar: Hilary Term: 11th–31st January, Easter Term: 15th April–18th May, Trinity Term: 22nd May–12th June and Michaelmas Term: 2nd–25th November. The shortness of the terms, whether ecclesiastical or civil, led to the need for courts to sit out of term. By the Judicature Act, 1873, law terms as such were abolished, and court sittings regulated, as they still are, by the Rules of the Supreme Court, the 'term' being replaced by 'sessions' of the same names: Michaelmas, Hilary, Easter and Trinity.

42.2. The deserted Inn

'I went up Holbourn, and there the Street was full of People; but they walk'd in the middle of the great Street, neither on one Side or other, because, as I suppose, they would not mingle with any Body that came out of Houses, or meet with Smells and Scents from Houses that might be infected. The Inns-of-Court were all shut up; nor were very many of the Lawyers in the Temple, or Lincolns-Inn, or Greyes-Inn, to be seen there. Every Body was at peace, there was no Occasion for Lawyers; besides, it being in the Time of the Vacation too, they were generally gone into the Country. Whole Rows of Houses in some Places, were shut close up; the Inhabitants all fled, and only a Watchman or two left.'

—Daniel Defoe, describing 1665,
from *Journal of the Plague Year*, publ. 1722.

The Black Books contain a reference to one Council meeting only which minuted any decision as to action to be taken in response to the plague: that on 13th June 1666. A committee was appointed to consider the safety of the Inn, and to arrange for some persons to remain—a confirmation of Defoe's account of the desertion of the Inns. Readings were suspended on account of the present greate contagion.

My lord[1] *now quits his venerable seat*
The six-clerk[2] *on his padlock turns the key*
From bus'ness hurries to his snug retreat
And leaves vacation and the town to me

Now all is hush'd, asleep the eye of Care
And Lincoln's Inn, a solemn stillness holds
Save where the Porter whistles o'er the Square
Or Pompey barks, or basketwoman scolds

Save that from yonder pump and dusty stair
The moping shoe-black and the laundry maid
Complain of such as from the town repair
And leave the usual quarterage[3] *unpaid*

In those dull chambers where old parchments lie
And useless draughts in many a mould'ring heap,
Each for parade to catch the client's eye
Salkeld[4] *and Ventris*[5] *in oblivion sleep.*

—'Jemmy Copywell of Lincoln's Inn' (William Woty),
Vacation in Lincoln's Inn, 1758.

> C W Heckethorn, *op. cit.*, 1896.

1 My lord: the Lord Chancellor.

2 The six-clerk: see 18.2.2.

3 quarterage: charges or payment to the Society.

4 William Salkeld: the editor of *Reports of Cases Adjudged in the Court of King's Bench, 1689-1712.* His tombstone under the Chapel is still clearly legible.

5 Sir Peyton Ventris: the editor of *Choice cases Adjudged in the Common Pleas, 1669-1691.*

Oliver Goldsmith's essay, 'A description of the Courts of Justice in Westminster Hall', 1760, two years later, explains the standing enjoyed by these two members of the Bar at that time:
—'"My lawyer tells me," returned he, "that I have Salkeld and Ventris strong in my favour, and that there are no less than fifteen cases in point."
—"I understand," said I, "those are two of your judges who have already declared their opinion."
—"Pardon me," replied my friend, "Salkeld and Ventris are lawyers who some hundred years ago gave their opinions on cases similar to mine; these opinions which make for me my lawyer is to cite; and those opinions which look another way are cited by the lawyer employed by my antagonist: as I observed, I have Salkeld and Ventris for me; he has Coke and Hale for him; and he that has most opinions is most likely to carry his cause."'

The lines quoted above are, of course, a parody of Gray's *Elegy*, 1751, a favoured source of inspiration at the time. Indeed, a theatrical member of the Society with chambers in the Inn, Arthur Murphy, published a version of the *Elegy* in Latin.

Editor's notes.

'It is the long vacation in the regions of Chancery Lane. The good ships Law and Equity, those teak-built, copper-bottomed, iron-fastened, brazen-faced, and not by any means fast-sailing Clippers, are laid up in ordinary. The Flying Dutchman, with a crew of ghostly clients imploring all whom they may encounter to peruse their papers, has drifted, for the time being, Heaven knows where. The Courts are all shut up; the public offices lie in a hot sleep; Westminster Hall itself is a shady solitude where nightingales might sing, and a tenderer class of suitors than is usually found there, walk.

The Temple, Chancery Lane, Serjeants' Inn, and Lincoln's Inn even unto the Fields, are like tidal harbours at low water; where stranded proceedings, offices at anchor, idle clerks lounging on lopsided stools that will not recover their perpendicular until the current of Term sets in, lie high and dry upon the ooze of the long vacation. Outer doors of chambers are shut up by the score, messages and parcels are to be left at the Porter's Lodge by the bushel. A crop of grass would grow in the chinks of the stone pavement outside Lincoln's Inn Hall, but that the ticket-porters, who have nothing to do beyond sitting in the shade there, with their white aprons over their heads to keep the flies off, grub it up and eat it thoughtfully.

There is only one Judge in town. Even he only comes twice a week to sit in chambers. If the country folks of those assize towns on his circuit could see him now! No full-bottomed wig, no red petticoats, no fur, no javelin-men, no white wands. Merely a close-shaved gentleman in white trousers and a white hat, with sea-bronze on the judicial countenance, and a strip of bark peeled by the solar rays from the judicial nose, who calls in at the shell-fish shop as he comes along, and drinks iced ginger-beer!

The Bar of England is scattered over the face of the earth. How England can get on through four long summer months without its bar—which is its acknowledged refuge in adversity, and its only legitimate triumph in prosperity—is beside the question; assuredly that shield and buckler of Britannia are not in present wear. The learned gentleman who is always so tremendously indignant at the unprecedented outrage committed on the feelings of his client by the opposite party, that he never seems likely to recover it, is doing infinitely better than might be expected, in Switzerland. The learned gentleman who does the withering business, and who blights all opponents with his gloomy sarcasm, is as merry as a grig at a French watering-place. The learned gentleman who weeps by the pint on the smallest provocation, has not shed a tear these six weeks. The very learned gentleman who has cooled the natural heat of the gingery complexion in pools and fountains of law, until he has become great in knotty arguments for term-time, when he poses the drowsy Bench with legal 'chaff', inexplicable to the uninitiated and to most of the initiated too, is roaming, with characteristic delight in aridity and dust, about Constantinople.

Other dispersed fragments of the same great Palladium are to be found on the canals of Venice, at the second cataract of the Nile, in the baths of Germany, and sprinkled on the seasand all over the English coast. Scarcely one is to be encountered in the deserted region of Chancery Lane. If such a lonely member of the bar do flit across the waste, and come upon a prowling suitor who is unable to leave off haunting the scenes of his anxiety, they frighten one another, and retreat into opposite shades.

It is the hottest long vacation known for many years. All the young clerks are madly in love, and according to their various degrees, pine for bliss with the beloved object, at Margate, Ramsgate, or Gravesend. All the middle-aged clerks think their families too large. All the unowned dogs who stray into the Inns of Court, and pant about staircases and other dry places, seeking water, give short howls of aggravation. All the blind men's dogs in the streets draw their masters against pumps, or trip them over buckets. A shop with a sun-blind, and a watered pavement, and a bowl of gold and silver fish in the window, is a sanctuary. Temple Bar gets so hot, that it is, to the adjacent Strand and Fleet Street, what a heater is in an urn, and keeps them simmering all night.'

—Charles Dickens, from *Bleak House*, 1852.

42.3. The appeal of remaining in, or of leaving, an Inn in the Long Vacation

...But now it's Long Vacation you will say,
The town is empty, and who ever may
To th' pleasure of his country home repair,
Flies from th' infection of our London Air.
In this, your errour. Now's the time alone
To live here, when the city dame is gone
T' her house at Brentford; for beyond that she
Imagines there's no land but Barbary,
Where lies her husband's factor. When from hence

Rid is the country justice whose nonsense
Corruputed had the language of the Inn;
Where he and his horse littered, we begin
To live in silence; when the noise o' th' Bench
Not deafens Westminster, nor corrupt French
Walks Fleet Street in her gown. Ruffs of the Bar
By the Vacation's power translated are,
To cut-work bands. And who were busy here
Are gone to sow sedition in the shire.
The air by this is purged, and the term's strife
Thus fled the city: we the civil life
Lead happily…

—William Habington, from *To my Worthy Cousin Mr E C, In Praise of the City Life, in the Long Vacation*, 1634.

> Lawrence Manley, *op. cit.*, 1986.

Come away with me, Tom,
Term and talk are done;
My poor lads are reaping,
Busy every one.
Curates mind the parish,[1]
Sweepers mind the court;[2]
We'll away to Snowdon
For our ten days' sport;
Fish the August evening
Till the eve is past,
Whoop like boys, at pounders
Fairly played and grassed.
When they cease to dimple,
Lunge, and swerve, and leap,
Then up over Siabod,[3]
Choose our nest, and sleep.
Up a thousand feet, Tom,
Round the lion's head,
Find soft stones to leeward
And make up our bed.
Eat our bread and bacon,
Smoke the pipe of peace,
And, ere we be drowsy,
Give our boots a grease.
Homer's heroes did so,
Why not such as we?
What are sheets and servants?
Superfluity.
Pray for wives and children
Safe in slumber curled,
Then to chat till midnight
O'er this babbling world—
Of the workmen's college,[4]
Of the price of grain,
Of the tree of knowledge,
Of the chance of rain;
If Sir A. goes Romeward,
If Miss B. sings true,
If the fleet comes homeward,
If the mare will do—
Anything and everything—
Up there in the sky
Angels understand us,
And no 'saints' are by.
Down, and bathe at daydawn,
Tramp from lake to lake,
Washing brain and heart clean
Every step we take.

Leave to Robert Browning[5]
Beggars, fleas, and vines;
Leave to mournful Ruskin[6]
Popish Apennines,
Dirty Stones of Venice
And his Gas lamps Seven—
We've the stones of Snowdon
And the lamps of heaven.
Where's the mighty credit
In admiring Alps?
Any goose sees 'glory'
In their 'snowy scalps'.
Leave such signs and wonders
For the dullard brain,
As aesthetic brandy,
Opium and cayenne.
Give me Bramshill[7] *common*
(St John's harriers[8] *by),*
Or the vale of Windsor,
England's golden eye.
Show me life and progress,
Beauty, health, and man;
Houses fair, trim gardens,
Turn where'er I can.
Or, if bored with 'High Art',
And such popish stuff,
One's poor ear need airing,
Snowdon's high enough.
While we find God's signet

Fresh on English ground,
Why go gallivanting
With the nations round?
Though we try no ventures
Desperate or strange;
Feed on commonplaces
In a narrow range;
Never sought for Franklin[9]
Round the frozen Capes;
Even, with Macdougall,[10]
Bagged our brace of apes;
Never had our chance, Tom,
In that black Redan,[11]
Can't avenge poor Brereton[12]
Out in Sakarran;[13]
Tho' we earn our bread, Tom,
By the dirty pen,
What we can we will be,
Honest Englishmen.
Do the work that's nearest,
Though it's dull at whiles,
Helping, when we meet them,
Lame dogs over stiles;
See in every hedgerow
Marks of angels' feet;

Epics in each pebble
Underneath our feet;
Once a year, like schoolboys,
Robin Hooding go,
Leaving fops and fogies
A thousand feet below.

—The Rev Charles Kingsley [of LI],
The Invitation (to Tom Hughes), 1856.

---

1 parish: although Kingsley (1819-75) had joined the Society as a student, he was not called but entered the priesthood of the Church of England. He was at this time, and for most of his ministry, vicar of Eversley in n.e. Hampshire; later he became Regius Professor of History at Cambridge, and then a Canon of Westminster Abbey, and Chaplain to the Queen. He is associated with the label 'Muscular Christianity'—understandable perhaps in the context of this poem, but not one which he chose for himself—and with that of 'Christian Socialism', on which his thoughts, expressed in his novels, and articles published in journals, were highly influential in their day.

These lines were reputedly written to and left for Hughes after Kingsley had called on him at his chambers in the Inn and found him out. The difference between the simple and safe pleasures of England and Wales, and the exotic, challenging and dangerous world beyond these shores can rarely have been more graphically expressed.

2 court: Hughes (1822-96), the author of *Tom Brown's Schooldays*, was at this time in practice at the Bar, with chambers at 3, Old Buildings in the Inn. He had joined the Society, and read for the Bar in the Inn, but was called by Inner Temple. He became a QC and a County Court Judge. He was particularly fond of country rambles, and there is a collection of his essays on that subject.

3 Siabod: Moel Siabod, 2851 ft., in Snowdonia.

4 The Working Men's College was founded in Red Lion Square, n. of High Holborn in 1852, by the efforts of the Rev J F D Maurice, Chaplain to the Society (noted elsewhere in this book), in the work of which both Kingsley and Hughes took a deep interest. It continues to this day, in Camden Town.

5 Browning: Robert Browning, the poet, was at this time living in Florence, where he and his wife Elizabeth Barrett had settled on their marriage in 1846.

6 Ruskin: *The Seven Lamps of Architecture*, 1848, and *The Stones of Venice*, 1851-3, John Ruskin's two influential works on architecture, written after extensive Continental travel.

7 Bramshill: in n.e. Hampshire, the next village to his parish.

8 harriers: no information has been found in the course of compilation of this book to indicate whether the St John's harriers were a pack of beagles or a cross-country running club. Neither would seemingly have been out of character.

9 Franklin: Sir John (1786-1847), Arctic explorer. All members of his last expedition to find the Northwest Passage in Canada died. Expeditions were sent out, including one by his widow, to investigate their fate and achievements. A statue to his memory stands in Waterloo Place, off Pall Mall.

10 Macdougall: Francis Thomas (1817-86), missionary in Borneo, made Anglican Bishop of Labuan and Sarawak in the year before these verses were written.

11 Redan: in 1854 the British Army captured from the Russians, but failed to hold against them, the Redan (a fortified salient) in the Crimea, during the war of that name. The Treaty of Paris concluding the war was signed in the same year as these verses were written.

12 Brereton: Sir William (1789-1864), campaigned in the Peninsular War, Mesopotamia, China and the Crimea.

13 Sakarran: taken to be a reference to the havens in Borneo which sheltered the feared pirates, known as the Sakarran Dyaks, who harried European shipping in the Far East.

Editor's notes.

42.4. Returning to the Inn from the country during, or at the end of, the long vacation

...But now 'tis time we should be gone,
And leave the Country for Town;
My Muse and I with easy pace,
Tow'rd London now have set our Face:
But had you seen, as we took notice,
Of such a numerous train of Coaches,
Both Hackney, Stage, and those of Gentry,
Who had upon the Road made entry,
Calashes[1] *made by Workmens Art*
A much more modish sort of Cart;
And ev'ry one of these 'forenam'd,
With Folks as thick as Bee-hives cram'd;
Of had you likewise seen beside,
The numerous company that Ride
On Long-tails, Bob-tails, Trotters, Pacers,
Pads, Highlers, Hawkers, Hunters, racers,
Who did with Whip and Spur repair,
To tast the Countries purer Air...
When we arriv'd...... 'twas my first desire
To visit Hall of Westminster,

Where oft till two a Clock I've staid,
Starving my Guts to feed my Head
With scraps of Law and bits of Lattin,
(Oh! What a Bliss is Learned Prating)...
No Judges learned in the Law,
Nor Serjeants who choice Pleadings draw,
Nor Councel who can split a Hair,
Were seen on Bench or at the Bar;
Not one Atturney with his Bags,
Stuft full of Law, or Rogues in Rags,
We justly Pettifoggers[2] *call,*
Were to be seen about the Hall;
Nor Affidavit-Men, nor those
In Temple-Walk with Straws in Shoes...
And Bookseller long time may snort,
Before he's askt for Cook's Reports;[3]
The place appear'd so Melancholy,
To stay there longer was a folly,
Therefore did most convenient judg it,
To Lincolns-Inn on Foot to trudg it;

...So passing on to King's-Bench Walk,
Survey'd a Num'rous crew were Talk-
Ing, hither, thither, to and fro,
As if they'd little else to do:
Poor Pettifogging Pimps o'th' Law,
Salt-water Trav'lers who ne're Salt-water saw,
Alsatian[4] *Biters*[5] *and their Cullies,*[6]
Pretended Wits and Sharping Bullies,
Projectors and their Undertakers,
News Writing 'Squires and Ballad Makers,
Were Walking here this Long-Vacation,
To give their thoughts some Recreation.

...Thank Heaven, I am at last return'd,
Tho no one for my Absence Mourn'd;
Pleasure should give to Business place
(Men do not use to feed on Sauce)
Not dawn of Light to People, where
'Tis Midnight Darkness half the Year,
More welcom is, than dawn of Term
To Lawyers, who to London Swarm.
The Nobles now and Gentry too,
To Country Pleasures bid adieu,
And with the Cities Conversation,
Supply the want of Recreation.

...Nay, I myself must take my leave
Of Cowly,[7] *Waller, Oldham, Cleave-*
Land, and beloved Hudibrass,
To study Actions on the Case,
And leave my Thought ere made an end on't,
To think of Plaintiff and Defendant;
And so farewell all Recreation
In this Dull, Tedious, Long Vacation.

—Richard Ames [of LI], from *Lawyerus Bootatus and Spurratus, or the Long Vacation, a Poem by a Student of Lincoln's Inn*, 1691 [a monograph, microfilm, BL].

The lines quoted above are but a few from a doggerel of epic length, written by a prolific author of other works of similar character and length. Whatever their literary limitations, there is no reason to doubt that they convey an accurate (if colourful) description of the traffic out of London at the beginning of the long vacation, and back again at its end, and of the country pursuits in between. They seem certain to be the authentic voice of a C17th law student, for the full text contains a score or more of colloquialisms which are contemporary with, or even a few years earlier than, to the date of their first quoted usage in the *OED*.

"WHEN THE CAT'S AWAY"——

42.a. Anon. artist: 'When the Cat's Away—Mr Blazer, KC, returns unexpectedly to his chambers in the middle of vacation', ? 1830s [Editor's coll.].

1 Calashes: light carriages, with a folding hood—*calèches*.

2 Pettifoggers: legal practitioners of the lowest status, normally men practising as though attorneys, but who had not qualified by service of a period of years in articles of clerkship.

3 Sir Edward Coke's *Reports*.

4 Alsatian: Alsatia was the colloquial name given to the lawless neighbourhood e. of the Temple (i.e. the 'frontier zone' over which neither Inner Temple nor the City Corporation exercised effective control) which in a later century was described in Sir Walter Scott's *Fortunes of Nigel*; and changed its character in the C19th only with the advent of the newspaper industry to Fleet St.

5 Biters: hoaxers.

6 Cullies: mates.

7 Cowly: Abraham Cowley (1618-67) poet, playwright and satirist.

Waller: Edmund Waller [of LI] (1606-87) poet.

Oldham: John Oldham (1653-83) poet, not least of translations or imitations of classical poets.

Cleaveland: John Cleveland (1613-58) poet, whose very successful writings appeared in some twenty-five editions in the second half of the C17th.

Hudibrass: *Hudibras*, the satirical poem by Samuel Butler, Part I published in 1662, Part II in 1663 and Part III in 1680.

Editor's notes.

43. THE WORLD OUTSIDE THE WALLS OF THE INN:

43.1. Intolerance outside the Inn, and refuge within

¶ Of the several bitter controversies over doctrine or ritual among Christian churches or sects, or between individuals, in C19th England, was one provoked by the Rev J F D Maurice, Chaplain to the Society (noted elsewhere in this book). In 1840, he was appointed to the academic staff of King's College in the Strand—at that time a staunchly and exclusively Anglican institution—and, in the following year, Chaplain of the Inn. Six years after his joining King's, he was installed in the Chair of Theology in that College, and in 1853 published his *Theological Essays*. The liberal views expressed in them on atonement and eternal life were repugnant to the authorities of the College and he was compelled to resign his post. The Inn, however, declined his offer of resignation from the chaplaincy of the Inn, and—a few hundred yards away from that College—continued for several more years to furnish him with a pulpit and a stipend, and a refuge from the orthodoxy of King's. His need for, and the availability of, refuge was also expressed in the year after his forced resignation by the then Poet Laureate, who offered him a domestic sanctuary to complement that in the Inn, thereby capturing the spirit of the times. It is not imagined that the Inn's offer of refuge would have been quite so elegantly expressed!

Come, when no graver cares employ,
Godfather, come and see your boy:
Your presence will be sun in winter,
Making the little one leap for joy.

For, being of that honest few,
Who give the Fiend himself his due,
Should eighty-thousand college-councils
Thunder 'Anathema,' friend, at you;

Should all our churchmen foam in spite
At you, so careful of the right,
Yet one lay-hearth would give you welcome
Take it and come to the Isle of Wight;

Where, far from noise and smoke of town,
I watch the twilight falling brown
All round a carelessordered garden
Close to the ridge of a noble down.

You'll have no scandal while you dine,
But honest talk and wholesome wine,
And only hear the magpie gossip
Garrulous under a roof of pine:

For groves of pine on either hand,
To break the blast of winter, stand;
And further on, the hoary Channel
Tumbles a billow on chalk and sand;

Where, if below the milky steep
Some ship of battle slowly creep,
And on through zones of light and shadow
Glimmer away to the lonely deep,

We might discuss the Northern sin
Which make a selfish war begin;
Dispute the claims, arrange the chances;
Emperor, Ottoman, which shall win:

Or whether war's avenging rod
Shall lash all Europe into blood;
Till you should turn to dearer matters,
Dear to the man that is dear to God;

How best to help the slender store,
How mend the dwellings of the poor;
How gain in life, as life advances,
Valour and charity more and more.

Come, Maurice, come: the lawn as yet
Is hoar with rime, or spongywet;
But when the wreath of March has blossomed,
Crocus, anemone, violet,

Or later, pay one visit here,
For those are few we hold as dear;
Nor pay but one, but come for many,
Many and many a happy year.

—Alfred, Lord Tennyson, 'To the Rev F D Maurice', 1854.

43.2. Murder or revenge, inadvertently let into the Inn

¶ Ralph Scrope [of LI] (called 1549, d. 1572) was appointed, with other members of the Inn, to investigate the disputes between the Principal and Ancients of its daughter house, Furnival's Inn. He reported in 1567.

It would seem that in making his investigation and report he made an enemy who resolved to invoke—so far as was in his power—a curse on him. The lead charm of which a line drawing is reproduced here was evidently made specifically with that object.

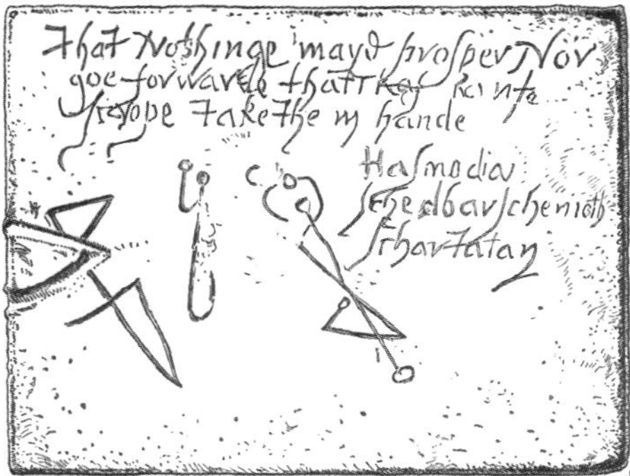

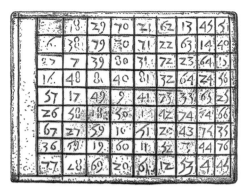

43.a. A mid-C16th lead charm unearthed in the Inn in 1899, in *Proceedings of the Society of Antiquaries*, 29th March 1900, transcript of paper delivered by W Paley Baildon [of LI] FSA [an off-print, HSLI].

The obverse of the charm has a table of numbers claimed to have occult significance, and on the reverse are the words: 'That nothing maye prosper nor goe forward that (Raf) Raufe Scroope takethe in hande—Hasmodai, Schedbarschemoth, Schartatan.' The words appear to be of Hebrew origin and cabbalistic significance. It was suggested by W Paley Baildon [of LI]—in his day the pre-eminent scholar of the Inn's history—that they invoke the spirit of the Moon, the king of the demons and the Devil. Paley Baildon observed that the text seemingly derives from Heinrich Cornelius Agrippa, *De Occulta Philosophia*, 1533.

> language: Professor C Abramski.

A

TrueRelation of a most desperate Murder, committed vpon the Body of Sir Iohn Tindall Knight, one of the Maisters of the Chancery;

Who with a Pistoll charged with 3. bullets, was slaine going into his Chamber within *Lincolnes-Inne*, the 12. day of Nouember, by one *Iohn Barterham* Gent:

Which *Barterham* afterwards hanged himselfe in the *Kinges-Bench* in *Southwarke*, on Sunday being the 17. day following. 1616.

LONDON

Printed by *Edw: All-de*, for *L. L.* dwelling in *Pauls* Church-yard, at the signe of the Tygers head. 1617.

43.b. 'A True Relation of a most desperate Murder' 1617 [title page].

The Black Books record the letting of the chamber late Sir John Tyndall's but say no more.

¶ Over the centuries, there have been several deaths within the precincts of the Inn known or suspected to be murder. Among them, the death of Sir John Tindall and the subsequent death in prison of his murderer are particularly well documented.

'Master John Barterham… a man so stricken in age, that so much hair as was upon his head (it being exceeding bald) with a long and comely beard, were all turned white, for three score and ten years at least sat upon his stooping shoulders… A long time had he suits depending in the Chancery, in which the law not running with so even and calm a stream as he did expect, or persuade himself that the justice of his cause did deserve: one Sir John Tindall, one of the Masters of the Chancery, a man grave for his age, reverenced for his wisdom, knowledge and authority, giving and awarding this Michaelmas term, by a certain report… a sum of money to the value of 200 marks, or £300, or thereabouts… as a full satisfaction: yet Barterham being of a haughty, turbulent and distainful spirit, full of rage, fury and headlong indignation; propounding to himself that Sir John Tindall was the only Caltrap thrown under his feet that to prick him and cast him down, sealed a damnable vow [that] as his state was confounded by Sir John Tindall, Sir John Tindall should be by Barterham confounded likewise in his. The means to make this vengeance sure much… troubled his cogitations and… at last the devil… stood whispering in his ear this word "report", upon which… it did him good to think, that as he found himself undone by the report of a lawyer's pen, so now by another report of his own devising, he should overthrow the lawyer.

He provides himself thereof a pistol, which charging with three bullets nothing wanted now, but place and opportunity. He made choice of Westminster for the place, and the returning of Sir John from the Hall, should in the open street, be the fatal hour of this desperate execution.

But whether the last of his life was appointed to run a little longer yet, or whether crossed by numbers of people, still walking up and down, so that Barterham could not stand conveniently to bring his purpose to pass, it is unknown: but howsoever, he constant in his resolution, followed close the old knight, until he came to Lincoln's Inn, where alighting out of his coach, and spying Barterham who, according to his custom and his vexation of spirit, grown into uncivil language with Sir John, upbraiding him, to be the utter undoing of him and his, and crying after him (into the knight's chamber door) for new compromise, arbitrements, and a great deal of frantic talk, which Sir John sleighted, bidding him to trouble him with his clamours no more, this in distain so to be cast off, Barterham out with his pistol, shot and killed him, his last farewell to the world being only a deepfetched groan. At which his servants about him crying out murder, murder, on a sudden Barterham was laid hold on, and being hauled away, to be led to some judge to be examined, and they who plucked him along, with reviling language, for the love they bore to Sir John, and odiousness of the fact, terrifying Barterham with threats of hanging etc., he glorying in the deed and in no way repenting it, but scorning to stand to the mercy of any more lawyers, on a sudden stabbed himself, but his hands being held, and the wound, though it bled much, not being dangerous, he was examined before the judge, and his wound being dressed, committed to the King's Bench Prison in Southwark, there to be kept prisoner, with a keeper attending upon him…'

—Anon., from *A true relation of a most Desperate Murder…*, 1617 [a tract, Folger; microfilm, BL].

43.3. Insurrection and disorder around the Inn:

43.3.1. The Peasants' Revolt, in 1381, and the destruction in Fleet Street, the Temple and the Savoy

'In the year 1381, the rebels of Essex and of Kent destroyed and plucked down the houses and lodgings of this Temple, took out of the church the books and records that were in hutches of the apprentices of the law, carried them into the street, and burnt them…'

—John Stowe, from *Survey of London*, second edn. 1603.

43.3.2. The Lollards' Revolt, in 1413, and the foregathering in Fickett's Fields, next to the Inn

¶ Fickett's Fields, or Templars' Fields, or latterly Little Lincoln's Inn Fields, were open land until the building of New Square. They are clearly shown in the early prospects of the area, reproduced in 1. above, from which it may be seen that they comprised the whole area of what is now New Square, and extended somewhat further w. When they were part of the demesne of the Knights Templar, the fields served for the exercise of horses and military training. After the Knights were expelled in the early 1300s, the Fields accrued to the Knights Hospitaller of St John of Jerusalem and thence to the Priory of the same Order, in Clerkenwell, until the dissolution of the monasteries.

An incident in the Fields in 1376 concerning law clerks is referred to in the Historical Essay.

In 1413, during the Lollards' Revolt, Sir John Oldcastle chose Fickett's Fields as the meeting-place for his band of followers. The rebels planned to march thence to Westminster and overthrow the King. After the attempted revolt, Sir John went into hiding, but after four years was captured, and executed at St Giles' Fields (to the n.-w. of Lincoln's Inn Fields), near the scene of his treason. These lines, drawn from one of several plays based on his life, evoke this place in those troubled times:

'*Sir Roger Acton*:

There are of us our friends, and followers,
Three thousand and three hundred at the least,
Of notherne lads foure thousand, beside horse,
From Kent there comes with sir John Old-castle
Seaven thousand, then from London issue out,
Of maisters, servants, strangers, prentices
Fortie odde thousands into Ficket field,
Where we appoynt our speciall randevous.

Murley (brewer of Dunstable, a rebel):

Fue paltry paltry, in and out, to and fro, Lord have mercie upon us, what a world is this, wheres that Ficket Fielde, sir Roger?

Acton:

Behinde saint Giles in the fielde neere Holborne.

Murley:

Newgate, up Holborne, S. Giles in the field,
and to Tiborne, an old saw: for the day, for the day?

Acton:

On friday next the foureteenth day of January.

Murley:

Tyllie vallie, trust me never if I have any liking of that day: fue paltry paltry, friday quoth a, dismal day, Childermasse day this yeare was friday.

Beverley (a rebel):

Nay maister Murley, if you observe such daies,
We make some question of your constancie,
All daies are like to men resolv'de in right.

Murley:

Say Amen, and say no more, but say, and hold master Beverley, friday next, and Ficket field, and William Murley, and his merry men shalbe al one, I have halfe a score jades that draw my beere cartes, and every jade shall beare a knave, and every knave shall weare a jacke, and every jacke shal have a scull, and very scull shal shew a speare, and every speare shal kill a foe at Ficket field, at Ficket field, John and Tom, and Dicke and Hodge, and Rafe and Robin, William George, and all my knaves shall fight like men, at Ficket field on friday next.'

—Michael Drayton, from *Sir John Oldcastle*, 1598 in *Collected Works*, ed. J William Hebel, 1961 [BL].

> H B Wheatley, *op. cit.*, 1891.

43.3.3. The Gordon Riots, in 1780, and their way along High Holborn past the Inn and thence to a *bencher's town-house*

'The accounts which the papers will have given you of the religious mobs which have infested us for some days will make you desirous to know in what state we now are. I have the satisfaction to tell you that from the appearance of to-night everything seems likely to subside, and we may sleep again as in a Christian country. Lincoln's Inn has been surrounded with flames on all sides.'

—William Pitt the younger [of LI], from Letter to his mother, the countess of Chatham, 8th June 1780.

'1, New Square, Lincoln's Inn,

I have not time nor words to describe the horror and anxiety of mind I have lately felt at the villainies practising in this devoted city, which I greatly fear are yet much short of what is to be expected. I have been but five hours in bed for both the two last nights. On Tuesday I was a spectator of the detestable conflagration at Lord Mansfield's house, where I heard and saw such things as nothing less than the evidence of my own sight would have convinced me could have happened... Last night I saw seven fires raging at once in different parts of the town: a horrid and affecting spectacle after what I had seen on Tuesday night, the memory of which never will be effaced from my mind. This night we are quiet and I hear no attempts at fire have been made, but I have too good reason to fear that further mischief is still to be expected, and that the authors of these infernal practices have laid their schemes very deeply.

American treachery and English treason I believe are at the bottom of it, and religion is the pretext. However, say nothing of this beyond your own family.

We of this Society, as well as the Temple and Gray's Inn, are associated for our protection, and I have by me a musket and bayonet and am to patrol at 2 o'clock for an hour. We are 120 strong besides servants.'

—? John Batt [of LI], from Letter to James Harris, MP, 8th June 1780.

So then—the Vandals of our isle,
Sworn foes to sense and law,
Have burnt to dust a nobler pile
Than ever Roman saw!

And Murray sighs o'er Pope and Swift
And many a treasure more,
The well judg'd purchase and the gift
That graced his letter'd store.

Their pages mangled, burnt and torn,
Their loss was his alone;
But ages yet to come shall mourn
The burning of his own.

—William Cowper [of IT], *On the Burning of Lord Mansfield's*[1] *Library Together with his MSS by the Mob in the Month of June 1780.*

[1] John Murray, first Earl of Mansfield [of LI], LCJ, had a private library of exceptional size and quality in his town-house in Bloomsbury Square, half a mile n.w. of the Inn. The house was attacked and the library destroyed by the Gordon rioters, on account of Mansfield's reputation for toleration towards Roman Catholics. The path of the rioters was along Holborn and High Holborn but mercifully did not deviate to the Inn. As LCJ, Mansfield presided at the ensuing trial of Lord George Gordon, and remarkably exculpated him on the grounds of insanity.

43.3.4. The Great Reform Act Riots, in 1832, and the Duke of Wellington's refuge in the Inn

'The bitter resentment and anger generated by opposition to the Bill was still fiercely burning eleven days after its passage—June 18, 1832, seventeenth anniversary of Waterloo. On the evening of each Waterloo Day the Duke's custom was to give a great dinner at Apsley House to some of the officers who had been present, but otherwise he did not treat the day as a holiday. On this particular anniversary he had official business at the Tower of London, to be followed by an interview with the Solicitors to the Treasury in Lincoln's Inn, where he had appointed a meeting with Lord Eliot and Lord Granville Somerset.

The Duke set out with his unvarying punctuality, riding a horse and accompanied by a mounted groom. He dispatched his business at the Tower, and had just started back when he was recognized and almost instantly surrounded by an angry and rancorous mob. Attracted by the hoots and threats, members of the City police attempted a rescue but were swept aside; one man even seized the Duke's bridle, but was forced away by the groom. The Duke refused to put his horse to a gallop, and continued on his way at a walk, looking steadily to his front and paying not the slightest attention to the screaming and murderous throng. Luckily for him, passers-by came to the aid of the reinforced police; and a man driving a phaeton (or tilbury) kept close behind, so that the crowd could not press too heavily on the Duke.

With this singular escort for a Field-Marshal, he arrived at Lincoln's Inn, transacted his business, and then started home, guarded by Lincoln's Inn lawyers. A zealous solicitor seized a "bawling butcher" with one hand and knocked him down with the other, to the intense gratification of the assembled citizens. A *cortège* was then formed, with (the future) Lord St Leonards walking in front of the Duke's horse, a peer at each stirrup, and the groom behind. Policemen came in to swell the little force, but St Leonards forbade them to draw their truncheons and sent a body of them on ahead to occupy a place where street repairs were in progress and therefore plenty of stones available for mob ammunition. In this manner they proceeded as far as St James's Palace, and "there being only a few stragglers left, the Duke and his companions shook hands" with their rescuers and trotted off to Apsley House.'

—Richard Aldington, from *Wellington*, 1946.

>> Guy Green [solicitor in LI].

43.3.5. The Chartists' Marches, in 1848, and the preparations for the defence of the Inn

¶ In 1848, there was great apprehension as to a march arranged for the 10th April of that year by the Chartists, in pursuit of the demands of their Charter. The lines quoted below, written by a Lincoln's Inn man, evoke a day on which many members of the Society, under the orders of their elders, prepared themselves in the approaches to the Inn to assist in preventing a riot, and armed with staves having white ribbons attached, to defend the gates of the Inn. Some eight hundred special constables were sworn-in in the New Hall. The full set of verses from which these lines are drawn conveys a strong sense of class war—which was, of course, exactly how most of the professional and land-owning classes saw the situation. Although the demands of the Chartists seem in retrospect rational and unrevolutionary, it will be recalled that 1848 was a year when several crowns fell in continental Europe—France having had a revolution earlier in the same year.

Of Parker and the Bar, sing the glorious day's renown,
That array'd for civil war
All the pride of wig and gown,
In good trim for a freak or a fray:
From the Inn's remotest nook,
How all rush'd to kiss the Book,
And be marshall'd in warlike array.
... Great unwash'd! you'd better shy us!
If you venture to defy us,
You'll have Selwyn's Nisi Prius
'Mong your snobs;
And, if taken in the fact,
Oh! beware of Denman's Act,
And of Smith's Chancery Practice *on your knobs!*

For the rest I have not time,
Tho' we all were brisk and prime,
And our bearing quite sublime,
As we stood;
Whilst our Adjutant, Sir Walter,
At his post ne'er known to falter,
Would shed alike his ink and his blood.

Now the day wore on apace,
But no rioting took place,
And of tumult not a trace
Met our eyes:-
So, without a coup de truncheon,
Our brave forces went to luncheon,
And pitched into the beef, ham, and pies!

At four the news arrived,
That the monarchy survived,
And bold Feargus had decamped with his crew;
While our band, from Trafalgar,
Tho' well drench'd, without a scar,
Brought us word that we had nothing to do.

But lo! at half-past five,
'The game is all alive!' Cried Blunt, as he rushed into Hall;
'Down in Holborn there's a fray,
And the dev'l and all to pay, So the Magistrate has sent for you all!

'In the philo-chartist mob,
Lo! each sanguinary snob,
Has found out a new dodge in his game;
From the amateur police,
They have wrench'd the staves of peace,
And are punching all our heads with the same!'
... By the archway in Old Square,
Bold we sallied forth, to dare
All the snobs collected there
To the last!
While we march'd, with warlike tramp,
Up the Lane, full many a scamp
Thrust his tongue into his cheek as we pass'd!
... Then, from half-past six till nine,
Those who had not,—strove to dine;
Those who had,—discussed their wine,
All at ease;
While a few patrolled the Square,
All alive and debonnair,
But beginning to despair
Of a breeze.
... And so, God bless the Queen!
May her days be still serene!

In her realm be never seen
Strife or War!
And may London snobs,[1] *at peace*
With the Guards and New Police[2]
Live in salutary fear of the Bar!
Vivat Regina!

—Martin Archer Shee [of LI], from 'The Lay of the Lincoln's Inn Legion' (to the tune of 'The Battle of the Baltic'), 13th April 1848 [a monograph, BL].

---

[1] Snob: A person belonging to the lower classes of society; or ? a person not of the Inns, a townsman, from Cambridge slang—*OED*.

[2] The New Police: The Metropolitan Police established in 1829 by Sir Robert Peel [of LI] (1788-1850), PM.

These dire verses may be found to be unreadable without a melody. However, a reader not familiar with the tune of the patriotic ballad by Thomas Campbell to which they were intended to be sung is encouraged to try fitting them to Don Von Tress' 'Achy Breaky Heart', the American country music success of Billy Ray Cyrus in the early 1990s. The words more-or-less scan, and the song comes alive.

43.3.6. The General Strike, in 1926, and the safeguarding of Chancery Lane

Last week we had a dreadful strike
We went to school by bus and bike
By tube and train and underground
So everyone at school was found.

—Hugh Barrett-Lennard [later the Rev Sir Hugh, sixth baronet],[1] 1926.

---

[1] The author of these unpublished lines, then aged 8, was living in the residential chambers at 25, Old Square of his father, a member of the Society. They refer to the difficulties overcome in reaching his preparatory school, Mr Gibbs' in Sloane St., when for a brief period the public transport system was kept running by untrained undergraduate volunteers. From the windows of those third-floor chambers, overlooking Chancery La., he saw First World War armoured vehicles deployed as a precaution against feared consequences of the strikers' marches, and had a close view of the officer-in-charge addressing the crowd assembled there by loud-hailer from his vehicle, stopped outside the Great Gatehouse.

> David Long [solicitor formerly in LI].

44. WARS AND THE THREATS OF INVASION:

44.1. The Society's Volunteers from the C16th to the C20th: their recruitment and training in the Inn:

44.1.1. Their precursors from the mid-C16th to the mid-C18th

¶ The Inn's military volunteers are usually said to have had their formal initiation in 1584, when in the face of the threat of the Spanish Armada, ninety-four members of the Society, under Sir Thomas Egerton (later Lord Ellesmere, LC) signed a Declaration of Association, pledging their lives in the defence of their queen, Elizabeth I.

However, half a century earlier, the Report of Henry VIII's Royal Commission of *ca.* 1540 clearly envisaged the availability of the students from the Inns of Court and Chancery to serve him under arms. Indeed, from the C13th, judges had raised bodies of men from the Inns of Court for the defence of the realm or of London.

'And whereas we think it very expedient, that such men should also besides their studies aforesaid, have more knowledge and practice in martial feats, whereby they may be able to doe the King's Grace and the Realm service both in time of peace and warre also. First therefore, that it shall be lawful for every the King's students to occupy and exercise at his pleasure shooting in a Cross-bow and Long-bow without Licence and Placard; so that it be not prejudicial to the King's Highness' games.'

—from the *Report* of Henry VIII's Royal Commission to Thomas Denton, Nicholas Bacon and Robert Cary on legal education, *ca.* 1540.

> D S Bland, 10 *Journal of the Society of Public Teachers of Law*, 1969.

At earlier dates, occasions of civil unrest would surely have led to the Society's members organising themselves for the protection of the Inn's perimeters, as evoked at a later date in 43.3.5.

¶ The earliest recorded form of physical military or quasi-military training of students in the Inn (rather than the expression of aspirations) is thought to be of 'barriers'. These were staged mock combats with staves, the origin of which lay in medieval jousts, whence the origin of the word—referring to the palisades around (or along the middle of) the tilt-yard. By the early C17th, they had acquired something of the elaborate and artificial character of the Inns' masques, with music and an acted script. In November 1616, the Royal Court invited the young members of the Inns to perform barriers in the yard at Whitehall. They did so, but on that occasion at least their performance was much criticised by members of the Court present there—presumably for being ill rehearsed or undisciplined. The following lines celebrate the event. However, it has been suggested that a lasting consequence of the disorganised production may have been the issue some four months later of Letters Patent by James I, which are quoted below, leading to the formal establishment *inter alios* of this Society's Volunteers (under their various successive names).

Brave Mars and mighty Pallas
Come help me to remember
The noble acts, and worthy facts
Performed in November.

By Barriars stoute and sturdie
Young Gentlemen for propper
Whoe had their Hose, as men suppose
bedawbed with lace of Copper.

This proiect was invented
their purses beinge shallow
Sure by a Prince, a subiect since
I meane the owld Prince Swallow.

Confirmed by the Benchers
soe spruce, soe wise, soe wittie
With a trick i'th'lawe, not a strawe
to cousen Court and Cittie.

Bid understandinge blinde you
or eye sight dotinge asses
To thinke your owne, better than ours
which lookes but thorough your glasses.

But happie was this Proiect
thrice happie was this Monday
To Jenninges owld, and Burbige[1]
Natt Feild, and Harry Cundy

—Anon., 'The Barriers', a poem in praise of the presentation on 4th November 1616 [MSS. Eng. poet. c. 11, *f.* 72, Bodleian].

---

[1] Richard Burbage (1567-?1619), Nathaniel Field (1587-1633), Henry Condell (d. 1627), 'Jennings' may be John Heming (d. 1630) the coeditor of the First Folio of Shakespeare (with Condell).

> D S Bland, 'The Barriers, Guildhall Library MS 4160', *The Guildhall Miscellany* (no. 6), 1956.

¶ James I embodied the Inns' Volunteers by Letters Patent:

'Right trustie and wellbeloved, wee greet you well, &c.
Whereas wee are well pleased and advised that out of the Innes of Court and Chauncery there shall 600 gent. (such as shall voluntarily offer themselves thereunto), being devided into tow equall portions or companies according to there Howses, be tollerated and allowed to practise

and exercise martiall discipline—the one company whereof to be under the patronage of our selffe, and to be instructed therein by Captaine John Fowler, and the other to be under the patronage of or welbeloved sonne, and to be instructed by Captaine Georg Allen:—These ar to require you to call before you such of the Benchers of every the said Howses (as you shall thinck fitt), and to acquaynt them with our said pleasure. Wherein wee doubt not both of there consent and assistance in the generall furthering of the same, as also in the more particular providing of such fitting orders for the setling and continuance thereof, as whereby the trewe uses of soe good a designe may be upheld, and all conveniences taken away and prevented. And so wee bidd you hartely farwell.

Given at our court of Whitehall this 10 of March, 1616 [=1616/7].

To our right trustiee and wellbeloved
Councellor, St Frauncis Bacon, Kt,
Lord Keper of our Greate Seale of England.

ORDERS conceaved for the setling and establishing of the Company of the Innes of Court and Chauncery in there exercise of military disceplyne.

For Matter of Religion:

1. First, that none be admitted but such as ar well affected in Religion.

2. Next, if any one be a common swerer or quarreller, and will not be reformed, he shalbe cashiered.

For the Comon Weale:

1. First, that there armes be not in theire owne custodye, but kept in some fitting place betweene tymes of exercise.

2. Next, that there tymes of exercise by lymited, both for terme and vacacion respectivelye.

For theire Government:

1. First, that the Benchers sett forth and appropriate what Howses shalbe of the Kinge's patronage, and what of the Prince's.

2. That for matters of great weight the Benchers determyne, and for matters of lesse weight, in tyme or place of exercise, twelve of the discretest young gent. chosen out of all the Houses shall, together with the Captaine, determyne.

3. Next, that for prioritie of place every Howse give there owne gent, theire ranke, and that the Howses take place first by chaunce of the dice, and afterwardes by course and turne.

4. Next, that the Officers be chosen by their Captaine.

For the Charge:

1. First, the peice of ground for exercise to containe fower acres with the inclosing of it, yf such a peece alredy inclosed may not be found.

2. Next, the Armes of the Pikequere.

3. Next, the charg of admission of every one into these bandes—what themselves thinck fitt.

4. Next, for dressing and keeping of there armes—some reasonable allowance to be given to an armirer.

5. Next, for the Capteines and other Officers—such allowance as the gent. shall think fitt.

And it is intended that no gent. ar to be injoyned to exercise in this kynde but such as shall voluntarie offer themselves to be tollerated to doe it at their owne voluntarie charg.

And as for the number of 600, it is not enjoyned, but a number lymited, beyound which they shall not exceed.

And yf the Benchers (fynding this exercise shall noe wayes withdrawe young gent. from theire studdyes, being moderately used, but fill upp that tyme which would otherwise be worse spent, and manyfold other benefittes shall arise thereby), shalbe pleased to advise if a further allowance to the Officers, to be made out of the Howses, it will give them the greater livelihood and incouragement; and yf they be not pleased soe to doe, they only pray the tolleration of voluntaries, *ut antea*.'

—James I, *Letters Patent* of 1617, copied into the MS Black Books.

> Vol. II, *The Black Books*.

44.1.2. In the French Revolutionary and Napoleonic Wars

¶ The next serious threat to London from beyond these shores to be noted here was that presented by the French Revolutionary armies, the responses to which are the subject-matter of several quotations and illustrations. A number of units with Inns connections were raised in 1797-8: those with particular Lincoln's associations being the Bloomsbury and Inns of Court Association Volunteers, and The Lincoln's Inn Association Volunteers. On the resumption of war in 1803 after the one year's Peace of Amiens, The Law Association Volunteers were formed, amalgamating The Lincoln's Inn Association and The Temple Association, under the Hon Thomas Erskine [of LI] (who is depicted in that capacity in the caricature here).

'Resolved that the following uniform be adopted:

Round Hat with Bearskin, White Feather, and Black round Cockade,
Black Leather Stock, bound with Velvet,
Scarlet Jacket, faced with Yellow, Gilt Buttons,

44.b. E Walker: 'To the Gentleman of the Bloomsbury and Inns of Court Association', 1803 [ICCEY].

The uniform is that adopted by the Committee in 1798, whose minutes are quoted here, replacing a blue-coated uniform worn at the time of the formation of the Association, in 1797. The building in the background is the Foundling Hospital, some three-quarters of a mile n. of the Inn, whose extensive grounds were used for drill. The Hospital was, incidentally, the nearest building to the Inn which functioned as a concert hall. Its governors had the enlightened practice of arranging fund-raising concerts in its hall, to assist in its work with foundling children, and in which Handel, among others, participated. It may be imagined that the audiences included members of this Society and Gray's, being nearer.

White Kerseymere Waistcoat, single breasted, Gilt buttons,
White Kerseymere Breeches, Gilt Buttons,
Black Cloth Gaiters (up to the Knee)
White Belts and Sling,
Metal Ornament on the Pouch.

The Pattern of the Cloth and Jacket to be seen at Mr Addington's Woollen Draper, May's Buildings, St Martin's Lane, and the Ornaments at Messrs Fleming's and Charlton's, Strand; where in order to preserve Uniformity it is particularly requested that the Cloth and Ornaments be got. It is recommended that the Members of the Association employ one of the following Taylors to make their Uniform, viz.

William Walker, Corner of Bream's Buildings, Chancery Lane, whose Estimate is £5 14s.6d.

Abraham Walker, King Street, Covent Garden, whose Estimate is £4 14s.6d.

The Pattern of the Hat to be seen at Mr Knowlton's, Hatter, Temple

44.a. G Thompson: The proclamation of Peace (by the Treaty of Amiens), on 29th April 1802 at Temple Bar [LMA].

It was customary, over the centuries, to make great announcements of public importance at Temple Bar, the grandest of the bars on the boundaries of the City.

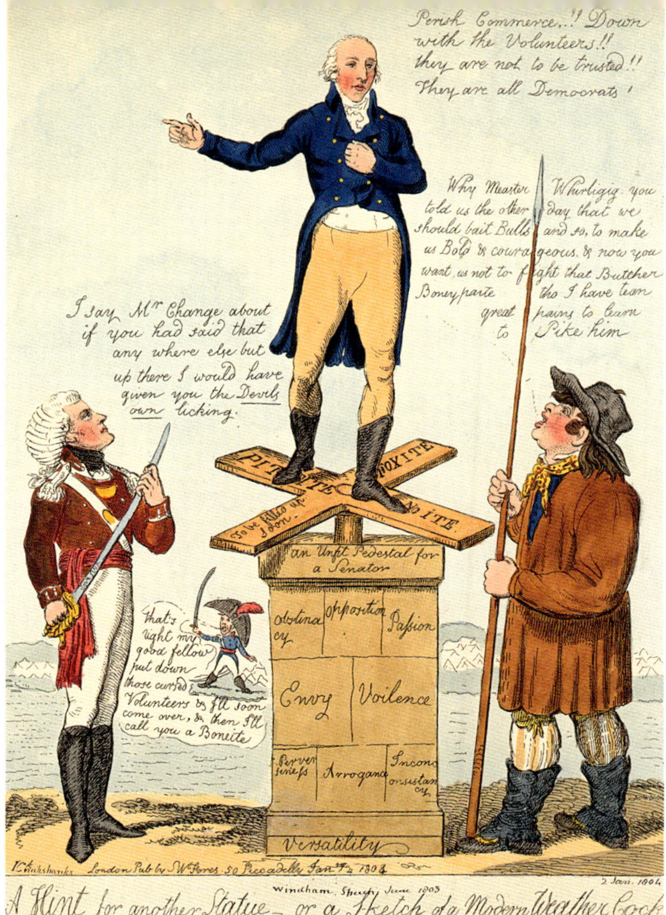

44.c. G Cruikshank: 'A Hint for another statue, or a sketch of a modern weather-cock', 1804 [BM *Catalogue of Satire* 10221] [ICCEY].

William ('Weathercock') Windham (who had been Secretary-at-war under Pitt and later, under Grenville, War secretary) stands on the weathercock, with Thomas Erskine [of LI] on the l. The latter was Lt. Col. of the Inns of Court Volunteers. The phrase 'Devil's Own' in Erskine's words is the nick-name of the Volunteers, bestowed on them by George III at the Hyde Park Review in 1803. Windham was unpopular for the doubts he expressed as to the ability of the Volunteers to defend the country on land against the French armies, if they had once been put on shore. In the background of the caricature is the Channel, the French coast and Napoléon I.

For the Inn's last word on Napoléon—unforeseeable then and surprising even now—see *28.1.iii.b.*

Bar. The Belts, Sling and Ornaments to the Pouch, to be had at Mr Clarke's, Maiden Lane, Covent Garden… The Gaiters to be had at Mr Savage's, Pimlico, opposite the Barracks, or Mr Warren's, Taylor, in the Colonade, near Upper Guildford Street.

The Committee appoint Saturday, the 10th of February next, for the appearance of the Association in the new Uniform.'

—from Minutes of the Committee of the Bloomsbury and Inns of Court Association, 29th January 1798 at Serle's Coffee House,[1] in Bryant Lillywhite, *London Coffee houses*, 1963.

[1] Serle's: by this date, located just outside the Inn.

NANCY DAWSON

TUNE

44.d. The air of *Nancy Dawson*: the march of the Inns of Court & City and Essex Yeomanry Band of the Royal Yeomanry, traditional, arranged *ca.* 1980 by Douglas Shewan [ICCEY].

> computer transcription: J H W Hamilton [solicitor formerly in LI].

'On days of general inspection or exercise, London presented the appearance of an immense garrison. In almost every square and street were to be seen parties or single files of well-appointed soldiers proceeding to their places of exercise; the Inns of Court especially appeared for the time to lay aside their character as retreats of study, and to assume that of barracks; at almost every staircase at an early hour in the morning might be seen the gay uniforms of the Bloomsbury or of the Inns of Court Associations, whilst the horses of the Light Horse Volunteers were waiting in the squares of Lincoln's Inn or the Temple till the troopers were ready to mount.'

—James N Collyer and John Innes Pocock, describing the 1790s, from *An Historical Record of the Light Horse Volunteers of London and Westminster*, 1843.

> D M Hatton, *The Devil's Own*, 1992.

¶ The Napoleonic Wars, in common with wars before and since, had their soldiers' marching songs and their sailors' sea shanties. The Volunteers seem to have adopted for this purpose a folk song and also a contemporary street ballad.

The folk song was 'Nancy Dawson'. This song, very popular in the 1790s, celebrated the actress and dancer of that name, famous at the time. Its music derives from the hornpipe in *The Beggar's Opera*, 1727 (performed in that work, but printed in the lesser-known sequel, *Polly*), but probably had an earlier origin. As noted above, the Opera was first performed in the Lincoln's Inn Fields Theatre. It was adopted as the regimental march, *ca.* 1798.

Of all the girls in our town—
The black, the fair, the red, the brown—
That prance and dance it up and down,
There's none like Nancy Dawson,
Her easy mien, her shape so neat,
She foots, she trips, she looks so sweet,
Her very motions are complete—
I'd die for Nancy Dawson.

> Jeremy Barlow.

The street ballad was 'Molly put the kettle on':

Molly put the kettle on, Molly put the kettle on
Molly put the kettle on, we'll all have tea.
Sookey take it off again, Sookey take it off again,
Sookey take it off again, they have run away.
... So Molly put the kettle on, we shall have a drop of dram,
Drink a health to Jack that's gone, for he oftimes spent galore.
Another health to Jenny too, with her petticoat fringed blue.
Now without any more ado, we'll have had tea.[1]

> John Wardroper, *Lovers, Rakes and Rogues*, 1995.

1 These are the first and last verses of the song. The middle four (no better written than them) refer to Jack the sailor's putting into St Katharine's Dock, Wapping. The song is essentially the same as the nursery rhyme 'Polly put the kettle on'.

44.1.3. During the fear of invasion by the armies of Napoléon III

¶ By 1858, fears of a threatened invasion of England by the French, under Napoléon III, had grown to such a point that lord lieutenants of counties were authorised to form volunteer rifle corps. In 1859, the Inns of Court Rifle Volunteer Corps was raised, some members

44.e. Jules Dranier: 'Angleterre: Inns of Court Volunteers', *ca.* 1860 [ICCEY].

One of a series of illustrations of the regimental costumes of Europe by this famous Belgian artist. As noted above, the Volunteers had just been sworn-in in Lincoln's Inn, in the expectation of a French invasion. The uniform is of the full dress 'rifle' pattern, with shako head-dress. The depiction of facial hair in the form of dundrearies was at that time a French (or francophone) visual *cliché* to indicate an Englishman or Scotsman.

of which were sworn in the Old Hall, during January 1860, by Lord Campbell, LC [of LI], who himself had seen service in the Napoleonic Wars, half a century later.

44.1.4. In the South African War

¶ In this, the largest colonial war in which the country was engaged in the C19th, the total number of British and imperial troops deployed from beginning to end approached half a million. The first of the quotations is a short extract from the writing of a distinguished literary member of the Society and expresses with a gentle cynicism imputed to his character, Nicholas Forsyte, the two unfortunate consequences of the scale of the war: the risks of loss of life and of damage to investors' capital.

44.f. H G Willink: 'The Inns of Court, 1890' [ICCEY].

The Inns of Court Rifle Volunteers, looking much the same as they would have done in South Africa, a decade later. The grey uniform dating from 1860, just after the foundation of the Volunteers, was changed to khaki in 1908 with the military reforms which saw the establishment of the Territorial Forces, and the Inns of Court OTC as part of them, in the place of Volunteers—six years before the mobilisation of the First World War.

'The possessive instinct, which, so determinedly balked, was animating two members of the Forsyte family towards riddance of what they could no longer possess, was hardening daily in the British body politic. Nicholas, originally so doubtful concerning a war which must affect property, had been heard to say that these Boers were a pigheaded lot; they were causing a lot of expense, and the sooner they had their lesson the better. *He* would send out Wolseley[1]! Seeing always a little farther than other people—whence the most considerable fortune of all the Forsytes—he had perceived already that Buller[2] was not the man—"a bull of a chap, who just went butting, and if they didn't look out Ladysmith[3] would fall". This was early in December, so that when Black Week came, he was enabled to say to everybody: "I told you so." During that week of gloom such as no Forsyte could remember, very young Nicholas attended so many drills in his corps, "The Devil's Own",[4] that Nicholas consulted the family physician about his son's health, and was alarmed to find that he was perfectly sound. The boy had only just eaten his dinners and been called to the Bar, at some expense, and it was in a way a nightmare to his father and mother that he should be playing with military efficiency at a time when military efficiency in the civilian population might conceivably be wanted. His grandfather, of course, poohpoohed the notion, too thoroughly educated in the feeling that no British war could be other than little and professional, and profoundly distrustful of Imperial commitments, by which, moreover, he stood to lose, for he owned De Beers, now going down fast, more than a sufficient sacrifice on the part of his grandson.'

—John Galsworthy [of LI],[5] describing 1899,
from *In Chancery—The Forsyte Saga*, 1920.

---

[1] Wolseley: Garnet, Viscount Wolseley, Field Marshal (1833-1913). At an earlier date he had military command of Natal and the Transvaal.

[2] Buller: Sir Redvers Buller (1839-1908), Lt.-General, Commander-in-Chief in the South African War.

[3] Ladysmith: the famous siege of this town was between 1899 and 1900.

[4] 'The Devil's Own': the nickname of the Inns of Court Volunteers.

[5] Galsworthy (1867-1933), the son of a solicitor, was called by the Inn, but did not practise long. He received the Order of Merit in 1929, and the Nobel Prize for Literature in 1932, probably the only member of this Society or any of the four to be thus doubly honoured. He was exceptionally and discreetly generous to charitable causes out of his substantial literary earnings. The Christian name of his character, Soames Forsyte, was inspired by the name of a solicitors' firm then in practice in New Square.

Members of the Inns of Court Rifle Volunteers—the corps mentioned here—were among the City Imperial Volunteers who set sail for South Africa on 20th January 1900, and who were part of an assembly of over 600 who were entertained to supper in the Great Hall of the Inn on the eve of their departure. The evening was presided over by a score or more benchers, and attended by the Lord Mayor, Sheriffs, Under-Sheriffs and the City Marshal. The report in *The Black Books* notes that one of the Inns of Court Volunteers who had offered himself for service had rowed stroke for Cambridge in the Boat Race.

The sharp falls in value of Stock Market securities provoked by the war caused, among many other consequences, the exposure of inadequate accounting by a small number of prominent solicitors acting as trustees or advisers to trustees of clients' funds. In the responses to these circumstances may be traced the creation of the Public Trustee (or Trust) Office, the trust corporations of several prominent banks, the institution of professional rules for the segregation of clients' money held by solicitors, and the enactment of statute law on 'white collar' crime.

Editor's notes.

¶ These lines, a surprising contrast to the mood of some of the author's other verses—most obviously 'Vitaï Lampada'—offer a different view of the emotions of the South African War. Were they a precursor to the recognition of conscientious objectors in the First World War?

Among a race high-handed, strong of heart,
Sea-rovers, conquerors, builders in the waste,
He had his birth; a nature too complete,
Eager and doubtful, no man's soldier sworn

44.g. F Hannam: City of London Imperial Volunteers, 1900 [LMA].

As noted above the Volunteers were entertained by the Benchers of the Inn, on the eve of their departure to South Africa.

And no man's chosen captain; born to fail,
A name without an echo: yet he too
Within the cloister of his narrow days
Fulfilled the ancestral rites, and kept alive
The eternal fire; it may be, not in vain;
For out of those who dropped a downward glance
Upon the weakling huddled at his prayers,
Perchance some looked beyond him, and then first
Beheld the glory, and what shrine it filled,
And to what Spirit sacred: or perchance
Some heard him chanting, though but to himself,
The old heroic names: and went their way:
And hummed his music on the march to death.

—Henry Newbolt [of LI], 'The Non-Combatant',
in *The Island Race*, 1898.

44.1.5. In the First and Second World Wars:

i. Their training

¶ Training for the First World War, in Stone Buildings:

'The problem of the supply of trained officers in numbers sufficient for the requirements of the new armies and the additional battalions of the Territorial forces raised since August last, besides replacing the heavy wastages of the war, is one which has presented itself to every mind as most formidable. It is here that the existing Officers' Training Corps such as the Inns of Court are proving of such inestimable value. When the great change was made some seven years ago and the Territorial force was created from the old Volunteers, the Inns of Court, among others, was formed into an Officers' Training Corps, and these corps became virtually the Sandhurst of the Territorial Forces… Originally composed only of barristers and their clerks, the corps is now recruited from the four Inns of Court, advocates of Scotland; Oxford and Cambridge Universities, and Public School men; and

(2) Inside the Preliminary Enquiry Bureau, where the officer recruits undergo preliminary examination and the main facts about each applicant for a commission are noted down on a card

(3) A Scene in the Armoury, where the recruits are waiting to be interviewed by the C.O.

(4) Shows the Fateful Interview Itself in which each officer recruit is being further examined by the C.O., who has before him the card giving particulars of the applicant

(6) The Attestation Takes Place in the Old Hall, Lincoln's Inn. A row of officer recruits are here seen taking the oath faithfully to serve their King and country

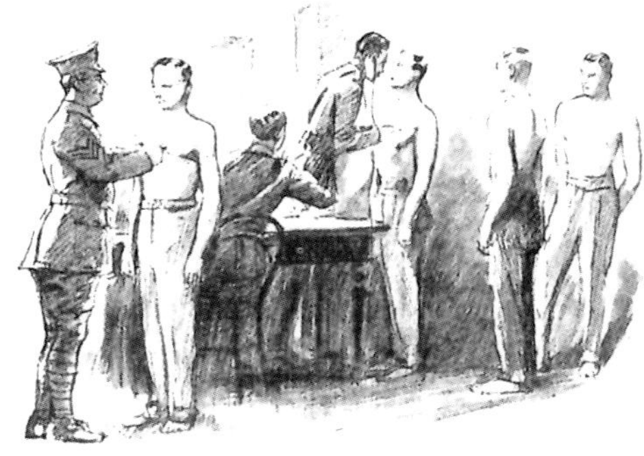

(5) If the Applicant has been Passed by the C.O. he then goes through the process of medical inspection, in the course of which he is very throughly examined and measured. If he succeeds in passing the doctor, he then proceeds to the next stage

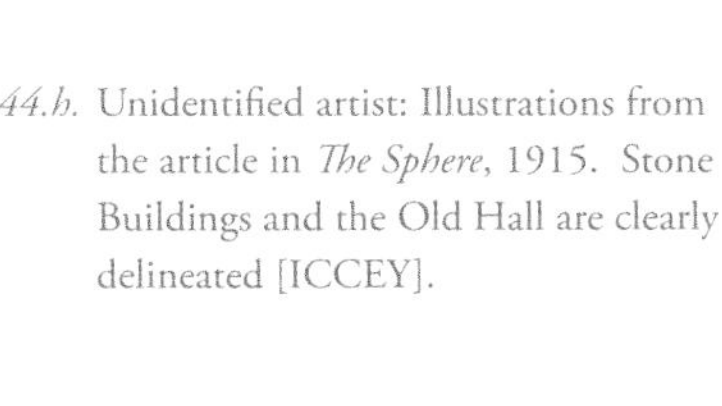

44.h. Unidentified artist: Illustrations from the article in *The Sphere*, 1915. Stone Buildings and the Old Hall are clearly delineated [ICCEY].

(1) Outside the Depot at 10, Stone Buildings, Lincoln's Inn, showing a group of officer recruits and officers waiting outside among kitbags and suit cases

Copyrighted in the U.S.A.
DRAWN BY F. MATANIA
THE ÉPÉE CHAMPIONSHIP AT LINCOLN'S INN—A DUEL BETWEEN TWO COMPETITORS

44.i. Fortunino Matania: 'The Épée Championship at Lincoln's Inn—a duel between two competitors', *The Sphere*, 1922 [press cutting, MoL].

The competitors are on the gravel walk at the foot of the raised bank to the Cherry Tree Walk. Matania, an Italian, was a much-admired illustrator and official British war artist. His work was valued for the accuracy of his depiction of humans, animals and landscape with emotion and compassion. He had a remarkable photographic memory, enabling him to draw a scene of a crowd of people, having simply glimpsed it momentarily.

gentlemen considered by the officer commanding as "specially suitable". As the foregoing sources of recruiting are not unlimited it has been found desirable to waive to some extent the strict qualification formerly adhering, and many desirable members are now admitted… who have not passed through the orthodox channels. Indeed, many of the later recruits, and some of the finest material of the corps, are men who have returned from the furthest limits of the Empire—from India, from China, from the Argentine, from almost every foreign country, travelling thousands of miles in order to qualify themselves to lead our soldiers in the field…

Sir Evelyn Wood, the honorary colonel, who reviewed the corps recently, said he had never seen a finer body of men, and described the corps as the best training school for officers in the country.

Major J A Hay is in command of the depôt which is the recruiting centre of the corps and has done yeoman's work in bringing the corps to its present important position. The acting adjutant, Mr Hugh K Ryan, who resigned a Government post in British East Africa to carry on the work, has built up and controls the now worldwide organisation of the corps, which is represented in every continent by some 21,000 bureaux, including shipping offices and so forth. In every country and township persons of local standing are its official representatives. Recruiting officers at the ports meet incoming ships and establish communication with men who have been sent home by the foreign bureaux. With this successful organising work is also associated Mr R Montagu Scott, cousin of Lord Montagu.

Captain Matthews, who commands the depôt company, has now the largest company a captain has ever commanded; 533 men await their turn to be drafted to camp. He is a stern taskmaster, with a great love for his men.

Quartermaster Sergeant Langridge gave up a large practice at the bar to carry out his present work at the depôt. Normally the training extended over four years, and members were under obligation to pass certain examinations. Since the war the system of examinations has been suspended, and the fact that the corps has been embodied has enabled the training to be more practical and thorough; it has now been found desirable to compress the whole into a period varying with the aptitude of the men themselves.'

—from 'The Training of an Officer, the work of the "Devil's Own"', in *The Sphere*, 1915 [press cutting, ICCEY].

¶ Training before the Second World War:

'I often think of the Templars jousting in Fickett's Croft when I see the gentlemen of the Epée club fencing in the Inn garden. On evenings of June the white figures have a magical effect—white made gold in the sunlight, pale mauve in the shadow, so that these two interlacing colours braid the green. Our nine-foot wall throws up its ghostly defence at this hour; the past is recreated; just so must the sun-dappled figures have danced in the heyday of the Inn. … Seen at a distance, as they so constantly recapture an attitude or play between two or three, they recall figures on Egyptian friezes—angular, repetitive, with an odd reminder of the law of frontality.'

—Margaret Ashworth, from 'On Living in Lincoln's Inn', in *Cornhill Magazine*, 1930 [an off-print, HSLI].

The scene described above is that of the exercise of the members of the Inns of Court School of Arms Club, founded in 1883 and which taught and practised the foil, épée and

44.j. Joseph Lee: London Laughs—Inns of Court Regiment: 'such a rush from the courts to this parade, Serjeant', *Evening News*, 3rd June 1938 [original cartoon, ICCEY].

A barrister is depicted wearing literally two forms of head-dress, and metaphorically two hats. This cartoon is included less for the sake of its ephemeral humour than for its record of the civilian population's beginning slowly to prepare itself for inevitable war, in the year of the Munich Accord, and thus the serious purpose of the military training in Lincoln's Inn. The suspension of the activities of the Epée Club in the same year, as noted in this section, was another example of the mood of the times. It may also be that the publication of the cartoon also showed, then as now, the general public's surprise at the juxtaposition of the practices of law and of arms.

sabre. It was, for half a century, one of the most famous fencing clubs of England. For many years, the English Amateur Épée Championships were convened at 10, Stone Buildings, the headquarters of the Inns of Court Regiment. The Club was suspended on 2nd March 1938, with the imminent approach of war, and the realisation that it would not be won by épées.

Trumpets again too soon have pealed
For us who dreamed release from war,
Asking that courage once before
Our fathers showed on Flanders field.

Not ours to judge their ill success,
Who won the war and lost the peace.
Enough if when our tired guns cease,
They deem our bravery not less.

No Lord of Hosts shall bear our trust,
Who face all fates with open eyes.
Straight home the unswerving bullet flies,
Unschooled to know whose cause is just.

No Angel's wings shall shield from harm,
Nor turn the swift resistless blow,
Stands only 'gainst a cunning foe
The cunning of our own right arm.

It may be, howsoever fain,
We shall not hold the last redoubt;
Stern steel shall wear our ardour out,
And all our soldiery be vain.

It may be when the fight is done,
And peace war's retinue reprieves,
We shall march home with laurel leaves,
As fruitless as our fathers won.

We ask not pity nor applause.
Say only 'In the narrow pass
Close comrades with Leonidas,
They broke a lance in freedom's cause.'

—Michael Albery QC [of LI], 'Trumpets Again ?', *ca.* 1939-40, in *Verses from Lincoln's Inn*, 1975.

---

ii. Their deaths

Out of the fields I see them pass,
Youth's own battalion—
Like Moonlight ghosting over grass—
To dark oblivion.

They have a wintry march to go—
Bugle and fife and drum!
With music, softer than the snow
All flurrying, they come!

They have a bivouac to keep
Out on a starry heath;
To fling them down, and sleep and sleep
Beyond reveilly—Death!

Since Youth has vanished from our eyes,
Who, living, glad can be?
Who will be grieving, when he dies
And leaves this Calvary?

—John Galsworthy [of LI], 'Youth's Own', in *Collected Poems*, 1934.

> Martin Stephen, *Poems of the First World War*, 1993.

They fell in the wilderness,
In that desolate place
Where no man dwells

They lie in the sand
With the fox, and the hare, the jerboa
and the gazelle
And where the dove lies broken in the cistern.
Like the creatures of the desert
Whose grave no man knows.

But my soul is torn for them, O God,
O Compassionate, O Merciful,
For they were my friends, and very dear to me;
Neither better, nor worse than another man's friends,
But very lovely and pleasant in their lives.

Grant them eternal rest O Lord
And light perpetual shine upon them.

—Lord Hailsham of St Marylebone [of LI],[1] 'Sidi Rezegh'[2] from *The Devil's Own Song, and other verses*, 1968, reprinted in *Verses from Lincoln's Inn*, 1975.

---

[1] Lord Hailsham: Quintin McGarel Hogg, sometime second Viscount Hailsham and latterly as a life peer, Baron Hailsham of St Marylebone (1907-2001), CH, FRS, barrister, writer, politician and member of Cabinet, LC, and son of an LC, the first Viscount Hailsham [of LI] (1872-1950).

[2] Sidi Rezegh: a battle in November 1941 in which the British and Commonwealth Army suffered a decisive defeat, but which led to their victory at El Agheila.

44.2. The aerial bombing of the Inn:

44.2.1. Its paradox in the First World War

¶ The bombing of the Inn in the First World War might be seen, in a specific context, to have been paradoxical. The Inn was first bombed on 13th October 1915 in a *Zeppelin* raid, when the worst damage was to the Chapel and its stained glass. Yet, seven years earlier a German scholarly journal, *Blätter für Architektur und Kunst Handwerk*, had published articles on the architecture of the Inn and two of the Inns of Chancery, entitled 'Altes in London': old [buildings] in London. These exemplified the best of German scholarship and technology, being illustrated with high-quality photographs. No illustrated journal article of a comparable standard was published in England until after that war, when in 1922 *Country Life* published one, prompted by the Inn's celebrations to mark the five-hundredth anniversary of the first entry in the MS Black Books.

The second bombing was on 18th December 1917, as part of *Operation Türkenkreuz*, by a *Gotha* G. IV aircraft (of the type illustrated here), belonging to *Bombengeschwade der Obersten Heeresleitung* 3 ('*Bogohl* 3'), based at airfields near Ghent in occupied Belgium. Technology had moved on from the *Zeppelins*, which were as dangerous to those in the air as to those on the ground. The principal damage was to the HQ of the Officers' Training Corps in Stone Buildings, which might have been a legitimate military target (as witnessed by the quotation in 43.1.5.i.), albeit that the bombing could hardly have been capable of being that accurately directed.

44.k. Sir Arthur Underhill [of LI]: 'Their Worships take cover—and refreshment, 1917' (the vaults under the Old Hall, during the air raid) [HSLI].

A light interlude in the deadly and damaging air raid, described in the adjacent quotation.

44.l. Sir Arthur Underhill [of LI]: 'Search lights over Lincoln's Inn, 1917' (n. view) [HSLI].

Search-lights over London in the Second World War are an image which forms part of the national memory or general historical knowledge—those of the First World War are perhaps neither.

'...but for an hour's grace [I might have died]. I was left sound, and the Stone Building scarred and pitted as by a pox, with marks to be carried while Lincoln's Inn endures. It happened that I took possession of the chambers on a certain December day whose history is told in a tablet on the Inns of Court School of Arms, opposite my door.

We left my chambers in disarray and went out through the dark streets to eat and drink and be merry. The raid warning came and found us indifferent. We talked the guns down, talked the moon another two hours' journey across the sky, talked till the restaurant put us to the door. On our way back to the Inn the raid began again. There were plenty of bombs falling and guns crashing, and shrapnel pattering freely about as we ran across the open space of the Fields to the west gate of the Inn. By some error it was closed and the postern gate locked. From a policeman standing under shelter of the coping I learned that a bomb had fallen in the Stone Buildings court, 'outside number four and five'. No one was hurt, all the residents being in the dugout. In a lull of the firing, one man helped another over the gate wall and drew the bolt.

As we rounded the chapel corner our feet were in a flood. The bomb had ploughed down into the water main, and Stone Buildings court seemed like a heaped seashore. Over masses of débris we crawled and gained the sorry shelter of the house, where stairs were strewn with shattered windows and frames and masonry; all the doors had sprung

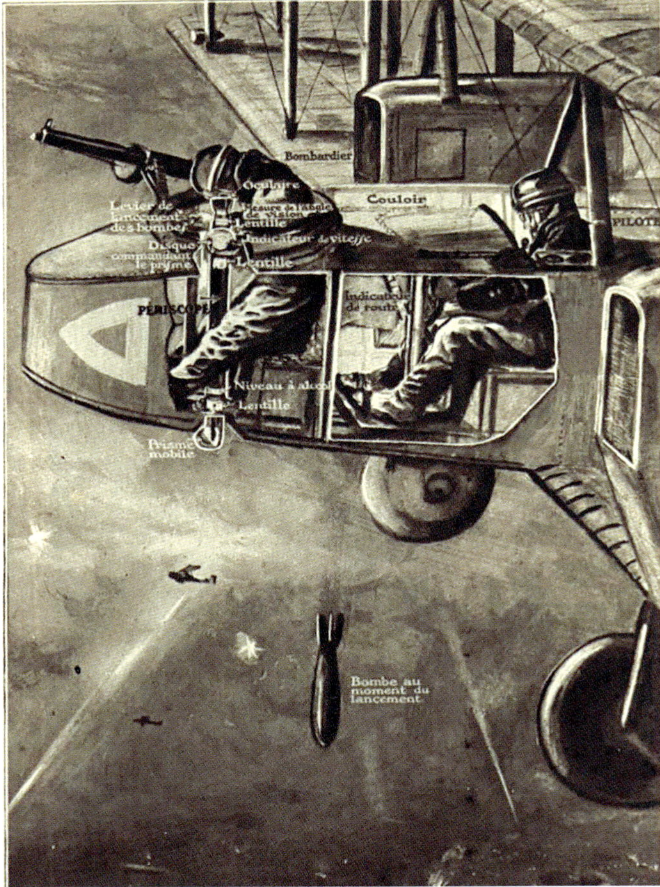

44.m. 'La guerre aérienne', in *Lectures pour tous*, 15 November, 1917 [Wikipedia].

The caption reads, in translation: "How the bombardier operates when in charge of the discharge of bombs on board a German 'Gotha', of the type of those which took part in the recent missions over London." Thus seemingly at that date London was the only field of battle in which these bombers had been deployed.

open, black entries yawned on us as we climbed. My own floors were thick with glass and wood. We groped for candles and I shuddered as I looked about. Glass had been hurled in long darts across a room of twenty-five feet, and, at a height level with my head, lay deeply embedded in walls and doors.'

—Margaret Ashworth, describing December, 1917, from 'On Living in Lincoln's Inn', in *Cornhill Magazine*, 1930 [an off-print, HSLI].

44.2.2. Its fortuity in the Second World War

¶ The bombing of the Inn in the Second World War might be said to have been fortuitous. Despite, according to the Society's records, its having been hit by explosive or incendiary bombs on twenty-seven occasions, less lasting damage was caused than in the other Inns, partly on account of the vigilance, endurance and courage of the night firewatchers. Of the other three Inns of Court, two had their halls irretrievably destroyed and new halls built in the 1950s. The Elizabethan hall of the third—Middle Temple—suffered a direct hit but was, with great skill, fully repaired. All three lost their library buildings. Lincoln's two halls and its library building, although damaged, have survived almost as though nothing had happened. A bomb which fell just outside the Inn in Serle St., between 11, New Square and the (then) Land Registry, so shook the former building that it needed to be almost totally rebuilt. But its original C17th oak staircase survived, and is still there. A notable literary figure of the time, quoted below, recorded the bomb in Chancery La. which would have destroyed the e. range of Stone Bldgs. had it fallen a few feet to the w.

An image of bomb damage and another of the repairs in this Inn are shown here.

¶ One of a series of similar reports on war damage from the Under Treasurer to each of the Masters of the Bench:

'Treasury Office,
Lincoln's Inn,
London, WC2

25th September 1940.

Sir,

I beg to inform your Worship that an Adjourned Council Meeting will be held on Monday 14th October at 3.45 p.m. An agenda will follow in due course.

It may be of interest to you to have a short account on the damage done to the Inn up to date.

Intense bombing started on the night of 8th September, when a large oil incendiary bomb fell in Lincoln's Inn Fields about 50 yards from my bedroom window. Huge fragments of the case were hurled against the garden wall, but though most terrifying, no damage was done. The next night, at 1.30 a.m., a 1,000 lb high explosive wrecked Lincoln House, High Holborn. This is the house north of Nos. 1 & 2 Stone Buildings. I was in my Office at the time with my wife and son; the building rocked, the windows were blown in, and my wife's reaction was distress at the amount of soot which smothered the room. Half an hour later a second bomb fell on the same spot, which caused casualties amongst the Wardens, Rescue Parties etc., and it is feared there were heavy casualties in the shelters under this House. The corner of Gt

Turnstile was hit at the same time, as also other buildings in Holborn. The Post Office in Chancery Lane (the property of the Inn), has been hit, much glass was broken in Stone Buildings, the Hall, Library, Chapel and other parts of the Inn, window frames have been blown out, but no serious structural damage was caused. Constant raids have since caused damage to surrounding property, but until today, when at 1.30 a.m., about 60 incendiary bombs were dropped in the Inn, nothing outstanding happened. We fought the bombs by every possible means, but one lodged behind the eaves of 13, Old Square and was not discovered until flames came through the roof. The top floors of 13 and 14 are burnt out. A serious fire was started on the roof of 6, Stone Buildings, and has spread northwards as far as No. 3. It is still burning, and the firemen inform me that it is likely to burn for some time.

Amongst those who worked so hard and well last night, I feel I must mention my son Robert, who is Acting Night Master, Mr Dodd a Solicitor, resident at 11, New Square, and two members of the A F S who saved the Old Hall. All your staff have done their utmost to meet the crisis.

I fear this narrative is sketchy and incomplete, but please excuse as I am fatigued and lack sleep.

I am, Sir,
Your obedient Servant,
N M Marriott
Under Treasurer.'

'Back from half a day in London—perhaps our strangest visit... He said the Jerrys had been over for 3 nights trying to bomb Kings X. They had destroyed half Argyll Street, also shops in Grays Inn Road. Then Mr Pritchard ambled up. Took the news as calm as a grig. 'They actually have the impertinence to say this will make us accept peace—!' he said; he watches raids from his flat roof & sleeps like a hog. So... we went on to Grays Inn. Left the car & saw Holborn. A vast gap at the top of Chancery Lane. Smoking still. Some great shop entirely destroyed: the hotel opposite like a shell. In a wine shop there were no windows left. People standing at the tables—I think drink being served. Heaps of blue green glass in the road at Chancery Lane. Men breaking off fragments left in the frames. Glass falling. Then into Lincoln's Inn, to the N[ew].S[tatesman] office: windows broken, but house untouched. We went over it. Deserted. Wet passages. Glass on stairs. Doors locked. So back to the car. A great block of traffic... In Chancery Lane I saw a man with a barrow of music books...'

—Virginia Woolf, from *Diary* for 10th September 1941, ed. Anne Olivier Bell, 1984.

> A N Wilson, *The Faber Book of London*, 1993.

[Specially drawn for THE SUNDAY TIMES by Hanslip Fletcher

Though the scars of the air raids remain, much of the old-time peace and serenity are still to be found in the Inns of Court, as this drawing of Stone Buildings, Lincoln's Inn, shows.

44.n. Hanslip Fletcher: Stone Buildings, showing bomb damage to the w. range of chambers, 1945 (n.e. view), in *The Sunday Times* [press cutting, HSLI].

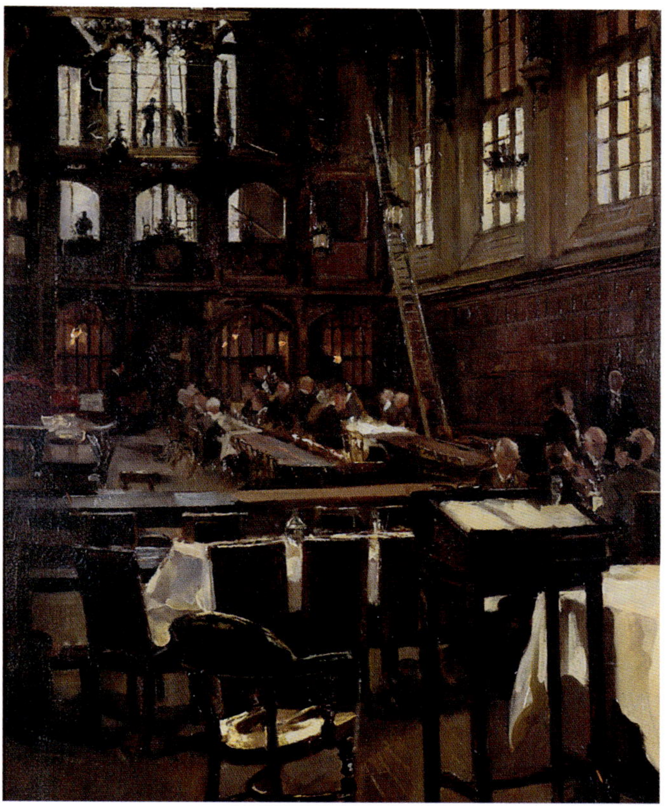

44.o. I Airy: 'Repairs to the New Hall, Lincoln's Inn, after bomb damage, 1944' (s. window of the Hall) [HSLI].

Among those members sitting at a trestle table in the Hall was known to be E H W Christie, later Head of Chambers in 13, Old Square, in succession to his father.

44.p. Charlotte Halliday: The Society's War Memorial (the w. end of the memorial: detail from n.w. view of the New Hall and North Lawns), 1994 [coll. Adrian Salter, QC [of MT]].

This was a particularly devastating bombing, striking photographs of the consequences of which are preserved in the Imperial War Museum. It affected the Inn both by shattering Stone Buildings on the night of the raid and also a few days later when the civil authorities, with excessive zeal, blew up the dangerous skeleton of the building in Chancery La. to avoid the risk of walls collapsing into the street.

The building destroyed was Lincoln's Inn Chambers, a large commercially owned late Victorian chambers building numbered 59-69, Chancery La., and facing Stone Buildings across the La. The site is now occupied by a post-Second World War building. The modern building accommodates some firms of solicitors (as did its predecessor) but is widely known to the general public for the London Silver Vaults in its basement: an adjunct to the London Safe Deposit, which had been housed there (the entrance to which had been on Chancery La.), and whose facilities had once been relevant to, among others, Inn solicitors for holding clients' valuables.

44.3. The War Memorials

¶ The Society's War Memorial, situated in the s.e. corner of the North Lawns, facing New Square, commemorated the lives of sixty-three members and thirty sons of members who died in the First World War. The names of members and sons of members from the Second World War were added in due time.

The Memorial is thus the Society's, and takes no account of the solicitors, barristers' clerks or solicitors' clerks of the Inn who gave their lives, nor those of the Inns of Court Regiment, if not also members of the Society or their sons.

'...though law is a profession whose function always has been, and is, to substitute in the controversies of mankind the arbitrament of reason for the crude ordeals of force, we have met to commemorate friends and associates bred in that tradition who, in obedience to a supreme and testing appeal, gave their own lives and in many cases the lives of their sons, on the greatest battlefield of history... They were not soldiers by profession or pastime. They had most of them, indeed, no previous training in arms. They were dedicated by choice and by practice to civil life, to a branch of civil life, it is true, which brings men into almost daily controversy, though in a bloodless arena, with a constant interchange of give and take, with ever-shifting vicissitudes of fortune, with alternating experiences of victory and defeat. ... among the traditions of Lincoln's Inn their memory will always hold and keep a separate and a treasured place, for it will be recorded and remembered of them that when the fortunes of humanity were in issue they staked everything either in achievement or in ambition which they had or hoped for, and gave to a righteous cause—gave without doubt gave without stint, all that they had to give.'

—H H Asquith (later Earl of Oxford and Asquith) [of LI] PM, from Speech of dedication of the Society's War Memorial on 17th March 1921 [HSLI].

These words have an even greater poignancy than might at first appear. Asquith, as Prime Minister, had been responsible for the Declaration of War on 4th August 1914—the first British military involvement in western Europe since Waterloo, ninety-nine years earlier. He had lost his brilliant eldest son, Raymond, who was killed in action in 1916, the same year as Asquith was forced to cede the rôle of head of the coalition War Cabinet to David Lloyd George. His second son, Herbert, had written some notable war poetry, not least of which 'The Volunteer', published the year his brother died, commemorating the clerks (amongst whom this book could number barristers' and solicitors' clearks) who had gone out from their offices, and fought and died in France and Flanders, and whom he saw as the descendants of those who fought and won at Agincourt and Crécy.

¶ There are now two memorial tablets on the walls of the Chapel. One records 'the Loyal service of the Inns of Court Officers' Training Corps during the War of 1914-18. The Devotion of the 12,000 Men who Passed through its Ranks to Commissions of whom more than 2,000 were killed in Action...' The other commemorates 'the Distinguished Service of the Inns of Court Regiment During the War 1939-45 at Home in France, Belgium, Holland and Germany. The Sixty-Four Officers and Men Killed in Action while Serving in it. And the Many Others who Received in the Regiment their Training as Officers and afterwards Fell in Action...'

45. SPIRITS OF THE SOCIETY'S MEMBERS:

45.1. In a lawyers' heaven

The time has come and I must shortly go
My destination? Ah, I do not know.
If I must travel to the Fields of Sleep,
Let my repose be dreamless and be deep,
But if I'm asked to live another life,
Let it be spiced with argument and strife!
(From what I'm told about a life of bliss
I judge that these are things I'd sadly miss.)
I'd like again, as once in youth, to find
That I could flex the muscles of my mind
And when my argument did not quite fit
Could barb the point with elegance and wit.
But when the strife and argument were done,
Why, I believe that I should find it fun,
If my opponents and my friends could dine.
We'd broach some bottles then of vintage wine,
Ambrosial Nectar 1959!

—Thomas Shelford [of LI], 'The Old Barrister', early 1970s,
in *Verses from Lincoln's Inn,* 1975.

45.2. In the Inn

Candlemas-Night![1] *and the moonbeams fall*
Cold and faint on the old white Hall,[2]
Square, and Chapel, and all about
Shuttered and barred from the world without;
Only a rumble, now and again
Heard through the portal of Chancery Lane:
'Lovell's gatehouse' of centuries four—
Good red brick, with its old oak door
Fashioned and hung, as the record saith,
Anno sexto, *Elizabeth.*

Twelve of the clock! and the New Hall's chime
Rings in the Old Hall's festival time.
E'en as the last stroke dies in air
Lutes and fiddles are merry there;
Painted windows of earlier days,
Flaunt their heraldries, all ablaze;
Candlemas Revel the screens affirm;
Great Grand-night of Hilary Term
Marred no longer by stucco or slate,
The Old Hall shows like the old brick gate;
Free tonight to welcome its dead,
In Tudor habit, mulberryred.
Shadows trooping to meet their kin:
Oldtime members of Lincoln's Inn;
Legal phantoms, an endless train,
Flocking to dance in their hall again.
Many a serjeant brave in fur,
Many a wizened conveyancer,
Chancellors ranging from Selborne to More,
Masters in Chancery, many a score,
Countless judges in erminepile,
Hordes and hordes of the rank and file.

Lutes and fiddles are bending low;
Masterfiddler dips his bow;
Squeal the fiddles; and off they go
Innermost, outermost, every sprite
Tossing and turning, left to right;
Those of the middlemost, madly gay,
Turning and tossing the other way.
Romping the measure with leap and bound,
Quicker and quicker they fly around;
Shrilling forth, in a Bedlam choir—
Here we dance round our seacoal fire
Thrice they circle, and thrice they shrill—
Scatter—vanish And all is still
Only a cock crow, faintly borne,
Hails a streak of the coming morn.

Vapours rising clammy and cold
Wrap the Inn in an icy fold;
Spectral trees on gravel and lawn,
Drip—drip—drip to a murky dawn.
But daylight flares over Chancery Lane,
And the wind smites down upon louvre and vane,
Gust upon gust, with a lashing of rain.
Candlemas-morrow comes in with a squall,
To a work-a-day world and an old white Hall.

—'Christian Tearle' (E T Jaques[3]), from 'The Ghosts of Lincoln's Inn',
in *The Gardens of Gray's Inn and other verses,* 1911 [HSLI].

---

1 Candlemas: 2nd February.
2 white Hall: a reference to the then exterior of the Old Hall, cement-stucco'd, in contrast to its original appearance 'mulberry-red'.
3 Jaques practiced as a solicitor from his eponymous firm in Gray's Inn.

And last of these, dear Theo,[1] *you*
Well-earned rest at length have sought,
Wittiest of spectres who
Haunt the leafy Inns of Court.

Hands clasped backwards, tilted hat,
Humming voice, abstracted pose,
Pince-nez spectacles that sat
Halfway down the lifted nose.

Master-pleader, plead once more
For your leafy Inns of Court
That peace returning may restore
The havoc[2] *lawless hands have wrought.*

—Lord Hailsham of St Marylebone [of LI] 'Legal Ghosts', in *The Devil's Own Song and Other Verses*, 1968, reprinted in *Verses from Lincoln's Inn*, 1975.

---

[1] Theo: Theobald Mathew (1866-1939), in his day celebrated as a wit and after-dinner speaker, as a cartoonist and greatly respected as a Chancery junior, was the pseudonymous author of the series of *Forensic Fables by O.* Much of his wit has stood the test of three quarters of a century, but a few of his fables are unacceptably racist by modern standards. The title of these verses refers to a chapter which evokes shades of former members of the Society, in Mathew's *For Lawyers and others*, 1937, thereby adding him to that list.

[2] havoc: the bombing of the Inn in the Second World War.

45.3. At home

Oh Lord Cozens-Hardy[1]
Your mausoleum is cold,
The dry brown grass is brittle
And frozen hard the mould
And where those Grecian columns[2] *rise*
So white among the dark
Of yew trees and of hollies in
That corner of the park
By Norfolk oaks surrounded
Whose branches seem to talk,
I know, Lord Cozens-Hardy,
I would not like to walk.

And even in the summer,
On a bright East Anglian day
When round your Doric portico
Your children's children play
There's a something in the stillness
And our waiting eyes are drawn
From the butler and the footman
Bringing tea out on the lawn,
From the little silver spirit lamp
That burns so blue and still,
To that half-seen mausoleum
In the oak trees on the hill.

But when, Lord Cozens-Hardy,
November stars are bright,
And the King's Head Inn at Letheringsett
Is shutting for the night,
The villagers have told me
That they do not like to pass
Near your curious mausoleum
Moon-shadowed on the grass
For fear of seeing walking
In the season of All Souls
That first Lord Cozens-Hardy,
The Master of the Rolls.

—John Betjeman, 'Lord Cozens-Hardy', in *Collected Poems*, 1958.

---

[1] Herbert Hardy Cozens, Baron Cozens-Hardy [of LI] (1838-1920), MR 1907-18. Caricatures of him by 'Spy' in *Vanity Fair* have been widely reproduced. One was captioned: 'Fair if not beautiful'—a reference to his physiognomy.

[2] Grecian columns: Cozens-Hardy inherited from his uncle Letheringsett Hall, near Holt in Norfolk. It is an C18th gentleman's house, notable for its striking and powerful early C19th addition of a façade in a pure Grecian style, a replica of a temple on the island of Delos, incongruous among the brick-and-flint of north Norfolk. The evocation is of the Hall itself: there is not, in fact, a *separate* mausoleum in the grounds.

I: PLANS OF THE DEVELOPMENT OF THE INN

1612

LINCOLN'S INN

Development 1230-1953

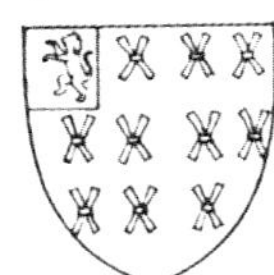

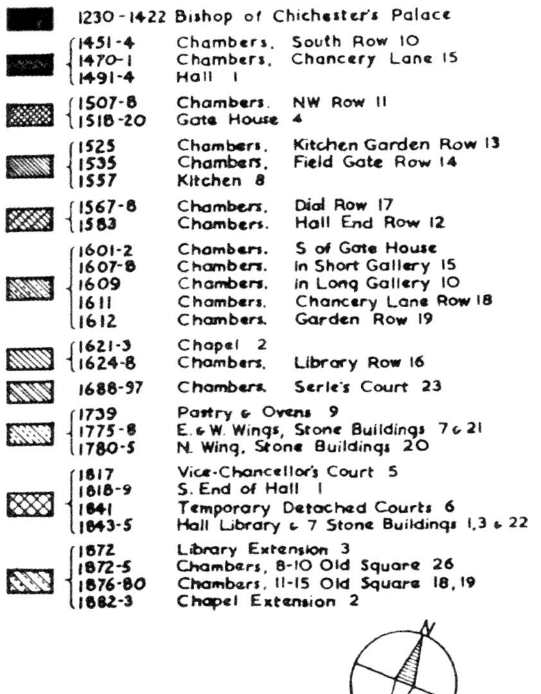

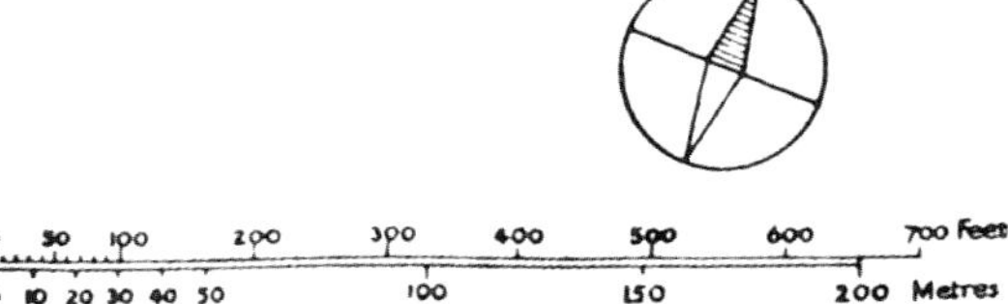

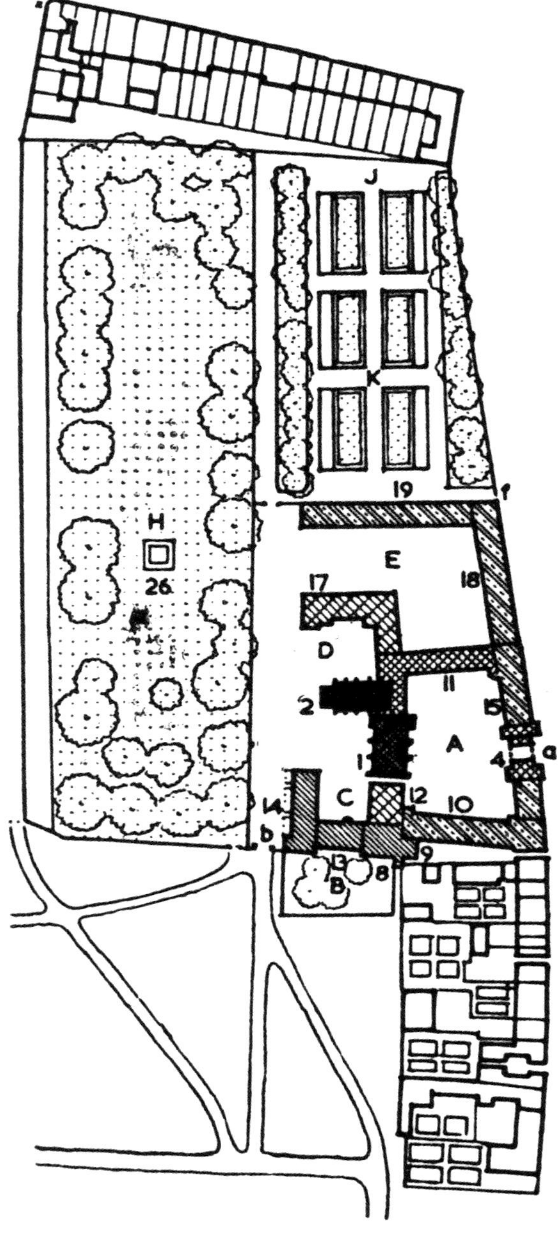

I.a. Lawrence Baker M Sc, FRIBA: Plans showing the development of Lincoln's Inn in 1612, 1628, 1697, 1785, 1845, 1883 and 1953 [HSLI] [L. Baker].

Plans by an academic architect at London University, published as 'Lincoln's Inn Development, 1230-1953' in *Journal of the RIBA*, 1955, were based on his extensive research in *The Black Books* and from maps, plans and views then available to him. They are the most thorough produced to date for this Inn and perhaps for any of the Inns, and constitute a remarkable study in historical topography. The four earliest of his plans—those for 1230-1422, 1518, 1535, and 1568—have been omitted here as predating the images of the Inn's buildings included in this book. Mr Baker recently bequeathed the originals to Honourable Society.

1628

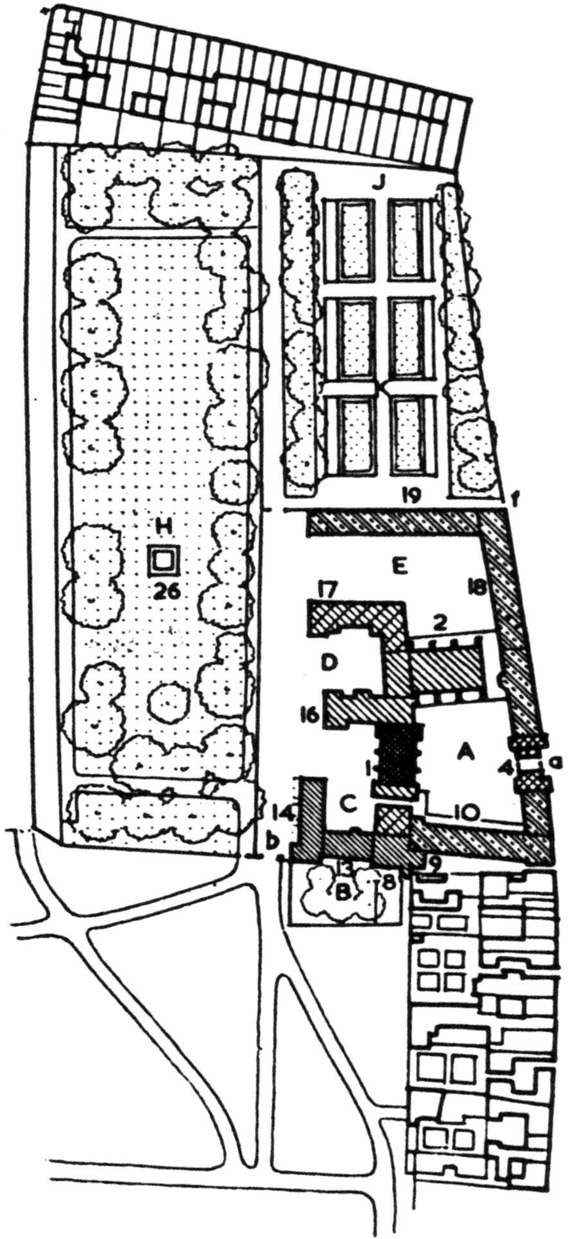

1697

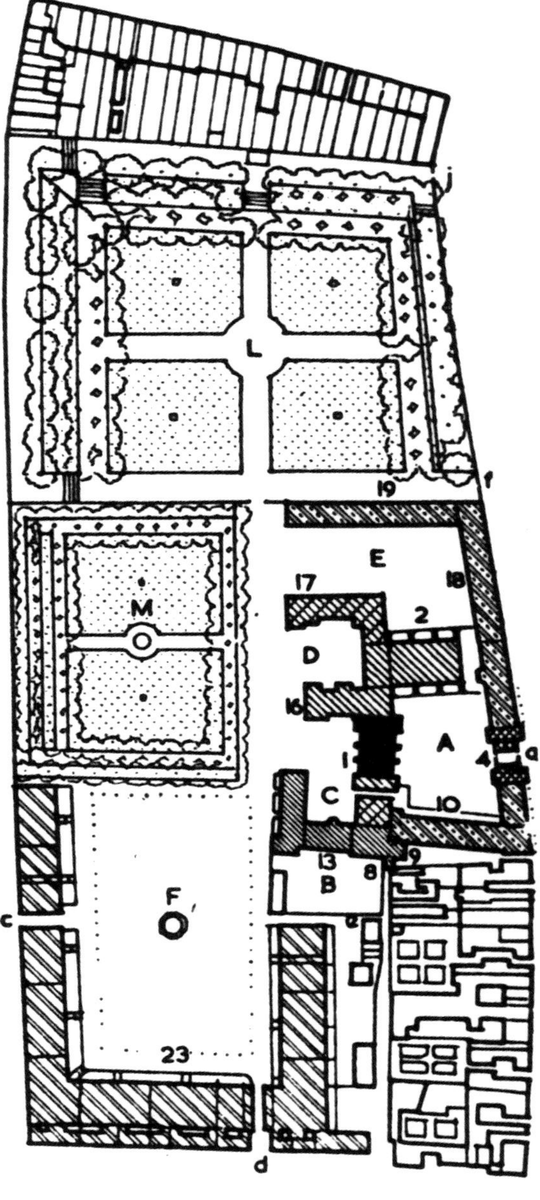

KEY

Buildings and Rows: 1, Hall; 2, Chapel; 3, Library; 4, Gate House; 5, Vice-Chancellor's Court; 6, Temporary Courts; 7, Register's, Accountant-General's and Six Clerks' Office; 8, Kitchen; 9, Pastry and Ovens; 10, South Row, Long Gallery or Stone Pace Row; 11, North-west Row; 12, Hall End Row; 13, Kitchen Garden Row; 14, Field Gate Row; 15, Short Gallery; 16, Library Row; 17, Dial Row or Chapel Row; 18, Chancery Lane Row; 19, Garden Row; 20, 1 and 2 Stone Buildings; 21, 3–6 Stone Buildings; 22, 7 Stone Buildings; 23, 1–11 Serle's Court; 24, 11A Serle's Court; 25, 8–10 Old Square; 26, Red House.

Courts and Gardens: A, Chancery Lane Court, Gatehouse Court or Old Buildings; B, Kitchen Garden Court; C, Field Gate Court; D, Middle Court or Chapel Court; E, Garden Court, Dial Court, or Old Square; F, Serle's Court or New Square; G, Stone Buildings; H, Coney Garth 12th C.; J, Long Garden or Cotterell's Garden 13th C.; K, The Walks 1608; L, Upper Garden 1662; M, Lower or Benchers' Garden 1662; N, Long Walk 1760; P, New Square Garden 1845.

Gates: a, Chancery Lane or Great Gate; b, Field Gate or Postern Gate; c, Postern Gate, Serle's Court; d, South Gate; e, Gate to Chichester Rents; f, Gate to Chancery Lane; g, Gate to Lincoln's Inn Fields; h, Garden Gate; j, North Gate.

1785

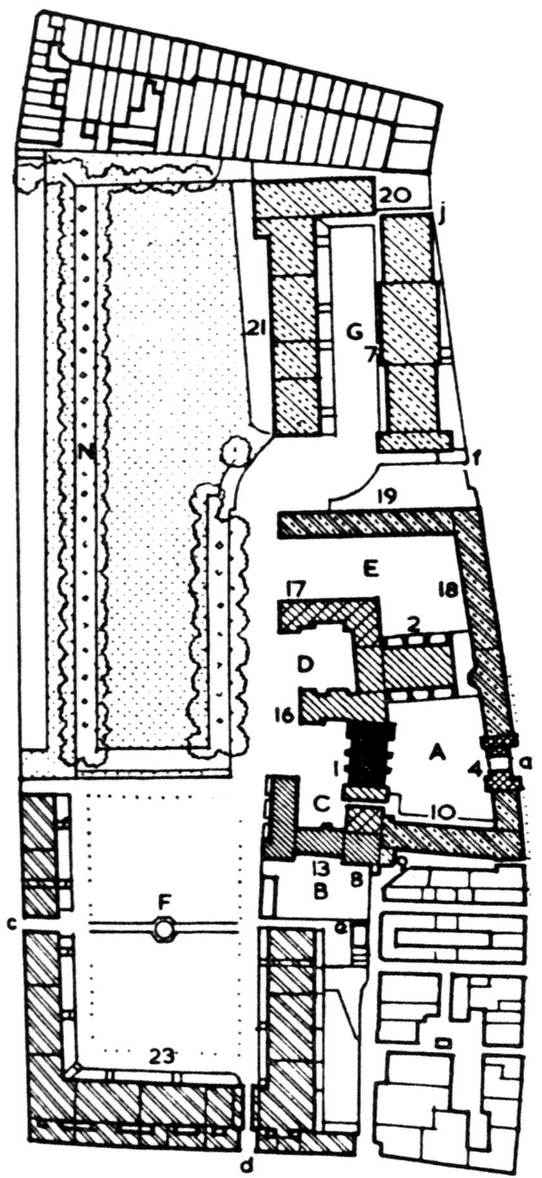
20
j
21
G
7
N
f
19
E
17
18
2
D
16
1
A
4
a
C
10
13
B
8
e
c
F
23
d

1845

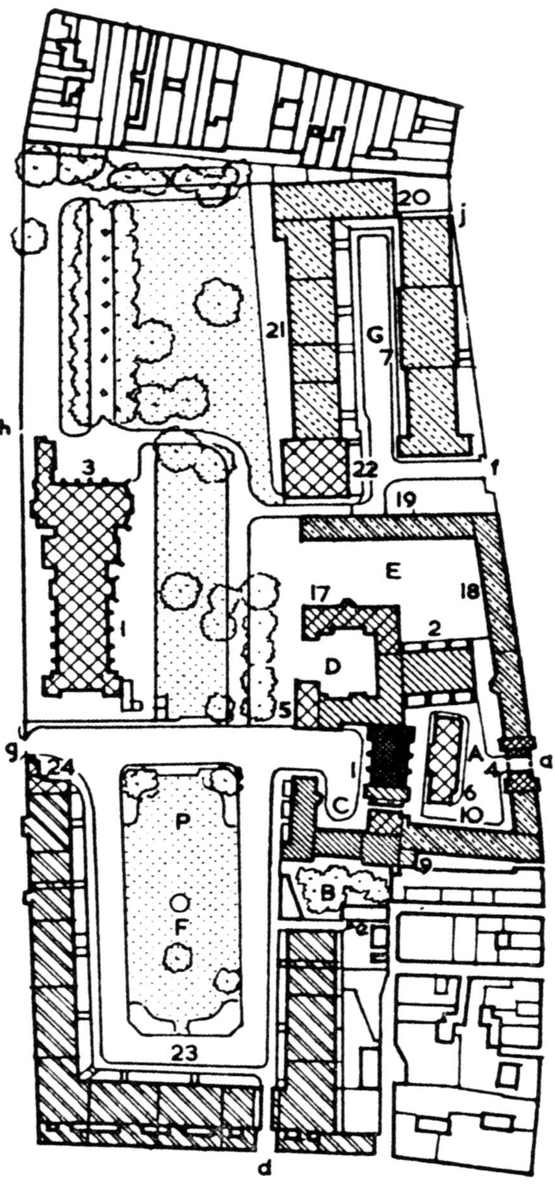
20
j
21
G
7
h
3
22
f
19
E
17
18
2
D
1
5
g
24
P
1
C
A
4
a
6
10
9
B
e
F
23
d

1883

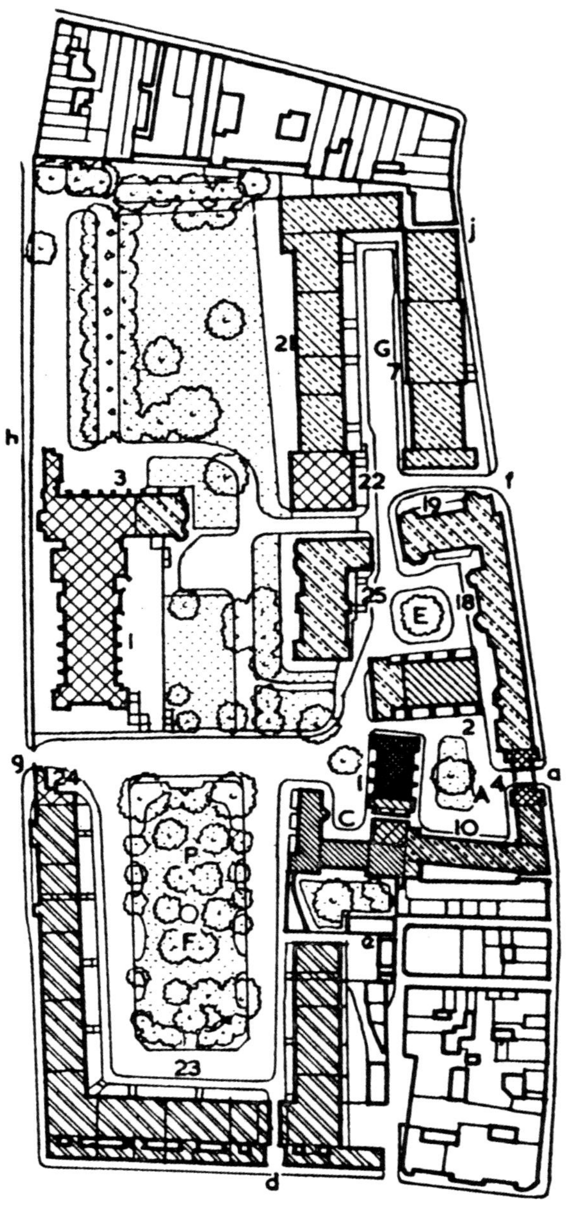

1953

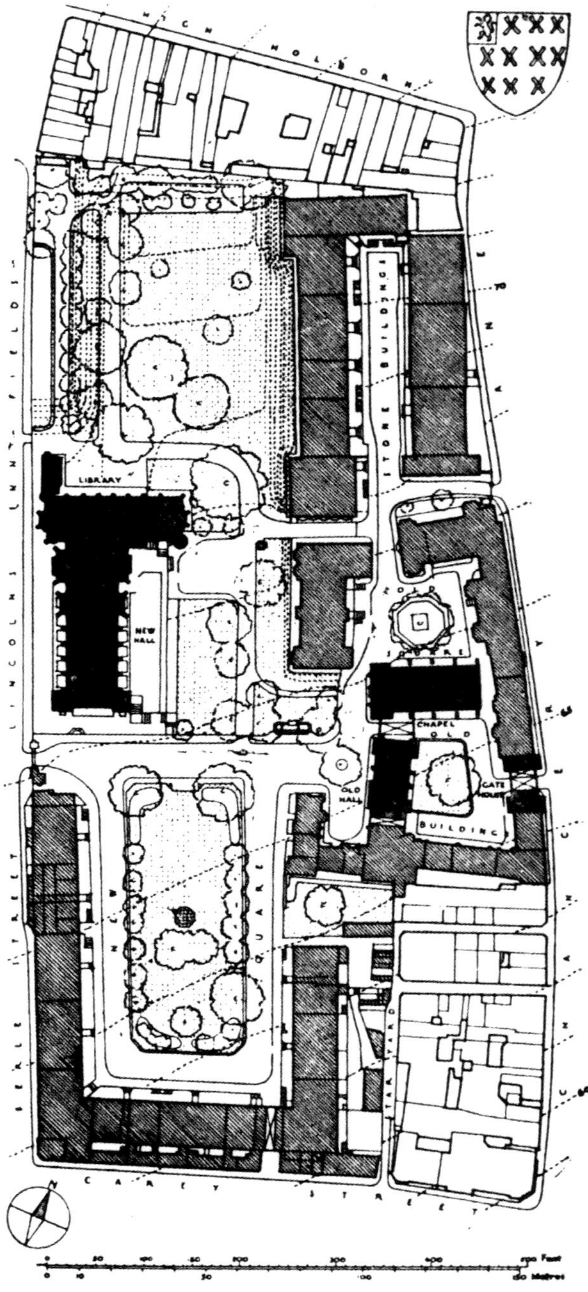

KEY

Buildings and Rows: 1, Hall; 2, Chapel; 3, Library; 4, Gate House; 5, Vice-Chancellor's Court; 6, Temporary Courts; 7, Register's, Accountant-General's and Six Clerks' Office; 8, Kitchen; 9, Pastry and Ovens; 10, South Row, Long Gallery or Stone Pace Row; 11, North-west Row; 12, Hall End Row; 13, Kitchen Garden Row; 14, Field Gate Row; 15, Short Gallery; 16, Library Row; 17, Dial Row or Chapel Row; 18, Chancery Lane Row; 19, Garden Row; 20, 1 and 2 Stone Buildings; 21, 3–6 Stone Buildings; 22, 7 Stone Buildings; 23, 1–11 Serle's Court; 24, 11A Serle's Court; 25, 8–10 Old Square; 26, Red House.

Courts and Gardens: A, Chancery Lane Court, Gatehouse Court or Old Buildings; B, Kitchen Garden Court; C, Field Gate Court; D, Middle Court or Chapel Court; E, Garden Court, Dial Court, or Old Square; F, Serle's Court or New Square; G, Stone Buildings; H, Coney Garth 12th C.; J, Long Garden or Cotterell's Garden 13th C.; K, The Walks 1608; L, Upper Garden 1662; M, Lower or Benchers' Garden 1662; N, Long Walk 1760; P, New Square Garden 1845.

Gates: a, Chancery Lane or Great Gate; b, Field Gate or Postern Gate; c, Postern Gate, Serle's Court; d, South Gate; e, Gate to Chichester Rents; f, Gate to Chancery Lane; g, Gate to Lincoln's Inn Fields; h, Garden Gate; j, North Gate.

II. GLOSSARY OF INNS OF COURT TERMINOLOGY, ESPECIALLY AS USED IN LINCOLN'S INN

compiled by Professor J H Baker

References in the form GI, IT, LI and MT are to the printed records of the Inns so designated. 'Dugdale' means W. Dugdale, *Origines Juridiciales* (1666; 2nd edn. 1680).

Abbot. Colloquialism used in IT for the most senior members of clerks' commons (*q.v.*). Dugdale 158. IT 1609 (p.42).

Admission. The act of joining an Inn. The date of admission governs seniority until call to the Bar; for those called on the same day it governs seniority at the Bar as well.

Admission Bond. Bond, with sureties, given by a student on admission as security for the payment of commons and dues. In LI such bonds were proposed in 1609, but not introduced until 1663.

Admittance. (a) A synonym for Admission (*q.v.*): as in MT 1509 (p.27). (b) Admission to chambers. LI 1526 (p.213).

Aid. A tax on members. IT 1528 (p.91).

Aid Roll. Roll of members liable to contribute to an aid (*q.v.*). LI 1585 (p.439).

Amercement, see Vacation Amercement.

Ancient (L. *antiquus*). (a) Senior barrister of an Inn of Court: a term more often used in GI and MT than in the other houses. In GI the ancients had a special part in the constitution of the Inn, and were 'called' as such. MT 1503 (p.8); GI 1514 (*Pension Book*, I, 498); LI 1558 (p.325). For Ancient Company, see GI 1574 (p.18). (b) Member of the governing body of an Inn of Chancery.

Ancienty (L. *antiquitas*). Seniority.

Apparels. Debit balance of an account (*cf.* Emendals). Furnival's Inn 1407 (p.22); LI 1442 (p.11); MT 1504 (p.9); IT 1527 (p.89); GI 1573 (p.14). The term was still used in IT in the mid-C17th. See Bland, 198 *N. & Q.* 3.

Apprentice of the Law. This term has undergone changes of meaning.
By the C17th it denoted a reader in court, or (according to some authorities) a double reader: see Baker, *Collected Papers*, i. 34, 56. It was not a term used within the Inns themselves.

Assistant of the Bench. The original term used in LI for an associate of the bench (*q.v.*). LI 1530 (p.226). In the other Inns certain benchers were appointed to attend each reading as assistants to the reader; but this is not the same thing.

Associate of the Bar. Mentioned in IT 1597 (p.419), but apparently not used in LI.

Associate of the Bench. Members of an Inn admitted to the rank and privileges of benchers, but without having a voice in the government of the Inn. IT 1545 (p.139); LI 1558 (p.325); MT 1577 (p.217). The rank seems to have originated when benchers were elected who had not read; but most of those elected were senior officers of the courts, such as prothonotaries. The last recorded election in LI was in 1769 (p.399). *Cf.* Honorary Bencher.

Autumn Vacation (L. *vacatio autumnalis*). The second of the two learning vacations, kept in August; this was usually the time when a first reading was delivered. Furnival's Inn *ca.* 1450 (p.29); LI 459 (MS Black Book I, fo.119); IT 1505; MT 1507. In 1436 it is referred to as Harvest (*BB*, I, 6). *Cf.* Summer Vacation.

Avant Commons. The same as Devant Commons (*q.v.*).

Bar (L. *barra*). (a) The place in hall representing the Bar of a court of moots, marked out by rearranging the forms. (b) The members of the Inn who argued moots at the Bar; the barristers. LI 1469 (p.48, fellows of the Bar). In the second sense often used in composite phrases, such as 'Bar table' (i.e. the table where barristers dine); and the following.

Bar Bond. Bond, with sureties, entered into on call to the Bar, for the performance of offices and the payment of dues. First mentioned in LI in 1577 (p.402).

Bar Council. Short form of The General Council of the Bar of England and Wales. See under Senate of the Inns of Court and the Bar.

Bar Moot. Moot performed by newly called utter barristers. LI 1622 (p.257).

Barrister (L. *barrestarius*). Member of an Inn who has been called to the Bar. LI 1466 (MS Black Book I, fo. 144v, 'utterbarresters'); IT 1481 (71 Selden Soc. 170, 'barester'); MT 1502 (p.2). The title is also found in the statues of Clifford's Inn and Clement's Inn. For the various forms of this word in the C15th, see 105 Selden Soc. liv. 'Barrer[ius]' occurs in LI 1455. When used without a qualifying epithet, it usually denotes an utter barrister (*q.v.*) of one of the Inns of Court. A more precise synonym introduced in the C16th for this kind of barrister was 'barrister at law': 105 Selden Soc. lv.n.277. This became the usual title and remained in general use until about 1969, when the Bar Council sanctioned the omission of the words 'at law'; but it must still be correct to use the full title, which is sanctioned by ancient usage. See also Inner Barrister.

Batells. Payment in an Inn of Chancery for additions to commons. Clifford's Inn statutes *ca.* 1505 (nos. 2, 3, 7, batelles). This term is still used in Oxford.

Bench (L. *bancus*). (a) High table in hall, where the senior members of an Inn sit; it seems to be so called because it represented the bench of a court at moots. (b) By extension it also denotes the company of benchers (as in 'call to the Bench'). LI 1442 (MS. Black Book I, fo. 45, bancum); IT 1495 (Brit. Lib., MS. Harley 1691, fo. 147); GI 1496 (Brit. Lib., MS. Harley 5103, fo. 56v). The 'high bench' (*haut banke*) is mentioned in GI *ca.* 1500 (93 Selden Soc. 233). There was a Bench in the Inns of Chancery also: *CITR*, I, 192.

Bench Table. (a) The table at which the benchers sat, and the commons there. Benchtables cases were argued by utter barristers after call: IT 1620 (p.121). (b) Meeting of benchers. This term is still used in IT (whose Bench Table Orders commence in 1668).

Bencher (L. *bancarius*). Member of an Inn elected to the Bench. Also known as Master of the Bench; but the shorter title is older, and is not a diminutive form. LI 1475 (MS. Black Book II, fo. 30v, 'bancariorum'); IT *ca.* 1490 (94 Selden Soc. 133; 105 Selden Soc.

1v); GI *ca.* 1502 (93 Selden Soc. 41); MT 1507 (p.21). The title does not seem to have been used in the Inns of Chancery: but *cf. CITR*, I, 192 (puisne of the bench). 'Bencher in court' was used in the C16th: Order in Council 1574 (*CITR*, I, 277); IT 1591 (KB 27/1318, m. 682).

Black Books (L. *libri nigri*). Books, originally bound in black leather, containing the principal records of LI, from 1422 to the present day. LI 1441 (MS. Black Book I, fo. 45v, 'in magno nigro libro').

Blowing of the Horn, see Winding of the Horn

Board of Green Cloth. The governing body of Serjeants' Inn, Chancery Lane.

Board's End Cases. An exercise found only in the IT, though GI had Board Cases: 105 Selden Soc. 1xxiv.

Bolt. A learning exercise involving argument, similar to what is now called a moot, but not strictly so because it did not involve the formulation of pleadings. LI 1556 (p.316); GI 1570 (p.4). See also 105 Selden Soc. lxxivlxxv.

Boltable Day. Day on which a bolt was held. LI 1572 (p.381).

Boltfail. Default in performing a bolt. LI 1560 (p.332).

Bonds, see Admission Bond; Bar Bond

Boyer. Allowance of ale, which benchers and barristers were entitled to draw from the buttery for their supper. LI 1541 (pp.257, 259); GI 1619 (Dugdale 278). Also called 'livery'.

Breaking up of Commons. Cessation of commons, for instance because of insufficient numbers in residence or because of plague. LI 1519 (p.196); Furnival's Inn 1551 (p.43). For the breaking up of the house, see Dugdale 197 (MT 1539).

Butler (L. *pincerna, arius*). Servant of an Inn in charge of the buttery. LI 1450 (p.20, 'butellarius' in MS.), 1464 (p.39, 'pencerna' in MS.); MT 1507 (p.16); IT 1508.

Butler for Christmas. Member of an Inn appointed to take charge of the buttery during the Christmas period. LI 1460 (p.35, 'botillarius' in MS.); MT 1051; IT 1505.

Buttery (L. *promptuarium*): LI 1428 (p.3, 'botery' in MS.), LI 1482 (p.74, 'promptuarium'); Clifford's Inn statutes *ca.*1505 (no. 4, 8, 'boterie'); IT 1521 (p.60). MT 1523 (p.72).

Call (L. *vocatio*). Graduation in an Inn of Court. Call to the bench: LI 1466 (p.43); IT 1507 (p.7). Call to the Bar: LI 1516 (p.179); IT 1563 (p.225); GI 1588 (Dugdale 280). Call to masters' commons: IT 1513 (p.28). Call to be an ancient: GI 1514 (*PBGI*, I, 498)

Call Day, Call Night. Day on which students are called to the Bar. There is now one Call Day each Term. The ceremonies vary from Inn to Inn. LI 1563 (p.339).

Calves Head Roll. Roll of contributions towards gratuities for the Inn's servants, originating in a calves' head breakfast at which the servants were treated. The term seems to have been confined to MT. Dugdale 201.

Chambers (L. *camera*). Rooms, or a set of rooms, in an Inn. At first these were for residential purposes, but in modern times they are for the most part in professional use only. It is a rule of etiquette that barristers may only practise from recognised sets of chambers; but there are now sets outside the Inns of Court, and indeed outside London. LI 1450 (p.20).

Chancery, see Inns of Chancery.

Chapel Moots. Moots argued in the mean vacations by students appearing before barristers: 105 Selden Soc. 1xxiv. MT 1539 (Dugdale 195); LI 1553 (p.305). They were discontinued in LI when the new chapel was consecrated in 1623. They seem to have been equivalent to the Library Moots held in GI and IT.

Chapel Silver. Charge levied on members for support of the chapel. It was apparently intended primarily to defray the expense of candles: see *BB*, I, 241 (custom of paying 12d. for that purpose on admission, 1535). LI 1429 (p.3).

Clerk (L. *clericus*). Young student member of an Inn admitted to clerks' commons rather than masters' commons. Clerks were given financial concessions; for instance, they might be able to dine at lower charges (with one extra person to a mess), or be exempt from pensions: Dugdale 193. LI 1439 (p.9); MT 1501.

Clerks' Commons (L. *Communes clericales*). That part of the membership of an Inn comprising new entrants designated as clerks rather than as masters. It was possible to move up to masters' commons while still below the Bar; but sometimes the move coincided with call to the Bar (e.g. *BB*, I, 188). In 1539 it was said to be usual to move from clerks' commons to masters' commons after about two years: Dugdale 239. LI 1449 (p.20); IT 1505; MT 1506. 'Clerks of the third table' are mentioned in GI *ca.* 1500 (93 Selden Soc. 233). *Cf.* GI 1576 (p.26, *mensa clericorum* = clerks' table).

Coal Gatherer (L. *Carbonarius*). Member of LI appointed to collect contributions towards the provision of fuel. LI 1444 (p.15, 'colegaderer'). Also known as the Collector of Coal Money (L. *collector grossorum carbonum*): LI 1451 (p.21). Or the Fuel Collector (L. *collector pro focale*): LI 1454 (p.24). In 1461 the same member is called both 'carbonarius' and '*escaetor denariorum focalium*' (p.36). In the C16th, the title is usually Escheator. In GI the title was Collector of Fuel Money: GI 1579 (p.34).

Common Serjeant. An officer of the Christmas revels in IT. IT 1521 (p.58).

Commoner. Member of an Inn in commons. Furnival's Inn 1408 (p.23); LI 1596 (p.46). *Cf.* Fellow Commoner.

Commons (L. *communes*). (a) The privilege of eating in the society of an Inn. (b) The payment therefor. Commons were paid to the steward on a weekly basis by those who were 'cast into commons' (residents). Some members, who were in town but not resident in the house, were allowed to be in Half Commons. A frequent punishment for minor offences was to be put temporarily out of commons. Furnival's Inn 1408 (p.23); LI 1428 (p.2); MT 1502; IT 1505.

Commons Roll. Nominal roll of members in commons. IT 1527 (p.89); LI 1546 (p.273, rolls of commons).

Compotation. Another name for a Drinking (*q.v.*). LI 1697 (p.197).

Constable. An officer of the Christmas revels, who held a mock constable's court. Clifford's Inn statutes *ca.* 1505 (no. 20); LI 1513 (p.173).

Constable Marshal. An officer of the Christmas revels. GI *ca.* 1500 (93 Selden Soc. 233); IT 1512 (p.25); LI 1519 (p.190); MT 1519 (p.60). *Cf.* Marshal.

Constable of the Tower. An officer of the Christmas revels: MT 1501.

Continuance (L. *continuatio*). Remaining in residence for the purpose of participation in the learning exercises. LI 1445 (p.15).

Continuer. Student who continued in residence and participated in learning exercises. LI 1529 (p.223).

Council. Governing body of an Inn; a term now used only by LI. FI 1452 (p.29); LI 1509 (p.153).

Council Chamber. Room where the Council of LI meets. LI 1509 (p.154).

Council of Legal Education. Body formed in 1852, following the Select Committee on Legal Education 1846, to organise teaching and examinations for Bar students. In 1967 it became a committee of the Senate of the Four Inns, and an Inns of Court School of Law (*q.v.*) was founded. In 1997 it ceased to operate and its records were transferred to the General Council of the Bar.

Cross Table Ancient. A GI term, used for Ancients (*q.v.*) who were appointed to sit at the Cross Table under an order of 1593: GI 1593 (p.98); Dugdale 276, 289.

Cupboard. The table in hall which, when not used for serving, was a place at which certain exercises and business might be performed. GI *ca.* 1500 (93 Selden Soc. 233); MT 1503 (p.8); LI 1546 (p.273, order promulgated at the cupboard). *Cf.* GI 1570 (p.7, 'at a pencion or cubbard').

Cupboardmen. In the MT, four Ancients appointed to perform certain functions in connection with learning exercises; they were understood to be barristers destined for readership. Dugdale 203.

Dean of the Chapel. Bencher responsible for the chapel. LI 1505 (p.139); GI 1569 (p.3). Also found as 'Clerk of the Chapel': LI 1452 (MS. Black Book I, fo. 88, 'clericus capelle'). And 'Keeper of the Chapel': LI 1460 (ibid., fo. 122, '*custos capelle*'). Since 1823 it was the usual for a bencher to be appointed Dean of Chapel in the year prior to becoming Treasurer. At the present day, the office may be also held by the Keeper of the Black Book.

Devant Commons. Commons paid in advance. In New Inn there was a 'devant roll', with the names of those who had paid.

Devil's Own. Nickname said to have been conferred on the Inns of Court Volunteers (*q.v.*) by King George III. The regiment still has a representation of the Devil on its buttons and collar badges.

Dining Term. Period during which a student may keep term by eating dinners in hall. There are four dining terms (Michaelmas, Hilary, Easter and Trinity), each of which used to last for several weeks.

Disadmission. (a) Revocation of admission to an Inn. IT 1595 (p.405, 'disadmitted'). (b) Revocation of assignment of chambers. IT 1593 (p.389).

Disbarment, Disbarring. Revocation of the degree of barrister. LI 1609 (p.118 'disbarred'). Referred to in LI 1571 (p.380) as 'uncalling'.

Disbenching. Revocation of call to the bench.

Discontinuance (L. *discontinuatio*). Cessation of continuance (*q.v.*). LI 1438 (p.8). Whence 'discontinuer': LI 1545 (p.269); IT 1614 (p.84).

Domus. The House or Society. The expression is found in e.g. the Domus Dinner (IT), or the toast 'Domus' (GI).

Door Tenancy. Tenancy (*q.v.*) which does not include the personal occupation of space in chambers: e.g., where the tenant has principal working place elsewhere.

Double Reader (L. *duplex lector*). Reader elected to give a second (double) reading. A double reading was usually given during the Lent Vacation, unless adjourned. GI 1550 (Dugdale 276); LI 1560 (p.329); IT 1590 (p.367).

Drinking (sb.; L. *potatio*). Reception with drinks, such as that given for the members of MT by LI in 1441 (p.11). See also Reader's Drinking.

Dues (L. *debita*). Debts owed by a member of an Inn.

Easter, see Term.

Emendals. Profit balance of an account (*cf.* Apparels). LI 1477 (p.62); Furnival's Inn 1494 (p.35); GI 1577 (p.28). See Bland, 198 *N. & Q.* 23. In *BB*, I, 4 (1431), it seems to mean simply the improvement of a balance.

Escheator (L. *escaetor denariorum focalium*). The later title of the member assigned to collect money for fuel: cf. Coal Gatherer. LI 1461 (p.36n).

Exercises, *see* Learning exercises.

Failer. Default in performing an exercise or duty. Dugdale 160, 213. *Cf.* Boltfail; Mootfail.

Fellow (L. *socius, consors*). Member of the fellowship of an Inn, apparently meaning anyone not in clerks' commons: a reference in LI 1439 (p.9) seems to assume that admission can only be as a fellow or clerk ('in socium sive clericum'). LI 1427 (p.2); GI 1469 (inscription formerly in the Greyfriars, London); MT 1470 (inscription formerly in Temple Church, '*medio templo sociatus*'), 1501. *Cf.* Clifford's Inn statutes *ca.* 1505 ('compaignon'). 'Fellow in court' (L. *socius curie*) meant a member of an Inn of Court: LI 1468 (MS. Black Book I, fo. 148v).

Fellow Commoner (L. *commensalis*). Fellow of an Inn in commons. MT 1505 (p.14). *Cf.* Commoner. The term is used differently in Cambridge to mean someone who, though not being a fellow, takes commons with the fellows.

Fellowship (L. *societas*). Membership of the 'society' of an Inn; probably including all those in masters' commons: see Fellow. LI 1431 (p.4, 'felawschip'); GI *ca.* 1500 (93 Selden Soc. 233, 'fellowshipe'); IT 1519 (Dugdale 173, 'commitivus'), 1557 (KB 27/1183, m. 190, 'consortium'); MT 1539 (Dugdale 197).

Fine (L. *finis*). A person elected as an Ordinary Bencher is required to pay a Bench Fine on election.

Fire Cases. Learning exercises which took place at the fire in the centre of hall. The term is found (from *ca.* 1580) in all the Inns except LI: 105 Selden Soc.1xxv.

Fueller. Synonym for the Collector of Fuel Money: see under Coal Gatherer. GI 1580 (p.41).

Gardener's Roll. Roll of contributions to the wages of the gardener. LI 1610 (p.131).

General Council of the Bar, commonly called the Bar Council. Body formed in 1894 (superseding a Bar Committee formed in 1873) to represent the interests of the Bar and to maintain professional standards. It is a body representing the practising members of the Inns of Court rather than the Inns of Court themselves. Its function was recognized by Parliament in the Courts and Legal Services Act 1990.

Governing Bencher. A recent term introduced to distinguish benchers who serve on the governing body of Inn of Court from retired, honorary or academic benchers.

Governor (L. *gubernator*). In the C15th and early C16th centuries the executive government of at least three of the Inns was committed to a group of governors, numbering between three and six. LI 1425 (p.2); IT 1484 (CP 40/888, m. 220d); MT 1498 (CP 40/946), m. 543).

Grand Company (*magna societas*). Term used in GI for the body of readers and ancients, as distinguished from the company of masters and clerks: GI 1570 (p.5); CP 40/1447, m. 2428d. Also in Furnival's Inn 1541 (p.42).

Grand Day, Grand Night. Festival day, when there were special commons and entertainments in hall. LI 1590 (p.18); IT 1628 (p.170: a reference to singing in the hall on grand days). There is a reference to four festival grand days in LI 1622 (p.235), probably All Saints, Candelmas, St Erkenwald and Midsummer. In recent times they are less frequent and are the occasions for the principal dinners held in each Inn to which distinguished guests are invited by the treasurer.

Grand Moots. Solemn moots held in the Inns of Chancery during the learning vacations, and attended by members of all the other Inns. GI 1577 (p.27); LI 1596 (p.45).

Grand Vacations (L. *magna vacatio*). The two principal periods of learning in the Inns, when readings were given, in Lent and during the Autumn. MT 1539 (Dugdale 194); IT 1570 (p.257); GI 1581 (p.49, 'magnae vacationes').

Grand Weeks. Weeks when the principal revels were held. LI 1614 (p.166); GI 1666 (Dugdale 278). *Cf.* Petty Grand Weeks.

Half Commons, see under Commons.

Head of Chambers. Senior barrister appointed by the members of a set of chambers to act as their administrative head.

Hitcham. Drink passed in a loving cup in Serjeants' Inn, Chancery Lane. Named after Serjeant Hitcham (d.1636), who gave the cup (now in the Wallace Collection).

Honorary Bencher. Bencher elected *Honoris causa* without payment of a fine, and sometimes without prior membership of the Inn. MT 1761. Honorary benchers rank according to their dates of election, but do not vote or hold office. The commonest categories are Commonwealth judges and academic lawyers, though the latter are sometimes elected as ordinary benchers.

Hove, Howe. Ring dance as performed at revels in an Inn of Court.

Imparlance Exercise. Formalised moot, involving the repetition of pleadings. Survived in IT until 1778 (p.352).

Inn (L. *hospicium*, Fr. *hostel*). The original meaning of the word is townhouse, and the word was widely used in the C14th for the houses of bishops and noblemen who maintained London residences. Its first mention in connection with the lawyers seems to be in the year books for 1355. See also Inns of Chancery; Inns of Court.

Inner Barrister. Student below the Bar, perhaps so named from his position inside the Bar at moots. Clifford's Inn statutes *ca.* 1505 (no. 46); IT 1535 (p.109); GI 1574 (p.17).

Inns of Chancery (L. *hospicia cancellariae*). Collective name for the lesser Inns, which in the C15th were under the superintendence of the lord chancellor, perhaps because some of them had been associated with the household of the Chancery; they became colleges for younger students, and provided chambers and commons for practising attorneys. The Latin term is found in a charter of 1432 (105 Selden Soc. xxxi n.107); and in Fortescue, *De Laudibus Legum Anglie* (*ca.* 1470), c. 49. In the early C16th they became associated with particular Inns of Court, who provided their readers and a recourse in case of disputes. The number of Inns of Chancery settled at nine before 1500: In alphabetical order, with their allegiance to an Inn of Court, they were: Barnard's Inn [GI], Clement's Inn [IT], Clifford's Inn [IT], Davies (or Thavies) Inn [LI], Furnival's Inn [LI], Lyon's Inn [IT], New Inn [MT], Staple Inn [GI] and Strand Inn [MT].

Inns of Court (L. *Hospicia curie*). Collective name of the greater Inns; Gray's Inn, the Inner Temple, Lincoln's Inn and the Middle Temple. The English expression is found *ca.* 1425 (*Arnold's Chronicle* (1811 edn.), 291, 'ynnes of courte'); 1437 (Nicolas edn., *Acts of Privy Council*, V, 74). The Latin '*hospicia curie*' is used in Fortescue, *De Laudibus Legum Anglie* (*ca.* 1470), c. 49. The longer Latin form '*hospicium hominum de curia*' (Inn of men of court) is found in a plea in bar of maintenance by members of IT and Outer Temple in 1448 (KB 27/750, m. 105) and in an undated plea in bar of maintenance by a fellow of LI: W Rastell, *Collection of Entrees* (1566), 396 ('*hospicium hominum de curia legis temporalis et hominum consiliariorum legis predicte*'). The same expression is used for a member of IT 1589 (E13/373, m. 25). But 'domus curie' is used for GI 1585 (CP 40/1447, m. 2428d). In 1479 Clement's Inn claimed to be '*hospicium hominum curie*': ibid., 108.

Inns of Court School of Law. Law school founded in 1967 by the Council of Legal Education to provide vocational training for students reading for the Bar. It consists of a number of readers, lecturers and tutors, presided over by a Dean. Its headquarters are in Gray's Inn Place, but lectures are held in other places, including at one time Lincoln's Inn Old Hall. It was taken over in 2008 by City University and renamed the City Law School.

Inns of Court Volunteers. Various military associations have been formed in the Inns of Court for the defence of the realm, and although they have not strictly possessed a continuous history there is some claim to regard them as a single entity. Loyal 'Associations' were formed for the protection of Queen Elizabeth I, and ninety-two members of LI joined such a band in 1584. Inns of Court Volunteer Associations were formed during the invasion scare of the 1790s, but lapsed when the immediate fear had passed. In 1859 the Inns of Court Volunteer Rifle Corps (23rd, later 14th, Middlesex Regiment) was raised; it saw service in South Africa and was reformed in 1908 as the Inns of Court Officers' Training Corps. Though at first its recruits were drawn largely from members of the Inns, before 1914 most were coming from the public schools.

Junior (a) In the Inns, especially in the form 'Mr Junior', the term denotes either the Junior in Hall (the most junior student), or the junior bencher. In this sense it has replaced Puisne (*q.v.*). (b) In general professional parlance, a junior barrister (i.e. one who has not become a Queen's Counsel); but this is not a term used officially in the Inns of Court.

Keeper of the Black Book (L. *custos nigri libri*). The bencher of LI responsible for keeping the Black Books (*q.v.*). Since 1812 it has been usual for a bencher to hold this office in the year prior to his becoming Dean of Chapel (*q.v.*) (and therefore two years before becoming Treasurer).

Keeping Term. Before being called to the Bar a student must 'keep' a certain number of terms. A term was traditionally kept by dining in hall on the prescribed number of occasions (three or six) during Dining Term. Eating was not strictly necessary; the duty was performed by being present in hall between the graces which are said before and after dinner. Modern regulations provide for alternative ways of keeping term, for instance by attending lectures.

King. Member of an Inn elected to preside at the Christmas revels. Furnival's Inn 1450 (p.28); GI *ca.* 1500 (93 Selden Soc. 233); LI 1519 (p.189).

King's Counsel, see Queen's Counsel.

Lammas Vacation. Synonymous with Autumn Vacation. Lammas Day is 1st August.

Laundress (L. *lotrix*). Woman servant whose main function was to wash the Inn's table linen, but who also cleaned chambers. LI 1482 (p.78); MT 1539 (Dugdale 196, the laundress of the clothes of the house); GI 1571 (p.9, 'landrisse'), 1581 (p.47, 'lotrice').

Learner Student attending learning exercises: MT 1539 (Dugdale 194); IT 1557 (pp. 194, 204).

Learning Exercises (L. *eruditiones*). Exercises, such as readings, moots and bolts, for the promotion of legal learning. IT 1521 (p.63). *Cf.* LI 1544 (p.269, 'larnyngs'). *Cf.* 'Exercises of learning': Orders of PC 1574; GI 1574 (p.19).

Learning Vacation (L. *vacatio eruditionis*). Vacation when learning exercises were held. There were two (Autumn and Lent). LI 1512 (p.166); MT 1516; IT 1520 (p.55); GI 1574 (p.18). *Cf.* GI 1572 (p.11, 'lerned vacations').

Lent Vacation (L *vacation quadragesimalis*). One of the two learning vacations (*q.v.*) falling in March and part of February or April depending on the date of Easter. Lent is the forty-day period preceding Easter.

Library Moots. Moots argued by students before barristers in the vacations. The term is apparently limited to GI and IT, but is equivalent to Chapel Moots in LI and MT: 105 Selden Soc. 1xxiv.

Livery (L. *liberatura*). (a) Allowance of ale which benchers and barristers were entitled to draw from the buttery for their supper. Later called boyer (*q.v.*). LI 1469 (p.49). (b) Allowance of clothing for an Inn servant. E.g. LI 1613 (p.161, livery cloak for the porter).

Mainprise (L. *manucaptio*). Surety for the good behaviour of a member or the payment of his dues. LI 1427 (p.2). The person giving mainprise was called a mainpernor (L. *manucaptor*).

Manciple (L. *mancipium*). Servant of an Inn responsible for administration, particularly in relation to the provision of commons and other services. LI 1464 (p.39); IT 1532 (p.101); MT 1539 (Dugdale 196, defined as the students' servant). The title has been replaced by Under-Treasurer.

Marshal (L. *marescallus*). Member of an Inn appointed as an officer for the Christmas revels. Furnival's Inn 1476 (p.31); GI *ca.* 1500 (93 Selden Soc. 233). MT 1501; IT 1505; Clifford's Inn statutes *ca.* 1505 (no. 20). *Cf.* Constable.

Marshal Pence. Money due to the marshal from cards and dice at Christmas. GI *ca.* 1500 (93 Selden Soc. 233).

Master (L. *magister*). This title is now used only for Masters of the Bench (*q.v.*), and (in the Temple) for the Master of the Temple. It was formerly used for all members of the Inn above clerks' commons: see Masters' Commons. Thus, it was used of someone on his admission to the MT in 1515 (p.46). At moots in the IT the benchers were addressed in the C17th as 'Your masterships'. Titles such as Master of the Bench and Pupil Master (*q.v.*) are accorded to men and women alike.

Master of the Bench (L. *magister de banco*). Bencher (*q.v.*) of an Inn of Court.

Master of the Game. Officer of the revels in IT: IT 1539.

Master of the Revels (L. *magister revellorum*). A barrister elected to preside over the Revels (*q.v.*) in hall, especially at Christmas. LI 1455 (p.27); MT 1501; IT 1505. According to C17th accounts, he carried a white wand or staff and conducted the measures around the hall: Dugdale 158, 200.

Master of the Temple. The incumbent of Temple Church, appointed by the Crown.

Master of the Walks. The bencher of LI responsible for the Walks (or gardens) of the Inn. Since the early C19th it has been usual to hold this office in the year prior to serving as Keeper of the Black Book (*q.v.*).

Masters' Commons (L. *communes magistrorum*). That part of the membership of an Inn designated as masters, as opposed to clerks; all the masters may originally have had the same commons, although in later times the Inner barristers, utter barristers and benchers (Masters of the Bench) came to have separate dining arrangements. In 1539 it was said to be usual to move from clerks' commons to masters' commons after about two years: Dugdale 239. LI 1469 (p.50); MT 1506 (p.17); IT 1510 (p.21). In IT 1666 (Dugdale 162) the term seems to be used only for the students above clerks' commons. *Cf.* GI 1576 (p.26, 'societas magistrorum' = masters' company).

Mean Vacation. Vacation or part of a vacation falling outside the learning vacations. IT 1518 (p.43); LI 1520. Meanvacation moots are mentioned in MT 1539 (Dugdale 195).

Measures. Stately dances, probably derived from the hove (*q.v.*) or ringdance, and performed at the solemn revels by all the members of an Inn in their gowns. Even in the time of Charles I they were known as the 'old' measures. They were last performed in 1733 at IT.

Mess. The original meaning of 'mess' (L. *missa*) is a dish sent from the kitchen, but in the Inns of Court it denotes each small group of diners who share the same allowance of food. In former times the number of members to a mess varied, and was larger in clerks' commons than in masters' commons: MT 1539 (Dugdale 193). The present number is four. LI 1523 (p.207); GI 1556 (Dugdale 276).

Michaelmas, see Term.

Midsummer Term. Another name for Trinity Term. GI 1574 (p.16).

Mirth and Solace. The old song sung at revels in IT and LI, and perhaps in all the Inns.

Mixed Dining Night. An evening during Dining Term when benchers and barristers dine at the same tables as the students. A modern innovation.

Moot. Disputation involving an imitation lawsuit. In its original sense, it denoted an exercise which required the framing of pleadings appropriate a set case, and ensuing argument. This kind of moot largely died out in the C17th. The modern moot is a disputation on points of law, usually by students or young barristers appearing before a panel of benchers.

Moot Book. (a) Book containing set cases for use in moots. Perhaps the sense of LI 1528 (p.219), 1592 (p.27, 'liber mote' rebound); IT 1621 (p.126, rebound). (b) Book recording the participation of members in moots. GI 1631 (p.309). The reference in the records are not always clear, and no book of either kind seems to have survived in the records of the Inns themselves. See Baker, *Collected Papers*, i. 147-8, 330-1, 335-41.

Moot Day. Day on which a moot is held. IT 1519 (p.46).

Mootable Day, Night. Day or night on which a moot is held. LI 1552 (p.301); GI 1571 (p.9, 'tempus motabilis'). *Cf.* Moot Day.

Mootfail. Offence of failing to perform a moot. Furnival's Inn 1465 (p.29); LI 1559 (p.326). Cf. LI 1560 (p.332) 'chappell mootefayles').

Mootmen. Students who took part in moots.

Musicians' Roll. Roll of contributions towards music at Christmas. LI 1586 (p.442).

Outer Bar. (a) A synonym for utter bar: *see* Utter Barrister. IT 1528 (p.90). Cf. GI 1576 (p.22, outer barrister). (b) In modern times it has come to denote junior barristers, in contradiction to Queen's Counsel (who have been called within the Bar of the courts).

Pannierman. A servant who blew the horn for dinner, laid the table, cut the bread, and waited in hall. LI 1482 (p.78); IT 1546; GI 1571 (Dugdale 276), 1580 (p.42). The word probably derives from 'pannier' (breadbasket) and therefore primarily denotes a pantler (L. *panetarius*), an officer of the pantry.

Parliament. Governing body of IT and MT. MT 1501; IT 1505. Hence Acts of Parliament, a term still in use in the Temple.

Parliament Chamber. Room where the benchers of IT or MT meet for parliaments. There is also a reference to a Parliament Chamber in LI 1519 (p.191). *Cf.* Parliament House IT 1507.

Pecunes, Pekynnes. A raised space in the Court of Common Pleas where students were accommodated. LI 1483 (p.80, 'pekynnes'): as explained in Baker, *Collected Papers*, i. 308-14. Etymology uncertain.

Pension (L. *pensio*). (a) the pension of the house is the total sum of money due from its resident members as a payment for permission to reside in chambers. (b) Each individual contribution was also called a pension. Pensions were paid annually, and collected by the Pensioner; they were applied towards the payment of the Inn's rent, servants' wages, repairs of chambers, and other general outgoings. LI 1433 (p.4); Clifford's Inn statutes *ca.* 1505 (no. 2); IT 1505; MT 1507. They have long since been replaced by rent. (c) In GI the term was also used by the C16th for the governing body of readers (later the benchers); and this is now the only sense which survives; (d) the same usage formerly obtained in Barnard's Inn (which preferred the spelling Pentin) and Staple Inn.

Pension Chamber. The meeting room of the Pension of GI. The records of such meetings are kept in the Pension Books.

Pension Roll. Nominal roll of members liable to pay pensions. IT 1507 ('roulle of pencions', 'pencions roull'); LI 1509 (p.159); GI 1577 (p.28).

Pension Writ. Writ of debt brought by an officer of the Inn (usually the treasurer or pensioner) to recover arrears of pensions. IT 1537 (p.115); LI 1552 (p.301); GI 1577 (p.27). There are many examples of such writs in the plea rolls of the Common Pleas.

Pensioner (L. *pensionarius*). (a) The member of an Inn elected to perform the duty of collecting the Pension (*q.v.*) from the members in residence. LI 1427 (p.2); Lyon's Inn 1484 (CP 40/887, m. 262); IT 1505; Barnard's Inn 1517 (CP 40/1020B; m. 100); GI 1552 (Dugdale 284). (b) In some of the Inns of Chancery (as in the universities) a pensioner was someone who paid a pension: Furnival's Inn 1451 (p.28); Clifford's Inn Statutes *ca.* 1505 (no. 35).

Petty Grand Weeks. Festival weeks other than those when the principal revels were held, defined in 1623 as Whitsun, Midsummer, Shrovetide, and Easter, together with the weeks of readings. GI 1623 (Dugdale 278). *Cf.* Grand Weeks.

Petty Moots. Lesser moots performed in termtime in the Inns of Chancery. LI 1596 (p.45); IT 1617 (p.101); GI 1621 (Dugdale 275).

Post Revels. Dancing performed in hall by the Inner barristers after the solemn revels or measures (in which more senior members took part). LI 1528 (p.222). See also Dugdale 161 (IT), 205 (MT). They consisted in the C17th of galliards, corantoes and country dances.

Preacher's Roll. Roll of contributions to the stipend of the preacher or reader of an Inn. LI 1585 (p.442).

Principal (L. *principalis*). Head of an Inn of Chancery; often quite a junior member. LI 1514 (p.172, reader of Furnival's Inn). Furnival's Inn 1411 (p.23); Clifford's Inn 1471 (CP 40/840, m. 467); Thavies Inn 1477 (CP 40/863, m. 451d); Clement's Inn 1477 (CP 40/864, m. 394); New Inn 1486 (CP 40/898, m. 506d); Strand Inn 1489 (CP 40/910, m. 486d); Barnard's Inn 1511 (CP 40/996, m. 454); Staple Inn 1514 (CP 40/1004, m. 89d).

Puisne. Junior, or most junior: e.g. puisne bencher, puisne butler. LI 1560 (p.329, 'puisne of the Benche'), 1565 (p.342, 'pewney' utter barristers); GI 1578 (p.32, 'pune reder').

Pupil Master. Barrister who has accepted a pupil to read in chambers. The title has recently been replaced by Pupil Supervisor. At present a pupil master must be a practising junior barrister (male or female) of not less than six years' standing who has undertaken a course of training for that purpose.

Pupillage. Vocational training in the chambers of a practising barrister. Within living memory it was customary to pay 100 guineas to the pupil master for the privilege, but it is now mandatory for pupils to be paid and many sets of chambers now pay substantial remuneration to pupils.

Puts. Unpaid debts transferred from the steward's account to the treasurer's account. LI 1504 (p.133). See *BB*, I, xxiii.

Quatuor. Senior mess of four. Quatuor of the bench: LI 1663 (p.24).

Queen's Counsel. Barrister appointed by letters patent under the great seal as one of Her Majesty's Counsel Learned in the Law. This is a public office but not a degree in the Inns of Court, and so technically Queen's Counsel remain barristers until called to the bench of their Inn. Most Queen's Counsel are called to the bench of their Inn within about seven years of appointment. They wear a distinctive gown, both in court and in hall.

Reader (L. *lector*). Member of an Inn who has given a reading. Furnival's Inn 1408 (p.23). A reader is still elected in IT and MT, but no reading is now expected, and the title is retained only during the year of office.

Reader in Chancery. Reader in an Inn of Chancery.

Reader in Court. Reader in an Inn of Court; the title was retained in GI after giving the reading. GI 1584 (p.62); IT 1591 (KB 27/1318, m. 682).

Reader (of the Chapel or Temple Church), **Divinity Reader**. Minister appointed to say daily offices in the chapel or church, in the absence of the Preacher (LI) or Master (Temple). Also called the chaplain (LI): LI 1581 (p.421).

Reader's Dinner. Feast provided by the reader of an Inn during his reading. LI 1479 (p.69); IT 1557 (p.193).

Reader's Drinking. Reception, or compotation, given during a reading. LI 1539 (p.227). It was an entertainment provided after one of the exercises, also known as the reader's supper: LI 1584 (pp. 436, 437). *Cf.* LI 1614 (p.166, 'reader's drinkinge night').

Reading (L. *lectio, lectura*). Lecture in an Inn; in the Inns of Court readings were always on a statute, but in the Inns of Chancery there may have been a wider choice of text. LI 1466 (p.42).

Reading Vacation. Another name for grand vacation. MT 1503 (p.6).

Red Books. A LI term for books of admittances to chambers and orders touching chambers; comprising six volumes from 1598 to 1891 (extant). LI 1614 (p.169).

Repaster. Member of an Inn allowed to be at repasts. LI 1596 (p.46); GI 1615 (Dugdale 278).

Repasts (L. *repasta*). Meals taken on a casual basis, and charged *ad hoc*, without being cast into commons. LI 1428 (p.2) Clifford's Inn statutes *ca.* 1505 (nos. 2, 44); IT 1521 (p.57); GI 1577 (p.29).

Repetition (L. *repetitio*). An exercise forming part of a reading. LI 1614 (p.166).

Report. A learning exercise of uncertain character in an Inn of Chancery. Clifford's Inn statutes *ca.* 1505 (no. 40).

Rerecommons. Commons paid in arrears. Clifford's Inn statutes *ca.* 1505 (no. 3).

Reresupper. A late supper, some time after supper (which corresponded to the modern dinner). GI *ca.* 1500 (93 Selden Soc. 234).

Revels (L. *revelli*). Festivities, including dancing and games, held at special religious seasons; the most elaborate were at Christmas. LI 1431 (p.4); GI *ca.* 1500 (93 Selden Soc. 233, 'revells'). Note also 'solempne revelz' (ibid. 234).

Round about the Fire. Ancient song accompanying the ringdance in GI *ca.* 1500 (93 Selden Soc. 234).

Royal Bencher. Members of the Royal Family are customarily admitted to an Inn and called to the Bar and to the Bench on the same day; they then take precedence over the other benchers. The earliest instance seems to be the election of James, Duke of York (later King James II) as a bencher of IT in 1661 (p.4). At present the Royal Benchers are: the Prince of Wales, the Duchess of Cornwall and the Duke of Gloucester (GI), the Duke of Edinburgh and the Princess Royal (IT), the Dukes of York and Kent (LI) and the Duke of Cambridge (MT).

Ruler. An early synonym for Governor. LI 1447 (p.18, reulour).

Sage Company. The governing body of Barnard's Inn and Staple Inn, later called Pension.

Scanning. A learning exercise, perhaps the examining a moot case to ascertain the points. GI *ca.* 1500 (93 Selden Soc. 234: 'le case serra assigne et nient skanne'); GI 1571 (p.9, '*bis argumentaverit super scann' in librario*').

Screens. A wooden partition separating the hall from the buttery or kitchens, and commonly used for posting notices. LI 1549 (p.295); GI 1571 (Dugdale 281). Names of candidates for call to the Bar are still required to be 'screened'.

Senate of the Four Inns. Body formed by agreement between the Inns of Court in 1967, to coordinate policy and practice, especially in relation to education and discipline. It was reconstituted in 1974 as part of the Senate of the Inns of Court and the Bar.

Senate of the Inns of Court and the Bar. Body formed in 1974 by amalgamating the Senate of the Four Inns (*q.v.*) and the General Council of the Bar of England and Wales, to oversee the structure, organisation, finance and practice of the profession. The Bar Council also retains an autonomous existence as the body responsible for representing the Bar and ensuring the maintenance of professional standards.

Senior in Hall. In GI, when the benchers withdraw after dinner, the senior barrister present, as senior in hall, presides over the proceedings customary in that Inn.

Serjeant at Law (L. *serviens ad legem*). The highest degree in the law, formerly qualifying the holder to practise in the Court of Common Pleas and to hold a judgeship in one of central courts of common law. Until the C17th, with few exceptions, only readers in court were made serjeants. A serjeantelect automatically became reader of his Inn (though if several new serjeants were called from the same Inn, the duty fell to the puisne), and then had to leave the society and join one of the Serjeants' Inns. In LI (in later times) a serjeant was 'tolled out', by ringing the chapel bell as if for a funeral. The last serjeant called from LI was Sir Richard Amphlett (1874), appointed a Baron of the Exchequer. The last serjeant of all (Lord Lindley, formerly of MT) was created in 1875 and died in 1921.

Serjeants' Feast (L. *festum servientium*). Feast, in medieval times lasting several days, given by new serjeants at law for the legal profession. From the C16th it was usually held in the halls of one of the Inns. Fortescue, *De Laudibus Legum Anglie* (*ca.* 1470), c. 50; LI 1503 (p.132); MT 1503 (p.7); IT 1521 (p.59). The first one held in LI was in 1547 (p.278).

Serjeants' Inns. The Inns established for the serjeants at law; unlike the Inns of Court and Chancery they had no educational or public functions. From the C15th until 1730 there were two Inns, one in Fleet Street and one in Chancery Lane. In 1730 they merged as Serjeants' Inn Chancery Lane. The buildings of the Inn were sold in 1877, but the society continued until the serjeants died.

Serjeants' Roll. A roll of contributions to the leaving present of a serjeant at law. MT 1507 (p.19). A serjeant was usually presented on leaving with a purse or a pair of gloves containing a 'regard' of money: LI 1463 (p.38).

Single Reader. A reader who has only delivered one reading. LI 1539 (p.255); GI 1550 (Dugdale 276). *Cf.* Double Reader.

Solace. The old song of Mirth and Solace (*q.v.*).

Special Admission (L. *specialis admissio*). Admission on special terms, such as dispensation from learning vacations or offices. IT 1519 (p.45); LI 1562 (p.338); GI 1576 (p.21, speciall admittans), 1581 (p.47, specialis admissio).

Steward (L. *senescallus*). Servant of an Inn responsible for the provision of commons. Furnival's Inn 1407 (p.21); LI 1420 (MS. Black Book II, fo.); MT 1500 (CP 40/953, m. 67d); IT 1502 (CP 40/959, m. 44d); GI 1514 (CP 40/1008, m. 783d).

Steward for Christmas. Member of an Inn appointed to take charge of commons over the Christmas period. LI 1495 (p.105); GI *ca.* 1500 (93 Selden Soc. 234); MT 1501; IT 1505; Clifford's Inn statutes *ca.* 1505 (nos. 20, 43).

Student (L. *studens*). This is now the term in universal use for members of the Inns who have not been called to the Bar; a wide range of synonyms were formerly in use, including Inner barristers, learners and mootmen.

Students were originally divided into clerks and members of masters' commons; but there has long been only one category, who dine separately from the barristers and benchers and wear distinct gowns. Fortescue, *De Laudibus Legum Anglie* (*ca.* 1470), c. 49 (L. *studentes*); GI *ca.* 1520 (105 Selden Soc. lxxxiii, 'un studyent'); MT 1539 (Dugdale 194); LI 1556 (p.315, 'studient').

Sub-Treasurer (L. *subthesaurarius*). Synonym for Under-Treasurer (*q.v.*); its use is now confined to IT.

Summer Vacation. Another name for the Autumn (or Lammas) Vacation. MT 1507 (p.21).

Tenancy. Full membership of a set of chambers, as a practising barrister rather than as a pupil. Tenants have their names painted on boards on the door casement of their chambers.

Term. The legal year is divided into four terms: Michaelmas, Lent, Easter, and Trinity. These were the periods in which the superior courts used to sit. They are also the names of the dining terms in the Inns of Court.

Treasurer (L. *thesaurarius*). Bencher of an Inn elected as the principal financial officer, nowadays serving for one year as the presiding bencher. LI 1454 (p.25); MT 1479 (CP 40/870, m. 440); IT 1484 (CP 40/888, m. 220d); Lyon's Inn 1486 (CP 40/897, m.31); GI 1530 (*Pension Book*, I, 495). The treasurer is now addressed within his Inn as 'Master Treasurer'.

Treble Reader (L. *triplex lector*). Reader who has given a third reading; this usually happened only in the case of a serjeant at law who read a third time as serjeantelect. LI 1531 (p.229).

Trinity, *see* Term.

Turnbroach. A kitchen servant, turnspit. IT 1555 (p.180); LI 1562 (p.338); MT 1666 (Dugdale 200).

Under Treasurer (L. *subthesaurarius*). Chief executive officer of an Inn of Court. Originally an assistant to the individual treasurer: MT 1524 (p.76); LI 1567 (p.358).

Utter barrister. (a) Member of an Inn called to argue at the Bar in moots. (b) Someone who has been called to the Bar; the adjective 'utter' distinguishes him from an Inner barrister. Clifford's Inn statutes *ca.* 1505 (no. 46); MT 1501; GI 1570 (p.4). The term has given way to 'Barrister at law', and (in very recent times) simply 'Barrister'.

Vacation (L. *vacatio*). Interval between terms. LI 1436. The Autumn and Lent vacations were important in the Inns of Court and Chancery as a period of learning.

Vacationer. Member of an Inn keeping a vacation. MT 1507 (p.20); GI 1596 (p.121); LI 1615 (p.174).

Varlets' Commons. Another name for Yeomen's Commons (*q.v.*). LI 1544 (p.269, 'verlettes comens'); GI 1569 (p.3, varlett in comens); 1579 (p.39, 'varletts comons').

Visitors. The Inns of Court are under the appellate supervision of Visitors with respect to their disciplinary jurisdiction. This visitatorial function is exercised, by a custom dating at least from the C17th, by the judges of the High Court; and the present practice is for visitatorial hearings to take place before three judges who are not benchers of the Inn appealed from, or before a single judge if the appeal is not against disbarment. The Inns of Chancery did not have Visitors, but were probably under the supervision of the Chancellor before they fell under the superintendency of the Inns of Court. Baker, *Collected Papers*, i. 238-52.

Visus in villa. If a member was 'seen in town', he was liable to be cast into Commons (*q.v.*) or Half Commons, whether he attended hall or not. Dugdale 205. LI 1581 (p.422); IT 1606 (p.21); GI 1612 (Dugdale 277).

Walks. Gardens of an Inn. LI 1555 (p.312, 'walke'). *Cf.* Master of the Walks.

Washpot. Menial servant of an Inn who washed the pots. LI 1569 (p.373).

White Books. Books instituted in LI in 1619 (p.214) to contain provisional orders and 'remembrances'.

Winding of the Horn. Dugdale 200. The ancient mode of summons to dinner or supper. LI 1544 (p.269). The custom was kept up within living memory in the Temple.

Yeomen's Commons (L. *communes valettorum*). The tables in hall set aside for the yeomen, or servants of the barristers and benchers. LI 1465 (p.39). The term seems to have gone out of use in LI in the C17th. But there was still a Yeomen's Table in IT 1666 (Dugdale 162).

III. LIST OF SUBSCRIBERS

David Ainger
His Honour Ian Alexander QC
Philip Ardley
Jalil Asif QC

Md Tariq Bin Aziz
Amanda Bailey
Tess Bain
Ms Horejah Bala-Gaye
Zoë Barton
Terence Bate
Professor Graham Battersby
Sir William Blackburne, Treasurer 2015
Mark Blackett-Ord
Leslie William Blake
Peter Blincow
John Brisby QC
Michael Brodrick
Jacqueline L Brown
Michael Bruce
Roy Anthony Burgess

Murray Campbell, Assistant Under Treasurer
James Matthew Oliver Carter
Edna Chayen
Cheong Soo Han
Nicholas Chew Soon Yew
Ian Clarke
Virginie Bontoux Clausen
His Honour Judge Andrew Collender QC
Sir Jeremy Cooke
The Hon John D Cooke SC
Michael Corkery QC
Rosemary Craig JP LM BA LLB LLM AFHEA
Anne-Marie Craven
Commander W L Critchley RN
Daniel Curzon

Professor Gillian Davies DL PhD
A N Dobson Esq
Nick Doherty

Nicholas Easterman
Sir Chief (Dr) Alfred O Eghobamien
Barry C Ellis
Andrew Ezsias

Sir Francis Ferris
Georgia and Joshua Fieldsend
Dr Jon Fistein
Roy Fitzsimmons
James Flynn QC
Vernon Flynn QC
Andrew Francis
Michael Furness QC

His Honour William George
Dr Andrew Julian Gilbert
The Right Honourable Lord Gill
Joseph Goldsmith
Graham S Goodchild
Martyn Gowar
Mark Alexander Grimes

Stephen L Hall
Caroline Harrison QC
Mark Hatcher
The Hon Mr Justice David Hayton
(of the Caribbean Court of Justice)
Christopher Heath
Leonard Hedworth
Mark Herbert QC
Edward and Gabriela Hewitt
The Very Rev M J Higgins
Jason Hill
David Hodge QC
Guy Holborn
Justice Randy J Holland
Stephen Hunt

Dr William Thomas Jackson
Gloria James-Civetta
Geoffrey Jaques, Treasurer 2014

Lawrence Victor Jones
Philip Jones QC
Jong Yee Ling

Shivaan Kanag-Isvaran
Ann Kennefick
Sir Sydney Kentridge
Mary Anne Kerr, Under Treasurer
James Kessler QC
Paul Klaas
Darren N T Koh Esq
His Honour Dr Colin Kolbert

Wilson Lai Wai Shing
Toby Landau QC
Dennis Lau Yee Meng
Emily Louise Lauchlan
Professor Anthony Lavers
Nicholas Le Poidevin QC
Dr Brian Montague Leach
Peter Leaver QC
John Leeson
Edite Alexandra Izabella Ligere
C Lindsay
Timothy Lyons QC

Charles Henry Mack
Andrew William Mackenzie LLB (Hons) NP
Ola Malik
John Ross Martyn
Professor Stephen Mayson
Catherine McArdle
Denise McFarland-Cruickshanks
His Honour Judge Warwick McKinnon
Lord Millett
David and Jane Mohyuddin
Professor Dr John Warwick Montgomery
Wiebke Morgan
Gerald Moriarty QC
His Honour David Morris
The Rt Hon Sir Andrew Morritt CVO

Keith Morton QC
Linda J E Moss
Miss Alex Moyler
Richard Moyse
Mihir Kumar Mukherjee
Tonmoy Mukherjee
Mark Mullen
Bruce Ashley Mullins Esq
Warren J Murray

The Rev Canon William Norman
Rosemary Norris
In memoriam Edward Nugee QC

Jane O'Hare
Michele O'Leary
Mark Ockelton
Joseph and Esther Ollech

Howard Page QC
Ariranga G Pillay, Honorary Bencher of Lincoln's Inn
Nicholas Powell
Dr Michael J Powers QC
Amy Proferes

Puneet Rai
Tharuma Rajah
Arshad Tanveer Rajput
Mr and Mrs S Reevell
His Honour Robert Reid QC
The Rev Dr Peter and Mrs Elizabeth Rowe

R M A Sampson
Syamaprosad Sarkar
Reuben Scott Esq
Adrian Sedgwick
E M T Segar
Dr Colin Seymour
Shardi Shameli
Sir Christopher Slade
George Smedley
The Rt Hon Dame Janet Smith DBE

Mary Ellen Smith
Joseph A G Smyth BL
The Hon T C Smyth SC
David Southern QC
Chandra Sri Ram
Trevor R Standen
Andrew Stevens and Annalisa Tosdevin
Claire B Stevenson
Sir Thomas Stockdale Bt
Mark Studer

Leanne Targett-Parker
Paul Taylor
Athena R Taylor-Carroll de Mueller
Peter Trevett QC

Dato' Sithambaram Vairavan

Lord Walker of Gestingthorpe
Dr A Watson CBE
Robert S Webb QC
Nicholas Whitsun-Jones
Spencer Williams
Jonathan Winegarten
Hugh Woodeson
Jane Woosey
Yee Shin Ching
Michael Yin Esq
Yvonne Young Ai Peng

IV. MISCELLANEOUS ACKNOWLEDGEMENTS NOT ALREADY MADE IN THE TEXT

Specific Authors and Publishers

Aldington, Richard—*The Duke: A Life of Wellington*: reproduced by kind permission of the Estate of Richard Aldington c/o Rosica Colin Limited, London.

Asquith, H H—Speech of Dedication of War Memorial, 1921: Copyright © The Estate of Lord Bonham Carter

Betjeman, John—'Lord Cozens-Hardy' (from *Collected Poems*): Copyright © 1955, 1958, 1962, 1964, 1968, 1970, 1979, 1981, 1982, 2001. Reproduced by permission of John Murray Press, an imprint of Hodder and Stoughton Limited

'Caudwell, Sarah' (Sarah Cockburn)—*The Sirens sang of Murder*, 1989; *Thus was Adonis Murdered*, 1989: published by Little, Brown Book Group

Church, Richard—'The Bonfire', 1936; *Green Tide*, 1945; *The Voyage Home*, 1964: reprinted by permission of Pollinger Limited (www.pollingerltd.com) on behalf of the Estate of Richard Church

Cowper, Francis—*Prospect of Gray's Inn*, 1961: GRAYA, on behalf of Gray's Inn

Fookes, Robert & Wallington, Richard—*A Portrait of Lincoln's Inn*, 2007: Third Millennium Publishing, an imprint of Profile Books Ltd

Granville-Barker, Harley—*The Voysey Inheritance*, 1903: The Society of Authors as the Literary Representative of the Estate of Harley Granville-Barker

Hamilton, James—*Arthur Rackham, A Life with Illustration*, 1990: Copyright © James Hamilton, 1990. Permission granted by the author

Jones, E and Woodward, C—*Architecture of London*, 1983: The Orion Publishing Group, London

McLeod, Mona—*London Observed: A Polish Philosopher at Large…*, 2009: Signal Books

Newton, Douglas—*London West of the Bars*, 1951: Robert Hale Ltd

OED—Oxford University Press

Ockleton, Mark—*A Portrait of Lincoln's Inn*, 2007 as above

Partridge, Eric—*Dictionary of Slang and Unconventional English*, 1984: Copyright © Eric Partridge. Reproduced by permission of Sheil Land Associates on behalf of Eric Partridge

Piper, David—*Companion Guide to London*, 1992: Companion Guides, an imprint of Boydell and Brewer Ltd

Summerson, Sir John—*Architecture in Britain 1530-1830*, 1991: reprinted with permission from Yale University Press

Woolf, Virginia—*Diary*, 1941: From *The Diary of Virginia Woolf*, edited by Anne Olivier Bell, published by The Hogarth Press. Reprinted by permission of The Random House Group Ltd

---

The majority of the images in this book are from copies in the possession of the Editor, the location of the original of which is indicated by an accompanying abbreviation in its caption (expanded on pp. 33–34).

The publisher would like to extend its thanks to Jeremy Smith and the staff at the London Metropolitan Archives, and Nick Finegold and the staff at Tag Worldwide for their assistance.

All images captioned LMA are © London Metropolitan Archives, City of London, which *2.e.* and *2.d.*, which are © Guildhall Art Gallery, City of London.

For original paintings, drawings and manuscripts, and for unique or rare printed material, an acknowledgement is given as to location or ownership. The Editor acknowledges with gratitude permissions given to reproduce these works (in whole or in part) in this book.

For illustrations taken from second-hand printed books which are not rare, an indication is generally given as to the title, but not necessarily as to a library.

The Editor's reliance on printed secondary source material will be self-evident to any reader, among which books on the Inn, the Inns generally, and Holborn; the C19th and C20th encyclopaedias to the buildings and streets of London, architectural histories of London, guides to literary London, and literary anthologies—especially of poetry.

Perhaps the two most important guide-posts have been for text: D S Bland, *Bibliography of the Inns of Court and Chancery*, 1965; and for pictures Gabriel White and Stephen O'Malley, *Legal London*, 1971.

The staff of the numerous libraries, archives and galleries, the names of which are listed in the abbreviations, have been courteous and helpful, as have a few others not noted there such as the Technische Universität, Berlin. The book owes much to librarians and archivists now deceased, whose foresight preserved material to the present day.

Every effort has been made to obtain copyright permission to reproduce words or images here (including photographs in which there is copyright of works out of copyright). Apologies are offered for any oversights, and these will be corrected if there is a second impression of this book.

The persons and institutions named here generously made financial grants to The Lindum Trust to assist in the costs of picture research, art work and copyright fees: the late Mr P W E Brown, Mrs F B Laurence's Charitable Trust, the Golden Bottle Trust and the Skipton Building Society.

Whilst the publication of this book is not associated with Payne Hicks Beach, several of the retired or current partners and staff of that firm have been very supportive to the Editor in a variety of ways over the years and his gratitude to them is recorded here.